CONTENTS

MAPS

INFLATION ALERT: We don't have to tell you that inflation has hit Hawaii as it has everywhere else. For that reason it is quite possible that prices may be slightly higher at a given establishment when you read this book than they were at the time this information was collected in late 1984. This may be especially true of restaurant prices. Be that as it may, we feel sure these selections will still represent the best travel bargains in the islands.

A DISCLAIMER: Although every effort was made to ensure the accuracy of the prices and travel information appearing in this book, it should be kept in mind that prices do fluctuate in the course of time, and that information does change under the impact of the varied and volatile factors that affect the travel industry.

Readers should also note that the establishments described under Readers' Selections or Suggestions have not in many cases been inspected by the authors and that the opinions expressed there are those of the individual readers only. They do not in any way represent the opinions of the publisher or authors of this guide.

Introduction

HAWAII ON $35 A DAY

The Reason Why

THIS BOOK WAS WRITTEN for the express purpose of disposing of a couple of myths. The first is that a South Seas idyll—that longed-for journey to enchanted islands that everyone dreams of at one time or another—is beyond the means of the budget traveler. We're here to tell you that all that is ancient history. Less than five jet hours and as little as $169 away from the West Coast lie the islands of Hawaii, a name to conjure dreams, a place to explore on a shoestring budget.

People will tell you, of course, that the 50th American state is one of the most expensive areas on earth to visit. It is—and it isn't—depending on which Hawaii you care to see. If you choose prepackaged and preconceived Hawaii, you'll undoubtedly stay at plush hotels, dine at expensive restau rants, be herded around in sightseeing limousines with people just like the folks you left back home—and pay a pretty penny for it. But if you agree with us that travel is a do-it-yourself activity, if you'd rather leave the plush and nonsense to others and strike out on your own to find out how the islanders really live, you'll find that a vacation in Hawaii is one of the best travel bargains anywhere. For, contrary to legend, Hawaii has dozens of comfortable, clean, and reasonable hotels; scores of restaurants where the food is exotic and inexpensive; and most important, an almost endless list of free and low-cost entertainment—from beaches to bon dances, from museum browsing to mountain climbing, from hiking to dancing the hula. Add to that an incredibly cheap airfare, and you've got the ideal place for a budget vacation—even in these inflationary times.

WHAT $35 A DAY MEANS: As in most of the other books in this series, our aim is to show you how to keep your basic living costs—*room and three meals only*—down to somewhere around $35 a day. There's nothing fantastic or gimmicky about that goal. Since the costs of transportation, shopping, sightseeing, and entertainment are all in addition to that figure, our book prescribes reasonable methods of vacationing on a budget.

We think you'll agree that by keeping these room-and-meal expenses low, you can make a substantial dent in the overall cost of your trip. But more important, we believe you'll have more fun—and enjoy a more meaningful vacation—by relying on your brains rather than your pocketbook. Hawaii is one of the few places where you can still live comfortably on a limited budget, even in the face of tremendous inflation that is raising prices everywhere. In fact, many people who used to travel abroad for their holidays are finding Hawaii one of the best bargain areas anywhere. And considering that this is an enormously popular resort area, $35 a day is very little to pay. We'll give you specific tips on how to do it elsewhere in this chapter. But first, back to our debunking.

MYTHS AND PARADOXES: The second myth was neatly put by a friend of ours, a sophisticated woman who travels regularly to Europe. "Why go all the way to Hawaii," she asks, "just to find yourself at a beach?" Now no one in his or her right mind would dispute the glory of Hawaii's beaches, some of the best in the world. But anyone who looks on Hawaii as merely a seaside resort is missing some of the most profound, exciting, and exotic travel experiences available anywhere.

The essence of Hawaii, its special mystery, lies in its startling and subtle paradoxes. Take its people, as fascinating a mixture of mankind as you'll find on this planet. The children and grandchildren of Stone Age warriors, New England missionaries, and Oriental plantation workers mingled and intermarried to create nothing less than a new race. Scratch an islander and you'll find a Hawaiian-Chinese-Portuguese, a Japanese-American-Tahitian-Puerto Rican, or perhaps an English-Filipino-Korean. The typical islander—if such a creature exists—long ago gave up counting the racial strains in his background; it got too complicated. Hawaii's people, American in ideals, optimism, and drive, still retain the serenity of Polynesia and the Orient. They avidly follow the scores of baseball games played by fellow citizens 6000 miles away in Boston or Philadelphia, yet many of them dream of going to visit "the old country"—Japan, China, the Philippines. And as if in answer to the bigots who cringe at "mongrelization," the interracial democracy of Hawaii has produced the most attractive Americans anywhere. Hawaii's children are unbelievably exquisite, a mixture of the best the races can give to each other.

But the paradoxes don't stop here. They are even more astonishing on a sheer topographical level; Hawaii has the kind of scenery that all but overwhelms the senses. Steep cliffs tumbling down to coral beaches, tropical rain forests and woods that run a hundred shades of green, black sand beaches and pounding blue surf, scores of tropical blossoms, vying for attention at every turn—this is the landscape. Even more awe-inspiring, the volcanoes that created these islands from the vast nothingness of ocean are still alive. The land is still being born. Drive mile after mile on the Big Island of Hawaii and see where the lava flows have scalded their way to the sea and how slowly life renews itself over the years. Then go to Kauai and see what the centuries and the forces of erosion have done to a much older and extinct volcano. You will have a sense of the youth—and age—of the earth that you can get nowhere else.

The paradox that is Hawaii continues on a third level as well. In less than 200 years it has gone from Stone Age to Space Age, from a primitive island kingdom ruled by stern gods of nature to the fastest-growing state in the U.S., ruled by booming laws of economics. Industry soars, hotel and apartment construction grows apace, population and tourism increase astronomically, Space Age science and education become established, and wherever one looks, something new is being built, planned, developed. "Full speed ahead" are the words on every front. Still, despite the aggressive energy of the times, Hawaii somehow manages to retain its gentleness, its warmth, its relaxed nature. The spirit of aloha remains untouched, a calm center in the eye of the hurricane of progress. Which is perhaps why so many people who've been everywhere and back can't seem to get enough of Hawaii.

LIVING ON $35 A DAY: The trick in Honolulu is to stay at a small apartment-hotel or condominium complex, complete with a built-in money-saving device: a kitchenette. This doesn't mean, however, that you'll spend your vacation slaving away at a hot stove. It means only that you'll fix breakfast, maybe pack a sandwich or some marvelous fresh fruit for a picnic or a light supper, and dine out once a day (preferably at lunchtime, when prices are always low and values best). Many of Hawaii's visitors live just this way—but they live in expensive apartment hotels. We've scoured the city looking for *budget* apartment-hotels and have come up with a surprisingly large number of them.

To stay within the boundaries of a $35-a-day budget, you should be part of a twosome, which means that you will have a total of $70 per day to spend on room and meals. To stay on the low side of this budget, you will want to choose a room between $20 and $30 a day double. If you wish to live a little higher, then choose a room that goes between $30 and $40 a day. Whatever will be left over from your planned $70-a-day for two living expenses can be used for your meals; in our chapter on restaurants, we'll show you how to eat inexpensively and well, figuring about $7 to $8 for dinner, about $4 for lunch, roughly $3 for breakfast. Of course, whatever you save by eating in means so much more in the kitty for other pleasures.

THE SEASON, THE COMPETITION, AND THE PRICE: You should bear in mind another important fact about hotels in Hawaii: their rates usually vary according to season and business. The hotel industry is highly competitive, and room prices go up or down as conditions dictate.

In general, you'll get a much better bargain if you avoid the winter season—mid-December to mid-April; that's when *everybody* seems to want to go to Hawaii, and many visitors—especially those from cold areas like western Canada—often stay for a few months at the budget apartment-hotels. Many hotels routinely impose a surcharge of at least $5 per room during that period. The summer months of June, July, and August are also busy, but many hotels maintain "low-season" rates in those months, and during the months of October, November, and May all kinds of choice rooms are yours for the picking. If you think you'd like to spend the Christmas–New Year's season in the islands, make reservations as far in advance as you possibly can; many hotels accept reservations as much as six months to a year in advance for this insanely popular period. Reservations are a good idea, in fact, any time of the year. Budget accommodations do exist, but they are much sought after even now that the supply of hotel rooms has overshot the demand—few of the new hotels that have been built in Waikiki in the past few years have been in the economy category.

The high-season markup, incidentally, often extends to car rentals and other visitors' services as well. The motto seems to be, alas: "Get what the traffic will bear."

The Hawaiian "season," incidentally, has little to do with the weather, which is usually good year round. Hawaii's climate is subtropical, with spring-like temperatures averaging about 75 degrees and seldom going more than 6 or 7 degrees above or below this point. In midwinter you can occasionally get some "raw" days in the low-to-mid-60's and in midsummer some humid ones in the 80s. (August is probably the most humid month of the year; if your room does not have cross-ventilation to allow the trade winds to come through, air conditioning is essential at that time.) Cool waters drifting down from the Bering Sea make the islands ten degrees cooler than other places in the same latitude—and the trade winds provide balmy breezes. As for rain, we must admit that we have experienced some dreary, rainy days here, especially in the winter—anytime from November to March. But most of the time showers are brief and seldom heavy enough to spoil the pleasures of a vacation.

A BIT OF GEOGRAPHY: Most people think of Hawaii as synonymous with Honolulu and Waikiki Beach (they probably know they're on the island of Oahu), but they're a bit vague about the names of the other islands. Actually, there are 122 islands in the Hawaiian chain, a great volcanic mountain range spreading 1500 miles across the floor of the Pacific, from Hawaii on the southeast to Midway and Kure islands in the northwest. Many of these are just jagged rocks or sand shoals, however, and the term "Hawaiian Islands" usually refers only to eight: Oahu (on which you find Honolulu), Hawaii or the Big Island, Maui, Kauai, Molokai, Lanai, Kahoolawe, and Niihau. The first five are the ones of greatest interest to the visitor, and the ones we'll describe in this book. Of the last three, Lanai is a pineapple plantation island, almost completely owned by Castle & Cooke, the parent company of the Dole Pineapple Company; Kahoolawe, uninhabited, is a target range for American planes and ships; and Niihau, where an ancient Hawaiian community survives, is private property not open to the public.

ISLANDER ORIGINS: The Hawaiian Islands were settled about a thousand years ago by Polynesians who came most likely from Tahiti, crossing the Pacific in outrigger canoes and performing feats of navigation undreamed of by their European contemporaries. They were Stone Age men, blissfully unaware of the modern world until Captain Cook inadvertently discovered the islands in 1778 (he was seeking the Northwest Passage) and received a god's welcome. He named them the Sandwich Islands, in honor of the Earl of Sandwich. Then came fur traders, merchants, whaling men, adventurers from all over, to the crossroads of the Pacific and its languorous pleasure ports. In 1820, from Boston, arrived other travelers, those who would settle the islands and, more than any others, determine Hawaii's pattern of civilization. These were the missionaries, earnest men intent on converting the "childlike" heathen to the no-nonsense Calvinism of New England. The missionaries never went home; their children stayed to inherit the islands and their riches, to create the great business empires that still rule Hawaii. The Polynesians sickened and dwindled and refused to work the white man's sugar and pineapple plantations. But the poor of the Orient came, tens of thousands of them—contract labor pursuing the dream of a better life. (In the great mainland cities at the same time, the dispossessed of Europe were finding their America.) Somehow the welcoming aloha of the islands found a way to absorb them all. Now the era of settling the land is over, and today's "immigrants" are Japanese, Filipinos, and many, many mainland haoles: Westchester businessmen, California schoolteachers, tourists from all over who fall in love with the islands and forget to go home.

REQUIRED READING: Don't—this is a must—get on the plane without having read James Michener's great epic novel of the islands, *Hawaii;* not to do so would be as bad as forgetting your bathing suit. Michener has taken a leading figure from each of the groups who settled in the islands—the Polynesians, American missionaries, Chinese, Japanese—and through their stories, told the story of the islands. The book, which is available in paperback, will illuminate your trip as nothing else will. According to Michener, Francine du Plessix Gray's *Hawaii: The Sugar-Coated Fortress,* published by Random House, picks up where his book left off, and we agree with that judgment. It is not a novel, but an insightful, uncompromising look at what is really happening in modern Hawaii. (This one is no longer available in the bookstores, but you should be able to get it at the public library.) A new book, *Hawaii: An Uncommon History,* by Edward Koesting, published by W. W. Norton & Co., has received high critical praise and is well worth your time. So, too, certainly, is Gavan Daws's *A Shoal of Time,* a history of Hawaii from 1778 (Captain Cook) until statehood (1959), published by the University of Hawaii Press. For more about Hawaii's background, read Ben Adams's *Hawaii, The Aloha State,* a beautifully lucid history of the islands, published by Hill and Wang and available in any library, as is Lawrence Fuch's *Hawaii Pono,* published by Harcourt Brace Jovanovich, a masterful sociological study. *A Hawaiian Reader,* a delightful anthology of pieces on Hawaii past and present written by, among others, Jack London, Robert Louis Stevenson, and Somerset Maugham, also makes absorbing reading before, during, or after a stay in the islands. This one's in paperback too.

KNOWING SOME HAWAIIAN: You don't have to learn the language, since everyone speaks English. But the islanders do pepper their vocabulary with lots of Hawaiian words, and almost all place names are Hawaiian. So it's a good idea to bone up on a few pronunciation rules and learn a few words. The original Hawaiians spoke a Polynesian dialect but they had no written language; the missionaries transcribed it in order to teach them to read the Bible, and they made it as easy as possible. There are only 12 letters in the alphabet: the five vowels and seven consonants: *h, k, l, m, n, p, w*. Every syllable ends in a vowel; every vowel is pronounced no matter how many there are in the word (these have a frightening way of piling up one after another); and the accent is almost always on the penultimate syllable (the next to the last), as it is in Spanish. Consonants receive their English sounds, but vowels get the Latin pronunciation: *a* as in farm, *e* as in they, *i* as in machine, *o* as in cold, and *u* as in tutor.

Lists of Hawaiian words can be obtained in most tourist offices, but check out our Appendix—"A Hawaiian Vocabulary"—first. Do bear in mind that the name of the state is pronounced Ha-wye-ee (it does not rhyme with how-are-yuh). You are a newcomer, a malihini (mah-lee-hee-nee), and longtime residents of the islands are kamaainas (kama-eye-nahs). The haoles (properly pronounced ha-o-lays, but more commonly how-lays) are the whites, originally foreigners.

The mysterious lanai (lah-neye) that landlords are always boasting about is nothing but a balcony or porch. Kau kau (cow-cow) means food; you'll go to a lot of luaus (loo-ows); and people will say thank you—rather, mahalo (mah-hah-low)—for your kokua (ko-koo-ah), your help. It's kanes (kay-nays) for men, wahines (wah-hee-nays) for women. You already know that a lei (lay) is a necklace of flowers. And just as you expected, everyone says aloha (ah-low-hah)—one of the most beautiful words in any language—meaning hello, good-bye, good luck, and salud! It also means love, as in "I send you my aloha."

THE ALOHA SPIRIT: The warm, welcoming hospitality of the islanders is perhaps the thing that most impresses the visitor, who usually goes back home and reports to friends: "I couldn't get over the people—they're the nicest I've met anywhere." One celebrated visitor expressed it very well. Mrs. Jacqueline Kennedy Onassis, returning home after a visit here with her family some years back, wrote to the editors of the *Honolulu Advertiser and Star Bulletin* (who had asked the public to give the Kennedys privacy and assigned no reporters or photographers to follow them around): ". . . In this strange land everyone constantly goes out of his way to be kind to the other. From Governor Burns, who so kindly watched over us and asked people to help make our visit private, to the driver of a vegetable truck who went out of his way to lead us several miles, when we merely asked for directions, everyone in Hawaii has been the same. Now I know what the Aloha spirit means. I hope it is contagious—for it could change the world."

A FEW MATTERS OF USAGE: It's preferable to refer to the residents of the 50th state as "islanders," rather than as natives or Hawaiians—unless they happen to be of Hawaiian descent. You are from the mainland, not the States; islanders are very sensitive about this. And don't make the dreadful mistake of calling Americans of Japanese ancestry "Japs." They're as proud of being Americans as any descendants of the *Mayflower* passengers. During World War II, in fact, the Nisei volunteers so distinguished themselves in the bloody battles of southern Europe that their unit—the 442nd Regimental Combat Team—was designated "probably the most decorated unit in United States military history." One of its veterans is Daniel K. Inouye (of Watergate investigation fame), chosen as Hawaii's first representative in Congress, now its senior senator. Spark M. Matsunaga, now its junior senator, is also a veteran of the 442nd. Remember, too, that although statehood was achieved only in 1959, residents of Hawaii have been American citizens since 1898, when, five years after the Hawaiian monarchy was overthrown in a bloodless revolution (a triumph for the haole sugar and other commercial interests), the Republic of Hawaii was annexed by the government of President McKinley.

INCIDENTAL INTELLIGENCE: One of the nicest things about going to Hawaii is that you don't have to get one single shot, you don't have to fiddle with passports or visas, or have the slightest worry about unsanitary food or polluted drinking water. Standards of sanitation are very high, and the islands have an excellent supply of pure water. As far as health goes, Hawaii is way ahead of the rest of the United States: a male child has a life expectancy of 74 years compared to 66.5 on the mainland; a female child has a life expectancy of 78.1 compared to 73 for women in the 49 other states.

AREA CODE: All of the Hawaiian islands share one area code number: it's 808. The only area code numbers we list in the text are the 800, toll-free numbers.

A WORD FROM OUR READERS: As the years have gone by (this book is now in its 20th edition), we have printed hundreds of Readers' Selections and Readers' Suggestions. If you come across any particularly appealing hotel, restaurant, beach, shop, bargain—please don't keep it to yourself. We'll send free copies of the next edition of this book to readers whose suggestions are used. And this applies to any comments you may have about the existing listings: the fact that a hotel or restaurant is recommended in this edition doesn't mean that it will necessarily appear in future editions if readers report that its service has slipped, that bugs have gotten out of hand (something which, alas, happens now and then in this climate), or that prices have risen unreasonably. Send your comments to us, Faye Hammel and Sylvan Levey, c/o Frommer/Pasmantier Publishers, 1230 Avenue of the Americas, New York, NY 10020. We regret that we cannot personally answer the many hundreds of letters we receive each year. You can, however, be sure that your letter is carefully read and that we are grateful for your comments.

To those of our readers who follow the Readers' Selections listed at the end of most chapters, we should also add a word of caution: we cannot personally vouch for these selections, since we have not seen and tried most of them for ourselves. Our general experience, however, has been that 90% of them are excellent. We also try to give a cross-section of opinion on various establishments, knowing that somebody's great little discovery may be somebody else's great little disaster. But that's all part of the fun of traveling and discovering.

INFLATION: We don't have to tell you that inflation has hit Hawaii as it has everywhere else. For that reason it is quite possible that prices may be slightly higher at a given establishment when you read this book than they were at the time this information was collected in late 1984. This may be especially true of restaurant prices. Be that as it may, we feel sure these selections will still represent the best travel bargains in the islands.

And please don't be one of those nonunderstanding types (we understand there are some!) who become furious with proprietors whose current rates have gone up above the prices mentioned here. Remember that the prices we give here are the most specific the proprietors could project as we went to press. Remember too that this book is revised each year to keep prices as accurate as possible; always be sure you are reading the very latest copy available.

SAFETY: Yes, it's true; there is crime and violence in Hawaii, as there is everywhere else in the world. Only, because Hawaii was indeed a trouble-free paradise for so many years, people tend to ignore basic safety precautions. Our advice is: *Don't.* Don't go hiking on deserted trails except in a group; don't go wandering on isolated beaches alone; and don't go jogging in the canefields alone at the crack of dawn, as one recent crime victim did. Stay in well-lighted areas at night, travel with a friend if possible, lock your car and remove valuables from your trunk, and use your common sense—just as you would at home. Follow these precautions, and you should find a visit to Hawaii no more dangerous than one to your own hometown.

The $25-a-Day Travel Club—How to Save Money on All Your Travels

In this book we'll be looking at how to get your money's worth in Hawaii, but there is a "device" for saving money and determining value on *all* your trips. It's the popular, international $25-a-Day Travel Club, now in its 22nd successful year of operation. The Club was formed at the urging of numerous readers of the $$$-a-Day and Dollarwise Guides, who felt that such an organization could provide continuing travel information and a sense of community to value-minded travelers in all parts of the world. And so it does!

In keeping with the budget concept, the annual membership fee is low and is immediately exceeded by the value of your benefits. Upon receipt of $15 (U.S. residents), or $18 U.S. by check drawn on a U.S. bank or via international postal money order in U.S. funds (Canadian, Mexican, and other foreign residents) to cover one year's membership, we will send all new members the following items:

(1) *Any two* of the following books

Please designate in your letter which two you wish to receive:

Europe on $25 a Day
Australia on $25 a Day
England and Scotland on $25 a Day
Greece on $25 a Day
Hawaii on $35 a Day
India on $15 & $25 a Day
Ireland on $25 a Day
Israel on $30 & $35 a Day
Mexico on $20 a Day
New York on $35 a Day
New Zealand on $20 & $25 a Day
Scandinavia on $25 a Day
South America on $25 a Day
Spain and Morocco (plus the Canary Is.) on $25 a Day
Washington, D.C. on $35 a Day

Dollarwise Guide to Austria and Hungary
Dollarwise Guide to Canada
Dollarwise Guide to the Caribbean (including Bermuda and the Bahamas)
Dollarwise Guide to Egypt
Dollarwise Guide to England and Scotland
Dollarwise Guide to France
Dollarwise Guide to Germany
Dollarwise Guide to Italy

Dollarwise Guide to the Northwest
Dollarwise Guide to Portugal (plus Madeira and the Azores)
Dollarwise Guide to the Southwest
Dollarwise Guide to Switzerland and Liechtenstein
Dollarwise Guide to California and Las Vegas
Dollarwise Guide to Florida
Dollarwise Guide to New England
Dollarwise Guide to the Southeast and New Orleans
(Dollarwise Guides discuss accommodations and facilities in all price ranges, with emphasis on the medium-priced.)

Dollarwise Guide to Cruises (including Alaska, Canada, the Caribbean, Hawaii, Mexico, Panama and the U.S.)
(This complete guide covers all the basics for ships cruising the above areas: ports of call, selecting your ship, fly-cruise packages, what to pack, customs, types of cabins, cuisine—and more.)

Bed & Breakfast—North America
(An indespensable directory of all the major bed & breakfast organizations, the types & price ranges of accommodations they offer, plus nearby attractions—by one of America's top travel experts.)

How to Beat the High Cost of Travel
(This practical guide details how to save money on absolutely all travel items—accommodations, transportation, dining, sightseeing, shopping, taxes, and more. Includes special budget information for seniors, students, singles, and families.)

The New York Urban Athlete
(The ultimate guide to all the sports facilities in New York City for jocks and novices.)

Museums in New York
(A complete guide to all the museums, historic houses, gardens, zoos, and more in the five boroughs. Illustrated with over 200 photographs.)

The Fast 'n' Easy Phrase Book
(The four most useful languages—French, German, Spanish, and Italian—all in one convenient, easy-to-use phrase guide.)

Where to Stay USA
(By the Council on International Educational Exchange, this extraordinary guide is the first to list accommodations in all 50 states that cost anywhere from $3 to $25 per night.)

A Guide for the Disabled Traveler
(A guide to the best destinations for wheelchair travelers and other disabled vacationers in Europe, the United States, and Canada by an experienced wheelchair traveler. Includes detailed information about accommodations, restaurants, sights, transportation, and their accessibility.)

Marilyn Wood's Wonderful Weekends
(This very selective guide covers the best mini-vacation destinations

within a 175-mile radius of New York City. It describes special country inns and other accommodations, restaurants, picnic spots, sights, and activities—all the information needed for a two- or three-day stay.)

(2) A one-year subscription to *The Wonderful World of Budget Travel*

This quarterly eight-page tabloid newspaper keeps you up to date on fast-breaking developments in low-cost travel in all parts of the world bringing you the latest money-saving information—the kind of information you'd have to pay $25 a year to obtain elsewhere. This consumer-conscious publication also features columns of special interest to readers: **The Traveler's Directory** (members all over the world who are willing to provide hospitality to other members as they pass through their home cities); **Share-a-Trip** (offers and requests from members for travel companions who can share costs and help avoid the burdensome single supplement); and **Readers Ask . . . Readers Reply** (travel questions from members to which other members reply with authentic firsthand information).

(3) A copy of *Arthur Frommer's Guide to New York*

This is a pocket-size guide to hotels, restaurants, nightspots, and sightseeing attractions in all price ranges throughout the New York area.

(4) Your personal membership card

Your membership entitles you to purchase through the Club all Arthur Frommer publications for a third to a half off their regular retail prices during the term of your membership.

So why not join this hardy band of international budgeteers and participate in its exchange of travel information and hospitality? Simply send your name and address, together with your annual membership fee of $15 (U.S. residents) or $18 U.S. (Canadian, Mexican, and other foreign residents), by check drawn on a U.S. bank or via international postal money order in U.S. funds to: $25-A-Day Travel Club, Inc., Frommer/Pasmantier Publishers, 1230 Avenue of the Americas, New York, NY 10020. And please remember to specify which *two* of the books in section (1) above you wish to receive in your initial package of members' benefits. Or, if you prefer, use the last page of this book, simply checking off the two books you select and enclosing $15 or $18 in U.S. currency.

ABOUT THIS BOOK: And now, here's how to plan to handle the details of low-cost Hawaiian living.

Chapter I describes the easiest and the cheapest ways to get to the islands and gives you information on packing to save money.

Chapter II gets you off the plane, onto the island of Oahu and into the city of Honolulu, and outlines the best hotel bargains in Honolulu, especially in the heart of the tourist scene, Waikiki Beach.

Chapter III takes you to Honolulu restaurants, on and off the beaten tourist path, where an appetizing meal costs less than you would expect—and to the inexpensive nightspots all over town.

Chapter IV discusses the pros and cons of guided tours, taxis, bus trips, and auto rentals, and delves into the cheapest way of getting around the fabulous city of Honolulu.

Chapter V tells you about the enormous range of activities and entertainment available in Honolulu at little or no cost—with a rundown on beaches, sports, free classes, concerts, films, folk festivals, art galleries, and learning the hula, to mention just a few.

Chapter VI is devoted to shopping in Hawaii—where to buy items ranging from muumuus to orchids to macadamia nuts, concentrating on bargains, of course.

Chapter VII provides an alternative to the expensive guided tour: seven do-it-yourself bus and walking trips in Honolulu, only one of which should cost you more than $1 for transportation.

Chapter VIII takes you out of Honolulu, for a low-cost, never-to-be-forgotten drive around the island of Oahu.

Chapter IX outlines the ABCs of Honolulu living.

Chapter X gives you the basic orientation on traveling in the neighbor islands: Kauai, Hawaii, Maui, and Molokai.

Chapter XI introduces you to the Garden Isle of Kauai and gives you the essentials on hotels, restaurants, car rentals, and the night scene.

Chapter XII takes you sightseeing in Kauai.

Chapter XIII describes the biggest island in the 50th state—Hawaii. Essentials again: hotels, restaurants, car rentals, nightlife.

Chapter XIV takes you sightseeing on the Big Island.

Chapter XV provides all the basics about the island of Maui.

Chapter XVI shows you the sights on Maui.

Chapter XVII takes you to Hawaii's newest tourist destination: Molokai.

The *Appendix* offers a Hawaiian vocabulary.

ADDITIONAL SOURCES: For further information on traveling and living in Hawaii, you can contact the **Hawaii Visitors Bureau (HVB),** which has offices in the following cities:

Los Angeles—Room 502, Central Plaza, 3440 Wilshire Blvd., Los Angeles, CA 90010 (tel. 213/385-5301).

San Francisco—Room 615, Brooks Bros. Building, 209 Post St., San Francisco, CA 94108 (tel. 415/392-8173). *(Note:* The California offices request that you write to the main office in Honolulu—see below—instead of contacting them).

Chicago—Suite 1031, 180 N. Michigan Ave., Chicago, IL 60602 (tel. 312/236-0632).

New York—Room 1407, 441 Lexington Ave., New York, NY 10017 (tel. 212/986-9203).

Vancouver, B.C.—4915 Cedar Crescent, Tsawwassen, Delta, BC V4M 1J9

In Hawaii, the **HVB** offices are as follows:

Oahu—Suite 801, Waikiki Business Plaza, 2270 Kalakaua Ave., Honolulu, HI 96815; or P.O. Box 8527, Honolulu, HI 96815 (tel. 808/923-1811).

Hawaii—75-5719 W. Alii Drive, Kailua-Kona, HI 96740 (tel. 808/329-1782); or Suite 104, Hilo Plaza, 180 Kinoole St., Hilo, HI 96720 (tel. 808/935-5271).

Maui—25 North Puunene Ave., Kahului, Maui, HI 96732 (tel. 808/877-7822).

Kauai—Suite 207, Lihue Plaza Building, 3016 Umi St. (or Kauai P.O. Box 507), Lihue, Kauai, HI 96766 (tel. 808/245-3971).

READERS' TIPS ON BOOKS AND MAPS: "Your reading list should include *Plants of Hawaii National Parks* by Otto Degener, $4.50, paperback, available in most of the larger bookstores and in the National Park Service visitor centers. Far more than a botanical guide, it contains fascinating essays on Polynesian and modern uses of various plants. One can learn to make poi, tapa cloth, and many other things. It also goes into the history and religious practices of the Hawaiians. We used it every day. It is a gold mine" (David and Marilynn Rowland, Oakland, Calif.). . . . "The best, most comprehensive, and altogether most fascinating work on Hawaii is Frederich Simpich, Jr.'s *Anatomy of Hawaii* (Coward-McCann Geoghegan Inc., 1971; Library of Congress 78-146101). Mr. Simpich's discussion of early Hawaii, modern Hawaii, the land, the military influence, the social scene, tourism, politics, and island psychology and sociology is the most concise and interesting I have read anywhere" (Hobbs A. Brown, Mesa, Ariz.). . . . "As an addition to your recommended reading on Hawaii, I would suggest the 'on the spot' account by Lucien Young, U.S.N., in *The Real Hawaii, Its History and Present Condition, Including the True Story of the Revolution (American Imperialism—Viewpoints of U.S. Foreign Policy, 1898-1941)*, reprint edition published by Arno Press, N.Y., 1970, covering the author's personal observations of the political situation in 1892 and 1893 and later years. It provides another perspective (and background) to Michener's *Hawaii* and du Plessix Gray's *Hawaii: The Sugar-Coated Fortress*" (Donna Inguerson, Calgary, Alberta, Canada). . . . "For those who like books about the islands, might I suggest *Above Hawaii* by Cameron, with pictures from the satellite and then present-day and 50-year-ago pictures of the same site—really gorgeous photography" (Mr. and Mrs. B. D. Riley, Rockford, Ill.). . . . "For a background to the islands, we recommend Insight Guides' *Hawaii* by APA Productions, 1980, 413 pages, $7.95 in paperback. Hundreds of color photos. Sensitive and accurate text. A combination guide and history" (Larry Sprecher, Beaverton, Ore.).

"I would hope that you could include Euell Gibbons's *Beachcombers' Guide* and *The Rising Sun* by John Toland, or Gordon Prange's *At Dawn We Slept*, as further enlightenment. These last two are essentially historical rather than political and give quite a challenge and stimulus to some of the historical and geographical highlights to one's interest" (Bob Thompson, Stockton, Calif.). . . . "Let me say a word about the Hawaiian people. We found them to be some of the warmest, most gracious and delightful people we have ever encountered anywhere. They were truly a joy. They welcomed us with 'Aloha,' thanked us with 'Mahalo,' were helpful at every turn with information, answers, and advice we could benefit from. I don't recall encountering an Ugly Hawaiian—not just the waiters, waitresses, bellhops, and taxi drivers who depended on tips—but all of them. The rest of us Americans could benefit so much by their attitude!" (Jim Cox, Middletown, Ky.).

"For those who really want to get the feel of the history of Hawaii, but who have already read Michener and don't want to get into history books, there is no better source than the three beautifully written novels by O. A. Bushnell, which begin with Captain Cook and carry through until the end of the monarchy. They are exciting, enjoyable, and tremendously informative in a painless way. They are: *The Return of Lono* ($4.95, paper); *Kaawa* ($10, hardback only); and *Molokai* ($5.95, paper). Many public libraries carry all three volumes, but for those who would like to buy them, they are available from the Book Department of *Aloha*, The Magazine of Hawaii, P.O. Box 3260, Honolulu, HI 96801" (William S. McDonald, Houston, Texas). . . . "Thor Heyerdahl's book *Early Man and the Ocean* has an excellent section on Hawaii, pages 164 to 184. Reading these will make visits to the Bishop Museum and the Academy of Arts much more enlightening" (Mrs. Lydia Marie Matz, Lehigh Acres, Fla.).

"We think your suggestion to read du Plessix Gray's *Hawaii: The Sugar-Coated Fortress* was invaluable—such easy, fascinating reading! May we also recommend the American Wilderness/Time-Life Books' *Hawaii* by Robert Wallace. The photography and text are both outstanding, for those who are interested in the natural beauty of all of Hawaii" (Mary and Donald Lee, Chicago, Ill.). . . . "I would like to recommend the five beautiful pictorial books by Robert Wenkam; his photography is superb and his thoughts about the people and the environment are really excellent. *Honolulu Is an Island* is surely a book to reminisce with. *Hawaii* has 150 full-color photographs of Kauai, Oahu, Maui, Molokai, Hawaii, and Lanai. *Maui: The Last Hawaiian Place, Kauai and the Park Country of Hawaii,* and *The Big Island Hawaii* are the other three. These books cost about $25 each, but they are available in libraries and it's enjoyable to read them and look at the photographic beauty of Hawaii" (Margaret Niezgoda, Calumet City, Ill.). *[Authors' Note:* Agreed: These are books to treasure.] . . . "I picked up a most interesting historical novel of Hawaii, covering the period from approximately 1820 to 1850, called *To Raise a Nation,* by Mary Cooke, at the airport on the way home. I wish I had read it on the way to Hawaii instead" (Carole McIvor, Calgary, Alberta, Canada). . . . "The best maps of Oahu island are now available from the State of Hawaii, Department of Transportation, Highway Planning Branch, Honolulu. These maps are available to the public at nominal cost. There are also maps available from the Map Information Center, Denver, Colo., prepared by the U.S. Geological Survey" (David C. Moore, Phoenix, Ariz.).

Chapter I

GETTING THERE

1. The Fares
2. Inter-Island Travel
3. Packing to Save Money

WHAT WILL IT COST you to travel to Hawaii? We wish we could tell you precisely, but our crystal ball is cloudy. Ever since the federal government reduced its tight regulation of the airline industry, competition —and massive confusion—have set in. Fares can vary from airline to airline, and even within one airline, depending on when you're going, how long you're staying, whether you make land arrangements through the airlines, and how long in advance you book your ticket. Or fares can vary depending on what new, low-cost gimmick one airline might introduce to beat the competition. But you can rely on this: the airlines want your business, and the 2400-mile route from California to the Hawaiian Islands is a highly competitive one. A little smart shopping on your part and that of your trusted travel agent will usually turn up a good deal.

1. The Fares

Low fares to Hawaii can now be had from World Airways, which started Honolulu service just a few years ago. At this writing, their one-way rates were from $169 to $189 from Los Angeles, $199 to $219 from Oakland, $526 to $606 roundtrip from either Newark or Baltimore, with a seven-day advance booking. One-way fares from Newark and Baltimore are $283 to $333. There is also a special $476 roundtrip fare between Newark or Baltimore and Honolulu if you fly on a Tuesday or Wednesday. Flights are also available from Kansas City from $273 to $323 one way, $476 roundtrip Tuesday and Wednesday, $526 to $606 roundtrip with seven-day advance booking. World Airways flies 384-passenger DC-10s, serves meals, cocktails, and even shows movies—everything you expect from the better known airlines. The only problem is that they run only one departure a day from each of the above-mentioned cities, which means that booking a seat exactly when you want it is difficult.

As for flying on one of the new airlines that seem to crop up every six months or so with bargain fares to the islands, we can only repeat to you what a very wise person in the travel industry has stated: "To be perfectly sure that the airline doesn't go out of business and leave you holding your tickets, fly only on reputable carriers that you know have been in business for at least five years." Sounds like good advice to us.

The other major carriers flying into Honolulu are United, American,

Northwest Orient, Pan Am, Western, and Continental. All occasionally offer special bargain flights and excursions. United offers the most flights to Hawaii, and its "Hawaiian Excursion" fares offer real value, at approximately 60% of regular coach fare—the kind of fare that in the past has only been available to those flying in groups. Airfares change constantly, and it is highly likely that the fares you actually pay will be different than these, but for the record, and for purposes of comparison, United's 30-day excursion fares, to and from Honolulu, at the time of this writing were, for all cities Denver and east—including Boston, New York, Washington, D.C., Detroit and Chicago—$499 roundtrip Tuesdays and Wednesdays; $549 Mondays, Thursdays, and Fridays; $629 Saturdays and Sundays. To qualify for these flights, you must purchase your tickets at least 14 days in advance, stay at least until the first Sunday after your arrival, and for not more than 30 days. There are some holiday blackout periods. From the West Coast, it works this way: one-way fares from San Francisco to Honolulu are $239 Saturdays and Sundays, $219 other days; from Los Angeles, $209 and $189; from Seattle, $219 and $209.

Again, need we tell you—in these crazy inflationary times any prices quoted here are subject to change.

DIRECT TO THE NEIGHBOR ISLANDS: Here's good news for repeat visitors who may wish to drop Honolulu from their itinerary and go directly to Maui, Kauai, or the Big Island (or route their trips to start on the neighbor islands and end in Honolulu). United, the only carrier to go to all four major islands, now has three daily nonstops and one daily one-stop from Los Angeles to Maui; one daily nonstop and one daily one-stop from San Francisco to Maui; one daily nonstop from Seattle to Maui. To Kona, on the Big Island, they offer one daily nonstop and one daily one-stop from Los Angeles, and one daily nonstop from San Francisco. To Hilo on the Big Island, there is one daily nonstop from Los Angeles. And you can go directly to Lihue, Kauai, from Los Angeles, one daily nonstop. To figure the cost of these flights, add approximately $50 to one-way Honolulu fares (subject to change).

GROUP TOURS: Some excellent values are available on group tours, for short periods of one to two weeks. Of course, we prefer the do-it-yourself brand of travel, but if you do want a group trip, consult your travel agent for a variety of choices.

THE ROYAL TREATMENT: We gave up a long time ago counting how many trips we've taken to Hawaii in the past 20 years or so, but we remember very well the especially delightful one we made via United Airlines last summer. Still caught up in the big-city atmosphere of Los Angeles, it came as a pleasant shock to find ourselves surrounded at the gate by Kahili poles, tiki gods, tapa cloth, birds of paradise, and anthuriums, all part of United's Royal Hawaiian Service. Culture shock continued as we were welcomed aboard the wide-bodied 747 jet (United offers them on most flights from the West Coast) Hawaiian style, with island music, and greeted by flight attendants in muumuus and aloha shirts. (United always has at least one Hawaiian flight attendant on board.) Mainland tension disappeared quickly as we relaxed with island music and studied the attractive menu describing the Polynesian dishes that had been prepared for us. By the time dinner was served, home could have been at least a million miles away. Our salad of Polynesian mixed vegetables came served on a monkey-pod tray garnished with crispy vegetable sticks, pineapple wedges, and—shades of the islands!—an orchid. Our Polynesian entree was a delicately seasoned pineapple chicken—but it might have been teriyaki chicken, Hawaiian pork roast, or sesame pork. Dessert was macadamia nut carrot cake. (On other flights, diners are offered a choice of either a Hawaiian or a mainland style meal; we prefer the Hawaiian, with delicious island treats like vegetable sushi, coconut shrimp, beef teriyaki brochette, breast of chicken with plum glaze.) We watched a movie, noticed that the hours were skimming away, and by the time we were approaching the islands we knew again what aloha was all about.

JET LAG: If you're going all the way through from the East Coast to Honolulu or Hilo in one stretch—about ten air hours—you'll be crossing at least six time zones, and your normal body rhythms are going to be thrown out of sync. Here are some tips from the experts in avoiding jet lag. First, they advise that several days before your departure, you gradually accommodate your eating and sleeping times to be closer to those of your destination. You'll be heading west, so go to bed a little later each night and sleep a little later in the morning. When you come home, reverse that pattern. Second, avoid smoking, drinking, and heavy eating in flight—another reason to bring your own picnic lunch! You may have heard of the Argonne Anti-Jet-Lag Diet, which alternates feasting and fasting for several days before departure, and is effective for many people. To get a free copy of the program, send a stamped, self-addressed envelope to Office of Public Affairs, Argonne National Laboratory, 9700 South Cass Ave., Argonne, IL 60439. Our personal prescription for avoiding jet lag is to stop off at one of the airport hotels in either Los Angeles or San Francisco en route, have a swim in the pool and a good night's sleep, and arrive in Hawaii the next day refreshed.

THE TRIP BY SHIP: Forget about it. There is no crossing to Hawaii that costs less than the lowest air fares. Only luxury ships now call at Honolulu Harbor.

ANOTHER TIP: Try not to arrive in Hawaii on a weekend, when Honolulu is crowded with visitors from the outer islands. Everything is easier and less crowded on weekdays, especially checking into hotels, and air fares are lower during the week as well.

TIME TRICKS: Don't forget that you'll be flying into yesterday when you head for Hawaii from mainland U.S.. You pick up an extra five hours in flight (six during daylight saving time) if you're starting from the East Coast, three hours if you begin on the West Coast. Going home, of course, you lose the hours and can find yourself leaving this afternoon and arriving tomorrow morning.

2. Inter-Island Travel

THE FARES: Alas, the good old days when travelers coming from the mainland could book their inter-island flights for tiny prices are long gone. The Common Fare program has been phased out, and now there is a point-to-point fare, which means that each time you want to visit another island—and most people will want to see at least two or three—it can cost you as much as $50.

However, there are a couple of ways to play the budget game. The first is to book whatever flights you can on **Mid Pacific Air,** the newest of the inter-island carriers, which operates comfortable new 60-passenger turbo-props out of Honolulu Airport. Regular fares are $43 to Maui, the Big Island, or Kauai (as opposed to $50 on **Hawaiian Airlines** or **Aloha Airlines,** the major jet carriers). The best deal of all is to go standby, when the fare is a rock-bottom $28.95.

As for Hawaiian Airlines and Aloha Airlines, they also keep the budget traveler well in mind with a variety of price-savers. Hawaiian Airlines has two price structures: $50 to the major islands on jet equipment, $43.95 on De Havilland Dash 7 50-seat turbo props. Both Hawaiian and Aloha offer standby fares of $31.95 (on Hawaiian, standby for the turbo props is $28.95), and both offer Joint Fares at $47. Joint Fare means that you have a regular roundtrip or excursion ticket from the mainland; it does not apply to foreign flights. They also offer a $5 membership in their travel clubs, which brings the fare down to $47 (on Hawaiian, $39.95 for the turbo props). In addition, they have senior citizen, military, youth group and capacity-controlled fares (a certain number of seats are discounted). These quotes are one-way fares. Note that all three inter-island carriers offer periodic promotional fares and tie-ins with hotel and car packages, so it pays to do some personal research on this, either by calling the airlines direct, or with your travel agent before you book. Remember that rates change constantly, and that the rates quoted here are very much subject to change. Again, be sure to check with the airlines or your travel agent for the latest developments.

As for standbys, we've had good luck with them and so have many of our readers. Unless it's a very, very busy period, the planes do not fill up completely, and even if they do, flights are so frequent that you're sure to get one fairly soon.

Should you wish to call the airlines, here are their **toll-free numbers:** Hawaiian Air: 800/367-5320; Aloha Airlines, 800/367-5250; Mid Pacific Airlines, 800/367-7010.

SCHEDULING SECRETS: Now that United is running its big jets directly into Maui, Kona, Hilo, and Lihue, it's not necessary to both arrive at and depart from Honolulu; you can be more flexible with your itinerary. You might, for example, start in Honolulu, travel from there to Kauai, then to Maui, from there to Molokai, and on to Hilo, where you pick up your plane for your return flight to Los Angeles. Another routing that we have found very pleasant is to fly directly to Hilo from Los Angeles, then on to Maui, Molokai, and Kauai, making the last stop Honolulu, and departing from there to home. (Plan it this way if you want peace and quiet first, excitement later.)

3. Packing to Save Money

Another important way to save money on your Hawaiian trip is to give careful thought to the clothes you take and the way you pack. First rule is *not* to go on a big shopping spree in advance. If you need to fill out your wardrobe, do it in Hawaii, where the stores are packed with colorful island resort clothes at prices cheaper than those you'll probably pay at home (see our shopping chapter).

Second important rule: Pack a light suitcase and take only one piece of luggage per person (you can also carry a small travel bag for reading matter on the plane, then use it later as a beach bag). If you can carry your own bag, you are your own person and not dependent on expensive porters and bellboys and taxis. Having a light bag (or at least one of those wheeled luggage carriers) is practically essential, since it is often quite difficult to locate porters at the airports, and in small hotels you are usually expected to carry your own luggage. If you happen to arrive at a new place without hotel reservations, being able to manage your own luggage will enable you to look around instead of grabbing anything that gives you a chance to put your bags down. Therefore get yourself the lightest suitcase you can buy (the cloth ones are good, roomy bets), and leave at least one-third of the space for bringing back the things you'll buy in Hawaii. Do buy all your luggage before you go; it will be more expensive in Hawaii.

Most important, don't burden yourself with several large bags. By what we dub the Hammel-Levey Amendment to Parkinson's Law, the contents of a suitcase have a way of expanding to fit the space available.

CONTENTS: What will you need to take with you? Easy does it. It's much simpler to pack for Hawaii than it is for Europe or almost anyplace else. You need only spring or summer clothes and then of the simplest kind. There are no extreme variations in temperature between day and night, so you do not need the usual all-purpose travel coat or overcoat you'd take to Europe or Mexico—unless you're coming from the eastern United States and plan to spend a few days in San Francisco on the way back; then you'll have good use for it. A light raincoat is helpful, and so is a folding umbrella—and let's hope you won't need them! Women will find a stole or shawl useful at night. The only heavy garment that you will require is a warm sweater or hooded parka for exploring the volcano regions on the islands of Hawaii and Maui. Good canvas or other heavy-soled hiking shoes and socks are a must for hiking or for trekking over recent lava flows on Hawaii.

For Men

We're not going to give specifics on what to take, since you know what you like. We will tell you, however, that island dress is extremely casual, and many of our readers say they've never worn a suit in the islands! Some of the fancier places do require a jacket for dinner, however. It's easier to travel with drip-dry shirts and underclothing, but not necessary since the islands are dotted with quick-service launderettes (many apartment-hotels have their own), so you can have a stack of clothes washed and ready to wear in a few hours. Plan on buying a colorful aloha shirt when you're in Hawaii (it's worn outside the trousers and cut a little fuller than the usual sports shirt). You can use it back home for beach or country wear.

For Women

Before you begin to pack your bag, you'll want to know a little bit about what women wear in Hawaii. Allow us to introduce you to the muumuu, the most comfortable garment known to woman. Try one and see. They're loose enough to provide their own inner air conditioning, require a minimum of underwear underneath (the girdle industry must be nonexistent in Hawaii), and look pretty enough to flatter almost everybody —especially large women, who look positively graceful in them. (You'll see more than a few of these hefty Polynesian ladies, by the way, a carry-over from the days when the alii, the nobility, cultivated fat as a royal status symbol.)

The thing we love most about Hawaiian fashion is that many, many women wear muumuus or other long dresses outdoors, especially at night: it seems Hawaii discovered the maxi back in the days of the missionaries. You'll see full-flowing muumuus (the colorful Hawaiian version of the Mother Hubbards the missionaries forced on the natives); long, slim adaptations of classic Chinese tunics; or, prettiest of all, holomuus, long muumuus, slightly fitted at the waist. (The holoku—a fitted muumuu with a train—is worn mostly on formal occasions.) We strongly urge you to buy a long dress while you're in the islands. You can use it later for an at-home gown, and you'll have a great time walking through the streets with it swishing gracefully at your ankles. Be sure that the muumuu at least touches the instep if you want to look like a kamaaina. And unless you already own a couple of shifts, it's not a bad idea to wait until you get to Hawaii to pick up a few of the local equivalents: the short muumuu, or island-style sundress. The selection is tremendous (see our shopping chapter), and the prices are at all levels. Of course, many women visitors live in pants (and unflattering shorts) in Hawaii, and there's no reason why you shouldn't. It's just that long muumuus are so much more a part of the island scene.

So pack your bathing suits (or get a bikini in Hawaii), your favorite casual clothes, a sturdy pair of sandals (maybe some hiking boots if you're going to go out on the trails), a lightweight woolen sweater, stole, or throw to wear in the evenings, a warm jacket if you're going up into the mountains. Leave your stockings at home; nobody but businesswomen seem to wear them. You'll live in sandals or Japanese zoris, or go barefoot the way many islanders do, especially indoors. (Island kids, by the way, wear shoes as little as possible, usually not even to school, with resulting household crises when they need to find their shoes to go to a movie or restaurant.) The idea is to fortify yourself against the summer heat by wearing open shoes and sleeveless dresses. Leave all your city cottons and little dark dresses at home. Wash-and-dry clothes are helpful, but not crucial since the launderettes are so handy. As for jewelry, the only kind most people wear is island craft, shell or coral necklaces and the like, which can be picked up in any gift shop. The most beautiful jewelry of island women is the natural kind: blossoms in the hair, flower leis around the neck.

A final word on Hawaiian clothing: We don't want to give you the impression that island women never get dressed up. They do, especially for fancy social events. In downtown Honolulu, businesswomen wear more conservative summer clothing, and many men wear regular business suits with tuck-in shirts. But that's for work—not fun.

SUNDRIES: Bring a travel iron or ask if your hotel will let you borrow theirs (most have boards and irons for guests). Get plastic bottles for your liquid toilet articles; they won't break and they take up less space. Seal perfume bottles with wax for plane flights. Get little packets of cold-water soap and scatter them in odd corners of your suitcase. The plastic clotheslines, complete with miniature clothespins and soap, sold in most department stores, are very, very handy. Those inflatable or plastic hangers are good to have too, since you can't always count on finding wooden hangers on which to drip-dry your clothes in an inexpensive hotel. Disposable wash-up tissues are nice to carry with you, particularly on long plane or auto trips.

HOW TO PACK: Everyone's got his or her own theory on this, but ours is simply to put all the heavy things on the bottom—shoes, books, bulky objects—and lay everything else neatly on top. Then, roll underwear, socks, soft articles into the corners and empty spots (inside shoes, for instance). We think it also helps to have plastic bags for organizing underwear, handkerchiefs, sundries. You'll need one large one at any rate for carrying damp bathing suits. Folding tissue into your dresses does help avoid wrinkles.

SAFETY FIRST: Let's hope your suitcase won't get stolen, lost, or misdirected on the airlines to Australia. But it doesn't hurt to take a few sensible precautions, especially if you're flying in a huge group where bags often get shipped to the wrong hotels and you may have to go without them for several hours. Always tag your bags, inside and out, with your name and home address. Inside each bag, put a note that gives your address in Honolulu; if your bag should arrive at somebody else's hotel, it can easily be sent to yours. Carry with you your valuables, medicines, prescriptions, cameras, etc.—anything that you can't easily replace if your bag is among the missing.

READERS' TRAVEL SUGGESTIONS: "First-time visitors to Oahu (and even those who have been there before but are somewhat vague on their geography) will find a little folder titled 'Map of Waikiki—Hotels and Points of Interest,' available free at any **HVB** office, invaluable as they attempt to sort out the vast wealth of free tourist literature they encounter on street corners and in hotel lobbies. Major and minor hotels are indexed both alphabetically and by map reference number. All streets, no matter how short, are shown and clearly labeled; and the longer ones have street number indicators to help you locate the exact block where a non-hotel attraction (such as a restaurant) is located" (Leilani Moyers, Patterson, N.Y.).

"I visited Hawaii several years ago, and this year I decided to brighten up the winter by subscribing to the Honolulu Sunday newspaper. Perhaps other readers would enjoy this paper, either to help plan a trip or to read during a cold winter. You can get all the information about subscribing by mail to the *Sunday Star-Bulletin and Advertiser* by writing to Hawaii Newspaper Agency, Circulation Dept., P.O. Box 3350, Honolulu, HI 96801. Last year, the cost was $7 for a four-week period" (John Meyer, Sterling, Ill.). [*Authors' Note:* This rate is for ship mail; the airmail rate is

$18.25.]. . . . "A word of caution: Although we were very careful about leaving anything valuable in our car, we had no choice on one occasion, and someone broke into the trunk of the car and took two canvas bags containing all of our newly purchased snorkeling equipment, plus beach and swimwear. The policeman said the trunk can be opened with a screwdriver without damaging the lock. This theft occurred one block from the Pioneer Inn in Lahaina while we were on a sunset dinner sail" (H. Emil Johnson, Darien, Conn.). . . . "Regardless of where you stay in Hawaii—big hotel, little hotel—you might have a small number of roaches in your room. I found it a good idea to buy a Roach Motel for each hotel I stayed at. That way, I never had to see them" (Morgan E. Tallman, Wayne, Mich.).

"We went to Hawaii on a Western Airlines/TOTAL (Trans-Ocean Travel & Leisure) package deal of round-trip air and hotel room for a week for $499 per person, with additional days at $20 per day. Western Air and TOTAL came through with grace, precision, and absolutely no problems. As one man from TOTAL remarked, 'we don't leave anything to chance,' and apparently they don't. . . . It is amazing how finely the Hawaiians have honed their ability to handle great mobs of tourists so that you seldom feel taken advantage of or intruded upon. A great deal of this is probaby due to the pride people take in doing their work and in their state, from the lowest paid waitress to the captain of the DC-10 that takes you there. We are sure that Hawaii has its grim sides, since no place is paradise, but with a little common sense the visitor can enjoy the islands to a greater degree than most other places" (Robert and Jean Carroll, Helena, Mont.).

"We had the opportunity to take Mid Pacific Air from Honolulu to Hilo. We had number-one service and free fruit punch. The turbo-prop jet takes an hour to get there, but who's in a hurry? You fly lower so you can see the islands; many flights are offered. Again, excellent service" (Mrs. John Hoyt, Fountain Valley, Calif.). . . . "We brought two round plastic containers from home to fill with ice to put in our insulated lunchbag to help keep our lunches cold. We didn't have to purchase straw mats for the beach as a lot of people did, as I had packed a large sheet for our "beach blanket.' Certainly, a lot easier to pack for our trip home. A folding suitcase we had packed came in handy for all the souvenirs we had bought. Our most indispensable item turned out to be a ten-foot length of rope. Since most of our previous traveling has been camping, it just seemed like a natural thing to pack. It was used to secure the trunk of a small car when all the luggage wouldn't fit, to hang wet bathing suits outside, and last, to tie a suitcase when the lock broke" (Beverly Russo, N. Massapequa, N.Y.).

"T-shirts are very much a part of the island scene, worn by every age, it appears. I think it would be more interesting if people wore a T-shirt with the name of their hometown, or area, on it, instead of the local Hawaiian ones; that way tourists could say 'Hi' to anyone wearing a name from their own hometown and probably end up enjoying a great chat. We did see the odd person wearing a 'hometown' T-shirt, and noticed the way passersby obviously read it" (Joy E. Deeks, Victoria, B.C., Canada).

"Transportation from Honolulu Airport to Waikiki is good, but I have a suggestion. The limousines fill up very fast and it's not uncommon to have to wait a while. My suggestion is to wait by a taxi stand and share a cab with two or three other people. I did this, and within ten minutes, I had three other people and myself in a cab to Waikiki at a cost of $3 per person, right to our various hotels. I was on the way in 15 minutes, but I could have waited two or three hours for a motorcoach" (John Salmon, Antioch, Calif.).

"A terrific packing idea is an inflatable raft. It takes up no room in the suitcase, but can be used to lie on the sand and float in the water" (Mr. and Mrs. R. Bivona, Massapequa, N.Y.). . . . "For an inexpensive souvenir to take back home, just bring a cassette radio recorder and some blank tapes; you can record Hawaiian music from the local radio stations" (Roz and Jim Morino, Colma, Calif.).

"In three weeks in the islands I broke my watchband, my sunglasses' earpiece, my tote pocketbook strap, and my camera carrying-case strap. Therefore, my suggestion is to purchase carrying cases with secure handles, preferably straps that continue all around the bag, including the bottom. This is important for any type of vinyl or plastic bag that will be used for carrying more than a hanky. . . . I carried my film (40 rolls) in filmshield bags, which are lead-lined. They can be found in camera stores. Because I made several inter-island flights and went through numerous x-ray machines, the film was protected from the rays. They try to insist it won't damage the film, but professional photographers recommend using the bags because of the accumulative effect of the rays. Where possible I had them hand-examine the film carriers. Some places I was required to remove them from my baggage for examination because the lead lining made them show up as a black, unidentifiable blob on the machine" (Jane Kenney, Kingston, N.H.).

"It's nice to go to the airport early and ask for seating arrangements, as the first row of seats behind first class has more leg room, is less noisy, and has less vibration from the engines. We left three transistor radios at home, but wanted one so badly that we bought one in Honolulu. We recommend one for the packing list" (Mr. and Mrs. Rodney Phillips, Seattle, Wash.). [*Authors' Note:* More and more letters arrive every year agreeing about transistor radios. Many hotels include neither radio nor television, and the cost of renting a radio is about $3.50 a week. As for going to the airport early to get good seats, it's usually not necessary: try asking your travel agent to reserve seats for you or do so yourself by phoning the airlines a few days before your flight. Unless you've done so, three or four of you traveling together during a busy season may have to be split up, or you may not get to sit in the cabin (smoking or nonsmoking, movie or not) that you prefer.] . . . "I would like to suggest to your readers that they either bring with them or buy as soon as they get to the islands a can of good insect repellent. We were at Waimea Falls Park in June (which wasn't really all that great) and even though we never saw any, we were eaten up by insects. Our tram guide had sprayed himself and at the time I couldn't imagine why, until later when we started itching and scratching. This also happened to us on Kauai when we took the evening Wailua River Cruise to the Fern Grotto. At least that time we saw them flying around" (Muriel P. Maloney, Huntington Beach, Calif.).

"My husband and I agree that a tape recorder is a must for trips. We taped the songs and commentary at the Fern Grotto cruise on Kauai and plan to use the tapes as part of a background to our slides. We also taped our impressions of each day's events before we went to bed. It's so much easier and quicker than keeping a diary, and a great deal of fun to replay" (Joann Leonard, Los Angeles, Calif.). . . . "I suggest taking a feather-weight hooded nylon waterproof shell jacket. We were the only ones who could really enjoy the sights around the top of the volcano craters on the Big Island and Maui. Because of the wind, most sleeveless-dressed ladies were miserable" (Mrs. Richard K. West, Glenview, Ill.). . . . "Let me thank the reader who suggested taking a featherweight, *hooded* nylon waterproof shell jacket—that saved my day many, many times. It was for those sudden showers that it was invaluable during our trip. I had made a special shopping trip before I left home to buy the jacket and found it much better to carry and use than a plastic raincoat; it folds into such a neat package that I could tuck it into my purse. Another helpful item we took with us was a pair of binoculars, and we were the envy of lots of fellow travelers viewing the Waimea Canyon on Kauai, Haleakala on Maui, and the volcanic action on Hawaii—it was very active at that time. They have telescopes at some of the places, but the lines are long! Binoculars need not be expensive or heavy to carry; there are many compact glasses available" (Mrs. Lee Morgan, Vacaville, Calif.).

"In the ten days we were in the islands, my husband didn't have to wear a suit once. Visitors might be safe to bring one, but one is more than enough" (Terry and Lou Cicalese, South Ozone Park, N.Y.). . . . "One item that made our trip particularly enjoyable was a plaid insulated bag. It easily fit into my suitcase on the way over. We thoroughly enjoyed shopping for foods in Hawaii. The produce department was great fun. Each day we packed a lunch, which stayed fresh in our insulated container until we found a delightful place to stop for lunch. This bag saved us considerable time and money. We used it to transport leftover foods when we island hopped. And on the way home we stuffed it with souvenirs" (Marylin C. Haley, Watertown, Mass.).

And now, after a budget flight, we land in the islands. It's time to tour Hawaii on $35 a day.

Chapter II

HONOLULU: ORIENTATION AND HOTELS

AS YOU'VE ALREADY LEARNED, most planes and ships going to the Hawaiian Islands land first on the island of Oahu and deposit you in or near the capital city of Honolulu. For those of us on a budget, that's a marvelously appropriate choice, because Oahu happens to be the cheapest of all the Hawaiian islands—and one of the most fascinating to boot.

THE ISLAND ITSELF: Oahu means "the gathering place" in Hawaiian, and no other name could be so apt. Although it's merely the third largest of the islands in size (40 miles long, 26 miles wide), it boasts the most people (over half a million, and more arriving all the time), the most skyscrapers, the most construction, the most schools, hospitals, radio and television stations—and the most tourists. Honolulu, the capital city, is the center of island life, the metropolis of which youngsters from the other islands dream, a tremendous military stronghold (approximately one-quarter of the island is owned by the military, and defense is a major industry), a bustling boom town, and a cosmopolitan center plunked down in the middle of the Pacific Ocean.

Just about ten minutes away from downtown Honolulu is **Waikiki Beach,** a favorite resort of Hawaiian royalty long before the word "tourist" was invented. For the visitor, this is an ideal situation; it's as if Mexico City were just ten minutes away from Acapulco, Paris a short bus ride from the Riviera. You can, with such geography, have the best of both worlds—as much beach or city, laziness or excitement, as you choose.

The island is dominated by two mountain ranges: the Waianae, along the west coast, and the Koolaus, which form the spectacular backdrop to the city of Honolulu. On the other side of the Koolaus is **Windward Oahu,** which is what islanders are referring to when they talk of going to the country. Commuters tunnel through the mountains to pretty little suburbs that are developing here as the population booms. For the visitor, it's the closest thing you'll see—if you don't get to the neighbor islands—of rural Hawaii: tiny plantation villages, miles of red earth planted with pineapple and sugarcane, a breathtaking succession of emerald beaches, and gorgeous trails for riding and hiking. But we'll get to that later. First, let's get you settled in Waikiki, which in all likelihood will be your center of operations in Honolulu.

ARRIVAL: Honolulu International Airport is about five miles out of town. Although it's easy enough to hop right on the no. 8 Hickam-Waikiki bus that goes from the terminal to the beach area (fare: 50¢) there is one major problem: the bus has no special section for luggage, and even one large bag is no longer allowed on it. So unless you're traveling extremely light, or picking up a car at the airport, your best bet is to take one of the limousine services right into Waikiki. **Airport Motor Coach** (tel. 955-1446) makes trips to and from the airport and Waikiki hotels at a cost of about $3.50. Regular taxi fare into town runs a high $13 to $14.

Note: If you need to get to the airport *very early* in the morning (say, around 5 a.m.), your best bet is **Waikiki Express,** which will pick you up at your hotel and drop you off at your flight at a cost of $4.50. Call them at 942-2177.

If you're planning to rent a car, the rates are usually cheaper at places in town than at the airport. Better yet, make your arrangements in advance at one of the less expensive car agencies in town (see Chapter IV).

GETTING YOUR DIRECTIONAL SIGNALS: In order to get your bearings, you should know that no one ever refers to directions in the old-fashioned north-south, east-west way out here. Since the islands sit in a kind of slanted direction on the map, those terms just wouldn't make much sense.

This is how it's done in Hawaii. Everything toward the sea is **makai** (mah-kye); everything toward the mountains is **mauka** (mow-kah). The other directions are **Diamond Head** (roughly eastward) and **Ewa** (roughly westward), named after two of the major landmarks of the city. Once you move out beyond Diamond Head, roughly eastward directions are referred to as **Koko Head** (Aina Haina is Koko Head of Kalani Valley, for example). Once you learn how to use these simple terms, you'll be well on the way to becoming a kamaaina yourself.

HOTELS: Now, with the preliminaries done, we arrive at the initial, all-important, make-or-break project of your Hawaiian vacation—finding a good but inexpensive hotel. As we've discussed in our introduction, inflation is rampant in Hawaii—as it is everywhere else. Many of the cozy little guest houses that used to enable budget tourists to live comfortably on peanuts just a few years ago have been torn down as part of the masterplan for upgrading Waikiki. In their places, new, more expensive structures have been built. (Some of the remaining guest houses are in such a state of neglect that we won't bother mentioning them here.) However—and this is good news—because of the tremendous number of accommodations in Waikiki, it is still possible to find plenty of good rooms for a very few dollars. And because of the uncertain economic situation, Hawaii has been experiencing some periods of tourist decline, which can bring prices down more than ever—and give you some remarkable bargains.

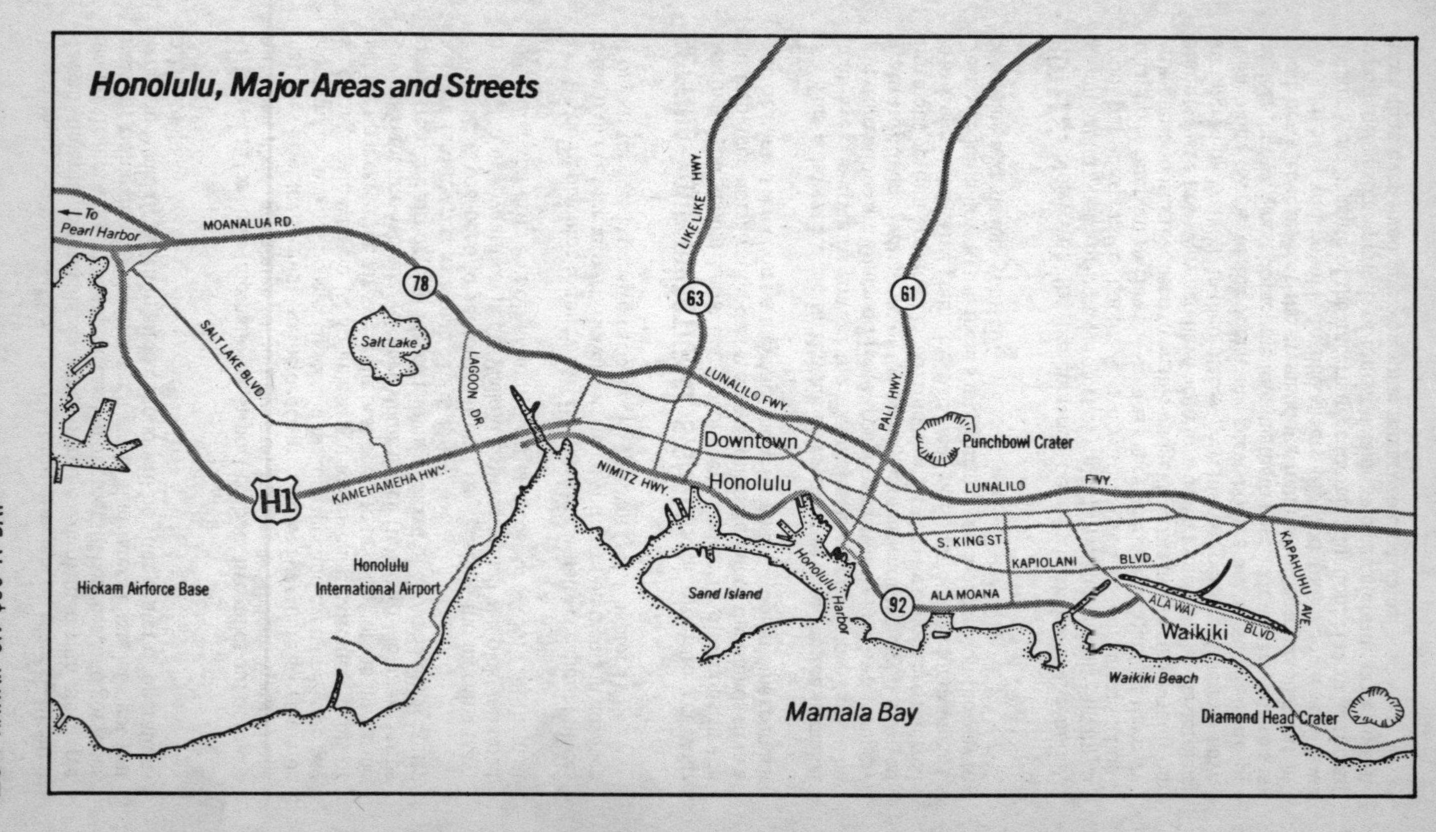
Honolulu, Major Areas and Streets
To Pearl Harbor
MOANALUA RD.
78
SALT LAKE BLVD.
Salt Lake
LAGOON DR.
LIKE LIKE HWY.
63
61
PALI HWY.
LUNALILO FWY.
Downtown
Punchbowl Crater
H1
KAMEHAMEHA HWY.
NIMITZ HWY.
Honolulu
LUNALILO FWY.
S. KING ST
KAPIOLANI BLVD.
KAPAHULU AVE
Hickam Airforce Base
Honolulu International Airport
Sand Island
Honolulu Harbor
92
ALA MOANA
ALA WAI BLVD.
Waikiki
Waikiki Beach
Mamala Bay
Diamond Head Crater

For the purpose of a $35-a-day budget, we will presume that you are part of a traveling twosome, and that between the two of you, you have a total of $70 to spend on a room and meals. If you want to stay on the low side of this budget, check out our selections under "Bargain Beauties." This section covers rooms that average between $20 and $30 a night for two. If you can afford to spend more, then consider the listings under "The Good Buys." These rooms begin at $30 and go to $40 and up. Whatever is left over from the money you spend on your room can go for food. Of course, if there are more than two of you traveling in a party, or if you are staying in Honolulu for more than a week or two, you can realize considerably savings on these figures.

Whichever your budget, you will be living sensibly and pleasantly—and far more inexpensively than most tourists, who are led to believe that a hotel in Waikiki under $60 or $70 a day just doesn't exist. It certainly does exist, particularly at that Hawaiian wonder of wonders: the apartment-hotel with kitchenette. So many tourists—especially family groups—are enamored of kitchenette units that accommodations of this sort have sprung up all over Waikiki. Many of them are individually owned condominium units. Invariably, they're cheaper than the rooms in the large seaside hotels; they have excellent locations near the beach and mountains; they are fully available to transients; they permit you to reduce expenses by cooking at least one meal in (dishes and utensils are always provided); and most important, they offer what we regard as the most relaxing and enjoyable type of accommodation in Hawaii. We offer names, addresses, and descriptions of several dozen of these establishments below.

If you plan to arrive in Hawaii during the summer season—June through Labor Day—advance reservations are a good idea. They are essential anytime during the peak winter season—roughly from December 20 to April 15. (During the Christmas holiday season, people have been known to reserve up to a year in advance at some of the more desirable places.) While not so imperative at other times of the year, reservations remain the best way of obtaining exactly what you want at the price you can afford to pay. But if you haven't done your homework, all is not lost. Thumb through the pages ahead and phone the likely possibilities from the airport. Or park your traveling companion and suitcases at a seaside bench in Waikiki (get off the bus at Kuhio Beach) and set out to do some serious scouting. That way you won't collapse with exhaustion at the first hotel you find.

A WORD ABOUT CAMPING: For details on camping permits, renting trailers, and where to camp on Oahu, see Chapters IV and VIII.

1. Hotels in Waikiki

Practically all tourists stay in Waikiki, mecca of the malihinis. This is a relatively small area of Honolulu, but within it are concentrated most of the town's best beaches, and therefore most of the hotels and entertainment facilities. Downtown Honolulu is only a short bus ride away.

As a point of orientation, remember that most of the fancy hotels are located right on the beach and on Kalakaua Avenue, the main drag; between Kalakaua and the Ala Wai Boulevard (which marks most of the makai and mauka boundaries of Waikiki) are dozens of tree-lined pretty streets containing the bulk of the smaller and less expensive hotels. Waikiki itself is small enough that you can easily walk or bus from any one of these hotels to the beach; they are also near each other, so you should have no trouble in getting from one to another if you have to do some hotel hunting.

A further word about prices: As we've pointed out above, prices are often cheaper if you stay for a week or more. Also, they can go up or down according to business pressures, so prices may vary slightly from these figures, gathered in late 1984, but give or take a dollar or two, they will be your best hotel buys on the island. Quite a few hotels up their rates during the busy winter months. But remember that in slow seasons you may be able to get rooms at lower prices than the going rates; you can do especially well on weekly rentals. The hotel may eliminate maid service (which is costly), but you may be able to get a very decent apartment (normally selling for $25 to $30 a day) for as little as $125 or $130 a week. Please note that we are not responsible for changes in prices: we simply quote the figures hotel owners give us. Also, please do not expect special rates at hotels unless we specifically indicate that the owners are willing to give them to our readers. In addition, and unless otherwise stated by us, all rooms listed below have private bath.

Since most tourists spend far less than a month in Waikiki, we have not covered the apartment buildings that take only monthly or seasonal rentals; if you do plan to stay for at least a month, it may be worth your while to investigate them too. And, of course, many of the apartment-hotels listed here will accept guests for several months or more.

THE BARGAIN BEAUTIES: Although the price range in this category is modest—averaging from $20 to $30 for a double room—the variety of accommodations is surprisingly wide. They range from simple motel-like apartment buildings to graceful small hotels featuring pools, lovely tropical grounds, air conditioning, private phones, and resort-living comfort. We've divided these hotels, and the ones in "The Good Buys" section to follow, into three general areas: **Diamond Head Waikiki,** that part of town closest to Kuhio Beach and Kapiolani Park; **Central Waikiki,** the area centering, roughly, around the International Market Place; and **Ewa Waikiki,** the section near the Hilton Hawaiian Village Hotel and Reef Hotel and the closest area to downtown Honolulu. Two additional subdivisions of the last will be called **Near the Ala Wai** and **Near Ala Moana.** Remember that all these areas are within a few blocks' walking or a short bus distance of each other and all are comparable in terms of comfort and convenience. And they're all near the beach.

Diamond Head Waikiki

We'll begin with an old standby in this part of town, the **Royal Grove Hotel,** 151 Uluniu Ave., Honolulu, HI 96815 (tel. 923-7691), one of the prettiest of Waikiki's small hotels. The six-story pink concrete building is about three minutes away from Kuhio Beach, but if you're really lazy you can dunk in the tiny pool right on the grounds. All told, the Royal Grove has about 85 rooms and a widely varying price range: you can get a room (single or double) starting at $28, a room with kitchenette starting at $34.50, a kitchenette unit with private lanai at $38 to $42—all air-conditioned. One-bedroom apartments average $38 to $70, and it's $4 for

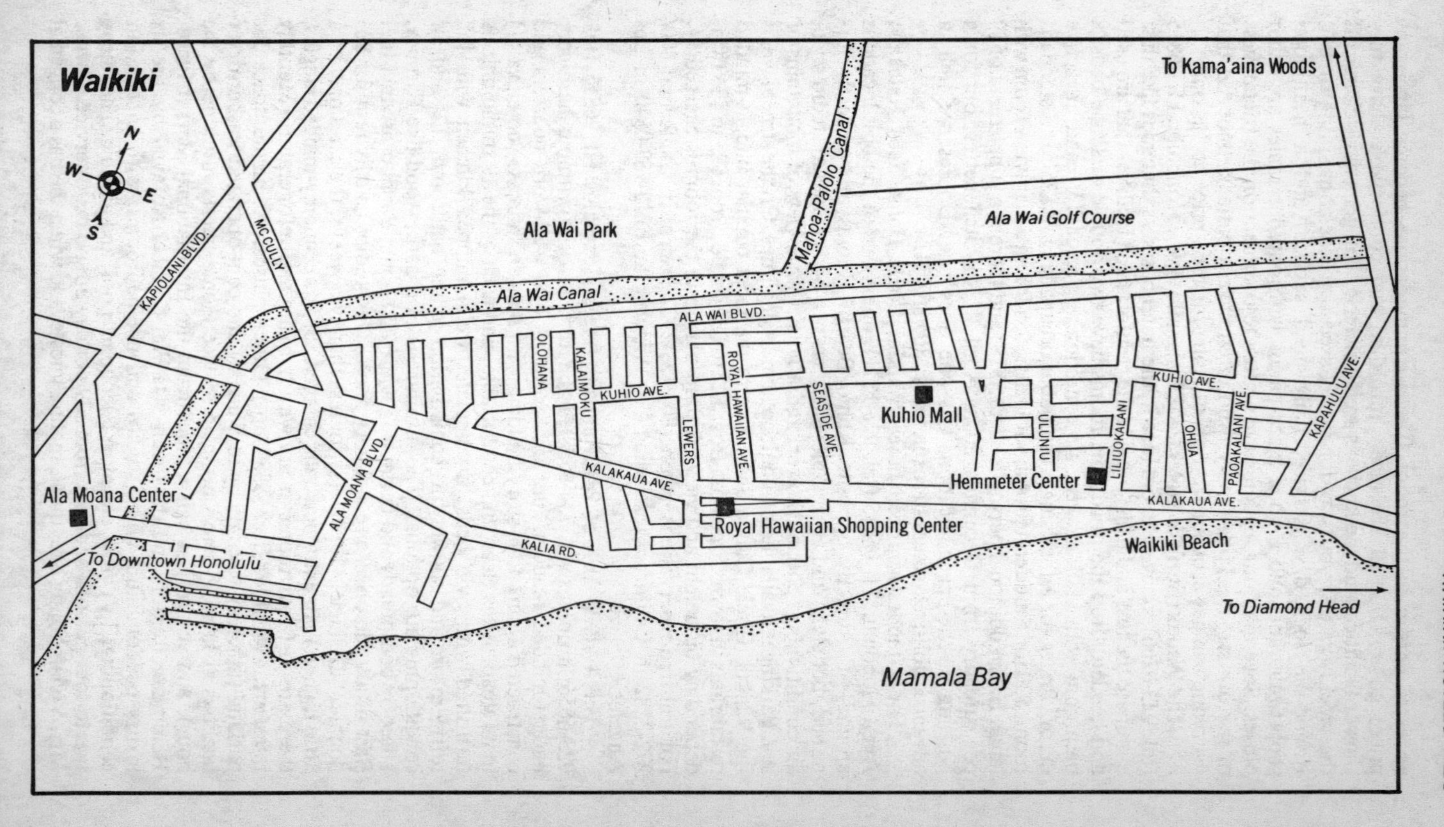
Waikiki
N
W
E
S
Ala Wai Park
Manoa-Palolo Canal
Ala Wai Golf Course
To Kama'aina Woods
KAPIOLANI BLVD.
MC CULLY
Ala Wai Canal
ALA WAI BLVD.
OLOHANA
KALAIMOKU
KUHIO AVE.
LEWERS
ROYAL HAWAIIAN AVE.
SEASIDE AVE.
Kuhio Mall
ULUNIU
LILIUOKALANI
KUHIO AVE.
OHUA
PAOAKALANI AVE.
KAPAHULU AVE.
Hemmeter Center
KALAKAUA AVE.
KALAKAUA AVE.
Royal Hawaiian Shopping Center
ALA MOANA BLVD.
Ala Moana Center
KALIA RD.
To Downtown Honolulu
Waikiki Beach
To Diamond Head
Mamala Bay

an extra person in the room. The accommodations become fancier as prices go up, but all are nicely furnished and comfortable, have tub-shower facilities, and the kitchens are all electric. You get a day's charge off the weekly rate if you stay for two consecutive weeks in spring or fall. Round-the-clock desk service, daily maid service, and a healthfood shop-restaurant, and a good pizza parlor with outdoor tables are other pluses. Several of our readers have written to comment on the friendliness of the owners, the Fong family, who often have a potluck dinner so that everyone can get acquainted. Lots of aloha for little price at this one.

The **Waikiki Surfside Hotel,** 2452 Kalakaua Ave., Honolulu, HI 96815 (tel. 923-0266), revived an old idea in the hotel business that goes like this: eliminate the fuss and frills; provide the comforts and facilities that are used and needed; drop the price. The rooms have two double or single beds, a bathroom with stall shower, air conditioning, color TV, and attractive decor. Prices for either single or double occupancy are $26 for a standard room, $30 for a moderate room with lanai, $36 for an ocean-view room with lanai. Each additional person is charged $9, and there is a supplement of $9 per category from December 20 to April 1. No kitchenettes, but for a bustling on-the-beach location, this one does fine. Do reserve well in advance. Toll-free reservations number: 800/367-5124.

For a modestly priced hotel, **Waikiki Circle Hotel,** 2464 Kalakaua Ave., Honolulu, HI 96815 (tel. 923-1571), offers one of the best locations around—it's directly opposite Kuhio Beach. Rooms are modestly furnished, but clean and acceptable; each has two beds made up studio style, air conditioning, phone, shower, and a lanai with a view of mountains or sea. Parking is available; no pool; no laundry facilities. On the street level is the Waikiki Circle Coffee Shop, one of the most popular budget-minded restaurants in town. Rates run from $22 to $31 single, from $25 to $34 twin, depending on height and view. A third person in the room is charged $4. For toll-free reservations, phone 800/423-2922, except in California; 800/272-3282 in California, excluding Los Angeles; and 213/988-0540 in Los Angeles.

The **Waikiki Lei,** at 241 Kaiulani Ave., Honolulu, HI 96815 (tel. 923-6656; if no answer, 734-8588), a longtime favorite with our hard-core budget-minded readers, has torn down its old, well-worn quarters and constructed a pink four-story building with outside staircase (no elevator) in its stead. All is clean and comfortable, and each of the 19 studio units is furnished with twin beds, a complete, well-equipped kitchen with full refrigerator, and shower-tub combination in the bathroom. TV and air conditioning are optional. The furniture is of a dark, wood-like Formica, offset by bedspreads and curtains in white and bone; the floor is vinyl tile. Best of all, the prices are still very good. The studios usually rent for $23 double, $21 single. (If you stay for less than two weeks, the rates may be a little higher.) An extra person is charged $3. For economy-minded singles, there are just four rooms at $19 with hotplate and refrigerator. (Monthly rates are available, from $350 up.) Other pluses: Adequate space for parking (not easy to come by in Waikiki) and coin-operated washer-dryer facilities at hand. There's no maid service (some guests hire one by the hour), and you're just half a block from the International Market Place, Hemmeter Center, and the lovely Ala Wai Canal. Also available are six luxury condominium units, studios and one-bedrooms, with kitchen, air conditioning, TV, view, elevator, telephone, pool, and parking. They sleep two to four persons and rent from $29 per day up, no maid service. Owner Mrs. Vivian Young likes quiet, mature guests, and when she has a congenial group she often plans an outdoor party, especially to celebrate the Chinese New Year. Reserve a few weeks in advance.

Our next recommendation in the Diamond Head area is a good bet for families: the two-story apartment complex **Venture Isles Apartments,** 2467 Cleghorn St., Honolulu, HI 96815 (tel. 923-6363). All units here have been renovated within the last few years. Studio apartments usually go for $20 to $25 a day, single or double. The considerably larger one-bedroom apartments—they can accommodate up to six people—go for $25 to $40 a day, single or double, with an extra charge of $2.50 a day for each additional person. Owners Ed and Agnes Cordeiro will grant readers of this book a 10% discount. Weekly and monthly rates are also available. Make reservations well in advance.

The **Continental Surf,** 2426 Kuhio Ave., Honolulu, HI 96815 (tel. 922-2755), is an attractive high-rise with a big, airy lobby and comfortable rooms. The rooms all have color TV, telephones, and individually controlled air conditioning, but no lanais. The decor is tasteful Polynesian, using earthy browns and golds. Prices are reasonable: rooms without kitchenette are priced from $25 to $30 single and double during the off-season, April 16 to December 20. The rest of the year, add $8. Should you want a room with a nicely equipped kitchen, expect to pay $34, single or double. One-bedroom suites with kitchenette go for $53 for up to four people during the low season. An extra person is charged $6, but children under 12 may stay free with their parents. The Continental Surf has no pool, restaurants, or recreational facilities; guests use all the facilities of its sister hotel, the Miramar, which is just 1½ blocks away. For reservations, call toll free 800/227-4320 from mainland United States, or 800/663-9671 from Canada.

There's nothing at all fancy about the **Lealea Hale Apartment Hotel,** 2423 Cleghorn St., Honolulu, HI 96815 (tel. 922-1726), but there's a friendly feeling about this unpretentious little place. There are just 30 units: studios, one- and two-bedroom apartments. All units are fully but modestly furnished with a full kitchen, bath, and private lanai. Most units have wall air conditioners and color TV. A coin-operated laundry facility is on the ground floor. Parking is extra. During the low season, from April 15 to December 15, the studios go for $20 to $25 single or double, $125 to $160 weekly. One- and two-bedroom units are $25 to $35 daily, $160 to $225 weekly. Each additional guest is charged $6.50 per night. During the winter season rates are about 20% higher. Group rates and monthly rates are available on request. The management prides itself on personal service, and is available to make travel and recreation arrangements. You can also inquire about their "semi-deluxe vacation apartments" in other locations. Be sure to see the room before you take it.

Amy Lau, the owner of **Edmunds Hotel Apartments,** 2411 Ala Wai Blvd., Honolulu, HI 96815 (tel. 923-8381), has been making newcomers to Hawaii feel at home for well over 20 years now. Amy's establishment is very modest, a small guest house with long lanais curving around the building and fronting each of the small, very well-worn, but still okay studio rooms. Best news of all, these rent daily for just $18 single, $20 double, and $22 triple. All rooms have twin beds, private baths, small kitchenettes, plus toasters, ironing boards, and television sets—good values for this price category. The hotel faces the cool and breezy Ala Wai Canal and provides a lovely vista, especially at night, of Manoa Valley and the mountains, which goes far in making up for the fact that you do hear automobiles buzzing by.

Again, undemanding types might check in at the **Waikiki Prince Hotel,**

2431 Prince Edward Ave., Honolulu, HI 96815 (tel. 922-1544), which offers small studios at $24 per day; with refrigerator and stove, these are $27. Medium studios with kitchenette begin at $30. The location, just two blocks from the beach and in back of Hemmeter Center, is excellent, but the rooms need redoing. There is no maid service.

Central Waikiki

Choicely located a block from the beach and a block from the main drag in Waikiki, the **Coral Seas Hotel,** 250 Lewers St., Honolulu, HI 96815 (tel. 923-3881), is one of the inexpensive hotels in the empire of Roy Kelley, the Henry Ford of Hawaii hotels. Like Ford, Kelley believes in operating on a big scale and offering standard quality, an attractive package, and a good price. At the Coral Seas, spacious rooms are done in blues and greens with tan carpeting; all have private lanais and air conditioning to keep things cool. Small kitchenettes (with rather minimal cooking equipment) are available upon request. Doubles without kitchenettes are priced at $20 to $24. Doubles with kitchenettes are $22 to $26. And there are some larger rooms starting around $40 that can comfortably accommodate four, a real family find. The beach is just down the street, and right in the hotel is a branch of Perry Boys' Smorgy, which offers such good bargains that you may never bother cooking in your room at all.

An important thing to remember about the Coral Seas: If there are no rooms available here, the management will easily be able to place you in any of several hundred equivalent rooms a few blocks away, all part of the Kelley chain. For reservations, call toll free 800/367-5170.

Another of those ubiquitous Roy Kelley outposts, the **Waikiki Surf,** 2200 Kuhio Ave., Honolulu, HI 96815 (tel. 923-7671), is well set up for comfortable living. The rooms are spacious, with compact kitchenettes if you ask for them, usually studio beds, air conditioning, and a long narrow lanai that is shared with the next room. The accommodations vary according to the prices—$24 to $30 single and $24, $26, and $30 double—but all are comfortable. The comfortable chairs in the lobby afford a view of the swimmers in the pool or passersby on the sidewalk. The bustle of Kalakaua is just one long block away; the Pacific, two. The **Waikiki Surf East** and **Waikiki Surf West** are part of the same complex, all located close to each other and the beach. A nice plus: Waikiki Surf guests are welcome to use the oceanfront beach and pool of the Waikiki Outrigger Hotel, run by the same management. For toll-free reservations, phone 800/367-5170.

The **Edgewater,** one of Hawaii's Reef Hotels, at 2168 Kalia Rd., Honolulu, HI 96815, corner of Lewers (tel. 923-3111), has long enjoyed one of the best locations in Waikiki. Halfway between the ocean and Kalakaua Avenue, the hotel is a two-minute walk to either the peace of sun and surf or the bustle of restaurants, shops, and nighteries. It's a big hotel (200 rooms), but the prices are fairly low: $22, single or double, for the smallest rooms with the least to look out at. The deluxe rooms, with more space and more view, are $38, single or double, with kitchenette. It's $10 for each additional person. Rooms are pleasantly furnished; the bathrooms have stall showers but no tubs. Your lanai will be furnished, but nothing will separate you from your neighbor's porch. This is a homey place, with lots of space to stroll around the building, plenty of lobby area and public rooms. The Trattoria Restaurant, right on the grounds, is a Waikiki favorite for northern Italian food. There are three other Reef hotels in town: the Reef, Reef Towers, and Waikiki Towers, and guests may use the facilities at all three. Reservations: Reef Hotels, Honolulu, HI 96815, or call toll free 800/367-5170.

Ewa Waikiki

Families are made especially welcome—but then so is everybody else—at the cozy **Malihini Hotel,** at 217 Saratoga Rd., Honolulu, HI 96815 (tel. 923-9644). Situated in an ideal location, across the street from the right-of-way to the beach, the Malihini is a small, older hotel, a homey place with a brick courtyard with barbecue facilities where guests gather to eat and talk. The rooms in the older building, once a private home, are super-plain and the furnishings are well worn, but everything is clean. During the long off-season—from April to December 15—studios are $20, single or double. The lanai rooms in the newer building are very well maintained and go for $22 to $20, single or double; one-bedroom apartments are $32 to $40 for two to four people. During high season, studios are $18 to $20, lanais are $26 to $30, and one-bedroom apartments run $36 to $40. There is no air conditioning, but fans keep things cool. Weekly rentals are available, and families are always given the best rates possible. Owner Richard C. Sutton, a cordial host who likes to make everyone feel at home, advises reservations 60 days in advance.

The management of the **Reef Lanais,** 225 Saratoga Rd., Honolulu, HI 96815, is the same as that of the Coral Seas and Waikiki Surf hotels, which we've told you about in the section on "Central Waikiki." The Reef Lanais and the Coral Seas have the same telephone number: 923-3881. The Kelleys call this one their "family hotel." Doubles here start at $24 for a good-size room. The same type of room with a refrigerator and hotplate for light cooking $31 on a lower floor, $27 on one of the higher floors. Add $8 for each extra person. There are also one-bedroom family suites, with refrigerators and hotplates and a total of four beds, for $43. The beach is a hop-skip-and-a-jump away, since there is a public right-of-way to the beach just across Kalia Road. There is no pool on the premises, but the Reef Lanais' guests may use the one at Waikiki Village, right around the corner on Lewers Street. The hotel is 100% air-conditioned, and although it lacks some of the frills of its two sister hotels, and could benefit from some spiffier house cleaning, it is an excellent value for the price. Oh, yes, as its name would imply, each unit has a big lanai. For toll-free reservations, call 800/367-5170.

One of our favorite streets in Honolulu is Beach Walk, a tiny street running from Kalakaua smack into the ocean and relatively—for Waikiki—quiet. Here you'll find the **Niihau Apartment Hotel,** 247 Beach Walk, Honolulu, HI 96815 (tel. 922-1607), a relaxing place in which to kick off your sandals. The 11-story, 31-unit hotel consists of only one- and two-bedroom apartments, small but cozy, all with air conditioning, cable TV, private telephone, and lanai. The decor is pleasant enough, varying in each apartment: bathrooms (showers only, no tubs) are prettily wallpapered; the modern kitchens are immense and very well equipped. And although the rooms are small, the fact that each apartment has several provides a sense of privacy. Prices are good: during the off-season (April 15 through June 15 and September 1 to December 15), one-bedroom apartments for a party of two are $24.50; two-bedroom apartments for up to four are $39. The rest of the year, one-bedrooms are $29; two-bedrooms, $43. An additional person is $5 a day; parking next door at $2 a day. Manager Hyacinth Hesson (everybody calls her "Hy") runs this place with a firm hand, aims to keep it quiet, and turns away noisy guests. Bravo! Advance reservations advised.

Many of the guests at **Hale Pua Nui,** 228 Beach Walk, Honolulu, HI 96815 (tel. 923-9693), are returnees, coming back year after year to this lovely little complex of some 20 large studio apartments run by the very hospitable Fay Heady, who cares for you as if you were a guest in her own home. She also takes loving care of this place, and, despite its 25 years, it looks spanking new. The studio apartments are of good size, with either two twin beds (arranged studio fashion) or a queen-size bed. They are nicely furnished with artistic touches (notice Fay's paintings on the wall), have cross-ventilation, acoustic walls and ceilings, are thoroughly equipped (even to ironing boards), and have good, complete kitchens. Rooms go for $28.50, $32.50, and $35.50. There's a courtesy phone in the office. Children are accepted over the age of 12, but only one to a room. Fay recommends the excellent swimming at Fort DeRussy—just around the bend.

The **Pacific Palms Hotel,** at 441 Lewers St., Honolulu, HI 96815 (tel. 922-1522 and 923-4020), is one low building away from the Ala Wai Canal, so it offers abundant mountain and aquatic views. The beige building is ten stories high, and its sidewalk elevator allows you to go in and out without having to enter the lobby area. The hotel recently became a condominium; however, all the renovated and refurnished rooms can be rented as hotel rooms. The twin beds are covered in bold Polynesian prints that harmonize nicely with the new carpeting and attractive furniture. The kitchens are all electric, and the bathrooms are papered in beautiful silvery wallpaper. Rooms here are $29 to $33, single or double occupancy, and $5 for each additional person (less in low season). Weekly and monthly rates are available on request. Write manager Mrs. Rita Medeiros for reservations, or call the toll-free number: 800/367-5176.

Near the Ala Wai

A small luxury hotel at budget prices is the **Waikiki Holiday,** 450 Lewers St., Honolulu, HI 96815 (tel. 923-0245), where your willingness to walk about ten minutes to the beach will save you a nice few dollars. This is at the Ala Wai Canai end of Lewers, so don't expect an ocean view, but there is plenty of mountain view—and lots of view inside, where the handsome decor and appointments are the work of Tom Hirai, a top Honolulu designer. All rooms are air-conditioned and have private lanais. There's a perfectly beautiful free-form pool and a tempting Indian restaurant, Shalimar. Now about those attractive rates: singles or doubles without kitchens are $22 to $34; with kitchens, $28 to $58; an additional person is charged $6.

Just Beyond Waikiki

Our last recommendation in this category is technically just over the Waikiki border, but not far enough out to be inconvenient. The **Central Branch YMCA,** 401 Atkinson Dr., Honolulu, HI 96814 (tel. 941-3344), is a five-minute bus ride from Waikiki on the no. 8 or Ala Moana bus to Ala Moana and Atkinson Drive. It's a beautiful place, with an outdoor swimming pool and lovely grounds. Rooms are small but adequate—"Y-style." Singles without bath are $14 daily; with bath they're $16. Without bath a double is $13.50 per person daily; and with, $14.50 per person. It is likely that these rates will go up in the near future. The Y has a reasonably priced snackbar and no end of recreational activities. The single male tourist could hardly do better than stop here. No reservations are accepted.

THE GOOD BUYS: Prices in this category range, roughly, from $30 to $40 and up for a double. Again, savings can be realized by those staying for more than a week and by groups of more than two people traveling together.

Diamond Head Waikiki

A big, bright, modern hotel, the **Aloha Surf,** 444 Kanekapolei St., Honolulu, HI 96815 (tel. 923-0222), is a 15-story, 204-room building offering cheery accommodations in a variety of sizes and shapes. Best suited for our budget are the standard rooms, which go for $32, single or double. They are sunlit, brightly decorated, and air-conditioned. Located higher up, with better views and private lanais, are the superior rooms, at $37. If you want a kitchenette, you'll have to pay $44. Traditional Japanese suites or "ozashiki" are available at $50 double. Each additional person in a room is charged $7. There's a nice pool, good service, a coffeeshop serving breakfast and lunch, and the beach is just a few blocks away.

Readers of past editions of this book who remember the Kuhiolani Hotel will be surprised—very pleasantly—to discover its metamorphosis into **Kaulani Kai,** 2425 Kuhio Ave., Honolulu, HI 96815 (tel. 922-1978). Located in a great spot three minutes away from Kuhio Beach, the tall, modern pyramid-like building designed by Scandinavian architect Jo Paul Rongstad has been repainted and remodeled inside and out. A strong blue-and-white color scheme predominates, starting in the tasteful lobby, working its way up through elevator and hallways, and into the attractive rooms (58 are available for tourists in the 100-room, partly condominium hotel). These are not large, but they are attractive, done primarily in white, with a white table, white dresser-desk, a white spread with red and blue accents, tasteful prints on the wall. Each room is fully carpeted, with twin beds, small lanai, and a tidy two-burner kitchenette, with refrigerator underneath the range. Studio rooms start at $44 and $49, one-bedroom suites (two beds in one room, a double in the other, plus a larger kitchenette), are $67 for up to four people. Parking is available at $2.50 per day. Attractive and pleasant, this is a bright new find. For toll-free reservations, phone 800/367-5252 from the U.S. mainland.

Very welcome in this area is the **Quality Inn,** 175 Paoakalani Ave., Honolulu, HI 96815 (two blocks from Kalakaua, one block from Kapahulu, near Kapiolani Park; tel. 922-3861). It's cheerful, sparkling, and radiates aloha, which you'll notice the minute you approach it. It's smart looking, with a waterfall at the entrance, a golden lobby, and friendly people behind the desk. Prices are lowest in the Diamond Head Tower: $32 single, $35 double, with $10 for each additional person. There are no kitchenettes, but you'll still enjoy your lanai and the view. In the Pali Tower, all rooms have partial kitchenettes; here the rates go up to $37 single, $40 double. The air-conditioned rooms are standard size, equipped with call-out phones, dressing areas, and stall showers large enough and deep enough for a bath too. There are two small pools on the third floor. Call, toll free, for reservations: 800/228-5151.

The **Waikiki Grand,** at 134 Kapahulu, Honolulu, HI 96815 (tel.

923-1511), is one of the most popular places in town for the flocks of Japanese tourists who've discovered Hawaii, and for us that's an extra inducement to stay at this attractive hotel. You can get all the comforts of this hotel at its standard rate of $34, single or twin. At this price you'll get a room with a view of the center of Waikiki and the mountains in the distance; you'll have to go a few dollars more ($39, single or twin) for a breathtaking view of Diamond Head in the other direction. Studio rooms with kitchenettes are $44, single or twin. An additional person is $7. "Premium" rooms go for $46, single or twin. Super views or not, the rooms are pleasant if small (very little closet space), feature tub-showers, direct-dial telephones, and air conditioning. There's a pleasant swimming pool in a secluded court, a Japanese restaurant is on the premises, Kapiolani Park and its activities are across the street, and good old Kuhio Beach is just around the bend.

You'll find the **Park Shore Hotel,** 110 Kapahulu St., Honolulu, HI 96815 (tel. 923-0411), a large, cheery place up near Kuhio Beach, Kapiolani Park, and all the goings-on at this end of Waikiki. The Park Shore does have stunning views of the beach and Diamond Head, but these are reserved for the more expensive, more spacious rooms, with small refrigerators. These run from $50 to $70. Best we stick with those rooms without a view, facing the Holiday Inn; they go for $40, single or double, in summer, for $45 in winter. It's $7 for an additional person. Tub-shower combos, air conditioning, color TV, and radios are added attractions, while the bright blue and green interior creates a cheery ambience. For reservations, phone toll free 800/426-0580 or 800/421-0680.

If what you care about in a hotel room is space, comfort, and lovely furnishings and you don't mind doing without a swimming pool, sundeck, shops, and restaurants, then you'll enjoy the accommodations at **Tradewinds Plaza,** 2572 Lemon Rd., Honolulu, HI 96815 (tel. 922-4555), an attractive condominium building very near Kapiolani Park. Since the hotel is about half a block from the beach, it really doesn't need much more than very good rooms, and that it does have. The most inexpensive rooms are the hotel rooms, which rent for $30 a night double, off-season (April 1 to December 24), and $35 the rest of the year; they all have color TV, air conditioning, large closets, and beds are either twin or queen-size. Go one step up to the standard condo studios, which have a refrigerator and sink, for $35 and $40. Deluxe condo studios, which boast a full kitchen, are $40 and $45; and one-bedroom suites, with full kitchen, are $50 and $55. All rooms are furnished in handsome light woods, are fully carpeted, decorated in tones of sand and red with silkscreens on the walls; some have small lanais. Mrs. Marie Martin, a former reader of this book who relocated to Honolulu, manages the largest number of these apartments, and she will see that you get settled in comfortably. For reservations, write her directly at the hotel.

The **Pacific Monarch Hotel and Condominium,** 142 Uluniu Ave., Honolulu, HI 96815 (tel. 922-4359), is right across the street from one of our old favorites, the Royal Grove (see above), and in fact the Fong family manages several of the attractive units here. Most of the units, however, are managed by Silver, Ltd., at the address above. The rooms in this high-rise are small but nicely decorated, and there are superb facilities: secured building, sky-top pool, sauna, Jacuzzi, and sundeck. The beach is half a block away. Studios with kitchenettes and walk-out lanais begin at $49 double. One-bedroom apartments with full kitchens and large lanais begin at $65 for three people.

The towering new **Royal Kuhio** condominium building, 2240 Kuhio Ave., Honolulu, HI 96815 (tel. 923-4441), is one of the growing number of such places that has a great number of apartments in the "hotel pool"—which means they are available to visitors for short- or long-term stays. These apartments are quite attractive, nicely decorated, with a bedroom with twin beds that can be closed off from the sitting room or opened to make one big area. The sitting room has sofa beds, and rollaways are available for extra people. The kitchens are all-electric (with dishwashers), the closet space is ample, and every apartment has its own color TV and lanai. A pool and sundeck area, billiard room, Ping-Pong, a shuffleboard court, and a huge laundry room and recreation area all make for easy living—not to mention the location close to the beach. For families, the standard apartments are quite a bargain: off-season they are $43 a day single or double, $50 for three, $57 for four. Weekly rates range from $271 for two to $360 for four. During the busy season (December 16 to March 31) rates go from $57 to $71 per day, single or double, for the same apartments. Reservations: Paradise Management Corp., Suite C-207, 50 S. Beretania St., Honolulu, HI 96813.

Central Waikiki

A place that has just about everything going for it is the **Marine Surf,** 346 Seaside Ave., Honolulu, HI 96815 (tel. 923-0277). Located about a block and a half away from the beach, the Marine Surf is a 23-story luxury hotel featuring smartly decorated studio apartments, each of which boasts two double beds, lots of drawer space, expensive-looking furnishings, phone, dressing room, and bath with both tub and shower. Best of all, each studio has a full electric kitchen, just in case you're not prepared to spend the rarified prices at Matteo's Italian Restaurant, one of the finest in town, right on the lobby floor. (Jameson's Irish Coffee House, also in the building, is more modestly priced.) From your private lanai you'll have a view of Diamond Head, and if you're too lazy to get to the beach you can swim and sun at the lovely pool on the fourth floor. Now for the rates: during the long spring-summer-fall season (from April 15 through December 14), standard rooms are $40, single or double; superior are $46; and deluxe, $52. During the winter, rates jump another $7. A third person is charged an extra $8; children under 12 are free unless a crib or rollaway bed is required. A rate increase is expected. On-site parking is $2 per day. For toll-free reservations, call 800/367-5176.

There seem to be Outrigger hotels wherever you look in central Waikiki: one beachfront hotel right opposite the International Market Place and several others nearby. For the budget-minded, we think the most suitable of the Outriggers is the **Outrigger Surf,** 2280 Kuhio Ave., Honolulu, HI 96815, on the corner of Nohonani Street (tel. 922-5777), a short walk from the beach. We like it because it has the greatest number of standard units, kitchen facilities, and the most reasonable prices of the lot: $35 single and $39 to $43 double. For $4 more, you can get a "superior" unit; the room is identical, but the view is of Diamond Head and the morning sun.

All Outriggers are tall, modern buildings, and the Outrigger Surf is no exception—there are 16 floors of comfortable studios, each with a lanai, TV, shag carpeting, air conditioning, beds in studio arrangement providing a living-room look. There's a stall shower in the bathroom, his-and-her closets for storage, a two-burner range and base-cabinet type of refrigerator for light cooking. The lobby is small but comfortable, and green Astroturf surrounds the lobby-level pool.

Reservations for the Outrigger Surf should be made through the central office: Outrigger Hotel, 2335 Kalakaua Ave., Honolulu, HI 96815. The toll-free reservations number is 800/367-5170.

We've always considered the **White Sands Garden Hotel** at 431 Nohonani St., Honolulu, HI 96815 (tel. 923-7336), to be one of the prettiest of the smaller hotels in Waikiki. It's nestled in an acre of tropical plants, and boasts a big, beautiful swimming pool; in such a setting, it's easy to forget that you're in the midst of bustling Waikiki. All rooms have complete kitchenettes, color TV, telephones, lanais, and, of course, air conditioning. The decor is soft Polynesian, with floral prints. Rates here go from $35 to $46 single and from $39 to $50 double. The less expensive rooms are in the main building facing the street; higher priced and quieter ones are in the garden buildings. A third person in the room is charged $6; a fourth, $4. One-bedroom suites offer a bit of luxury at $52 single, $56 double. Guests receive complimentary newspaper and coffee in the morning and rum punch on Monday evenings. The staff is friendly and courteous. For toll-free reservations, phone 800/421-0680. *(Note:* White Sands is basically a time-sharing condo, but they do rent empty rooms to the general public.)

It was love at first sight when we saw the **Sherry Waikiki,** 334 Lewers St., Honolulu, HI 96815 (tel. 922-2771), one of the newer hotels in town, with a high standard of taste and quality in all its public areas and rooms. Its studio rooms are beautifully decorated units with a double bed, deep-blue carpeting, tasteful paintings on the wall, wicker and bamboo furniture, spacious closets and vanity-dressing room area, full tub-showers, private phones, and long and narrow lanais. And these rooms, like all in this hotel, have a nifty little kitchenette unit with stove and sink on top, refrigerator underneath, toaster, utensils, dishes—everything you need to keep the home fires burning. They are priced at $50 for one or two persons. Larger studios—which can accommodate four people—are $60 double, and the handsome one-bedroom apartments are $75 for up to four people; they can accommodate one more, and the extra charge is $7. Parking is $2 a day, and there are washer-dryers on alternate floors. There's an open, airy feeling throughout. It's a short block to the heart of Waikiki Beach. For reservations, call toll free 800/367-2373, or locally, 923-0222).

The **Waikiki Village Hotel,** 240 Lewers St., Honolulu, HI 96815 (tel. 923-3881), is the first hotel we've ever seen with a swimming pool in the center of the lobby! The lobby is a quadrangle built around the pool and there's no ceiling in the center, so you can swim and sunbathe while checking out the new arrivals. The hotel is decorated from lobby to rooms in a bright blending of contemporary and Polynesian styles. Each of the 450 units has air conditioning, a television set, at least one lanai—some rooms have two! Rooms are all the same, although those on the lower floors are cheaper; the prices, bottom to top, are $36 to $44, single or twin. Kitchenette units—standard, moderate, and deluxe—go for $48 to $50. Family suites are $50 to $54 for up to four persons. These have half-size refrigerators and hotplates. The Village boasts its own restaurant, cocktail lounge, and several attractive shops—and a superb location right in the middle of everything and close to the beach. See the Readers' Selections for a personal report. For reservations from the U.S. mainland, phone toll free 800/367-5170.

The **Waikiki Malia Hotel,** 2211 Kuhio Ave., Honolulu, HI 96815 (tel.

923-7621), is a bright and beautiful new hotel in town. The rooms in the Malia wing, the taller of the hotel's two sections, contain two double beds with Polynesian print bedspreads in soft, muted colors and russet wall-to-wall carpeting. All rooms in the hotel have color TVs, telephones, and lanais, both tub and shower in the bathrooms, as well as small refrigerators and ironing boards. Handicapped people will be glad to know that there are 16 rooms in this wing especially designed for them, with wider doorways, grab bars in the bathrooms, and twin-size rather than double beds for greater wheelchair mobility. Rooms in the Malia wing rent for $36 single, $46 double from April 1 through December 15, $42 and $52 the rest of the year. Differences in rate depend on the floor; and an extra person in the room pays $7.

Then there's the Luana wing, with its junior suites. These contain a sitting room with two couches and a bedroom with two double beds. The lanais in the suites are much larger than those in the bedrooms in the Malia wing. Junior suites, which can accommodate four guests comfortably, go for $42 single, $47 double from April 1 through December 15, for $52 and $56 the rest of the year. An extra person pays $7. Pluses for guests at both wings include a Jacuzzi whirlpool, a rooftop tennis court, and the excellent Wailana Malia Coffeeshop, open 24 hours a day (see Chapter III). And, of course, the beach is just a block away.

You get a really large room at the **Coral Reef,** a modern high-rise hotel at 2299 Kuhio Ave., Honolulu, HI 96815 (tel. 922-1262), directly behind the International Market Place and a short walk from Waikiki Beach. The 310-room hotel boasts every facility—swimming pool, garage, restaurants, shops—and nicely furnished, air-conditioned rooms that have either one or two double beds (or a double and a single), private lanais, and cable color TV. Prices run from $38 for doubles all the way up to $64 for one-bedroom suites on the higher floors. A third person in the room is charged $7; during the winter season, from December 20 to April 10, add $6 per category. For reservations, call Hotel Corporation of the Pacific toll free at 800/367-5124.

Ewa Waikiki

Brand new and beautiful, **Maile Court,** 2058 Kuhio Ave., Honolulu, HI 96815 (tel. 947-2828), is a welcome addition to the Waikiki scene; it's reasonably priced, designed for the easy life, and well located at the "Gateway to Waikiki," across the road from the well-known Nick's Fishmarket Restaurant—which means it's within easy walking distance of the beach and all the attractions of Kalakaua Avenue. There's a very pleasant feeling here, evident as soon as you walk into the open-air lobby, so pretty with its statuary, fish pond, maroon-and-beige rugs, and dusty-rose and rattan sofas. With over 500 rooms, this 43-story Colony Resorts condominium resort has a variety of accommodations to offer: 322 hotel rooms, 900 studios, and 88 one-bedroom suites. Rooms are of modest size, but most have views (some, from the higher floors, are spectacular), all have attractive furnishings, flower prints on the walls, cable color TV, and individually controlled air conditioning. There are clocks, radios, tub-showers, phones, but no lanais. Even the hotel rooms boast small refrigerators; studios and suites add a two-burner electric range for light cooking. Prices were modest during the opening season—$35 and $40 for hotel rooms, $40 and $45 for studios, $75 for one-bedroom suites (perfect for two couples or a family, with two bedrooms, two bathrooms, and two refrigerators), and although they will be going up, the hotel manager has promised that there will always be low-budget rooms available. Children under 12 stay free if they use existing beds; rollaways and cribs are charged at $8 each. There's lots to keep you busy in-house: a pool and a huge, hot Jacuzzi on the large, carpeted sundeck; a croquet court; a small fitness center; and Dalt's Restaurant, a lively watering spot for three meals a day. For reservations at Maile Court, phone, toll-free, 800/367-6046.

A favorite oldtimer in Hawaii, the **Hawaiiana Hotel,** 260 Beach Walk, Honolulu, HI 96815 (tel. 923-3811), just keeps getting more and more mellow year after year. One of the few low-rise, garden hotels left in Waikiki, the Hawaiiana is wonderfully located just half a block from good swimming in front of the Reef Hotel and Fort DeRussy. Ninety-five rooms are situated around a gorgeous tropical garden and two swimming pools in the two- and three-story buildings, so you can just step out of your door for a swim in the pool or a complimentary breakfast of juice and coffee out on the patio. Comfortable chairs at poolside are occupied most of the day by guests too content to go out and do much else. Rooms are simply furnished and not fancy, but all have electric kitchens, excellent beds, air conditioning, phones; most have lanais. During the summer (April 20 to December 17), rates are $41 to $56 single, $44 to $58 double for studios with kitchens; one-bedroom suites are $80 to $83 with kitchens; an additional person is charged $11. During the winter, rates are about $3 higher. Several package deals offer good value; inquire of the management. The real charm here is in the grounds, and especially in the all-Hawaiian staff, who treat each guest with true aloha, and dispense such welcome extras as pineapple upon arrival, flower leis on departure, free newspapers in the morning or afternoon, Hawaiian shows twice a week, free use of washing and drying machines, free parking at the rear of the hotel on Saratoga Road. A real taste of oldtime Hawaii. For reservations, phone toll-free 800/367-5122; from Canada, call collect, 808/922-8188.

The modest-looking **Kai Aloha Hotel,** at 235 Saratoga Rd., Honolulu, HI 96815 (tel. 923-6723), is the kind of place whose faithful fans return year after year. They prefer the homeyness of this simple little hotel, the friendliness of the management, and the feeling of intimacy rare at the more impersonal concrete high-rise hotels. The location, very close to the beach and shopping area, is convenient, and the lush tropical plantings add an island flavor. Every unit has either a modern kitchen or kitchenette; apartments have full-size refrigerators, and the studios, half-size ones. All units have garbage disposals, toasters, and ironing boards. There are coin-operated laundry facilities available on the premises. Every unit has air conditioning, although on our last visit the trade winds alone made the rooms delightfully cool on a very hot day. Lanai studios, all with their own little porches, are $36 to $38 double; the one-bedroom apartments are $44 to $46. The latter can comfortably accommodate families of four or five, with twin beds in the living room as well as living-room furniture. There is a charge of $7 for each additional person, and children are welcome.

Although it looks better from the outside than it does inside, **Ambassador Hotel of Waikiki,** 2040 Kuhio Ave., Honolulu, HI 96815 (tel. 941-7777), is still good value for the money. All the of the rooms in this high-rise building are approached from outside walkways, and all studios from the second through seventh floors boast private lanais, contemporary furniture, air conditioning, and deep *furo*-type shower-tubs. You can relax at the big pool and sundeck on the second floor, eat at the Café Ambassador, and you're close to all the attractions of Waikiki. Rates for studio rooms range from $32 to $40 single, $36 to $44 double, and there are also deluxe one-bedroom suites, with full electric kitchens, from $58 to $74. Studios with kitchens on request.

The **Waikiki Gateway Hotel,** at 2070 Kalakaua Ave., Honolulu, HI 96815 (tel. 955-3741), manages to stay within our budget for most of the year—from April 15 to December 20. The theme throughout is the Hawaii of bygone days, before the arrival of the missionaries. A well-known island artist is responsible for the murals that decorate the lobby and all of the rooms. Studio rooms are priced from $30 to $38 double, and each has a private lanai, TV set, luxurious bath with both tub and shower, and air conditioning. During the winter months, it's $8 to $9 more per category. An additional person is charged $8 to $9. Rooms have refrigerators and hotplates. A recent million-dollar renovation has included new furniture, drapes, carpeting, bedspreads, and painting. The beach is less than a ten-minute walk, but if you'd rather swim at home, try the beautiful pool backed by a volcanic rock wall and a spacious sundeck. Adjacent to the pool area is a room with laundry facilities. Toll-free reservations: 800/367-5124.

Near the Ala Wai

The **Hawaiian Monarch,** 444 Nui Rd., Honolulu, HI 96815 (tel. 949-3911), is Japan Air Line's entry into the Honolulu hotel scene. The skyscraper is situated very close to the Ala Wai Canal and halfway between the Ala Moana Shopping Center and the beaches of Waikiki. It's a well-run first-class hotel, with a mixed Japanese-haole international clientele, complete with all the amenities of tourist life: a huge sundeck and regular pool, plenty of shops in the arcade, two popular restaurants (Serena, known for prime rib dinners, and Cast 'n' Kettle for seafood and steak), and the cozy Piko Bar in the main lobby, where there are free pupus during he Happy Hour, plus Hawaiian-style entertainment every night. A shuttle bus runs on a frequent schedule to shepherd guests to Ala Moana Shopping Center and the heart of Waikiki. Parking is available at a nominal fee.

The Hawaiian Monarch is part hotel, part condo, and the hotel rooms, which occupy the 7th to 24th floors, all have individually controlled air conditioning, color TV, telephone, tub/shower combinations. They are small and pleasantly furnished, of no particular charm, but comfortable enough. The nicest views are those overlooking the Ala Wai Canal. In the off-season, April 1 through December 20, standard rooms are $36 and $42, superior rooms are $40 and $46, deluxe rooms are $48 and $50, and suites are $80. A third person in the room is charged $8; children under 12 stay free with their parents. For reservations, call toll free (except in New York) 800/221-4872; in New York and Canada, call collect, 212/867-1092; in Los Angeles, call 213/488-9917. Reservations can also be made through any Japan Air Lines office.

Near Ala Moana

One of the most attractive of the new chain of Colony Hotels is **Inn on the Park,** located at 1920 Ala Moana Blvd., Honolulu, HI 96815 (tel. 946-8355). A five-minute walk from Fort DeRussy Beach, the inn is across the big road from the Hawaiian Village. This is a 230-unit, all-condominium hotel, with smallish but very pretty rooms attractively decorated with floral spreads, nice prints on the wall, and white furniture. Very helpful for those wishing to eat breakfast in and fix a light lunch are the refrigerators under the sink, toasters, and electric coffeepots in each room. (For more serious cooking, you'd have to get one of the kitchenette units.) This place would be most suitable for twosomes; families might find it a bit tight. The lobby is wood-paneled, with Oriental rugs and candelabra-style chandeliers. There's a nice pool and sunning area on the fifth floor next to the Inn Beer Garden, another bar on the second floor, and the Liliane Chinese Restaurant on the ground floor, which has built a sizable reputation for gourmet Chinese cooking despite its plain looks. The Pantry Store provides groceries and sundries.

Accommodations here are in three classes: superior, deluxe, and kitchenette. The superior rooms, most with twin beds, do not have lanais; they run $38, single or double. Deluxe rooms with lanais are priced at $44, single or double. Kitchenette units are $54, single or double. All rooms have color TV with 11 channels of programming. For toll-free reservations, phone 800/367-6046, except in California; 800/272-3282 in California, excluding Los Angeles; and 213/988-0540 in Los Angeles.

A new skyscraper in this area, the **Waikiki Hobron,** 343 Hobron Lane, Honolulu, HI 96815, at Discovery Bay (tel. 942-7777), has 600 attractive accommodations to its credit. The 43-story condominium hotel was already bustling with many tour groups about three months after its opening when we first inspected it. There are 160 hotel rooms, 140 studios, and 150 deluxe studios. Most of these rooms look similar, the major difference being in height. All rooms have attractive blonde wood furniture (desk, vanity, chair), multicolored drapes and bedspreads, air conditioning, TV; they are small but well appointed, and many offer very good views of ocean, city, mountains, and the nearby Ala Wai Yacht Harbor. Most rooms have twin beds; only four on each floor have queen-size beds, which must be requested in advance. There are also differences in housekeeping facilities: the hotel rooms, which rent for $30 superior, $35 deluxe, have refrigerators only; the studios, which go for $35 superior, $40 deluxe, have mini-kitchenettes. Rates are expected to rise about 15%. There's a nice pool on the mezzanine level, a sundeck plus Jacuzzi and sauna on the fifth floor. A restaurant was being planned at the time of this writing. Parking is available to hotel guests at $3 a day. All the excitement of the Ilikai and Hilton Hawaiian Village complexes are about five minutes away. For toll-free reservations, phone 800/367-5124.

The **Waikiki Marina,** 1956 Ala Moana Blvd., Honolulu, HI 96815 (tel. 955-0714), is a handsome hotel, just a few steps away from the Hilton Hawaiian Village and Rainbow Bazaar complex, boasting a large swimming pool and sundeck, plus central air conditioning, and cable color TV. The most inexpensive accommodations here are the standard hotel rooms, which go for $30, single or double, from April 20 to December 19, and $41 the rest of the year. If you want to cook in, however, it's worthwhile to go a little higher to get one of the deluxe, full-kitchenette studios at $36 in summer, $47 in winter. The studios are adequate in size, accented in blues and greens, with sliding glass doors opening onto a small lanai that seats two. Inside are a kitchenette with base refrigerator and two-burner range, a tub-shower combination, television, and phone. Apartment suites for up to four persons are available at $45 during summer,

$55 in winter. An extra person is $8. For toll-free reservations, phone 800/367-6070.

The **Hawaiian Colony,** at 1946 Ala Moana Blvd., Honolulu, HI 96815 (tel. 941-3302), is in the process of a total renovation after having taken over from the old Waikiki Blue Sky Hotel. The three-story building is built around a swimming pool and offers a sundeck overlooking Fort DeRussy (which has one of the best beaches in town). The accommodations are cozy studio apartments with all-electric kitchenettes, cane furniture, and Polynesian print spreads and drapes. Newly renovated courtyard rooms are priced at $31 and $41, and have new carpeting and all new kitchenette units. Until renovations are completed on the rooms at the front—facing Ala Moana, and not as quiet as those in the courtyard—low prices of $25 double prevail. All rooms have color TVs.

Another good choice in this neighborhood, the **Hawaii Dynasty Hotel,** 1830 Ala Moana Blvd., Honolulu, HI 96815 (tel. 955-1111), is a high-rise hotel with an inn atmosphere. The accent is on comfort, with medium-size rooms and oversize beds. Twin beds are as big as most doubles, the doubles enormous. Rooms are tastefully furnished, with combination tub-showers in the bathroom, TV, and individual air-conditioning units. There are no cooking facilities, but a laundry room is available. The pool on the second floor is one of the largest in Waikiki. Now for the prices: doubles from $33 to $44, plus a high-season surcharge of $7 from December 21 through April 10. An additional person is $7. For reservations, call toll free 800/421-6662.

A Reminder: Unless you want to spend most of your time in this area around the big Ilikai and Hilton Hawaiian Village complex of hotels, stores, restaurants, and beaches, you'd better have a car or be prepared to take the bus; it's a healthy ten-minute walk to either the center of Waikiki or the Ala Moana Shopping Center and Ala Moana Beach Park.

To compensate for not being right where the action is, the **Pagoda Hotel,** 1525 Rycroft St., Honolulu, HI 96814 (tel. 941-6611), keeps a free bus shuttling back and forth between the hotel and the Pacific Beach Hotel in Waikiki. But you won't be isolated here: not only are you near the shopping center, but right on the grounds is one of Honolulu's most spectacular restaurants, the Pagoda, with its colorful displays of flashing carp. Most important, though, is what you'll get for your $38 single or $42 double: a studio room nicely set up for housekeeping, with a full-size refrigerator, four-burner range, and all the necessary equipment. Additional persons are charged $8. Rates may rise by $2 or $3 soon. You can pay more to go higher up in the building ($4), but don't expect spectacular views here, as you're about a third of a mile from the water (in view over the Ala Moana Shopping Center). The rooms are air-conditioned, and a swimming pool is here for the dunking. Color TV in all rooms.

2. Hotels in Downtown Honolulu

Tourists who prefer to stay in downtown Honolulu (an easy bus ride from Waikiki) rather than in the beach area will have somewhat tougher sledding; there are so few hotels outside Waikiki that most tourists never hear about them at all. They are primarily occupied by businesspeople. But there are a few in our budget category, and because this area is ideal for serious sightseeing, you may want to consider them.

There are only 41 units in the **Nakamura Hotel,** 1140 S. King St., Honolulu, HI 96814, just off Piikoi Street (tel. 537-1951), but you may be lucky enough to find a room on the spur of the moment since it's off the tourist mainstream. We say lucky because rates are only $22 to $24, double or twin, in this clean and quite comfortably appointed building; and because each and every room has wall-to-wall carpeting, large, tiled bathroom with a tub-shower combo, good drawer and closet space, even a telephone. We prefer the rooms facing the mountains; even though they do not have air conditioning, they do have those refreshing trade winds. In the air-conditioned rooms, the machine also has to drown out the traffic on King Street (so keep those jalousied windows closed). All these rooms are too small for a third person, but there are a few larger rooms in which a third person is permitted for an additional $4. Mrs. Winifred Hakoda, the personable desk clerk and day manager, advises that no late arrivals (after 10 p.m. on weekdays, after 9 p.m. on Sunday) are accepted.

Also pleasant is the tastefully modern **Kobayashi Hotel,** 250 N. Beretania St., Honolulu, HI 96817 (tel. 536-2377), a Japanese establishment where you'll mingle, so the management promises, "with important personages and travelers of every race." All this cosmopolitanism costs $24, single or double. Don't expect to sleep on the floor Japanese style: the bedrooms are as Western as the air conditioning. The inexpensive restaurant, however, serves authentic Japanese (and American) dishes.

For men, the **Nuuanu YMCA** is a good downtown bet at 1441 Pali Hwy., Honolulu, HI 96813, near South Vineyard Boulevard (tel. 536-3556). It is a modern, $1.3-million facility with 70 dormitory rooms; singles go for $14 to $15 a day. Weekly rates are available, and advance reservations are accepted. There's a cafeteria here, and excellent athletic facilities are made available to residents.

For women tourists who'd like to stay at a **Y,** Honolulu has a terrific answer: the **Fernhurst YWCA,** an attractive tropical residence at 1566 Wilder Ave., Honolulu, HI 96822, about halfway between downtown Honolulu and Waikiki (tel. 941-2231). Women can stay overnight, or for up to one year, as the residence accepts both short- and long-term visitors, many of the latter from countries around the world. So staying here is a good way to get to know people from many countries and backgrounds. The accommodations are double rooms, nicely furnished and decorated, each joined to another room by a common bath. At times single rooms are available. For a double occupancy, each person pays $14 a night with YWCA membership ($16 without), and that includes two meals a day—surely one of the best buys in town! The room and board charge for a single room is $20 a night. Linens may be rented for a nominal fee if you do not wish to provide your own. Pluses include a swimming pool, garden, laundry room, and a lounge area. Also available for use: typewriters, piano, TV, sewing machine. Advance reservations are accepted with a one-night deposit. Fernhurst recommends that you write first and inquire about future accommodations.

Both military and nonmilitary men and women are welcome to stay at the **Armed Services YMCA,** 250 S. Hotel St., Honolulu, HI 96813 (tel. 524-5600), an older, well-equipped building downtown. Rates range from $15 in a single, community bath only, to $22 in a double with private bath. Active-duty military and dependent discounts are available. There's an outdoor swimming pool, gym, and restaurant right at hand—and bus service in front of the building to all of Oahu.

3. Hotels in Windward Oahu

Windward Oahu, as you'll recall from the introduction to this chapter, is the area on the other side of the mighty Koolau mountain range, which serves as a backdrop to Honolulu. The scenery is comparable to what you'll find on the neighbor islands. This is "the country," where many local people spend their vacations, but it's far off the usual tourist track. Although this is a good jumping-off spot from which to visit many of the attractions of the windward side, it's essentially a place where you sit on the gorgeous beach surrounded by sea, sky, and fragrant blossoms and do absolutely nothing at all.

If you're not going to the neighbor islands and you find Waikiki too much hustle and bustle, **Pat's at Punaluu,** 53-567 Kamehameha Hwy., Hauula, HI 96717 (tel. 293-8111), might be just the antidote to civilization you're looking for. Pat's enjoys an idyllic setting: the 140-room, nine-story condominium apartment building directly overlooks a glorious, reef-protected beach and lagoon, ideal for swimming and snorkeling. There's a seaside restaurant right on the premises (Hawaiian-style entertainment most nights, a good $6.95 buffet lunch every day), plus a big freshwater pool, gym, sauna (imagine jumping from the sauna right into the ocean!), and other recreational facilities for the comfort of its long-term residents. But about 30 of the apartments are available for short stays; they all have lanais (some rather large) overlooking the ocean, are attractive and comfortable (each has been individually decorated by its owners), and decently priced. All studios and apartments can comfortably accommodate up to four people. The smallest unit—called the Lodge ($48 a day)—is definitely not small; it has 622 square feet, and is so arranged that the living area is entirely separate from the sleeping alcove. The Deluxe Lodge ($52) adds another 100 or so square feet of space and boasts wrap-around lanais with ocean and mountain views. The one-bedroom apartments ($56 to $60) are even more spacious. Rates go down several dollars a day if you stay more than one day; monthly rates are also available. Except for the Lodge units, which have limited cooking facilities, all units have full kitchens, complete with dishwashers, washer-dryer combinations, and garbage disposal units. You could easily live here for a long time, and many people do. Waikiki and the excitement of the city are about an hour's drive away.

For reservations, and to inquire about apartment/car-rental deals, call, toll free, 800/367-2686, or write to the manager, Jack Chafee, at Pat's at Punaluu, P.O. Box 359, Hauula, HI 96717.

Located right next door to the Polynesian Cultural Center, the **Laniloa Lodge Hotel,** 55-109 Laniloa St. in Laie, HI 96762 (tel. 293-9282), is a modern, motel-like building offering lots of comfort and a good location not far from many of the attractions of the North Shore. Right at home is a sandy ocean beach and pool; a short drive away is all the swimming, surfing, windsurfing, diving, horseback riding, and the like available in the Sunset Beach and Haleiwa area. Waimea Bay offers some of the world's best swimming (in summer) and best surfing (in winter); Waimea Falls Park is delightful, and Haleiwa has many shops and restaurants and an artsy-craftsy atmosphere. Rooms at Laniloa Lodge are nicely furnished, all with refrigerators, private lanais, cable color TV, and air conditioning, and they all look out on the pool. Rates, subject to change, are $39 single, $43 double, $47 triple, $51 quad. Family rates are $43 per room; children must be under 18. Inclusive hotel-car packages are also available.

SOME FINAL WORDS ON LODGINGS: If you'd like to exchange your own home or apartment for a place to stay in Honolulu, it can probably be arranged. Get in touch with the **Vacation Exchange Club,** 12006 111th Ave., Unit 12, Youngstown, AZ 85363 (tel. 602/972-2186), a worldwide home-swapping group. You can be listed in their directory for $22.70 (or receive their directory without being listed for $15) a year and find out what's available in Hawaii (a recent listing, for example, offered a three-bedroom, two-bath house, along with two cars and two bikes, in the posh Kahala region, for a three-month exchange), as well as many other places in the world. Rentals are also available. Vacation Exchange Club provides information only (it is not a travel agency); the actual arrangements are all up to you.

The bed-and-breakfast concept is gaining in popularity all over the United States, and Hawaii is no exception. Evelyn Warner and Al Davis started **Island Bed & Breakfast Hawaii** a few years ago, "not as a big business operation, but as a low-key, intimate way for people to visit Hawaii." They offer accommodations in private homes and apartments on all the islands, for rates ranging from $15 to $35 single, $20 to $60 double, including continental breakfast. If you think you'd like to live in a private home in the islands, this might be for you. Write for a free brochure to Bed & Breakfast Hawaii, P.O. Box 449, Kapaa, HI 96746 (tel. 822-1582). Members pay a $5 membership fee and then receive a directory of homes and apartments that can be rented.

The **Shower Tree** at Honolulu International Airport is something every traveler should know about—just in case. In case your plane departure is delayed, or you have to wait several hours to make a connecting flight, or you simply need a place to be if you've checked out of your hotel early and have a late-night flight. That's where the Shower Tree comes in. This clean and pleasant new facility offers showers and eight beds where you can catch a nap for an hour or two or more. The cost for a shower, including soap, towels, shampoo, deodorant, shaving equipment, and hairdryer is $7.50; resting facilities cost $3 an hour, $18 for any eight-hour period, which includes a shower. A sitting room and kitchen are available. Reservations are advised for sleeping space. The Shower Tree is tucked away behind the ticket counter for Continental Airlines, on the second level of the main terminal (tel. 836-3044). A refreshing idea.

READERS' HOTEL SELECTIONS: "Might I suggest to your readers that they visit Hawaii as I did. I spent six weeks in Honolulu as a student at the **University of Hawaii** at Manoa. The cost of dorm room and board was very economical. Many tours, at special prices, were provided through the university. Our summer student identity cards even got us 'kamaaina' rates at various clubs and attractions. We were often roomed with local students and were thus able to share our different cultures. This is not just meant for single students; there were some dorm facilities for couples. The course selection is wide, ranging from golf and tennis to more academic studies. By the end of six weeks, I was referring to the dorm as 'home'" (Susan McEwin, Stratford, Ontario, Canada). . . . "There was a big robbery in our hotel, which occurred only because people on the 12th floor kept their lanai doors open, thinking no one could get in. The robber crawled from the stairway, went from one lanai to another, entering and stealing from purses. Please keep your doors locked at night! We were lucky, as ours was locked" (Dorothy and Mike Capellani, Chicago, Ill.).

"Three cheers for the **Waikiki Towers Hotel,** 200 Lewers, adjacent to the Edgewater! Since we went to Hawaii to be outdoors, the small, $33 room was just perfect! The rooms (we moved a couple of times before and after our outer-island trips) were clean; the maid service was cheerful; the front desk staff *most* accommodating; the in-house Happy Hour the best we found in Waikiki; the restaurants excellent in terms of food, service, and atmosphere; the location excellent; and all-around the best accommodation of our entire trip" (Mr. and Mrs. Lorne Alton, Edmonton, Alberta, Canada). . . . "I stayed at **Edmonds Hotel Apartments** ($20 now), near the beach, quite homey and helpful, right by the Ala Wai Canal, which not only provided a nice view of golf course, mountains, and cityscape from my lanai, but a jogging course along the canal with observations of local crab fishing" (Margaret H. Mills, Albuquerque, N.M.). . . . "The cheapest way to get from Honolulu International Airport to Waikiki, if you are in a party of two or more and have luggage, is just to walk upstairs to the passenger departure level and catch a cab there. The taxis that bring people to the airport are not allowed to use the lower level (passenger arrival). So after the cab drivers drop someone off at the airport, they are very eager not to have to drive back to Waikiki empty. Depending on the driver, they'll usually take up to four people back to Waikiki for about $7" (Morgan Tallman, Wayne, Mich.). . . . "A fellow Army captain and myself were en route to Australia and waiting in Hawaii for a flight. We took your advice and stayed at both the Malihini and Reef Lanais. Both were very reasonable—$20.80 a night. A special note might be included for military readers. Both these hotels are only minutes from the Fort DeRussy complex and the military exchange store, and the prices of these rooms on Saratoga Road are almost half those of Hale Koa, the military hotel" (Capt. Don Huskey, Hinesville, Ga.).

"We arrived at Honolulu at the height of Hurricane Iwa. All was chaos—no power, no telephones, streets flooded and closed. It took us three hours to get from the airport, the final 300 yards wading through knee-deep water buffeted by high winds, carrying luggage, and trying to find the **Hale Pua Nui** on Beach Walk, when out of the darkness came a flashlight and people calling our name. It was the Headys: with no idea whether our flight had even landed, they waited and watched for us, truly outstanding hosts, having stayed on over six hours past their office closing time. Our top rating for their aloha spirit" (John and Maureen Royle, Pitt Meadows, B.C., Canada). . . . "Of all the places I have seen in the world, Waikiki is the one to which I hope to return, mainly due to the wonderful people and services at the **Outrigger.** I found it possible to ignore the slums of Pearl City, the condo salespeople, and other irritants, because the good things far outweigh the bad. At the Outrigger, right on the beach, we asked for the cheapest room and received a very large room containing a bedroom, sitting room (with convertible bed), balcony, bath, and powder room. There were two large closets, one containing a personal safe, so guests have the choice of using the room safe or individual deposit boxes at the desk. Amenities include an unlimited supply of postcards, stationery, refrigerator in each room, coffee maker, and a large amount of coffee, tea, sugar, and creamer packets, which made waking up a pleasure. Coffee and juice on the balcony with a view of the beach became part of our Hawaiian experience. The Outrigger also provides an outdoor laundry area, unlimited beach towels, sand chairs, chaise lounges, and beach showers between the beach and the palm-lined sun patio. In future, I would always head for the Outrigger!" (W. J. Murphy, Falmouth, Mass.). *Authors' Note:* Doubles at the Outrigger, 2335 Kalakaua Ave., are currently going for $60 to $125.]

"The only lodging place we could find in Kaneohe was the **Bayview Apartment**

Hotel, on Kaneohe Bay Drive (tel. 247-3635) toward the east end of town. Furnished suites for two are $32 a day, with cooking and laundry facilities" (Dorothea Smith, Wilmington, Ill.). . . . "We stayed at the **Royal Grove Hotel** and loved it. Not only was it economical, but the Fongs made our stay at their hotel pleasurable and a Hawaii 'learning experience.' Occasionally they have a barbecue complete with Hawaiian song and dance. And on our last night there we attended a luau at their home on Diamond Head. The food was delicious and the company was the best! I've been to Hawaii before, but I've never gotten to know Hawaii until this visit" (Jackie and Keith Fannin, Akron, Ohio). . . . "The best thing about the **Edgewater Hotel** is that it is cooled by fans in the lobby and trade winds in the rooms; the windows open, and the panels on the louvered doors can be opened for cross-drafts. Since the hotel is away from traffic and surrounded by high-rises, it is quiet so you don't have to suffer in drafty, noisy air conditioning. The staff is very friendly, the rooms are spacious, clean, and comfortable, and you are a block from the beach. Terrific!" (Betty and Bud Eldon, Los Altos, Calif.).

"We studied your descriptions of the hotels in Honolulu and the **Kai Aloha Hotel** at 235 Saratoga Rd. seemed to offer what we wanted. We decided on the lanai studio apartment at $36 a day. We couldn't have made a better choice! The room was large, airy—air-conditioned, but not needed—and immaculate. The large closet and dressing area adjoining the bath was a plus not often found in hotels. The daily maid service was a benefit usually lacking in an apartment dwelling. The manager, Miss E. Chang, is a pleasant, helpful hostess who obviously cares about the comfort of her guests. The location of the Kai Aloha, less than five minutes' walk from uncrowded Fort DeRussy Beach, made it more attractive to us than many of the large hotels with their limited beach facilities. We can understand why so many of her guests return year after year" (Anne and Arthur Desmond, Braintree, Mass.). . . . "I paid $126 per week at **Mrs. Na'ai's** at 53-224 Kam Hwy. (tel. 237-8169). This is an efficiency apartment with small kitchen and shower, no tub. It is one of 14 apartments on landscaped grounds. They were built about 1950, but are clean and comfortable. Rates run from $325 per month, and some are available by the week. Hawaiian friends, residents in Punaluu, helped me find this place; there's access to a beautiful, fine, soft sand beach with swimming and fishing privileges. It is located just eight-tenths of a mile southeast of Pat's at Punaluu, right on the Kam Highway. Packages of dried noodles in Styrofoam cups are available in the small local groceries; these are easily prepared, and with fresh fruit, also available locally and inexpensively, provide very reasonable food; one can splurge occasionally on a nice dinner or luncheon" (David C. Moore, Phoenix, Ariz.).

"Please warn people against free offers by employees of **time-sharing companies.** Tourists are assaulted with offers all over Waikiki. They promise you free transportation and free breakfast, which turns out to be coffee, orange juice, and doughnuts. What they don't tell you is that transportation is one-way. We were subjected to high-pressure sales tactics. Three different men with three different approaches worked on us in turn. The 90-minute presentation turned out to be three hours, and then we were informed that we had to find our own transportation back to our hotel at the other end of Waikiki. I strongly feel that if people want to take advantage of the free offers, fine. But they should be prepared for some wicked sales pressure" (Pat Barnes, no address given). . . . "We were very quick to discover the variety and intensity of competition among time-share promoters in Waikiki to enlist visitors to attend 'no obligation' sales presentations. We were very cautious and avoided all the associated discounted tours, sunset sails, etc., until we succumbed to what appeared to be a very generous discount on a compact convertible rental and a 'promised' soft-sell pitch. The next morning we spent 2½ hours subjected to a steadily intensified hard-sell of a condominium time-share on Waikiki. The salespeople tried every approach thinkable to convince us of the affordability of the time-share and the variety of ways we could pay for it. We are both very experienced and skilled at resisting a hard-sell, but this eyeball-to-eyeball team concept tried our intelligence and ingenuity. Only accidentally did we happen upon what we believe to be a foolproof response to such pressure. We ascertained from the sales staff that by

Hawaiian state law the time-share property can only be offered for sale within the state of Hawaii. The parties also have five days within which to finalize or negate the contract. So these companies are pressured into completing the sales quickly, at the presentation if possible. We asked them for a property report to take with us (which they repeatedly refused to provide) and told them our attorney back home would have to examine a property statement and all other details of the proposal. This quickly ended the pitch as there were no copies of the property report available and our attorney's involvement would put the sale out of the legal time frame as well as out of the state. If we had known this at the beginning of the presentation, we would have had another morning of our vacation to enjoy in addition to our discounted car rental" (Philip and Vicki Hodgen, Milwaukie, Ore.). [*Authors' Note:* Our own personal reaction to the time-sharing peddlers: Avoid them unless you're seriously interested in buying, or unless you have unlimited time and very strong sales resistance. Otherwise, vacation time is too precious to waste on this sort of hustle.]

"I stayed at the **Waikiki Surf East,** 422 Royal Hawaiian Ave. (tel. 923-7671). For my $24 single (doubles are $24 to $30), I had a wall-to-wall carpeted room with kitchenette and bath, maid service, TV, telephone, full air conditioning, mail delivered to room" (Mrs. Lorace Gray, Vallejo, Calif.). . . . "We certainly enjoyed the convenient, quiet **Hawaii Dynasty Hotel;** it was all you said. Our $38 spacious double looked down on the pool. The no. 8 bus stops right in front and goes directly to the airport for 50¢. The number of Japanese staying there added to the delightfully polite Oriental atmosphere of this completely American hotel" (Pat Diehnelt, Menomee Falls, Wisc.). . . . "We stayed at a hotel recommended by a friend who lives in Hawaii and found it a terrific bargain. It was the **Holiday Surf Apartment Hotel,** 2303 Ala Wai Blvd. (tel. 923-8488). Clean as a whistle! Daily maid service, modern electric stove and fridge. Daily rates for a studio apartment are $24 to $36 per day; for a one-bedroom, $27 to $40; $3 for each additional person, and so forth. This place is very popular with the military, so it is recommended to write well in advance. Only five short minutes to the beach and parking beneath the building" (John Creighton, Vancouver, B.C., Canada). [*Authors' Note:* The annex at 2231 Ala Wai Blvd. charges $20 to $25 a day on stays of at least five days.]. . . . "We stayed at the **Hawaiiana Hotel,** 260 Beach Walk, where the rates are high, but well worth the money. The hotel has 95 units overlooking the garden and two pools (one for children). Also included: complimentary pineapple juice and Kona coffee in the mornings, an island staff for hospitality, hula shows twice a week, a movie once a week, full beach facilities, travel and sightseeing service, complimentary newspaper each morning and evening, daily maid service, etc." (Jim Hart, Jr., Everett, Wash.). [*Authors' Note:* We agree; it's a super hotel. See our comments in the text.]

"We spent five weeks on Oahu, having previously arranged to exchange homes with a couple who lived in a delightful home in Manoa Valley. Surprisingly, many island people do like to have excursions to the mainland, and home exchange is an ideal way of providing the basis for a really inexpensive vacation. A government employees' bulletin circulates in Honolulu and elsewhere, and at the University of Hawaii; this provides a good place to advertise" (David Brokensha, Santa Barbara, Calif.). . . . "We got to Honolulu on a Saturday with no reservations and a lot of misgivings, correctly placed. *Everything* was full, including the superdollar places. In the event any of your readers should get stuck thus, the **Pacific Marina Inn** (tel. 836-1131) near the airport nearly always has something available. We wound up in a small room that went for $40 single, $42 double, not bad, with shower and air conditioning, a decent café, and a swimming pool. The free shuttle service to the airport saves money, and it's near several car-rental places" (C. R. Snyder, San Diego, Calif.). [*Authors' Note:* Kitchenette suites are available, and so are weekly rates.] . . . "We stayed in the **Ilima Hotel** (tel. 923-1877) at 445 Nohonani St. We paid only $39 a day for a studio unit with two double beds and complete kitchen. There was plenty of storage in the apartment, the kitchen included all the plates, etc.—even a toaster—and everything was very clean. It was only two blocks from the beach. We will stay there again on our next visit, if rates and quality stay the same" (Mrs. Lew Fisk, Greenwood, Ind.). [*Authors'*

Note: Rooms run from $31 to $48.] . . . "Some hotels will give a 25% to 50% discount off their published room rates for military personnel and their families. We stayed at three- and four-star hotels at half the normal room rate. I believe that many of your readers are in the U.S. military and would be happy to know about this benefit!" (Joe and Robin Gruender, Wright-Patterson AFB, Ohio).

Chapter III

HONOLULU: RESTAURANTS AND NIGHTLIFE

CAN THE AVERAGE TOURIST still find romance, happiness, and a good inexpensive meal in Hawaii? Well, we won't make any rash promises on the first two counts (that's up to you), but on the third we can be quite positive: despite inflation everywhere, Honolulu's restaurants still do very well for the tourist. Although the price for dinner at one of the really elegant restaurants can easily zoom into the stratosphere, most of the good restaurants are in the middle range, which means soup to nuts averaging $9 to $14. And there are also quite a few—praise be—where a good dinner need average no more than $7 to $8. That's where we come in. Even if you wish to spend as little as $15 a day on food, you should have no trouble figuring about $8 for dinner, $4 for lunch, and $3 for breakfast. To keep on a really tight budget, plan to eat breakfast and at least one meal a day at home; that's when your kitchenette apartment more than pays for itself. Remember that lunch is always cheaper than dinner—often for much the same meal.

THE FOOD ITSELF: The food of Hawaii, like its people, reflects a wide cultural diversity—a lot of American, quite a bit of Japanese, a little less of Chinese, a smattering of Hawaiian, Korean, Filipino, and you-name-it thrown in for good measure. You quickly get used to the ubiquitous sign "Japanese Delicatessen" and to the fact that saimin (a Japanese-type noodle soup with a seaweed base) is just as popular as a hamburger and is often served at the same counter. You soon learn that the exotic-sounding mahimahi is Hawaiian for dolphin, a bland and pleasant-tasting fish—not to be confused with the intelligent mammal of the same name, the porpoise. You'll be introduced to poi, the staff of life of the early Hawaiians, at your very first luau, and you may develop a liking for this purple-gray goo that's one of the most nutritious foods known to man, so high in Vitamin B and calcium that it's fed to babies and invalids. Just ignore the old joke that it tastes like library paste; the Hawaiians, and quite a few malihinis, think it's delicious.

Hawaii's fruits are among the islands' special glories. Pineapple, while not exactly invented here, might just as well have been. It's well priced in the markets, served everywhere, and as good as you'd imagine. Pineapple juice is kind of a national drink, something like tea for the English. If you hit the mango season in July, when the local trees are bursting with this succulent fruit, you're in for a great treat. Guavas, coconuts, papayas (one of the most common breakfast foods) are all superb, as are guava juice and passion fruit juice, which you'll often see listed under its Hawaiian name, lilikoi (lilikoi sherbet is wonderful). Macadamia-nut pancakes, as well as coconut ice cream and syrup, are special treats that taste better in Hawaii than anywhere else in the world. We should warn you coffee addicts right here and now—the kind of coffee you'll get everywhere is Kona coffee, grown on the Big Island of Hawaii, and it's so good that you may find yourself drinking innumerable cups a day.

Don't miss the chance to try Hawaii's game fish, caught fresh in local waters, and served up in fish houses under "Catch of the Day." If you're lucky, the catch that day will be ahi (a kind of tuna and a personal favorite), or aki (another tuna), marlin, ulua, opakapaka, rock cod, or a special island delicacy called ono. That word has, in fact, slipped into local parlance as meaning "delicious"—or even "great"—as in "ono ono." At this writing, "Catch of the Day" was selling for about $12 to $14 in most restaurants; save this for a "big splurge" meal.

As for the preparation of these foods, you may not find haute cuisine, but you will find good eating. It is no hardship at all to eat in the budget establishments. Standards of sanitation are very high, and you need have no worries that your food will be anything less than clean, tasty, nourishing, and more often than you'd expect, surprisingly delicious.

1. Restaurants in Waikiki

The most exotic, and the most numerous, budget restaurants are located outside Waikiki. But that doesn't mean you can't have a very good time eating in the beachside area. We'll tell you first about our particular favorites, some three dozen places we call the "fun" restaurants; then move on to the "old reliables," where you can always have a good and inexpensive meal with a minimum of fuss and bother. We've also thrown in a few big splurges—for those moments when you don't mind going slightly beyond your food budget.

THE "FUN" RESTAURANTS: We'll begin with **Perry's Smorgy Restaurants,** which have been offering hearty, American-style buffet meals for as many years as we can remember. They're perhaps the only place in town to offer buffets three times a day. The food here is known to vary: it can be very, very good, and then again, it can be just so-so. But at prices like $6.75 for dinner, $4.75 for lunch, and $3.75 for breakfast, it's always worth a try. Choose either of the two Perry's: one at the **Outrigger Hotel,** with gorgeous oceanside views and tables for watching the world go by, the other at the **Coral Seas Hotel,** across from the Reef Towers at 250 Lewers St. At both, the help-yourself buffet is the same. The table is stacked with about 30 different selections; many fruit and vegetable salads; gelatin combinations; hot vegetables; rice or potatoes; homemade corn muffins and dinner rolls; and lots of hot entrees including southern fried chicken, mahimahi, and Italian spaghetti. Dinner adds a hand-carved round of beef au jus and golden fried shrimp. Fresh island pineapple and local Kona coffee are served at each meal. Breakfast features french toast, blueberry and banana muffins, hotcakes, smoked ham and sausages, and more. You can have as many refills as you like, but no take-home packages, please. Breakfast is served from 7 to 10:30 a.m., lunch from 11 a.m. to 2:30 p.m., dinner from 5 to 9 p.m.

Jameson's Irish Coffee House, 342 Seaside Ave. (tel. 922-3396), is a darlin' place, a wee touch of the old country transplanted to Honolulu. In the attractive pub-like atmosphere—dark woods, low, low lights, stained glass, tufted velvet booths, and Tiffany-type lamps—you dine on the same menu throughout the day. Monday through Saturday from 11:30 a.m. to 1 a.m. and on Sunday from 5 p.m. to 1 a.m., you can always get one of the three main dishes: Mulligan stew, corned beef and cabbage, or seafood quiche at $7.95, and a quiche Lorraine at $6.95, each served with clam chowder (Boston style, of course) or house salad and freshly baked biscuits. There's also a slew of tasty omelets (ham and cheese, cheddar, mushroom, crabmeat, etc.) from $5.95 to $7.75; a huge chef's salad with everything, plus a few burgers and meat sandwiches. Dessert is limited to apple pie or cheesecake. And to be sure, after your meal, or in place of, there's Irish coffee made with Jameson's Irish whisky and a tall layer of whipped cream. Local people like Jameson's as much as the tourists do, and make it a popular after-theater, movie, or symphony hangout—not many nice places like this serve dinner so late.

There's another Jameson's downtown at 16 Merchant St. that's also full of atmosphere and hearty spirits. It's open 11 a.m. to 11 p.m. weekdays only: phone 531-4666 for reservations.

If you can bring yourself to walk past the huge stuffed moose head with a lei around its neck—the first thing you see when you walk in—you'll love **Moose McGillicuddy's Pub-Café,** 310 Lewers St. (tel. 923-0571). It's big and airy—in fact, it's open to the street, with huge rattan Mama-san chairs and shiny ceramic tile floor. This place is very popular among the local folks, since portions are large and prices very reasonable. Their Early Bird Breakfast Special, served from 6:30 to 9 a.m., is one of the best buys in town: two eggs, bacon, toast, rice or potatoes, orange juice, and fresh fruit, all for $1.99. Lunch and dinner menus are the same, and feature "hot 'n' juicy" pizzas ($4.95 to $6.50 for small sizes), gourmet hamburgers (most at $4.50 to $5.40), hearty four-egg omelets served with fries or rice, Texas toast, and fruit ($5.50), hot soups, sandwiches, and salads. We especially like their Munchies: nachos, deep-fried zucchini in beer batter, fried potato skins with beef or cheese, fish 'n' chips, yummy hot Texas chile ($3.50 to $5.95). Along with your meal you can have some far-out exotic drinks, including terrific margaritas and daiquiris at $3.50. A rock 'n' roll band plays nightly for dancing in the upstairs pub. McGillicuddy's is a lively spot, the crowd is congenial, and the menu descriptions an entertainment in themselves (look up, for example, the description of the "Anita Bryant Omelette"). There's another Moose in Lahaina, Maui. Open every day, from 6 a.m. to 2 p.m.

Near the Reef Hotel is the **Buccaneer,** 2164 Kalia Rd. (tel. 923-8186), a great place to know about for a casual-but-intimate lunch or dinner. The pirate mood begins with the torches out front and continues inside with the ship's wheel and lanterns, but the reasonable prices on the menu for the very good steak and seafood specialties are hardly what you'd call piracy. You can get by with a $6.75 entree, or up the tab to only $7.95 for a top sirloin. The nightly entertainment comes gratis and is one of the big draws here—hula dancers, Hawaiian vocalists and instrumentalists. The drinks are just as exotic. Up until 6 p.m., mai tais are only $1.25.

So popular has the Buccaneer become that it has recently doubled its size by adding a picturesque patio complete with a waterfall and palm-covered umbrellas. This might be just the place to have breakfast when you like it—and that means daily until 5 p.m. Then you can order, among other things, a pancake sandwich for $3.45; or you can fill up on the Jamboree Special (two eggs, bacon, sausage, or ham, and all the pancakes you can eat) for $3.95.

The budget crowd is kept well in mind at the **Waikiki Broiler,** in the Waikiki Tower Hotel, 200 Lewers St. (tel. 922-6424), a cozy nautical place lit by ship's lanterns and candles, with old seafaring prints and paintings on the wood-paneled walls. The dining room overlooks the pool area of the Edgewater Hotel; in fact, two of the tables are practically in the pool! The Broiler offers low-priced dinner entrees like fish and chips, Hawaiian chopped steak, teriyaki chicken breasts, and mahimahi steak, from $6 to $7.95—in addition to such higher priced offerings as crab legs, scallops, and roast beef, the specialty of the house. At lunch, there are special sandwiches served with soup or salad (around $5), burgers, and a chef's special salad. Breakfast is served all the way from 7 a.m. to 2 p.m.; waffles or buttermilk pancakes with syrup are a good bet at $1.95.

And there's a long daytime Happy Hour too: mai tais for $1.25 and chi chis for $1.50, from noon to 5 p.m. Plus entertainment on Friday from 9 p.m. until 2 in the morning.

The **Hau Tree Lanai** of the New Otani Kaimana Beach Hotel, 2863 Kalakaua Ave. (opposite Kapiolani Park; tel. 923-1555), is one of those sparkling, over-the-water spots where the atmosphere and food contend for honors. It's so nice to dine here under the hau tree, watching the waves wash up to the shore, and even though a million-dollar refurbishing has recently upped prices, you can still get by with a nice salad bar and soup dinner for $6.95. Since most dinners are in the $11 to $16 range here, stick to the Kapiolani Jogger's Menu; sauteed brook trout, broiled ground beef steak and boneless chicken breast are offered for $8.50 to $10, including green salad and vegetable. Lunch has many reasonably priced sandwiches, several specialties between $4.25 and $6.25, and a refreshing papaya and chicken salad (a fresh papaya half, topped with chicken salad and garnished with fruit slices) at $4.75. For a picturesque beachside breakfast, a full menu is available, starting with pancakes at $2.95.

Just because you're saving money, it doesn't mean that you can't dine in style. If, for example, you'd like to have breakfast at one of the most glamorous tropical settings in town, at coffeehouse prices, simply take yourself over to the **Tahitian Lanai Restaurant** of the Waikikian Hotel, 1811 Ala Moana Blvd. (next to the Ilikai Hotel; tel. 946-6541). Seat yourself at an umbrellaed table overlooking the pool, the tropical lagoon, and the Waikiki surf out beyond (or in the atmospheric lanai dining room), and prepare yourself to feast both eyes and palate. Palm trees ring the pool, and waitresses are clad in Polynesian costumes, and jungle-like island decor is everywhere. While you're soaking it all up, you can order, as we did, coconut waffles or fresh banana griddle cakes for about $2.95, two eggs for $1.85, and Hawaiian banana muffins for $1.25—recommended! If you're a little hungrier, you could have, perhaps, "Half A Benedict"—eggs Benedict served with hash browns, banana muffins, or a scrumptious popover, $4.50 (a "Whole Benedict" is $6.25). Coffee is robust, and served continuously. Come as early as 7:20 a.m.; they stop serving breakfast by 11 a.m.

It's not hard to figure out why the **Shore Bird Beach Broiler,** beachfront at the Reef Hotel, 2169 Kalia Rd. (tel. 922-2887), quickly became one of the most popular restaurants in Waikiki. First of all, you can't beat the location: the large, attractively decorated open dining room is right on Waikiki Beach. Second, the food is good; and third, the price is right: that's because you're the chef, broiling your own portion of teriyaki chicken or ribs, seafood or filet mignon kebab, New York steak, ground or top sirloin. Prices run from $4.95 (for mahimahi) to $10 (for steak and seafood). While the fire is doing its work, you can have a few drinks, then fill up on salad bar, chili, plain or fried beans. Coffee, tea, or iced tea are included with the meal; dessert (heavenly Bob Busch chocolate-chip cheesecake) is extra. Perfect for sunset drinks and dinner. The broiler is hot from 5 to 10 p.m.; from 10 p.m. on the heat is provided by nonstop video, and music and dancing continue until about 2 a.m.

Walk from the Reef's beach to its pool and you'll find more bargain dining: that's at **Sadie Thompson's Poolside Bar and Grill** (tel. 923-3111). Sadie starts the day (every day but Sunday) with a $2.75 breakfast special: eggs, pancakes, bacon, Kona coffee, served up with the morning paper. In the evening the special is barbecued ribs, chicken, and spaghetti, at $4.45. On the regular menu it's spaghetti at $3.95 and $4.95, barbecued chicken at $4.95, and a chicken-and-ribs combination at $6.95, as well as the usual soups, salads, sandwiches.

Owner-chef Richard Shimizu took the name for his restaurant from his chili-stuffed potatoes, but **Richard's Stuffed Potato,** 2109 Kuhio Ave. (tel. 122-1012), is not the fast-food operation its name conjured up for us. Nor does the very casual decor—a counter, most tables out in the courtyard—give a hint of the high quality of food Richard whips up in his tiny kitchen. Pasta meals are the best buy here; they include salad with house dressing and garlic bread. You could have fettucine noodles Alfredo or marinara for $5.75. We thoroughly enjoyed our pesto and pasta primavera at $6.50. Daily specials are usually in the $7 to $10 range, and they might include Italian sausage, calamari, chicken, or fresh fish: fish of the day is usually $9.95; so is filet mignon. These entrees too come with salad and garlic bread. Richard is at the range from 6 p.m. until midnight, Monday to Saturday.

Godfather's Pizza (tel. 922-5748), at 2139 Kuhio Ave., claims they'll make you a "pizza you can't refuse." You might as well accept, since the pies are good, and the atmosphere—with a big garden in back, trees all lit up, and many gays parading about—is lively, to say the least. A mini deluxe cheese pizza is $2.29; taco pizza and vegetarian pizza, each $3.09. An all-you-can-eat salad bar is $2.79. And you can have a six-inch mini-pizza, salad bowl, and soft drink for all of $3.50. Open late.

We've had several letters recently about **Caffè Guccinni,** also in the 2139 Kuhio Ave. cluster (tel. 922-5287), raving about the superiority of its Italian food ("the best we've enjoyed at any restaurant, regardless of price," according to Jim Hedstrom of Diamond Bar, California) and the delectability of its desserts. We sampled both recently, and we're impressed too. This is a modest place with a counter inside, tables outside, and the menu posted beside the counter. Right now, owner Jocelyn Battista is serving dinners only; hopefully, by the time you read this, lunch will be added as well. Among her main courses, we're partial to the manicotti stuffed with five kinds of cheese and the wickedly fattening stuffed chicken (its filling consists of zucchini, garlic, and cream cheese!), each $6.25. Among the desserts, we're at a loss to choose. Who can decide between the merits of a heavenly crème brûlé or chocolate torte, a Sicilian cannoli, or a light and lemony cheesecake? The best solution is to bring a group of friends and share. Desserts are $2 to $2.50. (If you've eaten elsewhere, come here just for dessert.) Along with your feast, have some of the best espresso and cappuccino in the islands, $1.25 to $1.50. Everything is homemade in Jocelyn's own kitchen. Open from 4 p.m. to midnight daily.

While wine bars have become all the rage in sophisticated New York and San Francisco, Honolulu has not been asleep. A wine bar, in case you hadn't heard, is a place where one may sample fine wines by the glass—no need to order a whole bottle—and accompany these wines with appropriate light food. The **Grape Escape,** in the lobby of the Waikiki Trade Center, 2255 Kuhio Ave. (tel. 923-0438), is a sparkling example of the genre. The decor is contemporary, the music classical, the ambience refined. And the food will not jade the palate of the dedicated oenophile. Cheese appears often on the menu here, from a warm and melting baked brie (a $4.95 appetizer) to the platter of fresh fruit and cheese, to the quiche of the day. If you've brought your Omar Khayyam with you, have the Poet's Dinner: soup of the day, green salad, a good hunk of imported cheese, some crusty french bread, and a glass of house wine, all for $7.95. For a hot entree, there's lasagne at $7.50; for something cold, Caesar salad with bay shrimp at $5.50, or spinach salad at $5.25. A glass of wine begins at about $2.50. Different for Waikiki, and very enjoyable. The Grape Escape is open every day from 11:30 a.m. to 11 p.m. or midnight.

If you'd like to dine in a fern grotto by a sparkling waterfall, or in a lush formal garden beside a pond, make a reservation for dinner at **Banyan Gardens,** 2380 Kanekapolei St. (tel. 923-2366). This is a new building of lava rock with a steep shingled roof. Inside there are wooden fences and cobblestone paths, tables arranged so that there is little difference between indoors and outdoors. The food here is exceptional and has made the place very popular with Honolulu residents as well as visitors. While dinner, the only full meal served here (5 to 10 p.m. daily), is a bit out of our budget range, it's well worth a splurge. The lounge opens at 11 a.m. for cocktails, and you can order from the pupu menu all day. Priced from $2.25 to $5.95, delicious pupus include nachos with chicken and shrimp, a sliced raw beef and vegetable salad, Caesar salad and crab, fried cheese with barbecue sauce. A soup specialty is the Soup Bake, seafood chowder or soup of the day sealed in puff pastry and baked in a crock, $3.25. Complete dinners are served with your choice of soup or salad, steamed rice, rice pilaf, or potatoes. Prime rib is a specialty here; a ten-ounce portion is $14.95. Scallops, sauteed or tempura, cashew chicken and pineapple, and barbecue of baby back ribs are all hearty and good, priced from $9.95 to $11.95. The Wok Cookery specials—stir-fried vegetables, with chicken, shrimp, or a combination of both—are delicious, from $9.95 to $11.95, and nicely served in miniature earthenware fry pans. There's a special dessert menu; macadamia-nut cheesecake, triple chocolate torte, and coconut cake are all good, but the adventurous among you should try the Pineapple Surprise—fresh fruits marinated in several liqueurs over strawberry Häagen-Dazs ice cream, slathered in meringue, and baked in a pineapple shell. Fantastic! Reservations are a must at this utterly delightful spot.

Not far from Banyan Gardens is another very popular new dinner spot, the **Blue Water Café,** at 2350 Kuhio Ave. (tel. 926-2191). It's a big, busy place decorated with a nautical flair—captain's chairs and lots of brass. Complete dinners are priced from $10.95 to $16.95—and $21.95 for lobster—and include soup, a trip to the marvelous salad bar, and a choice of steak fries, steamed rice, baked potato, and french bread. Entrees of note are beef short ribs, top sirloin steak, scallops, mahimahi, teriyaki chicken, and combinations of steak and one of the seafood specialties. Calorie-counters and budget-watchers can have the soup and salad bar for $6.25. And you haven't lived until you've tasted their chocolate-chip cheesecake. Blue Water Café is open for dinner only, 5 to 10 p.m., every day.

Tony Roma's—A Place for Ribs has long been popular in a few cities on the mainland and now there's a new one in Waikiki at 1972 Kalakaua Ave. (tel. 942-2121). It's big and comfortable, decorated in western style, with lots of wood and leather, walls of brick, shuttered windows, oil paintings on the wall. The staff is energetic and friendly. The menu (which, by the way, is your placemat) carries a disclaimer: "Not responsible for meat ordered well done"! All entrees here are served with rice or french fries and cole slaw; add 50¢ if you'd prefer a baked potato. The house specialty, of course, is ribs, a generous serving for $8.95. Barbecued chicken is really inexpensive, at $5.45; and a chicken-and-ribs combination is $8.50. Steak fans swear by the filet mignon, served on a skewer, at $6.95, and the big 12-ounce sirloin at $11.95. Be sure to order the loaf of onion rings at $2.95. Daily specials are $4.55: Tuesday's is veal parmagiana; Thursday's, roast loin of pork. The same specials are just $3.85 at lunch. The only dessert on the menu is cheesecake—but who needs anything more? With your cheesecake, have some espresso or cappuccino, or French, Irish, or Mexican coffee. Tony Roma's is open from 11 a.m. until 2 a.m. Monday through Saturday; Sunday and holiday hours are 4 p.m. to 2 a.m.

When was the last time you had a real Japanese breakfast? Well, you needn't go as far as Tokyo for an authentic Japanese waker-upper (rice, fish, dried fish, miso soup, raw egg, nori, pickled vegetables, and tea, at $7 complete) or for other authentic Japanese meals, either. Go right to **Maiko Odoriko,** in King's Village, 131 Kaiulani St. (tel. 923-7368) in the heart of Waikiki. This very spacious, lovely Japanese establishment, with many dining areas, including some large tatami rooms, sushi and robata bars, specializes in high-priced steak and seafood specialties, but for those who are counting their yen, they offer "Odoriki" specials from about $7.95, and satisfying they are. Here's what we got for $7.95: grilled chicken on skewers, broiled salmon with butter, soup, salad, rice, pickled vegetables, and tea. Portions were dainty, but the chicken and fish were delicious, and while we would have preferred miso soup to clam chowder in this setting, and an Oriental to an American salad, they were not bad. We had a choice of guava sherbet or vanilla ice cream for dessert (extra), and a big pot of tea was brought to the table. For $8.95 we could have had the chef's special: broiled beef in teriyaki sauce or broiled butterfish, with all the side dishes.

Maiko, which has a sister restaurant at the Ilikai Hotel, is a good place to try a meal at the sushi bar, or have some of the robata-yaki appetizers: broiled baby cuttlefish, broiled dried mushrooms, broiled butterfish, and the like, about $2.85 each. Waitresses wear Japanese costumes and service is cordial. Maiko is open daily from 6 a.m. until 2 a.m. From 10 p.m. on, you can listen to kara okae—i.e., entertainment without an orchestra: an entertainer sings Japanese songs with a taped music background.

For a true Japanese budget restaurant in Waikiki, your best bet is the

Sushi Tora Hyakumangoku, on the seventh floor of the Kalakaua International Center, 2155 Kalakaua Ave., corner of Beach Walk (tel. 926-3070). Following the custom of Tokyo restaurants, this Sushi Tora displays plastic replicas of its dishes up front, so you can window-shop your meal. For lunch, look over the jumbo shrimp tempura at $4; as you'll see, it is served in a large bowl of soba (buckwheat noodles), with sliced vegetables and fishcake all sitting in the broth. The sushi soba ($5.50) is served on a tray; how neatly they tuck a cup of miso soup in the corner and arrange the fishcake around the noodles. Eating here is a treat; this place is Japanese—from lanterns to kimonos. At dinnertime, this means dishes like tekka don (raw fish and seaweed) at $8, and edomae (shrimp and rice cakes) at $7.50. Little salad tastes and pickled vegetable treats are included. Prices begin at $4.

The only non-Japanese foods here are the desserts: perhaps a strawberry frappe with mandarin orange slices, pineapple chunks, strawberries, and cherries. Cooling, but at $2.75 we'd call the copy better than the original. Open daily from 11 a.m. to 9:30 p.m.

In this same part of town, across Beach Walk at 2131 Kalakaua we found **Satsuma Rahmen,** a wonderful little Japanese noodle shop, where we could cheerfully have dined every day. Its huge bowls of rahmen (which the Hawaiians call saimin) were delicious and inexpensive, and the decor—an impeccably clean, U-shaped counter around which the customers sit on wood-and-straw chairs, Japanese lanterns, open door with pennants—was straight out of Tokyo. We tried both the vegetable rahmen, a soup base topped with stir-fried vegetables ($4 regular, $4.50 jumbo), and the yaki soba, stir-fried buckwheat noodles, topped with vegetables, pork, shrimp, and octopus in a special sauce ($3.50 and $4), and found each a complete and filling meal in a bowl. Since this is the kind of food that works well for breakfast, lunch, snack, dinner, or midnight munchie, it's good to know that Satsuma Rahmen is open every day from 8 a.m. to midnight and until 1 a.m. Friday and Saturday. There are two others, Satsuma Rahmens, at 1035 University Ave. (tel. 946-6055) and 1103 S. King St. at Pensacola (tel. 533-2033).

There's a cute little corner of Mexico at the corner of Kalakaua and Saratoga, and **Popo's Mexican Restaurant,** 2112 Kalakaua (tel. 923-7355), is the name. Popo's has both decor (white walls, tile floors, stucco, serapes, native pottery) and food that is *muy auténtico,* and the prices are right. Come at lunch and you can have dishes like a good and snappy chile relleno for $3.75, or machaca—shredded beef sauteed with bell peppers, tomatoes, eggs, and onion—for $5.95. Combination plates are just $6.50, and regular entrees of enchiladas, burritos, etc., are $3.95 to $4.95. Here's your chance to try some new specialties of the native-born Mexican chef: perhaps flautas (deep-fried corn tortillas stuffed with shredded beef and topped with cheeses, guacamole, and sour cream); or chalupa (a boat-shaped flour tortilla filled with picadillo-seasoned beef, cheeses, tomatoes, and guacamole). There's usually a special, like the tasty chicken poblano at $6.95. Dessert? *¿Cómo no?* Guava sherbet with coconut and honey is great, and, of course, there are margaritas, sangría, and Mexican beer at the ready. A *simpático* choice.

So popular has the original Popo's become that two new branches of the same family have opened up, both in Waikiki and both offering good food and good bargains. **Popo's Cantina Mexican Food,** at the corner of Ala Moana Boulevard and Ena Road (tel. 955-3326), usually has a fresh catch of the day, served with rice, beans, and tossed salad, at both lunch and dinner for $5.95. **Popo's Margarita Cantina** at the International Market Place (tel. 923-8373) is a relaxed spot for sipping margaritas, of course, and for enjoying such inexpensive luncheon and dinner specials as tacos, beans, and rice, served with tea or coffee, for just $2.95, lunch or dinner.

A Chaucerian dining spot in Honolulu? Of course! You'll think you're in Olde England (well, almost) when you step into **Tops Canterbury Coffee Shop & Tavern** at 1910 Ala Moana Blvd. (tel. 941-5277), what with its flowered tapestry chairs, lots of wood, and waitresses in period costumes and mob caps. But the modern menu and 24-hour service make this one briskly up-to-date. Lunch and dinner specials are well priced, and both food and service get good marks. You might have grilled beef with onion rings and mushroom sauce, grilled mahimahi, or chicken in a basket with french fries, corn bread, and butter, each $6.95 or under; shrimp and vegetable tempura for $7.75. Soup or salad, french fries or rice, vegetable, roll, and butter come with each entree. For dessert, try the tasty cheese or carrot cakes. The menu is extensive, ranging from very good burgers to kosher-style deli sandwiches to international specialties like quiche Lorraine, nachos, and lasagne, from 11 a.m. to 1 p.m. Strawberry daiquiris are a treat at $1.75. Breakfast is ready all day; we like the dollar-size pancakes at $2.25.

A *Honolulu Advertiser* columnist recently named **Emilio's Pizza** as "the best new pizza place in Honolulu." Well, we knew it all along. Emilio's has recently moved to a new location at 1423 Kalakaua, near the corner of King Street (tel. 946-4972), as cozy as ever, with interesting framed pictures and glass shelving giving it a homey atmosphere. This is pizza with a professional touch—deep-dish Sicilian style. They make their own tasty dough fresh every day and their own sausages and sauces. Hearty sandwiches, soups, salads, garlic bread, and the like are also available. But about those pizzas. . . .

There is a choice of 14 fresh toppings, which are piled abundantly on deep-dish crusts, making a ten-inch pie a filling meal for two to three people. Prices run from about $5.75 for the ten-inch cheese pies with one topping, up to $15.80 for the mind-blowing combo with six toppings. Emilio's is open from 11 a.m. to 11 p.m. Monday through Thursday, to midnight on Friday and Saturday, from 5 to 10 p.m. on Sunday. And, yes, they will deliver to all hotels and condos in Waikiki.

Pasta and salad are the big light food crazes these days, and the place to get both, very inexpensively, in Honolulu, is at the **Noodle Shop** in the Waikiki Sand Villa Hotel, 2375 Ala Wai Blvd. at Kanekapolei, behind King's Village (tel. 922-4744). With black booths, a bar, soft lighting, big wooden-and-rope chandeliers, the atmosphere could be called intimate cocktail lounge. You can try a variety of noodle dishes and help yourself to the all-you-can-eat salad bar, for about $4.95. Non-noodlers can fill up with dishes like chicken and fries, beef Stroganoff, filet of mahimahi, all in the $5.85 to $7.35 range, plus other entrees. The Noodle Shop is open daily from 7 to 10:30 a.m. for breakfast and from 5 to 8:30 p.m. for dinner. (No lunch is served.) There's entertainment nightly, plus a Happy Hour every day from 3:30 to 6 p.m.

At the International Market Place

Few tourists who set foot in Waikiki leave without at least one visit to the International Market Place, in the heart of the beach area at 2330 Kalakaua Ave. It's a tropical park gone commercial, but appealingly so;

dozens of merchants have set up their wares in a series of inviting small shops where you can buy anything from grass skirts to wooden idols. The place has quite a few restaurants, with perhaps a half dozen sensible enough for our budget. The first of these is the **Colonial House Cafeteria,** right at the beginning of the Market Place. Don't let the word "cafeteria" discourage you; they're different in Hawaii. This one is a semi-open affair, a bit worn looking, but still pleasant. The motto of the place is "Fine Food at Family Prices," and they mean it. You can easily put together a meal here for around $5. The last time we dined here we had clam chowder for 60¢, sweet-and-sour ribs for $3.15, and fresh pineapple spears with cottage cheese for 90¢; total: $4.70 for a delicious dinner. On other occasions we've had the meat loaf for $2.95 and the hot roast beef sandwich at $2.95. Salads are excellent; so are the pastries, fresh from the oven. Breakfast is served from 8 to 10:30 a.m., lunch from 11 a.m., dinner until 8:30 p.m. every night. There's a cocktail bar too, with a long (2:30 to 6:30 p.m.) Happy Hour every day.

If you've brought the kids along with you, you'll have even more fun in the Market Place at **Farrell's Ice Cream Parlour Restaurant,** a kicky Gay '90s affair that dispenses—in addition to the huge sundaes, sodas, and staggering banana splits—excellent one-third-pound fresh-ground and hand-made burgers with old-fashioned fries ($3.95 to $4.25), hot grilled sandwiches, various salad bar combinations, and well-priced lunch and dinner specials. Lunch, served until 4 p.m., features a different sandwich each day, plus either soup or fries, soft drink, and a sundae, for $4.50. Dinner entrees—filet of fish, chicken strips, hamburger steak, New York strip steak and mushrooms—include salad bar and toasted french bread, and cost only $5.95 to $8.95. Farrell's desserts are a meal in themselves—hot fudge ice cream puffs, mocha nut parfaits, and fudge mint marvel suggest the staggering possibilities. The place is open from 11 a.m. to midnight on weekdays, until 1 a.m. on Friday and Saturday. There are other Farrell's on Oahu and the neighbor islands. Good, sensibly priced family fare.

Our next choice in the Market Place is a bit of mittel-Europe in Waikiki. That's the **Bräuhaus,** a German biergarten-deli, where the guests sing along and drink along as the Hofbräu Band nightly belts forth polkas, waltzes, and the like. While you're humming along, you can dine (lunch or dinner) on inexpensive plates like bratwurst, knockwurst, and Polish kielbasa for around $3.95, or smoked pork loin for $5.50. Sandwiches, served on Jewish rye, with pickle and cole slaw, include pastrami, ham and cheese, and assorted German sausages, $2.25 to $3.50.

The culinary adventurers among you will want to experience something new indeed: the **Mongolian Bar-B-Que** at Kuhio Mall, which adjoins the International Market Place. Seems that a very special dish in the northern part of China is strips of beef, barbecued with vegetables and spices, and this is one of the few restaurants we know of in Honolulu that serves it. You select your own meats, sauces, vegetables, and spices, and they are then cooked as you like it in an open-fire pit. A Mongolian Bar-B-Que dinner, served with rice, tea, and dessert, costs $7.95. At lunch, the Bar-B-Que is $4.50. (True budget types will patronize the Mongolian Bar-B-Que in the Cultural Plaza downtown, where seconds on dinner are free.) Truth to tell, we find the Bar-B-Que a mite strange tasting, but many local people have become addicted to it. It's one of those things you have to experience for yourself to judge. Open daily from 11 a.m. to 10 p.m.

Although the very best Hawaiian shave ices are found elsewhere on the island (more about them later), the ices you can get at a little cart called **Island Snow** in the Market Place are indeed cooling on a sultry summer's day. The ice, doused with strawberry, banana, blue pineapple, or lemon syrup—or a bit of them all—is a long, luscious refreshment for about 65¢.

At the Waikiki Shopping Plaza

Time was when budget dining at the Waikiki Shopping Plaza, at 2250 Kalakaua (corner of Seaside), was limited to the basement snack shops (see "Old Reliables," ahead), while its upper floors harbored some of the more glamorous and expensive international restaurants in town. But then the **Marco Polo Eating and Drinking Establishment** took over one of these attractive enclaves and all that changed. Now budgeteers are scaling the heights (to the fourth floor) to meet "The Pasta Challenge": that's all you can eat of spaghetti à la marinara, house salad, and either garlic bread or Italian rolls (all baked on the premises) for a mere $2.95 at lunch, $3.95 at dinner. You may not be able to break the house record of six servings, but you can have a good time trying, as this is good food, and the intimate, multilevel setting is the type you expect in much higher priced restaurants. If you're not up to meeting this particular challenge, you can have other pasta dishes from $2.95 to $6.95, perhaps the very good baked lasagne with cheese and sausages at $6.25, or a variety of submarine sandwiches. Wine, beer, a lively bar—it's hard to beat this one. Open for lunch Monday to Friday from 11:30 a.m. to 2 p.m., for dinner every day from 5 to 10 p.m.

For a touch of opulence at the Waikiki Shopping Plaza, try **Lau Yee Chai** (tel. 923-1112), the famed Waikiki Cantonese restaurant, whose magnificent furnishings, irreplaceable today, come from the original Lau Yee Chai, which opened in 1929. The main dining room, big enough to hold 600 people with the full sanction of the Honolulu Fire Department, is decorated with gleaming lacquered furniture, rich woodcarvings, a huge brass gong that would put the J. Arthur Rank one to shame, and real gold in the exquisite wall panels. The golden calligraphy characters spell out poetry in the Cantonese dialect. Considering the splendor befitting an Oriental emperor, the prices are surprisingly democratic, and the food is very good. Most à la carte entrees run between $5.50 and $7.50, and in this price range you could have mushroom chicken, lemon chicken, scallops with vegetables, almond chicken or duck, stuffed duck, beef chow mein, and shrimp with vegetables. Should you favor shark's fin soup (a rarified taste), it's $3.95.

For the Steak Set

When the whole family wants to eat steak and you don't want to break the budget, there's a terrific answer: find the nearest **Sizzler Family Steakhouse.** Luckily, there are seven of them in the Hawaiian Islands, including one right in Waikiki, at the corner of Kalakaua and Ala Moana. The big round building has brown booths and tables, plants, a pleasant atmosphere, and it's open 24 hours a day; the Jamboree Breakfast, served from midnight until 11 a.m., offers eggs, bacon, and all the hotcakes you can eat for $3.99. For lunch and dinner, Sizzler serves steaks that are a good size and good quality, amazing values for the money, considering the cost of meat at the supermarket: an order of sirloin is $5.79; New York cut steak, $8.99. Along with your steak comes tangy, cheesey Sizzler toast, plus a choice of baked potato, french fries, or rice. All Sizzlers now have salad bars, soup, and serve beer and wine. There's also seafood, including steak and shrimp at $6.49. Salad, desserts, and coffee and iced tea are extra, but refills on the beverages are free. There are more Sizzlers elsewhere on Oahu and a very pretty one at Koko Marina, overlooking the waterskiing area.

The Exotic East

Up until a few years ago, the cooking of the exotic East—of India and Pakistan—was completely unknown in Hawaii. Now there's a lovely place where you can sample this cuisine right in Waikiki. That's the small and intimate **Shalimar Restaurant,** in the Waikiki Holiday Hotel, 459 Lewers St. (tel. 923-2693), with a gracious, subdued atmosphere, Oriental carpets on the wall, and at least one or two of the Karim brothers—who have owned and managed restaurants in Lahore, New York, and Chicago—on hand to explain the subleties of Pakistani-Indian cooking to you. We followed Tariq Karim's suggestions at a recent meal and chose the Khansameki Sifarish, a seven-course dinner consisting of mulligatawny soup, tandoori chicken, shish kebab, cubed lamb curry, vegetable curry, and rice pilaf, at $9.95; as well as a tasty Shakahari Thal vegetarian platter which included homemade yogurt with spicy potatoes, samosa vegetable patties, creamed spinach with potatoes, vegetable curry, and much more, at $9.50. (More inexpensive dishes run $6.50 to $8.95.) Flavors were subtle, the food gently and exquisitely spiced. With it we had a big order of naan—unleavened bread baked in a clay oven—as delicious a bread as can be found anywhere; we could have happily made a meal on that alone. A different dessert—each $1.50 to $2.25—is served every night. When you're there, you might be lucky enough to try their most popular dessert, the Ras Malai; it's made of unprocessed cottage cheese and sweetened condensed milk, and garnished with almonds and cashews. Well-priced wines are available by the bottle or carafe. If you have room for it, the pasha coffee—a combination of liqueurs, coffee, and whipped cream, looking like a pasha with a turban—is fine for leisurely, after-dinner dawdling. Dinner only, served from 6 to 10 p.m., seven days, and reservations are essential, as this small place is constantly growing in popularity.

At the Royal Hawaiian Center

If we had to take all our meals in Honolulu under one roof, we'd pick the roof of the Royal Hawaiian Center, right in the middle of Waikiki at 2233 Kalakaua. There, on the third floor, are three international favorites: The Great Wok of China, Restaurant Suntory, and La Mex. Downstairs, on the ground level, is another winner, It's Greek to Me.

Wok cooking is becoming almost as popular in the United States as it is in China. To see a master perform the art at your own table, take your chopsticks to **The Great Wok of China** (tel. 922-5373), a spacious and handsomely decorated room. The kitchen is largely Cantonese but various dishes also represent Mandarin and Szechuan cuisines. You'll be seated at tables for eight, with two woks in the center; you place your order for, perhaps, the Celestial Celebration Chicken at $8.85, the Shanghai Vegetarian (vegetables and tofu) at $7.25, or whatever the Wokmaster's Special is for that night, at $7.85. While the chef is busy in the kitchen with his cleaver cutting up the ingredients for your main dish, you'll be served, first, a delicious bowl of hot-and-sour soup, followed by a Chinese chicken salad—tiny shreds of chicken with lettuce and a sesame-based dressing—very tasty. Then the chef goes to work at the wok, tossing up a succulent (and happily, smokeless) meal. Of course, there's a pot of tea, and fortune cookies for dessert. Dinner is served daily from 4:30 to 10 p.m. At lunch, daily from 11 a.m. to 2 p.m., you can sample some Imperial Salads, like the Kwongung Tofu Salad (with shrimp, vegetables, and egg), the Hanchow Salad (cold meats and vegetables), and the Four Winds Salad (chicken, sprouts, mushrooms), all between $3.75 and $4.25. Sunday brunch, 11 a.m. to 2 p.m., is $2.95.

It's not hard to understand why **Restaurant Suntory** (tel. 922-5511) is one of the most popular Japanese restaurants in Waikiki. The service is gracious, the setting charming, the ambience altogether delightful. Decor is all soft lights and graceful Japanese pottery. And the food is exceptional. At lunch, you can choose from such cosmopolitan delights as sukiyaki teishoku, stir-fried vegetables and beef, prepared at your table and accompanied by miso soup, rice, and tsukemono, at $8.25; or beef teriyaki, marinated strips of beef served with tossed salad, tsukemono, and rice, at $4.50. We especially like the boneless broiled chicken on a bed of rice, with miso soup and tsukemono ($4.50). At dinner, the teppanyaki is the specialty. These are the dinners prepared at your table by chefs who perform wizardry with their sharp knives. All the teppan entrees are served with consommé, tossed green salad, assorted fresh vegetables, and either special flavored or white rice. Teppan choices include chicken, shrimp, fresh fish, and New York cut steak, from $7 to $9.25. Lunch is served weekdays from 11:30 a.m. to 2 p.m.; dinner is served daily from 6 to 11 p.m. Reservations are a must, especially for dinner.

Mexican restaurants are no longer a novelty in Honolulu, but any restaurant as beautiful and tasteful as **La Mex** (tel. 923-2906) certainly is. Stepping into La Mex is like entering another realm, one of mirrored ceilings, thick carpets, canopies over round tables, subtle Aztec designs on the walls. The room is done in the colors of adobe, of sand—very cool, very restful. Although the food is not quite as unique as the setting, it's very good, and served in copious portions. All of the dinners come with rice, refried beans, and tea. Beef enchilada, tamale, huevos rancheros, and burrito dinners go from $5.50 to $8.75. Lunch is served à la carte, with dishes like burritos at $4.95 and chimichangas at $4.65. Beer, wine, margaritas, of course, and a tasteful cocktail lounge adjoining. Strolling musicians serenade you at night. A good place to relax with friends. La Mex is open weekdays from 11 a.m. to 11 p.m.; on weekends, the doors open at 5 p.m.

Come down to earth now, to the ground floor and Building A, where **It's Greek to Me** (tel. 922-2733) provides the answer to a lot of dining needs. You can stop here anytime and get a quick sandwich at the counter, or sit down at one of the comfortable tables and enjoy a delicious meal. We have so many favorite lunch foods here—for example, the tasty gyro sandwich at $3.79, the falafel plate at $5.50, the light and flaky spinach pie at $3.15—that it's hard to choose. On our last visit, we went with a refreshing tabouleh salad at $3.75, and a wonderfully tasty chicken souvlaki sandwich at $4.15—that's a skewer of char-broiled marinated chicken breast, onions, and pepper rolled in warm pita bread and topped with tomatoes and lettuce—ummm! We like taramasalata (a fish roe spread) for an appetizer, an honest-to-Zeus baklava for dessert. At dinner, salads and sandwiches are a bit higher, and entrees run $6.50 to $9.85. One of our readers, L. Faulstich of Dallas, Texas, writes to recommend the great apple and cherry pastries made fresh on the premises every day. For liquid refreshment: wine, beer, espresso, and cappuccino in addition to the usual. Open daily.

A Honolulu friend of ours once described a trip to **Copenhagen Cones** as a religious experience, and she had the right idea. You'll find these ice-cream shops all over the island (there are three in Waikiki: here at the Royal Hawaiian Shopping Center, and also at the Outrigger and Outrigger East Hotels). The difference between these cones and all others are the cake cones made right on the spot; filled with Dreyer's ice cream and topped with nuts or sprinkles, they're a great treat. One scoop is $1.35.

THE OLD RELIABLES: Now we come to the standbys, the places you can always count on for fast service, and good, basic food. And if there's anything more basic than a McDonald's hamburger, we've yet to find it. There are two **McDonald's** in Waikiki, one at 2204 Kalakaua Ave. and another in the Royal Hawaiian Shopping Center at 2233 Kalakaua. Both are attractively decorated (outdoor tables at the first are great for people-watching), and staffed with employees who can give sightseeing advice as well as dish out the Big Macs. Breakfast, served from 6 to 10 a.m. (Egg McMuffin and Sausage McMuffin served until 11 a.m.) features inexpensive scrambled eggs, sausages, muffins, and hash browns. For the rest of the day, it's Big Macs at $1.45, Filet-O-Fish sandwiches at $1.05, single hamburgers at 65¢, plus other sandwiches, desserts, and drinks. A special blessing is the fact that both places close late (midnight on weekdays, 1 a.m. on weekends), so that the grownups can have a snack while junior and company are fast asleep.

Woolworth's, in the Bank of Hawaii Building on Kalakaua (tel. 923-1713), is another family-type spot that can be relied on for decent and inexpensive food. The atmosphere is pleasant and the prices are right: every day there's a $2.95 luncheon special like pineapple chicken, and regular luncheon entrees run $2.95 to $4.95. Franks with potato salad and cole slaw are $2.55; other sandwiches are $4.15 tops; a seafood salad bowl costs $3.95. Prices are also low at night—a turkey dinner is $3.70. Japanese and Chinese dishes are also served, and you can have pizza and southern fried chicken to go. Note, too, Woolworth's Oriental Snack Bar in the back of the store, where you can sample all kinds of strange goodies. We'll give you more details in our section on Japanese restaurants, ahead. You'll find a larger, equally bustling and cheerful Woolworth's restaurant at Ala Moana Center.

A number of readers have written to tell us how much they've enjoyed **The Surf,** a brilliantly decorated Polynesian coffeehouse at 2496 Kalakaua Ave., in the Pacific Beach Hotel. We heartily concur. Although the menu is standard, the ambience is anything but: canoe paddles, tiki masks, a huge primitive chandelier, and Hawaiian music in the background set an impressive scene. Complete dinners can be had for $6.25 to $11.50, including salad or soup, potatoes or rice; entrees like jumbo fried shrimp, mahimahi, veal cutlet; and the house's special toasted passion fruit bread, which really is a treat. Pineapple boats, double-decker Beach Boys with fries, a good breakfast menu, and reasonably priced drinks adds up to a good spot to remember. And it fronts the ocean, as well. Open most of the day, from 5 a.m. to midnight.

Princess Bernice Pauahi Bishop (the very lady after whom the Bishop Museum was named) is also honored in the **Princess Pauahi Coffee Shop Restaurant,** on the ground floor of the Royal Hawaiian Center, 2233

Kalakaua Ave. She and her husband once made their home on this location, near the enormous banyan tree in front of the Royal Hawaiian Hotel. The restaurant is tastefully decorated in Hawaiian monarchy decor, with prints and portraits on the walls; the food is nicely presented American fare with island accents, at very reasonable prices. Dinner specials like stuffed peppers or roast chicken or beef sukiyaki run from $6 to $8, and are served with a choice of soup or salad, vegetables, potato or rice, hot roll, and butter. Always available are offerings from the "Fry Kettle"—fish and chips, deep-sea scallops, seafood platter, from $4.95 to $7.25—as well as grilled items like beef liver and onions, and Hawaiian chopped steak. Specials like corned beef and cabbage with mustard sauce or shoyu chicken, from $4 to $5.75, will make for a filling lunch. Doors open at 7 a.m. for breakfast, close at midnight, seven days a week. Their outdoor Garden Bar is a relaxing spot for a drink. It's open from 11 a.m. to 11 p.m., with music and hula dancers every evening.

Local office workers praise the **Peking Garden,** 307 Royal Hawaiian Ave., for takeout food. It's a hole in the wall with a tiny counter and a few sidewalk tables; for $2.75, you can indulge in a plate lunch of shoyu chicken, Peking fried chicken, Korean beef barbecue, or sweet-and-sour pork. A big bowl of wonton soup is $2.75.

Denny's, in the Imperial Hawaii Hotel at 205 Lewers St. (tel. 923-8188), is a good-size coffeeshop-style operation that's always open. There are comfortable booths, silent ceiling fans, and abundant greenery. And the glass façade affords a panoramic view of the passing parade. Lunch or dinner entrees are priced the same all day. Such entrees as chicken fried steak or fried chicken, broiled rainbow trout, meat loaf, New York steak, or steak and shrimp range from $4.10 to $6.95, and are accompanied by vegetables and potato, roll and butter. Our breakfast favorite here is the french toast with strawberries ($2.75), but eggs Benedict is another winner.

The **Waikiki Beachcomber Veranda Coffee Shop,** one flight up in the Waikiki Beachcomber Hotel, 2300 Kalakaua Ave., looks more like a veranda than a coffeeshop, set back from the street as it is in a gardeny gazebo-like area, with striped wallpaper on the ceiling, old-fashioned soda chairs, potted palms all about, and the pool and patio right outside. At lunch it's $4.50 for a combination omelet, $4.75 and up for thick meat sandwiches. Dinner is a good buy in a good setting—your choice of, say, mahimahi at $6.75 or Oriental shrimp tempura at $8.25, with either salad or soup. And if you like spaghetti—how can you beat their all-you-can-eat spaghetti dinner for just $4.95? With salad bar, it's $6.95. Lunch is on from 11 a.m. to 2 p.m. and dinner is served until 9 p.m. Breakfast, served from 6 to 11 a.m., features Beachcomber french toast made with thick slices of Portuguese sweet bread.

There are two **Jolly Rogers** in Waikiki: the newer one is in the Outrigger East, at the corner of Kuhio and Kaiulani; the original has been holding forth at 2244 Kalakaua Ave. for just about as long as anyone can remember. The new place has red carpets, a leathery look, and a nice atmosphere; there's a cocktail lounge too, where a trio entertains nightly. The other place gives you a choice of sidewalk tables right out on the busy avenue or, more peacefully, tables inside under thatched umbrellas; there's also the **Crow's Nest** above the restaurant with nightly entertainment and a Happy Hour every day from 4 to 8 p.m. Both restaurants offer a casual nautical ambience and American coffeehouse-style food, quite tasty, at good prices. Complete dinners—served with soup or salad, potatoes or rice, and dinner roll—include such entrees as breaded veal cutlet, honey-fried chicken, or baby beef liver with onions or bacon, and most are under $8. There are also daily specials like beef curry casserole or baked meat loaf for around $6.50. Burgers, salads, sandwiches, and breakfasts are also available. The doors are open from 6:30 a.m. until around midnight, cocktails till 2 a.m.

Whenever you see a **Ron's of Hawaii** in the islands (in Waikiki, you'll find them at the International Market Place, the Outrigger West and Ilikai Hotels, at Ward Warehouse and Salt Lake Shopping Centers, and at 2323 Kalakaua Ave.), you'll know that you can get inexpensive, tasty food in clean surroundings. The mini-breakfasts—most items 50¢—the ice-cream specialties, and the fountain drinks (orange freeze, frosted coconut, milkshakes) are fine, but you'll also like the $1.50 hamburgers, the $1.30 chili, and the $2 french waffles.

Located just across Kalakaua from the International Market Place, **The Rigger,** in the Outrigger Hotel, 2335 Kalakaua Ave. (tel. 922-5544), is one of those places you can always depend on for a reasonably priced meal in attractive, comfortable surroundings. Hamburgers are a specialty here, and they're good. The surf burger is $3.50; the fancier variations—mushroom burgers, teriyaki burgers, chili burgers, and the like—slightly higher. If you want a complete meal, you can get an entree like mahimahi with soup or salad, french fries, rice or baked potato, and dinner roll, for $7.50 after noon. Other meat and fish dishes run up to $8.95. The doors stay open from 6 a.m. to 3 a.m. every day.

While shopping at the **Waikiki Shopping Plaza,** 2250 Kalakaua, corner of Seaside, can be expensive, and most of its upper-level restaurants are pricey, its below-street level is a veritable bonanza for the budget-conscious diner who wants something a little bit different. Start in the Japanese sector at **Ramen** for freshly made Japanese noodles. You can have them seated at the open tables or at the Japanese counter flanked by Japanese lanterns. Prices start at $3.75 for shoyu ramen and go to $4.25 for char siu ramen—Japanese noodles Chinese style—and to $5 for shrimp tempura; a combination plate is $5.75. You'll see Japanese visitors enjoying ramen at all hours of the day; in fact, this is one of the few Plaza spots that opens for breakfast. There are no tables at the next Japanese fast-food outlet, **Okazu-Ya Bento** (bento means take-out). Here, they custom-design your take-out lunch or dinner, filling the large plate with Japanese favorites at tiny prices: vegetable tempura, potato tempura, fish tidbits, shrimp tempura are each 40¢ and 50¢. All items are in view in a glass showcase, Japanese style, so you can just point. To round off this Japanese trio, there's **Plaza Sushi,** a tidy little restaurant that serves a mostly all-Japanese crowd, offers a complete sukiyaki lunch for $6.50; at dinner it's $7.75. You'll get chicken, beef, or pork sukiyaki, miso soup, rice, pickled vegetables, and tea. And they also have a cute little sushi bar, where you can choose from sushi stuffed with king crab, codfish roe, octopus, herring roe, and more. Two pieces of sushi go from $1.50 to $3.

Want more variety? You can have a deli lunch at **Plaza Deli,** perhaps a baked ham or roast beef sandwich at $3.95; barbecued or teriyaki chicken for $3.95 at **Plaza Chicken,** where a complete chicken lunch or dinner goes for $4.25.

Then there's the huge **Plaza Coffee Shop,** where a complete lunch can be had for $4.50, dinner for $4.75. The extensive menu includes daily specials such as soup and sandwich for $3.25 and island fresh fish cutlet for $4.50. Sandwiches, salads, pasta, and all sorts of hot dishes are available. The dinner menu offers a choice of eight to ten dinner plates for $5 to $6.

The Chinese Kitchen has lots of goodies like lemon chicken, sweet-and-sour fish, and roast duck, served in $3.95 and $4.95 Princess and Empress plates. **Plaza Burger** has a $3.25 burger platter. For $3.25 you could also have a hot ham-and-cheese sandwich. **Plaza Pizza** is one of the welcome few places around town where you can get pizza by the slice: $1.30. They also have daily specials like two slices of pepperoni/bacon pizza and tossed green salad at $2.95, plus hearty pasta dishes from $3.75. And of course there has to be a **Plaza Ice Cream,** with soda chairs and tables and cooling cones, sodas, and sundaes.

An always dependable establishment at the oceanfront in the Reef Towers Hotel is the **Islander,** at 247 Lewers St. (tel. 923-3233), famous for its fresh baked orange bread, served hot with dinner or as french toast or dessert. Copper trim and copper fixtures against a cocoa color scheme accent this impeccably clean and attractive place, open most of the day (6 a.m. to midnight). Breakfast is served all day; $2.75 buys a waker-upper of egg, two slices of bacon, and toast with jelly. Lunch and dinner menus and prices are largely the same. At dinner, along with your entree—perhaps teriyaki steak, mahimahi, or old-fashioned beef stew, at prices ranging from $4.45 to $6.95—you get homemade soup or salad, potatoes or rice, plus hot orange bread. Don't miss one of their great desserts, and if you order pie, ask them to heat it up for you.

For an authentic Japanese meal at a very low price, **Ezogiku,** 2038 Kuhio Ave. (tel. 941-1646), fills the bill. It's a tiny, lunch-counter-type place, with perhaps ten seats surrounding the cooking area and a limited number of menu items. The "menu" is posted over the counter. One of our readers, Lester S. Hyman of Washington, D.C., recommends this as a great place for kids; they not only love watching the chefs do their antics in front of a roaring stove, but they can also buy their fortunes for 25¢ from an English-Japanese machine on the counter, and skim the colorful Japanese magazines and comic books stacked beneath the counter. And the food is amazing considering the prices. Noodles, or ramen, is the specialty here; miso, butter, or shoyu ramen, which also contains bean sprouts, vegetables, and meat, is $3 for a big plate. There's a curry rice plate at $3.50 and a fried noodle plate at the same price. Lunch and dinner prices are the same. A find!

Spaghetti dinners at $3.95 are the big feature at the **Mr. Egro Restaurant,** at 2136 Kalakaua (tel. 923-9888), opposite Beach Walk. The atmosphere is red-checkered Italian, quite pleasant, and in addition to the spaghetti dinners, they also offer barbecued chicken, fried chicken, broiled mahimahi, and New York cut steak, from $4.25 to $5.25. Occasionally there's a Soup 'n' Sandwich luncheon at $2.95; the day we were there it was minestrone and grilled cheese, and not at all bad. There's an adjoining cocktail lounge. Mr. Egro serves lunch and dinner, from 10 a.m. to 10 p.m.

Unless somebody told you, you wouldn't think the **Wailana Coffee House** was a budget place, because it looks so imposing and expensive, located as it is in the exclusive Wailana Condominium at 1860 Ala Moana Blvd. (corner John Ena Road), opposite the Hilton Hawaiian Village dome. But go! It's never closed, and the prices will surprise you. The nicest thing about the Wailana is that lunches and dinners are the same price—the tab does not go up after 5 p.m. as it does in so many other places. So any time of the day you can have the soup and sandwich lunch for $3.50, or the delicious "broasted" chicken, juicy and tender, served with a generous helping of french fries, cole slaw or salad, roll, and honey, for $5.25. Other good buys are the old-fashioned beef stew at $5, the beef liver with fried onions or bacon at $5.50, the top sirloin at $9.50. All of these entrees are served with a choice of soup, salad, or fruit cup; and you get plenty of potatoes, hot rolls, and butter, as well as salad bar between 11 a.m. and 10:30 p.m. Prices subject to change here.

The attractive **Wailana Malia Coffee Shop** in the Waikiki Malia Hotel at 2211 Kuhio Ave. (tel. 922-4769) is owned by the same firm as the Wailana Coffee Shop on Ala Moana, and it too is open 24 hours a day. The food, again, is delicious and inexpensive. We like the breakfasts here a lot, especially the Irish breakfast: grapefruit juice, a three-egg omelet stuffed with corned beef hash and topped with cheddar cheese, grilled fresh pineapple spears, hashed brown potatoes, toast and jelly, and coffee, at $4.95, are guaranteed to put you on top of the morning. Lunches and dinners, served all day, include baby beef liver, knockwurst and cabbage, oyster-sauce beef with onions, and the like—all served with soup, salad or fruit cocktail, french fries, baked potato, or rice, hot vegetables, and rolls and butter, for only $5.25. Broiler favorites begin at $5.75 for hamburger steak and go up to $7.50 for teriyaki steak and $9.75 for top sirloin. There's a salad bar at lunch and dinner. Cakes and pies are good here, and best of all is the cheesecake with strawberries. Another Wailana winner for Waikiki.

It's rare in Honolulu to find a restaurant where you can get pizza by the slice (as well as by the pie), so we were happy to discover **Slices,** at 870 Kapahulu Ave. (tel. 735-6441), on the Diamond Head border of Waikiki, near the Honolulu Zoo. A mere 79¢ will buy you a very good-size slice of cheese-and-tomato pan pizza. You can pile on as many extras—meatballs or anchovies or whatever—as you like, for either 25¢ or 30¢ each. Sub sandwiches are also a treat, especially the steak sub at $2.50. And they also have a variety of plate lunches: teriyaki steak or beef tomato, kalua pig and cabbage, roast pork, from $2.69 to $2.99. You step up to the shiny-clean counter to order and pay for your food, then take it with you to sit at one of the little tables outside. Slices also slices up breakfast specials at 99¢—you can choose from pancakes, two eggs with rice and toast, or french toast. Open just about always, i.e., Monday to Saturday from 6 a.m. to 2 a.m., Sunday from 7 a.m. to 10 p.m.

There's a new sidewalk pizza-calzone parlor with seats at umbrellaed tables a block from Kuhio Beach, at 151 Uluniu St., at the side of the **Royal Grove Hotel** (tel. 922-1622). Carlton Fong, one of the owners of the hotel, has been having great fun creating pizzas that he swears are just as good as those in New York—and they really are. The pizzas are thick crusted, and can be had by the pie ($2.65 for an eight-incher) or by the slice ($1.25), either plain or with a variety of toppings; the veggie pie, with mushrooms, olives, bell peppers, zucchini, tomatoes, and green onions is a special treat at $4, small. And if you've never tried calzone—a stuffed pizza dough filled with ricotta, mozarella, sauce, and seasonings—here's your chance; they are $2.65 each, and the breakfast calzone with two eggs, Canadian bacon, cheese, tomatoes, green onions, plus coffee, is a winner at $3.50. Ask about their hot garlic bread and hot cinnamon bread, baked right on the premises. Open daily from 11 a.m. to midnight. Happily, they will deliver in Waikiki, between 5 and 10 p.m.

2. Restaurants Around Town (Outside Waikiki)

Once you leave the Waikiki area, your choice of restaurants—in all categories—becomes much greater. The following are all within easy driving or bus distance of Waikiki, and they're listed according to the type of food they serve and/or the geographical area in which they're located.

AMERICAN RESTAURANTS: These aren't necessarily your basic steak-and-baked-potato/hamburger-and-fries/fried-chicken-and-mashed-potatoes places. Not in Honolulu U.S.A., where teriyaki beef is as American as apple pie. So many ethnic specialties have come into the local repertoire that Japanese, Chinese, and Polynesian dishes (among others) are listed right along with—yes, steak, hamburger, and fried chicken. In a few pages we'll concentrate on the "foreign" restaurants—those that specialize solely in ethnic food. Right now, it's a little bit of everything.

From Waikiki to Downtown Honolulu

In this area, which stretches from the ewa end of Waikiki to downtown Honolulu (Kapiolani Boulevard is the main thoroughfare), we'll begin with the charming **Victoria Station,** 1599 Kapiolani Blvd. (tel. 955-1107), where it won't cost you more than a pittance to dine if you limit your visit to lunchtime only. You'll dine surrounded by mementos of the English railroad era—antique boxcars out in the front and on the side, red and gold railway signs all over. Inflation-fighting lunches feature cheeseburgers at $2.95, baked rainbow trout and teriyaki chicken at $3.65, quiche and soup at $2.95. Jumbo baked potatoes stuffed with Mexican or Italian or Californian (mushrooms, sour cream, sunflower seeds) toppings are great filler-uppers at $3.75, as are the Mexican dishes, nachos and enchilada pie, at $3.95 and $4.45. Soup-and-salad luncheons are $4.25. At dinner, the entrees advance into the $8 to $16 category, making it a bit of a splurge for us. Salad bar is included with most entrees at lunch and dinner. There are drinks for the grownups (you can have them in the bar and cocktail lounge with the huge "Waiting Room" sign or at table), and a separate menu that folds into a bright-red cardboard train for "Junior Engineers." A non-smoking section is available. There's another Victoria Station at Ala Moana and Hobron Lane, on the ground floor of the Ilikai Marina parking complex.

We always wonder why Honolulu's tourists haven't yet caught up with **King's Bakery and Coffee Shop,** 1936 S. King St. near McCully (tel. 941-5211), which has been a popular local rendezvous for years. Even though it's open practically 24 hours a day seven days a week, it's always jammed and you sometimes have to wait a few minutes for a seat at the counter, tables, or booths—that's how well liked it is. Certainly it's not because of the decor, which is perfectly plain with plastic-topped tables. It is because of the good service, the good food, and the fact that lunch and dinner menus are the same and are served around the clock. This means you can always count on a plate of hot, lusty beef stew, Hawaiian chopped steak, crispy fried chicken, sauteed mahimahi, or breaded veal cutlet, from $4 to $4.25. Daily specials at $4.50 include pot roast pork, short ribs, and mushroom chicken, served with a tossed green salad, vegetable, rice or potatoes, butter, and roll. We mention the roll last because this is also a bakery, and a good one. People come from miles around to shop for King's bread and rolls and their delicious pies and cakes. After you've had your fruit pie, or cream cheese pie, you may be tempted to join the crowd at the bakery counter and take some home with you—and don't forget the very special sweet bread, $1.55 per loaf. (Try it for french toast!) Send some home to your friends—King's has them already packaged—and they'll bless you forever.

You can also get the standard sandwiches here at low prices, plus soups, salads, and soda-fountain concoctions. Breakfast is served around the clock. King's also has two other locations, at the Kaimuki Shopping Center, 3221 Waialae Ave., and at Eaton Square, on Hobron Lane.

In the Ala Moana Area

Classical music lovers and/or lovers of Korean food should have a delightful time at the **Cosmos Piano Restaurant,** 1376 Kapiolani Blvd., about half a block ewa of the Ala Moana Shopping Center (tel. 944-1006). Cosmos is a handsome place with several dining rooms. In the main dining room, with its attractive leather booths, classical music prevails. If the talented proprietor, Mrs. Amy Ahn, is not playing the grand piano, you can watch videotapes of world-renowned symphony orchestras and soloists on the huge TV screen. And while you're listening, you can enjoy the very good Korean food which, contrary to popular opinion, is not highly spiced: that's only the kim chee. Dinner plates are accompanied by soup, rice, kim chee, and vegetables, with a choice of beef rib (kal-bi), chicken, beef sirloin, and pork, at $6.50 to $9. For those who do like hot food, there's a fiery kim chee stew at $5.50, or perhaps pan-fried octopus for $6.50. Luncheon plates, served with rice, kim chee, and vegetables, run from $3.50 to $5.50 for choices of chicken, beef, and combination. Cosmos is open from 10 a.m. until 2 a.m., seven days a week.

A most welcome addition to the Honolulu dining scene for calorie counters (and who isn't, these days?) is the **Guiltless Gourmet,** located a block from Ala Moana Center at 1489 Kapiolani Blvd. (tel. 955-6144). The calorie count of everything served is right on the menu at this cute little place done in pink and white with ice-cream chairs and tables. In addition to the yummy desserts made with "Skinny Delite" (their frozen ice milk), they offer several "lite meals." We like the Tasty Tostada, whole-wheat cracker bread covered with veggie chili, melted cheese, and salsa, 375 calories for $3.49; and the potato skins, four baked potato skins filled with either imitation bacon bits or vegetables, 350 calories for $2.99. The tuna or chicken pocket sandwich made of choice chicken or tuna tucked in an enormous piece of pita bread contains a tasty 297 calories for $2.97. Now, about those desserts. Skinny Delite is available in dozens of flavors, like English Toffee, Swiss Chocolat, Tootsie Roll, various fruit flavors, and many more. It tastes divine and it's only 20 calories per ounce! The Hot Fudge Cake (200 calories) is very popular; it's a chocolate brownie served with a scoop of ice milk and topped with hot-fudge sauce, $2.49. Our favorite is apples à la mode—steaming hot apples topped with Skinny Delite, 130 calories for $1.99. Skinny Delite also comes in cups, cones, and take-out containers. Guiltless Gourmet is open every day, usually until 10 or 11 p.m.

The **Original Pancake House,** at 1221 Kapiolani Blvd. (tel. 533-3005), is a pleasant place to have breakfast or lunch on your way to or from the Ala Moana Center. We especially like to sit out in the pretty little garden, where one is sure to be visited by English sparrows, doves, Brazilian cardinals, and mynahs, all looking for a handout. Pancakes and crêpes include cottage cheese pancakes (one of our favorites!), at $3.70; Kijafa cherry crêpes, made with liqueur, at $4.75; blueberry pancakes, at $3.70; and the house special, apple pancakes (allow 30 minutes), at $6.50. Among the many omelets, all served with three buttermilk pancakes, our favorite is the potato—made with green onions and bacon bits and served with a flavorful sour cream sauce, $5.50. Beef Stroganoff crêpes and crêpes Palestine (filled with sour cream and Triple Sec) are unusual and special; they're priced at $4.30. There are also hot sandwiches such as teriyaki, steak, and french dip in the $3.80 to $4.10 range, and daily specials like mahimahi, chicken-fried steak, spaghetti, and beef stew, priced from $3.95 to $4.30. The restaurant is open from 10 a.m. until 2 p.m. every day.

One of our favorite places to pick up wonderful, portable food for a picnic or the beach—or just to take back to our hotel—is **Chicken Alice's,** at 1339 Kamaile St. (tel. 946-3446). The stellar attraction here is Alice Gahinhin's flavorful fried chicken. It's ever-so-delicately spiced and definitely habit-forming. And you can't beat the price—$4.25 for a small box containing 10 pieces; $6 for the large box, 18 to 20 pieces; $20 for some 60 to 70 pieces (in case you're throwing a party or have a very large family to feed). We also like the combination Korean plate: kal-bi (tender barbecued ribs), chicken, rice, and kim chee, for $4.75. The plate lunches here are king-size, to say the least. Chicken Alice's is open seven days a week from 10 a.m. until 2 a.m. At night, it becomes Korea House, a cocktail lounge, but you can still stop in and order anything on the restaurant menu. If you call and order ahead, they'll have your food all ready to go when you arrive. Kamaile Street is one block up from Kapiolani, just off Keeaumoku.

Middle East food is new for Honolulu, so it's worth hopping aboard your camel and getting yourself to the **Middle East Delicatessen and Bakery,** 747 Queen St. (tel. 524-6823), a cute little "Mediterranean marketplace" with just six center tables for eating in, and lots of delectable food for taking out. Local hostesses swear by this place for catering their parties, and local lunch crowds keep it busy for those luscious plate-lunch sandwiches served on their freshly baked Middle Eastern bread. The only problem is making a selection; everything is so good. Our own favorites are the Happy Greek (peppered beef, onions, tomato, olives, and either Syrian cabbage salad or Greek salad with feta cheese), $3.35; Tears in Your Rye (liverwurst, Brisling sardines, and Bermuda onion), $3.85; Tongue Fu (beef tongue, pepper beef, and Swiss cheese), $4.55; and 50 ways to Leave Your Liver (chopped liver, cream cheese and chives, and onion), $3.95. The only solution is to come back several times to keep sampling more of these goodies. If you're cooking in, praise Allah for the deli, with its formidable array of exotic cheeses, meats, salads, and home-baked baklava and other traditional goodies.

A real haven for the hungry and high-price weary, **Hana,** 636 Sheridan St. (tel. 537-1523), is worth the five-minute walk from the Sears end of the Ala Moana Shopping Center (it's one block mauka of Kapiolani Boulevard). It wouldn't do Hana justice to call it just a delicatesssen—it's a combination deli, cafeteria, restaurant (although tiny, with fewer than a dozen tables), and a picnic kickoff spot. The main reason for coming here is their broasted chicken: nibble on a wing (67¢) or a breast ($1.09), or order either the regular chicken box (two pieces, french fries or rice, salad) for $2.29; the queen size with three pieces at $2.97, or the king size with four pieces for $3.89. You're ready for your picnic. There's another Hana at Pearlridge Center.

Although J.C. Penney's, the huge department store at Ala Moana Center, is right up-to-date with its fashions, the prices they charge at

Penney's Restaurant, on the third floor, went out of style years ago—which makes it a great place for us. Every year we get letters from readers telling us about the good, inexpensive meals they've enjoyed here. It is a good deal, for breakfast, lunch, or dinner. At lunch, for example, hot plates are mostly under $4.50; we like their teriyaki plate at $4.10. A roast beef sandwich is $3.25. At 4 p.m. some dinner items are added to the menu, like grilled beef liver or choice sirloin steak. Entrees, from $5.25 to $7, are served with potatoes, vegetable, dessert, and beverage. Try to avoid the peak lunch hour unless you don't mind queuing up for a few minutes' wait. Open from 8 a.m. to 8 p.m. on weekdays, on Saturday from 8 a.m. to 5 p.m., and on Sunday from 8:30 a.m. to 4 p.m. Early arrivals must use the special third-floor entrance.

Note: For a rundown of other restaurants at the Ala Moana Shopping Center, see Chapter V.

Close to Town

For years the Flamingo restaurants have been offering terrific quality for the money. There are two such restaurants close to town: the **Café Flamingo,** at 574 Ala Moana (tel. 538-6927), and the **Flamingo Kapiolani,** 871 Kapiolani Blvd. (tel. 538-6931). We have a slight preference for the latter if only because it's nearer Waikiki; both are attractive and specialize in good service and delicious food. There are something like 14 main dishes on the menu at $6.35 or less. And here's what a typical dinner for that price would be like. It starts with soup or fresh mixed fruit cup (we tried both: the soup was a very satisfactory chicken mulligatawny; the fruit cup was out of the ordinary since it was made with fresh papaya); an entree of grilled butterfish with lemon butter sauce; spinach, rice, and salad on the side; delicious banana pie or chocolate pudding for dessert; and coffee or tea, hot or iced (at no extra charge), orangeade, or fruit punch to drink. If you choose spaghetti with meat sauce for a main course, the price of the entire meal is only $4.90. The quality of the food and the variety of choices are remarkable for the prices. At lunch there's an equally good bargain—no salad, but the prices go down about 50¢. Note to late eaters: You can get dinner at the Café Flamingo until 1 a.m. weekdays, until 2 a.m. on Friday and Saturday; the Flamingo Kapiolani serves dinner until 9 p.m., cocktails until closing. The Café Flamingo opens at 6 a.m. for breakfast, the Flamingo Kapiolani at 6:30 a.m. weekdays and 7 a.m. on Sunday.

The same top-notch management also runs the **Flamingo Chuck Wagon,** at 1015 Kapiolani, where lunch starts at $3.50 and at dinnertime you can eat as much prime rib or fried chicken as you like, served chuckwagon style, for $9.25. The **Flamingo Royal Lanai,** at 1529 Kapiolani, is the newest addition to the group. Steak and seafood dinners start at $6.50 and include a serve-yourself salad bar. Lunches start around $4.95. A singer entertains every evening beginning at 6 p.m. In the central business district downtown, the **Flamingo Coffee Shop,** and **Arthur's Restaurant,** at 173 Merchant St., are big local favorites. Luncheon in the coffeeshop starts at around $3.75, and at Arthur's at $4.95.

News dominates the conversation at **Columbia Inn,** 645 Kapiolani Blvd. (tel. 531-3747), a favorite hangout for the staffs of Honolulu's two daily newspapers just a few doors away. The news about food is also good at this large, wood-paneled spot, with its leather booths; you can choose from 13 entrees for around $6. The last time we were there we had chicken livers sauteed with mushrooms, served with rice and also breaded sirloin cutlet. Appetizers, salad, dessert, and beverage are à la carte. At dinner, there are all of 11 choices for $7 or under! Columbia Inn is open 24 hours a day seven days a week—except during the wee hours of Sunday morning—but full meals are served only from 11 a.m. to 4 p.m. (lunch) and 4 to 10 p.m. (dinner).

Everything about **TGIFriday's,** at 960 Ward Ave., corner of King (tel. 523-5841), is delightfully different—from the *big* menu with some 160 items to the art-nouveau leaded-glass hanging lamps and lovely antique furniture and accessories. It's obvious that no expense was spared in making this a delightful place to dine or have a drink. Friday's is insanely popular, and since reservations are not accepted, it's first-come, first-served.

The food, too, is far from run-of-the-mill. It was here that we discovered potato skin plates, a TGIF specialty. The skins are baked, then fried to a delightful crispness. You can order them plain or with sour cream and chives for dipping ($3.95), or "loaded," i.e., slathered with a quarter pound of cheese and crumbled bacon, plus the sour cream dip ($5.95). Or try a potato skin dinner, with chicken and asparagus and cheese, also $5.95. Another tasty treat is chicken nachos (like the Mexican original but substituting chicken for refried beans), $5.75. The quiches, priced from $5.50 to $5.75, are exceptional. Even the salads are something out of the ordinary—how about an avocado-crab salad in a flour tortilla, for $6.95? Seafood selections include fried clams in a basket with wedge fries at $4.95, fried scallops at $9.50, and fried shrimp at $9.95. Omelets can be custom designed, and there are tacos and burgers of all descriptions, and sandwiches on the order of chicken, french dip, or steak, priced from $4.95 to $10.95. We like their steak on a stick too: a skewer of beef marinated in teriyaki sauce and served with fries and a big onion ring, $2.95. TGIFriday's is open every day from 11 a.m. until 2 a.m. We love it.

At Fisherman's Wharf

For a nautical meal in a nautical atmosphere, **Fisherman's Wharf,** 1009 Ala Moana (tel. 538-3808), is a Honolulu tradition. If you're counting pennies, though, it's best to go at lunch, since the menu on the whole is too expensive for our budget. At lunch, however, you can get dishes like fish 'n' fries for $5.50, or fried Pacific oysters for $4.95, and sandwiches from $3.75; a chowder and mahimahi sandwich lunch is $5.95. Fisherman's Wharf soup—a thick, delicious brew—is $2.95 a bowl. This place fully deserves its popularity; there are huge picture windows for viewing the sampan fleet outside, and the waitresses wear intriguing uniforms that look like French sailor suits. Happy Hour in the Snug Harbor Inn is from 4 to 6 p.m. daily, when pupus are served along with beer and bar drinks.

At Ward Warehouse

Just opposite Kewalo Basin is the delightful **Ward Warehouse** shopping complex and there are several charming restaurants here that match the appeal of the shops. The **Chowder House,** for one, is a bright, bustling, and inexpensive seafood house, where you can watch the boats of Fisherman's Wharf through the glass wall behind the bar and have a light seafood dinner for as little as $5.85. We recently lunched on a good-size fresh salad, two slices of french bread, and filet of red snapper with french fries for that price. Most of the other seafood dinners are $5.25 to $8.95 (prices stay the same in the evening; there's only one menu). Fish sandwiches, also served with fries, go from $3.10 for mahimahi to $3.75 for bay shrimp; there are salads, seafood cocktails, fish fries, and three kinds of chowder, all reasonably priced.

Upstairs at Ward Warehouse, the same management operates the much fancier **Orson's Restaurant,** a spacious dining room with a peaked roof, bamboo shades on the windows, a delightfully open and breezy feeling. Although fish and seafood dishes average $7 to $9.50 for the likes of Maryland crab cakes and creole shellfish, you could also dine more modestly on dishes such as fettucine Alfredo or baked lasagne at $7.25 and $7.75. Both restaurants serve continuously from 11 a.m. to 10 p.m. seven days a week.

If you like spaghetti and you like low prices, then you're going to love **the Old Spaghetti Factory** at Ward Warehouse (tel. 531-1513), which has to be the most stunning budget restaurant in town. It's worth a visit just to see the setting, which might be described as "fabulous Victorian," the rooms brimming with authentic European antiques and Oriental rugs, ornamental lampshades, overstuffed chairs, many mirrors, and huge chandeliers. You may dine in an authentic trolley car or, more likely, at large, comfortable tables on colorful plush velvet seats, some with backs made from giant headboards. So popular is this place that you can always anticipate a wait for lunch and dinner, even though the main dining rooms seats 350 and the bar upstairs about 125! The menu is modest, concentrating mostly on spaghetti, and the food is not as dazzling as the surroundings; but you will eat heartily and well for very little. Complete dinners, from about $3.75 to $6.45, include a good green salad with choice of dressing, french bread with marvelous garlic butter (a whole loaf is brought to your table with a knife, and there are seconds), beverage, and spumoni ice cream in addition to the main dish. It's fun to have either the Pot Pourri, a sample of the four most popular sauces, or the Manager's Favorite, which serves up two different sauces. Our favorite sauces are the clam and the browned butter with mizithra (a Greek cheese). Lunch runs from about $2.75 to $5.75, has smaller portions, and does not include beverage and dessert. Beer, wine, and cocktails are available. Note the hours: lunch from 11:30 a.m. to 2 p.m. Monday through Saturday; dinner from 5 to 10 p.m. Monday through Thursday, till 11 p.m. on Friday and Saturday, from 4 to 10 p.m. on Sunday.

The newest dining spot at Ward Warehouse is **Upstart Crow & Company** (tel. 533-1761), a quite marvelous coffeehouse/restaurant/bookstore. The menu here is like a little newspaper—and you get to take it with you. The inside pages detail the varied fare available, the two outer pages give news about new arrivals at the bookshop. Coffee and pastries are served from 10 a.m. until closing (10 p.m. Sunday to Thursday, 11 p.m. on Friday and Saturday), dinner selections from 5:30 p.m. until closing. Regular food service begins every day at 11 a.m. Brunch runs to eggs Benedict and quiche (Lorraine and quiche of the day), plus other egg dishes. Burgers—cheese, avocado, guacamole, or bacon cheese—are all served on a big English muffin, garnished with carrot curls, tomato, and onion, and served with a good potato salad, priced from $4.25 to $4.75. In the same price range are sandwiches both unusual and tasty, like croque monsieur (grilled ham and Swiss cheese with sour cream on french bread), Napoleon (grilled Italian sausage and tomato on french bread), and Sorrentino (avocado, bacon, and turkey). We're especially partial to the salads here, like the curried chicken with almonds, apples, ginger, and garlic, and the Greek salad, $6.45 and $5.95. For dinner, there's fettucine Alfredo or pesto, chicken Dijon (in a nicely balanced mustard sauce), and tarragon chicken, all served with a choice of soup or salad, bread and butter, fresh vegetables and rice—one of the best buys around for $6.95 and $7.95. For late evenings or just a shopping break, Upstart Crow & Co. always has hot spiced cider, cappuccino, café mocha, hot chocolate, and English teas at the ready.

Note: Upstart Crow's canvas totes are a useful souvenir of your visit here: $10, spacious, and very sturdy.

At Ward Centre

The elegant Ward Centre shopping/dining complex at 1200 Ala Moana Blvd. and Auahi St., Diamond Head of Ward Avenue, boasts a number of first-rate restaurants. We could spend weeks eating here and not needing to go anywhere else. A few of our favorites:

On the street level, inside the Le Pavillon shopping area, are two restaurants with the atmosphere of European cafés: Rox San Pâtisserie and Crêpe Fever. **Rox San Pâtisserie** (tel. 526-9533), open to the court, is a fine restaurant, dessert shop, and coffeehouse all in one sophisticated package. It's the kind of place where Honolulu-ites like to meet their friends for lunch and dine lightly, say, on a quiche at $4.95, a cheese plate with fresh fruit and nuts at $4.50, or perhaps a chicken galantine at $7.95. Join them then or at dinner. Some of the dinner items are a bit high for our budget, but unless you're really ravenous, you could make do quite nicely with one of the appetizers—like duck pizza (really!) at $6.50—plus one of the awesome desserts that are the specialty here (more about them below). Dinner entrees are served with potato and vegetable, and include chorizos (freshly made sausages) at $7.50; fresh fish of the day at $12.50; and coq au vin at $10.50. Salads, such as Greek, squid, or mushrooms, are mostly under $5. Rox San is a very popular after-symphony (or theater, or movies) place; that's the time to come by for a variety of exotic coffee-and-liqueur drinks—and treat yourself to one of the sinfully rich pastries, such delights as Linzer torte, apple strudel, Chocolate Decadence, strawberry poppy-seed cake, chocolate cheesecake, Viennese walnut cake—we could go on for pages—which are priced from $1 to $3.50 for a generous serving. Rox San is open from 11 a.m. to 11 p.m. Monday through Saturday; on Sunday they close at 6 p.m. There is an $8 minimum charge during peak hours.

The quality of the food and the charm of the surroundings make **Crêpe Fever** (tel. 521-9023), a few doors down from Rox San, quite special. Red tile floors, round black tables, red and orange pennants overhead set a sparkling background for a menu that is not limited to just crêpes. For example, our favorite lunch here is homemade soup—we had cream of broccoli—served in a bowl of scooped-out cracked-wheat bread; with salad, it's a satisfying lunch for $3.25. Crêpes are filled with the likes of crab and shrimp, tuna salad melt, and cream lemon spinach (with cream cheese), and so are croissants, and either can be had with soup or salad or both for an under-$5 meal. Desserts are yummy too: cheese blintzes topped with sour cream, an apple cinnamon crêpe, fresh strawberries and cream and bananas and cream crêpes, $3.95 and $4.95, plus luscious chocolate crêpes too. Since Crêpe Fever serves the same menu continuously, Monday to Saturday from 8 a.m. to 9 p.m., Sunday to 4 p.m., you can have breakfast anytime:

three-egg omelets, waffles, and (especially good) their french toast: thick slices of Hawaiian sweet bread, served with cooked apples, $2.95.

Monterey Bay Canners (tel. 536-6197) offers a tremendous variety of seafood specialties, many of which we've not seen elsewhere. It's a big, bustling, nautical-type place; you'll want to linger over dinner here. If you're lucky enough to get a table by the window, you can overlook Kewalo Basin, where the commercial fishing charters are berthed. Lunch fits better than dinner into our budget, since you could order a delicious seafood tostada (a tortilla stuffed with seafood, cheddar, avocado, etc.) for $6.25, a big bowl of bouillabaise for $7.95, or Pacific red snapper for $4.95. But dinner too has a number of entrees on the low side of the menu, like red snapper at $7.95, or mahimahi at $8.85. And at both lunch or dinner you can order catch of the day—which might be opakapaka, ono-wahu, ahe, or ula—priced according to availability (several of the local radio stations carry MBC's "Fresh Catch" report several times a day). Drinks are quite special here: when was the last time you had a watermelon daiquiri! Sunday brunch, 10 a.m. to 3 p.m., is the time for seafood crêpes and shrimp, scallop, and crab Mornay, priced from $5.45 to $6.95.

Monterey Bay Canners serves lunch from 11 a.m. to 4 p.m., dinner from 4 to 11 p.m. Sunday through Thursday, until midnight on Friday and Saturday; cocktails available from 11 a.m. to 2 a.m. all week.

Fans of the **Yum Yum Tree,** that delightful pie shop and restaurant at Kahala Mall (see below), are cheering the opening of its new branch at Ward Centre. That makes it all the easier to stop in whenever the urge—for, say, macadamia nut or lemon crunch or English toffee pie—becomes overwhelming to take home a whole pie, or just have a delicious slice here. The menu is the same as at Kahala, and the setting is charming, both inside and out, with the feeling of a big country house with a large porch, shady and cool, thanks to the big blue umbrellas. This Yum Yum Tree serves breakfast food from 7 to 11 a.m. and again from 11 p.m. to closing, lunch from 11 a.m. to 5 p.m., dinner from 5 p.m. to 1 a.m. (until 3 a.m. on weekends), and cocktails from 11 a.m. to 2 a.m.

To our mind, the dazzler here at Ward Centre is **Ryan's Parkplace** (tel. 523-9132), a big, rambling, stunner of a room with highly polished wood floors, gleaming brass, lazily revolving ceiling fans, windows all around, myriad lush plants, and a shiny kitchen open to view. What impresses most is the pride the attractive staff takes in this knockout place. The menu is incredibly varied, and everything on it is available all day, so even the fussiest of eaters will be hard put to find fault here. And prices, considering the quality, are quite reasonable. Consider, for example, fish and Maui chips, stir-fried chicken, fried yearling oysters, Mediterranean chicken salad, a sensational lasagne, linguine with fresh zucchini, tomatoes, and goat cheese—all between $5.95 and $7.95. All pastas are homemade, as are the pizzas, priced from $5.95 to $8.50 for a good-size pie. We're partial to the Three-Salad Sampler, which includes the Mediterranean chicken salad, Broadway pea salad (fresh peas and bacon in a heavenly herb dressing), and the pasta salad with pesto, quite a meal at $7.95. And we've also enjoyed "James Beard's Famous Chicken with 40 Cloves of Garlic," simmered in white wine and parsley at $9.25, and the chicken enchilada at $7.50. Like everything else at Ryan's, the bar list is generous: wines are available by the glass or bottle. Ryan's serves lunch from 11 a.m. to 5 p.m. and dinner from 5 to 11 p.m., every day; the bar is open until 1:30 a.m. Reservations are accepted. Try not to miss this one.

Mexico is represented at Ward Centre by **Compadres** (tel. 523-3914), which gets a resounding *ole!* from us. It's a big, very attractive place with comfortable rattan basket chairs and soft lights, and a young and energetic staff to serve you. The food is *muy bueno,* and the prices won't damage your budget. The same menu and prices are in effect all day long. The sandwiches, like the chicken and avocado at $4.75, are all served with thick-cut deep-fried potatoes and Mexican salad, but you'll probably want to sample such Mexican specialties as the various platillos, which include refried beans, Mexican rice, and salad; they run from $3.95 to $7.95, the latter price for our favorite, crab enchiladas topped with special green sauce and sour cream. A nice selection of burritos and chimichangas is priced from $4.25 to $7.75. Arroz con pollo and chicken mole at $8.95 are both good, as are the baby back ribs, at $6.95 and $12.95, and the barbecued chicken deliciously marinated in white wine at $8.95. As for the desserts, we can't resist the apple chimichanga—brandied apples in a flour tortilla, deep fried and topped with vanilla ice cream or cheese, at $2.45. Compadres serves the complete menu from 11 a.m. until midnight daily; brunch specialties are available from 10 a.m. until 3 p.m. on weekends.

Downtown Honolulu

A good place to eat in the downtown area is in the YWCA Building, 1040 Richards St. (tel. 533-7859), which houses **M's Garden Buffet,** a longtime bargain standby with Honolulu businesspeople. Inside, there's a lovely large room with beamed ceilings, a cool place to go when the sun has gotten to you. Outside there are tables under pretty awnings. You can easily pick up an inexpensive lunch from the cafeteria line here—there are plenty of fruit and vegetable salads, a tuna sandwich platter at $2.75, and lunch specials that include salad or dessert and beverage and cost from $3 up. Breakfast will run you from $2.50. M's also has a snackbar right outside the cafeteria for people on the run. M's is open Monday through Friday only, from 6 a.m. to 2 p.m. When you finish, stroll around the Y a bit; we especially like the scene at the pool, with mamas earnestly watching their serious-faced youngsters learning to swim.

A Cinderella treatment has transformed **George's Inn,** 1360 S. King St. (tel. 949-7222), an old kamaaina hangout, inside and out. But although everything has changed here, including the menu, value and quality are still first rate. The cozy restaurant is lit by hanging Japanese lanterns and furnished with shiny booths upholstered in black. Friendly waitresses wear bright happi coats over long pants; Oriental scenics and plants decorate the dining room. The menu features complete meals served with soup, salad, or fruit cup, mashed potatoes or rice, vegetables and bread, and dessert. No need to spend over $5 here, unless you want the seafood platter for $5.95 or the T-bone steak for $8.85; you can do very nicely with breaded mahimahi or hamburger steak teriyaki for just $4.65; boneless chicken or liver and onions for $4.85; a Hawaiian plate (lau-lau, lomi lomi salmon, rice or poi, haupia, and rock salt and onion) at $4.50. À la carte choices include breaded shrimps, oysters, or scallops at $4.25. Sandwiches and burgers too. George's is open from 7 a.m. to 9 p.m. every day except Sunday and holidays.

You'll have to look sharp to spot **Harold's Restaurant,** behind the Bank of Hawaii in the King Center, 1451 S. King St. (tel. 946-0295), but it will be worth the effort. This cozy place, with its curtain pattern on the walls, blue carpeting, and bright-red linen, serves good food at reasonable prices at all three meals. There are always luncheon specials priced around $4.95, like braised turkey wings or teriyaki chicken cutlet. The price includes fruit cup or soup, salad with choice of dressing, and rice, potatoes, or steak fries. Standard lunch-menu items range from spaghetti with meat sauce at $4.50 and roast turkey at $4.95 to the seafood platter at $6. Come dinnertime, many of the same dishes are served and the prices hardly change. Shrimp tempura is $5.95. Portions are generous and the menu is varied. You get a feeling of "home-cooked." And breakfast is good too, with eggs and omelets at $2 to $3. Harold himself will probably seat you or greet you at the cash register on the way out. Booths add privacy, and the bar is separate. There is plenty of parking in the bank parking lot. Harold's is open daily from 6:30 a.m. to 10 p.m.

Hawaiian Bagel—how's that for a marriage of concepts? This wholesale-retail delicatessen with a few tables for those who can't make it out the door is at 753B Halekauwila St. (tel. 523-8638), in a new contemporary-style building located in the rundown but picturesque Kakaako section of Honolulu. The sights and scents are surpassed only by the tastes. Needless to say, proprietor Stephen Gelson is not a full-blooded Hawaiian. Nor are the bagels, blueberry muffins, and homemade rye bread. But the little restaurant and takeout bakery deli is a hit with the local folk.

They carry ten varieties of bagels, including onion, sesame seed, and poppy seed, priced at 30¢ and 32¢ each. The sandwiches are typical deli variety: roast beef, lox or whitefish and cream cheese, corned beef, liverwurst, turkey, pastrami, and the like, from $2 to $3. In true deli tradition, they even serve celery tonic. You may want to take home a fragrant, round loaf of fresh-from-the-oven rye bread.

Hawaiian Bagel is open every day except Sunday from 6:30 a.m. to 5:30 p.m. There is parking on the premises.

Jake's Downtown Restaurant, at 1126 Bishop St. (tel. 524-4616), is a tremendous favorite with people who work downtown. Don't let the lunchtime line scare you away; the turnover is quick and the wait is never long. Jake's is a most attractive place of the brick-wall, stained-glass, cozy-booth, wood-paneled variety; the food is excellent and the service quick and courteous. Although the usual breakfast, lunch, and dinner items are here in abundance, the stars are the wonderful pancakes, waffles, crêpes, and blintzes: buttermilk pancakes, blueberry or strawberry crêpes, macadamia-nut pancakes, blintzes with fruit compote and sour cream, and strawberry and blueberry waffles, served with hot fruit compote and sour cream, and dusted with powdered sugar, are special favorites, from $1.95 to $3.50. Plenty of omelets too, and eggs Benedict served with home fries and sauteed zucchini, at $5.25. There's home-made clam chowder and Portuguese bean soup every day, as well as a variety of meat sandwiches, a "Vegetarian Exquisite," and crêpes Stroganoff, from about $3.75 to $5.75. Save some room for either the carrot cake or the cheesecake, plain or with fruit compote: heavenly! Jake's is open from 6 a.m. to 9 p.m. Monday through Friday, and 7 a.m. to 6 p.m. on Saturday and Sunday.

For a quick, inexpensive, and very good lunch while shopping or sightseeing in the downtown area, pop in at **Ann's Burger Factory** at 1148 Bishop St. (tel. 531-8663). You can tell it's good because of its popularity with the local office and shop workers. Daily specials are priced at $2.75 and include beef stew, shoyu chicken, meat loaf, spare ribs, hamburger steak with gravy, and teriyaki hamburger steak. The burgers are ample and priced at $1.50, cheeseburger at $1.70. There's a bento box (Japanese lunch) for $2.75. Ann's is open Monday through Saturday from 9 a.m. until 4 p.m.

There always seem to be huge lines of hungry people waiting to get into the **Orange Tree** in the Amfac Building, one of the two Amfac skyscrapers, at 700 Bishop St. They're attracted by the good food and the low prices. The roast beef sandwich is only $2.25. The daily special, perhaps a ham sandwich with potato salad, is $2.60. We enjoyed their syllabub—a concoction of orange juice, milk, yogurt, fruit salad, egg, wheat germ, and honey; it's $1.95, and a meal in itself. The soup of the day is hearty enough to make a meal on too; we sampled a thick and lusty bean and bacon soup, $1.10 for 12 ounces. This bright, cheerful spot opens at 6 a.m., closes at 4 p.m. weekdays, 1 p.m. on Saturday.

Not too long ago, *Aloha* magazine had an islandwide search for the best hamburger on Oahu. The winning burger was the one offered by the **Bakery Kapiolani Coffee Shop,** 1221 S. King St. (tel. 523-1291), and it only costs $1.35—$1.55 with cheese! The hamburger and cheeseburger deluxe are $1.60 and $1.80 respectively. Also available in this basic coffeeshop with lunch counter, booths, and bakery in the middle, are the likes of teriburgers, chili dogs, saimin, and coconut pies; and what must be the world's last surviving 40¢ hot dog. All sandwiches are served on home-baked buns or bread. Open 5:30 a.m. to midnight daily.

When a restaurant has been going strong for over 30 years, you know it must be doing something right. Such a place is the **Wisteria,** 1206 S. King St. (tel. 531-5276), very popular with the local crowd (at a recent lunch we and one other couple were the only haoles present). Save for a few murals painted with wisteria branches, there is very little decoration. The atmosphere is pleasantly businesslike, the service swift and professional, and the deep leather booths comfortable. The menu leans to the Japanese side, but there are also quite a few American-style specialties. If you're in the mood for Japanese food, you can choose from various sushi dishes at $5 to $6 (plastic replicas are displayed in a case at the entrance), or select from a wide range of donburi, tempura, and sukiyaki specials (sukiyaki dinners of chicken, beef, or pork are $5.20 to $8.20). Treading on more familiar ground, you might order such American-style dishes as roast young tom turkey, broiled rainbow trout with sauce meunière, broiled filet of mahimahi, or breaded tenderloin cutlet, from $4.95 to $5.55. The house special is an excellent roast prime rib of beef au jus with horseradish sauce and rice: $8.70. Our Japanese meal (we chose the daily specials of tempura soba and chicken araimo) included eggdrop soup garnished with scallions in dainty black bowls, pickled vegetables, rice, and a pot of tea. Two of us had more than enough to eat for $10.50.

The Wisteria is open daily from 6 a.m. until 10:30 p.m., on Friday and Saturday until 11:15 p.m.

If you're sightseeing by car and want a clean, reasonable, fast-service restaurant where the food is above "fast service" average, try **Kenny's Coffee House,** a local favorite at the Kam Shopping Center, Likelike Highway and North School Street (tel. 841-3733). How Kenny's manages to keep the prices so low is hard to figure out. Standard broiler items like steaks, chops, and chicken run from only $4.95 to $5.95, and most are accompanied by fruit cocktail, soup or salad, and roll and butter. Two daily specials at around $4 are noteworthy: the oxtail soup served with rice is a meal in itself, and the teriyaki butterfish melts in your mouth. The menu is the same all day, from 6 a.m. to 11 p.m., until 1 a.m. on Friday, Saturday, and Sunday. There's a dinner special each night, ranging from Swiss steak on Monday, to seafood platter on Friday, roast pork on Saturday, and roast beef on Sunday—all from $4.25 to $5.50. Whenever you go, you'll be well fed and well pleased. Kenny's is a bright, cheery place with high ceilings and wall-to-ceiling windows. The bright-green booths and yellow-and-orange color scheme reinforce the cheery mood.

If you prefer a picnic, try Kenny's take-out deli next door, where meat and chicken picnic trays are just $2.75 and $2.95, and the chicken isn't fried, but broasted. Tasty.

In the University Area

Now that the cafeteria at the striking East-West Center has closed, the best place to eat at the university is the **Student Activities Center,** close to University Avenue in the middle campus. Its huge upstairs cafeteria serves weekday breakfast and lunch from 7 a.m. to 2 p.m. Depending on the day, you may get lemon chicken, mahimahi, veal cutlets, or barbecued ribs, from $1.50 to $3.50. A variety of salads and desserts are available too, and more of the latter can be purchased at the Bake Shop (open until 1 p.m.) and the Ice Cream Shop (open until 4 p.m.). If you want to party with the students, **Manoa Garden,** right next door in Hemenway Hall, is open 10:30 a.m. to 9 p.m. weekdays and 11 a.m. to 3 p.m. on Saturday. There is often live entertainment in a bargain-priced pub atmosphere. You can get healthy sandwiches made to order, salad by the ounce, and assorted pupus. You can sit indoors or, if the sun is shining in Mano Valley, try the lanai and throw some crumbs to the Brazilian cardinals, sparrows, and doves.

The Buzz's restaurants have been popular with residents and visitors alike for as long as we can remember. Our favorite of these handsome places is **Buzz's Original Steak House,** just off University Avenue at 2535 Coyne St. (tel. 944-9781). The decor is art nouveau, with wood paneling, stained glass, and wonderful '30s light fixtures. Steak and seafood are the mainstays of Buzz's bill of fare, so prices run a bit above our budget, but they also have one of the best salad bars in town, at just $5.50. A perennial dieter friend of ours swears by it. This is one place where we wouldn't want to pass up the pupus: sauteed mushrooms, artichoke surprise, escargots ($2.50 to $4.50) and an appetizer-size order of kal-bi (Korean-style marinated beef ribs), $4.95. A dinner-size kal-bi platter is $8.25. Other specialties on the low side of the menu include Buzz's beef kebabs at $8.25, and top sirloin (six ounces) at $7.75. Combinations of steak with scampi, crab, or lobster can go from $13.50 up to $17.95. All entrees come with bread, veggies, and that salad bar. And don't miss Buzz's incredible ice-cream pies, at $2.50 a serving.

Buzz's in the university area is open Sunday to Thursday from 5 to 10 p.m., on Friday and Saturday to 10:30 p.m. There are three other Buzz's steakhouses, in Lanikai, Pearl City, and at Kona, on the Big Island.

The longtime mecca for pizza lovers in this area is **Mama Mia,** at 1015 University Ave. in Puck's Alley (tel. 946-2533), and real "New York pizza" it is too, since the owner is a transplanted New Yorker. There's a pie for every taste (even a vegetarian pizza with whole-wheat crust—$8.05); terrific spaghetti and lasagne dinners for under $7; some really lusty and crusty hero sandwiches; plus soda, beer, and wine. The place stays open until 1 a.m., so it's fun to come here—and sit at the sidewalk café if you like—after the evening's entertainment. Occasionally there's entertainment here too—perhaps a grownup puppet show, or just music.

One of our favorite places for submarine sandwiches in these parts is **Mr. Sub,** 1035 University Ave. in Puck's Alley, a clean and cheery spot that is very, very popular. (At a recent chic Honolulu cocktail party, the pupus turned out to be six-foot long Mr. Subs!) All the subs are good, but our favorite is the No. 4 supersub—prosciutto, pressed ham, salami, capicola, and cheese, covered (as are all the subs here) with lettuce, tomatoes, onions, and dressing, $1.95 for a half, $3.90 for a whole. The place closes at 10 p.m. The people here really work hard at maintaining quality, quantity, low prices, and super-fast service!

At Kahala Mall

A big favorite in the lovely Kahala residential area is the **Yum Yum Tree Restaurant and Pie Shop** (tel. 737-7938) in Kahala Mall. This is such a pretty place, with seating both on the lanai and in the wood-and-stone inside room. Service is fast and friendly, and the food is good: we like the grilled tuna, tomato, and cheese sandwich on sourdough bread at $3.85; the salads; and the main dishes—mahimahi, sirloin, jumbo fried shrimp, and the like, served with soup or good salad (choice of dressing), fries or baked potato, roll, and butter—all under $7.95. Best of all are the yummy pies for dessert, baked in their own kitchens; the pie display at center stage makes it difficult to resist taking a whole one back to your hotel. It's rumored that folks who stay at the posh Kahala Hilton Hotel a few blocks away like to come here now and then for a quick and inexpensive change of pace.

It's open for all three meals, starting at 7:30 a.m. with breakfast, until 11 p.m. daily. There's a lovely new Yum Yum Tree at Ward Centre (see above).

For a little bit of mittel-Europa in Kahala Mall, stop in at the **Pâtisserie** (tel. 735-4402), a bakery that also serves sandwiches and pastries (and a German dinner every Thursday evening) at its sparkling counter and several little booths. Sandwiches, served on their home-baked breads (we like the country Swiss), with sprouts or lettuce, run to the likes of Black Forest ham, head cheese, roast beef, bratwurst, pastrami, and prime rib; prices go from $2.75 to $3.95. And there's hot German potato salad, quiche Lorraine, and carrot salad too. If you don't want anything quite so heavy, Black Forest cake, dobosh, and freshly baked pies should be just right. Open weekdays from 7 a.m. to 9 p.m., until 7 p.m. on Saturday and Sunday. Check their shops too, at the Edgewater and Outrigger West Hotels in Waikiki.

THE NATURAL LIFE: There are lots of vegetarians and natural-food fanciers in the islands, and if you eat with them, you can save money while getting healthy. In addition to several good health-food store counters and, of course, salad bars and vegetarian entrees in many restaurants, we're happy to tell you that Honolulu now boasts three real gourmet natural-food restaurants. The oldest of these, and still very good, is **Laulima,** at 2239 S. King St. (tel. 947-3844). Come here for dinner for a real treat. For around $8.95 you can have the special of the day; it may be vegetable cheese pie or eggplant parmesan or a Mexican dinner or whatever the chefs dream up. Your entree comes with a delicious soup, fresh salad, whole-wheat bread, and herb tea. À la carte, entrees are priced from $5.20. Home-baked desserts (cream cheese pie, shortbread) are extra. Specialties available during the day include tostadas, nachos, bean burrito, vegeburgers and pita plate; and their homemade soups (especially the vegetable sweet-and-sour soup) are excellent. A locals hangout, Laulima is closed on Sunday.

The "gourmet vegetarian restaurant" is the way Sherrie Orr characterizes **Sherrie's White Flower Inn,** 2312 S. Beretania (tel. 947-2126), and we're inclined to agree. This is a health-food restaurant with a flair. Take, for example, the broccoli walnut cassoulet: fresh broccoli, mushrooms, and sauteed walnuts served over steamed rice, topped with yogurt and melted cheddar cheese, and served with a mixed salad. It typifies the special dinner plates that run from $4.75 to $8.25. Sherrie calls her potato fritata "the anytime meal": it's a three-egg potato omelet, open face, endowed with herbs and green onion and topped with melted Swiss cheese. Sandwiches, priced from $3.95 to $4.75, include salmon, tuna, and avocado with cheese, plus a dozen more, all with a special touch. Take the lowly peanut butter sandwich. Sherrie serves it on raisin bread with honey, raisins, shredded carrot, and a side of fruit munchies. There are equally glamorous soups, salads, side dishes, juices, and desserts, the latter including fresh carrot cake with a cream cheese frosting, and "lemon dream pie."

The country-store atmosphere at Sherrie's is almost as intriguing as the food. The restaurant is open until 9 p.m. seven days a week, starting at 11:30 a.m. on weekdays, at noon on Saturday, and at 10 a.m. on Sunday, when breakfast is served, featuring buckwheat waffles and real maple syrup. There is some off-street parking in front.

The food at **Johnny Appleseed,** 930 Ward Ave., just across from Blaisdell Center (tel. 536-2277), is so tastefully prepared and beautifully served that you might forget that you're dining in Honolulu's newest gourmet health-food eatery. The decor is airy and gardeny, with white trellises, many plants, and quiet ceiling fans. Everything on the extensive menu is served all day. The treats begin at breakfast time, with three-egg omelets served with a choice of Basque, Spanish, or sherried cream sauce, fruit garnish, ten-grain roll and butter, priced from $4.35 to $4.95. We find it hard to resist those ten-grain sourdough pancakes with berry topping at $3.35. Hot sandwiches have a special flair here: East Indian almond baked tuna and Far Eastern tofu ($5.45 and $4.75) are two examples. Of course there are salads, usual and unusual (watercress and mint tabouleh and New Age spinach salad are both great). But the chef really pulls out all the stops with the hot entrees: it's hard to choose between dishes like the Singapore chicken or beef, $8.75; chicken piccata, $7.50; fresh vegetable sauté with rice pilaf or spinach noodles, $5.95; or the curried shrimp or chicken sauteed with chutney, fruits, nuts, and spinach noodles or rice pilaf at $8.95. Vegetarian, chicken, or beef tostadas are $6.45 or $7.45. And along with your entree arrive soup or salad and ten-grain rolls. A bakery counter up front dispenses appetizing and healthful goodies.

Johnny Appleseed is open from 7 a.m. to 10 p.m. Sunday to Friday, to 11 p.m. on Saturday.

Wherever you see the name **"Vim and Vigor Foods,"** you can be sure you're getting very fresh, tasty natural food. There are several Vim and Vigors around town. Their take-out and drink counter at Ala Moana Center keeps huge lunch crowds happy with luscious sandwiches like falafel on Bible bread (the best), vegetable chicken salad on corn bread, and Mexican tostada, all around $2.45 to $2.90. Plenty of honey ice creams, fruit smoothies, and the like too. The Vim and Vigor at Puck's Alley, 1009 University Ave., near the University of Hawaii, has an all-day (10 a.m. to 8 p.m.) buffet that includes hot vegetarian dishes, fresh vegetable soup, brown rice, pastas, salad fixings, fresh fruit, breads, and desserts. It's a good buy at $3.50, but be sure you get there well before closing time or you're likely to find nothing much left. Sandwiches and smoothies are also available.

The newest Vim and Vigor, at Kalaha Mall, has a small salad-sandwich bar in back of the health-food store that dishes out big portions of very tasty food, plus lots of home-baked cookies and pies. Don't miss their wonderful breads up at the front counter, especially the whole-wheat cinnamon-raisin bread.

Ruffage and the Juice Factory has two locations: one in Waikiki at 2443 Kuhio Ave. in the Royal Grove Hotel (tel. 922-2042), and one at 824 Kaheka St., across from Holiday Mart (tel. 949-7009). Both have freshly squeezed juices; good fruit and vegetable salads; sandwiches like tofu tuna with tomato and sprouts ($2.95) and their version of a Reuben (natural Swiss cheese, mustard, sauerkraut, and sunflower seeds on rye); shakes and smoothies and frozen yogurt sundaes—all modestly priced. The atmosphere is health-food counter, but the food is fresh and good.

LUNCHING FOR A GOOD CAUSE: Now here's your chance to have two good lunches for two good causes in two picturesque settings. The atmosphere in both is decidedly tea-roomy, but men *are* allowed. The first of these is the **Garden Café**, at the Honolulu Academy of Arts, 900 S. Beretania, where the dining lanai is under the trees just outside one of the world's great art collections. The waitresses, the cashier, even the cooks are all volunteers, and all profits from your $5 (tax included) meal go to further the work of the academy. Lunch is served from Tuesday through Friday at either an 11:30 a.m. or 1 p.m. sitting, and every day there is a different soup, salad, and sandwich. Almost everything has a gourmet touch: the soups include chicken curry and crème mongole; you might get greenbean and bacon salad (delicious), or green salad with sliced fresh mushrooms; as for sandwiches, it's turkey, ham, and roast beef. The desserts, $1.25 extra, include ice cream with homemade chocolate sauce, brownies, or special dessert bars. Only one menu is served each day. Lunch reservations are recommended: call 531-8865.

Since there is usually a film or lecture at the academy at 7:30 Thursday nights, the volunteers also serve a Thursday supper at $6.50 (tax included) for a light meal of international cuisine. Wine and dessert are extra. Reservations are required. *Note:* The Garden Café is open from a week after Labor Day through the Friday before Memorial Day; closed Christmas and Thanksgiving.

Lunch at the **Waioli Tea Room,** 3016 Oahu Ave. in Manoa Valley, has been a Honolulu tradition since 1922. The food is good; the surrounding grounds are beautiful enough to justify the 15-minute bus trip (Route 5) from Waikiki; and all profits go to the Salvation Army. There are three entrees to choose from: Waioli fried chicken, coconut mahi, and Stevenson broil (beef patty with teriyaki sauce). Along with your entree, whose price should run about $4.85 to $5.25, comes salad and home-baked Waioli bread. Waioli's famous coconut cream pie or macadamia-nut cream pie, at $1.25, is a must for dessert. Lunch is served from 11 a.m. to 2 p.m. Tuesday through Sunday: on Sunday, it's a $7.95 buffet. Reservations are advised; phone 988-2131. Do walk around the grounds and view the Memorial Grass House of Robert Louis Stevenson, the chapel, and the stained-glass windows; this is some of the lushest, most exotic scenery in all Honolulu. Stop in too at the gift shop and bake shop for good things to take home.

KIDDIE TREATS: So you're traveling with the kids? By all means, take any youngsters up to age 12 or so to **Showbiz Pizza Palace** (tel. 373-3151), at the Aina Haina Shopping Center out on Kalanianaole Highway, not far from the Kahala Mall. There's a big stage at the front of the dining room, and every so often the curtains part to reveal very cleverly designed, life-size mechanical animal musicians and singers, such as Beach Bear, Mitzi Mouse, and Fatz the Gorilla. These ingenious creations appear most lifelike, and they "sing" and "play" instruments. There are also people in animal costumes who circulate in the dining room and talk with young diners. As if that weren't enough, there are myriad video games. This is a most popular place for local kids to celebrate birthdays. And the food isn't half bad. The pizzas—Super Combo (cheese, sausage, beef, pepperoni, etc.), Aloha Delight (cheese, ham, pineapple, toasted almonds), Vegetarian Favorite, and Taco Pizza sell for $8.50 small, $12.10 medium, and $15.45 large. There's a salad bar with a good variety of fixings, $2.54 for a bowl. You can even buy the kids—or yourself—a Showbiz Pizza T-shirt. Showbiz Pizza Palace is open every day.

SPLURGES: If you're a lover of musical comedy and light opera as well as excellent continental cuisine, you'll become an instant fan of **Villa Cabaret** (formerly known as Le Bon Restaurant), in its new home at the posh Eaton Square complex, 400 Hobron Lane (tel. 945-7880). It's a big, airy room with splendid rattan "throne" chairs, lots of plants, and an airy ambience. All of the extremely attractive young staff members are professional singers; don't be surprised if your waitress bursts into a tune from *Camelot* or *South Pacific* as she serves the salad. Requests are honored. Now, to the cuisine. If you order à la carte, consider this a big splurge, since entrees like coquilles St. Jacques and tournedos de boeuf maison are about $13.50 to $15.75, and accompaniments such as Caesar salad or shrimp or crab Louie are $6 and $9. It's more reasonable to order one of the complete dinners, which are served with soup de jour and a dinner salad; some of our favorite entrees are the demi poulet au Chardonnay (chicken sauteed in white wine sauce with grapes and mushrooms), $12.50; the filet of sole Bretonne, topped with shrimps, and mushrooms and cream sauce, $13; and the beef bourguignon, $12.75. You can also eat here quite reasonably by choosing from an imaginative assortment of appetizer crêpes, priced from $4 to $4.50; the chef does good things with the New Orleans crêpe, filled with shrimp and creole sauce; the Hungarian, filled with chicken in paprika sauce; and the Madras, stuffed with curried seafood. For dessert, there's ice cream or a superb mousse au chocolat, $2. Villa Cabaret also takes pride in its impressive wine list, with both domestic and continental wines.

Villa Cabaret serves dinner from 6 to 10 p.m., lunch from 11:30 a.m. to 2 p.m. Closed Monday.

Hackfeld's, on the ground level of Liberty House at Ala Moana (tel. 945-5243), is an elegant new place with modern decor and low lights. The food has a French-continental accent here, and the artful presentation makes dishes as pleasing to the eye as they are to the palate. Hot luncheon entrees are served with a choice of soup of the day or salad, and either garlic pasta (yum!), steamed rice, or french fries. Selections, which run from about $6 to $8.75, include chicken Cordon Bleu, Pulchu short ribs, and New England crab cakes. There's always a quiche Lorraine, served with fresh fruit. The dinner menu is equally promising. Escargots in mushroom caps and fettucine Alfredo are among the appetizers that might precede dinner. Entrees are served with soup of the day or salad, and garlic pasta, steamed rice, or potato pancakes. We like the lamb chops Provençal, baked in a buttery bread crust at $12, and the teriyaki steak at $8.75. Croûte Windsor, which is filet mignon on Canadian bacon, served on an English muffin with sauteed mushrooms, cheese, and hollandaise sauce, is a specialty at $7.75. For dessert, you owe it to yourself to try the crème caramel Chantilly.

Hackfeld's serves lunch from 11 a.m. to 2:30 p.m. Monday through Saturday; dinner, Monday through Friday only, from 5 to 9 p.m. Closed Sunday.

La Terrasse, 1855 Kalakaua Ave. (tel. 945-7766), gets our nod for one of the most charming French restaurants in Honolulu. Here you dine in a delightful garden atmosphere, with plants everywhere; the decor is light and airy, the table settings lovely, and the food superb. Lunch might begin with a bowl of cold vichyssoise, followed by such hot entrees as fettucine de homard (spinach noodles in lobster sauce with tender pieces of lobster) or steak Café de Paris, in herb butter sauce; each is $9. Salads are very well done here, like the avocado scampi, avocados filled with large ocean shrimp and topped with vinaigrette dressing, $7.50; or the papaye farcie (curried chicken breast, celery, green peppers, and almonds in a papaya half), at $6. Or you might choose soup and salad for $6. Dinner does tend to get quite pricey, but it's worth it, for creations like papillotes de veau with marsala sauce, $17; lobster in a pastry shell crowned with caviar, $18.50; or a variety of steaks at about $18. Have some wonderful French pastries, served from the rolling cart, to top it all off. With its garden of beautiful plants, the trellises that abound, and the tinkly piano music in the background, we'd have to call La Terrasse *magnifique.*

Lunch is served weekdays only, 11:30 a.m. to 2:30 p.m.; dinner from 6 to 11:30 p.m. weekdays, until midnight on Friday and Saturday.

The **Pagoda Floating Restaurant,** 1525 Rycroft St. (tel. 941-6611), is one of those rare places where the scenery alone is worth the price of admission. The glass-enclosed circular dining rooms—the informal Koi Room, which specializes in seafood, and the more elegant Lotus Room above, which offers Japanese cuisine—look out over a lotus-blossom pond stocked with almost 3000 brilliantly colored Japanese carp. Walkways lead out to individual pagodas seemingly floating in the pond. Although the individual pagodas are reserved for groups of eight or more, the view from the main dining rooms is quite beautiful. Both these places are a bit higher than our budget in the evenings, with entrees going from $9.95 to $18.95. The house specialty, roast prime rib of beef au jus, is $13.95. Lunch is more modestly priced, averaging $5.50 to $7. Try to plan your visit to catch the grand show at carp-feeding time—8 a.m., noon, or 6 p.m. Bring the kids and the cameras.

A dinner-only spot that combines a fine meal with an educational experience is the **Pottery Steak House and Seafood Restaurant,** in the

Waialae-Kahala area, at 3574 Waialae Ave. (tel. 735-5594). Not only is your meal served in unusual pottery—eating and drinking vessels fired in kilns right on the premises—but you can see the potters in action up front. And when you've finished your meal, you can buy the dishes and take them home! As you might expect, this attractive restaurant is decorated throughout with clay vessels that re-create some of the history and romance of early world pottery. And the food is excellent. If you want to stay on the low side of the menu, have the Potter's Delight, ground sirloin, at $8.50. Like all the other entrees, it comes with a choice of soup or salad, rice, or a baked potato with a variety of garnishes, vegetables, and loaves of garlic bread that continue to toast in their hot ceramic loaf-shape containers. Or splurge and order mahimahi at $9.75 or a variety of steaks from $10.75 up to $19.25 (for steak and lobster). We can recommend the Cornish game hen at $13.75, moist and tender and fired in its own clay vessel—you get to keep the pot. For dessert, go all out with the special potter's coffee, laced with rum, topped with whipped cream and served in a handsome mug. The Pottery Steak House is open from 5:30 to 10 p.m. daily, and reservations are advisable.

The dining critic of the *Honolulu Star-Bulletin* has called **Alfred's European Restaurant,** at 677 Ala Moana Blvd. (tel. 523-1602), "one of the top five restaurants in the city." We couldn't agree more. A visit to chef/owner Alfred Vollenweider's gracious blue-velvet dining room in the Ala Moana area, about halfway between Waikiki and downtown Honolulu, is like visiting a fine restaurant on the continent where every detail is handled perfectly, from the china on the table to the attentive service by the waiters to the superb French-continental cuisine. Everything is prepared fresh, using only the best market ingredients. And nothing comes out of the kitchen until Alfred—who spends part of each evening walking around the restaurant in his tall chef's hat, checking on everything—makes sure that it is perfect. While a meal here is not inexpensive, neither is it overly priced by today's standards, and it offers top value for the dollar. Dinner starts with four or five salad-relish dishes prepared according to the season, plus a basket of European-style breads. Soup de jour follows that, and then it's your choice of such dishes as a flavorful wienerschnitzel, coquille St.-Jacques au beurre blanc, Long Island duckling, tournedos de boeuf, live Maine lobster, or fresh fish taken from local waters and sauteed or steamed or poached in a light champagne sauce. Prices range from about $15.50 to $18.95 for the complete meal. Desserts are extra but more than worth the price, especially for creations like the soufflé glacé Grand Marnier, or the unforgettable strawberries Romanoff, fresh strawberries marinated in liqueur and topped with Häagen Däzs ice cream, served in a tall champagne glass. Irish, Swiss, and other specialty coffees, English and herbal teas, plus brandies and cordials top off the meal. Lunch is also pleasant and very reasonably priced, with egg dishes, salads, fresh fish, sandwiches, burgers, plus a daily chef's special which includes soup or salad, vegetables, and coffee, for $7.50.

Alfred's is open every day but Sunday, serving lunch Monday to Friday from 11 a.m. to 2 p.m., and dinner Tuesday to Saturday from 6 to 10 p.m. You can take the no. 2 or no. 8 ("Airport") bus from Waikiki. There is validated parking in the Gold Bond Building. Reservations are advised.

DRIVE-IN RESTAURANTS: One of the side benefits of renting a car in Honolulu is that it then becomes easy to join the throngs of local folk who swear by the drive-in restaurants. They've got a good reason: the price is right. We figure you can save about 50¢ at breakfast, from 75¢ to $1 at lunch, and from $1 to $1.50 on dinner at a drive-in compared to the same type of meals at a sit-down restaurant.

Chunky's, at the corner of Isenberg and King, just a block from University Avenue, offers a breakfast of fried eggs, potatoes, toast, and coffee for $2.20. The rest of the day there are hot plates like breaded beef cutlet, fried shrimp, and roast pork, from about $2.65 to $5.50, all served with side portions of rice or potatoes and a vegetable. And, of course, they have the inevitable hot dogs (75¢) and tuna sandwiches ($1). Drive-ins do not usually up their prices at dinnertime, so that's when you realize the biggest savings.

Quite close to Waikiki, **Like Like Drive-Inn,** is at 735 Keeaumoku St., at the mauka-Diamond Head corner of Kanunu Street. This is a sit-down place that tries to act like a regular restaurant; in the process prices have inched up a bit, but the values are still good. Daily specials like chicken tofu, tripe stew, and breaded mahimahi run from $4.65 up. Saimin is a specialty. Open 24 hours a day.

Across the street at 724 Keeaumoku is **Diner's Drive-In,** where the values are still old-fashioned. Hot plates are available any time of the day and they range from $3.25 to $3.40—and that's for teriyaki beef, shrimp tempura, and half a roast chicken. Steaks are available from $4.80 to $5.20. Sandwiches too, inexpensive breakfasts (try the banana hotcakes at $1.95), and sheltered tables as well. It's open 24 hours a day, as are most of the drive-in restaurants.

You'll see plenty of **Colonel Sanders Kentucky Fried Chicken** outlets around Honolulu. The local people queue up for the three-piece regular dinner for one person—with cole slaw, roll, gravy, and mashed potatoes; it's a tasty bargain at $3.64. For feeding a hungry family, what could be better than the nine-piece family dinner, enough for three or four, at $11.30? From Waikiki, the closest Colonel Sanders branches are at 645 Kapahulu Ave., 1124 McCully (corner Beretania), and 1460 Kapiolani Blvd.

HAWAIIAN RESTAURANTS: You'll probably have your first experience with Hawaiian food at a luau, and then you'll find the same dishes appearing again and again in Hawaiian restaurants and on the "plate lunch" menus of other restaurants all over town. We'll first tell you about the major Hawaiian food specialties, then give you some tips on a "poor man's luau," and finally show you where to find the budget-priced Hawaiian restaurants.

The Food and How to Eat It

You're already on speaking terms with poi. The other basic dishes are kalua pig (pig steamed in an underground oven, or imu), laulau (ti leaves stuffed with pork, salt fish, bananas, sweet potatoes, and taro shoots, and steamed), chicken luau (chicken cooked with coconut milk and taro or spinach leaves), sweet potatoes, pipikaula (jerked beef), and lomi-lomi salmon. The last is a triumph of linguistics over gastronomy: lomi-lomi means massage, and this is salmon "massaged" with tomatoes and chopped onions, then marinated. Haupia (coconut pudding) and a piece of coconut cake are the usual desserts, along with fresh pineapple.

Food is served on paper plates and the proper way to eat is with your fingers; plastic spoons are provided for the timid. The correct way to eat poi, by the way, is to dip one or two fingers in it (in the old days you could actually order "one-" or "two-finger" poi), scoop it up quickly, and attack. But nobody expects that of a malihini.

Poor Man's Luau

Luaus are fun affairs—everyone comes dressed in aloha shirts and muumuus, a great ceremony is made of putting the pig in the imu (camera buffs have been known to go wild with joy at this part), there's lively Polynesian entertainment, and of course there's the equally delightful food. But most of the commercial luaus cost from $20 to $30, enough to destroy a minimum budget for a week.

Here's our answer to the high cost of luaus: check the *Waikiki Beach Press* and the other local tourist papers for news of the frequently held church luaus. There's a neat irony about all this: the early missionaries forbade the Hawaiian songs and dances, and now, just a century later, the churches raise money by presenting them. At any rate, it's the local equivalent of a cake fair or card party, the price is usually about $10 for adults, $4 for children, and the food and entertainment is as good—or better—than at many a commercial shindig. Visitors are warmly welcomed.

Budget Restaurant Recommendations

The most down-to-earth Hawaiian restaurant is undoubtedly **Helena's Hawaiian Food,** 1364 N. King St. (tel. 845-8044), where you'll have a real experience in seeing nontourist Hawaii. The last time we were there, our fellow diners included an Oriental couple with an infant no more than a few weeks old asleep on the table; two Polynesian men of enormous girth; and a cheerful band of Japanese chatting away at a big table. The place is perfectly plain, and you'll sit on red wooden stools, dining on the likes of laulau ($1.45), lomi-lomi salmon ($1.20), or broiled butterfish ($1.20). The best idea is to have either the laulau plate (poi, laulau, salmon) for $3.25, or a kalua pig plate (poi, pig, salmon, or pipikaula) for $3.75. Helena's also has a "tourist's special"—a huge plate of native dishes for about $4 a person. Helena's food is also available for taking out, and lots of islanders who have never eaten a meal on the premises swear by it. We think it's a great place that should be seen—by the adventurous.

Close to Waikiki, a very popular place to find ono Hawaiian food is **One Hawaiian Foods,** at 726 Kapahulu Ave. (tel. 737-2275). It's a little place, with about ten tables, its walls covered with photos of popular local entertainers who are patrons. Try the kalua pig or laulau plate at $3.45, or just go mad and have the combination kalua pig *and* laulau at $4.30. These and other plates come with pipikaula (Hawaiian beef jerky), lomi salmon, poi or rice, and haupia. The atmosphere here is very friendly; the place may be short on size, but it's definitely long on aloha. Open Monday through Saturday from 10:30 a.m. to 7:30 p.m.

People's Café, 1310 Pali Hwy. (tel. 536-5789), is the most modern-looking spot for authentic, inexpensive Hawaiian food; the local office girls come here when they have a hangover and want some of that nice, soothing-to-the-tummy poi. This one has yellow plastic-leather seats and is much more modern than Helena's, but the crowd doesn't seem quite as colorful. Poi plate lunches go for $5.55 to $6.41, and the ingredients vary slightly every day; kalua pig and laulau are also served every day. The prices are the same at lunch and dinner. A good place to remember for take-out orders; there's a $2.75 bento box. Open every day, except Sunday, from 10 a.m. to 7:30 p.m.

JAPANESE RESTAURANTS: Japanese cuisine has so permeated the islands that you'll find Japanese dishes—beef hekka, shrimp tempura, saimin—on menus everywhere. Hekka is a kind of poor man's sukiyaki (a beef and vegetable stew) and tempura means anything fried in batter. Saimin (known in Japan as *rahmen*), the seaweed-chicken-noodle soup that we mentioned earlier, is just the thing for the starvation budget; a large bowl, which will cost about $1.50 to $2.50, will do for a whole meal, and you can get it almost anywhere. You can even make it at home: instant saimin, direct from Japan, is sold in the food departments of most Japanese stores, like Shirokaya at Ala Moana. Sooner or later you'll be introduced to sushi or sashimi, probably served among the pupus (hors d'oeuvres) at a bar, and you'll think it's delicious unless somebody spoils the fun first and tells you it's raw fish. Forget your prejudices and enjoy it. Sushi bars are great favorites, and can be found in many Japanese restaurants.

A good place for your first experience with Japanese food—and for one of the best bargain lunches in Honolulu—is the **Oriental Snack Bar** at Woolworth's on Kalakaua Avenue in Waikiki or at Ala Moana. Both are big hits with office workers and shoppers, and both offer you a chance to sample authentic Japanese dishes for just pennies. The prices vary minutely at the two; an order of beef hekka will be about 95¢, butterfish is $1.10, and a bowl of saimin is $1.50 to $2.25. The Kalakau Avenue store has a Sushi Bar and bento (take-out) lunches. We slightly favor the Ala Moana Woolworth's since, after filling up your paper plate, you can go out and sit in the pretty mall watching Hawaiians mill about you as you nibble. Incidentally, two "cone sushis" (cold, marinated rice cakes) tucked in your bag make a tasty lunch-on-the-run.

When you dine in a regular Japanese restaurant, all you order is your main course; it will come served on a tray with several small dishes like pickled vegetables, soup, rice, and tea. Nobody will think you're a square if you ask for a fork, but why not live dangerously? You'll get the hang of chopsticks, more or less, by the end of your first Japanese meal.

Many of Hawaii's Japanese restaurants are pretty expensive affairs, complete with kimono-clad waitresses and lavish settings. We have a couple of favorites, however, where you can dine quite reasonably at lunch and pay an average of $7 to $8 for complete dinners.

First, we've always liked **Suehiro,** at 1914 King St. (tel. 949-4584). Try to get one of their ozashiki or tatami rooms, where you sit on the floor and dine at a low lacquered table (you take off your shoes before you enter, of course); the setting will immediately put you in a tranquil mood, ready for a different kind of experience. You usually need a party of eight and a reservation for these rooms, but if a room happens to be open you may double up with other waiting guests. On one visit we teamed up with a big, charming family of Japanese-Americans, and had dinner at $10 per person that included a tasty miso soup (a clear broth made with soybean paste), namasu (pickled cucumber), lobster salad, sashimi (raw fish), shrimp tempura, fried lobster, and beef sukiyaki. All of this was served with several side vegetables, sauces, rice, dessert, and plenty of tea. It was a colorful and memorable experience. At the regular restaurant tables, you may order a similar dinner special for $20 for two people, and there are several "combination dinners" at $6.95 per person, again with all the extras. At lunchtime, the combination plates are an especially good buy: shrimp tempura and broiled fish or barbecued chicken at $3.95, both served with tossed green salad, soup, and rice. *Note:* You can also get a tasty Japanese box lunch here, for picnics and trips.

To sample a full range of Japanese seafood at a reasonable price, the name to remember is **Teruya's,** at 600 Kapiolani Blvd. (tel. 538-6078), a fair-size, no-nonsense Japanese restaurant smack in the middle of the Civic Center. Every night from 5:30 to 9 p.m. a buffet is laid out with steamed clams, crab legs, fish miyosaki, shrimp tempura, miso-style pork, sashimi, nishime, teriyaki, yakitori, sukiyaki, yaki soba, assorted sushi, shrimp gyoza, lomi-lomi salmon, and salad bar. Eat as much as you like: it's $10.95 for adults, $5.95 for children. If you're here at midday, join the downtown working crowd and get a bento (lunch) box to take out: the price is right, and the food is good, from $2.75 to $3.75.

Our favorite of the new Japanese restaurants is **Kamigata,** in the Manoa Marketplace, 2756 Woodlawn Dr. (tel. 988-2101), a very attractive spot, all reds and golds and low lights. Come at lunch and try one of their three combination specials: each starts with shrimp tempura. Add shoyu chicken and the price is $3.90; with beef teriyaki, it's $4.45; and with broiled butterfish, $4.25. These are served with rice, tsukemono, and soup. Other complete lunches run up to $6.50. At dinnertime, you can have sushi plates, from $3.75 to $9.25, yakiniku dinner for $8.95, a king crab legs dinner for $12, New York steak for $9.50. If there are at least four of you, call ahead to reserve one of Kamigata's lovely tatami rooms: here you can have their festive Bun Raku or Kabuki dinners ($11.75 and $12.75), in addition to the choices mentioned above. Kamigata is open for lunch from 11 a.m. to 2 p.m. Monday through Saturday, and dinner is served nightly from 5:30 to 9 p.m.

Should you get a craving for Japanese food at an odd hour—say, at 2 o'clock in the morning—be advised that **Restaurant Jiro,** at 1551 Kapiolani Blvd. (tel. 941-3940), is almost always open (8 a.m. to 3 a.m. Monday to Thursday, to 5 a.m. on weekends). This is a pleasant place with deep-red carpets and booths, friendly, bustling Japanese waitresses, and soft Japanese music. You can really save money here with the noodle dishes, priced from $2.50. Tempuras, served with rice and miso soup, are interesting, since you can be quite specific about the fish (or vegetable) you want deep-fried; they include shrimp, scallops, squid, eggplant, and oyster, and most are between $5.20 and $6.50. For a good, filling meal, try one of the Jiro Specials: accompanied by rice, miso soup, and salad, they are priced from about $8.30 to $8.70, and include sliced beef, barbecued teriyaki steak, pork or chicken yakiniku, and beefsteak with butter sauce. And a variety of fish dishes is priced from $5 to $6.

CHINESE RESTAURANTS: Cities with large Chinese populations always have enough inexpensive restaurants to keep you going for some time, and Honolulu is no exception. It's especially good for us budgeteers, since many of the restaurants are quite lavish and yet offer a number of surprisingly reasonable dishes. The problem here is choosing from an embarrassment of gourmet riches: local friends each swear that their favorite is "the best." Remember that since most of Hawaii's Chinese came from the southern districts, most restaurants feature Cantonese dishes; but happily, the more subtle Mandarin cooking of the northern provinces and the fiery Szechuan cooking that's so popular on the mainland have found their way to several of our budget choices.

One of the most popular Chinese restaurants in town is **Yong Sing,** 1055 Alakea St. (tel. 531-1366). It's a huge place occupying all of a recently renovated downtown building, and the vast dining room is nicely, if not elaborately, decorated in red and gold. There's a huge menu from which to choose, and the selections run the gamut from a $3.75 luncheon plate—pork chop suey, fried shrimp, sweet-and-sour spare ribs, pot roast pork, crisp wonton, and fried rice—to a $125 nine-course dinner to feed a party of ten. In between, there are loads of well-priced goodies. The last time we were here we had a succulent almond duck ($4.75) and chicken with oyster sauce, the house specialty ($4). An excellent $17 dinner for two people includes egg flower soup, almond chicken, and sweet-and-sour spare ribs with tomatoes and fried rice. For something unusual, ask the waiter for a dim sum lunch. This consists of many different varieties of Chinese dumplings: either steamed, baked, or fried, some filled with sweetmeats and served as main dishes; others, dainty pastries for dessert. Five or six of these and plenty of the free-flowing tea—and you've had a lovely, inexpensive treat. But be sure to get there between the hours of 11 a.m. and 2 p.m. for the dumplings; otherwise: so sorry, all sold out today. Yong Sing also has cocktails at reasonable prices, take-out orders anytime, and plenty of parking available. It's open from 7:30 a.m. until 10 p.m. seven days a week.

The **Ming Palace,** 1272 S. King St., between downtown Honolulu and the university area (tel. 538-1985), used to be relatively unknown to the haoles. Not that it was waiting to be "discovered": the Chinese population came in droves for some of the best Chinese food anywhere. Now that the word's out, people are flocking here from everywhere. The restaurant is elegant inside and out, adorned with Chinese art and plaques on the outside, with elaborate woodcarvings within. The food is equally elegant: if you're a seafood lover, don't miss the fried shrimp at $4, or the lobster at $9. The chef also does magical things with specialties like Peking duck and sharkfin soup, as well as the more common Cantonese fare. Prices are reasonable, and most dishes—like the chicken and duck entrees at $3.25 to $4.50, and the pork and beef dishes at $3 to $3.75—are big enough to serve three. And there are noodle dishes galore in the $3 range. Ming Palace is open every day from 11 a.m. to 8:30 p.m., and the same menu holds all day long.

There are precious few North Chinese restaurants in the islands, so praise be for **King Tsin,** 1486 S. King St. (tel. 946-3273), an attractive, pleasantly decorated place popular with both visitors and local folk. The food is reasonably priced, subtly flavored, and most fun to eat with a group, as we did the last time we were there. A Chinese friend had ordered for us over the phone, and our soup and appetizer were whisked to our table moments after we arrived. Our party of four began with pot stickers, small dumplings stuffed with pork, two orders at $2.95 each, and two orders of sizzling rice soup at $2.95 per order. For our main courses, we had mu shu pork, a kind of crêpe assembled right at the table by spreading it generously with plum sauce and stuffing it with a marvelous pork concoction, $5.25; dry fried beef—superhot— at $5.50; King Tsin chicken, $5.25, a delicate combination of tender white meat of chicken and pea pods; braised bean curds, $4.95; and sweet-and-sour fish, and entire rock cod, complete with tail and head, smothered in sauce, around $12, depending on size. We all ate until we couldn't manage another bite—and still had a huge doggie bag to take home. The bill for this veritable banquet was $38.25 for the four of us, but one could, of course, dine much more modestly, since most dishes are $3.95 to $4.95. Lunch prices are about 10% cheaper than dinner. Steamed rice and tea were in abundance, and the service was fast and friendly. With the exception of the aforementioned beef—about which the menu warns you—the food here is not overly spicy, as it can be at other northern Chinese restaurants. Open daily for lunch from 11 a.m. to 2 p.m. and dinner from 5 to 9:30 p.m.

Vegetarians who love Chinese food swear by the **Yen King Restaurant** in the Kahala Mall Shopping Center, near the Kahala Hilton Hotel (tel. 732-5505)—there are at least 25 meatless dishes on the menu! So do lots of other folks who've discovered this attractive restaurant that specializes in the cuisines of Peking and Szechuan. There's a lot to choose from here (most dishes run $3.95 to $6.50), but two dishes that we never miss are their famous Singing Rice Soup (it "sings" when the hot broth is poured into the crispy rice), and Chinaman's Hat, which consists of very light "pancakes" that you stuff and wrap at the table with a luscious filling of pork and vegetables. From then on, choose what you like: crackling chicken, lemon beef, sauteed clams—they're all good. As for those vegetarian dishes, we found the lo hon chai vegetable dish delectable, and vegetarian chicken with celery, braised bean-curd balls with mushroom, and five-spiced bean-curd are all intriguing. Desserts at Chinese restaurants are usually unimaginative, but not here. If they're not too busy, they might make you their fried apple with honey: flaming apple cubes covered with a honey-maple syrup sauce are dipped into ice water right at your table. The result? A treat you won't forget. Everything on the regular menu is available for take-out, and take-outs during the dinner hours (5 to 9:30 p.m.) are only charged lunchtime (11 a.m. to 2:30 p.m.) prices. Yen King has full bar service, and is open seven days a week.

Both local people and tourists have been singing the praises of **Fat Siu Lau,** at 100 N. Beretania St. (tel. 538-7081), ever since it opened in the Cultural Plaza. A large place, traditionally decorated with red and gold dragons on the wall, it has a huge selection of tasty dishes, many at low prices—for example, boneless chicken with cashew nuts, $4.75; shrimp with broccoli, $5.50; beef with ginger and onion sauce, $4.50. One of our favorite things to do here is to make an entire meal of the dim sum, or stuffed dumplings, simply pointing to the dishes you choose as the carts with bamboo baskets are rolled among the tables. Platters of stuffed chicken roll, beef balls with watercress, pork hash, or fresh shrimp look funn roll ($1.20 to $1.70 per platter) could be your "main course" and, for dessert, how about a lotus sugar bow, egg tart, or a black sugar doughnut—two or three for $1.10.

Seafood is the specialty of the house at **Won Kee,** another very popular spot in the Cultural Plaza (tel. 524-6877). The dining room is pleasant enough, decorated in cool greens with scenics on the wall that depict birds; the carpeting is thick and plushy, and wind chimes tinkle faintly. But the star attraction here is the food. The menu abounds with such fish and seafood delicacies as sauteed Dungeness crab with ginger and garlic sauce, $13.50; steamed island prawns with bacon, $9.75; and a 1¼-pound Maine lobster, Won Kee style. Delicious! Steamed island fish is highly recommended; at various times they have kumu, golden perch, sea bass, opakapaka, and other varieties, priced according to the current market value. On the low side of the menu ($6.95 to $7.95), you can feast on the likes of deep-fried crispy oysters, sweet-and-sour crispy fish filet, or seafood casserole. And if you'd rather not have fish or seafood, you'll be happy with dishes like sliced beef with seasonal vegetables, sweet-and-sour pork, golden crispy chicken. Won Kee serves lunch from 11:30 a.m. to 2:30 p.m. and dinner from 5 to 10 p.m. every day.

Also in the Cultural Plaza on the block bounded by Beretania, Maunakea, Kukui, and River Streets, is the downtown branch of the **Mongolian Bar-B-Que Restaurant** we told you about at the International Market Place (see above). This is a very tidy, neat little place; lunch is served from 11 a.m. to 2 p.m. Monday to Friday; dinner from 5 to 9:30 p.m. daily.

Rating high with the local Chinese community is **Maple Garden,** at 909 Isenberg St. (tel. 941-6641), a small, most attractive dining room with Chinese decorations on the walls, wood paneling, and soft lights. The Szechuan dishes are so tasty and authentic that a doctor friend of ours from Taiwan says that he takes all of his visiting friends and relatives there. Mr. Robert Hsu, the owner, is constantly adding new delights to the menu. The house specialty is Szechuan Smokey Duck, crispy on the outside and tender on the inside, served with steamed buns—you tuck the meat into the buns. A very generous order (you'll probably need a doggie bag) is $5.50. If you really like the super-hot Szechuan-style cooking, you'll love the eggplant with hot garlic sauce or the pork with hot garlic sauce, $4.25 each; they're real eye-openers. There are more than 100 entrees on the menu priced at less than $5.50, including hard-to-find singing rice—actually it's more of a whistle—served either with pork and vegetables or with shrimp, $5 in either case. Lunch is from 11 a.m. to 2 p.m. Monday through Saturday; dinner from 5:30 to 10 p.m., seven days. There's ample parking space; and you can phone for easy bus or auto directions from Waikiki.

One of the most elegant Chinese restaurants in the islands, **House of Hunan** in Eaton Square, 444 Hobron Lane (tel. 943-1188), specializes in the spicy delicacies of northern China. You can have your meal on the terrace, or in the rather formal dining room. The combination lunch specials here all include spring rolls and rice; entrees like moo goo gai pan, chicken with cashew nuts, sweet-and-sour pork, and beef with green pepper are all priced at $6.45. At dinner, if you fancy something quite spicy, you might want to try the chicken, beef, pork, or shrimp Hunan style—sauteed with broccoli, mushrooms, bamboo shoots, and hot peppers, priced from $5.75 to $5.95—or even the "firecracker" beef, sauteed with red hot peppers, $5.95. If you prefer something milder, order the exceptional lemon chicken at $5.95. House of Hunan is open daily for lunch from 11:30 a.m. to 2:30 p.m., and for dinner from 5:30 to 10:15 p.m.

Just about ten minutes away from Waikiki, in the area of McCully and King Streets, are two restaurants very popular with the locals. The first is an old favorite of ours that recently underwent a major renovation. Now the **New Golden Duck,** 930 McCully St. (tel. 947-9755), is back again and better than ever. It's a tremendous dining room furnished with red leather booths and chairs, extremely popular with local Chinese families for big parties and receptions. Almost everything on the large and varied menu is under $6, with most items about $3 to $4. Some of our favorites include lemon chicken and shoyu chicken, shrimp with broccoli, beef with sweet-and-sour cabbage, shrimp vegetable noodle, and oyster roll. The portions are so generous and the food so good that you'll want to visit this one again and again. New Golden Duck opens at 10:30 a.m. daily and closes at 1:30 a.m. on Friday and Saturday, at 12:30 a.m. the rest of the week. From Waikiki, take the no. 2 bus to Kalakaua and King, transfer to a no. 1 bus going Diamond Head on King Street (or walk) four blocks to McCully Street.

The other place on this street is the very plain **McCully Chop Sui,** 2205 S. King St., at the corner of McCully (tel. 946-4069). The only decor to speak of is the crowds of happy families lapping up the good food. Prices are super-low. Reader Phyllis Montague of San Diego, Calif., wrote about this place: "We had the *best* sweet-and-sour pork we have ever had for $3.50, and pot roast was $2.95; beef with oyster sauce, $3.25." McCully Chop Sui is open daily from 10:30 a.m. to 1:30 a.m., until 2:30 a.m. on Friday and Saturday.

One of the best budget Chinese restaurants in town is just out of Waikiki in the Diamond Head direction, near the Honolulu Zoo. That's **Hee Hing,** at 477 Kapahuhu (tel. 734-8474), and it's one of the few places left the haoles have not yet discovered. It's a bright, colorful spot, with good-luck murals, paintings, and collages adorning the walls, menus that practically light up in your hands, and plates brilliantly bordered with Chinese "Walls of Troy." The brightest news of all is the prices for the delicious, authentic Chinese dishes. Most Chinese restaurants have special lunch and dinner plates, but this one has a breakfast plate as well. It's $3.65, consists of sliced Chinese sausage, two fried eggs, and fried rice, and it's a hefty meal to start the day with. The lunch plate, at $3.35, is overflowing with sweet-and-sour spare ribs, hot roast pork, pork chow mein, steamed rice, wonton, and fried Chinese meatballs. Or come for the $3.85 dinner plate, more of the same plus a crispy chicken stick. And there are something like 100 à la carte items reasonably priced between $2.95 and $4.25. Almond chicken is good at $3.95. Don't miss those delicious dim sum (dumplings) at 30¢ to 40¢ each. A great find for dollar-watchers.

When local Chinese families want to celebrate a special occasion, they gather up at least ten friends, call **The Chinese Menu** a few days in advance, and gather for a banquet of crispy, crackling Peking duck. But even if there are just a few of you, a visit to this highly praised restaurant at 2600 S. King St., in Puck's Alley (tel. 946-1633), is well worth your while. It's a big, attractive, local place, full of scurrying waiters and people chomping down the delectable dishes that owners David and Georgiana Li and their staff produce. Everything is reasonably priced: four of us ate dinner here recently, from soup to dessert, for just over $20. Wonton soup, at $2.50, enough for all of us, was outstanding; main dishes like lemon chicken at $4.50, fresh scallops sauteed with a choice of vegetables and green onions at $4.25, and sweet-and-sour pork at $4.25 were all delicately prepared. Fresh seafood, like Hawaiian prawns at $8.95, and king clams at $7.95, are house specialties. We finished our meal with cooling almond floats, turned our teapot top upside down to signify that we wanted more tea, and left feeling happy and contented. Lunch is also a good bet, with most dishes running around $2.95 to $4.50. Bar service is available. The Chinese Menu is open for lunch from 11 a.m. to 2 p.m.; for dinner, from 5 to 9 p.m., seven days.

Located in a bandbox-fresh, blue-trimmed white building between the

Ala Moana area and downtown, **Eastern House Restaurant,** 1102 Piikoi St. (tel. 533-4737), has a big local following. No wonder! Many of the dishes are unusual, the selections are vast, and the prices are modest. No need to stick with the usual eggdrop or wonton soups here: you can try tripes with sour cabbage, fishcake soup, or Szechuan meat-and-cabbage soup. Cold plates featuring spiced beef, tongue, or duck are all in the $3 to $4 range. Beef and lamb dishes ($3.95 to $4.75) encompass everything from the expected beef broccoli to the unexpected "stir-fried vegetables and the meat covered with eggs plus six pancakes." Seafood is the most extensive offering (46 choices), with prices ranging from $5.50 to $10 for the likes of sea cucumbers, squid, abalone, scallops, prawns, and crab legs. Eastern House is also a good place to try earthen pot specialties, like mutton, assorted seafood, or, for those who dare, fish head! Prices for these go from $5 to $10.

Gather a group of at least four people to go with you to Eastern House to maximize your taste experiences. It is open for lunch from 11 a.m. to 2 p.m., and for dinner from 5:30 to 10 p.m., every day except Tuesday, offering the same menu all day. Advance reservations are a must: phone 955-8706.

A PHILIPPINE RESTAURANT: At last there is a restaurant offering Philippine cuisine that we can recommend enthusiastically. At 750 Palani Ave. in Kapahulu (tel. 735-0400), **1521** (named for the year in which the Philippines were discovered by Magellan) is a handsomely appointed place. The walls are "papered" with woven straw fans, the tablecloths are lavishly embroidered cotton, and a beautiful mural depicts Magellan's galleon *Victoria.* The attractive staff members are very proud of their heritage and their restaurant. As the menu states, the food here is "just like the Filipino people, partly Malaysian, Spanish, Chinese, Japanese, European, American. It is, at the same time, very Filipino." We suggest that you start your meal with soup, so you can sample such delicacies as the tinolang manek (a ginger-flavored chicken soup) or the pancit molo, a stuffed noodle soup with chicken, pork, and shrimp. Salads are equally interesting: the Mindanao salad consists of cucumber slices dressed with a coconut-cream vinaigrette and tossed with fried fish flakes; char-broiled eggplant with onions and tomatoes and a coco-ginger dressing comprise the Bicolono salad. Entrees are accompanied by vegetables and a choice of either garlic fried rice or steamed rice. There are all kinds of authentic selections to choose from: we like the chicken and pork adobe, flavored with garlic and pepper; the bistek Tagalog, grilled filets of beef in a soy-lemon sauce topped with butter-fried onions; and especially the prawns in coco—giant prawns sauteed in coconut cream, braced with chili peppers and garlic. These are priced from $4.50 to $8.50. House specialties include roast duckling with mango sauce, paella, and solomille Manileño, (beef tenderloin with an oyster, cream, and brandy sauce (these are priced from $9 to $19). Desserts are unusual and luscious: we find it hard to choose between Manila Holiday (mango crêpes stewed in liqueur with chantilly cream and chocolate sauce), $4.50, and cassava Bibingka, a pudding of cassava baked with a topping of sweetened coco cream, $2.50.

1521 is located in a cluster of handsome buildings modeled after those on the famous Parker Ranch on the Big Island; they were built several years ago by Richard Smart, the owner of Parker Ranch. The little complex is known as Plaza Manile, and a Philippine clothing shop and grocery shop will open here soon. 1521 serves dinner from 5:30 to 10:30 p.m. daily; reservations are advised. By time you read this, they should also be serving lunch from 11:30 a.m. to 2:30 p.m. daily.

AN INDIAN RESTAURANT: **India House,** at 2632 S. King St., near Puck's Alley (tel. 955-7552), is owned by Ram Arora, formerly the specialty chef at the elegant (and super-expensive) Third Floor Restaurant at the Hawaiian Regent Hotel. His new place, besides being very much more within our reach, is attractive, cool, and relaxing. Brass lamps and lush plants abound in the small dining room that accommodates perhaps a dozen tables. A sari-clad hostess will greet you, make you welcome, and assist you in ordering. At dinner, the only meal served, you'll do well with boti kebab, fish tikka, or tandoori chicken, priced at $9.75, and served with pullao (rice pilaf) and wonderful naan bread from the tandoor—that's a clay oven which imparts a delicious flavor to the food baked within. Combination dinners run $7.95 to $11.95. There are plentiful à la carte choices—curries, keema, chicken, shrimp, and lamb or vegetarian dishes, from $4.75 to $5.75. A particularly good dessert choice is the gulab jaman, a "dairy delicacy served in rosewater syrup." We'd call this one a thoroughly delightful dining experience. India House is open for dinner Tuesday through Sunday from 5 to 9:30 p.m.

THAI: Every now and then one discovers a place where the food is exotic and delicious, the staff cordial and attentive, the atmosphere warm and cozy, and the prices painless. Such a find is the **Mekong Restaurant,** a charming bit of Thailand at 1295 S. Beretania St. between Keeaumoku and Piikoi (tel. 521-2025), where a meal is a cultural experience. The small dining room sparkles with yellow linen tablecloths, posters on the wall, and a pretty latticed ceiling. An upstairs room is usually open. The voluminous menu will explain the basics of Thai cooking to you, but you'll do just as well to tell your waiter what you like and follow his suggestions. Thai cooking is a cross between East Indian and Chinese, and while it can be highly spicy, almost every dish can be ordered either mild, medium, or hot. Our waiter explained to us that the hottest—and most popular—dishes are Thai green curry (beef, pork, or chicken sauteed in green chili and curry in fresh coconut milk), $5.25; and Evil Jungle Prince (beef, pork, or chicken sauteed with hot spices with either hot or sweet basil leaves), $4.50. We chose, however, a number of mild dishes which were exquisitely spiced: not-to-be-missed spring rolls (you "sandwich" them at table in fresh lettuce and mint, top with a flavorful carrot-based sauce, and sprinkle with ground peanuts—incredible!) $4.95; a memorable chicken ginger soup in a fresh coconut-milk base, $5.50; a dish of thin, crisp noodles with tiny bits of chicken, $4.95; water chestnut fried rice, $4.50; and the special of the day, king crab sauteed with green onions, eggs, and bean sauce, $6.95. Bring your own bottle if you want wine. Dessert was another unforgettable treat: tapioca pudding unlike any you've ever tasted, in a warm coconut milk; and half-ripe Thai apple-bananas, again cooked in coconut milk. Thai teas are just a little bit different, brewed with vanilla beans and served with condensed milk to make it quite sweet. Eating at Mekong is such a delight that you might be tempted to end your culinary wanderings right here.

Open for lunch from 11 a.m. to 2 p.m. Monday to Friday, and for dinner from 5:30 to 9 p.m. every day.

So successful has the Mekong Restaurant been, that owner Keo Sananikone has gone ahead and opened two more temples of Thai cuisine: **Mekong II** at 1726 S. King St. (tel. 941-6184), and the grandest of them all, **Keo's Thai Cuisine,** at 625 Kapahulu (tel. 737-8420 or 737-9250). So spectacular, in fact, is the latter, that if you're going to have only one Thai meal, we suggest you pay a little more for the same items this one time, and eat here, imbibing the beauty along with the luscious food. Keo has created what might be called a garden-jungle atmosphere: tiny lights strung into the plants, umbrellas over some of the tables, ceiling fans overhead, straw chairs with blue cushions, statues, carvings, portraits on the wall, orchids everywhere—it's a stunner.

While Mekong I and II serve both lunch and dinner, Keo's Thai Cuisine serves dinner only, every day from 5:30 to 11 p.m. Reservations are a must.

KOREAN RESTAURANTS: So few cities in the world give you a chance to sample good Korean cuisine that you shouldn't pass up the opportunity in Honolulu. Koreans make up a relatively small part of the islands' population, but their culinary tradition has left its mark, especially in the ubiquitous kim chee—pickled cabbage seasoned with red-hot peppers. You'll find it in grocery stores, on menus everywhere in Honolulu, and even at the beach stands along Waikiki where they serve kim chee dogs. But the cuisine has much more to offer: barbecued meat dishes, hearty noodle soups, tasty meat dumplings, fish filets sauteed in spicy sauces, and daintily shredded vegetables are some of the other standbys. A few, but by no means all, of the dishes are served with fiery hot sauces; if you're not accustomed to that sort of thing, check with the waitress before you order.

Honolulu has only a handful of Korean restaurants, and the oldest and best of these, the **House of Park,** at 2671D S. King St. in Moiliili, on the way to the university (tel. 949-2679), is the kind of family-style place that gives you a real experience in nontourist dining. Small and tidy with white walls and flower arrangements—an attempt at decoration—it caters to local Korean and other Oriental families (lots of cute keikis spill about), and a smattering of university students. There are a few booths and tables up front (at one, a man may be rolling dumplings for the soup), from which you can see the big open kitchen in the back. We love the combination of mon doo and kuk soo—hot noodle soup with Korean dumplings stuffed with beef, pork, and vegetables. The waitress once explained to us that this is "New Year's Soup, but so popular we make it every day." The house specialty is kal-bi, barbecued short ribs, and it's excellent. Most dishes run $3 to $5. The plate lunch—barbecued meat, na mul (Korean-style vegetables and fish fried in an egg batter), and rice is a buy at $3.60. The latter two dishes come with mon doo and hot soup for 50¢ extra. Kim chee and hot sauce come with all orders. While you're here, try the famed Korean ginseng tea. The restaurant closes each night at 8 p.m. and all day Sunday. While you're in Moiliili, by the way, note that there are a number of similarly small, family-style Oriental restaurants, with low prices and, we suspect, good food.

Ted's Drive-Inn, 2820 S. King St. (tel. 946-0344), is a small Korean lunch-counter operation that features, in their words, "Seoul food."

Although the spelling differs here and there, the dishes are quite similar to those at the House of Park. You could have bul gogi (barbecued beef) at $2.98 kal-bi (barbecued meat) at $3.99, and kal-bi with mon-doo (dumplings) at $3.67. Non-Korean offerings include beef curry plates and a teri-beef burger. A recent *Honolulu Advertiser* survey rated Ted's as serving "among the top 10 best plate lunches in Honolulu."

Small, sparkly clean, and friendly pretty much sums up **O-Bok** in Manoa Marketplace, 2851 East Manoa Rd. (tel. 988-7702), a little Korean place that serves wonderful food at very moderate prices. All entrees here are served with na mul (vegetables), kim chee (best described as a fiery cole slaw), and rice. The most popular Korean specialty in Hawaii seems to be kal-bi, tender barbecued short ribs. They are particularly good here, and priced at $5.99. Other very good dishes, priced from $3.85 to $4.80, are the barbecued chicken, the fish or meat jun (breaded with an egg batter), and the bi bim bap, mixed vegetables, beef, and fried egg on rice. Very tasty too are the mon doo (a kind of Korean wonton); try them in soup or fried, as a side dish. To explore several of these taste sensations, order one of the mixed plates: the special plate at $4.35 includes kal-bi, barbecued chicken, mon doo, tae-ku (dried codfish), and na mul. The lunch plate (which you may also order at dinnertime), consists of barbecued beef, chicken, na mul, kim chee, and rice. Westerners tend to think of Korean food as being extremely spicy; in reality, it is only the kim chee that makes your eyes water. Open every day, from 11 a.m. to 8 p.m.

A MEXICAN RESTAURANT: One of the most *simpático* of Honolulu's Mexican restaurants, we think, is **La Paloma,** at 1216 Kapiolani Blvd. (tel. 533-1272). Owners Joe and Laura Martinez, a delightful California couple of Mexican descent, decorate their walls with Mexican murals and paintings, put candles on all the tables, and know how to whip up a mean enchilada or tortilla. We usually come at lunch (11:30 a.m. to 2:30 p.m. weekdays), when there are nine entrees on the menu, all served with coffee or tea, for $4.95. Our favorite is the sour cream enchilada with beans and rice. Their guacamole, a spicy avocado dip with chips, is excellent at $3.75. Combination plate dinners start with albondiga soup (vegetable and meatballs) or salad, include beverage and dessert, and average about $7.95. Or try one of their specialties like the tangy chimichanga—a flour tortilla stuffed with shredded beef or chicken, deep-fried and covered with guacamole and sour cream: $6.35. There are a number of unusual egg dishes (with an average price of $6), like enchiladas New Mexico style—flat enchiladas stuffed with beef, onions, cheese, olives, and topped with fried eggs. Note for los niños: a child's plate of hamburger or taco, beans, rice, plus dessert, is $3.75. Wine or Mexican beer or a pitcher of margaritas will go nicely with your meal. Other cocktails too.

La Paloma is open from 11:30 a.m. to 10 p.m. Monday through Thursday, until 11 p.m. on Friday and Saturday, and from 5 to 9 p.m. on Sunday.

ITALIAN: **Marino's Italian Restaurants,** at Manoa Marketplace (tel. 988-2969), reminds us of the little trattorias one sees everywhere in Rome and Florence—even though you more likely than not will be served by a friendly Oriental or Polynesian waiter. There are Chianti bottles suspended from the walls and bright red-and-white checked cloths on the tables. Best of all, the food is terrific and the prices reasonable. You can get big submarine sandwiches here, and pizza, as well as complete meals. Among the appetizers, we like the Italian clam chowder or minestrone soup, $2 for a big bowl. Spaghetti dinners include bread and tossed salad and range from $6.50 to $8—the latter for an anchovy-garlic sauce. Most other dinners run between $7.50 and $9: again, along with entrees like veal parmagiana or lasagne, scampi or chicken Sicilian, come bread and tossed salad. This is one of the few places in Honolulu where one can find cannoli, those flavorful ricotta-filled pastries. Try this, or the lovely ricotta cheesecake, for dessert. To take back to your kitchenette apartment, there's Marino's excellent meat sauce and their home-baked Italian bread. Marino's is open from 11 a.m. until 11 p.m., seven days a week.

FROM RUSSIA WITH LOVE: A Russian snackbar in downtown Honolulu is a cultural anachronism, but we don't mind a bit. **Rada's Piroshki,** 1144-1146 Fort Street Mall, specializes in the piroshki—a delicate, flaky bun stuffed with beef, cheese, cabbage, mushrooms, whatever combination suits your fancy. Whenever we're downtown, we simply can't resist the chicken, mushrooms, and cheese piroshki, but the other combinations are also delicious. Along with a drink, one big piroshki—$1.30—makes a satisfying meal. The chicken soup is also marvelous, and the Russian fried squids, 85¢ a bag, are . . . uh, different. Rada's is a family operation, and the people in charge make you feel welcome. But alas, they close at 5:30 p.m. every day, and all day Sunday. Warning: Piroshkis may be habit-forming.

TWO RESTAURANTS THAT NEVER CLOSE: If you get the hungries at, say, 3 a.m., there's no need to despair in Honolulu, for this is definitely not a place that shuts down tight at 9 in the evening. Take yourself to one of the following two restaurants where the menus run the gamut from breakfast fare to lunch and dinner and cocktails and back to breakfast again.

Slightly Polynesian in decor and with an open feeling, **Coco's Coffee House,** at Kapiolani Boulevard and Kalakaua Avenue, is attractive, squeaky clean, and enormously popular. Luscious blueberry pancakes at $2.25, and other breakfast dishes are available all day long—or choose an old-fashioned beef stew for $4.95, or a deluxe burger for $2.75. Everything is good here. The keikis have their own special menus of complete dinners from $1.95 up, and you can have ice-cream sodas or stronger beverages served to your table from the Calabash Bar.

Top's Beachwalk Coffee Shop, at 298 Beach Walk in Waikiki, is another 24-hour mecca run by the same management as Coco's. It's a nifty coffeehouse with a touch of Tiffany decor, breakfasts served around the clock, and lots of daily specials: many breakfast specials are under $3; complete dinners begin at $4.75. The pastry shop with fresh baked goods is also open 24 hours a day. You might have seafood dishes like mahimahi and deep-fried shrimp or a big Hawaiian pineapple fruit boat for $4.25, or a tasty light-eater meal from $3.75. Fanciful burgers—such as the Ranchero Burger with green Ortega chiles and cheese and french fries, topped with a fried egg, and served on a sesame seed bun—run under $4. Lunch is served in a unique pub, open from 11 a.m. to closing; and there's a daily Happy Hour from 11 a.m. to 6:30 p.m.

And remember, as mentioned above, these other Waikiki 24-hour favorites: **Top's Canterbury Coffee House and Tavern, Sizzler Steak House, Wailania Coffee House, Wailana Malia Coffee House,** and **Uncle John's Family Restaurant.**

3. And Elsewhere on the Island

RESTAURANTS IN WINDWARD OAHU: Family restaurants often have that special warmth and conviviality that other restaurants find hard to match, and that's part of the success story behind **Florence's,** 20 Kainehe St. (tel. 261-1987), in suburban Kailua (just across the Pali). Florence—Mrs. Gerardo Jovinelli—is an Italian-American woman who learned all of mama's recipes and has translated them into a superlative cuisine that's been keeping the local people coming for the past 30 years. We promise you won't forget Florence's giardiniera, a mouthwatering combination of lasagne, eggplant, ravioli, spaghetti, and beef ragoût that's served with minestrone and side dishes: $6 at lunch, $8.75 at dinner. Every night, there's an $8.50 Bohemian dinner that consists of minestrone soup or tossed green salad, vegetables or spaghetti, french bread, beverage, and an entree of the day, which could be anything from scampi veneziana to veal scaloppine to lobster Marseilles! Desserts are special too; try the lemon cheesecake at $1.25. Lunch features lots of salad 'n' sandwich meals (meatball sandwich, $2.50; crabburger on toasted bun, $3.50), but do try the Italian dishes; they're too good to miss. The place is uncrowded and unpressured, far from the milling tourist scene. From downtown, take the Pali Highway, which becomes Kailua Road, and watch for the intersection of Kailua with Kaneohe; Kainehe is the first street on the left before entering Kailua.

A newer Kailua restaurant that's become deservedly popular with the local residents is **Bib's Family Restaurant,** at 315 Uluniu St. (tel. 261-8724), on the ground floor of an attractive neighborhood shopping plaza. We heartily recommend that you bring your family here too. They offer keikis luncheon and dinner dishes at just $1.95, and for the grownups, food with a gourmet touch. Bib's is a small place, with four tables under a lovely gazebo hung with plants, and perhaps six more tables around the gazebo. The sparkling kitchen is open to the dining room. For a restaurant of this size, the menu is surprisingly varied: we enjoyed our lunch of ratatouille in cheese sauce served with a small tossed salad and homemade whole-wheat bread for all of $3.65 (it's $3.85 at dinner, when you get the choice of soup or a big salad to go with it), but we could also have chosen a variety of three-egg omelets (including an open-face fritatta), lots of tasty burgers, chicken or veggie crêpes, and veggie delight sandwiches like spinach, mushroom, and cheese melt; most items are in the $3 to $4.50 category. Dinner prices are positively relaxing: combination plates, for example, with a choice of two entrees like mahimahi and sliced teri sirloin, soup or salad, rice or beans or vegetable, are just $6.55. Full dinners are bargain priced at $5.50 to $6.95.

As for those $1.95 keiki plates: a young friend of ours lunched royally with us on chicken and chips, and a big glass of fresh lemonade for 60¢ (we could have had a whole pitcher for $1.95). Other choices include fish and chips, hot dogs, or mini-burgers.

Bib's is open from 7 a.m. to 9 p.m. every day, serving all three meals.

There's another interesting place to eat in Kailua, should you happen to be out this way. That's the cafeteria of the **Castle Memorial Hospital,** 640 Ulukahiki St., over the Pali at Waimanalo Junction. Everything served is vegetarian, delicious, and at old-fashioned prices. All the hot entrees—like meatless Oriental stew and herb loaf—are 85¢ to $1; an abundant choice of salads go from 55¢ to $1.75, and generous-size sandwiches are 85¢ to $1.75, so you can easily put together a very reasonable meal. Take the elevator or stairs down one flight as you enter the hospital and you'll see the cafeteria. It faces a rear garden and a beautiful view of the Pali. Meals are served to the public Monday through Friday from 11 a.m. to 1:30 p.m. and from 4:30 to 6 p.m. À la carte breakfast—pancakes, eggs, fresh fruits, and beverage, at $2.25—is served between 6:30 and 9:30 a.m.

AROUND THE ISLAND: The very cheapest way to eat on your round-the-island journeys is to bring your own picnic lunch, but there are also a few restaurants that make fine, budget-wise refueling stops. For a meal in a splendid setting, turn mauka just past Kaneohe and proceed about a mile toward the mountains and **Haiku Gardens,** an oldtime kamaaina favorite surrounded by two acres of gorgeous gardens and grounds that you may want to tour (see details in Chapter VIII). Lunch is a very pleasant and not expensive affair; you can have an open-face sandwich of barbecued teriyaki, hot beef, or mahimahi, served with cole slaw, coffee, or tea for $3.75 to $3.95. At $6.95 for adults, $4.95 for children, you get a serve-yourself Haiku buffet special—all you can eat of four hot entrees, salad, fruit, vegetable, dessert, and beverage. Dinner entrees run about $8.50 to $12.50.

Farther along, you'll find **Swanzy Beach Park,** a scenic picnic spot. If you haven't packed your own, don't despair: **Hana's Kitchen,** recommended by the local people, is across the street, and it has a small counter with a few seats, plus lots of take-out items, like $3.35 to $3.45 plate lunches of teriyaki or steak with onions, or fried chicken. Tacos too, and a dessert called Apple-Annie. It's next to the Kaaawa Post Office.

The **Texas Paniolo Café,** 53-146 Kamehameha Hwy., in Punaluu (tel. 237-8521), is our favorite fun stop on this route, even though we still can't quite bring ourselves to try the specialty of the house—rattlesnake chili! The place has a rustic, western appearance inside and out; it's a wooden frame building with a front porch and the interior walls resemble adobe. Country-western wails from the jukebox during the day; at night, there's live entertainment. You'll just love the stuffed rattlesnake on the walls! And if you're braver than we are, you can also have that rattlesnake chili at $4.95, whose menu notation states "in season (?) when available." If the rattlers are not available, however, there is plenty of other very tasty Tex-Mex food. Among the appetizers, we vote for the chili con queso—a crock of melted cheese, tomatoes, and green chilies with tostitos for dipping, $3.95. A big bowl of beef chili with rice or beans and crackers is $3.25; a chiliburger or jalapeño burger with cheese is $4.95. You can get a taco or enchilada plate for $6.95, chicken-fried steak with fries and cole slaw for $6.95, and strip sirloin steak, another house specialty, at $13.95 for a 12-ounce cut. Dessert offerings are such Texas treats as beer-batter deep-fried bananas with honey and pecan pie. Open Sunday through Thursday from 11 a.m. to midnight, Friday and Saturday until 2 a.m.

At the **Hauula Shopping Center,** near Laie, be on the lookout for the **Lotus Inn Chop Suey,** 54-316 Kam Hwy. (tel. 293-5412). The place is plain, but the service is good and the food tasty. There are scores of items on the menu (the same at lunch and dinner) ranging from $3.50 to $6. We particularly liked the ginger chicken, the pork fried rice, and shrimp Cantonese. Abalone lovers will enjoy their abalone soup at $3.75. There's a good bento lunch special at $2.50. You can pop in for a good, filling meal any day except Monday from 11 a.m. to 9 p.m. If you're driving by during Happy Hour time (3 to 7 p.m.), you can have a standard drink at $1.25 or a mai tai at $2.50, with free pupus to boot. Readers have praised this one often.

Where can you get the best sandwich on the North Shore, maybe in all of Oahu? We'd cast our vote for **Kua 'Aina** (tel. 637-6067), a sparkling sandwichery across the street from the courthouse in Haleiwa. It's tiny, neat as a pin, with wooden tables, framed pictures of local scenes, a few tables on the porch. And the atmosphere is casual, with people coming in off the beach. We haven't stopped raving yet about the sandwiches we had on our last visit: mahimahi with melted cheese, Ortego pepper, lettuce, and tomato at $3.95, tuna and avocado ("the tastiest combo in the Pacific") at $3.40, and a great baconburger at $3.85. Sandwiches are hearty enough to be a whole meal, and are served on either a Kaiser roll, honey wheatberry bread, or earth rye. Kua 'Aina is open daily from 11 a.m. to 9 p.m.

The most beautiful restaurant in Haleiwa town has to be **Steamer's Restaurant & Bar** (tel. 637-5071) in the Haleiwa Shopping Plaza on Kamehameha Highway. It's a big, low-lit, wood-paneled place with shiny brass accents, and a very cozy outdoor dining area. And the food lives up to the decor. The specialty here is seafood, with or without steak. The luncheon menu offers a hearty seafood omelet, bursting with king crab, shrimp, mushrooms, and Swiss cheese, topped with sauce mornay, at $6.25. This and the other omelets, priced from $4.95, are served with rice or fries and blueberry or French crumb muffins. A good variety of hot sandwiches —opakapaka, teriyaki, french dip, Reuben, and good old hamburgers—is priced from $4.50 to $6.50. All the hot sandwiches are accompanied by salad and rice pilaf or fries, so they make quite a satisfactory meal. One of our favorite dishes here, the Steamer's Delight Platter, is a tasty assortment of tempura vegetables: onion rings, zucchini, artichoke hearts, and mushrooms deep-fried in batter, $7.50. Save dinner for a splurge; red snapper is low on the menu at $9.75, petite top sirloin steak is $10.25, steak and seafood crêpes are $13.95, and other steak and seafood combos go up to $16.50. All entrees are accompanied by seafood chowder or house salad, Steamer's bread, rice pilaf, and fresh steamed vegetables. Save room for the special cheesecake or carrot cake. Steamer's is open from 11:30 a.m. to 11:30 p.m. (food service until 10 p.m.), seven days. The bar is busy until 2 a.m.

To give yourself a very special treat at the end of your around-the-island journey, stop in for dinner at **Kemoo Farm,** 1718 Wilikina Dr. (tel. 621-8481), overlooking Lake Wilson in Wahiawa, holding forth in these parts for 65 years and still going strong. And no wonder: this is a place where the spirit of Old Hawaii still lingers, with excellent food and drink, gracious service by caring waitresses, a gentle mood. If you come for lunch on Wednesday or Sunday, you can catch a show by noted island entertainers like Emma Veary and Charles K. L. Davis. The price of your entree includes a complete dinner, and that means a delicious soup (the seafood chowder we sampled recently was thick with potatoes and chunks of shrimp, crab, and mahimahi), excellent salad bar, even dessert and coffee. You might order fresh rainbow trout, sizzling ground sirloin with onion and rice, sauteed red snapper, or mahimahi, all on the low side of the menu at

$8.50 to $9.50. And if you're really watching the budget, just have the salad bar and soup for $6.50; it's quite special, including local favorites like lomi-lomi salmon that you otherwise find only at luaus. Nice little extras on the regular meals include a loaf of hot bread on its own serving board that arrives as soon as you sit down (and keeps being replaced), and crispy wontons. Add another $1.25 to the price of your meal and have Kemoo's pine-mint tea; they make it right here by marinating the pineapple in a simple syrup with fresh mint—quite wonderful.

At lunchtime, you can get some unusual salads (the Japanese somen, the Mexican taco), in addition to regular entrees and sandwiches, from about $4.50 to $7.50. And Sunday brunch is special, with many eggs Benedict and Florentine dishes, and an unusual filet of trout and eggs. Kemoo Farms serves lunch from 11 a.m. to 2 p.m. and dinner from 5 to 8:30 p.m. every day of the week.

A WORD ABOUT SHAVE ICE: A unique treat that's loved by just about everyone in the islands is a phenomenon called shave ice. Not "shaved" ice—shave ice. When it's pointed out to them, mainland visitors often sneer, "Oh, we have that at home—we call them snow cones" (or ices, or slushes). It isn't any of those things, it's just wonderful Hawaiian shave ice. Half the fun of having it is watching the ice being shaved. You can have "plain" shave ice—that's just the incredibly fine ice particles bathed in syrup—and there are all kinds of syrups. Strawberry is the most popular, but there's also vanilla, guava, lemon, cherry, orange, root beer, coconut, and combinations of the above, known as "rainbow." Or you can have ice cream on the bottom, or azuki beans (a sweet Japanese bean used in desserts); or throw caution to the winds and have ice cream and beans on the bottom. Shave ice is served in a cone-shaped paper cup, with both a straw and a spoon.

Shave ice places abound, but after years of diligent sampling and research, we offer our four favorites: **Matsumoto's Grocery** at 66-087 Kam Hwy. in Haleiwa, across from the intersection of Emerson Street, is a family operation and on weekends the lines can be long, because the local people drive out from all over the island; it's a pleasant wait, everyone is friendly. **Malia's** lunch wagon parks across from Sandy Beach at the intersection of Kalanianaole Highway and the Kalama Valley road every day except Wednesday and Thursday. The effervescent Malia has created a new shave ice called "The Snowy Delight." Then there's **Mr. John Vannatta's** little wooden kiosk at Koko Marina, which has great shave ice, but no ice cream or beans. Finally, the tiny **K-Y Delicatessen,** at 1320 N. School St., is about the most centrally located of the four. Prices at all these places vary slightly, from about 40¢ for a small plain shave ice to 95¢ for the large size with ice cream and beans. There's usually a 5¢ extra charge if you want rainbow—that's three or more flavors in a fetching striped motif.

Caution: Shave ice is definitely habit-forming.

4. The Night Scene

Contrary to what you'd expect, the night scene in Honolulu is not all hula girls in grass skirts and sentimental songs on the ukulele. Sure, there are palm trees and schmaltz aplenty, but there are also ultrasophisticated jazz groups, authentic Polynesian music and dances, songsters, psychics, comedians, discos, sing-alongs at the piano, and no dearth of gorgeous seaside gardens where you could easily while away a few years. We'll tell you about the free shows first, then take you on a tour of the "in" bars and cocktail lounges, and on to a rundown of what we consider the most exciting entertainment in town.

But you really don't need any planned entertainment to enjoy Waikiki at night. There's a great show going on wherever you look: you can observe the people, browse in the shops, or stand in front of the clubs and dig the sound, free of charge, at the International Market Place. Or watch the newcomers parade up and down Kalakaua Avenue, survey the scene at the big hotels, or take our favorite walk, the "scrounger's stroll."

THE SCROUNGER'S STROLL: Here's how you do it: at the Diamond Head end of the Surfrider Hotel, there's a paved path leading to the ocean. Follow it along the back of the Surfrider Hotel and onto the beach in back of the Moana next door; here you can gaze at the floodlit shore and listen to the music drifting from the Moana's romantic Banyan Court, just behind you. You can even have a nighttime swim if you want to; no one will stop you (all beaches are public property up to the high-water mark), or just meander barefoot along the sands ewa until you come to the beach of the Royal Hawaiian Hotel. If you've timed your scrounger's stroll correctly, you'll arrive in time to watch from afar the show at the Royal's fancy Monarch's Room; it's not exactly a ringside table, but it's fun.

Wander down the beach to the Outrigger Hotel, where the very popular **Chuck Machado Luau** takes place Sunday at 6 p.m. There'll be lots of people watching the show from the sand. Emcee Doug Mossman usually acknowledges the scroungers; he calls them the "graduating class." Join the fun and see the $19.50 entertainment gratis.

A free beach show gets rolling every Sunday at 8 p.m. on the beach in front of the **Reef Hotel.** A crowd of young people comes to watch the professional beach boys (you'll see them on the beach during the day) sing, play the uke, and try to impress the girls. Girls who have taken hula lessons get up and perform too, and there's often a noisy community sing. It's all done by amateurs, but it's friendly fun—and always packed. The show may be cancelled in poor weather; you may want to check with the hotel.

BARFLY'S TOUR: If you'd like to watch the sunset in luxury, arrive early (about 6 p.m.) at the cocktail lounge of the **Reef's Three Torches Bar** for a front-row seat. Drinks start at $1.50. The most intriguing bar at the Reef? That's **Harry's Underwater Bar,** reached via the basement and located right under the swimming pool. You can watch the swimmers above while you drink up.

Head mauka on Kalakaua Avenue to the smart-looking Princess Kaiulani Hotel for a pleasant drink poolside at the **Kahili Bar.** Cross the street (Koa Avenue) to King's Village for a drink at an English pub, the **Rose and Crown.** Brews from the mother country, of course, plus an assortment of beers and cocktails, sing-along piano, darts, ladies' night on Tuesday, tequila night on Thursday, and tropical drink specials on Aloha Sunday. Plus all-day Happy Hours. Or try the open and pretty **Garden Court Lounge** of the Hawaiian Regent Hotel, where you'll usually find a vocalist to help you while away the night. Their **Lobby Bar** is also pleasant, and so is **The Library,** a contemporary wine bar and lounge overlooking the beach, where it's fun to meet people and discuss wines or relax over a drink.

There's a snug feeling about the **Sandwich Island Pub** at the Holiday Inn, an intimate room serving drinks and pupus. You'll probably hear a guitarist or other entertainer Tuesday through Saturday nights, starting at 8:30. No cover, no minimum.

A big favorite with the Honolulu theater crowd is **South Seas Village** at 2112 Kalakaua Ave.; they come to hear John Saclaua at the piano bar, every evening except Sunday from 9 p.m. until closing. John plays, people get up and sing, and everybody has a good time. Wine coolers are $2.

Viewpoints

Waikiki is full of gorgeous rooms with a view, but for the most sensational of all, take the glass elevator (on the outside of the hotel; it's eerily exciting going up) to **Annabelle's** at the top of the Ilikai. This 30-story-high, glass-walled aerie is to Honolulu what the Top of the Mark is to San Francisco: the place to see the million lights of the metropolis dazzlingly spread out before you. Before 9 p.m., standard drinks are $1.25; after 9 p.m. they're $3.25. Dancing starts at 5 p.m. with Big Band sounds and favorite oldies; from 9 p.m. until closing at 4 a.m., the sound is disco. Alas, there's a $4 cover. But even if you're not a drinker or a dancer, don't miss the ride up in the darkened elevator, from which the view is also spectacular, and at least peek at the room. (Incidental note for parents looking for ways to amuse their kiddies: They love a ride in the glass elevator.) More about discos ahead.

Another thrilling view is to be had from **La Ronde Restaurant** atop the Ala Moana Office Building, a merry-go-round for sybarites. Twenty-three stories up, and affording an almost identical view to that of Annabelle's, the room slowly revolves, affording spectacular views of mountain, sea, and city. Cocktails are served until midnight.

At the center of Waikiki is another glamorous revolving restaurant, the **Top of Waikiki,** in the Waikiki Business Plaza Building at 2270 Kalakaua Ave. The top tier of this gigantic wedding-cake of a restaurant is the cocktail lounge, very glamorous by candlelight and starlight. Views of all of Waikiki are yours for the price of a drink: beer from $2, exotics from $4.

At the Sea

For one of the most majestic views in town, try the glorious **Hanohano Room** of the Sheraton-Waikiki; the panorama stretches all the way from Diamond Head to Pearl Harbor. Drinks are pricey: beers will cost you $3.25, imported beers are $3.95, and mai tais cost $4.95. There's entertainment and dancing nightly, from 9:30 on.

If ever you've dreamed of picture-perfect Hawaii, treat yourself to sunset cocktails at **The House Without a Kay,** the oceanside lounge at the newly rebuilt Halekulani Hotel. Here, under a century-old kiawe tree, you can watch the waves splash up on the breakfront, the sun sink into the ocean, and hear the music of two top island groups—either Sonny Amahele and the Islanders (Tuesday through Sunday, 5 to 7:30 p.m.), or the Paradise Serenaders (Monday through Wednesday). Kanoe Miller, a former Miss Hawaii, does some beautiful dancing Monday through Saturday. Beers start at $3.50, exotic drinks higher. Don't miss this one.

The Moana, one of the classic oceanfront hotels in Waikiki, is another neat place for a drink near the water's edge. Its **Beach Bar** offers mixed drinks from $3, beer from $2.50. You can also get a sunset drink at the **Captain's Galley** of the same hotel, which is primarily a steakhouse. Bottled beer goes from $2.25, mixed drinks from $3; the lanai overlooks the water.

At some of the Waikiki hotels, the cocktail gardens overlook the lagoon—and one of our favorites is the **Tahitian Lanai** in the Waikikian Hotel (a superb example of modern Polynesian architecture; as you walk through to the garden, note the hotel's cave-like lobby with the roof of an ancient spirit house). Beer is $1.75 and up; gin and tonic, $2.25 (about a quarter more when music begins at 8:30).

Another romantic spot we favor greatly is the **Hala Terrace** of the Kahala Hilton, a short drive from Waikiki. You can sip your drinks on the beachside patio and watch the surf roll in. At 9:30 p.m. a cover descends for the Danny Kaleikini dinner show, about which more later.

Pupus and Happy Hours

Now we come to the more practical side of pub-crawling: how to drink at half the price and get enough free food for almost a meal at the same time. The trick here is to hit the bars during their Happy Hours (usually from 4 to 6 p.m. but sometimes greatly extended), when they serve free pupus or lower their prices, or both. Note that these hours and prices are apt to change often, but these places always offer a good deal of one sort or another.

There's a generously long Happy Hour (4 to 8 p.m.) at the **Crow's Nest,** located above the Jolly Roger at 2244 Kalakaua Ave. Several readers have written to praise this place for being "the friendliest and cheapest bar in Waikiki." No cover, no minimum, entertainment nightly from 8 p.m., and plenty of free peanuts, whose shells cover the floor. . . . **Coco's,** at the corner of Kalakaua and Kapiolani, is another spot with a long Happy Hour, from 2 to 6:30 p.m., seven days a week; mixed drinks are $1, and the pupus last a long time (note that exotic drinks here are the regular price, $2.75, during Happy Hour).

Free pupus, hot and cold, are offered during the 4 to 7 p.m. Happy Hour Monday to Friday at **Hunter's Bar** in the Holiday Isle Hotel, and drink prices are low (standards from $1). . . . Tropical drinks at Happy Hour prices are offered from 11 a.m. to 6 p.m. (hot pupus from 4 to 6 p.m.) at the **Rigger** in the Outrigger Hotel. Readers Christine Joly and Dave Beck of Ontario, Canada, wrote to tell us about their discovery at the Rigger: its rooftop bar offers chi chis and mai tais for 99¢ during a rather late 7 to 9 p.m. Happy Hour, along with pretzels and guitar music, to boot. At 9, you can stay and listen to a four-piece island band for only an additional $1. . . . The **Warrior Bar** of the Miramar Hotel, fifth floor, poolside, keeps its Happy Hour going all day, from 11 a.m. to 7 p.m. It offers beers at $1.50, standards and mai tai punch at $1.75. There's another very long Happy Hour in the **Plaza Lounge,** downstairs at the Waikiki Shopping Plaza, from 11 a.m. to 9 p.m., standard drinks are around $1.

Marco Polo, on the fourth floor of the Waikiki Shopping Plaza, has one of the longest Happy Hours around—from 11:30 a.m. to 11:30 p.m. That's when standard drinks start at 95¢. On Monday there are tequila specials for everybody; on Wednesday, drink specials for the ladies only. . . . **Sadie Thompson's,** poolside at the Reef Hotel, offers standard drinks, beer, and wine at $1.50 during the 2 to 5 p.m. Happy Hour. Fresh-fruit daiquiris are $2.50, and pizza is available too. . . . Happy Hour runs from 2 to 6 p.m. at beautiful **La Mex** in the Royal Hawaiian Shopping Center, and delicious pupus are free. . . . During the 4 to 6 p.m. Happy Hour at the **Great Wok of China** at the Royal Hawaiian Shopping Center, standard drinks are $1; mai tais, $1.25; and pupus free. There's dancing from 4 to 6:30 p.m.

From noon to 6 p.m., the **Waikiki Broiler** in the Waikiki Tower Hotel, 200 Lewers, brings out the mai tais and chi chis at standard drink prices. There's entertainment afternoons and evenings. . . . There's a long Happy Hour every day at the **Reef Broiler** in the Reef Hotel. From 11:30 a.m. to 5:30 p.m., bar, standard, and exotic drinks are all $1.50 or less! . . . The **Buccaneer Restaurant,** across from the Reef Hotel, comes up with low-priced mai tais—only $1.25 until 6 p.m. They go up just a little bit in the evening, when live Hawaiian music begins at 8:30 p.m. No cover, no minimum. You'll often find beachboys and Hawaiian entertainers relaxing here.

There's an all-day Happy Hour, 11 a.m. to 7:30 p.m., which means 95¢ for beer and standard drinks at the **Surfboard Bar** of the Waikiki Beachcomber Hotel. On your way up the escalator to the bar, note the handsome woodcarvings that tell the Hawaiian story; you may not be able to fully appreciate them on the way down. . . . **La Ronde,** the lovely revolving restaurant atop the Ala Moana Office Building, observes Happy Hour Monday through Friday from 3:30 to 6 p.m., with wine or beer at 95¢ and bar drinks at $1.25.

THE DISCO SCENE: If you're still into the disco scene, Honolulu has plenty of places to go. A recent look around revealed something like a dozen clubs packing them in, and more on the way. Besides offering plenty of exercise, the local discos are mostly inexpensive; usually they have a modest cover charge or none at all, and just a few insist on a two-drink minimum and/or a fee. Live bands usually alternate with disco, and the action gets under way between 9 and 10 p.m. in most clubs and only ends when everyone drops from exhaustion—anywhere between 2 and 4 a.m. Here's a rundown on the action, with some "inside tips" provided by reader Sue Abrego of Brea, California, and her friends, who tried them all.

One of the most popular disco spots is **D.B.C.'s Dance Menagerie** in the Waikiki Beachcomber Hotel. D.B.C.'s goes into action at 9:30 p.m. (when Don the Beachcomber has stopped serving dinner), and continues until 2 a.m. Friday and Saturday night. Cover charge is $2, plus a two-drink minimum. . . . Perhaps the biggest singles scene in town is **The Point After** at the Hawaiian Regent Hotel, with plush rust sofas, twin dance floors, and live music alternating with disco that features popular rock tunes as well as "oldies but goodies." $2 cover charge. . . . Nothing shy about the people who run **Hula's Bar and Lei Stand,** a touch of old Waikiki tucked under a giant banyan tree on Kalaimoku Street opposite the Kuhio Theater. They claim their "Megasexual Club" is "the best video dance club in the Pacific." $3 cover on weekends, no minimum. . . . The weird, way-out costumes worn by the staff at **Bobby McGee's Conglomeration** in the Colony East Hotel really seem to turn the guests on. It's a lively spot also known for good food. Disco is open until 2 a.m. . . . **Spats,** in the Hyatt Regency Hotel, is a handsome and immensely popular room, where you're likely to run into (or bump into) a big crowd on weekends.

Other popular discos that sometimes impose either a two-drink minimum and/or a cover charge include **Annabelle's,** atop the Ilikai, a disco affiliated with Juliana's of London; **Da Sting** at the Princess Kaiulani Hotel; and **Atlantis,** in the Pacific Beach Hotel, big and bright with some 800 square feet and 1200 shining lights. There's a fancy feeling and dress code to match at **Rumours,** at the Ala Moana Americana Hotel, which also has a game room for the backgammon crowd. Disco is on from 8 p.m. until 4 a.m., with a cover charge of $2 on weekdays, $3 on weekends.

Should you want to get started on your dancing early, try the **Shore Bird Bar** of the Reef Hotel, which opens each day at 9 a.m. and closes at 2 in the morning. There's live entertainment from 4 to 8 p.m., dancing to nonstop videos from 10 p.m. on. The Shore Bird Broiler is great for a broil-your-own meal.

JUST DANCING: Remember the Big Band days of the '30s and '40s, when people actually did the fox trot, the tango, and the waltz? Well, they still do, thanks to the Royal Hawaiian Hotel Monarch Room's Saturday afternoon Tea Dances. From 3 to 6 p.m., Del Courtney and the Royal Hawaiian Hotel Orchestra provide the sounds. You don't even need to order a drink; tea and coffee, as well as harder stuff, are available. Cover charge is $3.

ACCENT ON ENTERTAINMENT: Let us be perfectly honest. To see the top nightclub shows in Hawaii, you're going to have to break your budget—and then some. When a big name is entertaining, the local clubs usually impose a cover charge of a few dollars, plus a minimum of two drinks, which can swiftly add up to more than you'd think. On top of that many of them prefer to accommodate their dinner guests only—and dinner at these places is usually in the $25 to $35 and up bracket. However, for those times when you're willing to go all out, here's the information on the top names and places. Check the local tourist papers when you're in town for exact details; a top star might just happen to be on the mainland when you're in the islands, but somebody new and unknown might be making a smashing debut. Prices quoted here are subject to change.

Don Ho, who is probably Hawaii's best known entertainer, has been moving around a great deal lately, but it looks as if he's found a comfortable home at the Hilton Hawaiian Village Dome Showroom. Don heads up an exciting Polynesian extravaganza, for which you'll have to pay $35 for adults, $22 for children, if you want dinner. It's still expensive—but more sensible—to come for the Friday or Sunday 10:30 p.m. cocktail show, which will set you back only $17.50 for adults, $12 for children, and includes a tropical drink, tips, and taxes. Don is not our personal cup of tea, but if he's yours, you'll want to splurge for this one. Reservations: 947-2607.

Again you'll have to splurge to see the **Danny Kaleikini** show at the Hala Terrace of the Kahala Hilton Hotel, but this time we second the motion. Danny is undoubtedly one of the islands' top entertainers, a brilliant musician who dances, sings, plays a variety of instruments (including the nose flute), and watches over a talented company of Hawaiian entertainers. The show is held nightly, except Sunday, at 9:30 p.m., with a $9 cover charge. If you have dinner (seating at 7:15 p.m.), expect to pay $33 for the table d'hôte selection; it's a lot cheaper to be seated at 8:45 p.m. for the cocktail show, with a two-drink minimum in addition to the cover. Danny is an authentic Hawaiian entertainer, and the show is deliberately low-key, in excellent taste. Reservations: 734-2211.

Again, try the cocktail show—it's $18.50 as against $38 for the dinner show—to catch the **Royal Hawaiian Revue** at the Monarch Room of the Royal Hawaiian Hotel. The cocktail show is on Friday and Saturday at 11 p.m. This one's a dazzler, with some of the top island entertainers: the Brothers Cazimero and songstress Emma Veary. Reservations: 923-7311.

Al Harrington, the "South Pacific Man," can always be counted on for an excellent show; he's an island favorite. You can catch him at the Polynesian Palace of the Cinerama Reef Towers at $16 for adults, $13 for children for the cocktail shows, Sunday through Friday at 5:45 and 8:45 p.m. Should you want to dine beforehand, the price is $35 for adults, $17 for kids under 12. Reservations: 923-9861.

There are several good Polynesian shows at the beach, but one of the most consistently well received is **Tihati's South Seas Spectacular** in the Bora Bora Showroom of the Waikiki Beachcomber Hotel. Although the tab is $33.50 for grownups, $20 for kids, the value is excellent: an hour-and-a-half-long authentic Polynesian show, an excellent prime rib buffet, one drink, and even an $8 record album of the show and a pamphlet on how to do the hula! Buffet seating is at 6 and 8 p.m. Or have just cocktails and see the show at $18 for adults, $17 for children. Reservations: 922-4646.

It will cost you $16 to see another long-running Polynesian spectacular: that's **Kalo's South Seas Revue** at the Hawaiian Hut of the Ala Moana Hotel. This price entitles you to watch the show and have one drink: if you want to feast on a lavish prime-ribs buffet beforehand, the cost is $29.50. Reservations: 941-5205.

In one of the prettiest beachfront locations of all, the **Moana Hotel Polynesian Revue** takes place out under the stars in the hotel's Banyan Court. Buffet and the show (seatings at 6 and 8:30 p.m. nightly) will cost $34 for adults, $25 for children under 12. For the show plus two drinks, it's $18.25 and $13.50.

Praise be for small favors. There still are places that levy no cover or minimum charges where you can watch the show for the price of a few drinks. One of our favorites among these is the **Blue Dolphin Room,** a cozy place with a turn-of-the-century atmosphere, poolside at the Outrigger Hotel. There's always outstanding, old-style Hawaiian entertainment. During the show, from 9:30 p.m. to midnight, beer is $2.75, mixed drinks from $3; exotics are $4.50. All meals are served here, indoors and outdoors, right beside the sands of Waikiki beach.

Fast becoming known as "The First Lady of Hawaiian Music"—and a terrific comedienne, to boot—**Karen Keawehawai'i** performs every Friday and Saturday from 8 p.m. to midnight at the Surfboard Lounge of the Waikiki Beachcomber Hotel. Again, no cover, no minimum. Come and enjoy. Reservations: 922-4646.

There is also no cover or minimum at the Kumu Lounge of the Pacific Beach Hotel, where two outstanding singers, native Hawaiians Marge Akana and Pauline Kumalaa, known as the **Kuhina Serenaders,** make beautiful music every night except Sunday. Known for their outstanding warmth and aloha, as well as their musicianship (see the Readers' Selections, ahead, for a detailed comment), they write and record many of their own songs and are fast gaining a place among the islands' "in" entertainers. Their show is on 7 to 11 p.m. Monday through Wednesday, 6:30 to 9:30 p.m. on Friday and Saturday.

A traditional Bavarian biergarten in Waikiki? Of course! For an inexpensive evening of doing the polka and the waltz and singing along to the oom-pah-pah band, head for the **Bräuhaus** in the International Market Place. Between sets, the waitresses, in authentic costumes, dance polkas with the customers. Food and drinks are inexpensive, and there is no cover or minimum.

READERS' RESTAURANT AND NIGHTLIFE SELECTIONS: "The **Hau Tree Lanai,** across from Kapiolani Park, was a highpoint. We ate a very good, yet inexpensive lunch under the tree overlooking the beach, then joined the sunbathers for the afternoon. A nice change from the rest of Waikiki" (Jeff and Chris Jacobsen, Rinton, Wash.). . . . "We had a five-star dinner at the Hau Tree Lanai; its food, service, view, and all are almost indescribable. We will remember it forever" (Cathie and Jim Sutler, Sykesville, Md.). . . . "Everybody in Hawaii has their own favorite shave ice place . . . and we have ours. We all agree that **Uptown Sundries—Bottles and Bric-A-Brac,** 1149 S. Beretania St., next to Safeway, is worthy of your book and compares with your other listings. It is located in the Makiki section of Honolulu, not far from Waikiki or downtown. Its proprietor is a charming "local" named Wally who is known as 'The King of Ice.' He makes his own delicious syrups from personal formulas which are very rich—but not too sweet. Also, he uses a special blade, he proclaims, that makes a unique shave ice, 'like cotton candy.' He proudly serves a huge mountain of this fine shaved ice in a small bowl rather than in the usual cone. Lemon, lime, and coconut are especially good. Also, chocolate fudge flavor!" (David Friedman, Honolulu, Hi.). . . . "Dinners were superb at both **Perry Boys:** the one in the Outrigger and the other on Lewers St. They were the best we had on Oahu. The prices were right—$6.75 for dinner buffet, $3.75 for breakfast buffet—and the food was marvelous, with lots and lots of island specialties. Mahimahi, tropical fruits and juices, vegetables, and meats fixed the Hawaiian way were all features of the house. And one could make as many trips to the food lines as he wished. Needless to say, we did" (Jim Cox, Middletown, Ky.).

"Be sure to see some of the island entertainers; they are extremely talented. **Andy Kimura** writes and performs his own music. **Society of Seven** does music and comedy. **The Beamers** are fantastic singers. I would highly recommend all of these performers" (Nancy Grant, South Easton, Mass.). . . . "The **Wailana Malia Restaurant** became a real favorite with us. The service was excellent, the food delicious, and the prices were almost unbelievably low. For that matter, with specials, coupons, and Early Bird meals, budget dining is no problem at any time of day or evening" (Mr. and Mrs. Lane Alton, Edmonton, Alberta, Canada). . . . "We made a new discovery this time—the **Shore Bird,** beachfront at the Reef Hotel. We used a coupon and had the mahimahi for $3.95. This included a nice salad bar and our beverages. The total bill was $7.90, and the meal was delicious. They do not serve lunch. Dinner starts at 5 p.m., and it is really delightful, eating on the lanai" (Mrs. Dorothy Astman, Levittown, N.Y.). . . . "At the poolside bar of the **Waikiki Village Hotel,** it is Happy Hour from 10 a.m. till closing. Beer is 50¢ and 75¢ for draft. Mai tais are 95¢ and standard drinks are $1.25 and $1.75 for doubles. The **Village Restaurant,** where you get two eggs, hash browns, two slices of toast with jelly, and a bottomless cup of coffee for $1.50, offers the best breakfast and value in the area. . . . At the Royal Hawaiian Shopping Center, **It's Greek to Me** has good food and a Happy Hour when you can buy any kind of bottled beer and get the second one for a penny. The **Great Wok of China** at the Royal Hawaiian Shopping Center has a Happy Hour from 4 to 6 p.m. when beer and standard drinks are $1. **Lani of Hawaii** plays—would you believe—mostly classical music on a grand piano and sings pretty well too. Besides that, you get plenty of deep-fried hot pupus. The place was full the times we were there" (Ray and Ruth Wiltse, Burnaby, B.C., Canada).

"We decided to take our chance without a car on Oahu and use the bus. We went to one of the big hotels for dinner, but discovered the price was a bit steep for us that night, so we decided to go back to our hotel. We didn't realize how sporadic the bus service is, got hungry while waiting for the bus, and wandered into the **Yakiniku House Tokyo** at 1910 Ala Moana. We had a delightful meal, and Mr. Neal Goya, the manager, came over and chatted with us for a long time—then refused to hear of our waiting for the bus and drove us to our hotel! He showed us the meaning of aloha" (Laura and Bob Gross, Bolingbrook, Ill.). . . . "We had a five-star dinner at the **Hau Tree Lanai:** its food, service, view and all are almost indescribable. We will remember it forever" (Cathie and Jim Stutler, Sykesville, Md.).

"Right next to the Sheraton Moana Hotel in Waikiki is the greatest fudge store around. Although the sign says they close after 10 p.m., we were allowed into the **North Shore Fudge Store,** 2379 Kalakaua, after closing hours and were treated to homemade Hawaiian ice cream with melted fudge poured on top. Their selection seems never-ending, ranging from chocolate macadamia nut to piña colada. Definitely a must for all chocolate lovers" (Scott Mosko and Debby Brown, Santa Clara, Calif.). [*Authors' Note:* North Shore Fudge now has a second location at 2370 Kuhio in the Food Pantry, and is open 9:30 a.m. to 10:30 p.m. daily.]. . . . "One place we found having good inexpensive food and a great view is the **Fifth Floor Cafeteria** in the Federal Building across from Aloha Tower. It's a beautiful cafeteria with balcony eating for a view of Diamond Head or Ewa. Open to the public from early morning to midafternoon" (J. R. Grimm, Centerville, Ohio). . . . "Our favorite restaurant on Oahu was **The Pottery,** 3574 Waialae Ave. All of the plates, goblets, and decorations are made right there and you can watch the potters at work. We had an excellent lunch. Some of the dinners are cooked right in the kiln, along with their special cheesecake—the best we've ever had" (Susan and Steve McDill, Wayzata, Minn.). . . . **Bobby McGee's Conglomeration,** 2885 Kalakaua, is fun and has good food. The waiters are dressed in a variety of costumes to make for an interesting atmosphere. We went for their Early Bird dinner (Sunday to Thursday from 5 to 6:30 p.m.) and had prime rib for $8.95. They also have a good salad bar. This is an easy 15-minute walk past the zoo. For Elks members, two doors down is the Elks Club, where we enjoyed having dinner. Cocktails are inexpensive, and they have a nice ocean view" (Larene and Al Olson, Sherwood, Ore.).

"We broke the bank one night and splurged at the **Seafood Emporium** on the second floor of the Royal Hawaiian Center. Complete dinners for both, including beverages, came to $32.50. The service and food here were the best of the entire trip, and well worth the expense. We had dinner at **Perry's Smorgy** at the Outrigger Hotel, and had a beachfront table where we looked out over Waikiki Beach and Diamond Head. Below us was the luau by Chuck Machado at the Outrigger Hotel. We had better food, and more of it, for $6.75 each, and we had a front-row, elevated seat for the luau entertainment" (Frank Castor, Ephrata, Penna.). . . . "The **Seigetsu Japanese Restaurant,** on the sixth floor of the Kalakaua International Center, at 2215 Kalakaua, near Beach Walk, had a placard outside advertising a 'special dinner' for $5.95, served from 5 to 6:30 p.m., so we decided to try it. Our meal was a veritable feast, a truly excellent, authentic Japanese meal for an incredible price. First, our kimono-clad waitress brought us a dish of pickled vegetables and a small bowl of pickled beef—absolutely delicious. Next came a bowl of miso soup. The main course consisted of a generous portion of beef teriyaki, a big helping of deep-fried chicken, two jumbo shrimp tempura, eggplant and green beans tempura, a small helping of both potato and macaroni salad, lettuce, and tomato. There was also some fruit, plus a heaping bowl of rice and all the tea we could drink. The Siegetsu is attractively decorated and paneled in wood. There are two rooms, and one has a choice of dining either American or Japanese style. The food was wonderful, and the Early Bird dinner a true bargain. Telephone number is 922-8686" (Roberta Rosen, Long Beach, Calif.).

"Regarding the time-sharing boom currently going on. We contacted the Better Business Bureau to inquire if we really would receive all the freebies mentioned in various tourist literature if we sat through the condominium time-sharing presentations. They assured us that while the presentation was very hard-sell, we would receive the premium of our choice. So we decided to attend the presentation that would give us free tickets to the **Don Ho** show. We were perfectly honest and above-board with the time-sharing people when they asked why we came to their presentations. We stated that we wanted the free tickets. They accepted our answer graciously, indicated that they were willing to pay that price for our attention to their pitch, and proceeded to try and sell us. The pitches last for 90 minutes and are very hard-sell. If one's sales resistance is not substantial, better not go. Ours is, and thanks to time-sharing, we had a lovely dinner, drinks, etc., all for free, at Don Ho. We felt sorry for the people who were paying $60 and $65 a couple, who received no better seating or treatment than we did, when we saw the shows for free" (Sheila Pritchett, Villanova, Penna.). . . . "Please tell your readers to beware of time-sharing offers. I and many of my friends have been rudely treated. People think they are getting a free meal or free tickets, etc., and a lot of vacation time is taken and ruined" (Diane Buzby, Swarthmore, Penna.). . . . "**Al Harrington,** who once played on TV's 'Hawaii Five-O,' has one of the most special and entertaining shows on the island. I truly felt that I had received my money's worth. The show price was about standard for the dinner shows in Honolulu, $35 per person, but the meal was very good, there were no bad seats and Mr. Harrington took time to talk and pose for pictures with each person there. The show is very one-on-one" (Diana Morgan, Santa Rosa, Calif.).

"For authentic Hawaiian music, both old-style and contemporary, our all-time favorites are the **Kuhina Serenaders,** who perform in Pacific Beach Hotel's Kumu Lounge. This is a little gem of a showroom with deep, comfortable armchairs and sofas. There is no cover or minimum and the drinks are standard price. But the true gems are the Serenaders—Marge and Pauline—two part-Hawaiian ladies who render island songs in voices so sweet it makes your heart ache. Marge, in addition, is a composer of considerable talent, and quite a few of the selections you will hear are from her pen. Some graceful and lovely young local gals add to the festive air with their hula artistry throughout the evening, culminating in a group hula lesson for any onlookers who wish to return home with a handsome certificate verifying that he or she learned the hula at Kumu Lounge. Best of all, though, is the sincere warmth and aloha that Marge and Pauline impart to their audience. You are only a 'stranger' in Kumu Lounge for as long as it takes you to walk in and sit down. After that, whether it be next day or next year, you receive a greeting befitting an old and treasured friend. These girls are very forthright and genuine about the high value they place upon their fans; as a result, they have an enviable circle of international devotees for whom returning to Kumu Lounge is like coming home!" (Leilani Moyers, Patterson, N.Y.).

"Harold, who used to be the turkey chef at the old Continental Restaurant at Ala Moana, now has his own restaurant in the Bank of Hawaii Building at 1451 S. King St., and a busy place it is. Among the 20 or so dinner choices, you can get a full-course turkey dinner for around $5. An average lunch is under $5. Service is excellent and Harold is always on hand to see that it stays that way. . . . The best Portuguese bean soup in the islands is served every Wednesday at **King's Bakery and Coffeeshop,** at Eaton Square on Hobron Lane. . . . Just down Kam Highway from Pearl Ridge Shopping Center in the Waimalu Shopping Center is **Shiro's Saimin Haven.** Local people flock here for their favorite variety of saimin—there are 57 varieties, and the bowls are almost big enough to swim in!" (Ruth Rulon, Whiting, N.J.). . . . "When in Oahu, make sure to dine at one of the **Kim Chee Restaurants.** They serve the best kal-bi in the islands. You start with seaweed soup. Then comes the kal-bi (Korean short ribs), a side dish of vegetables, and the fiery cabbage and cucumber relish, kim chee. A lot of diners, including myself, found it difficult to finish dinner. The restaurant offers paper plates and foil to take leftovers home. All this for about $6. There is one restaurant in Kaneohe at 46-10 Kam Hwy. (tel. 235-5560), another in Kaimuki at 3569 Waialae Ave. (tel. 737-6059), and a third near Blaisdell Center at 1040 S. King St. (tel. 536-1426)" (Kaz Okuda, Rosemead, Calif.).

"For cocktails and pupus, I would highly recommend **Top's Bar and Restaurant** at Kalakaua and Beach Walk. The pupus are unusually excellent and plentiful, bar booze is $1.25 between 1 and 6:30 p.m., and they have Hawaiian drink specials. Pupus are served from about 3 to 6:30 p.m., and the regular bartender, whose name is Zee, is so nice and pleasant that she makes a rainy day seem sunny" (Ronald Hohenstein, Chicago, Ill.). . . . "The **Caffè Guccinni,** 2139 Kuhio, serves the best Italian food we have enjoyed at any restaurant, regardless of price. Entrees go in the $3 to $6 range, and are truly gourmet in quality. The minestrone is superb. The owner served us personally and made us feel at home" (Jim Hedstrom, Diamond Bar, Calif.). . . . "Many good buys are advertised on restaurant windows or on signs in front of the restaurants; we found them all worthwhile and good for a budget. For example, we had an 'Early Bird Special,' from 5 to 6:30 p.m., of fish and fries plus salad bar for $3.95 at **Buzz's Steak and Lobster** on Saratoga. We also had several 'two-for-one' breakfasts at **Burger King** at Lewers and Kalakaua, and at the lovely new **McDonald's** in the Royal Hawaiian Shopping Center, with seconds on coffee, free. For these you need coupons from the beach papers. With all these bargains, we can't see why people always say Hawaii is expensive" (Dorothy Astman, Levittown, Long Island, N.Y.).

"Since we returned from Hawaii a couple of years ago, I have read your books almost cover to cover, waiting to see if anyone else would mention the food and service at the **Holiday Inn** on Kalakaua Avenue. We were there for ten days and waited until the last day to eat at their main restaurant, the Captain's Table, because we thought it would be expensive. It wasn't, and we missed several really good meals by not eating there sooner. This is not to take anything away from their coffeeshop, which also had very good food at a sensible price. We would recommend this hotel any time for anyone on a first trip to Waikiki. It is right across the road from the beach and our room on the 18th floor had a beautiful view of Waikiki Beach and the hotels on it" (Kenneth and Joann Johnson, Vernon, Vt.). . . . "On the windward side of Oahu we recommend the **Kim Chee Bar B Q** at 16 Kainehe St. in Kailua, a large, clean restaurant serving hearty portions of Korean food at reasonable prices: from $2.80 for kook-soo noodles to $6.25 for a combination plate with four kinds of meat plus dumplings and veggies, that takes two plates to serve up!" (Larry Spencer, Beaverton, Ore.).

"My old favorite standby has been **Chuck's Cellar** in the Outrigger East for many years. The walls are decorated with old pictures of Diamond Head; their salad bar is one of the best anywhere, and they often have reasonable specials for a complete dinner. . . . My favorite Sunday Brunch: **Don the Beachcomber!** You simply hate to stop eating, the variety is so great. You don't have to eat again all day! . . . This year I discovered the **Noodle Shop** in the Waikiki Sand Villa Hotel. Great for a mai tai or chi chi during Happy Hour, $1.50, and as good or better than any I had at any price. Rather small bar, though, with only a few bar stools" (Beverlee Lindberg, Marcola, Ore.). . . . "We particularly enjoyed lunch at the **Chinese Kitchen** at Temple Valley Mall. Two of us had large, delicious lunches for less than $6 total, including soft drinks. Everything is on display, so we selected our three choices each from how they looked as well as from the name; the friendly proprietor listed the ingredients in each" (Sharon Wells, Anchorage, Alaska). . . . "For a splurge, a waitress in Honolulu recommended **John Dominis.** It's tucked away behind the canneries on the western edge of Kewalo Basin. It's unadvertised, and the average tourist would not find it. The menu is mostly fish, but there are a few other choices, plus an excellent cold seafood appetizer bar. You can watch the sailboats glide by and enjoy an exquisite view of the Honolulu skyline. The crabs and lobsters swim in lagoons right inside the restaurant. Excellent food and service for a truly memorable evening!" (Mr. and Mrs. Morris Pengilly, South Euclid, Ohio). [*Authors' Note:* John Dominis is at 43 Ahui St. (tel. 523-0955), reservations advised; dinner for two should be in the neighborhood of $50 or more.]

"**Steamer's Bar & Restaurant** in Haleiwa, Haleiwa Shopping Plaza (tel. 637-5071), turned out to be a delightful spot for luncheon. We each had a Midori daiquiri, choice of a super seafood chowder or salad, and a fresh fish entree, including delicious potatoes, for $10.95. it was a perfect stop after taking a glider ride at Dillingham Air Force Base. . . . The **Chowder House** at Ward Warehouse serves the best strawberry daiquiris we've ever tasted, and the fresh island fish, which varies daily, is never priced over $7 or so, and is fixed in your choice of style—a great buy. **Waioli Tearoom** was exactly as mentioned—delightful—and one of the fun things to do is to watch the almost constant weddings going on in the little chapel. Apparently, package tours are sold in Japan, including a traditional church wedding, music, pictures, videotaping the ceremony, honeymoon, etc. The only people present at the ceremony we observed were the minister, his wife, and the photographer. However, the bride and groom were in traditional formal attire and we found ourselves wanting to wave as they were leaving the chapel. We saved **The Willows,** 901 Hausten St., for our last night in the islands and what a perfect choice. It was expensive—$50 with wine, tax, tip, etc., but worth every cent of it. The atmosphere outside is incredible; the three-piece ensemble playing 'Hawaii City Lights' reduced me to tears. The food was superior, as was the service; all in all, a must" (Sheila Pritchett, Villanova, Penna.). . . . "**The Willows** serves a most delightful Sunday Brunch, complete with roast pig, mahimahi, a multitude of fresh fruits and salads, and of course, superb desserts. The cost is $13.95 per person and reservations are recommended. They serve from 10:30 a.m. until 1 p.m." (Wende L. Hower, Monte Sereno, Calif.). [*Authors' Note:* The Willows is one of the islands' most gracious 'Old Hawaii' restaurants, situated on a beautiful pond amid garden surroundings. Try it for a big-splurge meal; at dinner, most à la carte entrees are in the $14 to $18 range; a complete dinner is $28.50. Lunch runs about $6.25 to $8.95. Perhaps the nicest time to come here is for the Tuesday or Thursday Hawaiian luncheons, with entertainment by oldtime kamaainas who get up to share a song or dance or tale—a real glimpse of pre-plastic Hawaii. Call 946-4808 for reservations.]

"I'd like to share with you a Korean restaurant on the North Shore called **Dong Yang,** 542 Oliver St., Wahiawa (tel. 621-5031). Five of us ate complete dinners plus an extra appetizer for only $19 plus tip. The restaurant lacks an appealing atmosphere—it is plain and overly lit—but is very clean and has friendly, courteous service. Our dinners included combination BBQ beef and chicken, rice, assorted Oriental vegetables, kim chee, dried shredded cuttlefish, potato and macaroni salad, soup, and tea" (Janet Locher, New Freedom, Penna.). . . . "Re: Pupus and Happy Hours: **Coco's,** with each $1.10 scotch-and-soda, gave me an unbelievable split English muffin, each half topped with ground beef with melted Swiss cheese on top!" (Richard Rosicahn, Miami, Fla.). . . . "As a family of four teens and three adults who live in Honolulu, we can recommend the following places to your readers: **Dickens,** 1221 Kapiolani Blvd., is a great British pub. Food and drink are medium-priced, great fish and chips and clam chowder. **Fast Food,** 75 S. Kam Hwy., Wahiawa, has great heroes and about 200 food items, great homemade foods. This is a mom-and-pop place—clean, inexpensive, filling" (Donald and Helen Martin, Ewa Beach, Hi.). . . . "We like Sunday brunches and tried three: the **Terrace Grill** at the Hyatt Regency, **Don the Beachcomber,** and the **Captain's Table** at the Holiday Inn Waikiki. The Captain's Table was outstanding; we went twice. The Sunday champagne buffet, served from 10 a.m. to 2 p.m., has a wonderful selection of delicious dishes. Some of them never appear at other buffets, and tempt one to eat so much that a light snack is all you can manage for the rest of the day. You seem to be dining right over the colorful Pacific with its surfers and sail boats. An outstanding gourmet budget experience. . . . Another lovely place to eat is **The Trellises** at the Outrigger Prince Kuhio Hotel, 2500 Kuhio. Entrees run from $5.75 to $11 for dinner. They also have sandwiches and snacks and serve lunch and breakfast" (Mr. and Mrs. C. W. Dynes, Nashua, N.H.).

"We were introduced to a good Japanese restaurant by university students. It is **Sekiya Restaurant and Delicatessen,** 2746 Kaimuki Ave., opposite Kaimuki High School. We had complete meals for $3.95, $4.95, and $5.50. The food was delicious. We were there on weekends, and it was busy, as it's very popular with the locals, and university people" (Mrs. Joseph R. Astman, Levittown, N.Y.). . . . "My favorite Chinese restaurant in this world is now the **Mandarin Restaurant** at 942 McCully St. (tel. 946-3242). The sweet-and-sour pork is the best I've ever tasted. The dessert, a form of apple fritters dipped in ice at the dinner table, was worth the whole trip. The price was not cheap, so I'd consider it a splurge after saving money on housing: $19 for two" (Charles B. Carlston, Palo Alto, Calif.). . . . "The **Queen Kapiolani Hotel** serves a mini-luau buffet luncheon Monday through Saturday from 11 a.m.

to 2 p.m. It's $7 for all you want to eat, and this sampling of the food usually found at luaus should let people know what to expect if they plan to spend $25 to $35 for both entertainment and food" (Linton Lum, San Leandro, Calif.). . . . "I highly recommend the sweet-and-sour cabbage (sin-choi) at **House of Dragon** in the Pearl City Shopping Center, Pearl City" (Pat Chong Lum, Berkeley, Calif.).

"For a splurge I'd like to suggest **Hy's** in the Waikiki Park Heights Hotel. It's a steakhouse; the food is excellent, and so is the service. Besides the usual steak selection, they also have freshly caught fish of the day; red snapper was pronounced excellent by the member of our party who sampled it. Our bill, including drinks and a bottle of rather expensive wine, came to over $100 for six of us. I feel six people could dine very well for about $80" (Ann and Howard Thoen, Edmonton, Alberta, Canada).

"We have visited the islands 16 times and are familiar with a lot of the restaurants. No finer, more reasonable Chinese food can be had than at **Kelly's,** on Kam Highway at Puuloa Road, in the vicinity of the airport (it sits just off the highway). The chicken chow mein with crispy noodles comes on a big plate; it serves two, but is considered a single serving. They also have a wide and varied American menu and their own bakery. Open 24 hours a day" (J. L. Roster, Kansas City, Mo.). . . . "For great decor with your meals, try the Chinese and Japanese restaurants in Waikiki; they are all authentic. We were warned against going into the Chinatown area at night because of the thefts. Please inform your readers that it is not a safe place after dark" (Barbara Smith, Winnipeg, Manitoba, Canada). . . . "The best economical Oriental food I found in Hawaii was at the **Dynasty Restaurant,** 1830 Ala Moana Blvd. I had a Chinese platter for $4.50, which included fried rice, chicken, and vegetables, and a small vegetable garnish. It was delicious and served promptly" (Pat Diehnelt, Menomonee Falls, Wisc.).

"**Horatio's at** Ward Warehouse provided a lovely lunch. At around $8.50, including tip, I suppose this would be considered a minor splurge. Interesting decor—it looks like an old sailing ship—friendly staff, and great food made it the best meal of the trip. . . . For me, the **Waioli Tea Room** filled the gap left by the removal of our old favorite, the Snack Shop, where we so enjoyed the birds frolicking about as we dined. The coconut fried mahimahi was the most delightful way I've had that fish served to me anywhere in Hawaii in three trips!" (Mary Risdon, Calgary, Alberta, Canada).

"We had a wonderful experience at **Cathay Inn Chop Suey,** 86-088 Farrington Hwy. (tel. 696-9477), near the Waianae Mall Shopping Center. Dinner for five of us ran less than $19. I can especially recommend the shrimp with pineapple. We were amazed at the size of the portions for the money; the plain crispy wonton was plenty for the five of us, and the bowl of steamed rice was so large that we questioned the girl to see if she had made a mistake and brought the larger size" (Mrs. Caryl Roberts, Tinley Park, Ill.). . . . "We enjoyed eating at the **Ocean Terrace** at the Sheraton Waikiki. They have a huge lunch and dinner buffet, with never less than three different meats, all kinds of salad fixings, vegetables, bread, fresh fruit, cheeses, cakes, and pies. We felt it a real bargain compared to other eating places. They have roast baron of beef, carved, at lunch, when the cost is $8.95, and prime rib, carved, at dinner, $12.50" (Amanda Anderson, Florence, Ala.). . . . "The **Jolly Roger** restaurant and lounge at the street level of the Outrigger East have very good food, very good service, and low-priced mai tais from 10 a.m. to 7 p.m. The food, service, and atmosphere were well worth the prices which were no more than for such fare at many nontourist meccas in northeastern Ohio" (The Ed Glassner Family, Kent, Ohio). [*Authors' Note:* In addition to complete dinners under $6, Jolly Roger also offers live entertainment nightly with no cover, no minimum.] . . . "We had a great meal at **Kenny's** in the Kam Shopping Center on Like Like Highway: a roast pork dinner, including fruit salad and dessert, for $5.75" (Mrs. M. Hunt, Jr., Monroe, Mich.). [*Authors' Note:* Kenny's is a local favorite that serves amazingly inexpensive dinners from about $3.50 to $5.75—the top price going for teriyaki or tenderloin steak. They also serve some Japanese noodle dishes.]

"We particularly enjoyed **Buzz's Steak & Lobster House,** 225 Saratoga. Mahimahi dinner was $8.95, and the salad bar was excellent, with great potato salad. The host was quite cordial, especially to the children" (Joseph Koh, Cerritos, Calif.). [*Authors' Note:* Buzz's is a longtime Waikiki favorite which specializes in fresh fish; catch of the day is usually $10.95 to $12.95. The menu includes a wide variety of beef and seafood. Their salad bar and fresh bread meal is only $4.95.] . . . "The **Reef Broiler,** the **Pagoda Restaurant, Victoria Station,** and **Chuck's** all have marvelous salad bars—all you can eat in a beautiful atmosphere. **Victoria Station I** and **Sizzler Steak House** have no smoking—a real blessing not to have someone blowing smoke in your face" (Mr. and Mrs. Michael F. Henely, Honolulu, Hi.). . . . "Perhaps the highlight of eating was **Chuck's Steak House** at Waterfront Village. A couple of dollars over budget, but well worth it" (John E. Salmon, Antioch, Calif.). . . . "For a splurge, I recommend the luau at the **Royal Hawaiian Hotel.** At $31 each, the meal is unspectacular, but the scenery and entertainment are outstanding. I especially enjoyed the talented young girls who performed a variety of dances; they were much more professional than but just as charming as the girls in the Ala Moana Show" (Sissy Waggoner, Rittman, Ohio).

"Our hint: We took from home silverware, paring knife, can opener, two-cup coffee pot, and the makings for morning coffee. Every one of our hotel rooms had a small refrigerator. We bought orange juice, papaya, Danish, whatever, and had breakfast on our lanai each morning before leaving. Many days we stopped in the grocery store and got sandwich fixings, canned ice tea, and fruit, and had a picnic on the beach. We not only saved money, but time as well. Many days we saw the tourists lined up at the coffeeshops trying to have breakfast before catching a tour bus" (Mary Lou and Davie Bregitzer, Cleveland, Ohio). . . . "When you cannot get a hotel with a kitchenette, take along the following equipment, which will fit right in with your clothes in the suitcase: a four-cup percolator or hotpot; an eight-inch electric frying pan; one pancake turner; one sharp paring knife; plastic or stainless-steel cutlery; coffee mugs; a plastic pot scraper; paper plates; two or more plastic margarine dishes to use for soup, cereal, salad, or dessert dishes; salt and pepper shakers. With these utensils I cooked up some really adequate meals. The little frypan holds four eggs at a time, and if you cut bacon strips in two, you can fry up a good panful. Two small steaks can be cooked, and then add and cook some frozen vegetables in a bit of water, and you have a meal in a dish. The little hotpot is for beverages as well as instant soup or porridge. One night I cooked an exotic creamed shrimp and hot rice dish by buying frozen 'boil in a bag' food. The extra plastic trays used for the meat become service trays, etc. It is a challenge to cook up imaginative meals and it can be done!" (Mrs. Margaret Springett, Moose Jaw, Saskatchewan, Canada). . . . "If you're going to be doing some cooking, save your pill bottles, remove the prescription labels, and fill them with all the spices you will need (salt, garlic salt, pepper, etc.), and label the containers. These take very little room and won't break. (Mrs. I. Hodgeman, Bloomington, Minn.). . . . "We discovered **Pâtisserie LeBon,** Fine International Pastries, 655 Keeaumoku St., Dean Asao, manager. The pastries are outstanding, and there are always good specials. A good buy is the orange chiffon cake which comes in two sizes, small for $1.85 and large for $2.85. It is very good, moist and light, and I believe they have this all of the time" (Charles and Mary Woodard, Ojai, Calif.). [*Authors' Note:* Try their lemon crunch cake too. They also do special packaging for gifts.]

"We recommend the buffet luncheon at the **Royal Hawaiian.** We went up to the front of the waiting line 15 minutes ahead of time and spoke to the waitress and were seated right along the oceanfront facing Diamond Head. The very friendly waitress encouraged us to help ourselves as often as we wished. For about $15.25 per person you get a good variety of foods and the best desserts and selection in the islands, with the exception of the Mauna Kea Beach Hotel on the Big Island. . . . Here are some ideas that have worked beautifully on our Hawaii trips and have saved us well over $100 on breakfasts alone. (1) Buy one of those small Styrofoam beer coolers, put in a few cubes of ice, and you have a refrigerator you can use in your room, or take with you on day trips, to keep your milk, butter, sandwich meat, etc., fresh and sweet. It can be easily carried from one island to another too. (2) On King Street in Honolulu, **King's Bakery** makes a Hawaiian sweet bread that has the unique quality of not drying out even after being cut. The taste is delicious, something like a sweet roll, and it will keep fresh in your room for days. (3) In the islands, orange juice comes in a quart glass 'milk' bottle. Fill this almost full of cold water, put in a few spoonfuls of instant coffee, insert one of those pigtail immersion heaters (made for heating liquid in a cup and available in most variety stores), using a clothes pin to stop it from going too far down, plug in, and voila!—a quart of excellent coffee in about five minutes" (Sheldon Myers, Berkeley, Calif.).

"The food at the **Reef Broiler** in the Reef Hotel, 2169 Kalia Rd., is excellent. You start out at their large help-yourself salad bar, with various types of salads, fresh island fruit, and hot bread. The white-hatted chef at the open broiler prepares your entree—steaks, chicken, and mahimahi—to order. We dined here a few times, always ordering the mahimahi, which was the tastiest we had enjoyed anywhere. We saw many people taking home doggy bags, as the meal—which will probably run $7 to $10—is very filling. . . . A local Chinese acquaintance recommended **China House** at 1349 Kapiolani, just mauka of Sears' second-level parking area at Ala Moana Center. They serve a delicious Chinese luncheon specialty, hot dim sum dumplings, filled with various meats and fish. Ask the waitress to make a selection for you. For dessert, they serve a lovely flaky, tender custard tart. Although I had seconds on the dim sum, our tab was just $7.50 for two. The dumplings are so filling that you will not want a big dinner that day. All the diners were local Oriental businessmen; we were the only haoles in the place" (Evelyn and Don Grewar, Bobcaygeon, Ontario, Canada). . . . "For a delightful splurge, we recommend **Little George's** on Ala Moana. The menu is basically seafood, entrees start at $7.50 and go up to $26.95 for live Maine lobster dinners. We enjoyed the decor, service, and delicious food. For reservations, phone 536-7344" (Howard and Marjorie Ackerman, Richmond, Calif.).

"Besides the service being excellent at the **Wailana Coffee House,** they have french toast that is out of this world. The bread is sliced thicker than usual and loaded with egg, with a pocket cut in for guava jelly. It melts in your mouth" (Mr. and Mrs. Leonard Dziedzic, West Allis, Wisc.). [*Authors' Note:* The Wailana Malia Coffee House also has the same delicious toast.] . . . "Tell your readers about **Pearl City Tavern.** The food is rather expensive, but you can go sit in the bar/lounge area watch the squirrel monkeys in the glass cage behind the bar. It may sound uninviting, and but it really was fun to see. Also, you can go upstairs to see their exquisite bonsai trees. For anyone interested in plants, this is a must" (Theresa Vasseli, Rome, N.Y.). [*Authors' Note:* We have received many letters of praise for this excellent family restaurant serving American and Japanese food and live Maine lobsters. Besides the Monkey Bar and rooftop bonsai garden, they also have spectacular saltwater aquariums. And there's a wonderful new Sushi Bar. They're in Pearl City; call 455-1045 for reservations.] . . . "The **Straub Clinic Cafeteria** on Ward and King Streets, across from the Honolulu International Center and near the Academy of Arts, serves very fine food at low, low prices, and is open to the public for all three meals. Entrees like beef Stroganoff teriyaki range from $1.50 to $1.95. Vegetables are 60¢, sandwiches from $1.50, salads and diet plates at $2.50. Breakfast is served from 6:30 to 10 a.m., lunch from 11 a.m. to 1:30 p.m., and dinner from 4 to 6:30 p.m. daily" (Mr. and Mrs. Sam Rubin, Honolulu, Hi.).

"I recommend the **Pieces of Eight Restaurant,** 250 Lewers St., across from the Reef Towers Hotel. The place is clean and the food is good. Help yourself to all the salad you want at the salad bar. Servings of fish and french fries were large. When I could not eat it all, they gave me a doggie bag—without my even asking for it!" (Alan G. Fragg, Corona del Mar, Calif.). [*Authors' Note:* Prices for complete dinners, with entrees of fish or steak, average $5.50 to $17.95. Catch of the day comes from their own fishing boat. Open from 2 p.m. daily for cocktails and free pupus, dinner from 5 to 11 p.m. Piano bar.] . . . "If you're planning to splurge at some of the fancier restaurants in town, here's a way to ease the high cost. You can buy a booklet of four $5 gift certificates (dining value: $20) from the **Aloha Dinner Club** for

$8. One certificate will be honored by any participating restaurant when the total bill for a party of two or more goes over $20. We used this successfully at Nick's Fishmarket and at several less expensive restaurants, where dinner was in the $8 to $14 range. To get the booklet, you send $8 to Aloha Dinner Club, 2131 Kalakaua Ave., Suite 212, Honolulu, HI 96815" (Beatrice Solomon, Philadelphia, Penna.).

Chapter IV

TRANSPORTATION WITHIN HONOLULU

From Buses to Cars to Rickshaws

IN THE CHAPTERS immediately following we'll discuss the sightseeing and activities of Honolulu and its suburbs. In this chapter, we deal with the cheapest ways to get to those activities and see those sights.

So many people think it's difficult to get around the islands that they succumb in advance to those package deals that wrap up your whole vacation in advance: transportation, hotels, sightseeing from the limousine window, all for one flat—and unnecessarily high—fee. And even if they've already discovered the do-it-yourself trick of staying at budget hotels and eating at low-cost restaurants, panic strikes when it comes to sightseeing—and how else to "do" Honolulu unless someone takes you by the hand on a guided tour?

Tours are okay, of course, pleasant and useful if you have only a day or two and want to pack in as many sights as you can. And you may want to take one (or else rent a car) when you circle the island of Oahu (see "Guided Tours," below). But for sightseeing in Honolulu, at your own pace, there's a method that's much cheaper, and much more fun—

THE BUSES: We refer, of course, to the MTL buses (known as TheBUS) owned by the City and County of Honolulu and operated under contract by the private firm of MTL, Inc. MTL has routes all over the island, which gives you a chance to mingle with the island's nontourist population. (You'll really feel like a kamaaina when someone asks you how to get to a certain place!) The friendliness of the Hawaiian drivers too will be quite an experience, especially if you come from an overcrowded city on the mainland where every passenger is a potential enemy. In a bus dispute a few years ago, the drivers figured out a novel way to show their dissatisfaction with the company: they just refused to collect fares from the passengers!

But don't count on that. You'll pay 50¢ for a ride on TheBUS. Exact change in coins is required. Children pay 25¢. Free transfers, which can extend your ride considerably in one direction, must be requested when you board and pay your fare.

Bus schedules are not, unfortunately, available on the buses themselves, but if you have any questions about how to get where, simply call TheBUS information number at 531-1611. Keep in mind, though, that the buses that you will take from Waikiki to Ala Moana Shopping Center or to downtown Honolulu must be boarded on Kuhio Avenue; buses on Kalakaua go only in a Diamond Head direction.

Note: Senior citizens (65 or over) who live here may ride free on the buses at all times. Visitors may also do so by presenting appropriate proof of age (driver's license, or birth certificate, or passport, or baptismal certificate with seal), but must wait three to four weeks for processing of their pass. Apply at the MTL office 725 Kapiolani Blvd. (tel. 531-7066), or 650 S. King St. (tel. 524-4626).

If you're staying in Honolulu and doing extensive bus riding for any length of time, it may pay you to buy a monthly pass. They cost $15 for adults, $7.50 for youths up to high school age (generally considered 19 or younger). Bus passes are available from the 16th of the month preceding the month in which they are valid to the 15th of the month in which they are valid. They are available at TheBUSPass Office at 725 Kapiolani or 650 S. King St., at the Manoa Campus Center of the University of Hawaii, at Foodland and Emjay Supermarkets, Satellite City Halls, and at most Bank of Hawaii branches. All purchases must be made in cash: checks or credit cards are not accepted. Fares are subject to change.

RENTING A CAR: This alternative to the buses is more expensive, of course, especially with the inflationary cost of gas, but it's awfully nice to have a car at your disposal. And you can save money on meals by driving to inexpensive restaurants or drive-ins outside the tourist area. If you do decide on one, you'll have your choice of just about any type of vehicle, foreign or domestic, from the numerous U-Drive agencies in town. The most inexpensive cars are Gala Jeeps and foreign compacts like the Datsun, both with manual shifts; if you want an automatic shift, you'll have to pay about $2 to $3 more. Prices are also higher for standard-size cars. As for the car-rental agencies themselves, they are very much in competition for your business, and since rates are constantly changing and new attractive deals are offered all the time, a little comparison shopping at the time of your arrival will pay big dividends. We'll give you the names of the top budget companies and their rates as of this writing, and we'll pass on the warning they gave to us: "Rates are subject to change at any time without notice." Most of the companies also offer flat rates with unlimited free mileage; we've found this most useful if you're going to do a great deal of driving—say, driving around the island of Oahu. If you're just doing in-city sightseeing or going to and from beach, hotel, and restaurants, it's cheaper to get the regular rates. The flat rates may not always be listed, so be sure to ask.

All-Island Rentals

If you're going to visit several of the major islands, the easiest way to rent your cars is to make one telephone call to a company that provides service on all of them. One of the biggest in the islands, and one that we've always had good luck with, is **Holiday Rent-A-Car Hawaii,** whose slogan "We Drive You Happy" makes sense practically (if not grammatically).

You'll be happy with the reputable cars, thoughtful service (they have Hospitality Rooms in which you can have a glass of juice while going over maps and sightseeing and restaurant recommendations with a friendly Hawaiian employee), and best of all, their very low flat rates (no mileage charges). For a compact manual, it's $18.95 daily; for a compact automatic, it's $19.95 daily. An air-conditioned sedan is only $21.95 daily. Comparable weekly rates are also available. Six- and nine-passenger station wagons and Lincoln town cars are also available. Call them on the courtesy phone when you arrive on Oahu or Kauai, and they'll come and get you, wiki wiki. On Maui at the Big Island, they're right at the airport. Holiday Rent-A-Car Hawaii is at 2918 Ualena St., Honolulu, HI 96819 (tel. 836-3944), but it's easier to give them a call on their toll-free reservations number: 800/367-2631.

The biggest budget car-rental operation on the islands? That's the local branch of the always-dependable mainland firm **Budget Rent-A-Car,** 2379 Kuhio Ave. (tel. 922-3600). They have a huge selection of foreign automatic American automatic compacts and sedans, sports sedans, and convertible Jeeps—a total of over 6300 new cars. Since rates fluctuate so much, Budget does not care to quote them, but you can be sure that they will be competitive. On the neighbor islands, Budget has offices at the Maui, Hawaii, and Kauai airports. And free admissions to major attractions on all islands, free meals, and free gifts are provided with each rental. Budget will rent to 21- to 24-year-olds with major credit cards. There are seven locations in Waikiki, and four at Honolulu Airport. For instant confirmation, call toll free 800/527-0700, or write to Budget Rent-A-Car of Hawaii, Central Reservations, P.O. Box 15188, Honolulu, HI 96815.

Friendly service and good deals are available at **Tropical Rent-A-Car Systems,** 550 Paiea St. (tel. 836-1041). They offer flat rates only (no mileage charges), compacts for as low as $19.95 a day, $108 to $120 "Super Saver" weekly specials; air-conditioned cars for $24.95 a day, $139.95 a week. They also have station wagons. Tropical has offices on all the neighbor islands, and rents to drivers 25 to 70 only, and not to campers. Tropical has two offices in Waikiki (call 922-2385) and a toll-free reservation number: 800/367-5140. Tropical can pick you up at all the airports; call them on the courtesy phones when you arrive in the baggage claim area. Rates are subject to change.

A variety of good deals are available from **American International Rent-A-Car,** which is the local affiliate of the fifth-largest worldwide car-rental company. American International services four major islands and offers their standard-transmission cars—Datsun, Toyota, and Mazda—for $17.95 a day, $92 weekly; these same cars with automatic transmission are $19.95 daily, $96 weekly. Written reservations should be sent to their Central Reservations Office at 3049 Ualena St., Honolulu, HI 96819 (tel. 833-3355). Again, they do not have airport space at Honolulu International Airport (they do at all the other airports), but they'll pick you up when you arrive and take you to their offices half a mile away.

Dollar Rent-A-Car of Hawaii is another enterprising outfit. They rent on Hawaii, Maui, Kauai, and Oahu at flat rates. For their compact cars with standard transmission, it's $22.95 daily; for the same cars with automatic transmission, it's $24.95 a day. They will rent to drivers over age 21 who have a major credit card. Their central reservation number is 922-6415.

Aloha Fun Cars, 2160 Kalakaua (tel. 836-2561), started small in Maui, and has recently expanded to all the major islands. They rent automatic compact cars at $21.95 daily, $131.70 weekly, with unlimited mileage. They are located at the airports in Honolulu, Maui, Kauai, Hilo, Kona, and also in Waikiki. For reservations from the mainland, the toll-free number is 800/367-2686.

National Car Rental of Hawaii, 2160 Kalakaua Ave. (tel. 922-3331), has locations at the airports on Oahu, Hawaii, Kauai, and Maui, and offers competitive unlimited-mileage rates for all types of cars, including station wagons and vans. The toll-free number is 800/CAR-RENT.

Thrifty Rent-A-Car has locations on Oahu, Maui, and Kauai (but not on Hawaii). They have direct-line courtesy phones at all baggage-claim areas. Usually, standard compacts rent for $19.95 daily, $109 weekly. New models, no mileage charge. Call 808/833-0046 for reservations, or write to them at 3039 Ualena St., Honolulu, HI 96819.

Royal Rainbow Rent-A-Car (tel. 836-3301) recently expanded from its Kauai operations (it's the only one to serve the Princeville area there) to an all-island service. Economy automatics rent for $23.99 daily, $129.99 on a weekly basis. Occasionally there's a discount offer that lowers the rates to $19.99 and $103.99. You can write them at 3049 Ualena St., Honolulu, HI 96819, or phone, toll free, 800/367-2651.

Avis Rent-A-Car, Honolulu International Airport (tel. 836-5511), serves all five major islands, and offers an "Aloha Special" for seven days of driving an automatic Chevy, Chevette, or similar car on a combination of two or more islands—about $119 a week. With every weekly rental, they offer Avis Unlimited Coupon books which, they say, can add up to $1500 at-home or on-the-road savings. Note: Avis will rent to 18-year-olds who have a major credit card. For toll-free reservations, phone 800/331-1717.

Hertz Rent-A-Car, 233 Keawe St., Room 625 (tel. 523-5181), features an All-Island touring rate that covers seven days or more on any combination of the four major islands. Days do not have to be consecutive and there is no mileage charge. The seven-day rate starts at $99.97, or $22.99 for one day. Daily rates offer free unlimited mileage. For toll-free reservations and information, call 800/654-8200; in Honolulu, 836-2511. Hertz has offices at airports and hotels on all the major islands, and will rent to 18-year-olds who have major credit cards.

General Note

Remember that automatic-shift cars always cost more than the standards and that there's a state tax of 4% added to all charges. Check, too, whether your rental charges include insurance and if so how much. Insurance should include public liability, property damage, fire, theft, and collision (usually $100 deductible, although many companies have much higher deductibles). If you carry insurance on your car at home, you might want to use your own insurance coverage for the rented car; this is sensible if your policy provides higher limits and if your company can furnish fast claim service in the islands. Using your own insurance can save you as much as $3 to $5 per day on rental charges. It would be a good idea to obtain the name of your company's local claim representative in Hawaii before you come; also bring your policy or identification card if you plan to do this.

You can arrange to have the car delivered to your hotel and picked up when you're finished with it. Usually, though, most people pick up and return their cars at the airport. A further tip: Since cars may not get regular servicing during the busy season, it would be a good idea to give yours a test run of a few hundred yards before the agency representative leaves you. They've been known to have quirks.

Also, it's a good idea to jot down the mileage on your car before you start out with it and just before you return it to the rental agency. This is a useful check on mileage charges.

And a final, important, word of warning. Don't be misled by those companies that offer cars for "$1 a day." Add to that mileage charges, plus a *50-mile daily minimum,* plus the cost of gas and insurance, and you're paying as much, probably more, than you would at the other agencies.

Advice for Younger Drivers

In the course of the years this book has been published, we have occasionally received letters from young readers who have had trouble renting cars in the islands. We have checked into the situation, and have come up with the following findings. Hawaii state law prohibits anyone under 18 from driving with an out-of-state license (even though islanders can get licenses at 15!). As far as we know, there are only two agencies willing to rent to those 18 to 20: **Hertz** and **Avis,** mentioned above. Major credit cards are necessary, and there is usually a daily charge for overall collision insurance. The same conditions apply to those under 25. There may be special stipulations for 21- to 24-year-olds. When you reach 25, of course, you can just sign the papers anywhere and drive away.

RENTING CAMPERS AND TRAILERS: Renting a camper in Hawaii used to be the ideal way to save money on both car rentals and hotel rooms. But now, with gas prices up so high, you'll have to do some careful figuring to know if it will really be a money-saver. But the camping areas on Hawaii's beaches and mountains are truly lovely, and immensely popular. All of the campers come fully equipped with good beds, pillows, blankets, pots and pans, stove, refrigerator or icebox; more deluxe models come with toilets and showers. You provide the gas. Costs are quite feasible for a large family or two couples traveling together. The best budget choice here would be **Beach Boys Campers,** 1720 Ala Moana (tel. 955-6381), which has a variety of recreational vehicles for rent on the four major islands. These start with a mini-cabover, which sleeps four, at $45; mini-motor homes begin at $55. Add 6¢ per mile to all prices. They service their clients seven days a week, but ask that there be no check-ins or out on Sunday or holidays. The price includes linens, dishes, and cookware. Collision insurance is $250 deductible.

The other major camping outfit is **Travel/Camp,** P.O. Box 11, Hilo, HI 96720 (tel. in Hilo: 935-7406). The oldest camper company in the business but serving only the Big Island, Travel/Camp has chassis-mounted motor homes, and mini-homes that are fully furnished and contain propane stoves, ovens, refrigerators, johns, hot-water showers, etc. Excellent U-Drive camper-oriented maps and complete itineraries are provided. Prices for recreational vehicles range from $50 to $90 a day for up to six sleepers, depending on the size of the vehicle. Be sure your reservations are all set before you go. They also rent cars, station wagons, vans, pickup trucks, and four-wheel-drives.

Note: See Readers' Selections in Chapter X for more details.

BIKING AROUND: Honolulu, like big cities everywhere, has become very cycle conscious. Bicycles used to be available for rental at a number of locations, but lately most of the hotels and rental agencies (like Hertz) have stopped renting them because of the high equipment mortality rate. "We kept finding them in the ocean," said one supplier. But we did find *one* place where they can still be rented: **Aloha Funway Rentals,** at 1982 Kalakaua Ave. (tel. 942-9696), offers them from $10 to $15 per 24-hour day; they also have tandems, Mopeds, and motorcycles, as well as snorkel equipment, underwater cameras, and boogie boards.

SKATING AROUND: Roller skating is no longer a big fad here, but should you get the urge, you can rent a pair from the above-mentioned **Aloha Funway Rentals** for moderate fees—$5 for 24 hours.

RICKSHAWS: Here's a novel—if not exactly inexpensive—way to get around Waikiki! **Pacific Pedicabs** has a number of them traveling on Kuhio and Kalakaua Avenues and connecting streets, between the Hawaiian Village Hotel and the Colony Surf Hotel (which covers a good part of the main part of Waikiki). Each Pedicab driver is an independent contractor and may charge passengers as he pleases. The ones we talked with asked $5 to $7 for 15 minutes, but they love to haggle and, if business is slow (as it often is due to the large proliferation of Pedicabs), you can ride for much less. Just be sure that you and the driver agree on price and distance before you hop in. The young people who sit on the bicycle seats and pedal you around, incidentally, all appear to be in excellent physical condition, tanned and handsome—making rickshaw drivers, unlike their counterparts in the Orient, altogether Hawaiian.

TAXIS: Honolulu taxi fares are not as rigidly regulated as they are in many other cities. No company may charge more than $1.40 for the first flip of the meter (Charley's, listed below, charges $1.20); it's usually $1.20 for each succeeding mile. Although they are not cheap, taxis are useful for emergencies and short trips and could be practical if four or five of you are traveling together. It's not always easy to find a cab cruising around (they have to report back to their stands when they don't have fares), but you can get one simply enough by calling any of the numerous companies listed in the telephone book. And you can often pick one up at the big hotels.

Here are the telephone numbers of a few taxi companies:

Charley's Taxi—531-1333 or 955-2211
Aloha State Cab—847-3566
Sida of Hawaii—836-0011
SR's Taxi and Tours—949-6444

GUIDED TOURS: If you're traveling alone, you'll have to invest about $18 (maybe more) for a guided tour around the island of Oahu. But, if there are at least two of you, renting a car slices the per-person expense considerably.

Even more cheaply, you can travel almost all the way around the island of Oahu for a mere 50¢ bus fare (details in Chapter VII). And economics aside, we believe there is no travel thrill like that of a do-it-yourself exploration of a new part of the world, where you make your own discoveries at your own pace, free to follow the intriguing bypaths that don't always appear on a planned itinerary. Best of all, you can throw your lunch and bathing suit in the back seat for a picnic or swim whenever you feel like it.

ADVICE FOR DRIVERS: A few words about driving in Honolulu. First of all, there's a remarkable extension of the aloha spirit to pedestrians, who are often considered fair game elsewhere in the world. The custom dates back to an old law from the days of the Hawaiian monarchy when the pedestrian had the right to lie down in the street. We doubt if you'll see anyone doing that, but traffic does stop for pedestrians crossing the street, provided they stick to the lights and the painted crosswalks at intersections and, of necessity, even if they don't. However, progress is catching up with the islands, and as it does, traffic—and manners—can get almost as bad as in the big mainland cities. But not quite—at least not yet.

Many of the major thoroughfares of Honolulu are now one-way streets, which helps the flow of traffic, but often makes it seem that you are driving miles out of your way to reach a specific destination; downtown Honolulu is an especially confusing place to drive in. You may want to keep in mind that in this area Beretania Street is ewa, King Street is Diamond Head, Pensacola traffic now heads makai (to the sea), and Piikoi cars go in a mauka (to the mountains) direction. In Waikiki, Kalakaua traffic is Diamond Head most of the way, with a short stretch downtown running in both directions; Kuhio Avenue and the Ala Wai Boulevard are ewa for most of their lengths.

Those painted white arrows on the various lanes are not to be ignored. They indicate in what directions you are permitted to drive from each lane: right only, left only, left and straight ahead, or right and straight ahead. It's legal to make right turns when the light is red at most intersections—but not all, so read the signs first. And if you come across a sign reading "We appreciate your kokua," it's not an invitation to pay a toll. Kokua means cooperation in Hawaiian.

Parking for the night can be a problem in the Waikiki area, where you may find yourself driving around and around the block. *Tip:* Ala Wai Boulevard, along the canal, is less crowded than other main thoroughfares (but cars must be off one side of the street by 6 a.m.). In the downtown area, there are both municipal and private parking lots. Street meters allow 20 minutes for a nickel, 40 minutes for a dime, one hour and 40 minutes for 20¢. In some busy locations the meters allow no more than 12 to 24 minutes. Read each meter carefully.

Mainland driving licenses may be used until expiration date. After that you'll need a Hawaiian license, obtainable from the Department of Motor Vehicles for $8.50, for those 18 and older.

READERS' TRANSPORTATION TIPS: "If a person is going to visit some of the attractions and/or plans to eat even one meal at other than the Jack-in-the-Box, and intends to rent a car for a drive to points around the island, rent the car before seeing the attractions. The freebies and discounts that come with many of the car rentals add up to some real savings. In other words, don't do something like taking a dinner cruise on a catamaran at full price and then learn you could have gone for free or at a substantial savings with a coupon that comes with a car rental" (The Ed Glassner Family, Kent, Ohio). . . . "We rented a small car from **Budget Rent-A-Car.** Their cars are of excellent quality, good prices, you get coupons for dollars off on other island attractions. We were very pleased and found Budget to have the best prices. Several of those places that advertise 'used cars' to rent for $7 to $9 a day are using false advertising—telling us that they don't have any of those types of cars in now and that they expect one in three weeks or so—a come-on!" (Paula Fisk, Greenwood, Ind.). . . . "We rented from Budget Rent-A-Car, $30 a day for an automatic Datsun 210—kind of high. They give out a lot of coupons, but please tell your readers you can only use your coupons while you are renting the car. You must show your car keys and/or your contract when you try to use a coupon. I don't really know if the free coupons were worth it. It might be cheaper to rent from a different agency without coupons" (Carl and Debbie Adams, St. Louis, Miss.). . . . "We felt the best deal on car rental was **V.I.P. Car Rentals,** 2463 Kuhio Ave., Honolulu, HI 96815 (tel. 946-1671). Basic rental on an automatic shift was $14.50 per day, unlimited mileage, and the car even came with a full tank of gas. (We did have to return it with a full tank of gas.) We asked for and were cheerfully given permission to return the car late—midnight" (Ken and Dorothy Gimblin, Sacramento, Calif.) [*Authors' Note:* Minimum age is 25. There's also a V.I.P. agency on Maui with the same low rates (tel. 887-2054).] . . . "I rented cars on all the islands except Lanai, and found parking at hotels and motels was quite limited in some cases. Fortunately, I always managed to get a spot. It would be wise to check that a hotel has parking available if you plan to rent a car. Also, be aware that some of the hotels, particularly in Honolulu, charge for parking" (Jane Kenney, Kingston, N.H.). . . . "If you're parking your car in Waikiki, try Fort DeRussy's huge parking lot (it's free) or the side streets near Kapiolani Park" (Jack Nakamoto, Ottawa, Ontario, Canada).

"Suggestions to drivers: You will be tagged for even one or two miles over the speed limit, and watch parking directions carefully. We parked in a driveway, in the evening, that had a closed fence around a vacant lot and obviously wasn't being used for anything that year—and received a ticket. Also watch the meters: around Fisherman's Wharf, for example, they *do not* stop at 6 p.m." (Sheila Pritchett, Villanova, Penna.). . . . "I thought you might appreciate hearing about the good service and product of a company I discovered on my recent trip to Hawaii. Following the advice of friends in Oahu, I arranged to rent a car from **United Car Rental Systems, Inc.,** at 234 Beach Walk in Waikiki. The representative I dealt with, Mr. Donald Asam, was exceptionally cordial and did not rush us in our decision like many other rental agencies in the other Hawaiian islands. Mr. Asam also knew a great deal about Oahu and gave me several suggestions about what to visit, where to dine, and the best—i.e., least crowded—times to go places. The rental car was clean, dependable, and, above all, reasonably priced" (Jay Adelstein, Washington, D.C.). [*Authors' Note:* United rents cars on the four major islands, and has a fleet of the latest model cars, from compacts to Cadillacs, vans, and Jeeps. Compact standards are $18.95 daily (sometimes they will go lower), $113.70 weekly; automatic compacts are $21.95 daily, $131.70 weekly.]

"Please remind people to lock rental cars even if leaving them just to take a picture. We met several people who stopped just to see a particularly scenic view and came back in less than five minutes to find coolers, cameras, whatever gone" (Sandy Abramovich, Thomaston, Conn.). . . . "It was interesting to take **TheBUS** to the New Windward Mall in Kaneohe (take no. 56 "Kailua-Kaneohe" or no. 52 "Kaneohe-Kailua." The mall has a Liberty House (with lunch specials), Penney's, Sears, etc., and is enclosed. The bus route over the Pali and Kaneohe Bay on no. 56 is scenic" (Marge O'Harra, Portland, Ore.). . . . "We found TheBUS quite difficult in Honolulu—usually crowded, slow, and uncomfortable, as well as hard to determine schedules. However, the "Guide" from a local paper helped. TheBUS is considering raising rush-hour fares to $1, and eliminating senior passes during those periods—

both moves strongly protested by riders" (Melvin H. Boyce, Corte Madera, Calif.). . . . "You are absolutely right about TheBUS. We could have gotten along without a car for a few more days by using TheBUS. It's easy to catch onto the routes as plenty of free information is available, and for price, TheBUS has to be one of the last bargains left on earth" (Robert and Jean Carroll, Helena, Mont.).

Chapter V

SHOPPING IN HONOLULU

MUUMUUS AND MACADAMIA NUTS, koa woods and calabashes, tapas and tiki figures—these suggest the exotic items for which you'll shop in the islands. Although Hawaii is not one of the great bargain shopping areas of the world (no free-port prices or favorable money exchange for dollar-bearing Americans), it still offers a fascinating assortment of things Polynesian, Oriental, and American for the inveterate browser and souvenir hunter. We'll skip the expensive items—jewelry, objets d'art, Oriental brocades and silk, elegant resort wear—and stick to the good buys for the shopper who wants quality and low prices—which is where you, the $35-a day'er, come in. Lately, a number of new shopping complexes, some of them geared to the affluent Japanese tourists, have opened in Honolulu and elsewhere on Oahu; we'll cover them here and tell you about shopping in the neighbor islands when we get to them.

1. Shops in Waikiki

Much of your island shopping can be done right in Waikiki: along Kalakaua Avenue and in the hotel gift shops, and at the International Market Place, King's Village, Royal Hawaiian Shopping Center, Hemmeter Center, the Waikiki Shopping Plaza, the Rainbow Bazaar, and the Kalakaua International Center. First we'll cover Waikiki in general, listing our recommendations by type of merchandise. Then we'll head for the special shopping areas and see what's up.

HAWAIIAN WEAR: Begin on the Avenue if you're looking for island muumuus, holomuus, aloha shirts, and such, which we've suggested you plan to buy here, in our earlier section on packing. Almost every shop carries these items, but be sure to take a look at the reliable Waikiki branches of Honolulu's major department stores—**Liberty House, Watumull's,** and **McInerny's**—where there are extremely attractive selections of clothing for men and women, and children too. There's nothing provincial about Liberty House, by the way; it has everything from swimsuits for baby at $6 up to designer sportswear separates at $300 and more. There are so many stores, on Kalakaua and in the hotels and shopping centers, that you could spend days and days just going from one to another. The manufacturers of Hawaiian clothing we like best include **Malihini of Hawaii, Bete, Lilia, Sun Babies, Nali'i, Princess Kaiulani, Dano, Tori Richards, Hilda,** and **Malama;** you'll find these brands all over town. Note too that most of the specialty shops will make up muumuus for mother, aloha shirts for dad, and junior versions of both for the kiddies in matching fabrics, and will also make clothes to your special size. (We should tell you that locals consider this very "touristy.") Many will make bikinis to order, or at least allow you to match the top of one to the bottom of another. Made-to-measure work usually takes just a day or two and in most cases costs no more than ready-made garments.

Prices for Hawaiian clothes are pretty standard everywhere: better muumuus average $30 to $40 short, $50 to $70 and up long. To realize substantial savings on aloha wear, your best bets are three places we'll tell you about under "Downtown Honolulu," ahead: Hilo Hattie's Fashion Center, Warehouse Showroom, and Muumuu Factory.

SOUVENIRS AND SMALL PRESENTS: Scads of Honolulu tourists swear by the low prices at the **ABC Discount Stores.** There are 18 ABC stores in Honolulu, in all the tourist areas. You can usually expect to save 20% to 25% here on small items, sometimes more. Hawaiian perfumes and macadamia nuts are always a bargain at ABC stores. Most are open seven days a week, from 7:30 a.m. to midnight. Most ABCs also have drugs, cosmetics, grocery sections, gift packages ready for mailing, deli, fresh produce, and liquor, and usually the lowest prices anywhere on Hawaiian scenic postcards.

A number of other stores cut the regular prices on standard items—perfumes, cosmetics, souvenirs—and you'll find quite a few of these shops on Kalakaua in the area just Diamond Head of Uluniu Avenue, up toward the Queen Kapiolani Hotel. You can also count on good buys at **Holiday Mart,** which you'll read about ahead. **Woolworth's,** in the Bank of Hawaii Building on Kalakaua, now charges more for some standard souvenir items than ABC and some of the other shops, but their discount on jade, coral, opal, and 14-karat gold items is good. (It's nice to know that they'll mail your gifts and souvenirs home for you.) **Long's Drugstore** in Ala Moana is another excellent, low-priced source for small items.

What to buy? Hawaiian perfumes make delightful small presents. Royal Hawaiian and Liana are the leading brand names for island fragrances—pikake, ginger, orchid, plumeria—all of them sweetly floral and worlds away from the sophistication of Paris. Gift packages complete with artificial orchids begin around $2.50. Royal Hawaiian's higher priced perfumes have a real orchid right in the bottle.

For Hawaiian jewelry that's both unusual and inexpensive, take a look at Pele's Tears and olivine, two stones found in fresh lava. Pele's Tears are drops of natural silica in dark-brownish to black shades; they make interesting earrings, which can be found for about $3.50 and up. Olivine has a lovely green cast and is sometimes called green diamond. Earrings run from about $4, and the stones are also used to decorate compacts and cigarette lighters.

The latest fashion in island jewelry is real flowers dipped in gold; prices start about $15 for orchid pins. We've also seen plumeria preserved in plastic so realistically that it looks natural, about $6.

Back to stones: Black coral, mined in the waters off Maui, is handsome in small tree shapes (about $10), and in numerous other pins and pendants. An exquisite pink coral called angelskin has also been found off Maui waters. Blue coral is the "look" with jeans and casual tops. You'll see all of these, in abundance, at jewelry stores all over the islands.

For carved wood, try **Blair's** with the largest selection in Hawaii. It's in the Outrigger Hotel on Kalakaua Avenue. Nothing here is a "bargain"; the woods are crafted with respect for the ancient Hawaiian traditions (all done in freehand) and that's what counts here. Blair's also makes to order superb free-form coffee tables in monkeypod or koa wood. For good buys in seconds of Blair's fine products, visit the factory store at 404 Ward Ave.; some items have small flaws, but they can be repaired, and the savings are huge. (Many of our readers have been happy with their purchases here.)

You can buy Hawaiian delicacies—such exotic tastes as guava jelly, coconut syrup, passion fruit ambrosia—at almost any grocery store, but should you want to send a package home, the best and most reasonably priced places are **Long's Drugs, ABC Discount,** and the **Waikiki A-1 Superette.** Prices for gift packages average $10 or $12.

There are shell stores in every beach city in the world, but to see shells treated as objects of art is something else again, and that's where **Shellworld Hawaii,** 2381 Kalakaua (near the Surfrider-Moana Hotel), comes into its own. Some of the shells are rare, some are simply naturally beautiful, many are mounted for sculptural display, and all come from Pacific waters—the Philippines, Japan, Australia, the Hawaiian Islands. Most shells are not inexpensive, but you could surface with a cowry shell for 60¢. Beaded shell curtains, $4 a strand, look nice in a doorway; you'll need about 25 to make a curtain—but what a curtain! There are more Shellworld shops at the Royal Hawaiian Shopping Center and the Kahala Hilton Hotel.

INTERNATIONAL MARKET PLACE: The oldest and most colorful shopping area in Waikiki, this place is still the most fun, despite the fact that its prices are apt to be a mite higher on the same items than they are in the department stores or Ala Moana Center. Still, with its enormous range of Hawaiian and Polynesian specialties—lauhala hats, shell and ivory earrings, woven placemats, tiki figures, woodcarvings, scrimshaw pendants, resort wear for the whole family, as well as other items ranging from T-shirts to Oriental rugs—there's nothing quite like it anywhere else. Informal, semi-open shops set around a giant banyan tree and interspersed among tropical plantings stay open until 11 at night, giving you plenty of time for al fresco browsing. A very entertaining scene, especially in the cool of evening.

You should be aware of two things when you shop at the International Market Place. One, comparison-shopping pays off; one booth might be selling T-shirts for $12, another one around the corner for $8 or $9. And lately we've noticed a bit of bargaining going on—it doesn't always work, but it could be worth a try.

There are two items in particular you might want to look for at the Market Place. One is polished kukui nuts, which resemble large black jewels, and sell for about $3. They usually come with their own black chain and make a handsome pendant. For around $25 to $35 you can treat yourself to a kukui nut lei (the same kind the male nightclub entertainers wear), a true island treasure. The other is tapa, an unusual fabric made from the bark of a tree and stenciled in handsome patterns; it was the original clothing of the primitive Polynesians. It can be worked into handsome tablecloths or draperies, but in quantity it's expensive. You might, however, pick up a two-foot square, back it with wood when you get home, and have an unusual wall hanging for just a few dollars. You can usually find tapa—as well as many other Polynesian crafts—at **Kalo's Polynesian Handicrafts.** Note the Tonga tapa bags, which start at $16, and the South Seas pareaus for about $27.

Shops come and go at the Market Place with great rapidity, so our best advice is simply to roam where fancy leads you. But do stop in at **Diamond and Ivory;** you can't miss it—you'll hear its windchimes tinkling in the wind. Wonderful windchimes go for all prices here, beginning with ones of ceramic pineapples at $8, of dolphins at $10. . . . **Diamond Palace** has everything from Playboy Bunny watches on up, including 14-karat gold Hawaiian charms from $10. They also offer a 40% discount on 14-karat gold chains. . . . **Harriet's Custom Made and Ready to Wear** has good selections of resort wear, and custom service if you desire. . . . They seem strange in Hawaii, but **NIJI** offers a good collection of western boots, cowboy hats, and an interesting collection of buckles. . . . We liked the straw baskets at the **Moon Lite Shop** on the second floor, and the mirrored good-luck elephants (from $2.75) at **Capricorn,** which also has a good selection of lamps, windchimes, jewelry, and dolls from Thailand. . . . You can watch carvers at work at several booths selling handmade candles, bedeck yourself with necklaces of "genuine fruit pits" (about $2.95) at others, watch the glassblower at work at **Little Glass Shack,** and pick up a new bag, if need be, at **That's My Bag,** to tote home all of your goodies.

ROYAL HAWAIIAN SHOPPING CENTER: Across Kalakaua from the International Market Place is Waikiki's newest shopping center, and in many respects its most exciting and sophisticated. "An oasis of green in Waikiki" is what the builders promised when ground was broken a few years ago, and despite the outcry against the lavish use of concrete, it's pretty much what they've delivered. Occupying three city blocks along Kalakaua Avenue between the Outrigger Hotel and Lewers Street, this stunning 6½-acre, 120-store complex is indeed graced with flowers and trees, ferns and shrubbery, and hundreds of trailing vines and Hawaiian plants. A high level of taste is evident in the shops, restaurants, and huge variety of entertainments, enough to keep the visitor happy and busy for a long time.

Number one on anybody's list here has to be the **China Friendship Store,** occupying the entire third floor of Building C. With its unique collection of affordable gifts and apparel from the People's Republic of China, this could well be the biggest Friendship Store anywhere ("Friendship Store" is the name the Chinese give to tourist stores selling arts-and-crafts merchandise). There are over 21,000 different items here, ranging in size from jewelry to furniture, in price from a few dollars up to the thousands: carvings, clothing, carpets, lacquerware, hand-embroidered linens, pure silk fabrics, bamboo, Peking glass, hand-turned vases, just to name a few. Even if you're just looking, thanks, be sure to drop by: frequent lectures (we wandered into one on acupuncture), arts-and-crafts demonstrations by artists from the People's Republic, travel films on China, fashion shows, and cooking demonstrations can be entertaining.

Chinese goods, sold on a much smaller scale, but all of excellent taste and at very fair prices, can be found in **China Marketplace** in Building C and **Peking Marketplace** in Building A. At China Marketplace, note the hand-painted goose eggs and Ping-Pong balls, $2.75 each; the whimsical animals—turkeys, owls—fashioned of split bamboo, from $2.95; and the cut wheat-stalk pictures at 95¢. Stop in to pick up a paper fan perhaps, only 25¢, at Peking Marketplace.

Although **Aki International** gives the impression of being an expensive shop, prices are quite reasonable for the quality handicrafts and embroidered wear imported from all over the world. Perfect for gifts are their hand-carved and hand-painted fish from the island of Bali, beginning at $2.95, and their Pacific mother-of-pearl pendants, starting at 50¢.

Look for the big quilted letters spelling out "Bazaar" on the third floor, Lewers Street end; this is **Handcrafter's Bazaar,** a quality showcase for arts and crafts handmade in Hawaii, a big cut above the ordinary. We loved the framed prints, the quilts, the Hawaiian dolls, the pottery, candles, and batiks. And there's much more—windchimes, hand-painted fabrics, jewelry, designer T-shirts, fish prints—at a wide range of prices. Shells mounted as nightlights were selling for $5.75 to $7.95.

Andrade's, long known for fine clothes for both men and women, has its largest store here on the second floor. Stop in to browse through its Princess Street, a collection of small boutiques. You can visit the White Butterfly and Backstreet boutiques for clothing, examine the nautical curios at Peddler's Port and the jade at House of Treasure, then stop for some refreshments—perhaps a pastry and a 25¢ cup of Kona coffee—at the Sweet Shoppe. For the bargains here, visit the Bargain Attic, which shows both local and mainland beachwear at discounts of 30% to 50%.

In the mood for browsing luxury shops? Take some time to browse through **McInerney's** big flagship store here, with a Hermès Boutique and a Sports Fashion Boutique too. . . . Visit **Lancel of Paris** (French luggage and leather goods) and **Les Must de Cartier** (jewelry and small gift items) on the first floor.

Be sure to visit the **Little Hawaiian Craft Shop,** where a fantastic assortment of unusual finished jewelry sits alongside buckets and barrels of raw materials, the same kind that were used by the ancient Hawaiians. This is a workshop for craftspeople using natural island materials in both traditional and contemporary styles. Replicas of museum pieces sit among $4 hand-carved tikis and buckets of 50¢ shells. They have some wonderful hard-to-find sandalwood necklaces—fragrant, lovely, and well priced, from about $18. Almost everything here is handmade in Hawaii.

Adjoining the Little Hawaiian Craft Shop and under the same management is the **Hawaiian Wood Shed,** an outstanding wood gallery that shows museum pieces from New Guinea as well as authentic replicas of Hawaiian artifacts: we liked the tapa beater ($35) and the poi pounder ($40), framed and ready to put on the wall. All their work is done in cooperation with the Bishop Museum, which receives part of their profits.

Particularly nice on the first floor is the **Hawaii Country Store,** a tasteful modern rendition of the old general store. It's a good place to pick up fresh fruit, cards, macadamia nuts, monkeypod carvings, and the like. We doubt if you could get a cup of espresso or cappuccino in a real country store, so its tiny café is most welcome, as is the snackbar, which dishes out sandwiches for about $1.75 and plate lunches under $3. This may be just the time to experience a real Hawaiian shave ice. The snack counter is open daily from 7:30 a.m. (8 a.m. on Sunday) until 8:30 p.m.

Where else can you eat here? We've already told you about some of our favorite sit-down restaurants in Chapter III (**Great Wok of China, La Mex, Suntory,** and **It's Greek to Me**). For a drink outdoors under the umbrellas, it's **Princess Puahi;** for a look at a private collection of Hawaiian art, it's **McDonald's,** on the second level. And for a unique ice-cream cone, it's **Copenhagen Cones,** which bakes waffle-like cones in an old-fashioned oven brought all the way from Scandinavia to Honolulu, stuffs them with ice cream, and tops them with home-made whipped cream and strawberries. Skol!

Plenty of free entertainment, arts and crafts exhibitions, hula lessons, and the like take place at the center on a continual basis; check the local papers for a schedule. Hawaiian entertainment is usually held on Monday, Wednesday, and Friday evenings from 6 to 8 p.m. and on Saturday from 9 to 11 a.m. Should you need information on where to find any of the shops or restaurants, or where to locate particular items, you can talk to a computer—or a real person on the computer screen—at the first-floor **information booth.**

Note: **Waikiki Medi-Mart,** in Building A-401A, is open 24 hours every day to provide medical treatment on a walk-in basis, no appointment necessary.

AN ORIENTAL EXCURSION—RAINBOW BAZAAR: Can't make it to Hong Kong or Tokyo for a shopping spree this year? Honolulu has a substitute of sorts: the Rainbow Bazaar at the Hilton Hawaiian Village Hotel. Authenticity has been stressed in the creation of this unique shopping complex, both in products and atmosphere; you enter through a Chinese moon gate, are serenaded by Japanese music in the background, and can shop for an intriguing selection of gifts from Japan, China (both the mainland and Taiwan), Korea, and the South Pacific. While some of the objets d'art, jewels, and brocades can get quite costly here, there are also loads of small things you can pick up, and it's certainly well worth your while to come and browse. You can have an inexpensive lunch or dinner at **Hatsuhana** or **J's Pancake House** while you're here. Have a look, too, at the grounds of the Hilton Hawaiian Village Hotel, which we always consider an entertainment in itself.

It's nice to wander where fancy leads you here, but let us tell you about a few of our personal favorites. **House of Jade** has beautiful baubles at fantastic prices, as well as pretty trivia like coral stickpins: black, $5, and pink, $6. . . . You'll find real Japanese fans, from $1, as well as resort wear, at **Lani Wear.** . . . **Nautilus of the Pacific** is the place for all manner of shells and items crafted from shells; you can't go wrong with pink coral "trees" at $2.98. . . . **Exotic Fair** is known for their footwear; if you need an extra pair of shoes for touring the islands, have a look here. They also feature locally made, one-of-a-kind, crocheted tops. . . . **Far East Antiquities** is best known for its miniature 25¢ brass abacuses, ivory and jade carvings, netsukes and antique silk embroideries. The price range is wide here, from "pearly necklaces" made in Japan over 20 years ago, 5¢ an inch, to Mandarin necklaces from 18th-century Tibet, in silver, coral, jade, and turquoise, $200. . . . We saw beautiful woodcarvings—bowls, figurines, wood roses—at **House of Kea.** . . . Trusty branches here, too, of Honolulu's better known stores like **Alfred Shaheen** and **Liberty House.**

KING'S VILLAGE: It's supposed to look like a 19th-century European town, with its cobblestone streets and old-fashioned architecture, but

King's Village is very much a part of modern Honolulu. Behind the gates at the corner of Koa and Kaiulani Avenues (across the street from the Hyatt Regency Waikiki, at Hemmeter Center) is a cozy bazaar that contains a variety of shops, several restaurants, and an open market—all done up in a style that recalls the 19th-century monarchy period of Hawaiian history, when royal palaces were built in Honolulu, and Hawaiian kings and queens journeyed to London to be presented at the court of Queen Victoria.

The shops, however, are not so much European as the typical Honolulu-international mix, with lots of Oriental and Polynesian crafts, plus plenty of Hawaiian resort wear and souvenirs. All are small and in good taste; King's Village is a commercial venture, certainly, but there's no commercial ugliness about it. We think you'll enjoy browsing here.

As at Rainbow Bazaar, prices go from just a little to quite a lot. Despite its name, **Harriet's Custom Made Ready to Wear** is not necessarily expensive; prices begin at around $20 for short muumuus, $40 for long ones. You select your material and your size, and they make your garment in a day or two. (See the Readers' Selections, at the end of this chapter, for a report on their outstanding work.) . . . Gift items galore—scrimshaw, nautical accessories, buckles, and a wide selection of brass decorative items—abound at the **Royal Peddlar,** starting at just a few dollars. . . . You can get a mushroom candle for $2 at **Candle Odysseys. . . . Jacqueline's Bikini Shop** (Jacqueline is the wife of an island entertainer Danny Kaleikini) has luscious resort wear in addition to those teeny bikinis, starting at around $24. . . . You can take home a cute Hawaiian love god for all of $1.98, courtesy of **Hime,** an intriguing woodcarving shop, which also has a milo woodcarving of Madame Pele for $400. . . . **Cal-Oahu Fabrics** features vibrant prints with which to make your own aloha clothing, plus patterns. The fabric is hung in the shape of a dress and matched with appropriate necklaces. Two panels, enough for a dress or a skirt, begin at $16.50. . . . Need suntan oil, perfume, bath soaps, and such? Stop in at **Good Scents of America**. . . . There's a large branch of the ever-popular **Crazy Shirts** here: we love the hula-dancing cat design. . . . If you've locked your real diamonds in the vault while you travel, visit the people at **Windsor Jewels.** They specialize in fake diamonds "that won't tell unless you do."

Unless you've wisely chosen to visit King's Village early in the morning or after the sun goes down—it tends to get very hot in midday—you may want to sit around the fountain up top and cool off for a bit under the canopy. You can also cool off very nicely and have a pleasant lunch or snack at **Café Old World,** a pâtisserie full of European charm, with tiled floors and lace tablecloths, white soda chairs, a mural of Venice on the wall. Displayed outside in a revolving case are the luscious European pastries—Black Forest cake, gâteau St. Honoré, napoleons (here they're strawberry kiwi napoleons), and more. Inside, to go with them, are coffee, espresso, and cappuccino, and sandwiches in the $4.50 to $5 range. And it's always good fun to stop by for a drink or a meal (steak-and-mushroom pie, quiche Lorraine, a variety of salads, and hearty sandwiches, in the $4.50 to $6.50 range) at a new-old English pub, **The Rose and Crown.** There's a long Happy Hour here, from 11:30 a.m. to 7 p.m.

There's more to do at King's Village than shop and eat. There are the King's Village Honor Guards to watch, so wax-like that they should be at Madame Tussaud's. The changing of the guard ceremony takes place every night at 6:15, followed at 6:30 by a drawing for free gifts donated by King's

Village merchants. There are often free shows; watch the papers for specific times. You can also hop the Bishop Museum's doubledecker London bus for the trip to the Bishop Museum here.

HEMMETER CENTER: Towering 44 stories above Kalakaua Avenue between Kaiulani and Uluniu Avenues, the multi-million-dollar Hemmeter Center, topped by the very posh and expensive Hyatt Regency Hotel, houses a beautiful and elegant shopping complex. You may do more sightseeing than actual shopping here, but see if you must. The shops surround the central courtyard in three tiers; a spectacular waterfall splashes from the third tier into a crystal pool in the courtyard below. The center part of the courtyard is open at the top, a massive metal sculpture hovers above, and beyond that is the sky. Striking metal sculptures inhabit the pool too. At night the courtyard is lit by massive polished brass lampposts. Combined with the brick-red ceramic tile floor, it all creates an effect that is at once modern Hawaii and Hawaiian monarchy, each style complementing the other superbly. Sweeping staircases lead to the two upper tiers of shops, as do unobtrusive escalators.

As for the shops, they are a quality collection, and many—like the elegant **Paris Boutiques, Gucci,** and **Bugatti**—are in line with the pricey atmosphere of this place. But there are several others for the budget-wise: **Watumull's** offers family-priced clothing, as do **Leilani, K. & K. International,** and **Hawaii Fashions.** . . . **Sure Things** has some of the loveliest dresses, long and short, that we've seen in Honolulu. Owner Jacqueline Kaleikini (who runs Jacqueline's Bikinis at King's Village) picks up French material in Tahiti and has the dresses created here. Not inexpensive, but very, very special. . . . **Cotton Cargo** has some neat togs for women. . . . **Tots 'n' Teens** has lots of clothes for keikis, as well as accessories for teens and younger. . . . The **Royal Peddlar** is known for gifts-in-depth, including handsome chess sets and nautical curios. . . . Pick your favorite gems: there are plenty of sources to choose from. The **Coral Grotto, House of Opal, House of Jade,** and the **Pearl Factory** are all here. . . . There's lots of fancy footwork to be seen at **Islander Thongs.** . . . Discover the intricate folk art of the People's Republic of China at **Camelot East.** . . . And ogle the handsome sculpture at **Bennett Sculpture,** the works of international and Hawaiian artists at **Center Art Gallery.**

Hemmeter Center shops are open daily from 9 a.m. to 11 p.m.

WAIKIKI SHOPPING PLAZA: The first impression one gets on seeing the enclosed Waikiki Shopping Plaza, 2250 Kalakaua Ave., corner of Seaside, is that it more properly belongs in New York or San Francisco or some sophisticated European city. Shops like Roberta di Camerino, Courrèges, Bally of Switzerland, Ferragamo, and many versions of the ubiquitous Paris shops have little to do with the islands. But as you ascend the escalators to the four shopping floors, it gets better and more versatile, with more of an island flavor. The traffic-stopper here is the five-story fountain by island designer Bruce Hopper, a wondrous, half-million-dollar creation with lights that change colors, and fascinating Plexiglass spheres and bubbles that make the waters dance. There's a different point of interest at each level, creating new surprises as you ride the escalators.

As you walk in, you can check out those pricey boutiques in the **Yokahama Okadaya** store, and then turn to the serious business of buying all kinds of souvenirs, food, aloha wear, and more at the enormous **Hawaii Discount Mart.** . . . More acres of souvenir-type items, including their own hand-carved candles and carved woods, await at **Polynesian Fair.** . . . Check the racks at **Villa Roma,** a high-fashion shop for women (they often run clearances on sports items for women) and also ogle the pretties at their other shop, **Chocolates for Breakfast,** with delectable designer women's clothing. . . . **Maleka's Attic** has charming women's clothing too, with a lot of crochet work. . . . You can pick up some cute Japanese children's novelties at **Okadaya:** a darling T-shirt reads "Hello, Kitty." . . . **Ocean Sports Wear** has good bargains: factory-direct purchases, special buys, and closeouts. . . . Stock up on some reading matter at **Waldenbooks,** which has a very large selection. . . . Collectors and investors can find museum-quality antiquities from the lands of the Bible at **Ancient Art.** Prices begin at $15 for Roman coins and go up into the thousands. . . . At the **Center Art Gallery,** they were featuring paintings by Red Skelton, which only prove that, as a painter, he is a very good comic!

No shopping complex is complete these days without an electronic games area: this one is no exception. **Plaza Games** has Space Invaders and the rest of the beep-beeping diversions.

While most of the shops at the Waikiki Shopping Plaza are not budget-oriented, the basement restaurants certainly are, with a bevy of fast-food counters offering varied ethnic foods. **Marco Polo,** on the fourth floor, also has great prices (see Chapter III's restaurants). And in the fourth-floor showroom, nightly at 6:30 and 8:30 p.m., there's a hula show, **Waikiki Calls.** You and your cameras are welcome, free.

BEATING THE HIGH PRICE OF POI—FOOD SHOPPING: If you're going to do any cooking in your kitchenette apartment, you're also going to be shocked when you do your first shopping for groceries. Food costs in Honolulu are substantially higher than in big cities on the mainland (almost one-third more, in some cases), and if you pick up your groceries in the hotel shops, sometimes much more than that. (We were stunned recently to have to pay almost $1 more on a quart of grapefruit juice in a hotel shop than it cost in a nearby supermarket.) The hotel shops are a convenience, and we're glad to have them, but if you're going to do any serious shopping, you're far better off to take your U-Drive and head for the supermarkets. The big Honolulu chains are **Star, Times, Safeway,** and **Foodland** (and **Emjay's,** a subsidiary of Foodland.) There are several of each of these, with addresses in the phonebook. **Parkview-Gem** on Ward Ave. and **Holiday Mart,** 801 Kaheka St. (two blocks mauka of the Ala Moana Shopping Center), also offers low prices. In Waikiki, best food prices (albeit on limited selections) are at the **ABC Discount Stores.**

Natural foods are generally not inexpensive, so we were delighted to find "healthy food at prices that don't make you sick" at **Down to Earth Natural Foods,** 2525 S. King St. (tel. 947-7678), near University Avenue. A recent poll taken by *Honolulu* magazine rated this friendly place as the best overall natural-food store in Honolulu. The markup is low, with prices consistently cheaper than at other stores. All products, including vitamin and mineral supplements, are totally vegetarian. And a full-service snackbar is open from 10 a.m. to 8:30 p.m., serving tasty, healthy food at low prices.

Terrific baked goods—freshly baked whole-grain breads (oatmeal, raisin, cinnamon, sprouted wheat), pies, and cakes—are the main reason for tracking down one of the popular **Vim and Vigor** stores: there's one at Ala Moana Center (in the rear of the complex), another at 1009 University Ave., near the University of Hawaii campus, and a third at Kahala Mall. They also have good prices on an extensive selection of dried fruits, nut butters, fresh produce, and many other natural and organic items. Their snackbars are great too.

If you'd like to shop for produce, fish, and meat with the local people, be sure to visit the **Ala Moana Farmer's Market** (a block in from the Ala Moana–Ward intersection at Auahi Street), where the atmosphere is pungent and the prices low. It's a great place to get acquainted with local Hawaiian foods and taste sensations. The long, low building is lined with a number of stalls, some with ready-to-eat items. Here you can sample poi, raw fish, and other delicacies such as ogo, palu, and tako. In case you're not feeling all that adventurous, you can settle for a 12-ounce can of New Zealand corned beef or imu kalua pig, both cooked and ready for your own private luau. At **Haili's Hawaiian Foods,** in business since 1867, we saw one-day and two-day poi and even sour poi, all quite difficult to find.

Get yourself downtown to **King's Bakery** at 1936 S. King St. (tel. 941-5211), which makes an incredibly delicious sweet bread that they will package and mail to the folks back home. There's a charge of $1 for a sturdy box to hold six loaves; loaves are $1.50 each. You can sometimes find them sold at the airport, just before you reach the gate to board your plane.

Need cookies for dessert or a nibble? The **Waikiki Chipyard,** centrally located at 2301 Kuhio Ave., uses all pure ingredients in its chocolate-chip cookies, charges around $2 a dozen, and will also sell you some ice-cold milk. You may recognize the place from its sister shops in Fanueil Hall Market in Boston and in Newport Beach, California.

SHOPPING FOR SURFERS: If you're really serious about surfing, or learning to surf, let us point you in the direction of **Lightning Bolt Unlimited Surf Company** at 1503 Kapiolani Blvd., near the Ala Moana Shopping Center (tel. 941-1502). Any surfer will tell you that in order to learn to surf safely and joyously you need good instruction and a well-constructed board. Many of those for rent at beach stands are outdated. Hence the need for a service like the one at Lightning Bolt, which will sell you a board and agree in writing to buy it back when you leave for $35 to $50 less for every week that you've used it. If you want to invest in a board to take home, this is also the place. All boards bear the Lightning Bolt name and are handcrafted to exacting standards. Owner-manager Jack Shipley will be happy to advise you, if he's not off somewhere judging an international surfing meet. All the friendly staff members, in fact, are surfers.

Store hours will most likely be from 10 a.m. to 7 p.m. Monday to Friday, until 5 p.m. on Saturday, and from 11 a.m. to 3 p.m. on Sunday.

2. Ala Moana Center

Honolulu's fabulous modern shopping center (one of the world's largest), just across the Ala Moana Beach from Waikiki, is an example of island architecture at its best. Landscaped with trees, flowers, fountains, and meandering stream down its Central Mall, which is graced with large works of sculpture, it's always packed with enough island families to make it worth seeing for that reason alone. But the stores are, of course, the main attraction—more than 150 of them, an international bazaar full of intriguing wares. We'll mention just a few, but shopping buffs will come back here many, many times. (From Waikiki, take the no. 8 bus or the Ala Moana shuttle bus from Kalakaua Avenue, in the block of the Princess Kaiulani Hotel.) The center is only ten minutes away.

One of Hawaii's biggest department stores, **Sears Roebuck,** is here, with the usual mainland amenities and the unusual Hawaiian specialties—like orchid plants (Sears will ship to the mainland and guarantees live delivery), and a tremendous selection of muumuus and island clothing at very reasonable prices. **J.C. Penney** is known for fashion and for excellent value in all departments. The flagship store of **Liberty House** is here, and most striking it is, its eaves decorated with Hawaiian tapas. **Watumull's** the **Ritz,** and **McInerny** (at 132 years, Hawaii's oldest specialty store) are represented too, and there are good selections and buys at all these places.

But we prefer to browse around the large Japanese department stores, **Shirokiya, Iida's,** and **Hotei-Ya.** Shirokiya has superb and often elegant wares: beautiful fabrics; good buys in cameras and radios; unusual women's jewelry, Hawaiian and Oriental, starting at low prices. You can also stock up here on Japanese cosmetics, should the mood strike you. Its Shibui Art Gallery has exquisite art objects, and a large selection of Japanese woodblock prints at reasonable prices. In another section is the kind of Oriental supermarket you'd find in Tokyo, offering such fascinating staples as a bottle of powdered sea urchins. As for the Hotei-Ya store, its nicest feature is the Japanese music you hear throughout. It's coming from the record department in back, a fascinating place where you can stare at the record jackets and wonder what music goes with what album. You might want to pick up a few recordings of Japanese popular songs; Toshiba and King are the labels. *Fashion note:* Shirokiya stores also carry stretch socks, with a separate space for the big toe, to wear with zoris.

There are also dozens of small shops in the center, reflecting just about every interest and taste. **Summer's Place** is a lovely gift shop full of precious stuff, notably scrimshaw, dollhouse miniatures, windchimes, and unusual greeting cards. They have another shop at Pearlridge Center. . . . **Paniolo Trading** has clothes and accessories for the equestrian (paniolo means "cowboy" in Hawaiian). . . . For the must-be-modern set, there are some marvelous boutiques here. **The Daisy Pot** is full of utterly feminine clothes, exciting sportswear, and accessories, as well as whimsical boutique gift treasures. Not a bargain store, but everything of great quality for the price.

Quality is also the word at **Villa Roma,** the fashion boutique always first with the newest—be it the classic, contemporary, or nostalgic looks, local crafts, what-have-you. The Japanese high-fashion designers are all the rage here at the moment. Tops, dresses, jewelry, and one-of-a-kind finds make this shop a big hit with the local people. . . . **Chocolates for Breakfast** has the sort of elegant clothing for women that never goes out of fashion. . . . **Prides of New Zealand** seems a bit incongruous in hot Hawaii, selling woolen sweaters, sheep-skin rugs, and sheepskin car seats, but the people here swear that sheepskin is cool. . . . **Louis Vuitton** luggage is, of course, the tops in elegance. . . . Stop in at **Musashiya** for wonderful patterns and fabrics, or pick up a surfboard at lively **Hawaiian Island Sports.** . . . You'll find a great selection of hand-carved pipes at **Tobaccos of Hawaii.**

Tahiti Imports, one of the most ubiquitous clothing shops in the islands, takes Tahitian pareu prints of their own design and makes them into muumuus (short muumuus average $30, long ones around $40), aloha shirts, bikinis, and pareaus. They also sell their exquisite hand-printed fabrics by the yard.

Need some decorating ideas? Stop in at the **Art Board,** which shows striking posters, many with an Oriental motif. Prices begin low: we saw Japanese block prints at $8, three for $20. . . . **Carol & Mary** is tops on our personal list, with sophisticated clothing that looks at home in Honolulu—or anywhere on the mainland. Hard-to-find junior lines are available here, and they have some really gorgeous full-tilt tutu (granny) muus in distinctive fabrics. Everything is nicely priced. . . . **Fumi's** is another show-stopper for women's clothes, with a line that might be described as demure but come-hither. . . . Best known for conservative men's and boy's wear, beautifully made and well priced, **Reyn's** also features good-looking women's clothes as well. Many shops on Oahu, Maui, and Kauai. . . . **Irene's Hawaiian Gifts** features unusual carvings from native woods and collectors' items made in Hawaii at good prices. . . . Candles in the shape of Hawaiian tikis and pineapples make novel presents. You'll find them at the **Hale Kukui Candle Shop**. . . . Check in at the big **Vim and Vigor Health Food Store** for excellent selections of honeys, nut butters, whole grains, organic foods, superb home-baked goods that should not be missed, and other healthies. . . . Stop in, too, at the **Crackseed Center,** if you want to know what island youngsters clamor for (crackseeds, originally a Chinese confection, are a cross between seeds and candies, very sticky, very tasty).

Chocaholics will find the temptations at Ala Moana hard to resist. If you're trying to break the habit, pretend you don't know that there's usually a woman working in the window at **La Maison de Chocolate,** hand-dipping plump, luscious, fresh strawberries into chocolate, and that you can buy one, sold by the weight, for about 60¢. Ignore the information that McInerny's harbors a branch of **Krön Chocolatier,** the famous New York store, whose chocolates are right up there at the top with Godiva's. And forget we ever told you about **Mrs. Field's Chocolate Chippery,** which turns out warm and moist cookies studded with chips, sold individually, or by the pound at $4.19.

One of the most intriguing stores at Ala Moana is the **Foodland Supermarket.** It's like an international food fair, reflecting the cultures that make up Hawaii—and the rest of the world. You walk along seemingly endless aisles of exotic foods: fresh-frozen coconut milk, a Hawaiian laulau all ready to take home (pork, taro leaves, or butterfish wrapped in ti leaves), packages of weird-looking Japanese dried fish, kosher foods, health foods, tortillas, English biscuits, French cheese, you name it—if it's edible, this place has got it. You can, in addition, pick up some okolehao, Hawaii's potent ti-root drink, in the large liquor department. If life has become boring in that little kitchenette of yours, don't miss a visit here. There's also an inexpensive souvenir section.

For more bargains in souvenirs and small items at Ala Moana, it's trusty old **ABC Discount Stores, Long's,** and **Woolworth's.**

The best bargains at Ala Moana are available when the stores take to the sidewalks—the ground-floor level that is—displaying racks and racks of clothing for very low prices.

Remember the center, too, for free entertainment during local holidays and at special ethnic celebrations; you may catch a Japanese or Philippine dance group, a Hawaiian show, or some of the island's top nightclub entertainers. For years now, the **Young People's Hula Show,** presented every Sunday at 9:30 a.m. on the Centerstage has been a

Honolulu institution. Don't miss it. Hawaiian entertainment by **Hookalei's Hula Halau** is often presented during the summer months on Tuesday and Thursday at 2 p.m.

RESTAURANTS AT ALA MOANA: Since most people don't want to take time to leave the area to eat, Ala Moana has quite a few eat-and-run and take-out places; you can eat either in the tiny restaurants themselves, or take a plate to the mall outside. The food is typically an island mix, prices are modest (and do not usually rise at dinner), and you may find it cheaper to eat your meals here than at home in your kitchenette apartment. Most of the restaurants are located at the street level, not too far in any direction from the center escalator.

A big favorite (readers keep writing and praising the food year after year) is **Patti's Chinese Kitchen,** where you can dine at attractive tables inside the restaurant, or pick up your food from the cafeteria-style counter and take it out. Plate lunches with rice or noodles and a choice of any two items are $2.55; with three items, it's $3.15; and with four, $3.75. Selections might include Peking-style roast duck, beef with broccoli, shrimp roll, shoyu chicken, sweet-and-sour fish, crispy almond duck, ad delicious infinitum. You can take home a half pint of duck for $2.45, as well as orders of the other dishes (prices are subject to change). As for us, we simply can't pass this place, mealtime or not, without stopping in for som(ıanapua at the bakery counter. Fill up a bag with the likes of black sugar moon cakes, bow ties, or coconut joi doi, each 30¢, grab a cup of coffee at the counter, sit down at a bench, and feast. They also have goodies like candied Chinese squash, lily root, and water chestnuts, for snacking at home.

Two doors away from the original Chinese Kitchen is **Patti's Noodle Kitchen,** featuring noodle-and-rice dishes and casseroles. The house special is old-fashioned kai see min at $3.25; another favorite, cake noodle with boneless chicken, is also $3.25.

Crowds also flock to **Lyn's Delicatessen,** one of the best kosher-style delis in town. There's lots of space here, and the hungry throngs will be lapping up $2.25 corned beef sandwiches or lox and bagel; most sandwiches are served on rye or a roll, and they come with pickles and cole slaw. You can custom-build your hot plate by selecting items like chicken thighs, wonton, corn on the cob. For the best buy on a steak dinner in town, come to Lyn's any Monday through Friday evening from 4 to 8:30 p.m. when, for $3.59, you'll get a New York–style steak with dinner rolls, tossed salad, vegetable, and broasted potato or rice.

Adjoining Lyn's is **Little Sicily Pizza,** which serves up New York–style brick-oven pies by the slice (95¢). Subs on Italian bread are $1.75, and a whole bambino vegetarian pizza is $2.75.

Lovely, strong-smelling cheese and salamis suspended by ropes from the ceiling make the **Bella Italia** look like a real Italian trattoria. Here's a place to sit down and relax. A hearty lunch could consist of a big meatball sandwich on a french loaf at $2.95, or a big submarine and a bowl of thick soup at $3. Come for dinner too: the veal dishes—parmigiana, piccata, and scalappine at $7.25—are well prepared, and the shrimp scampi is tasty. Complete meals begin at $3.50 for spaghetti with meat sauce, and include salad, garlic bread, and beverage.

Eat Mexican on the cheap at **La Cocina Mexican Food.** Most complete dinners include soup or salad, rice, refried beans with melted cheese, plus entree and beverage, and only cost between $5.50 and $6.95. À la carte you can have chile rellenos, huevos rancheros, burrito verde, and other Tex-Mex tasties. This is an attractive place with booths and partitions. There's a take-out booth for Mexican food next door.

There must be plenty of natural-food enthusiasts in Honolulu; they mob the wonderful take-out counter at **Vim and Vigor** every lunchtime. Enchiladas, quiches, salads, and natural-style pizza are ready to go, not to mention sandwiches made of tofu steaks, zucchini parmesan, Vigor burger, and the like—all bulging with sprouts, shaved carrots, and sunflower seeds, and only costing $2.45 to $2.90. There's a hot soup and a vegetarian chile every day. Try one of their cooling fruit smoothies in the middle of a hot Honolulu afternoon. Too bad there's no seating area, but there are benches outside. If you like unusual breads, take home a loaf of whole-wheat sweet bread, sprouted wheat, or carrot-onion!

There's a fresh, natural feeling about **The Haven,** a charmingly decorated place (tile floors, murals on the wall, banners hanging from the ceiling), and the emphasis here is on natural foods as well as on more traditional sandwiches like meat, turkey, and shrimp. It's one of the few places at Ala Moana where you can sit down at booths and tables to enjoy your meal. They feature freshly baked quiche, baked stuffed potatoes, and thick, homemade soups. Among the unusual natural sandwiches, all served on a choice of breads with lettuce or sprouts and tomatoes, are combinations of mushrooms, olives, parsley, and sour cream at $3 and avocado and tomato at $3.20. There are also good meat sandwiches, salads, and super desserts, like banana-nut bread at 75¢. End your meal with hot spiced apple cider, herb teas, fresh juices, or a 50¢ cup of Kona coffee with as many free refills as you like.

On that same rear level, you can join local Japanese families having dinner, from 4 to 8 p.m., at **Wong's Okazu-ya.** That's when they prepare such Japanese specialties as shoyu butter fish with tofu and vegetables, sukiyaki, and combination tempura plates, from about $5 to $8. Meals include soup, tsukemono, rice, and tea. The rest of the day, from 8 a.m. to 4 p.m., they'll fix you up with a hearty bowl of wonton min, saimin, or special rahmen for $2.75 to $3.95.

Not in Ala Moana Center itself, but on the mall level of the Ala Moana Building next door, is **Heidi's Bread Basket,** which offers gourmet sandwiches with a German flavor. It's a cute little place with red-checkered tablecloths where you can have your braunschweiger, Bavarian liverwurst, or Westphalian ham, among others, served on Heidi's stellar home-baked breads. Sandwiches go from about $2.50 to $3.50. German applecake for dessert, of course. There are also good breads to take home.

VITAL STATISTICS: Most Ala Moana Center establishments stay open seven days a week, opening at 9:30 a.m. Monday through Saturday, at 10 a.m. on Sunday. They close at 9 p.m. Monday through Friday, at 5:30 p.m. on Saturday, and at 5 p.m. on Sunday. From Kalakaua Avenue in Waikiki, you can take the no. 8 bus and you'll be at Ala Moana in about ten minutes. Parking areas are numerous—and they even have coconut palms coming through the concrete!

3. Around Town

WARD WAREHOUSE: One of the most eye-catching of Honolulu's shopping centers is Ward Warehouse, located at Ward Avenue between

Auahi Street and Ala Moana, across from Fisherman's Wharf. More than 70 shops and restaurants occupy the handsome two-story structures fashioned out of great rough-hewn planks, and there seems to be a higher-than-usual level of taste and selectivity here. Many are decorator shops of interest primarily to residents, but there is an equal number to delight the visitor.

Right up at the top of the list is **Rare Discovery,** a gallery-shop of collectibles. While most of the magnificent handcrafted works here—art glass, English enameled boxes, hanging stoneware fish tanks, ceramics, hand-sculpted jewelry, fine woodcarvings, Russian lacquer miniature paintings—are a bit out of the budget range, there are many small gift items: stationery, sachets, ceramic mugs, stained-glass nightlights, sculptured boxes of domestic and imported woods. On every visit, we marvel again at the high standard of taste here. Try their Hawaiian Plantation preserves and cookies. Rare Discovery will ship anywhere in the U.S. mainland, as well as to Alaska, so no need to worry about getting these lovely things home. . . . Another dazzling showplace for handcrafts is the **Artist's Guild,** a working gallery and outlet for many local craftpersons: you'll see beautiful ceramics, leaded glass, macramé, fine furniture made of local hardwoods, scrimshaw, jewelry, modern and traditional metal sculpture, soft sculpture, and finely detailed leather goods. Have a look at the Gyotaku—fish rubbings by island artist Michael Hemperly. These are framed prints of local schools of fish done in iridescent colors, according to the ancient Japanese technique. From $50, framed—not bad for a fine home decoration. Note the Old Hawaiian prints (from $9), and the lovely Japanese pillows, too. . . . There's a wheel and kiln in the back of **Exhibit,** where you're welcome to watch Charles Higa, the featured ceramicist, and several other associates turn out lovely handmade a mug, $12 pottery, mugs, plates, and planters. Prices start at $5 for a mug, $12 planters and $100 and up sculpture. Unusual necklaces studded with porcelain and Egyptian beads are about $20. They also have "oshibana"—handmade note cards featuring pressed Hawaiian flowers and leaves secured with rice paper in the Japanese manner, for $1—and chopstick rests in the shape of fish for $2.

Those weary of seeing the same clothing in every store should stop in to see **Kinnari,** where Yupin, a lissome Thai lady, designs creative dresses, skirts, and blouses; a touch of appliqué floral design, patchwork, or hand-embroidery sets each apart from the others. Considering the quality and the fact that minor alterations are included in the price of the garment, the price for long dresses—$80 and up—is competitive. There are dresses for children too, from sizes 1 up to 9 or 10. . . . **Birkenstock Footprints** is the place to buy those ugly-looking, marvelous-feeling naturally contoured Birkenstock sandals that give you a "barefoot on the beach" sensation even on hard surfaces. They're for men, women, and kids of all ages, and the average price is $50 for adults, $40 for children.

With your feet all nice and comfy, you're ready to continue your explorations of Ward Warehouse. You may want to pick up some Christmas ornaments from **Kris Kringle's Den,** some fine music boxes at **Erida's,** or lovely Japanese clothing and prints at **Manyo Gallery.** . . . A local friend reports she has found a jeans shop that discounts famous-name jeans, ladies' tops, and men's shirts and tops as well. It's **Jeans Warehouse,** where tops can run as low as $5. . . . The **Executive Chef** is for the compulsive cook: we saw wine glasses, cookie molds, French copperware, and other kitchen joys, at good prices. . . . And **Pause 'n' Paw** has the veritable something for everyone, from stuffed animals and pop-art home decor to scrimshaw jewelry.

If you like to collect, or just like to look, don't miss **G. D. Peters, Inc.,** purveyors of Hawaiian collectibles, which can help you collect Hawaiian money and stamps, books and scrimshaw. . . . Conscientious Honolulu mommies shop **Child's Play** for creative play and learning materials, educational toys, and books. An excellent selection. . . . And they find precious children's clothing at **Giggles**. . . . Don't miss **Strawberry Patches** if you're handy with needle and thread. With their beautiful fabrics and patterns, you could put together a batik dress for about $20. And they also have Hawaiian quilting thumb thimbles at $20, should the need arise. . . . **Spanky's** has some attractive Sansei T-shirts of silky cotton, made in China, plus clothing for men and women. . . . You can get gorgeous fans among the Chinese arts and crafts at **Chien Ho Gallery,** the traditional pottery of Okinawa at **Arts of Okinawa.**

End your excursion, perhaps, at the **Coffee Works,** a charming little shop that purveys all manner of imported coffees, teas, and chocolates, as well as some very attractive vessels from which to sip them. Coffee makers too. Happiness is a slice of carrot cake and a cup of Café Vienna, served from their tiny coffee bar.

We've told you about the **Chowder House** for a quick seafood meal, the *Old Spaghetti Factory,* for pasta in a fabulous setting, **Yum Yum Tree** for good food in a lovely open atmosphere, and **Upstart Crow & Co.,** a combination bookstore/restaurant, for good food and good reading to a soothing background of classical music. For light snacks, choose among **Yami Yogurt, Harpo's** for pizza, the **Cookie Kitchen** and **Fudge Works** for calories. There are outside tables on the lower level.

Ward Warehouse shopping hours are 10 a.m. to 9 p.m. Monday through Friday, until 5 p.m. on Saturday, and from 11 a.m. to 4 p.m. on Sunday. Restaurants stay open late into the evening. It's a 15-minute ride from Waikiki on bus no. 8.

WARD CENTRE: Down the road a block at 1200 Ala Moana Blvd., Ward Centre is a worthy follow-up to Ward Warehouse, another sophisticated collection of boutiques and restaurants, all with a high level of charm and taste. And speaking of taste, you may find it hard to leave **Napa Valley Grocery Company** without bringing home lots of goodies to indulge in. This is Honolulu's ultimate gourmet store, with a mind-boggling selection of imported cheeses, wonderful croissants and pastries, imported vinegars and herbs, cold pasta salads, and many dishes that you can take home for dinner in your kitchenette apartment. If you find the prices a bit high, settle for some freshly baked butterscotch cookies by Unknown Jerome. Umm! Thus fortified, you can proceed to explore other attractive shops, like **Peony Arts,** full of exquisite, hand-embroidered linens from the People's Republic of China. All the embroidery or "drawnwork" here—tablecloths, pillow cases, cushions, lace wear, pure silk blouses—is handmade. Treat yourself, at least, to a handkerchief—from $1.79 to $9, depending on the workmanship. . . . Moms-in-waiting or those who've already delivered will find **In Bloom** just what they've been looking for: attractive maternity and baby clothes under one roof. . . . When the kids are a little bigger, you can get them some clothes at **Chocolate Mousse,** then start their collection of dollhouse miniatures at **My Favorite Things.**

Some of the most beautiful arrangements of protea we've seen in the islands can be found at **Jenny's Garden;** they'll mail their floral arrangements and plants anywhere, and they also have attractive cards and novelties. . . . You can pick up a swimsuit from a dazzling selection at **Viva,** attractive women's shoes, handbags, and sportswear at **The Shop for Pappagallo,** and spend big bucks for those little polo player emblems at **Polo/Ralph Lauren.**

Of course you should eat at Ward Centre: the only problem will be in deciding among **Rox San Pâtisseries, Crêpe Fever, Monterey Bay Canners,** and **Ryan's Parkplace** (see restaurants, in Chapter III, for guidance). Again, take bus no. 8 from Waikiki, a 15-minute ride.

DOWNTOWN HONOLULU: Downtown is where the local people do most of their shopping, and we'll let you in on a kamaaina secret known to very few tourists. Head for 1 N. King St., where **Liberty House's Penthouse** is located. Discounted merchandise from all the Liberty House stores around town is brought here, and the initial reduction is a whopping 50%. On top of that, the price is automatically dropped 25% every 14 days. Most of the items consist of women's and children's clothing and women's designer shoes, but occasionally you'll see men's aloha shirts and other men's wear, as well. On a recent shopping foray we found $40 leather handbags at $20, $50 dresses at $25, a $45 peignoir and nightie at $22, and an $8 half-slip for $3.99. Enough said? This is one of those places where on some days you'll find nothing suitable, on other days you'll strike it rich!

The rest of Liberty House and the other Fort Street stores have merchandise similar to what you find in their Waikiki and Ala Moana branches, but perhaps a shade more citified, since they cater mostly to a local trade. It's fun to come here during the lunch hour, when island people are shopping, eating lunch on the many stone benches and seats that dot this fountained area, and watching their kids play in the sand. Traffic is closed off, creating one long window-shopping promenade. If you're hungry, stop off at any of the restaurants or fast-food stands mentioned in Chapter III (**Rada's Piroshki** is at 1144-46 Fort Street Mall).

We promise you'll come out smiling after a visit to **Rainbows and Smiles,** 1105 Bishop St., an enchanting little gift and toy shop in the heart of downtown Honolulu. The specialty of the house is bears. There are all sorts of stuffed bears, bear pictures, and teddy bear posters, and best of all, an adorable array of stuffed bears wearing costumes to fit their names: Amelia Bearheart (in her flight jacket and goggles); Bearishnikov, garbed in tights and ballet slippers; Scarlett O'Beara, the southern belle; Running Bear, in jogging suit and running shoes; and Green Bearet, in military garb. There's even Bare Bear, in the altogether (horrors!) in bright yellow, red, blue, or green. These big, beautiful, very well-made bears cost about $39. We know several adults who would love one of these. There are also well-priced items in glassware, jewelry, accessories, and boutique-y household ware—and the largest selection of rainbow-related gift items in the state!

If garment factories appeal to you, there's one you can be taken to, free and with extras thrown in. The **Hilo Hattie's Fashion Center,** at 440 Kuwili St., offers something like 20,000 Hawaiian fashions to browse through, all for sale at factory prices, plus free refreshments, free alterations, a lei greeting, and even a free bus trip to its doors. (They'll also take you to the Dole Pineapple Cannery.) Phone 537-2926 or check the tourist papers to find out where you can pick up the Fashion Center Fun Bus, or simply take bus no. 8 marked "Airport" from Waikiki or Ala Moana.

THE CHINATOWN LEI SELLERS: When local people need to buy leis, they usually head for Chinatown—and so should you. Although leis are sold all over town, especially at the airport and on the ocean side of Kalakaua Avenue, the best prices and finest quality can usually be found among the Chinatown lei sellers. There are several stores on Maunakea Street; three of our favorites are **Cindy's Lei Shoppe** at no. 1034, **Violet's** at 1110 Maunakea, and **Jenny's Lei Stand** at no. 1036. Cindy's carries the largest selection of flower leis in the state, and all three make up orchid, plumeria, double carnation, and other leis, at prices ranging from $2 to $8 and up, depending on the season and the availability of flowers. Should you want to send leis to your friends back home—a lovely but no longer inexpensive gift—the price, including shipping charges, ranges from $10 to $12 and up. We also like the flowers—and the low prices—at **Chiyo's,** located inside and at the front of the Thrifty Drugstore at 3610 Waialae Ave. in the Waialae-Kahala area. You can shop by phone (tel. 734-6337 or 737-5055), and be assured that your order will be well and speedily taken care of. They'll bill you later.

Sending leis to the West Coast is perfectly safe (they should reach their destination in about two days), but to the East Coast it's chancy; we've found that they sometimes sit around the post office and arrive in a rather droopy condition. So it's best, if you'll see your friends within a day or two of your arrival, to carry them yourself. Better still, give your friends the flower leis your Hawaiian friends will doubtless drape around your neck as they bid you aloha—if you can bear to part with them.

Buyers beware: The most expensive times to buy leis are May Day, the graduation season (end of May), and New Year's; that's when $2.50 vanda leis can suddenly become $12!

FOR RENT: If you need to rent something while you're in Honolulu—maybe a TV set or a radio, a stroller, even wheelchairs or crutches, we have a terrific place to recommend: **Dyan's Rental.** Their rates are low, they deliver to your hotel cheerfully and promptly, and they're very nice to do business with. Just call them at 531-5207 and a delivery boy will emerge from their huge downtown warehouse with exactly what you need.

BARGAIN HUNTERS' HEAVENS: A mecca for penny-pinchers, **Holiday Mart** is in a residential neighborhood at 801 Kaheka St. (two blocks mauka of the Ala Moana Shopping Center). It's a huge discount store, jammed with local people busy buying everything from groceries to books to toys to toasters, all at fat discounts. Buys are especially good in Hawaiian wear for men, women, and keikis. We also spotted a swim board for which we had paid $6.95 at a gift shop on Kauai for $3.99 here; a boogie board on sale for $40 here, regularly $55 (and $59 in other stores); macadamia nuts at $2.79 for a five-ounce tin; kukui-nut leis for $4.49; and Hawaiian records for $6.99—all very good prices indeed.

Those who sew should note the selection of Polynesian fabrics from about $4.49 a yard. And while you're here, stock up on groceries and booze—the prices are excellent, much better than in the smaller stores at the beach. If it's time for lunch, you can join the crowd at the outside Chinese cafeteria deli, which has a good take-out department as well as some 20 items on the steam table. Holiday Mart is open every day, from 8:30 a.m. to midnight, until 8 p.m. on Sunday.

The best place in Honolulu to buy monkeypod and koa pieces—which make wonderful gifts for friends or yourself—is the new **Warehouse Showroom** at 501A Cooke St. in the Kakaako industrial area, not far from the Civic Center. It's easily located on any street map. The Warehouse is a bit off the main drag, it's true, but you can't beat the bargains anywhere. We saw the kind of big, beautiful monkeypod serving bowls that start elsewhere at $25, for $12 and up here. Individual salad bowls are priced from $3.50, intricately carved candleholders decorated with dolphins are $6.25 each, and elegant footed compotes are priced from $10.75 to $15. Charming monkeypod animals are about $10. There are items made of Koa, mango, and milo wood as well. We compared similar items in one of the best department stores and found the prices twice as high and the quality and grain of the wood less pleasing.

As if all that weren't enough, Warehouse Showroom has recently begun to offer its own original casual-wear designs, which are made right on the premises in their upstairs loft. They make very attractive aloha shirts in tapa and other prints, and you can't beat the price—$15 to $25 for shirts that would easily cost twice that much elsewhere. We saw some lovely long dresses in very tasteful prints and solids priced from $15 to $22.50, and a stylish street-length dress with matching jacket for $20—a steal! Adorable aloha shirts and shorts sets for little boys are priced at $9.50. The clothing is also wholesaled to other outlets under three labels: Summer Palace, Chief Honolulu, and Rainbow Rags. The prices, of course, are lower here, since the middleman is eliminated.

Warehouse Showroom belongs to Ivy and Gale Gabbard, who have a wonderful shop called **Tramp Steamer on Kauai;** eventually, the Honolulu shop will have even more good things, among them appliquéed and embroidered hangings from China, reproductions of antique Hawaiian bottles, paperweights, and much more. The Warehouse Showroom is open from 8:30 a.m. to 5 p.m. Monday through Saturday. Some local friends of ours definitely plan to do their Christmas shopping here!

Women who like the attractive Nali'i Fashions muumuus, which sell for $60 to $80 in the regular stores, should hie to the **Muumuu Factory** at 818 Keeaumoku St.: it's the factory outlet for this manufacturer, and here the prices are never more than $35 for long dresses. During their very frequent sales—which seem to last for weeks—prices are even less: all long muumuus are $25; all shorties, $19. This is a good-size shop with wall-to-wall muumus, and while the number of styles is limited, each style comes in a variety of fabrics in all sizes, so you're very likely to find the dress you want in the fabric you like best.

AT THE ZOO: Honolulu Zoo has a little gift shop called the **Zootique,** filled with toys, books, kites, apparel, jewelry, and novelties with birds and animal themes. Our special favorites are the T-shirts made especially for the zoo with sayings like "Lion on the Grass at Honolulu Zoo" or "See You Later, Alligator," with appropriate line drawings underneath. Ceramic brooches of lions and tigers and parrots are fun, and so are the charming little gold gecko (lizard) pendants. Perhaps you'll walk away with some pop-up books, a stuffed animal or two, and the tote bags and backpacks sporting the zoo's logo. The Zootique is open until 3:30 p.m. every day, and all proceeds go to the Honolulu Zoo Hui, a nonprofit organization of friends of the zoo who raise funds for zoo improvements and educational programs. Since volunteers run the shop, prices can be kept lower than at many other establishments.

AT FOSTER BOTANIC GARDEN: A small gift shop at the entrance to Foster Botanic Garden is worth your attention if you'd like to stock up on film, postal cards, and cuttings and seeds of Hawaiian flora—all properly inspected by the Department of Agriculture—to take home and plant. They also have some very pretty T-shirts, silkscreened with designs of various Hawaiian flowers, praised from $9 to $10.50, as well as note cards, jewelry (we like the fragrant sandalwood beads), and a good selection of botany and gardening-related books.

THE CAT'S MEOW: Feline fanciers will have a cat fit when they see all the wonderful cat-related items at **The Cat House,** on the ground floor of Century Center, 1750 Kalakaua Ave. at Kapiolani Boulevard (tel. 949-3119). Owner Larry Goulet (a delightful, red-haired gentleman who is undoubtedly the cat's pajamas) has assembled a tremendous assortment of wooden, ceramic, metal, and anything-else-you-can-think-of cat ornaments, ranging in price from $3 to $5000. There are museum reproductions of sacred Egyptian cats, a cuddly variety of stuffed toys (Garfield and Felix are well represented), not to mention cat stationery, notebooks, stickers, mugs, plates, and what-have-you. Larry is also the only distributor we know of in the islands who has memorabilia of that smash London/Broadway musical entitled—you know. He has the T-shirts ($14), sweatshirts ($21), the beach towel ($30), and the book of the show. And even if you don't love cats, it's a trip just to go in and chat with Larry on just about any subject.

KAHALA MALL: Still haven't had enough of shopping malls? Hop into your U-Drive, go up Kapahulu to Lanalillo Freeway East, exit at Waialae, and you'll find yourself at Kahala Mall, part of the big Waialae Kahala Shopping Complex which the local folks love. Kahala Mall is an enclosed shopping center, with a main lobby like that of a hotel—carpeted and decorated with a beautiful fountain and plantings. Stretching out in various directions from the lobby are a bevy of interesting stores. The big chains like **Liberty House, McInerny, Carol & Mary, Andrade, J.C. Penney, Long's Drugs,** and **Woolworth's** are represented, of course, but there are also smaller, unusual stores, like **Hickory Farms,** a fascinating gourmet mart where you'll find everything from meat products to kosher dills to Danish cheeses to old-fashioned apple butter and stick candies. It's a good place to get picnic supplies, as well as gift packages of jams, jellies, cheeses, etc. . . . **Cotton Cargo** bursts at the seams with lovely, pricey clothes—mostly from Mexico and India. . . . Both custom-made and ready-to-wear couture clothing, plus accessories and jewelry, draw the cognoscenti to **Fabrications.** . . . Unhappy with the high price of most muumuus? Try **Especially for You,** which has beautiful ones, and all at reasonable prices: $22.95 to $39.95. They have five other shops around town. . . . The **Curious Porpoise** is chock full of tasteful and unusual gifts. . . . Thai silk,

Java batiks, antique chests, obi table runners, gorgeous caftans—all represent "the very best of Asia" at **Fabulous Things Ltd.,** an offshoot of the San Francisco emporium. Prices start at under $1 and go up into the thousands. . . . **Jennie's Garden** has a good selection of leis, cut flowers, arrangements, and quality houseplants. . . . The size range goes up to 14 at **Familiar,** which has darling clothes for children. . . . A full line of silk-screened and iron-on decal shirts are a specialty at **India Imports International.** . . . And **Morrow's Nut House** can supply you with macadamia nuts—freshly roasted every day.

Worth a special trip is **Following Sea,** a shop-gallery which represents the work of some 350 professional craft artists from 40 states, and sponsors outstanding monthly exhibitions. Everything is unique, and the inventory changes constantly. Prices range from a little to a lot, but there is a fine selection of ceramics, woodwork, and jewelry in the $15 to $20 range. Their most popular items are hand-blown oil lamps, from $34. On a recent visit we saw heavy glass paperweights from San Francisco in gorgeous colors and designs, from $20, and exquisite leaded-glass boxes each with a beautiful seashell set into the top, from $25 to $38. They are working with local crafts people to develop new and unique items. Save this place for gifts for some special person—or for yourself.

After you've explored the mall, go outside and see the other stores in the shopping complex; **Vim and Vigor,** for example, has one of the best assortments of natural-food items in the city. Top off your shopping excursion with a snack or a meal at the **Yum-Yum Tree,** a restaurant enormously popular with the neighborhood people for its well-priced food, deft service, and friendly atmosphere. Be sure to try a slice of their incredibly good pies—strawberry cheese and English toffee are among the choices; you'll want to take a whole pie home with you. Or enjoy a delicious northern Chinese meal at **Yen King,** one of the best such restaurants in these parts.

KILOHANA SQUARE: A far cry from the sleek modernity of Kahala Mall, **Kilohana Square** looks as if it comes right out of Hawaii's past. Drive up Kapahulu Avenue from Waikiki to the 1000 block (one block makai of the H-1 Freeway), and you'll come to a cluster of buildings surrounding a square and a parking lot. The atmosphere is more European flea market than shopping center, and indeed Kilohana Square seems more devoted to arts and crafts than to ordinary commerce.

You'll have fun browsing through the antique shops, galleries, craft stores, and boutiques, whose wares spill out into the street. Most of the items at **Something Special!** are just that: bamboo chopsticks with burnt-in designs ($1.50 for a bundle of ten); colorful tableware from China and Japan (from 50¢ to $10); hand-screened T-shirts of favorite local foodstuffs ($6.95 for children, $9.95 to $16.95 for adults), sushi refrigerator magnets, and their charming ceramic manapua (Chinese dumpling) paperweight, packed in a Chinese restaurant take-out container, are just a few of the selected items from at least ten different countries.

Needlepoint, Etc., could get you interested in the art if you're not already addicted. They have hundreds of beautiful needlepoint kits and canvases, with both Hawaiian and Oriental themes. . . . **The Trunk** specializes in muumuus and casual wear for queen-size ladies—size 16 and up. It's the only store in Hawaii that does so. And they also have a full line of swimwear and lingerie for "big, beautiful women." . . . And the **Flower Mill** abounds in things decorative, with the accent on exotic dried flowers and foliage.

AT MANOA MARKETPLACE: One of the most charming shops in Honolulu has to be **Distractions,** in a neighborhood shopping center at 2752 Woodlawn Dr. This browser's paradise is the only place we know in Hawaii that carries those elegant Caswell-Massey toiletries from England, such as cucumber soap, lotion and skin creams, English rosewater, and bewitching essential perfume oils. Teddy bears are a big item here (we're partial to the pastel rainbow-striped ones with blank faces), as are teddy bear T-shirts, posters, and stationery. There's a varied collection of unusual greeting cards and gift wraps, as well as beautifully designed writing paper. English jams and relishes abound, as do all sorts of bright desk accessories, including hand-painted wooden letters and ornaments to glue onto plaques for signs. Prices are modest. We never seem to be able to leave here without getting something new and different.

EATON SQUARE: Talking garbage cans are the big attraction at pretty little Eaton Square, a neighborhood convenience shopping center for residents of the village condominium complex on Hobron Square (near the Ilikai Hotel, two blocks mauka of Ala Moana Boulevard). Although the shops here are mostly of the utilitarian variety, with the exception of an art gallery and a jewelry store, the talking garbage cans could well be rated as a kiddy tourist attraction. Toss them something or put your hand inside to activate the device that sets the recording off and you will hear any of a dozen or so kooky messages spoken in pidgin. For example: "Thank you much—to you it's garbage, to me it's cash in the bank" or (bugle call) "Charge, people, charge into Eaton Square. But please, leave your garbage with me."

NEAR THE BISHOP MUSEUM: **Nake'u Awai,** at 1613 Houghtailing St., is a bit out of the way—unless you combine it with a visit to the Bishop Museum—but it is worth a trip if you like the unusual in fabrics and design. Joel Nake'u Awai is a young Hawaiian designer whose beautiful silk-screened fabrics are a blend of the traditional and the contemporary in Hawaiian art. After he designs and executes the textiles, he has them whipped up into long skirts, shirts, muumuus, bags, and sun dresses. While not cheap, the prices are certainly competitive with those of the better department stores and specialty shops; and the designs are exclusive. We also saw some very good-looking T-shirts with Hawaiian designs for $10 and up, and some pretty brooches made of clay with bright glazes—a fish, an anthurium, a lei-seller—for $4.16 and up. The shop is open only until 2 p.m., and is closed on Sunday.

PEARLRIDGE SHOPPING CENTER: Out in Aiea, about a half-hour drive from Waikiki, is Pearlridge Shopping Center, a multi-million-dollar complex that tops even Ala Moana in size and is a big favorite with the local people. Its design is unique. The two, huge, air-conditioned malls at Pearlridge are built on opposite sides of an 11-acre watercress farm.

Shoppers travel between the two malls in Hawaii's only monorail train, "The Pali Momi Express." From your perch in the Hawaiian-looking, orange and yellow monorail, you enjoy a panoramic view of Pearl Harbor along the way.

As at most of the shopping centers catering to the local trade, familiar names like Liberty House, Sears, J.C. Penney, and Long's Drugs dominate the scene. But the largest retailer in Tokyo is also represented here, and you'll feel as if you're right in Tokyo when you walk into **Daiei.** There's no attempt at artful display here; everything is just put out and people paw through it happily. This place is really an adventure. Its first floor is a supermarket of Oriental foods, plus a Japanese bakery that offers such authentic goodies as an pan (a bean-filled roll) and shoku pan (Japanese white bread). The second floor features kimonos, books, records, Japanese housewares, and popular character toys from Japan—as well as a huge Japanese restaurant and snackbar. And Daiei's third floor is a catalog showroom whose prices are not to be believed! Here you'll find some of the best prices in town on Hawaiian heirloom jewelry, jades, toys, cameras, TVs, stereos, and appliances.

In between the big stores, you'll find some fascinating smaller shops. The **Little Hawaiian Craft Shop** features handmade jewelry of natural Hawaiian materials: shells, nuts, and replicas of ancient island hieroglyphics (individual nuts and shells are in the $1 to $5 range). They also have a large selection of rare Niihau shells, Hawaiian woodcarvings, feather hatbands, lauhala weavings, plus other native handcrafts from Fiji, the Solomon Islands, Tahiti, and Tonga. . . . **Seed City** is filled with island delicacies like candied fruits and spicy crackers, all favorites with local people.

For those who must have the very latest in far-out fashions, Pearlridge is an embarrassment of riches: **San Francisco Rag Shop, Jazzy Boutique, Wildflowers, Pepperkorn,** the **Body Shop, American Denim Company, Ethel's Jeans West,** and **Foxmoor Casuals** all stock the foxiest of threads.

The kids will love **Playwell,** jammed with just about every imaginable kind of toy. The new $750,000 **Fernandez Fun Factory,** in the Pearlridge Makai (toward the sea) Mall, must be one of the world's fanciest "penny arcades." It features the newest, most elaborate electronic games. This is the main one; there are four branches around the island.

Shirokiya in one mall and **Fortuna** in the other feature captivating art objects from the Orient.

Hungry? Pearlridge "brings the world to you" with **Chuck's Steak House; Monterey Bay Canners; Anna Millers** coffeeshop, with a fancier restaurant, the **Round House,** downstairs; two Chinese restaurants: the **Pearlridge Chinese Kitchen** and **Shanghai Restaurant;** a Mexican café, **La Paloma.** For lighter meals, there's **Arby's, Hana Chicken, Uncle John's Pancake House,** and **Central Park.** And with two **McDonald's, Orange Julius, Soft Frozen Yami Yogurt,** a health-food cafeteria, **Vim and Vigor,** and **Farrells and Swensen's Ice Cream Parlours,** plus **Häagen Däzs and Baskin-Robbins,** there's something for every taste.

Official store hours at Pearlridge are from 10 a.m. to 9 p.m. weekdays, 10 a.m. to 5 p.m. on Saturday, and 11 a.m. to 4 p.m. on Sunday. You can easily squeeze your visit to Pearlridge into your trip to Pearl Harbor or to Makaha. If you're driving to Pearl Harbor on Kam Highway, you see it on your right just after you reach Pearl Harbor's entrance to the *Arizona* Memorial. If you're driving out the H-1 Freeway, take the Aiea exit. When driving out the Lunalilo Freeway from downtown, you'll see Pearlridge on the freeway directory signs. By bus, take the no. 20 from Waikiki to Pearlridge.

READERS' SHOPPING SUGGESTIONS: "My favorite shop in Kilohana Square is the **Pacific Book House.** The shop of rare and out-of-print books, with its attractive display cases, its friendly proprietress, and vast selection kept me happily occupied during one rainy afternoon. . . . A plus at the Kodak Hula Show: after the show I purchased all the shell necklaces I needed for gifts at the stands by the exit, at the same reasonable prices as the discount stores, but more variety, and I received a bonus for buying so many. Beautiful silk hibiscus leis were reasonably priced; I did not see these anywhere else" (Elizabeth C. Greer, El Cerrito, Calif.). . . . "We shopped several places for leis and found the best price was the booth in front of United Car Rental at 234 Beach Walk. This very friendly lady made sure our flowers were fresh the morning we left. Full orchid leis—up to $8 elsewhere—were $3 each. Coming back from the Polynesian Cultural Center we bought delicious pineapples from a roadside stand for 75¢ each. Since we were returning to Alaska we had no agricultural inspection and brought ten home for gifts. Perhaps one could take some to the airport ahead of time for inspection to see if they could be taken to other parts of the country. Anyway, at this price, you can eat your fill" (Sharon Wells, Anchorage, Alaska).

"We saw the process of living within a budget as a challenge and with your help did well with our program. We found the prices jumping about as we went from store to store, with the best prices at the newly opened **Waikiki Plaza Discount Mart.** It's well worth the bus ride to go to **Holiday Mart, Foodland,** or other major markets to beat prices like $1.05 per quart for milk, $1.67 for frozen peas in butter sauce, and $1.69 for bread, especially when one shopping was largely sufficient for the week. That's because restaurant prices are incredibly low in many places. Imagine $1.50 for breakfast at the **Village Tavern** in the Waikiki Village Hotel! The **Buccaneer,** around the corner, has the same hotcakes and eggs with bacon plus coffee for $1.99" (Melvin H. Boyce, Corte Madera, Calif.).

"I'm a size 44, and it took me six visits to find a place where I could get the kind of aloha wear I want, in a size that will fit me. **Harriet's Custom Made Ready-to-Wear,** on the top level in King's Village, doesn't have large sizes on its display racks, but they will take your measurements and specifications (length, diameter of sleeve opening, do you want a vent and how deep, pockets or not and where, where you prefer the first button, etc., etc.) and make up your garment from your selection of fabric. The finished product is ready for pickup in two days, and they make sure that a seamstress is standing by in case you decide you need any sort of alteration or adjustment. I had two made for me out of tapa pattern material—almost impossible to find in on-the-rack styles—and couldn't have been more pleased. The material was matched so well by the seamstress that it was difficult to see where the two side patch pockets were! The cost was $35 each, but the material and workmanship will last for years to come. They make everything: shirts, long and short muumuus, etc." (Leilani Moyers, Patterson, N.Y.)

"After taking the free bus tour to Hilo Hattie's Fashion Center at 440 Kuwili St., we noticed the **Salvation Army store.** We asked if they minded if we walked over there after visiting their factory, and they said, 'Of course, not, just come back anytime for the free bus trip back to Waikiki.' I found three muumuus and three Hawaiian skirts for $20. Wow—what a good deal, and fun to boot!" (Mark and Kay Irwin, Phoenix, Ariz.). . . . "We shopped nearly everywhere but found our best buys and variety of selections at **Luau Sportswear,** way back in the International Market Place. T-shirts were $4, short muumuus began at $18, and men's shirts began at $15" (Trish Donaghey, Garland, Texas). . . . "If you can cook, see if you can find uncooked macadamia nuts and roast them yourself: 12 ounces cost me $4, considerably cheaper than 5 ounces for $2 in a can. They are unsalted, and will keep in a refrigerator or freezer. Occasionally there are sales on macadamia nuts at the **Macadamia Nut Factory** on Kalakaua which even beats the prices at Long's Drug Store and other comparable places. I purchased six cans of five-ounce whole nuts for $10.95" (Barbara Karchin, Naperville, Ill.). . . . "We found the shopping centers to be well planned, very modern and quite expensive. We discovered that the **Swap**

Meet at Aloha Stadium was a bargain hunter's paradise. So very many new items, never before used, with prices sometimes at only one-fifth the cost of what the downtown shopping centers were asking. It was open each Saturday and Sunday from 6 a.m. to 3 p.m." (Jerald R. Borgie, San Diego, Calif.).

"Being a collector of militaria, I was thrilled to find the **Military Shop of Hawaii,** 1921 Kalakaua Ave. (tel. 942-3414). It is the best I have ever seen; the clerk told me it is the largest in the United States. They mail-order all over the world and are open every day. One whole wall is covered with military patches from all the services—a beautiful and interesting sight, even for the noncollector. They also have a large military book section—truly a fascinating place. It was formerly part of Fort DeRussy Museum" (David M. Banks, Paxtons, Mass.). . . . "We discovered **Mrs. Field's Chocolate Chip Cookie Store** on the lower level of Ala Moana. It sells the most delicious chocolate-chip cookies we have ever tasted—and we have tried them all. You can buy them with milk chocolate, dark chocolate, nuts, no nuts, etc., etc., and they are all fabulous" (Barbara Pocras, Lincoln, Neb.). . . . "**Gifts by Ko,** a shop in the Grand Hyatt Hotel, has beautiful ceramic mugs with your name written on one side and translated into Hawaiian on the other. The cost is only $3.99; 24 hours' ordering time is required" (Randi Bernstein, Woodhaven, N.Y.).

"A tip for people who want to buy leis to bring back: Don't buy them at the airport; the airport lei shops will rip you off for about $7 to $10 a lei. **Sears** at Ala Moana sells single orchid leis for about $5 that should last up to four or five days after you get back if you keep them refrigerated in plastic bags. The florist shops near the university will sell leis for $2 to $2.50 if you walk in trying to look local. . . . Clothing is very reasonable compared in price to the Ala Moana Shopping Center shops at the **Family Resort Shop,** 2276 Kalakaua, ground floor in the Waikiki Business Plaza. They are very polite and have a good general selection" (Randy and Bette Watson, Topeka, Kans.). . . . "For shopping, I like **Arakawa's,** on Depot Road in Waipahu. I've bought kukui nut necklaces for $3.95 and $4.95 (and also loose kukuis, already drilled, 30 for $3.95), shopping bags with wheels for $4.95, the popular tapa print tote bags with Velcro closings at $3 each, two for $5. The same type bag was $7 all over town, and the shopping bags with wheels were selling elsewhere for $10. I watch the local papers for the Arakawa ads" (Dorothy Astman, Levittown, N.Y.). . . . "I am writing about a real problem at the airport. I hope not too many Canadians are ripped off as we were. We bought a sealed anthurium plant which was stamped, supposedly cleared to take anywhere. We asked the shop owner if we could take it to Canada—she said no problem. When we got to Toronto, it was confiscated. This plant was okay for the U.S., but would not pass Canadian Customs. We asked other shop owners at the Kona airport and Honolulu—same answers. Somewhere, someone is wrong" (Jane Bowden, Oshawa, Ontario, Canada). . . . "I recently began a series of allergy shots and, to continue their effectiveness, decided to take my serum along. My physician suggested contacting one of the Kaiser hospitals. I did so and had my weekly shots in the outpatient section each week. It was low cost and very accommodating to me" (Mary M. McAndrew, Farmington, Minn.).

"**Deeni's Boutique,** 66-079 Kam Hwy., Haleiwa, carries small sizes which, for some unknown reason, no one else seems to; and a discount of up to 50% may be your bonus. She also carries all kinds of bikinis and swimwear, plus one-of-a-kind original tops and gowns, etc." (Mrs. H. N. Lormor, Escondido, Calif.). . . . "A tip for those who intend to take pineapples home: Many places take orders for pineapples to be delivered to the airport or shipped home—often for as much as $5 each. We waited until we were ready to depart, then picked up three in a handy carrying case at a good price at the **Aero Shop** in the Honolulu airport" (Jeffrey S. Campbell, Colorado Springs, Colo.). [*Authors' Note:* Aero's pineapple stands are located by the baggage check-in counters of the major airlines. They sell pineapples in three-packs, six-packs, and 12-packs, and the latter two can be checked with your baggage.] . . . "Visit the swap meets on weekends at drive-ins around the island. You can find monkeypod bowls, etc., for much less than at 'tourist traps' and also soak up the local feeling. Check the classified section for swap announcements" (Mrs. Christine Newman, Kaneohe, Hi.).

"Generally, we found that prices were much lower in Waikiki than at the tourist attractions. For example, we bought kukui-nut leis for $5.95 at **Woolworth's;** the same leis were $14 at Paradise Park. Other souvenir and gift items were similarly priced" (Fred C. Nagelschmidt, Ventura, Calif.). . . . "On our last trip, we bought a small pair of bamboo tongs for $1 at **Iida's** in the Ala Moana Shopping Center. It became the most useful item in the kitchen for removing stubborn toast from the toaster. This time I bought about a dozen pairs of inexpensive souvenirs for our friends. For a buy on macadamia nuts, watch the papers for the sales at **ABC** or **Long's.** We got them for $1.98 for the five-ounce can, and we saw them all over for $2.50 and up in the hotel shops" (Mrs. H. W. Rulon, Matawan, N.J.). . . . "The **ABC Discount Stores** are all you say. I purchased a package of four lahuala mats, four woven coasters, and four napkins for $2.22. I priced them from $4.95 to $5.95 in other gift shops" (R. L. Hilldale, Indianapolis, Ind.). . . . "The eight **Goodwill** stores on Oahu are great places to find good, 'gently used' muumuus from such stores as Liberty House, McInerny, Watumull, etc. They have a large selection, all dry-cleaned, for $7.95, sometimes less on sale. . . . I stopped in at the **Salvation Army** store at 711 Keeaumoku one day, and enjoyed it so much I went back. It was very clean and neat, and they had a big selection of muumuus, priced from $1.55 and up, about $10 for lovely Oriental brocades! I bought many, some just for the materials, others to wear. One day, I got five long muumuus! They also have bathing suits for 89¢ and up, and monkeypod from 49¢. [*Authors' Note:* There are eight Salvation Army stores on the island.) . . . I also liked the Thrift Shop at the **University of Hawaii** for books, Hawaiian clothes, jewelry, household items. It was open only Tuesday, Wednesday, and Thursday, so check before going (also closed during the month of August). . . . One inexpensive gift to take back home is a package of saimin. We bought a box of 30 packages for about $5 in a food market on South King Street, got Oriental soup spoons in **Long's Drugs,** and our friends were fascinated with this, as most of them had never heard of saimin" (Mrs. Joseph Astman, Levittown, N.Y.).

"My husband and I both wear large sizes, and we have never enjoyed shopping anywhere as much as we did in Honolulu. We could walk into almost any store and find racks of attractive things to fit us" (Mrs. Norman Cohen, Swampscott, Mass.). . . . "The **Hookano Sportswear,** 922 Austin Lane, can be reached by the 1-R Kalihi bus. It has some very inexpensive shifts and muumuus, along with men's shirts, children's clothes, etc. They sew their own clothes and sell yard goods. My mother bought an attractive shift for $15, while I bought a piece of beautiful 45-inch cotton print at $4 a yard. The selection is quite large" (Mrs. Peter Gerum, Wahiawa, Oahu). [*Authors' Note:* The last time we visited this factory-retail outlet, we saw some exceptional safari-style shirts for men in solid colors and prints for $18; that was the regular price, and it was about half of what one might expect to pay for similar quality shirts.] . . . "I found **Tropical Fruits Distributors of Hawaii, Inc.,** P.O. Box 1286, Honolulu, HI 96807 (tel. 847-3234), offered a very reasonable deal for shipment of pineapples back to the mainland with you. The pineapples are agriculturally inspected prior to your arrival at the airport and are boxed for shipment. The price for six medium pineapples is around $10, tax included. An invoice for payment from home is attached, which makes it a financially reasonably 'buy now, pay later' investment (Donna M. Corsale, Saratoga Springs, N.Y.).

"We purchased a lovely ukulele from **Kamaka Hawaii, Inc.,** 550 South St., where factory seconds are priced $83 and up. [*Authors' Note:* Visitors are welcome to visit their small factory, where they hire predominately handicapped workers and train them as craftspeople.] . . . Shopping at the Japanese department store at Ala Moana Center is a must if you are a short person—my wife found racks and racks of size 5 dresses; the average Japanese being short, it follows. However, when shopping, we had to watch ourselves when it came to style. Many things that were conservative there are considered wild by mainland standards" (William D. Devlin, San Francisco, Calif.). . . . **"Blair's,** at 404 Ward Ave., will give a 20% discount on first-quality items, as well as generous discounts on damaged goods" (Judith Jacobus, Long Beach, Calif.). . . . "There is so much to photograph that one can easily run out of film. In spite of our good stock of film, we had to buy more. We strongly recommend **Long's Drugstore** in the Ala Moana Center, where we found the best bargains in town. Long's price on both the film and the processing was lower compared to others, resulting in a net saving of $1.40 per film. Slide films were also cheaper than elsewhere. An excellent place for this kind of shopping" (B. K. Mehra, Massissauga, Ontario, Canada). . . . "We found some great jewelry bargains at the **Little Craft Shop** at Pearlridge; they have lots and lots of individual 'pendants,' with the nuts or pieces of shell, or whatever, with the jewelry ring attached. These run about $1 each. You buy one chain and you have a whole bunch of jewelry! By the way, the view of Pearl Harbor from the monorail at Pearlridge is great. My two-year-old nephew really loves it. He thinks 'Pearlridge' and 'monorail' are synonyms" (Florence Klemm, Colorado Springs, Colo.). . . . "We found the shops and the people at **Ward Warehouse** gave the most unusual selections and friendliest service of anywhere we've traveled" (Mrs. Eric Jones, St-Eustache, Québec, Canada).

Chapter VI

HONOLULU ON THE HOUSE

1. Something for Everybody
2. Ethnic Hawaii

THE FANTASTIC BARGAIN of Honolulu is the enormous amount of entertainment and activities—free or at low prices—that are available to the visitor. Probably no other community in the world (with the possible exception of Copenhagen) shares its activities so wholeheartedly with the newcomer.

Part of the reason for this, of course, stems from Hawaii's real need to attract tourists—for tourism is one of the islands' largest industries. But commercial motivations aside, there's enough genuine aloha to go a long way—and to give you so much to do that it becomes hard to decide what to sample and what to pass up!

There are three vital areas where the action takes place; they surround each other like concentric circles.

First, there's Waikiki, the heart of the tourist scene. Some people never leave it and feel they've had a marvelous vacation. Just beyond that is the big, exciting world of Honolulu, one of the great cities (the 12th largest in the United States, in fact). And beyond that, Windward Oahu and the joys of country life and rural beauty. We think you ought to try some of the doings in all three areas—as much as you have taste and inclination for.

The activities described below will give you the broad, overall picture. For up-to-the-minute, day-by-day news of what's going on, consult the *Waikiki Beach Press, Guide to Oahu, This Week on Oahu, On the Go in Oahu, Spotlight Hawaii,* or *Where,* free papers given away in most hotel lobbies, on Kalakaua Avenue, and elsewhere. (These papers also carry many bargain discount coupons which could add up to considerable savings on shopping, restaurants, car rentals, and the like. Be sure to check them out.) The "Aloha" section of the *Sunday Star Bulletin* and *Advertiser* provides a rundown of events for the coming week. *Oahu Drive Guide,* available at the offices of the U-Drive companies, has plenty of information, plus excellent driving maps. Finally, you can pay a visit to the Information Office of the **Hawaii Visitors Bureau,** on the eighth floor of 2270 Kalakaua Ave. (tel. 923-1811); they also have a booth at the Royal Hawaiian Shopping Center.

1. Something for Everybody

ON THE BEACH: The best place, of course, to get your basic training for a Hawaiian vacation is on **Waikiki Beach,** that fabled stretch of sand that curves from the Ala Wai Canal to the shadow of Diamond Head. Stretched out among other bodies in various states of pose and repose, you can calmly watch the frantic traffic out in the breakers where the surfboard and outrigger-canoe crowds are busy trying to run each other down. The blue Pacific, the coconut palms, the trade winds—everything around you induces a lotus-land lethargy that has caused more than one vacationer to tear up his return ticket home ($35-a-day'ers, naturally, should cash theirs in). The best part about all this is that it's absolutely free; there's no need to stay at any of the lush seaside caravanserais to use the beach. All of the beach area is public property, up to the highwater mark, even though some of the big hotels do rope off special areas for their guests. Swim in front of the hotels if you like, but you'll have just as much fun at **Fort DeRussy Beach,** near the ewa end of the beach (a good bet for families, but you can't buy anything at the snackbar unless you have a military card), and at **Kuhio Beach Park,** one of the best natural beaches in Waikiki and headquarters for the surfing and bikini crowd. The beach has been considerably widened, and now it's better than ever. However, we should warn you that there is at least one 22-foot-deep hole in the midst of otherwise knee-high (for an adult) water, and there is no way such anomalies in the ocean floor can be corrected—fill them in one day and they'll be back the next. Parents of small children and non-swimmers should exercise caution here. In fact, Ken Mesa, director of water safety for the City and County of Honolulu, suggests that visitors always check with the lifeguard on duty at a beach before swimming.

Kuhio Beach begins Diamond Head of the Surfrider Hotel, at Uluniu Avenue. Incidentally, it is named for Prince Jonah Kuhio, who once lived on the site. He was the last titular prince of Hawaii, a hereditary high chief and for ten consecutive terms the territory's delegate in Congress. We like the name the Hawaiians gave him: Ke Alii Makaainana—the People's Prince.

Unfortunately, there are no longer any beach services concessions at Kuhio Beach, so if you'd like to learn to surf, try the concessions in front of the Sheraton Waikiki, Moana, or Hawaiian Village Hotels, or inquire at the Recreation Desk of any large hotel. (See also information on Lightning Bolt Surfboard in Chapter V, "Shopping.") A beach boy will teach you (and one or two others) for about $10 an hour. You've got to be a strong swimmer. According to the experts, you'll need three months to become a real surfer, but if you're reasonably well coordinated, you should be able to learn enough to have some fun in a day or two. If you're not, don't torture yourself. Take a ride in an outrigger canoe instead. With six or seven others in the canoe, you paddle out to deep water, wait for a good wave, and then, just as the surfer does, ride its crest back to shore. It's a thrilling experience, slightly strenuous, but with little possibility of broken bones.

Looking for a beach far from the madding crowd (well, as far as you can get)? Take the bus going Diamond Head on Kalakaua Avenue (on the Makai side) to **Queen's Surf,** just across from Kapiolani Park, a lovely beach area frequented mostly by island families (and, at the Diamond Head end, mostly by the island's gay population.) There's a snackbar here, plus locker rooms, showers, and picnic tables. Another good family beach, practically surfless, is the one at **Ala Moana Park.** And if you drive out to the marina behind the Hotel Ilikai, all the way to the left, you'll find a delightful beach between the Hilton, Hawaiian Village and the marina. It's kind of an "in" spot for Kamaainas, but tourists don't seem to know about it. There's also plenty of space for free parking here (a rarity in Waikiki).

Want to see how the other half lives? Here's a chance to get a ride to one of Hawaii's most elegant resort hotels—the **Kahala Hilton**—and to spend as much time as you want at Waialae Beach Park next door—at minimal expense. A shuttle bus drives back and forth between the hotel and the Ala Moana Hotel every hour on the hour from 8 a.m. to 11 p.m. (with the exception of Sunday, when the last shuttle is at 9 p.m.). The charge is $3 each way, and en route to the Kahala, the shuttle stops in front of the Surfrider Hotel in Waikiki. It then takes you along a lush tropical route spilling over with trees and flowers, past millionaires' villas (Clare Boothe Luce had her residence here), to the Kahala Hilton Hotel in the residential section of Kahala. The hotel's architects and decorators have done a masterful job of translating the old Hawaiian motifs into a contemporary setting; the splendid round rugs in the lobby are an example. You can stroll around the lovely grounds and watch the mini porpoise show in the lagoon near the swimming pool. Feeding times are at 11 a.m., and 2 and 4 p.m. daily. If you get hungry, there's the **Hala Terrace** surfside for food and drink, and the new and lovely **Plumeria Café,** a courtyard café, for sandwiches, ice cream, snacks, and full meals. After you've explored the grounds, you're off for a swim at **Waialae** a bit rocky, however), reached by walking in an ewa direction from the Kahala sands. Buses will take you back to Waikiki from the Kahala every hour. If you're driving, parking charges are modest.

SNORKELING: Once you start traveling around the island, there are literally dozens of beaches, one more beautiful than the next, which we'll tell you about in Chapter VIII. One of the nearest of these beaches, and an ideal one for snorkeling, is **Hanauma Bay** (you can rent snorkeling equipment at many places in Waikiki, and other snorkelers are always willing to help beginners). And you don't need your own car to get to Hanauma Bay, or to Sandy and Makapuu Beaches, which are big favorites with the surfing set. Simply board the **Beach Bus.** It runs every day during June, July, and August, the rest of the year on weekends and holidays, departing from Monsarrat Avenue near the Kapiolani Park bandstand. Departures: 9:20 and 10:20 a.m., and every hour on the hour from 11 a.m. to 4 p.m. You can also take the no. 57 bus, "Hawaii Kai—Lunalilo Home Road" and walk up to the bay. (For more details on Hanauma Bay, see Chapter VIII, "Around Oahu," and the Readers' Selections, ahead.)

HIKING, TENNIS, AND OTHER SPORTS: If you'd like to discover what those mountains are actually like across the Ala Wai, the **Hawaiian Trail and Mountain Club** will take you on a hike any Sunday along one of the numerous beautiful trails around Honolulu, where you'll feel far removed from both city and beach. You pack your own lunch and drinking water on these hikes, which usually start from the Iolani Palace grounds at either 8 a.m. or 1 p.m. The fee is minimal, usually about $1 to cover the cost of the drive to the hiking site. For information, phone 734-5515, 247-3922, or 488-1161, or check "Pulse of Paradise" and "Calendar" in the daily papers. . . . **Tennis** in Honolulu? Certainly. It's free at 126 **public courts.** Pick up the brochure called "Golf and Tennis in Hawaii" at the Hawaii Visitors Bureau for complete listings. If the public courts are too crowded, call the **King Street Tennis Club,** which will pick you up at your Waikiki hotel and take you to their courts at 220 S. King St. They also have three covered racquetball courts, a complete pro shop, and rentals. Reserved court time is $5 per person per hour for doubles, $6 per person per hour for singles (tel. 947-2625). . . . The **Ilikai Hotel** has a lot of tennis action: seven specially surfaced courts, one court lit for night play until 10 p.m., ball machines, a full-time tennis pro, private lessons, daily clinics. The pro shop rents racquets and does overnight stringing. They'll even help you find suitable partners (tel. 949-3811). . . . Jogging is big in Honolulu, as just about everywhere else. You're welcome to join those getting in shape for the Honolulu Marathon (it's held the first or second weekend in December) at a free **Jogger's Clinic,** every Sunday at 7:30 a.m. at the bandstand in Kapiolani Park. . . . There are 14 public golf courses on Oahu, most with surprisingly low greens fees. The nearest one to Waikiki is the 18-hole **Ala Wai Golf Course** at 404 Kapahulu Ave. Reservations are taken by phone (tel. 732-7741) one week in advance starting at 6:30 a.m. All reservations are usually given out by 7 a.m. Huge lines of local people start to form before dawn to take advantage of any cancellations. Ala Wai is the busiest golf course in the world, with over 500 persons playing daily. Visitor rates are $8 weekdays, $12 weekends. Cart rental is $10; club rental, $6. With a car, you can drive to Hawaii Kai and the **Hawaii Kai Golf Course,** 8902 Kalanianaole Hwy., in about 20 minutes. Phone 395-2358 for information and reservations. For a listing of golf courses elsewhere on Oahu, see again, "Golf and Tennis in Hawaii," available from the HVB. . . . **Kapiolani Park** is certainly one of the world's most active recreational areas. It has archery and golf driving ranges, fields for soccer, rugby, and softball, courts for tennis, and volleyball, a jogger's circuit training course, and lots more. For details, call the Department of Parks and Recreation headquarters at 523-4631 (they can also give you information on swimming lessons). . . . Oahu also has loads of facilities for riding, waterskiing, skindiving, plain and fancy fishing, even birdwatching. The Hawaii Visitors Bureau can direct you to the right places. . . . You can even go glider riding, out at Dillingham Airfield on the north shore, using the facilities of the **Honolulu Soaring Club.** You can get instruction in doing it yourself or go for a joy ride on a sailplane ($39 for two passengers, $29 for one). Look ma, no engines! Phone Bill at 623-6711 for information. No reservations are required, and things glide along here seven days a week, 10 a.m. to 5:30 p.m. Bring your camera.

We realize that you probably didn't come to Hawaii to go **ice skating,** but if that's your pleasure, Honolulu has a beautiful new rink: the Ice Palace Chalet. Located in the new Stadium Mall, across from Aloha Stadium and Castle Park, this place has really caught on with the local folk. Admission is $5 for adults, $4.50 for students, and $3.75 for children 11 and under; the admission price includes rental of skates. The rink is open Sunday through Thursday from 9 a.m. until 11 p.m. (On Monday, Wednesday, and Friday, you can't skate between 5:45 and 6:45 p.m. unless you're taking a lesson. Fortunately, there's a diverting snackbar and dozens of video games to occupy those not skating.) On Friday, the hours are 9 a.m. until midnight and on Saturday 10:30 a.m. until midnight. For more information, phone 487-9921.

SPECTATOR SPORTS—THE SURFING SCENE: Some visitors to Hawaii find that watching others exert themselves is the most fun of all—and this usually means gazing at the surfers on Waikiki Beach. It's an incredible and never-ending show, especially enjoyable if you've brought your binoculars. If you'd like a closer view, try to catch one of the surfing movies that are shown frequently in the summer at places like the **Waikiki Shell** and **McKinley Auditorium.** They're instructive and thrilling—and much more dramatic than watching the scene from afar at the beach.

Surfing, by the way, was the favorite sport of Hawaiian royalty and originally had religious connotations; in the early part of this century, Jack London, among others, helped revive the sport, and today it's an absolute passion with every ablebodied islander, far surpassing the interest of the mainlander in, say, baseball or skiing. Radio weather reports always include a report on the latest surfing conditions. A special phone (tel. 949-9922) also gives the latest reports. And the proudest possession of any island teenager is, naturally, his surfboard. (There's been much medical talk about surfer's nodules, callus-like bumps on the feet and knees caused by too much contact with the board; since it becomes impossible to wear shoes, more than a few surfers were deferred by the army until the condition was treated.)

From time to time, special surfing clinics free to the public are held at Kapiolani Beach Park. Subjects include body-surfing, canoeing, skindiving, and the like. For information, phone 523-4361.

Other island spectator sports that you might like: football, baseball, and soccer at the **Aloha Stadium** in Halawa (tel. 487-3877); auto racing Friday and Saturday nights at **Hawaii Raceway Park** at Ewa Beach (tel. 682-4494). World-class polo is played each Sunday during polo season at **Mokuleia Polo Farms.** Basketball, karate, wrestling, boxing, Japanese sumo wrestling, and such are held at the **Neal S. Blaisdell Center Arena.**

THE HULA AND OTHER ETHNIC DANCES: Just as you expected, everyone in Hawaii does the hula except the lame (being old or blind is no hindrance). Island youngsters learn the hula just as mainland children take ballet or tap lessons. Social directors and hotel instructors patiently instruct the malihinis, and wherever you look there's a hula show underway. All this is fun and some of it is good dancing, but much of it is a bastardization of a noble and beautiful dance, Hawaii's most unique contribution to the arts.

The original hula dances were sacred, performed in honor of the goddess Laka (who supposedly entertained her sister, the volcano goddess Pele, with the first hula). Laka's devotees lived under a strict system of kapus, studying the hulas as well as the chants and meles, by which the myths of the race were transmitted from one generation to another. In the whaling days, some of the hulas became a bawdy entertainment for the sailors, and the good missionary fathers, who would have found dancing sinful on any account, naturally forbade it. But the hula managed to survive. Today the styles of hula range from the most serious to the most comic—the so-called hapa-haole hulas.

Some of the ancient hulas still live on too, and if you're lucky you may get to see them at some of the better nightclub shows or at concert presentations. True devotees of hula should visit the islands during the latter part of April. That's when the **Merrie Monarch Festival** is held in Hilo, on the Big Island of Hawaii, a week-long virtual Olympics of hula, with dancers from all the various hula halaus (schools) of the islands competing in both ancient and modern hulas. You probably won't be able to get tickets to the events themselves (they are usually sold out by the preceding Christmas), but they are fully covered on television, and are a true joy to watch. On a recent trip, we sat enthralled for nights in a row viewing the competition and the judging—as did just about everyone else on the islands.

One of the most delightful hula shows, in our opinion, is the **Young People's Hula Show,** presented every Sunday morning at 9:30 on the Centerstage at the Ala Moana Shopping Center. The children, all students of Ka'ipolani Butterworth, ranging in age from about three to the teens, are talented nonprofessionals bursting with charm and aloha. It's all free and more enjoyable than many an expensive nightclub show.

You'll note, by the way, that hula dancers—who can just as well be men as women—tell the story with their hands while their feet keep up a steady rhythmic pattern. They often use instruments to help them: the smooth stones or pebbles that they click together, that sound like castanets, are known as ili ili. The seed-filled gourd that sounds like a South American maraca is known as the uli uli. The hollow gourds are called ipus. Pui li, splintered bamboo sticks, produce a rattling sound, and kalaau are hard wooden sticks struck together to make a noise like that of a xylophone.

According to the experts, probably the best ethnic dancing in the islands is that done by the dance group at the **Polynesian Cultural Center,** which we'll tell you about in Chapter VIII. Watch for outstanding programs of Japanese and other Asian dances at the University of Hawaii.

DO-IT-YOURSELF DANCING: You too can do the hula! Hula-dancing lessons are given everywhere—at the Ys, at the university, and at any number of private dance studios. Best bets are the free lessons given occasionally at the various hotels. The **Ilikai Hotel** offers free hula lessons on the mall by the fountain each Monday, Wednesday, and Friday at 10 a.m.; and the **Hyatt Regency Waikiki** usually has hula lessons Tuesday and Thursday at 10 a.m. in Spats. For the specific lesson schedule, phone the Hyatt Hostess Desk at 922-9292. . . . Wednesday and Friday at 10:30 a.m., Auntie Mai'iki Aiu Lake gives lessons on the fourth floor of Building A at the Royal Hawaiian Shopping Center. (*Note:* Since the times of these lessons change with the season, check local papers before you go.) The **Department of Parks and Recreation** (tel. 523-4631) offers hula classes for a nominal fee.

For square-dancers, there's something going on almost every night of the week. The locations change frequently, so the best thing to do is to call the Hawaii Visitors Bureau (tel. 923-1811), or the Department of Parks and Recreation (tel. 523-4631) for information. The **Square Wheelers** is an excellent group that welcomes visitors (tel. 941-1607). Often, park programs are not held during the summer because of the Summer Fun programs that are held there for local schoolchildren.

MUSIC: Classical music lovers have no cause for complaint in Honolulu. Western concert artists of the stature of Andrés Segovia and Emanuel Ax stop here en route to the Orient or on round-the-world tours; Japanese soloists and orchestras pay frequent visits. You might catch opera companies and the like from China. You can enjoy subscription concerts by the **Honolulu Symphony,** which performs under the baton of its music director, Donald Johanos, and famous guest conductors. Soloists include internationally acclaimed virtuosos, and programs include choral works and appearances by the San Francisco Ballet. Pops concerts and the Starlight Festival in the Waikiki Shell are among the most widely attended symphony events, as are the annual presentations of *Nutcracker* and *Messiah.* Associate conductor Henry Miyamura conducts the very popular Youth Concerts, Youth Opera, and the annual Keikis' (Children's) Concert at the Waikiki Shell where guest stars have included Big Bird from "Sesame Street."

Try to attend a performance of the **Hawaii Opera Theater,** which holds a yearly Opera Festival in January and February, featuring world-renowned opera stars and lavish sets. And the islands' most gifted young musicians play with the **Hawaii Youth Symphony,** which performs during the year under the baton of Grant Okamura.

Also very exciting is the renaissance of traditional Hawaiian music in the islands. Watch the papers for concerts of Hawaiian music given at the local high school or by groups like the **Hawaiian Music Foundation** (Hui O Na Opio), which presents fantastic young performers in programs of true island music and dance.

THEATER: Hawaiian theater, long of the tired-businessman, light-entertainment school, is getting more mature and more varied all the time. Very popular here is the **Honolulu Community Theater,** an able group that presents a year-round program of current Broadway shows, revivals, and musicals old and new. Performances are held in the Ruger Theater on the slopes of Diamond Head. Tickets range from $4.50 to a top of $8.75 (for musicals). For further information, call 734-0274.

Now in its 14th season, the **Hawaii Performing Arts Company (HPAC)** provides an intimate setting for a broad spectrum of theatrical offerings. Their 100-seat Manoa Valley Theater at 2833 E. Manoa Rd. brings the lights up 42 weeks of the year on a variety of productions ranging from the Bard to Broadway, from classics to musical comedy. Tickets are priced at $8 and $9 for musicals, $7 and $8 for nonmusicals. Call 988-6131 for dates and availability of seats.

Up at the **John F. Kennedy Theater,** the University of Hawaii's outstanding Department of Drama and Theater presents the great classics of the Orient and the West—Shakespeare, kabuki, and modern plays, as well as ballet and modern dance. Besides the eight or so major productions staged each year, they present at least six shows produced by Kumu Kahua, a theater group that performs plays written by Hawaiian residents. For information on tickets and productions, call 948-7655.

Should you find yourself on the windward side of the island, you might stop in to see an offering by the **Windward Theater Guild,** a good local company. Performances are held in the Kailua Elementary School auditorium, tickets are $6 for adults, $5 for all others, and you call 261-4885 for information and reservations. Also outside of Honolulu, Broadway theatrical productions and name entertainment shows, some of them free, are presented at **Schofield Barracks** and **Fort Shafter.** Call 655-9081 or 438-2831 for information and reservations.

HUNA PHILOSOPHY: The old Hawaiians were very practical psychologists, and some of their ancient Huna practices are gaining the attention of psychologists and educators today. If you'd like to learn some of the secrets of that ancient wisdom, updated for today's world, try to catch one of the free evening lectures on Ho'Oponopono (the art of problem-solving and stress reduction), given by Morrnah Simeona and her staff at **Pacifica Seminars,** 1649 Kalakaua Ave. A native Hawaiian, Morrnah is renowned throughout the islands as Kahuna Lapa'au, a healer, herbalist, and authority on the Hawaiian teachings; she has recently been named a "Living Treasure of Hawaii." Among her colleagues is a clinical psychologist, Stanley Hew Lin, Ph.D. We attended one of these free lectures and a Ho'Oponopono workshop (for which there is a fee) on a recent trip and found it fascinating. For information, phone 955-1236.

THE JAPANESE TEA CEREMONY: As refreshing as a quick trip to Japan, the twice-weekly demonstrations of the Japanese tea ceremony held at 245 Saratoga Rd. (near Fort DeRussy), offer a fascinating look at the ancient "Way of Tea." Sponsored by the **Urasenke Foundation of Hawaii, a** nonprofit group whose goal is "to find friendship in a bowl of tea," the demonstrations are held every Wednesday and Friday (excluding holidays) from 10 a.m. to noon, and are free. Seated in a formal Japanese tatami room in a garden setting, guests are introduced to the proper customs for the preparation and partaking of tea, and are served a sweet and powdered green tea from exquisite "tea bowls." You may ask questions and take pictures if you wish. A must for lovers of Orientalia. For information, phone 923-3059.

THE STUDENT LIFE: Here's a tip that can save you literally scads of dollars. The **University of Hawaii at Manoa** sponsors any number of low-cost activities and tours (even including 20 different Oahu tours costing from $3.50 to $34, plus low-cost weekends in the neighbor islands) for the benefit of its students. But nonstudents can join in the fun and savings simply by paying a $5 activity fee that covers a six-week summer session. Inquire at Campus Center, Room 212, on the Manoa Campus of the University of Hawaii.

FREE SHOWS: There are quite a few of these, and most of them are worth your time. The best known, the **Kodak Hula Show,** takes place next to the Waikiki Shell in Kapiolani Park. Even without benefit of a light meter, you should enjoy this big free show of authentic music and dance by talented performers. Naturally, it's nirvana for photographers. Show times: Tuesday through Friday at 10 a.m. Get there early for a good seat. . . . The **Waikiki Shopping Plaza** presents an entertaining 45-minute show every night, at 6:30 p.m. and again at 8:30 p.m., in its fourth-floor showroom. . . . Everybody loves the **Young People's Hula Show** at the Ala Moana Shopping Center (details above). And from mid-June through August, free Hawaiian entertainment is also scheduled at 2 p.m. on Tuesday and

Thursday at Ala Moana. . . . Check the papers for dates of free entertainment at Pearlridge Shopping Center. . . . The Lilikoi Sisters perform every night at the splendid Fountain Mall setting of the **Hotel Ilikai.** First there's a torch-lighting ceremony (at 6:30 p.m.), and the ladies sing until 8. . . . Don't miss the free show at the beach in front of the **Reef Hotel** every Sunday, from 8 to 9:30 or 10 p.m. Lots of bright amateurs get into the act. . . . Free concerts and cultural shows are given in the Great Hall of the **Hyatt Regency Waikiki,** often at noon or 5 p.m., but since the schedule varies greatly, you should check with the Hyatt Hostess Desk (tel. 922-9292) for exact ties. . . . Free concerts are generally held Sunday afternoons at 2 at the **Kapiolani Park Bandstand.** Entertainment includes Polynesian revues, ukulele clubs, visiting mainland troupes, jazz and rock musicians, and sometimes the famed Royal Hawaiian Band. Call 922-5317 for more information. . . . You can nearly always be sure to catch the Royal Hawaiian Band at its Friday noontime concerts at the **Iolani Palace** bandstand. These lunchtime concerts are very popular with the local people who work nearby; bring a lunch and have a listen. . . . On Wednesday evenings during June, July, and August you can see "The Wildest Show in Town" at the **Honolulu Zoo.** The zoo stays open until 7:30 p.m., and there's a show at 6 on the stage in the main courtyard. Most families bring a picnic supper to eat during the show. We've seen the Honolulu City Ballet, a troupe of Scottish bagpipers (many of them Japanese and Hawaiian!) in full regalia, the Honolulu Boys' Choir, puppet shows, kabuki theater, and a New Orleans jazz group. . . . The Waikiki-Kapahulu branch of the **Library of Hawaii,** 400 Kapahulu, offers films, art shows, and chamber music programs for grownups, weekly story hours for 4- and 5-year-olds. It's also pleasant to just sit and read in the bougainvillaea-shaded lanai at this library in a coconut grove at the foot of Diamond Head. Visitors are also welcome to borrow books, free of charge. . . . There's free entertainment galore at the Royal Hawaiian Shopping Center: check the local papers for the schedule.

THE ART SCENE: A lot of good artists are coming out of Hawaii—young people with a mixture of backgrounds whose work shows a mixture of influences. Perhaps because of the natural beauty that surrounds them, their paintings tend to be more representational here than in other art centers, but ways of seeing are as modern as they are in Paris or New York. Not a few have married Oriental atmosphere with Western techniques, another example of the fortuitous cross-fertilization that goes on in every area of Hawaiian life.

The distinguished **Royal Gallery** in the Royal Hawaiian Hotel is a good place to catch the work of top island talent, as is the impressive **Contemporary Arts Center,** on the first floor of the News Building at 605 Kapiolani Blvd. The gallery is a showcase for leading island artists and specializes in individual exhibitions. . . . The **AMFAC Plaza Exhibition Room** at AMFAC Center, Fort Street Mall and Queen Street, has interesting group exhibitions of contemporary painting, crafts, sculpture, and photography, as well as cultural and historical presentations. Exhibits are scheduled the first two weeks of every month, 8:30 a.m. to 5 p.m., weekdays only (tel. 523-1440). . . . Island artists like David Lee, William De Shazo, and Margaret Keane, who have won international reputations, are shown at the prestigious **Center Art Galleries** (locations at the Waikiki Shopping Plaza, Ala Moana Shopping Center, and Hemmeter Center, two more on Oahu, and several in Maui), along with originals by old and new masters like Marc Chagall, Joan Miró, and Salvador Dali. Anthony Quinn and Red Skelton also star. . . . John Young, one of the islands' most outstanding artists, displays his own paintings and prints, along with a superb collection of primitive art, at the **John Young Studio,** Poka Place (tel. 732-2496). . . . On Saturday and Sunday mornings local artists exhibit and sell their work on the zoo fence near **Kapiolani Park**—sort of a twice-a-week Greenwich Village Art Show. . . . When you travel to the north shore, stop in to see works by local artists and craftsmen at the **Fettig Art Gallery,** 66-051 Kam Hwy., in Haleiwa (tel. 637-4933).

Art is, in fact, everywhere in Honolulu; the builders of large public facilities are becoming more and more art-conscious, and you will find monumental pieces of sculpture, some outstanding, some mediocre, in such places as the Ala Moana Shopping Center, Hemmeter Center, Royal Hawaiian Center, the Waikiki Shopping Plaza, the University of Hawaii, the State Capitol Building, and at Sea Life Park in Windward Oahu. The fountain sculptures at Ala Moana are particularly worth a look.

To see some excellent works by Hawaii's talented craftspeople (and perhaps to pick up some distinctive small presents), pop into some of our favorite places. **Following Sea,** at the Kahala Mall Shopping Center, 4211 Waialae Ave. (tel. 734-4425), is a visual experience. It represents the works of many American craftspeople in ceramics, glass, jewelry, fiber, woodwork, etc., and one piece is more glorious than the next. Many island artists are represented. . . . Some 13 craftspeople—potters, stained-glass makers, metal sculptors, painters, jewelrymakers, leatherworkers, and woodworkers—are busy at their studios in the **Foundry Craftsmen,** 556B Kamani (tel. 538-7288), and they won't mind if you come by to browse. They sell retail to visitors, wholesale to galleries and shops. Most studios are open Monday through Saturday from 9 a.m. to 6 p.m. It's fun to wander through the ancient building, which once was, and still resembles, a steel and iron foundry—a reminder of another epoch of the islands. . . . At Ward Warehouse, **Rare Discoveries, Exhibits,** and the **Artist's Guild** show outstanding handicrafts.

Keep an eye out for these artists: Randy Hokushin in pottery; Bumpei Akaji in welded sculpture; Marjorie W. Hee and Charles Higa in watercolors; Louis Pohl in mixed media; Barbara Engle and Dorothy Archer in prints and drawings; Hiroshi Tagami, David Lee, Richard Kolath, and Allen Akina in oils; Ronnie Kilpatrick and Pegge Hopper for Polynesian portraits. This is but a partial list of the talented island artists whose works are increasingly being recognized outside the islands. Incidentally, Hawaiian art is considered a good investment and is being scooped up by mainland people.

Crafts Fairs

Hopefully, you'll be in town for one of the several arts-and-crafts fairs that happen in Honolulu at odd times throughout the year. The Mission Houses Museum hosts two of them, one on Kamehameha Day (June 11) and one around Thanksgiving. There are two big, beautiful fairs at Thomas Square Park, one right before Christmas, the other before Easter. Several two-day fairs are held at Ala Moana Park, and there is usually a fair in July, at Kapiolani Park. On the North Shore, there are two two-day fairs each year—one in late June or early July and one in November—at Waimea Falls Park. (You needn't pay the park admission fee to go to the fair.) All of these are held on weekends. Some talented artists and craftpersons to watch for are: Linda Iwamoto (Hawaiian Sea Prints) who makes lovely, delicate pictures and notecards using many of the hundreds of varieties of seaweeds found in Hawaii; Joan Rose, who does beautiful batiks, notably of Hawaiian fish and shells, and finishes them as wall hangings and pillows; Deborah Woodford (Pegasus I), known for beautiful hand-wrought gold jewelry; Shirley Miller, with her whimsical Hawaiian dolls; ceramists John and Linda Bade; Lisa Starr Tong (Loveable Lumber), a gifted young woodworker; Larry Lee, who creates exquisite boxes of leaded glass, many embedded with seashells; Nonie, who crafts hat leis of dried flowers in soft colors; Kathy and Kathy, who do beautiful patchwork and appliqué clothing in calicos and provincial prints; and Mary Louise Kekuewa, the great lady of Hawaiian featherwork.

The Art Establishment

Hawaii, of course, has her art establishment, names that are known in art circles everywhere. Perhaps the greatest of these is the muralist Jean Charlot, who, along with Orozco, Siqueiros, and Rivera, brought the art of the mural to revolutionary heights in Mexico in the '20s and '30s. An islander by choice since 1949, Charlot has contributed much to Hawaii's art world. Other prominent figures include the painter and muralist Juliette May Fraser; painters such as Reuben Tam, Ben Norris, Tadashi Sato, Edward Stasack (also known for sculpture), the late Harry Baldwin, and Isami Doi; and the brilliant young ceramist Shugen Inoye, a Buddhist priest who died not long ago at the age of 29. John Kelly, who died a few years ago in his 80s, was Hawaii's master printmaker; his colored etchings of the Polynesians are considered the best of their kind ever done. They are widely reproduced and frequent exhibitions are held. Kelly's wife, Kate, was a sculptor; you'll see her monument to Amelia Earhart on the road to Koko Head and some of her other sculpture in the Honolulu Academy of Arts.

Another great lady of the arts in Hawaii was Madge Tennent, who came to Hawaii at the turn of the century via South Africa and Paris and broke away from the academy and its conventions to record on canvas her massive portraits of the Hawaiian people. You can visit her gallery, the **Tennent Art Foundation,** at 203 Prospect St., from 10 a.m. to noon Tuesday through Saturday, 2 to 4 p.m. on Sunday, or by special appointment: call Elaine Tennent at 531-1987. Closed Monday.

Don't leave Hawaii without a visit to the **Honolulu Academy of Arts,** 900 S. Beretania St., where you'll see the work of island artists and much more as well. The academy is one of the most beautiful art museums in the world and one of the most important; it offers a look at the best of both Eastern and Western art. The physical plant is ideal for viewing art, divided as it is into a series of small galleries that open into tranquil courtyards; the Chinese garden, in particular, is exquisite. There's a superb collection of Asian art—a magnificent sculpture of Kwan Yin, the Chinese goddess of mercy, Chinese scrolls and carvings, Korean ceramics, Japanese screens—as well as a good representation of Western masters, including works of Picasso, Braque, Monet, and Van Gogh. Note also the Kress Collection of Italian Renaissance painting. Stop in the bookshop for prints and other distinctive gift items and have a lovely lunch in the Garden Café (seatings at 11:30 a.m. and 1 p.m., September through May, $5 lunch, reservations suggested). The museum is open Tuesday to Saturday from 10 a.m. to 4:30

p.m., on Sunday from 1 to 5 p.m. Supper is served in the Garden Café on Thursday evening at 6:30, about $6.50. Reservations required (tel. 531-8865).

Admission to the academy is free. Locked lockers are provided, free of charge, for visitors' parcels. The academy is about a 15-minute ride from Waikiki on the no. 2 bus. Closed Monday.

MISCELLANEOUS ACTIVITIES: Need to exercise? It's not so bad when there are lots of other knee-bending and deep-breathing along with you. There's always a good crowd at the entrance to the **Honolulu Zoo** weekday mornings at 8:30, on Saturday at 9, getting into shape with **Ursula Hare.** You're welcome to join them. Ursula is a colorful lady, her classes are sponsored by People for Pets, and it's all free. There's also a free exercise and fitness class every day except Sunday, from 9 to 10:30 a.m., at the beach at **Fort DeRussy.** . . . The **Honolulu Senior Citizens Club** welcomes newcomers to its social and recreational activities every Wednesday from 9 a.m. to 2 p.m. at the Ala Wai Clubhouse. There's a bridge, canasta, and checkers. Membership is only $5 a year, and it's certainly worth that to go on some of the club's regular outings—sightseeing tours, picnics, etc. These usually start from the Ala Wai Clubhouse (on the other side of the Ala Wai Canal) on Wednesday mornings, under the auspices of the city Recreation Department. For information on other activities for senior citizens, contact the **Hawaii State Senior Center** (tel. 847-1322). . . . There's a group for just about every interest in Honolulu, from barbershop quartet singers to coin collectors, and they all extend their aloha to the visitor. Check the papers for news of their meetings. Bridge buffs will find duplicate bridge games at local hotels practically every night of the week. Meetings of mainland fraternal organizations take place constantly.

MEDICAL SERVICES: We hope it won't happen, but should you need medical assistance while you're in Honolulu, you have several possibilities. Quick medical attention is available at the **Waikiki Medi-Mart** in the Royal Hawaiian Shopping Center, which is open from 8 a.m. to 8 p.m. seven days of the week. No appointment is necessary. Should you need a house call—or hotel call—contact **Doctors on Call (DOC).** They're on duty every day, 24 hours a day, and a phone call to 923-9966 will bring them to your hotel room promptly; the charge is $54. **Waikiki Medical Services** also makes house calls around the clock, and their fee is $35; phone them at 922-2323. They also see patients during office hours, and have had an excellent reputation with visitors for many years. They are in Room 203 of the Waikiki Medical Building, 305 Royal Hawaiian Ave. Of course, in a medical emergency you can always call 911 and get an ambulance, or go to the Emergency Room at the Queen's Medical Center, 1301 Punchbowl St. (tel. 538-9011). See also, under "Readers' Activities Suggestions" at the end of this chapter, information on Waikiki Medical Services.

FREE AND LOW-COST CLASSES: You can learn to cook up those wonderful island flavors at the **Gas Company's** free demonstrations. Programs are held at their Penthouse auditorium at 1060 Bishop St. Call 547-3177 for date, time, and more information. . . . The **Hawaiian Electric Company** at King and Richards Streets has occasional free cooking demonstrations in the evening featuring the foods of one of the major ethnic groups in Hawaii each time. Call 548-3511 for further information. . . . Free classes in hula, fresh flower lei making, and Hawaiian ti-leaf hula-skirt making, as well as displays of the art of Hawaiian quiltmaking, are featured in the Great Hall of the **Hyatt Regency Waikiki** at various times. Specific information is available by calling 922-9292. . . . You can learn how to slice a pineapple, make a flower lei, weave a coconut frond, and lots more, in the huge array of classes presented at the **Royal Hawaiian Shopping Center.** Consult the local papers for schedules. . . . Check with the city's **Department of Parks and Recreation** (tel. 523-4631) about its recreation program for adults, teenagers, and children. Visitors are welcome to participate in classes (of up to ten sessions) in such subjects as quilting, Hawaiian, ukulele, and hula. At **Paki Park,** just behind the zoo, there's usually a free program for children 6 to 13 (3 to 5:30 p.m.) which includes sports, hula, arts and crafts. For details, call Paki Park (tel. 737-0990); the best time to call is between 2 and 2:30 p.m.

If you're staying in town for a month or two, you may want to sign up for one of the short-term, low-cost, noncredit classes at the **University of Hawaii at Manoa.** On the agenda one summer: Kundalini yoga, batik, folk guitar, occult numerology, belly dancing—and then some!

FREE AND LOW-COST TOURS: Free refreshments and more than 40,000 fashions to select from at factory prices are available at **Hilo Hattie's Fashion Center,** 700 Nimitz. Call them at 537-2926 and they'll tell you where their free bus will pick you up in Waikiki. . . . It's always Christmas at the **Emgee Corporation,** 3210 Koapaka St., in the airport industrial area. You're welcome to take a free tour of the factory and see artists handcrafting unique and whimsical wooden Christmas ornaments from over 400 original designs. Then you can browse in their Christmas Shop. A catalog is available. Call 836-0988 for details. . . . If you'd like to see how Hawaiian gift items—toys, hula skirts, jewelry, Hawaiian dolls, and kitchen accessories, etc.—are made, you can take a free tour of **Lanakila Crafts** at 1809 Bachelot St. Lanakila is a private, nonprofit organization that provides vocational training and employment for many handicapped adults. Their products are sold in the finest gift stores. Call 531-0555 for information on the tours, which are held on Tuesday and Thursday at 1 p.m. . . . Don't forget the **Dole Cannery** tour which we described in full in Chapter VII. Admission is $2.

2. Ethnic Hawaii

Now we come to perhaps the most colorful aspect of the Hawaiian scene—the life of its various cultural groups. For us, this is what most makes Hawaii a marvelous place to visit. All the ethnic festivals and celebrations are exciting; just take in whatever is going on when you're there. Some people even plan their trips to the islands around the festival calendar; we wouldn't go that far, but we would advise you never to miss a festival that's going on when you're there—it might be the best part of your trip.

THE FESTIVAL CALENDAR: Now we'll turn to the ethnic events, plus other events of interest, that take place only on certain dates. We've set them forth in roughly chronological order.

New Year's Eve. Celebrations are much like those on the mainland, except that the firecrackers are noisier (Oriental style), costume balls are held at the leading hotels, and purification ceremonies are performed at Buddhist temples, to which visitors are welcome. January 1st is open house among island Japanese families.

Narcissus Festival. For three weeks before and five days after the Chinese New Year (which usually falls in the first week of February), the community blows its collective top in a running series of lantern parades, fashion and flower shows, banquets, house-and-garden tours, the crowning of the Narcissus Queen, and dancing in the streets.

Cherry Blossom Festival. A Japanese cultural and trade show, in February or March, complete with a queen, pageant, and a coronation ball, plus demonstrations of tea ceremonies, flower arranging, and more.

Japanese Girls' Day. Japanese girls are presented with dolls on the first March 3rd after their birth and every March 3rd thereafter. In accordance with this delightful custom, public displays of dolls—usually costumed in the dress of a royal court—can be found in windows of the big Japanese department stores.

Prince Kuhio Day, March 26. Hawaii's beloved "people's prince" and first delegate to Congress is honored with impressive ceremonies first at Iolani Palace and later at his tomb at the Royal Mausoleum. At Kuhio Beach in Waikiki, the site of his home, a memorial tablet is decorated with leis. Hawaiian societies hold special programs and events.

Japanese Boys' Day. You needn't be Japanese to have your family fly a brightly colored paper and fabric carp in your honor. Many island families have taken up the custom; watch for the flying fish each year on May 5.

Lei Day. On May 1, everybody wears a lei, and there are contests for the most beautiful leis (judging at Kapiolani Park) and a wonderful Lei Day concert at the Waikiki Shell by the Cazimero Brothers in the evening. Tickets are about $8 for general admission. Come early, bring a picnic supper and a blanket, and join Hawaii's people for a joyous event.

Kamehameha Day, June 11. This is a state holiday (many offices will be closed) and one of the biggest celebrations of them all; there are parades and festivities all over the islands.

Japan Festival in Hawaii, June 13 to 15. One of the newer annual events in Honolulu, it includes a Bon Dance Festival (see below), a Tabishibai of the samurai period, a Japanese folk dance show, and, of course, a parade.

Bon Odori Festival, late July. One of the most colorful events in the islands, these traditional dances are done to welcome the arrival of departed souls in Paradise. The dances are usually sponsored by Japanese temples whose members practice their steps for months. Watch the local papers for dates.

Aloha Week. Mid-September to mid-October. Take the celebrations of all the ethnic groups, roll them into one, and you'll get some idea of Aloha Week—or Aloha Weeks, as they should more properly be called, since this is a moveable festival, taking place on different islands in a more-or-less progressive order. The Oriental, Polynesian, and Western groups all get together for this hoolaulea (gathering for a celebration), each vying to demonstrate the warmth and beauty of the wonderful Hawaiian aloha. The eight-day-long spree features music and dance events, demonstrations of ancient arts and crafts, a beautiful orchid show, water sports, an enormous flower parade, pageants, the crowning of both a king and a queen, and even a Molokai-to-Oahu Canoe Race (terminating at the Hilton Hawaiian

Village Beach). This is a great time to come to the islands. Check with the Hawaii Visitors Bureau for the exact dates of Aloha Week celebrations; as stated, they vary from island to island.

Bodhi Day. On the nearest Sunday to December 7, the enlightenment of Buddha is commemorated with religious observances in the Buddhist temples and with Japanese dance programs and ceremonies elsewhere.

Festival of Trees, November 30 to December 5. This very popular local event is held at the Neil Blaisdell Center and features glorious exhibits of decorated trees, wreaths, many Christmas items. All are for sale. Traditional Hawaiian carols are sung.

Princess Bernice Pauahi Bishop's Birthday. Hawaiian societies and schools state a moving expression of remembrance for the beloved princess at the Royal Mausoleum on December 19.

Christmas. What could be nicer than a Polynesian Christmas? There aren't any chimneys, so Santa might arrive in an outrigger canoe or on a surfboard. He might—it's not as bad as it sounds—be wearing a hula skirt. Carols are sung to ukulele accompaniment. If you happen to be in Lahaina during the Christmas season, you'll see two imaginative coral Christmas trees. Elsewhere, Christmas lights are hung on everything from evergreens to bamboo. There are special programs for the children at the Honolulu Academy of Arts. The stores are jammed, just as they are on the mainland, but surprisingly, a view of the bustling crowds (thronging the mall at Ala Moana Center, for example) is one of the prettiest of holiday pictures. The Christmas greeting: **"Mele Kalikimaka!"**

READERS' ACTIVITIES SUGGESTIONS: "The latest craze to hit the beach? **Aqua-bikes,** which everyone nicknames 'wheelies.' These contraptions have huge inflated wheels on either side and a flotation device out front to stabilize them. They're propelled by pedal power—two people sitting side by side—and are capable of going way out where the surfers hang out. The nonswimmers in my crowd went nuts about them, because it gave them a safe way to get some authentic water-sport thrills. One gal swore that it was the highlight of her visit, and she wasn't a stick-in-the-mud by any means! The concession is on the beach in front of the Reef Hotel. Cost is $10 per half hour, $15 for a full hour—per vehicle, not per person. . . . For summer visitors who like baseball, the best bargain in town is a $2.50 adult general admission ticket to Aloha Stadium to watch the **Triple-A Hawaii Islanders.** We used to pay a buck or so more to sit right down behind homeplate until we realized that the same location—only in the top row—gave us a much better overall view for less money. Also, it's only a step from there to the concession stands—yes, they sell saimin in addition to the standard hot dogs and beer—and rest rooms. The games are never crowded, you catch some fantastic sunsets over the Waianae Mountains, and there are a lot of door prizes and giveaways. One cute wrinkle: A fan who catches a foul ball on the fly not only gets to keep the ball, he also wins a free chicken dinner. This one has to rank high on any list of 'don't bust the budget' family outings because kids, of course, are admitted at reduced rates" (Leilani Moyers, Patterson, N.Y.).

"I would like to share a very tropical and beautiful hike to **Manoa Falls.** Few maps show it, but the trail starts at the end of Manoa Road, just beyond Paradise Park. There was only one other car parked in the area, and the trail is unmarked, but it is on the left near a gate. It is a muddy trail, often following a stream, so shoes should be worn in this jungle setting. It's about a 50-minute hike to the bottom of the falls, where there's a small, refreshing pool in this lush, secluded area. It's so secluded, in fact, that when I got to the bottom of the falls there was a beautiful girl having pictures taken with nothing on except an orchid lei" (Mark and Julie Martini, Huntington Beach, Calif.).

"On Sunday we went to the worship service sponsored by **Waikiki Beach Chaplaincy** on the shore outside the Hilton Hawaiian Village hotel. It ran from about 10:30 a.m. to noon and included a good deal of music and a sermon. People were there in every form of dress and undress imaginable—perhaps 300 to 400 persons. The services have been conducted there 14 years. We decided that it was one of the best services we had ever attended. Certainly God could be worshipped in this way in this beautiful place, and it was fitting to pause and thank him for his gifts to us, including the particular one of being in Hawaii. The preacher, in his early 30s, told us afterward that he was not a Southern Baptist, but for all the world he sounded like one!" (Jim Cox, Middletown, Ky.). . . . "Do not carry extra money to the beach—leave your wallet with a friend, or put your money and keys in a waterproof wallet that you can wear swimming. Thieves seem to love Waikiki Beach" (Nancy Grant, South Easton, Mass.).

"There are many ads for snorkel rentals and shuttle transportation to Hanauma Bay in the tourist papers. We found the best value to be **Budget Snorkel Rental** at 296 Beach Walk, next to Tops Coffee Shop. For $6, one can rent a mask, snorkel, fins, fish food, and a mesh carrying bag, and for the same $6 you can ride Budget's 7 or 8 a.m. shuttle van to the bay. The return trip is also included, every hour on the half hour from 10:30 a.m. to 5:30 p.m. Masks with corrective lenses are available for an additional $2. Minolta underwater cameras complete with a 24-exposure roll of film may be rented for $10 for the day. Later shuttles to the bay are available, but then the price rises to $7.50. Also, note that there is now a train, 55¢ a ride, that goes from the parking lot to the beach and back at Hanauma Bay. Be sure to look at the display on the patio of the snackbar. The bay is described, the fish found here are identified, and there is information on what level of snorkeling or scuba skills are needed in various areas of the bay" (Roberta Rosen, Long Beach, Calif.). . . . "Since there are no snorkel rentals at Hanauma Bay, we suggest that you rent snorkeling equipment at the 'yellow umbrella' stand (it has no name) on the beach in Waikiki near the intersection of Kalakaua Avenue and Kapahulu Avenue, near the zoo. Among the various things they rent, the snorkeling equipment goes for $5 for mask, fins, and snorkel for a full 24-hour day! If you have a coupon from one of the free Waikiki publications, it's $1 off that price. Also, *no* deposit, other than your name and hotel were required. They are open 9 a.m. to 5 p.m. From their stand, it's just a short walk up Monsarrat Avenue to catch the Beach Bus to Hanauma Bay, which runs weekends, holidays, and school vacations only" (Jan and Mike Cobb, Evanston, Ill.). [*Authors' Note:* Renting snorkeling equipment is one of the most competitive businesses in Waikiki. Rates change faster than the tides: do some local checking before you put your money down.] . . . "Our son had a lot of fun swimming at Hanauma Bay in the clear water. A professional scuba diver told him to feed cheese to the tropical fish and it worked great, better than bread. The cheese that comes in a tube and squeezes out is the best" (Ingo Platzer, Omaha, Neb.).

"Should medical assistance be required, **Waikiki Medical Services** (tel. 922-2323) is excellent. The cost is $35 for an office visit, with follow-up visits at no charge. They also make 'house' calls,' and are available 24 hours per day. They are located in the Waikiki Medical Building at 305 Royal Hawaiian Ave., Room 203. . . . Persons wishing to take noncredit courses should inquire from **University of Hawaii at Manoa,** College of Continuing Education, 2530 Dole St., Box N, Honolulu, HI 96822, for course information, schedules, and fees. They will mail a copy of their brochure about a month before the classes are scheduled—timing basically follows the quarter system. One would not have to be in Honolulu for a long stay to take advantage of some of these courses; some are one-day seminars" (Dian Presmanes, Atlanta, Ga.). . . . "We each bought an inflatable raft for $3.99, and loved going way out where the waves were breaking. It took practically no room to bring the rafts home. We felt sorry for the people who bought beachmats; many had to hand-carry them on the plane because they were too wide to fit into suitcases" (Carl and Debbie Adams, St. Louis, Mo.).

"Bishop Museum has a program of classes in such things as Ancient Hawaiian Featherwork (hatbands), lauhala weaving, Hawaiian quilting, etc. The classes are usually from 9 a.m. till 2 p.m., at the new Atherton Halau, on the museum grounds. The cost is $2 per class, and you can purchase needed supplies right there. Good for people who are just in town for a week or so, and want to learn a Hawaiian craft" (Mrs. Joseph G. Astman, Levittown, N.Y.). [*Authors' Note:* Evening classes are also held in all the crafts. For information, call 847-1443.] . . . "For those planning to be in Honolulu for Christmas, we would recommend attending **Christmas Eve services** at historic **Kawaiahao Church** in downtown Honolulu. The beautiful Christmas music is sung in both Hawaiian and English, giving the visitor a chance to sing along, and feel the island blend of cultures" (Mrs. John O'Harra, Portland, Ore.). . . . "My husband played **racquetball** for free almost every day at the court at the Diamond Head end of Fort DeRussy Park—Wilt Chamberlain beat him, though" (Diana Lofstron, Prince George, B.C., Canada). . . . "We enjoyed being in Waikiki for May 1st, **Lei Day.** There were lei-making exhibits all over and a contest at the park, where we saw the very impressive coronation ceremony of the Lei Day Queen and also a large craft show with many beautiful things, some very reasonable" (Kay Loesch, Cordova, Alaska).

"The beach at **Kailua** is great for children. There are good waves without dangerous undertow. . . . **Ala Moana Beach Park** is much more desirable for children than Waikiki. The water is shallow and there are no rocks or coral" (Kim Andrews, Lincoln, Neb.). . . . "I would like to suggest that your Protestant readers attend **Waikiki Baptist Church,** 424 Kuamoo St. They have a special Sunday School class for 'first-timers,' in which the history and culture of Hawaii are explained. We both found it the most interesting part of our trip" (Morgan and Kay Tallman, Westland, Mich.). . . . "Please check local papers the day you arrive. We did not do so and missed a beach fair on the one afternoon that we did not have rain when we were in Honolulu" (John Ruble, Hillsboro, Ohio). . . . "I would like to suggest that Hawaiian malihinis turn on their AM radios to 1420, **KCCN,** the only radio station playing strictly Hawaiian music. This immediately sets them in the mood for the Hawaiian experience" (Diane Miyazaki, Wahiawa, Hi.). . . . "Although it is often crowded, there are few places in Hawaii that can offer such fine scuba and snorkeling as **Hanauma Bay.** The coral reef here has formed in a sunken volcano crater, and the oceanward side of the reef is isolated from the open sea by the rise of the crater bowl. The reef has been made an underwater state park. Fishing or sample collecting is prohibited. As a result, the marine life has become so tame that schools of colorful fish will dart between your legs and inches in front of your mask as you swim through the warm, clear water" (Timothy Doherty, Latrobe, Penna.). . . . "Everyone should go to Hanauma Bay to see the big, beautiful tropical fish swimming in front of your face. However, be careful. The coral in the sea is beautiful, but the surf is strong; only strong swimmers go out past the coral. Walking on the coral (which has eels in the holes) to get to the deeper section is slippery, and surf can push you against the rocks; I got multiple bruises. Take a walk along the ridge to see the 'toilet bowl,' so called by the locals because it flushes you in and out. Wear shoes as you walk along the rocky path, and bring a camera" (Carl and Debbie Adams, St. Louis, Mo.). . . . "The **Hyatt Regency Waikiki** continues to provide great free entertainment. Check the tourist papers. On New Year's Eve in their Great Hall we danced to big-band entertainment with hundreds of balloons sailing down at midnight, vendors with Maui potato chips, pretzels, and other inexpensive treats—a very pleasant evening. Speaking of New Year's Eve, Waikiki was much quieter, with new fireworks regulations and great supervision by HPD. . . . The best fun is still free, wading in the warm surf at midnight in December while friends at home are shoveling snow" (Mrs. John O'Harra, Portland, Ore.).

"Those interested in other murals of Jean Charlot should stop off at the **Leeward Community College** exit and look at the mural painted in the lobby of the theater there. I think it's one of his best so far. You can see the fresco from the upper-level glass doors. . . . Check with the **State Department of Land and Natural Resources** for hiking maps, or check with the **Sierra Club** for information on local trails. To me, you haven't seen Hawaii until you have hiked up the mountains, eaten the wild fruits, and seen the magnificent tropical plants along the way. There is hardly any mountain trail where you will not find guava when it is in season. . . . The **State Foundation on Culture and Arts** can give you a schedule of what's happening culturally for the month. Some things are free. . . . If one wants to see Hawaiian dance and chant as it was, sans the ukuleles (imported) and shoobedoobedoo, accompanied only by the gourds, sticks, and stones, contact the above SFCA for time and location of their next **Annual Conference of Hawaiian Dance.** It's held twice yearly, usually in September and March. The show is fantastic. They will announce in advance that they are *not* here to *entertain you,* but to share the olapas (dances) and meles (chants) of their kapunas (grandparents)" (Shirley Gerum, Haleiwa, Hi.). . . . "One attraction that must not be missed is the annual **'Ho'onanea'** held early in August at Andrews Amphitheater. Four and one-half hours of beautiful kamaaina music presented by Hawaii's youth! Loyal Garner and Bill Haole were the most capable of MCs. When the entire crowd rose to close with 'Hawaii Aloha,' even this haole malihini was Hawaiian" (Susan McEwin, Stratford, Ontario, Canada). . . . "The **Prince of Peace Church** is an interesting attraction on Waikiki Beach; it's on the 12th—top—floor of 33 Lewers, and is referred to as 'the church with a view from the pew' and that is certainly true" (Jerald R. Borgie, San Diego, Calif.).

"I have a suggestion for vacationers who would like to make a very reasonable trip. My mother took two very interesting but not difficult courses at the University of Hawaii, one on the geography of Hawaii, the other on the botany of Hawaii. Both courses enhanced our trip very much. My mother is a teacher, and with these credits she moved up one notch in her income bracket—about $1000! Also, for the time she was in school (about two months), the trip was deductible from her taxes!" (Bonny Warner, Mt. Baldy, Calif.). . . . "In winter and spring, watch for the fairs and carnivals held at local schools such as **Punahou, McKinley High, Iolani,** or the **University of Hawaii.** They have lots of local color, good ethnic foods (great Portuguese malasadas), interesting white elephant and antique booths, carnival midway areas, etc. They are usually free and are fun to attend. There are sometimes local fundraising events at the **Blaisdell Center** or on the large stage at **Kapiolani Park,** at which the name Hawaiian entertainers, like Don Ho or Danny Kaleikini, appear, and these events cost around $2—much cheaper than going to see the same performers at a nightclub. We saw an excellent show with some of the best island talent and Don Ho as MC at the park, in a benefit for Life of the Land, the local ecology group" (Mrs. Joseph G. Astman, Levittown, N.Y.).

"You can now visit the **Kahala Hilton Hotel** by city bus. Take the no. 1 bus on South King Street, transfer on the corner of Wailie and Koko Head, and take the no. 14 bus to the corner of Pueo Street and Kahala Avenue. From here, turn left and walk a few blocks to the hotel. If you pack a lunch, there is a nice spot to eat before going home—the Waialae Beach Park—and the view of Koko Head is absolutely gorgeous. It's really a paradise on that part of the island" (Sharon Perna, Honolulu, Hi.). . . . "For about $2 to $3.50, you can enjoy musical concerts at the **Waikiki Shell.** You sit right on the grass. Bring a beach chair and a picnic dinner and spend a lovely evening under the stars" (Judy Tobor, Van Nuys, Calif.). . . . "I found the **Hawaii Trail and Mountain Club's Sunday walks** one of the most enjoyable parts of my vacation, introducing me to wild country that I should certainly not have seen on my own. An easy walk within Honolulu may be worth a mention. By getting prior permission from the National Guard in Diamond Head (open 8 a.m. to 4 p.m. Monday to Friday), we walked to the top of Diamond Head Crater, an easy 35-minute walk, although the last part involves a steep iron ladder, and needs a flashlight. Worth doing for fantastic views and orientation" (David Brokensha, Santa Barbara, Calif.). . . . **"Fort DeRussy Beach** is extra nice because of the grasses and trees and benches. True, it is primarily for the armed forces, but just walk up the beach and you can stay there all day. We watch the papers closely and always attend native celebrations and gatherings; sometimes news of one is passed on to us by a native. Enjoy them as an honored guest; you will be richly rewarded" (Mrs. S. R. Kranek, Brocksville, Ohio). . . . "Be sure to go early for the **Kodak Hula Show.** All the bleachers were full by 9:15 a.m. or so for the 10 a.m. show" (L. R. Walton, Utopia, Texas). . . . "The **Kodak Hula Show** is dated. Even though it is free, it simply is not worth it" (David Abraham, Forest Hills, N.Y.). . . . "We went to the Kodak show a half hour early because your book recommended going early and learned the hard way that this is not early enough. We went on a Tuesday, which is the first show of the week, and could be part of the reason it was so crowded; but whatever the reason, we had to sit on the ground. With people all around you, it is impossible to change your position, which is hard on the back, and you cannot get any pictures with heads in front of you on the same level. There were many people who were not admitted at all. If the show is always this crowded, it is a shame they don't enlarge the seating capacity" (Shirley Paulus, St. Louis, Mo.). . . . "Anyone planning to attend the free (great) **Kodak Hula Show** in Kapiolani Park has to be prepared to be annoyed by groups handing out candles, etc., and then asking for donations. They are persistent and hard to get rid of" (Sandy Abramovich, Thomaston, Conn.). . . . "The best beach we found on the whole island: **Waimanalo Beach Park**—*not* the State Recreation Area. It's recently opened, has beautiful sand with no rocks, waves that are perfect for bodysurfing, and very small crowds, so far, even on Sunday. The few people there were mostly families" (Sheila Pritchett, Villanova, Penna.). . . . "Square and round dancers can get a complete listing of square and round dance clubs from the HVB. At present, there are nine square dance clubs and two round dance clubs. The **Square Wheelers** meet every Monday at Kapiolani Park bandstand from 8 to 10 p.m., and visitors are welcome" (Diana Buzby, Swarthmore, Penna.).

Chapter VII

SIGHTSEEING IN HONOLULU

NOW WE COME to the serious center of any trip to a new place—seeing the basic sights. If you want to know what makes the 50th state tick, you must explore the city of Honolulu. And if you really want to experience the sights and sounds and feel of a city, the best way to do it is to get out and walk. Happily, it's also the cheapest way and the most fun.

Commercial tours are expensive and can only skim the highlights. We think the city merits more attention. The local buses of the MTL (Mass Transit Lines), a good pair of walking shoes, and the instructions that follow will get you to all the major places. And more important, you can go at your own pace, devoting the most time to what most interests you—and you alone.

These itineraries have been set up as basic touchstones for seeing Honolulu. Improvise at your pleasure. Take two days to do a one-day trip and spend the other half of each day at the beach, if that's what suits you. We've set forth eight different tours of Honolulu and vicinity, only one of which (the trip to Pearl Harbor) will involve more than $1 in transportation costs. In following our directions, please remember once again that makai means to the sea, mauka is to the mountains, Diamond Head is in the direction of Diamond Head crater, and ewa is away from Diamond Head.

If you have any questions about what bus goes where, phone MTL at 531-1611 for information. You may phone anytime between 5:30 a.m. and 10 p.m.—and the people here are really knowledgeable and friendly. Or visit the **Information Booth** at Ala Moana Center, on the street level, open daily from 9 a.m. to 5:30 p.m. (9:30 a.m. to 4:15 p.m. on Sunday). You should also note that traffic on Kalakaua Avenue, Waikiki's main thoroughfare, goes Diamond Head most of the way. Except for a short stretch between the end of Kuhio and the Ala Wai Bridge, buses running from Waikiki downtown should be boarded on Kuhio Avenue. Remember that bus fare is 50¢ (exact change in coins required), and that senior citizens can use the buses free at all times by showing a bus pass. (However, it takes four weeks to get a pass, making it meaningless for most tourists. Information: 531-7066.) Oh yes, they call it **TheBUS.**

Tour 1. Downtown Honolulu

Plan to spend at least a full day on this trip, which covers the major sights of the city: the Honolulu Academy of Arts, the Mission Houses, Kawaiahao Church, Civic Center including the State Capitol, Aloha Tower, the *Falls of Clyde,* the financial and shopping districts, Chinatown, and the downtown Japanese neighborhood. It's a long trip, but once you've done it, you'll have seen the heart of Honolulu. If you prefer, break the trip up into a two- or even three-day jaunt.

THE ACADEMY OF ARTS: Your first destination is the Honolulu Academy of Arts, which you reach by taking the no. 2 bus in Waikiki right to the academy at the corner of Ward and Beretania (that's how the early Hawaiians pronounced Britain), and you'll spot the low, pretty building of the academy. Magnificent art treasures await within. (See "The Art Scene," Chapter VI, for details.) Open Tuesday, Wednesday, Friday, and Saturday from 10 a.m. to 4:30 p.m., Thursday from 11 a.m. to 8 p.m., and Sunday from 2 to 5 p.m. Closed Monday and major holidays. Admission is free.

NEAL S. BLAISDELL CENTER: Now retrace your steps back across Thomas Square to King Street; coming into view is the dazzling Neal S. Blaisdell Center ("NBC" to the locals), a giant $1.25-million arena-concert-theater-convention-hall complex. There are no official tours of the building, but apply at the administration office if you are seriously interested in seeing it; they will have someone show you around. Don't forget to ask for a schedule of coming events while you're there; some big names in the entertainment world may be appearing. The Arena, which can seat up to 8800, was the scene of Elvis Presley's international television special; the Concert Theater, a smaller beauty, is now the home of the Honolulu Symphony Orchestra, and plays host to visiting orchestras, soloists, and theater groups. Happily for us, the best acoustics in the house are in the standing-room section! Blaisdell Center also hosts basketball games, rock shows, and such family-oriented entertainment as the Ice Capades and the circus. In the Exhibition Hall, you might catch a trade show, shows for bird and fish fanciers, and even the Hawaii Science Fair, in which Hawaii's future scientists (intermediate and high school students) display their projects. Admission to these events will be nominal or free. Since this is Hawaii, all is landscaped in a tropical setting with lovely gardens and a lagoon, a perfect natural backdrop to this modern-day marvel.

Note to Parents: Kids will enjoy feeding the tame ducks and geese that live in the ponds on the grounds. They are lovingly cared for by the staff of the City Auditoriums, but are always happy for a handout! You often see local keikis and their moms feeding them loaves of day-old bread.

THE MISSION HOUSES: Now we go back to the Hawaii of old. Cross Ward Avenue on the ewa side of the center, then turn left on King Street and walk ewa three short blocks to King and Kawaiahao Streets. There you will come across the Mission Houses Museum, three 19th-century buildings that will give you a tremendous insight into the lives of the missionaries in Hawaii—and the unlikely intermingling of New England and Polynesia. One of the houses, the home of missionary families, was built of ready-cut lumber that was shipped around Cape Horn from New England; a second, made of coral, houses a replica of the first printing press in the islands, which produced a Hawaiian spelling book in 1822; the third, also of coral, was the warehouse and home of the mission's first business agent.

A huge renovation and restoration project has been completed here and the museum is more attractive than ever. Restored to the period 1821-1860, the Frame House includes furnished parlors, bedrooms, kitchens, and cellar, a collection of original missionary furniture and other personal artifacts, documenting the lives of the families who lived and worked here. This house makes possible the study of a lifestyle and set of cultural values that had a profound influence on Hawaii's history. A new gallery in the 1831 Chamberlain House holds changing exhibits.

The Mission Houses are open daily, 9 a.m. to 4 p.m. If you happen to be in town in June for the Kamehameha Day celebration, don't miss the Fancy Fair on the grounds; about 50 booths are set up to sell local handicrafts, plus refreshing things to eat and drink. Admission, which includes a 45-minute guided tour, is $3.50 for adults, $1 for children 16 and under, free for children under 6. Be sure to pick up a copy of the Mission Houses' 50¢ booklet guiding you through "Historic Downtown Honolulu"; it's very helpful. Also note that a guided walking tour of that area leaves the Mission Houses Museum every weekday morning at 9:30. The fee, including museum admission, is $7, $2 for children 6 through 16. Reservations are advised (tel. 531-0481).

KAWAIAHAO CHURCH: Outside the Mission Houses Museum, turn left and cross Kawaiahao Street to Kawaiahao Church. Inside, the tall, feathered kahilis signify at once that this is royal ground. You're standing in the Westminster Abbey of Hawaii, the scene of pomp and ceremony, coronations, and celebrations since its dedication in 1841. On March 12, 1959, the day Hawaii achieved statehood, the old coral church was filled with ecstatic islanders ringing its bell noisily and giving thanks for the fulfillment of a dream long denied. The next day, the Rev. Abraham Akaka linked the spirit of aloha with the spirit of Christianity in a sermon that has since become a classic in the writings of Hawaii. Note the vestibule memorial plaques to Hawaiian royalty and to the Rev. Hiram Bingham, the missionary who designed the church. Note, too, the outstanding collection of portraits of the Hawaiian alii by artist Patric. If you have time, come back on a Sunday morning at 10:30 when you'll hear a Hawaiian-English service and some beautiful Hawaiian singing. You can visit the church from 9 a.m. to 3 p.m. weekdays, on Saturday from 9 a.m. to noon. Group tours can be taken during the week by appointment.

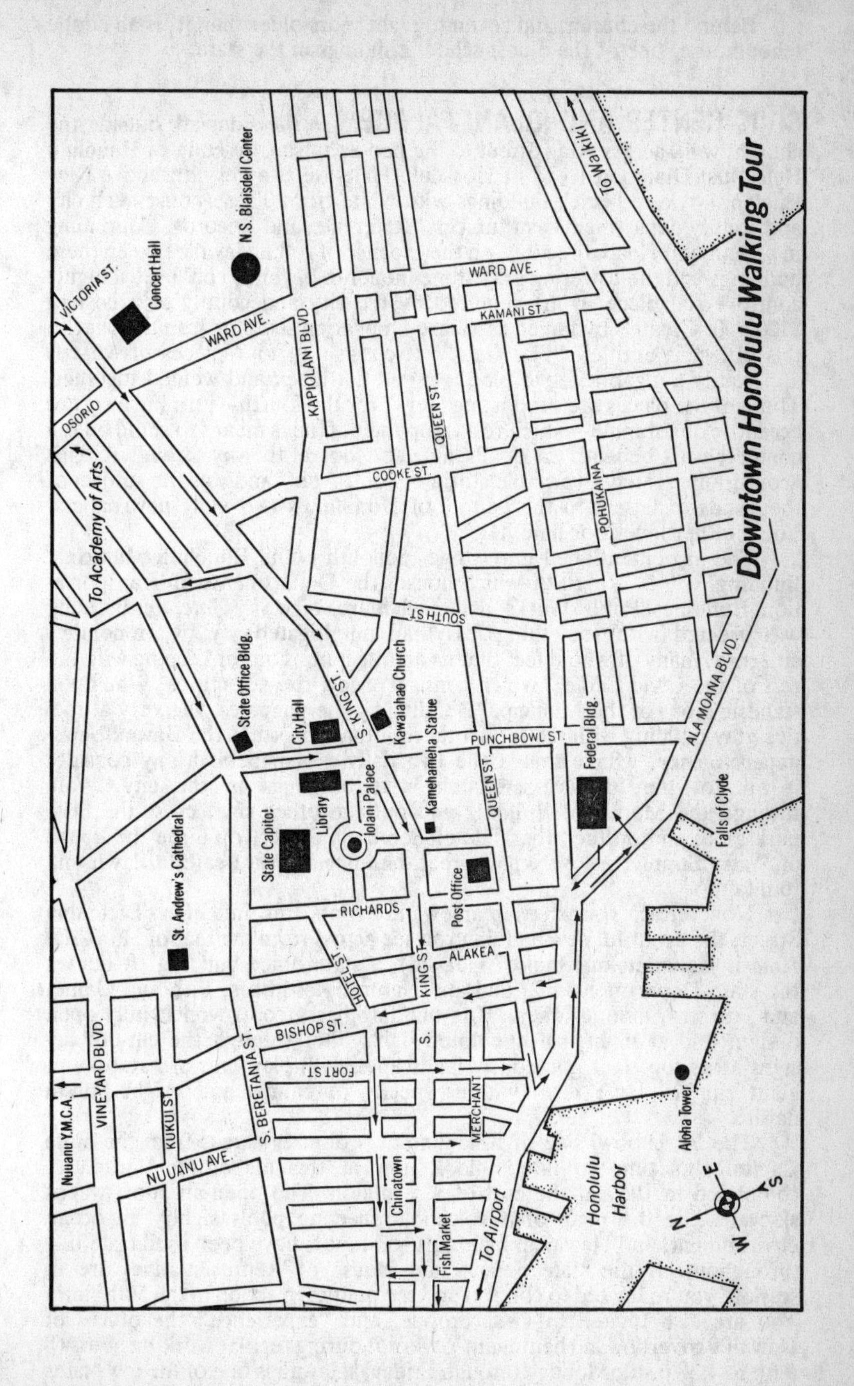
Downtown Honolulu Walking Tour
To Waikiki
N.S. Blaisdell Center
Concert Hall
VICTORIA ST.
WARD AVE.
KAMANI ST.
KAPIOLANI BLVD.
QUEEN ST.
OSORIO
COOKE ST.
To Academy of Arts
POHUKAINA
SOUTH ST.
State Office Bldg.
S. KING ST.
Kawaiahao Church
City Hall
Kamehameha Statue
PUNCHBOWL ST.
Federal Bldg.
ALA MOANA BLVD.
Library
Iolani Palace
State Capitol
St. Andrew's Cathedral
Falls of Clyde
RICHARDS
Post Office
ALAKEA
HOTEL ST.
KING ST.
S.
BISHOP ST.
FORT ST.
S. BERETANIA ST.
VINEYARD BLVD.
KUKUI ST.
Nuuanu Y.M.C.A.
NUUANU AVE.
MERCHANT
Chinatown
Fish Market
To Airport
Aloha Tower
Honolulu Harbor
N
E
S
W

Behind the church, and seven to eight years older than it, is an adobe schoolhouse, one of the oldest school buildings in the state.

CIVIC CENTER AND IOLANI PALACE: On the sidewalk outside the church, walk across King Street to the neo-Spanish City Hall, or **Honolulu Hale.** Just Diamond Head of Honolulu Hale are two very attractive New England–style red-brick buildings with white trim. These house such city and county departments as Municipal Reference and Records. Continuing in a Diamond Head direction, on the expanse of rolling lawn between these buildings and the towering gray stone monolith beyond, you'll see a highly controversial piece of art acquired by the city and county at a cost of $120,000. Created by famed Japanese-Hungarian sculptor Isamu Noguchi, this object is entitled **"Sky Gate."** It consists of four pieces of what is apparently a gigantic stove pipe, painted flat black and welded together. Three of the pieces are supporting "legs" for the fourth—forming a sort of eccentric quadrangle—which rests atop them. One is meant to stand on the concrete walk beneath the quadrangle and look at the sky through it. This acquisition created a veritable storm of controversy and was the subject of thousands of letters to the editors of Honolulu's two daily newspapers. You'll either love it or hate it!

The aforementioned gray stone monolith is the **Honolulu Municipal Building,** 650 S. King St., which houses the Departments of Transportation, Buildings, Public Works, and much more. Like *Sky Gate,* this building was greeted with something less than unmitigated joy by Honolulu's citizenry, many of whom feel that its architecture is out of keeping with the rest of the Civic Center, which consists of low-rise structures. When you stand in front of the Municipal Building by the flagpoles, the very attractive gray building with the terracotta roof that you see is the **Hawaii Newspaper Agency,** which houses the two daily newspapers. Many consider it one of the loveliest monarchy-style buildings in the city. Walk through the Municipal Building and out the other side, cross the little park area, and on the other side of Beretania Street you'll see the **Board of Water Supply,** a lovely pale-green building with a beautiful lawn and fountain.

Now retrace your steps in an ewa direction, this time along Beretania Street; the beautiful new building you see across from the rear of Honolulu Hale is **Kalanimoku** (Ship of Heaven), a state office building. It houses the state Departments of Land and Natural Resources, Fish and Game, and Forestry, among others. The building has a cool, wonderfully open design, and at night, softly colored lights filter through the cut-out designs at its top. It is gorgeously landscaped with plantings of natal plum, giant zinnias, lau'e fern, various species of palms, and bright Shasta daisies.

The Punchbowl side of Kalanimoku is directly across from the **State Capitol.** It's time to take a look now at this magnificent structure, completed in 1969 at the cost of $25 million. The open-air roof sweeps skyward like the peak of a volcano, reflecting pools signify an ocean environment, and Hawaiian materials and motifs have been used tastefully throughout. If the state Senate and House of Representatives are in session, you're invited to come in and see politics in action in the 50th state. You are also invited to visit, browse, and "experience" the offices of Hawaii's governor and lieutenant-governor during regular working hours (8 a.m. to 4:30 p.m., Monday through Friday); Hawaii is one of the few states that allows the public to visit its Executive Office without an appointment or on official business. Be sure, at least, that you see the building; it is a glorious architectural achievement. Note, too, Marisol's controversial statue of Father Damien, and other works of art in front of the building, facing Beretania Street. Just outside the makai side of the building are two new works: a replica of the Liberty Bell and a statue of Hawaii's last reigning monarch, Queen Liliuokalani.

After viewing the State Capitol, go back the same way you came in. Walk makai and you are at the central building of the **Hawaii State Library.** It's a Greco-Roman edifice with a delightful open-air garden court. Visit the Edna Allyn Children's Room to see Hawaiian legend murals by Juliette May Fraser, and take in the other paintings hung throughout the library; those by Madge Tennent are of particular interest. Library hours may differ with the season but are usually from 9 a.m. to 8 p.m. on Tuesday and Thursday, until 5 p.m. every other day, but closed on Sunday. Don't forget to ask about free programs at the State Library and other public libraries on Oahu. They include films, puppet shows, story hours, music recitals, and ethnic programs.

Directly across King Street is the **State Judiciary Building,** and right outside it is the famous statue of **King Kamehameha,** dressed in a royal feathered cape and a helmet that looks curiously Grecian. A symbol of Hawaii (you'll see it in countless pictures and on postcards), this larger-than-life statue of the unifier of the islands is not a great work of art, but it's appropriately heroic. On Kamehameha Day, June 11, the local citizenry decks the statue with huge leis.

Just ewa of the library you'll see a streamlined building, the **Archives of Hawaii.** Inside are invaluable documents, journals, photographs, and other records, the largest collection of Hawaiiana in existence. Visiting hours are Monday through Friday from 8 a.m. to 4:30 p.m.

The Archives are on the grounds of **Iolani Palace,** which is Diamond Head of the building, at King and Richards Streets. Take a good look at the only royal palace on American soil. Until 1969 the State Capitol, it was built during the glittering golden era of Hawaii by King Kalakaua and his queen, Kapiolani. But it housed its royal tenants for only 11 years, from 1882 until the monarchy was overthrown in 1893 by a group of haoles linked to American sugar interests. Kalakaua's successor, his sister, Queen Liliuokalani, spent nine months in the royal bedroom under house arrest after the abortive coup to restore the monarchy. (She is known for her song of farewell, "Aloha Oe.")

Now, after nine years of work and for a total cost of $6 million (the original palace came in for $343,595 in 1882), a massive restoration has been completed by the Friends of Iolani Palace and the Hawaiian flag flies over it once again. Many of the furnishings are still being restored, but several rooms are ready for the public, and the Victorian-Renaissance building is eminently worth seeing. The tour is conducted by extremely knowledgeable docents who will fill you in on plenty of Hawaiian history. While it becomes difficult to imagine the daily life of a royal household in such quiet, almost ghost-like surroundings, the splendid woods and carvings, the gleaming bannisters and shining mirrors, the remarkable plaster reliefs on the ceilings, have a hauntingly beautiful effect.

The Friends of Iolani Palace conduct 45-minute tours every 15 minutes up until 2:15 p.m. Wednesday through Saturday. Reservations are requested, and tickets not claimed 15 minutes before the start of a tour will be sold to anyone who happens to be waiting for a cancellation. The charge is $4 for adults and $1 for children ages 5 to 12 (children under 5 not admitted). You'll have to don enormous khaki "airplane slippers" over your shoes to protect the delicate wooden floors. We thought the tour overlong, but worthwhile nonetheless. Call 536-6185 for reservations.

Look ewa across King Street and you'll see a beautiful pink Spanish-style building with palm tree sentinels; it houses the U.S. Post Office and other federal agencies. Where else but Hawaii could a post office look positively scenic?

Ready for lunch? Check our "Downtown Honolulu" suggestions in Chapter III for some good restaurants.

HAWAII'S WALL STREET: The downtown shopping area is next on your tour. Walk back to King Street and turn right for a three-block walk to the **Fort Street Mall,** a lively shopping thoroughfare lined with fast-food stands and throngs of local people. You'll find Liberty House here, one of Hawaii's leading department stores, as well as a big, fascinating Woolworth's where you can buy grass skirts to send home to your niece—cheap. If you walk four blocks makai on Fort Street you'll come to the **Aloha Tower** at Pier 9 on the waterfront. The tower, open 8 a.m. to 9 p.m. daily, provides a good cool view of the harbor and city in all directions and is a fine spot for nighttime photography of harbor lights and the downtown area. On the ninth floor of Aloha Tower, stop in to see the new **Aloha Tower Maritime Museum,** housing such nautical arts and artifacts as the steam-whistle from the S.S. *Lurline,* flagship of the Matson luxury cruisers; a pictorial history of the development of Honolulu Harbor; and scrimshaw and other objects made by sailors. It's open Monday through Friday from 8:30 a.m. to 4:30 p.m., and admission is free at this writing.

Walk across Ala Moana Boulevard to see the newest (June 1977) buildings of the State Civic Center Mall. These are the $37-million **Prince Jonah Kuhio Kalanianaole Federal Building** and **U.S. Courthouse,** two unusual low-lying structures with terraced roofs in the style of Nebuchadnezzar's Hanging Gardens of Babylon. (They are situated on the ocean side of the Civic Center; the State Capitol is on the mountain side, and Iolani Palace is in the middle.) Two outdoor sculptures here have also caused quite a stir, mostly of the favorable variety. In the courtyard, George Rickey, known for his kinetic and moving sculptures, has fashioned the 31-foot-tall **"Two Open Angles Eccentric,"** and that's just what they are—two huge stainless-steel open and transparent frames that slice through the air but never collide as they frame buildings and sky. In the plaza is Peter Voulkos's 25-foot-long and six-foot-tall bronze called **"Barking Sands,"** composed of serpentine and geometric forms. Be your own art critic and give your verdict. Some lovely fiberworks by Ruthadell Anderson and Sharyn Amii Mills can be seen in the lobby and on the fourth floor of the courthouse.

Two blocks mauka of the Federal Building is Merchant Street—the Wall Street of Hawaii—where the "Big Five," the great financial powers of the islands, have their offices (money and the sea are always closely linked in seaport cities around the world). You'll see the handsome offices of Castle and Cook, Ltd., Davies Pacific Center, Dillingham Transportation, Amfac Center (at Merchant and Bishop), and the almost-Oriental decor of the Alexander and Baldwin, Ltd., building. (The Ltd. appearing after all these names is a remnant of the days when British influence was strong in the islands; so is the Union Jack, which coexists with the American Stars and Stripes in the Hawaiian flag.)

Now, retrace your steps and walk mauka on Bishop Street four blocks to Hotel Street; turn left here and walk ewa five short blocks to Maunakea Street. On the ewa corner you'll see the pagoda-like headquarters of Wo Fat, and you'll know you're in Chinatown.

THE ORIENTAL NEIGHBORHOODS: Now we leave money, power, and the affairs of state for a look at Oriental Hawaii. **Chinatown** begins at Maunakea Street (walk left), with its jumble of shops laden with crafts, herbs, and Chinese groceries. There are several Chinese acupuncturists and Hong Kong herb doctors here (the local people swear by them) should you feel the need. It's fun to poke around on your own, but if you want something organized, two tours are available. If you're free on a Tuesday morning, make arrangements for the **Chinese Chamber of Commerce** tour, whose leader is the well-known local TV and film celebrity, Yankee Chang. The four-hour tour includes visits to shops and two temples. The price is $3 (optional lunch, $4). The tour leaves at 9:30 a.m. from Chinese Chamber of Commerce headquarters at 42 N. King St. (tel. 533-3181 or 533-6967). The **Hawaii Heritage Center,** at 1026 Nuuanu Ave., has a tour on Monday, Wednesday, and Friday (except holidays), from 9:30 a.m. to 12:30 p.m. Cost is $4 per person. For information and reservations, phone 521-2749. If you're on your own and it's time for lunch, join the local folks at any of the plain little restaurants in the neighborhood, or at **Wo Fat,** where a window table will give you a good view of the goings-on below.

The **Cultural Plaza** itself—which occupies the block bounded by Beretania, Maunakea, Kukui, and River Streets—somehow never really took off as a major cultural-shopping area, and often seems half-deserted. This is not one of our favorite shopping centers, since many of the goods seem to be overpriced. We do, however, like **Hakubundo,** a Japanese "book shop" that sells many things besides books, like Japanese art supplies, ricepaper, martial art supplies, etc.; **Art of Japan,** with woodcuts, watercolors, and oils by Japanese artists (we saw some very pretty woodblock prints, nicely framed, for $6.95); **Dragon Gate Bookstore,** with dragon puppets, books, and calendars (in Chinese, of course); and several enjoyable restaurants that we've told you about in Chapter III: **Fat Siu Lau,** the **Mongolian Bar-B-Que,** and **Won Kee.** You might stop in at the Exhibit Hall to see the current show.

On to Japan. Walk three blocks mauka from King Street until you come to Beretania Street. Turn left and walk ewa a block or two to the Nuuanu Stream, where the ambience is slightly Southeast Asian. Across the stream on Beretania, half a block ewa, is the modern Kobayashi Hotel facing Aala Park. Much of the old Japanese neighborhood—scrubby little saimin stands and pool halls, fish and grocery stores under quaint Oriental roofs—has been torn down to make way for new construction. Here's where you'll find the **Kukui Market Place,** with its distinctive blue roof and a pretty courtyard to rest in.

Keep going now, for the best is yet to come. A few blocks mauka on River Street, on the other side of Vineyard Boulevard, is a green-roofed Taoist temple. Slip off your shoes and walk inside for a face-to-face con with Eastern religion. Joss sticks and incense burn at the altar, fo offerings calm the ancestral spirits, and the U.S.A. seems far, far away. This is the **Kwan Yin Temple.** (There's another statue of Kwan Yin—far more splendid, we think—in the Honolulu Academy of Art.)

Tour 2. Punchbowl, Lower Tantalus, and Nuuanu

Here's a compact tour that's typical of the variegated texture of Hawaii: a U.S. military cemetery, a summer home for Hawaiian royalty, some beautiful residential districts, the resting place of the Hawaiian nobility, two Buddhist temples, and one of the most exciting botanical gardens in the world.

To take this half-day ramble, start with a no. 2 bus on Kuhio Avenue heading for town (request a transfer). Get off at Alapai Street and walk a quarter of a block left, where you can pick up the no. 15 bus (Pacific Heights). This leaves every hour on the half hour, more frequently during rush hours. Get off at Puowaina Drive and walk for ten minutes to your first destination, the **National Memorial Cemetery of the Pacific** in Punchbowl Crater. Buried inside the crater of an extinct volcano (which had, with prophetic irony, been named the Hill of Sacrifice by the ancient Hawaiians) are some 20,000 American servicemen who perished in the Pacific during World War II, the Korean War, and the Vietnam conflict. Also listed here are the names of all Pacific war service people who have been recorded as missing or lost or buried at sea. (Visiting next of kin of any service person reported as missing during World War II, Korea, and Vietnam are urged to visit the Administration Office for information on obtaining, without cost, pictures of the Memorial and of the appropriate inscription recorded in the Tablets of the Missing.)

Parents from all over the mainland and from the islands come to Punchbowl on pilgrimages. The endless rows of gravestones of young men form a sobering sight, an awesome monument to the futility of war. When you've had enough, walk for another ten minutes to the lookout at the crater's rim for a sweeping panorama of Honolulu just below. Punchbowl is open to the public every day from 8 a.m. to 5:30 p.m. September 30 to March 1, until 6:30 p.m. the rest of the year.

Walking back to the bus stop, get another no. 15 bus and continue on it for a grand ride through the residential district of Pacific Heights. At the end of the line, another breathtaking view of the city and the Pacific awaits. When you pay for the return trip, get a transfer and leave the bus at Pauoa Road, along which you walk right two blocks to Nuuanu Avenue and bus no. 4R ("Nuuanu–Dowsett"). This bus will take you through damp, lush **Nuuanu Valley,** glorious in scenery and island history (here Kamehameha won the battle that gave him control of Oahu). Unfortunately, there's no bus to the Nuuanu Pali with its magnificent view of Windward Oahu.

The first stop on this leg of the trip is the white frame mansion on the left side, the **Queen Emma Summer Palace.** Emma and her consort, King Kamehameha IV, called this Victorian country retreat of theirs Hanaiakamalama, and it is faithfully maintained as a museum by the Daughters of Hawaii. Hawaiiana mingles comfortably with the 19th-century European furnishings of which Hawaiian royalty was so fond. Stop in at the gift shop for Hawaiian books, notepapers, postcards, and other tasteful items. The museum is open daily from 9 a.m. to 4 p.m. Admission is $3, $1 for ages 12 to 18, 50¢ for under-12s; there are conducted tours through the rooms for all visitors.

Ride on the same bus farther down Nuuanu Avenue, past the brightly colored Chinese Consulate to the **Royal Mausoleum,** on the right. Here's where the last of the Hawaiian alii, the Kamehameha and Kalakaua dynasties, and others of royal blood are buried. You can browse around from 8 a.m. to 4:30 p.m. weekdays. Closed weekends and most holidays except for Kuhio Day (March 26) and Kamehameha Day (June 11).

Resuming your makai trip on the no. 4 bus, ride down to the **Soto Mission of Hawaii,** a Buddhist temple of the Zen sect, at 1708 Nuuanu Ave., between School and Kuakini Streets; just look for its severe central tower and eight smaller octagonal ones (these represent Buddha's Path of Life). The interior is as ornate and Japanese as the exterior is austere, somewhat Indian. Walk in and have a look. They'll be happy to answer any questions. Free. Call 537-9409.

Leaving the temple, walk mauka to Kuakini Street, then turn right one block to Pali Highway, and right again for half a block to the **Honpa Hongwanji Mission Temple** on Pali Highway; this is the cathedral of the Jodo Shin Buddhist sect in Hawaii.

Now retrace your steps to Nuuanu Avenue and walk makai two blocks to Vineyard Boulevard. Turn right and you'll find the entrance to **Foster Botanic Garden** about one block away at 180 N. Vineyard Blvd. This is a marvelously cool oasis on a hot day and one of the most impressive botanical collections to be found anywhere. There are 15 acres of rare trees, flowers, plants, and unusual species of vegetation, many of them brought from the Orient. Orchids bloom throughout the year. Here you can measure the minuteness of man against a tree 20 times taller than you are, and ogle such rare specimens as the cannonball tree, the bombax, and the sunshine tree. On the grounds is a C-shaped granite monument, presented in 1960 to Honolulu by its sister city of Hiroshima, from which most of the first Japanese immigrants came to work the island plantations. A free, self-guided tour brochure is available at the reception office. There are also three free guided tours: a Hawaiian tour on Monday, and a general tour on Tuesday and Wednesday. All tours begin at 1:30 p.m., and reservations are necessary (tel. 531-1939). Foster Garden is open daily, 9 a.m. to 4 p.m. Admission is $1 for adults.

For the return, walk back to Nuuanu Avenue below School Street, board the no. 4 bus to Hotel and Bethel Streets, where you will transfer to a no. 2 bus back to Waikiki.

Tour 3. The University of Hawaii at Manoa, East-West Center, and Manoa Valley

Here's your chance to see what all those bikini-clad coeds are doing when they're not on the beach at Waikiki. Just as they do, take the Route 4 bus that runs from the corner of Kapahulu and Kalakaua right to the university campus. From here you can meander around the beautiful grounds of the university, one of the most relaxed institutions of higher learning we've seen anywhere. Nobody thinks it's unusual for that fellow in the library poring over the card catalog to be barefoot, so why should you?

Although many of Hawaii's socially conscious families still send their children off to mainland colleges (in the old days it was the Punahou-Yale route), the island's own university is the goal of thousands of other youngsters. Established in 1907 as a small agricultural and mechanical arts college, the university has grown into an important center for the study of tropical agriculture, marine biology, geophysics, astronomy, linguis and other fields. Its student body of more than 21,000 reflects multiracial composition of the population of Hawaii. In addition, students come from all 50 states (about 2000 per year) and more than 60 foreign countries (some 1200 each year).

The **East-West Center,** a separate institution at the Manoa campus, is particularly worth your attention. A meeting place of Oriental and Occidental cultures, it brings students, professionals, and research scholars here from Asia, the Pacific islands, and the mainland United States in an exciting exchange of ideas. All students have been given awards that send them first to the University of Hawaii and later out on field work—in the mainland United States for the Easterners, in Asia or the Pacific for the Americans. Later, most of the Asians will go back home to teach or work in government posts, and most of the Americans too will go to live and work in Asia.

Walk over to see the starkly simple East-West Center buildings, a masterful architectural blending of Eastern and Western styles. Free tours leave Monday through Thursday at 1:30 p.m. from **Thomas Jefferson Hall,** but it's easy enough to walk around yourself. The lounge area of Jefferson must certainly be one of the most interesting student centers in the world. Where else can you pick up copies of the *Phnom-Penh Press* (from Cambodia, in French), *Thailand Illustrated,* the *Wall Street Journal,* and *Social Casework,* all from one rack? Asian and other art exhibitions are frequently held in the lounge art gallery.

Walk now to the rear of Jefferson for a peaceful moment at the lyrical Japanese garden, with its waterfalls, stone ornaments, lanterns, and flashing carp. And be sure to see the **John Fitzgerald Kennedy Theater,** one of the best equipped in the world for staging both Western and Oriental dramas. It's the official home of the university's drama department, and a technological center that draws theater people from both sides of the Pacific to study teach and produce plays. Naturally, this is a great boon for the Honolulu theater-going community; a typical season might include productions of a Japanese Kabuki classic, Shakespeare, and a contemporary Broadway comedy.

You'll want to tour the rest of the University of Hawaii campus too. Stop in at the University Relations office in Hawaii Hall, Room 2, to get maps and directions for a self-guided tour. You'll find plenty to see, especially if you're interested in art—the university definitely is: there are two art galleries, and frescoes, sculptures, and works in other media are seen everywhere, from the **Campus Center** to the systems administration center, **Bachman Hall.** Begin on the first floor of that building with Jean Charlot's impressive two-story fresco depicting old and new Hawaii. At **Bilger Hall** are four more murals of old Hawaii, done by leading artists: Juliette May Fraser, Richard Lucier, David Asherman, Sueko Kimura. Artist Murray Turnbull is represented by a stained-glass window in **Keller Hall** and in a series of murals in the **Music Building.** A ceramic work graces one entrance to the Campus Center.

Students of modern architecture will want to see the **Biomedical Sciences Buildings,** designed by Edward Durell Stone.

Nature-lovers can have a treat here too, trying to identify the 560 or so varieties of tropical plants and trees that bloom all over campus. If you need help, check the **University Relations Office** at Hawaii Hall for a map showing names and locations. We'll give you a start: the tree on the side of Hawaii Hall, which looks as if it has large sausages dangling from it, is a native of West Africa, where the oddly shaped fruits are used externally for medical purposes. Here, however, they're just decorative.

Take a gander at the bulletin board in the Campus Center, the student union. You may pick up a tip on a surfboard, a plane ticket to Los Angeles, or someone with a room to share. Need a haircut? The barbershop at **Hemenway Hall** has women barbers; haircuts for both men and women are always a good buy.

Want to take a summer course? The university enrolls over 17,000 summer students in some 500 courses. Get into Hawaii's social and cultural mix with, perhaps, some Asian Studies courses in history, languages, literature, etc. For a physical view of the islands, try—Botany 105 (ethnobotany), Geography 368 (geography of the islands), or Oceanography 201. For a catalog and details, write in advance to the Summer Session Office, 101 Krauss Hall, 2500 Dole St., Honolulu, HI 96822.

The university's noncredit summer courses are also intriguing. How about sailing, stained-glass craft, Ikebana (Japanese flower arranging), hula, ESP, and self-hypnosis—for starters?

Lush **Manoa Valley,** in which the university is located, is one of the most beautiful residential areas in Honolulu and well worth an exploratory trip. You can see its flowering streets and graceful old homes from a no. 12 bus, which you board on University Avenue, back where you entered the campus. The ride up East Manoa Road to Woodlawn will take you past an interesting Chinese cemetery (marked with a big Chinese gate) at the intersection of Akaka Place, where there are often food offerings on the graves.

Taking the same bus back (on the opposite side of the road) toward the university, get off at the intersection of Manoa Road and Oahu Avenue. If you walk a little way to the right on Oahu Avenue, you'll discover the cozy **Waioli Tea Room,** a pleasant restaurant in a gorgeous large garden. The Little Chapel on the grounds was designed for the children of Waioli, and it's rumored that Robert Louis Stevenson courted the muse in the little grass shack (now rebuilt) nearby. You can stop here for lunch, for high tea, and delicious bakery goodies (see Chapter III for details). All proceeds go to the Salvation Army. Afternoon tea is served from 2:30 to 3:30 p.m. (by reservation only), lunch from 11 a.m. to 2 p.m.; the room closes on Sunday and holidays.

The shuttle bus will take you right back to Waikiki.

Tour 4. Bishop Museum and the Dole Cannery

Today's trip takes you to one of the Pacific's most important museums and then on to observe one of Hawaii's major industries in action. It takes half a day.

To reach your first destination, the **Bishop Museum,** go to their Waikiki Heritage Ticket Kiosk (tel. 922-1770), in King's Village, to buy your ticket. With that ticket you are entitled to a free round-trip ride on one of their restored London two-decker omnibuses, which shuttle back and forth at frequent intervals daily. Inside the stone walls at 1525 Bernice St. (which look more like those of a fortress than a museum) is housed a world center for the study of the Pacific—its peoples, culture, history, artifacts. Most fascinating for visitors is the Hawaiian Hall, where special exhibits illustrate particular aspects of early Hawaiian culture. Note the collection of priceless feather cloaks; one uses half a million feathers from the rare mamo b (each bird produced only a few feathers, so the kings built up feather treasuries—which were among the prime spoils of war). Other exhibits re-create the way of life of the Hawaiians, showing the outrigger canoes, a model heiau, weapons, wooden calabashes; trace the history of the Hawaiian monarchy; explore the marine and plant life of the Pacific. All this, plus the fascinating exhibits of primitive art, make for a rewarding visit, worth as much time as you can give it. You can have an inexpensive snack at the Museum Lanai Restaurant. Stop in too at Shop Pacifica for Hawaiian gifts, a cut above the usual: good books on Hawaiiana, children's games, a collection of Hawaiian ethnic dolls, and reproductions of Polynesian artifacts and ancient jewelry. The museum is open daily from 9 a.m. to 5 p.m., except Christmas Day. Admission is $4.75, $2.50 for those 17 and under. Admission includes a live **Heritage Theater** show at the adjacent Atherton Halau and admission to the planetarium. The serious work of the museum goes on behind the scenes and at expeditions in the Pacific. For information, call 847-3511 or 847-1443.

Sharing the museum grounds is the **Hawaii Science Center** (formerly known as **Kilolani Planetarium**), a great spot for anyone interested in space exploration and astronomy. The planetarium has the only observatory in the islands available to the public; it is open after the fascinating evening sky shows on Friday and Saturday at 8 p.m. Shows are also held weekdays at 11 a.m. and 3:15 p.m. Admission is included with your Bishop Museum ticket, the "Passport to Polynesia" tour, or $1.50 for adults, 75¢ for youths 6 through 17. Children under 6 are admitted free (with paying adults) on Saturday and Sunday.

To get to the Bishop Museum via public transportation, board the no. 2 "School–Middle Street" bus and ride it all the way past the center of town to School and Kalihi Streets, where you get off and walk one block makai on Kalihi, then turn left on Bernice Street. The museum complex entrance is at midblock. Or use the free Bishop Museum shuttle bus from major Waikiki locations. Phone 847-3511 for information.

After leaving the Bishop Museum grounds, you can face the modern industrial world again at the **Dole Pineapple Cannery.** To get there from the museum, board the no. 2 bus at School and Kalihi Streets, disembark at Hotel and River Streets, and transfer to the no. 8 bus on the opposite side of the street (make sure it reads "Airport-Hickam"). If you come direct from Waikiki, take the no. 8 "Airport-Hickam" bus on Kuhio direct to the cannery. The walk-through tour of the cannery is given only during the canning season; always call in advance to make sure that tours will be given that day (tel. 536-3411). The rest of the year, however, you can see a free film tour of the canning process. And you can be taken directly to the cannery—as well as to Hilo Hattie's Fashion Center two blocks away—by free bus from major Waikiki hotels. For information, call 538-3663.

Now, about that walk-through tour held during the canning season. The 45-minute tour, led by personable guides through the world's largest fruit cannery, is a fascinating one; the sheer size and efficiency of the operation is most impressive. You'll see thousands and thousands of pineapples bobbing along on huge conveyor belts, looking oddly like lambs for the slaughter. There's an amazing machine (the Ginaca) that can peel and core 100 pineapples in 60 seconds! And there are rows of workers checking and sorting the fruit before it goes into the cans; during the height of the summer harvest season, when the cannery operates at peak capacity, many of these workers will be high school and college students earning next year's tuition. Before the tour, you're free to imbibe as much pineapple juice as you like and you get a delicious fresh slice during the tour. That silly-looking pineapple on top of the building, by the way, is not filled with pineapple juice; it's the water tower. There is a charge of $2 for the tour, 50¢ for children under 17.

To return to Waikiki, take the no. 8 bus outside the cannery on Iwilei Road in the opposite direction.

Tour 5. Pearl Harbor

Anyone who remembers—or has heard about—December 7, 1941, should not leave the Hawaiian Islands without seeing Pearl Harbor. The cheapest way to get there is by TheBUS; bus no. 20 goes right from Waikiki to Pearl City. From Ala Moana Center, you can take no. 50, 51, or 52. The trip should take about an hour. Ask the driver to let you off at the **U.S.S. Arizona Memorial.** You can also take private bus services direct to the *Arizona* Memorial: the *Arizona* Memorial Shuttle Bus, $5 round trip (tel. 947-5015), and Airport Motor Coach, $3.50 round trip (tel. 955-1446). Reservations are necessary.

The new $4.2-million Visitor Center, administered by the National Park Service, provides an ideal starting point for your trip to the U.S.S. *Arizona* Memorial. Its museum relates the early history of the war at sea and life in wartime Hawaii. Step up to the Information Desk, where you will be given a tour number, which will tell you approximately when your shuttle boat will leave. Because the crowds can be enormous—up to 4000 on very heavy days—you may have to wait for two hours or more, unless you arrive before 9:30 a.m., when the wait should be short. While you're waiting, you can study a detailed mural of the *Arizona* or check out the books and souvenirs in the gift shop. When your number is called, you enter the theater to see a 20-minute film, and then are ferried on a navy boat to the U.S.S. *Arizona* Memorial.

Dedicated in 1962, the memorial is a covered white concrete bridge rising starkly above the hull of the battleship *Arizona,* victim of a direct hit on the day that bombs fell on Hawaii, and the tomb of 1000 American servicemen (some 2335 in all were killed that day). The outlines of the ship shimmer just below the water, and, as if warning that the story is not yet finished, oil slicks still rise from the rusting hulk. Like Punchbowl Cemetery, it is an eloquent witness to the fury and folly of war. A big experience.

Note: The Pearl Harbor Visitor Center is closed on Monday and navy boats that take visitors to the U.S.S. *Arizona* Memorial do not operate. If the weather is stormy, call the *Arizona* Memorial at 422-0561 to find out if the boats will be operating. Children under 6 are not permitted on the shuttle boats, but they are permitted at the Visitor Center itself; those 6 to 10 must be accompanied by an adult; bathing suits and bare feet are taboo.

If you have time, you can take a short walk from the *Arizona* Memorial to visit **Bowfin Park,** where the U.S.S. *Bowfin,* a World War II submarine launched one year after the attack on Pearl Harbor, is moored. Admission of $3 for adults, $1 for children 6 to 12, includes a guided tour. Open daily, 9:30 a.m. to 4:30 p.m.

Tour 6. Paradise Park

We recommend this place especially to families traveling with children; all of you can have a good time. Although it's easier to drive here, TheBUS can get you there within 45 minutes from Waikiki. Take the no. 8 bus to Ala

Moana, then transfer to the no. 8 with a card sign in the front window saying "Paradise Park." You can take the same buses back to Waikiki. Better still, take their free shuttle from Waikiki (tel. 988-2141).

The most exciting focus at Paradise Park is birds—mostly from South America and Africa (Hawaiian birds can be found in the Honolulu Zoo). You'll see rare birds as they are found in their natural habitats, in lush jungle and forest settings of great beauty. As you arrive, you'll descend into a mammoth cage with a circular walkway and all the parrots and macaws come up to you for a handout. Scheduled shows held at the Kamehameha Amphitheater offer birds that play poker, ride bikes across a tightrope, and do other amazingly human things. There is also a trained duck show on the grounds, and special shows at various times featuring different ethnic entertainment (the parks theme is a multicultural one) and children's entertainment. You can also take the marvelous jungle trails (don't miss the grove of Asian bamboos), see demonstrations of Hawaiian arts and crafts, gawk at and photograph what seem like millions of orchids, trees, flowers, and plants. And you're sure to enjoy the new "Dancing Waters" show. Plan on 3½ to 4 hours to enjoy it all.

Henri's Hawaii restaurant overlooking the grounds is a beauty, and prices are not overly expensive. They have a very pleasant Saturday and Sunday brunch, featuring a salad bar, at $7.95 for adults, $5.95 for children. Or you can fill up on hot dogs, soft drinks, and ice cream at the modestly priced snackbar. Admission to Paradise Park is $7.50 for adults and $3.75 for children 4 to 12. It is open daily, except Christmas Day, from 9:30 a.m. to 5 p.m.

Tour 7. Castle Park

This is another trip we recommend particularly to families with children, but we don't see why everybody shouldn't enjoy a visit to Castle Park, the first major theme amusement park—à la Disneyland—to hit the islands. Castle Park is much smaller than Disneyland—just 16 acres—but it packs a lot of fun into that space. The most exciting attraction, perhaps, is Water Country, which gives the daring a chance to ride one of two 400-foot water flumes or shoot the rapids on a white-water raft run (the rafts are huge truck inner tubes); the less adventurous can watch from the beach. Admission to Water Country alone is $6 for adults, $5 for children.

The rest of Castle Park also has plenty going for it: a real fairytale castle with drawbridge and moat (inside it's filled, paradoxically, with Space Age electronic and video games); three 18-hole miniature golf courses whose strange and wonderful obstacles include haunted houses and windmills; a batting range with authentic major-league baseball and softball pitching machines; the Grand Prix racing car ride, where you hope not to bump into other drivers, and Bumper Boat Lake, where you do. All in all, plenty to keep everybody in the family occupied for a full day's worth of fun. There's a snackbar on the grounds.

There is no admission charge to enter Castle Park. Each attraction has its own price, or you can buy a script card at $12.40, kids or grownups. To reach Castle Park, open daily from 9:30 a.m. to 10:30 p.m. weekdays, until 12:30 a.m. on Friday and Saturday, take the H-1 Freeway and follow the Aloha Stadium signs. It's about an eight-minute drive from downtown Honolulu.

Tour 8. A Waikiki Checklist

We're not going to map out any formal tour of the Waikiki area, since you'll be spending so much of your time here anyway. We'll simply remind you of some of the attractions you can see more or less anytime, before or after a swim at the beach.

The big hotels, of course, are great for strolling in and out of in the evening (see Chapter III). While you're at it, check out the sleek modernity of the **Ilikai,** the tasteful Polynesian architecture of the **Waikikian,** the graceful airs of the **Moana,** the old-world splendor of the **Royal Hawaiian.** The **Hawaiian Regent,** one of the newer hostelries, is done in beautiful taste, with its open-air lobby surrounding a central court aglow with a fountain and two lagoons. Walk up two flights of stairs to the pool and the Ocean Terrace, and you'll be rewarded with one of the most beautiful open daytime views in Waikiki. The hotel seemingly juts out right over the beach (even though it's across the street), and the glorious colors of ocean and sky surround you wherever you look. The famed **Halekulani Hotel,** the last of the low-rise, Hawaiian-style cottage hotels on the beach, has been totally rebuilt. The $100-million project has preserved the main two-story structure as an indoor-outdoor dining area and added five interconnecting high-rise buildings. It's luxury all the way here, in the first world-class hotel to be built in this area in 25 years. The **Hilton Hawaiian Village** represents Henry J. Kaiser's first contribution to Hawaii (he sold it to Hilton some years back and moved on to even bigger projects). It's a fascinating cornball beach city of its own, with 20 acres of tropical gardens, an artificial lagoon, three bars, seven restaurants, two nightclubs, six pools, a beautiful beachfront, its own post office, and a catamaran fresco by Jean Charlot in its Kona Koffee Shop and Beachburger. The array of fascinating shops here includes the Rainbow Bazaar, which we've detailed in Chapter V. Walk around for a few minutes and you'll view a cross-section of Hawaii's visitors—anybody from a group of Shriners on one side to a gaggle of blushing young Japanese couples on another.

Near the Hilton is the **Fort DeRussy Military Reservation,** a great low-cost recreation area for the military on a prime strip of Waikiki Beach. Fortunately, the beach is now open to the public, and many claim it's the best in Waikiki. You can usually park there too. (The 15-story Hale Koa Hotel here offers attractive, well-priced rooms to active and retired military, dependents, and widows of retired personnel.) You may want to stop in for a quick visit to the **U.S. Army Museum** in Fort DeRussy Park, which contains military memorabilia dating from ancient Hawaiian warfare to the present. It is housed in Battery Randolph, built in 1909 as a key installation in the defense of Honolulu and Pearl Harbor. Exhibits include "Hawaiian Military History," "Coast Artillery Defense," "The Pacific War, Korea, and Vietnam," and "A Hawaiian Gallery of Heroes." On the upper deck, the **Corps of Engineers Pacific Regional Visitors Center** graphically shows how the Corps works with the civilian community in managing water resources in an island environment. The museum is open Tuesday through Sunday from 10 a.m. to 4:30 p.m., admission free (tel. 543-2639).

You will, of course, want to spend a lot of time shopping and browsing at the **International Market Place, King's Village,** and the **Royal Hawaiian Shopping Center** (details in Chapter V). Whether you're shopping or not, though, you'll want to see the demonstrations of tapa clothmaking and other Polynesian handicrafts, presented daily at various times from 9 a.m. to 11 p.m. at the International Market Place. You'll spot the local girls working as you come in the main entrance—they'll be busy making dolls, weaving bracelets, or constructing shell or flower leis.

Of course you'll have to see **Hemmeter Center,** a stunning architectural landmark encompassing the super-luxurious Hyatt Regency Waikiki Hotel, plus a huge shopping center, restaurants, and cocktail lounges. The entire area is dramatically landscaped, with tropical foliage, trees and plantings, huge sculptures, many-storied waterfalls, flowing lagoons, picturesque kiosks, and Polynesian objets d'art. The Hyatt Regency, however, is slightly out of our range: penthouses at $550 per day. It's on Kalakaua, between Uluniu and Kaiulani Avenues.

There are more than a few things to see at the Diamond Head end of Waikiki, up near Kapiolani Park. Past Kuhio Beach, at Kapahulu Avenue, the **Honolulu Zoo** looms up on your left (the entrance is at 151 Kapahulu Ave.). It's noted for its collection of native Hawaiian and other tropical birds. You'll see Australia's national bird, the "Laughing Jackass" (more politely referred to as the kookaburra); gorgeously colored flamingos; handsome blue- and purple-crowned pigeons from New Guinea; and various bird-jungle habitats. The kids will get a kick out of the four primate islands surrounded by moats. There's also the usual array of African lions, Bengal tigers, two Asiatic elephants, and three adorable Himalayan sun bears. With Diamond Head providing the background, plenty of trees and flowers (including a giant banyan and date palms), white doves, and keikis tumbling about, it's one of the most charming zoos anywhere. Every half hour between 10 a.m. and noon and again between 1 and 4 p.m., you can take one of the Honolulu Zoo Hui mule-drawn trolleys around the zoo grounds; fare is $1 for adults, 50¢ for children 1 through 12. The zoo is open every day (except Christmas and New Year's Days) from 8:30 a.m. to 4:30 p.m. During June, July, and August, the zoo stays open until 7:30 on Wednesday evenings, with free entertainment starting at 6 p.m. at the stage under the earpod tree, just behind the flamingos. Take a picnic supper and join the fun. Local artists hang their work on the fence outside on Saturday, Sunday, and Wednesday. Be sure to stop in at Zootique, the charming gift shop (described in Chapter V). Admission to the zoo is $1 for adults, 50¢ for children.

From here on, Kalakaua Avenue is a regal, although narrow, tree-lined drive. And a little farther on, where Kalakaua meets Monsarrat Avenue, **Kapiolani Park** begins (those are the Koolau Mountains in the background). The 220 acres of the park have facilities for just about everything, from soccer to rugby to picnicking; also archery, a golf driving range, and tennis. The Royal Hawaiian Band plays frequently in the bandstand, and major musical events take place in the Waikiki Shell. For a particularly beautiful view, note Diamond Head framed in the cascading waters of the splendid Louise C. Dillingham Fountain.

Bordering the ocean on the right is a stretch of wide, palm-dotted grass lawn with a fringe of sand to let you know you're still at the beach. Swimming here is excellent, since the surf is quite mild; it's a big favorite with island families. **Kapiolani Beach Park,** with locker room, rest rooms, picnic tables, and snackbar, is just ahead.

The **Waikiki Aquarium** is also up here, just past the beach, and it's a lot of fun. Here's your chance to see, among other creatures of the deep like giant clams and sharks, the lauwiliwilinukunukuoioi; if you can't pronounce it, just ask for the long-nosed butterfly fish. The museum features an exhibit entitled "Hawaiians and the Sea," focusing on the early Hawaiians' love of and dependence on the sea. The aquarium is open daily from 9 a.m. to 5 p.m. Admission is free, but donations from adults are invited—to help them feed the fish.

Now it's time to rest your feet—and see something new—by hopping aboard a no. 14 bus going Diamond Head on Kalakaua Avenue. The bus will take you through the lovely **Waialae-Kahala** area and **Kaimuki** suburbs, and up the moutain to **Maunalani Heights.** From there, you can look straight down into **Diamond Head Crater,** Koko Head on the left, Waikiki slightly to your right. On your return trip, change to a no. 2 bus, and you'll be back in Waikiki. Or if you prefer, stay on the no. 14 and ride up to **St. Louis Heights** for a magnificent panorama of Honolulu. A forest of beautiful Norfolk pines with picnic tables and a splendid view of Manoa Valley awaits you here at the **Waahila Ridge State Recreation Area.**

Note: If you're making this little trip on wheels, you can actually drive right inside Diamond Head Crater—the only drive-in crater on Oahu, except for Punchbowl. Here's how you do it. Follow Kalakaua until it circles left, just past the Colony Surf Hotel; then make your first right to Diamond Head Road. Come up Diamond Head Road, past the lighthouse on the right. Take your first left before the triangular-shaped park; you are now entering the Fort Ruger area. Watch for the Diamond Head Crater sign on the left and follow the road to the left. Go through the tunnel, and you're in Diamond Head State Monument. Hiking trails go up to the rim of the crater. The area looks quite undramatic, but where else, but in Hawaii, can you drive into a volcano!

TOURS FOR THE HANDICAPPED: **Handicabs of the Pacific** offers special tours for handicapped passengers, in specially equipped vans that can handle six wheelchairs. Typical city tours cost $21 per person for four to five people; for under four, forget it: the tab is $110 per person! For information, phone 524-3866.

READERS' SIGHTSEEING SUGGESTIONS: "I would like to put in a good word for **E Noa Tours** (tel. 941-6608). We had a delightful city tour in a van with two other families for $13 each, $11 for children. We had a charming and helpful guide who gave us loads of tips for a great stay in Hawaii" (Ken and Dorothy Gimblin, Sacramento, Calif.). [*Authors' Note:* We get many letters each year praising E Noa and their warm hospitality that makes each passenger feel like a personal guest.] . . . "Perhaps you could suggest that people lock their cars, especially when stopping at scenic spots. This was the first thing my family in Hawaii warned us about, as there has been a lot of trouble with tourists' cars being robbed while they viewed the sights. One time when we were at the Blow Hole, we heard a police officer stop a couple and ask the woman if she had left her purse in the open car. When she said 'yes,' he politely but firmly told her to go back to get it, and lock the car. He also said, 'You people are careless, then you come to us and expect us to do something about it when your things are stolen'" (Mrs. Joseph Astman, Levittown, N.Y.). . . . "Please advise all visitors to do their sightseeing on their own. Bus sightseeing trips consisted of a few ten-minute stops at scenic points and too many long stops at tourist traps, always trying to sell something. Also, they *all* seem to arrive at a point at the same time, dumping hundreds of tourists together trying to see the same sight in the same ten-minute time limit, and generally raising havoc" (John C. Schmid, Line Lexington, Penna.).

"For those who *like* walking we would recommend the three-hour **walking tour of Historic Old Honolulu,** which includes the State Capitol Building, a worthwhile visit in itself. Here we were warmly welcomed by a receptionist who gave us a couple of very interesting and beautifully printed pamphlets on the capitol buildings, with terrific color pictures, including aerial shots of the grounds and Iolani Palace, and packed with facts on Hawaiian history, geography, culture. A really nice souvenir!" (Lloyd and Shirley Kilby, Hope, B.C., Canada). . . . "Just past Paradise Park on Manoa Road, the road ends. We parked and took a delightful 45-minute hike through the lush ferns and plants to a beautiful waterfall. This trail is mostly known only to locals and is well worthwhile" (Richard Marks, Lodi, Calif.). . . . "For what it's worth, we found **Polynesian Adventure Tours** on Oahu excellent—although the drivers were very, very loquacious!" (Richard K. Beebe, Litchfield, Conn.).

"Pearl Harbor was a disappointment because the U.S. Navy has turned the operation of the *Arizona* Memorial over to the National Park Service. We were exposed to a second-generation Japanese who took great pride in the "majestic victory of December 7th," and lectured us on why we should not live in the past. One of his statements was that Japan had no intention of starting a war, but was merely trying to prevent American interference in Japanese expansion through the Pacific. When I showed evidence of opening my big mouth, my wife gave me the elbow hard enough to sink my floating rib, explaining that since we were outnumbered by Japanese tourists, it was better not to start the war again after all these years. The memorial was impressive, but the lecture left me wondering who did finally win the war" (W. J. Murphy, Falmouth, Mass.).

Chapter VIII

AROUND OAHU

1. The Seaside Drive
2. The Pali and Makiki Heights
3. The Waianae Coast
4. Tips for Tourists

YOU HAVEN'T REALLY SEEN HAWAII until you've left the urban sprawl of Waikiki and Honolulu and traveled to the other side of the mountains for a look at Windward Oahu. And what a look that is! There are jagged cliffs and coral beaches; Stone Age ruins and tropical suburbs; a vast military concentration; backwoods country towns sleeping in the sun; endless stretches of breadfruit, banana, papaya, hibiscus, lauhala, coconut palms—the glorious vegetation of the tropics so ubiquitous as to be completely taken for granted. And best of all, some of the most intriguing sightseeing attractions in the 50th state are here: Sea Life Park, the Byodo-In Temple, and the Polynesian Cultural Center.

Not one advertising billboard defaces the landscape; they're kapu in Hawaii. The only signs you will see are those of the Hawaii Visitors Bureau's red-and-yellow warrior pointing to the places of interest. There are dozens of spots for beachcombing and picnicking, so pack your bathing suit and lunch. If you get an early start, you can certainly make this trip in one day, but there's so much to see that two would be much more comfortable. We'll provide a basic itinerary, around which you can plan your time.

TRANSPORTATION: You can now see a good part of the island by sticking to public transportation. The Wahiawa-Kaneohe bus no. 52, which leaves Ala Moana Center every 15 minutes from 6:15 a.m. to 6 p.m. daily ($1, including a transfer back to the beach area), will enable you to see many island points of interest: the big surf at Haleiwa, Sunset Beach and the North Shore, the Polynesian Cultural Center, to name some. Many of our readers make this trip and praise it highly. But since it is a commuter service, not a sightseeing bus, and would take you many, many hours, we personally believe it's not the best way to go. We therefore recommend that you part ways with the public transportation system and rent a car. If you're traveling alone or don't want to drive, you can, of course, take any of the standard around-the-island sightseeing tours. (We've had excellent reports, over the years, on those offered by **E Noa Tours**—tel. 941-6608; for a report, see the Readers' Suggestions at the end of this chapter.) But for two or more, it's far cheaper to rent a car for the day (total costs should come to about $25), and the really akamai way to do it is to find three or four other people and split the expenses down to practically nothing. But the main thing is to make the trip whatever way you decide. You might even consider hitching; since the bus strike a few years back, it has not been against the law to hitch, and many people do. If you're driving, remember to lock your car doors and take your valuables with you when you get out to look at the sights.

ON YOUR WAY OUT OF TOWN: You start at Waikiki, driving Diamond Head on Kalakaua Avenue past Kapiolani Park; this will lead you into Diamond Head Road, which runs into Kahala Avenue past the sumptuous residential area of Black Point (Doris Duke's seaside mansion is nearby). Sculptress Kate Kelly's monument to Amelia Earhart is just past the Diamond Head Lighthouse. At the end of Kahala Avenue, where it hits the Waialae Golf Course, turn left on Kealaolu Avenue; follow this road to Kalanianaale Highway (Route 72); the entrance will be on the right. Before you turn, you come to **Waialae Beach Park,** with modern facilities, covered pavilions, and wide, wide beaches, right next door to the prestigious Waialae Country Club. The swimming here, however, is not too good, since there are many rocks in the water. Next door is the splendid Kahala Hilton Hotel; you might want to have a look at the lovely grounds.

Just before you reach **Koko Head,** you'll pass the entrance to Henry Kaiser's once-controversial **Hawaii Kai**—a 6000-acre, $350-million housing development that's a small city in itself. You can drive in for your own tour of inspection. (A resident advises us that there is a beautiful view at the top of the hill past the Hawaii Kai Golf Course overlooking the ocean and the south end of Windward Oahu.) While you're in this area, you may want to stop in at **Waterfront Village,** a charming small shopping complex perched right out on the waters of Koko Marina, and just across the way from the much larger Hawaii Kai shopping center.

Koko Head and **Koko Crater,** now coming into view ahead, are reminders that Oahu, like all the Hawaiian islands, is a volcanic mountain spewed out of the Pacific. During Oahu's last eruption (volcanologists say it happened at least 10,000 years ago), these craters and the one that houses **Hanauma Bay** were born. One side of Koko Head has been washed away into the sea and the result is an idyllic beach, one of the most popular in the islands. Since the placid turquoise waters cover a cove in the purple coral reef, it is a perfect place for beginning and advanced snorkelers. (Rent snorkels in Waikiki or bring your own; none is available here.) Hanauma Bay is now a marine reserve, and so gentle have the fish become that parrot fish, bird wrasses, and others will eat bread from a swimmer's hand. There are dressing facilities, camping, barbecue and picnic areas. Although the beach is a very long walk from the parking area, the driver can drive all the way down to the beach, discharge his passengers, and then drive up to park. Or all of you can take a train from the parking lot to the beach for 55¢. Be sure to lock your car and remove any valuables! Needless to say, the islanders love this place, and the only problem is that you've almost always got to share it with quite a lot of them. (Before you begin this stretch, see "The Pali and Makiki Heights" below.)

1. The Seaside Drive

For the next few miles, you'll be driving along one of the most impressive stretches of rocky coastline in the islands. The black lava cliffs

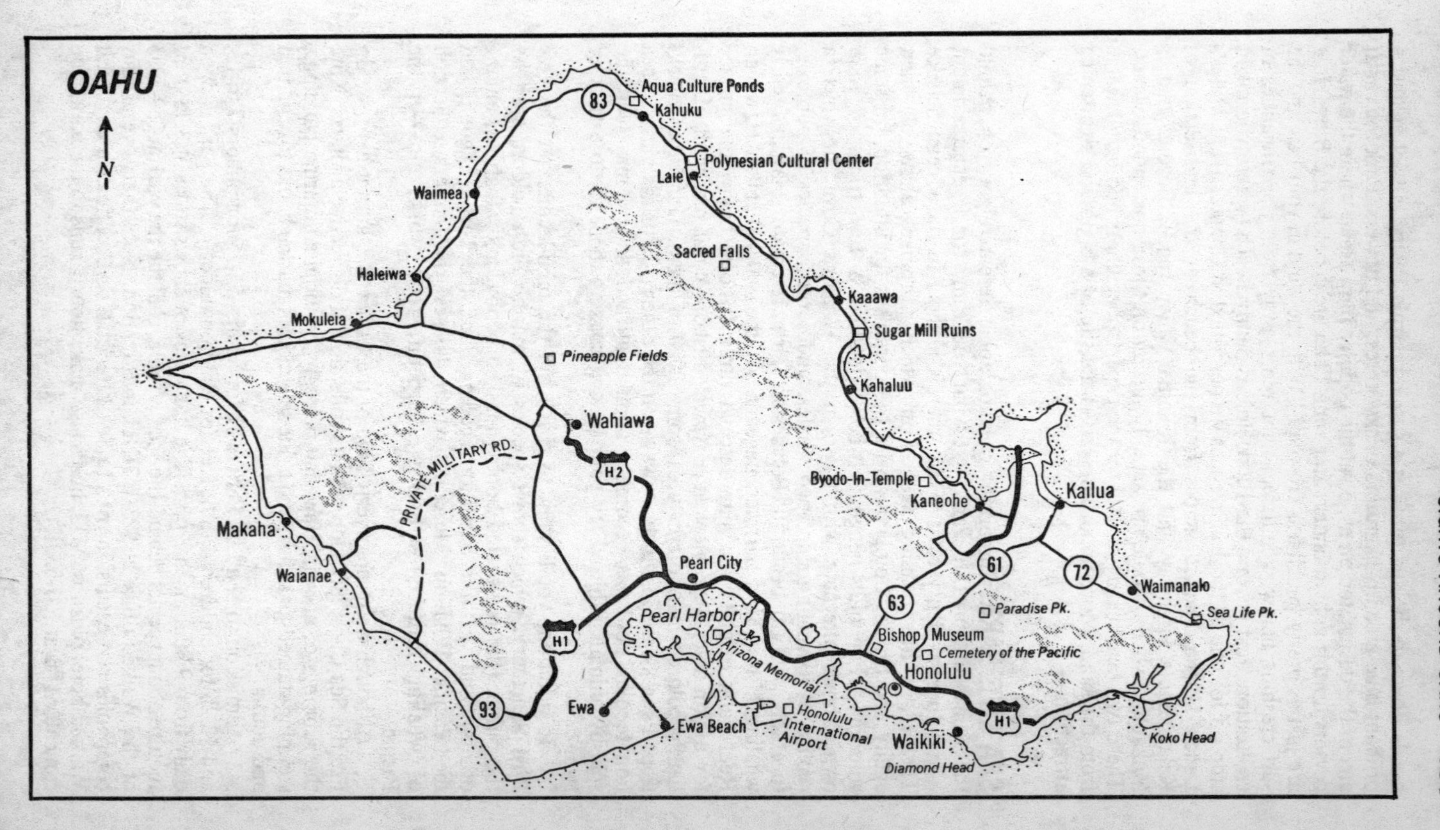
OAHU
N
Aqua Culture Ponds
Kahuku
83
Polynesian Cultural Center
Laie
Waimea
Sacred Falls
Haleiwa
Kaaawa
Mokuleia
Sugar Mill Ruins
Pineapple Fields
Kahaluu
Wahiawa
PRIVATE MILITARY RD.
H2
Byodo-In-Temple
Kaneohe
Kailua
Makaha
Waianae
Pearl City
61
72
63
Waimanalo
Paradise Pk.
Sea Life Pk.
Pearl Harbor
H1
Bishop Museum
Cemetery of the Pacific
Arizona Memorial
Honolulu
93
Ewa
Ewa Beach
Honolulu International Airport
Waikiki
H1
Koko Head
Diamond Head

hurtle down to the sea to meet a surging purple Pacific, all set against a brilliant blue-green background of sky, trees, and flowers. Park the car at any of the designated areas, or at the popular **Blow Hole,** where the water geysers up through an underwater vent. (The areas before the Blow Hole are just as pretty, much less crowded.) With the wind in your hair and the surf crashing below, you'll feel light years away from the trivialities of civilization. Just beyond the Blow Hole is **Sandy Beach** (where you might stop off for one of those shave ices we described in Chapter III at **Malia's Lunch Wagon,** parked across from the beach at the intersection of Kalanianaole Highway and the Kalama Valley road). Beyond that is **Makapuu,** where people are actually surfing on those horrendous waves. These two beaches are strictly for the experts; beginners had better watch from the sand. More important, this is the site of a big island sightseeing attraction—

SEA LIFE PARK: Important oceanographic research goes on behind the scenes at Sea Life Park, but what you came for is entertainment —and there's plenty of it. First, there's a show in the Ocean Science Theater, a live training session in which porpoises show off their agility and brains. Competing with the porpoises for attention are some winsome Humboldt penguins who've learned a few tricks of their own. Shows alternate with those in the Whaler's Cove, in which a replica of a whaling ship, two whales, and several species of porpoise, together with a beautiful Polynesian girl, re-create Hawaii's early whaling history in a narrated pageant. At the 300,000-gallon Hawaiian Reef Tank exhibit, you may descend three fathoms below the surface for a skin-diver's-eye view of a typical offshore coral reef, full of brilliantly colored marine creatures, some 2000 of them. Dangerous black-tipped sharks are just inches away—on the other side of the glass. A sea lion feeding pool has become a popular attraction: you may feed the splashy animals fish and try your luck at coaxing them to do a trick or two.

In addition, you'll want to check out the mini-lectures at the new **Bird Sanctuary,** which shows species of marine birds seldom seen by the public (the red-footed booby, masked booby, and albatross, among others); and visit the Sea Lion Feeding Pool, the Turtle Lagoon, and the Pacific Whaling Museum, which houses the largest collection of whaling artifacts—scrimshaw, harpoon, rope work, etc.—in the Pacific.

Although we're not overly fond of the Galley Restaurant here, we do like the Sea Chest gift shop with its collection of distinctive artifacts. Note the rubbings of ancient Hawaiian petroglyphs, original marine paintings, stunning stained-glass fish, and a fine selection of marine books for children and adults.

Admission to Sea Life Park is $7 for adults, $5.25 for juniors 7 to 12, and $2.25 for children 4 to 6; free for children under 4. The park is open daily from 9:30 a.m. to 5 p.m. The last series of shows starts at 3:15 p.m. Inquire about special behind-the-scenes tours. Call the the park at 259-7933 or the Waikiki office at 923-1531 for information. Note that several tour companies run excursion trips to Sea Life Park several times a day, with Waikiki hotel pickups. MTL buses also make hourly runs to the park. You can call MTL at 531-5321.

ON TO HEEIA: Off **Rabbit Island,** the water turns turquoise. The inland view along this coast is also spectacular, thanks to the towering **Koolau Mountains;** their corrugated slopes (an example of the forces of erosion at work on volcanoes) are a neat balance to the restless sea on your right.

Just past Sea Life Park, you'll find **Waimanalo Beach Park,** which many island families consider the best beach on Oahu: pleasant surf, grassy knolls, picnic tables, the works. You may want to come back here for a long stay. For now, drive on for a few more miles and you'll come upon what was long considered one of Oahu's most magnificent beaches by the few people lucky enough to enjoy it—the military. This is **Bellows Beach Park,** nestled against the mountains, a 46-acre strip of fine sand, lively but not dangerous surf, and wooded picnic groves of palm and pine. After long years, Bellows has been opened to the public, but on weekends only, from Friday noon to midnight Sunday; and on federal and state holidays. There are public bathhouses. (It's a favorite spot for tent and trailer camping; permits from the Recreation Department, City and County of Honolulu.) Bellows is a perfect place for a picnic lunch (bring your own, as there's nothing to buy), or a swim, the only danger (aside from occasional Portuguese man-of-wars) being that you may be tempted to spend the whole day and forget about your exploring. Keep going, for the best is yet to come.

Haiku Gardens

Your next stop might be a chance to stretch a bit at Haiku Gardens. The main house of this old kamaaina estate is the **Haiku Gardens Restaurant,** where you can stop by for a decently priced luncheon (see Chapter III for details). But you don't need to eat here or pay any other admission to tour the grounds, which are open during daylight hours. A lily pond dominates all, and from it, trails lead off which will take you to, among other things, a lovely grove of golden bamboo from Java, Hawaiian grass huts, a palm grove, a bird sanctuary, fragrant plantings of ginger and anthurium, and exotic fish ponds. To reach the gardens, turn left off the highway at Haiku Road and proceed mauka about a mile.

Byodo-In Temple

For devotees of Orientalia, we know of no more rewarding spot in the islands than the Byodo-In Temple in the Valley of the Temples, which should be your next destination. It's about two miles from Haiku Road, and you can reach it by driving back to Kahekili Highway from Haiku Gardens and proceeding north. (If you haven't stopped at Haiku Gardens, continue on Kamehameha Highway to Pineapple Hill, proceed to the intersection, then turn left the way you came onto Kahekili Highway; you'll come to Valley of the Temples in about half a mile.) Byodo-In is an exact replica of the venerable Byodo-In, reputed to be the most beautiful temple in Kyoto, Japan, constructed at a cost of $2.6 million and dedicated on June 7, 1968, almost 100 years to the day after the first Japanese immigrants arrived in Hawaii. The temple sits in a magnificently landscaped classical Japanese garden fragrant with pine, plum, and bamboo. Inside, you can gaze at the intricately carved screens and panels, and pay obeisance to the magnificent gold carving of Amida, the Buddha of the Western Paradise. Many of the Buddhist faithful in the islands come here, of course, but a visit is every bit as much an aesthetic, as well as spiritual, experience. While you're meditating, turn the kids loose in the gardens, supply them with a package of fish food (thoughtfully sold in a tiny teahouse gift store), and let them feed the flashing carp in the two-acre reflecting lake. The shop also imports religious items and other Japanese gifts from Kyoto. Have a look. Admission is $1 for adults, 50¢ for children.

Across the road is the attractive **Temple Valley Shopping Center** in Kaneohe, where you might stop to pick up some sundries, or have a Chinese lunch at the **Chinese Kitchen.**

Heeia

For a change of pace now, get back on Highway 83 and retrace your way to Heeia, on Kaneohe Bay. This is a good place to stop, stretch your legs, and switch to another mode of transportation. Glass-bottom boats at **Heeia Kea Pier** take you on 1½-hour narrated excursion at a charge of $12 for adults, $9 for children under 12. The price includes the use of snorkel equipment. Cruises depart at 3:15 p.m. Monday, Wednesday, and Friday. Make advance reservations by calling 247-0375. Also, check to see if the water is clear that day; if not, there's not much point in going out. The **Deli Snack and Gift Shop,** right on the pier, offers local-style plate lunches (around $3), as well as the usual snacks.

THE ROAD TO LAIE: Outside of Heeia, it's one awesome view after another as you weave along the coast, past acres of tropical flowers and trees whose branches frequently arch across the whole width of the road. You can't miss spotting **Pineapple Hut** on the right, which has a good selection of carved wood, shells, macramé planters, and the like, at reasonable prices. As you drive along, keep your eyes peeled for stands selling "Ice Cold Coconuts"; there's usually one out here, another on the road at Waimanalo.

You're now coming to the end of Kaneohe Bay, and the next HVB marker you'll see will point to an island that looks like its name **Mokoli'i** (little lizard); it's sometimes also called Chinaman's Hat. On the other side of the road, tangled over by weeds, are the ruins of a century-old sugar mill. Cane grown here was once shipped by boat to "distant" Honolulu.

In a short while you'll come to a rocky cliff that reminded the old Hawaiians of a crouching lion, hence its official name—**Crouching Lion!** The scenic **Crouching Lion Inn** is just in front. This area is fine for a picnic: **Kaaawa Beach Park** has good swimming, and so does **Swanzy Beach Park,** just before Punaluu and fully equipped with the amenities. The next beach, at **Kahana Bay,** is safe for swimming inshore, but there are no dressing facilities and the bottom is muddy.

Just past the lovely beach at **Punaluu Beach Park,** art lovers should get out and stretch at **Punaluu Gallery,** 53-352 Kamehameha Hwy. in Punaluu (tel. 237-8325). One of the oldest galleries in the islands (over 30 years in continuous operation), it shows only original works—paintings, drawings, etchings, watercolors, etc.—by local island artists, and the prices are very fair for professional work. Note the canvases of Hawaiian men, women, and legends by LeBranch. The friendly owner and resident artist Dorothy Zoller is proud to show the works to people who just come to browse, and she often has some reasonably priced gift items by local craftspeople. No tourist junk here. A refreshing interlude.

As you approach **Hauula,** you'll see the HVB marker pointing to a side road leading to the 87-foot **Sacred Falls.** Even though the trail is lined with impressive trees and flowers, our considered advice is to pass this one up; in order to see the falls and the mountain pool below, you have to hike for about an hour on a rough, rocky path. Coming up now, the beach park at Hauula is well equipped with the usual bathing facilities, and the swimming is safe inshore. But keep going; you're about to reach the picturesque village of Laie, one of the high points of your Windward Oahu sojourn.

Laie: Polynesia in Miniature

Laie is Salt Lake City with palm trees. No slouches at missionary work, the Mormons arrived in Hawaii not long after the first Protestants; over 100 years ago they founded a large colony of Hawaiian and Samoan brethren of the Church of Jesus Christ of Latter-Day Saints, whose descendants still live here.

In 1919 the Mormons established a Hawaiian Temple, the largest Mormon house of worship outside the mainland; in 1958, the Brigham Young University of Hawaii, a fully accredited liberal arts institution; and in 1963, the **Polynesian Cultural Center,** a loving re-creation of Polynesia in miniature. On beautifully landscaped grounds, seven authentic Polynesian villages—Tahitian, Marquesan, Samoan, Maori, Tongan, Fijian, and of course Hawaiian—have been built, peopled with islanders who demonstrate the ancient crafts of making tapa (barkcloth), pounding taro roots into poi (a Hawaiian food staple), weaving baskets of lauhala, woodcarving, and the like. All this is part of the church's effort to revitalize the ancient Polynesian cultures by giving them a dramatic showcase and, at the same time, to provide job opportunities for Polynesian young people who need to work their way through school.

A visit here (admission is $14 for adults, $7 for children 11 and under) is an absorbing excursion (albeit too expensive, we think) into long-ago, far-away culture. You'll find such curiosities as a splendidly carved Maori war canoe, all 59 feet of it carved from a single log (it took two years to make—in ancient times, it would have taken 20); a Tahitian queen's house; Tongan grass huts lined with tapa; and Samoan sleeping quarters for a high chief. Most striking of all, perhaps, is the Maoris' sacred house of learning, with its woven and cowrie-shell inside panels. The veddy British accent of the Maori guides, dressed in island costumes, may come as a bit of a shock until you remember that they are New Zealanders, Commonwealth subjects. As you make your way around, either on foot or by tram or canoe, you'll find that they and the other guides who explain their traditions with such deep feeling are the most impressive aspects of the Cultural Center.

Various events are scheduled through the day, like the "Aloha Festival" at 11:30 a.m., "Music Polynesia" at 12:30 p.m., and the "Pageant of the Long Canoes" at 3:30 p.m. (a floating panorama of island songs and dances). Buffet lunches and dinners are available at the Gateway House, but are not inexpensive ($9 and $13), so you can save money by bringing your own picnic. Be sure to check out the gift shops, laden with crafts that you don't see everywhere: fringed mats, striking wastebaskets and shopping bags of tapa; even Fijian "cannibal forks" (more politely used for the salad). The mailing department will send your purchases anywhere in the United States.

Six nights a week, the scenic open amphitheater becomes the site of a spectacular production of Polynesian dancing and singing. It's just a trifle showbiz (colored waters, tricky lighting), but the performers—people brought from Polynesia to man the villages, or students at B.Y.U. Hawaii—are quite good, and some of them, like the Fijian men in their traditional war dances, do probably the best ethnic dancing in the islands. Tickets are $15 for adults, $7.50 for children 12 and under, and although the seats are expensive by our budget, the show is sold out most of the time, and there's a daily waiting list; be sure to reserve in advance by mail. *Note:* Most tour companies can book you a package deal that includes a tour of the center, dinner, admission to the show, and transportation to and from Waikiki for around (ouch!) $46.50.

Hours at the Cultural Center are 10 a.m. to 7 p.m. and the evening show begins at 7:30. Closed Sunday. The phone is 293-3333 in Laie and there is a sales office at 2301 Kalakaua Ave., Suite 304 (tel. 923-2911), in Waikiki. If you are driving directly to Laie from Honolulu, take the Pali Highway and turn north on Kamehameha Highway. The North Shore shuttle bus can take you there and back for $2 each way (tel. 677-9600).

While you're here, you'll also want to see the **Hawaiian Temple;** it stands back from the road on high ground, above a pond, an illuminated fountain, and at the head of a long avenue of royal palms. Best approach for a Taj Mahal–like vista is to leave the highway at Halelaa Boulevard. A complimentary Historical Laie Tour is available. You'll tour the Mormon Temple, Brigham Young University Hawaii, and the Laie community on a re-created 1903 Hawaiian streetcar. By the way, not all the students here are Mormons; the school is open to others, provided they take the pledge not to smoke or drink, and "to live good Christian lives."

Laie Beach used to be the scene of the Mormon hukilaus, once considered one of the island's top visitor attractions. The ocean at **Laie-Maloo** is safe for inshore swimming, although the beach is not a public park and has no dressing facilities.

You won't want to leave Laie without a drive out to **Laie Point** (the turn-off is just past the entrance to the Cultural Center), where you get a dramatic view of the rugged coastline. Walk out over the porous lava rock as far as you can safely go for the best view of all. Some old Hawaii hands swear it's the best view in all the islands. Sunset devotees shouldn't miss this one.

THE HALFWAY POINT—KUILIMA, SUNSET BEACH, AND HALEIWA: Now the road runs inland through sugar country, starting with the village of Kahuku, the halfway point of your trip. (In summer, stop off at one of the roadside stands for the home-grown watermelon—the best on the island.) It reaches the shore again at Kuilima, where you might want to have a look at the sumptuous Turtle Bay Hilton and Country Club (formerly the Hyatt Kuilima Resort), one of the most beautiful in the islands.

Back to the car again for a drive along **Sunset Beach,** with its huge breakers crashing in at your right. It's safe for summer swimming, but in winter it's a wild, windy stretch, exciting to walk along; better still, you may be lucky enough to see some spectacular surfing here, for this is Oahu's North Shore, currently *the* place for the surfing set. If you're wondering whether you should try it yourself, be advised that the surfing areas range from pretty dangerous, to very dangerous, to one that's called "Banzai

Pipeline" (remember the war-time suicide cry of the Japanese?). **Waimea Bay,** just below Sunset, has the distinction of having Hawaii's biggest waves, sometimes crashing in as high as 30 feet. However, in the summer months Waimea Bay is tranquil, the waves are gentle, and swimming here is close to perfection.

While the surfers are tempting fate, you can survey a more primitive form of human sacrifice (and this time we're serious) if you have a four-wheel-drive vehicle. Then you can turn left on Highway 835, a steep, winding road, up to **Puu O Mahuka Heiau.** Here, on a bluff overlooking Waimea Bay (another view-collector's spot), are the ruins of a temple where human sacrifice was practiced. When Captain Vancouver put in at Waimea Bay in 1792, three of his men were captured and offered to the bloodthirsty gods. But the mile-long road leading to the ruin is so full of potholes, and the site is so poorly kept, that we'd pass this one up for now.

For a refreshing change of pace, head back to nature now at **Waimea Falls Park,** opposite Waimea Bay Beach Park, 1800 beautiful acres where you'll find an impressive collection of tropical and subtropical plants in the Waimea Arboretum, a bird sanctuary for many species including the rare Nene goose and Koloa duck, and hiking trails as well. It's fun to take the minibus up to the beautiful 45-foot waterfall (a three-quarter-mile walk), and then walk down; some of the lovely gardens cannot be seen well from the road. Of special interest is the site for ancient Hawaiian games (located near the upper meadow), where tour guides demonstrate and teach such games as Hawaiian checkers and spear throwing. Ancient hula and cliff-diving shows take place several times a day. Charlie's Country Store, with books on Hawaiiana, plus jams, jellies, and jewelry, is fun to browse. There are a number of natural picnic spots in the park; you can get sandwiches, snacks, and hot lunches from the Country Kitchen if you haven't brought your own. Guided walking tours go through the gardens and Hawaiian historical sites. The Proud Peacock Restaurant (medium to high prices and well recommended) has a soup, salad, and sandwich bar from 11 a.m. to 3 p.m. and dinner nightly. The park is open daily from 10 a.m. to 5:30 p.m. Admission is $6.25 for adults, $4.25 for juniors (7 to 12), $1 for children (4 to 6); 3 and under, free. Park phone: 638-8511.

Pupukea Beach Park in this area has good swimming and outstanding snorkeling in the summer months. A few miles farther along, at **Haleiwa Beach Park** on Waialua Bay, you'll find the last swimming spot before you strike into the heart of Oahu. It's a fine family-type place—lawns, play areas, pergolas, dressing rooms, showers, fishing, camping, and picnicking area.

The Youth Scene at Sunset Beach and Haleiwa

If you're seriously interested in—or part of—the youth culture, you'll be welcome among the inhabitants of Sunset Beach and Haleiwa, an area that attracts a number of young people who want to live close to nature. They're not putting on a show for sightseers or tourists, just quietly doing their thing—and an attractive thing it is. Haleiwa is like a very tiny version of Cape Cod's Provincetown, with its distinctively artsy atmosphere, small gift shops, and boutiques. Pottery, art objects, and paintings, most of them made in the area, are offered by Inga Jausel at **Oögenesis Originals** at 66-249 Kam Hwy. Note the low prices for handmade apparel in original custom designs. Inga's new store, **Rix,** 66-145 Kam Hwy., offers contemporary designs in hair and fashion. There are myriads of beautiful things at **Bebee's**

Boutique, 66-082 Kam Hwy. Bebee, a former fashion model and Playboy Bunny, designs some elegant muus at prices on a par with mass-produced dresses of like quality in the posh department stores. She's also made some lovely body ornaments of old pieces of quartz and jade which she has suspended from macramé neckpieces. These go from $25 and up.

Local Talent Unlimited is a tiny shop at 66-200 Kam Hwy. that features items crafted by people who live in the area. We recently saw some adorable aloha bears there—they're made of either aloha print fabric or palaka (Hawaiian plaid) and sell for $7 to $18, depending on size. We also liked the wild aloha print neckties, the quilted and appliquéd tote bags, $15; and the lovely airbrushed T-shirts for babies, $4.

Have a look, too, at the **Fettig Art Gallery,** 66-051 Kam Hwy., an important outlet for the local painters and potters. You might come up with a miniature for as little as $5; standard-size works run from $50 to $125. There are also handcrafted pottery, locally made candles, and sculpture.

Hungry? You've come to the right town. Some of our favorite North Shore restaurants are here (see Chapter III), like **Kua'Aina** for super sandwiches, **Steamer's** for island fish and seafood in a glamorous setting, and **Jameson's by the Sea** (a sister restaurant to the Jameson's Irish Coffee Houses in Waikiki and downtown Honolulu), open to beautiful views and breezes as it overlooks Haleiwa Harbor. Wherever you eat, skip dessert and drive over to **Matsumoto's Grocery** at 66-078 Kam Hwy. in Haleiwa (across from the intersection of Emerson Street) for the ultimate shave ice experience. Local people drive out from all over the island to queue up here, while no fewer than four girls from an "assembly line" to shave and season the ice. We won't swear that you'll really love shave ice with ice cream and azuki beans on the bottom ($1), but can you say you really know Hawaii unless you've tried it?

Since Sunset Beach is a spiritually attuned community, it abounds in centers for yoga, Zen, and other such disciplines; the people at any of the shops can give you information on any groups that may interest you. This area is a world apart from the urban crush of Honolulu, the tourist scene at Waikiki, and the rat race everywhere. Try to schedule your visit in time for the fantastic sunset, which turns the horizon to a brilliant blazing red.

THE RETURN TRIP: At the intersection of Route 82 (Kamehameha Highway), turn left and follow it as it climbs to **Leilehua Plateau.** Here the tall sugarcane gives way to seemingly endless miles of pineapple—dark-green and golden against the red earth. It's the largest pineapple area in the world. Just as you're beginning to feel like the Ancient Mariner (you can't pick any), you'll find a pineapple stand on the left side of the road as you come out of the pineapple area. Buy a whole "pine" or get a half-dozen delicious spears, fresher than any you've ever tasted. The custom here is to sprinkle a little unrefined Hawaiian salt on the pineapple; it helps cut the acidity. Unfortunately, Dole does not conduct tours through the fields, but many operations are visible from the highway. In case you're curious, the variety of pineapple grown here is called Sweet Cayenne.

In the midst of these Wahiawa pineapple fields, one mile past the pineapple hut, is the Del Monte Corporation's **Pineapple Variety Garden,** right at the junction of Highways 82 and 809. It's small, but well worth a brief stop to see a huge variety of species and pineapple plants from all over the world—Asia, Africa, South America, and various small islands. Just ignore the tremendous spiders that build their webs among the plants; they're nonaggressive and totally harmless—to people and/or pineapples.

Next stop is for the history-anthropology buffs: a Stone Age spot where the royal chieftesses of Hawaii gave birth. Just before **Wahiawa,** watch on the right for a dirt road leading into a clump of eucalyptus trees in a pineapple field on the Kaukonahau Gulch—the **Place of the Sacred Birthstone.** The large flat stone protruding several feet above the ground was a primitive delivery table; legend had it that a son delivered on this stone would be born with honor.

Now take Highway 99 into Wahiawa, a dreary-looking town that serves as a center for personnel stationed at **Schofield Barracks** (where James Jones met his muse) and **Wheeler's Field.** It's also a huge pineapple depot. The bright spot here is **Kemoo Farm,** a restaurant overlooking Lake Wilson that's been a big favorite with the kamaainas since 1927. Besides the very good food (see a complete review in Chapter III), Kemoo Farm sells some attractive gift items in its "country store" lobby, and its knowledgeable staff can help you plan a tour of the nearby points of interest. There are often lunch shows on Wednesday and Sunday with outstanding island entertainers. In this area you may also want to visit the **Schofield Museum,** with its military and historical documents; the **Wahiawa Hongwanji Temple** at 1067 California Ave., with its fascinating carving of Amida Buddha; and one of our longtime favorites, the **Wahiawa Botanical Garden,** at 1396 California Ave. (Diamond Head of the highway), 1000 feet high, where you can wander through four lovely acres of rare trees, ferns and shrubs, many orchid plants, and a Hawaiian garden. Don't forget your camera. Admission is free.

You'll pass through more sugar fields as you drive along the now four-lane Kamehameha Highway (Highway 99) or the new Interstate Highway H-2. From here on, it's fast sailing home. At the intersection with Route 90, take that road to the left; it will take you past Pearl Harbor (you might visit the U.S.S. *Arizona* Memorial if you have the time; see Chapter VII for details) and the Honolulu Airport. At Middle Street, turn right onto Route 92 (Nimitz Highway), which will take you past the harbor; take Ala Moana and Kalakaua into Waikiki.

But before you settle into your hotel, consider the following two points of interest, which you could take in at the start or at the end of your trip—or save them for another day.

2. The Pali and Makiki Heights

The only major attraction you haven't seen on this trip is the view from the **Nuuanu Pali,** a glorious panorama of Windward Oahu from the top of a jagged cliff. It's a historic spot too, because it was here that Kamehameha the Great vanquished the Oahuans in a fierce battle in 1795. Thousands of the defeated fell to their deaths on the rocks below. (You could start the round-the-island trip via the Pali, but you'd miss the scenery in the Koko Head area, which we find more appealing.) You can see the Pali by turning left off the Nimitz Highway in downtown Honolulu onto Nuuanu Avenue (or Bishop Street, which runs into Pali Highway), which you follow until it hits the Pali Highway, and on to the Pali.

Just before you reach the Pali, however, you might want to stop at one of the island's newest points of interest. If you drive about a mile up the Pali and turn left at Jack Lane, you come upon the beautiful **Tendai Mission of Hawaii** and its enormously impressive 25-foot statue of Senju Kannon, the Thousand-Armed Goddess of Mercy. The Tendai sect of Mahayana Buddhism ended 1200 years of confining its worship halls to Japan when it opened the Hawaii mission in November 1973. You're welcome to inspect the grounds and building any day during regular activity hours. (There are no specific times of opening or closing.) Occasionally, you'll see local groups using the facilities for flower-arranging, tea ceremonies, and handicraft exhibits.

Another spectacular view that we think you shouldn't miss is the one from **Makiki Heights.** In a way, we like it better than the Pali, since this is top-of-the-world view, completely unobstructed. Here's how to get there: from Waikiki, take Kalakaua Avenue until it ends at South Beretania Street; go past Makiki to Keeaumoku Street, turn right, go across Highway 1 and turn right on Wilder. Go one block, then make a left on Makiki, which runs into Round Top Drive, then Tantalus Drive, and up, up, up. The road, which is excellent all the way, goes through the Round Top Forest Reserve. Stop at **Puu Ualakka State Park** and have a look at the glorious view from Round Top. Back in the car, continue in the same direction you were going; you'll end up just about where you started, having come full circle.

3. The Waianae Coast

In past editions of this book, we have always suggested another excursion for those adventurous types who won't rest until they've seen everything, this one to the leeward side of the island, the area stretching from Ewa (the sugar plantation town whose name is used as a direction) to Kaena Point, the westernmost tip of Oahu. However, for some years now we've been suggesting that you skip the trip to the Waianae Coast. Sorry to say, a very hostile local crowd has recently taken to beating up tourists, and some very unpleasant incidents have been reported. So forgo Pokai Beach Park, Makaha Beach, Nanakuli, and Makua; we'll keep watch on the situation, and recommend the trip once again just as soon as it's safe.

4. Tips for Tourists

SWIMMING: Don't attempt to swim at any beach that is not also a public park; dressing-room facilities will give you a clue. Although dangerous areas are usually posted, the signs may be missing, or you may not see them. The following beaches on this drive are *unsafe* because of undertow or heavy surf: Koko Head Beach, Waimea Beach and Sunset Beach on the North Shore (in winter), and Light House Beach at Makapuu. Never swim where there is a steep beach, a rocky shoreline, or large waves. In case of trouble, call the police at 911 or dial zero.

CAMPING: If you want to join the island families camping on some of the beaches (besides the beauty, a really cheap way to cut overnight costs), obtain a permit from the Department of Parks and Recreation on the first floor of the Honolulu Municipal Building, 650 S. King St. Call 523-4525 for details, plus a list of the parks that have facilities: water, toilets, sometimes sinks and barbecue stoves. Note that all city beach park campgrounds are closed to camping every Thursday, except during the spring, summer, and Christmas vacation periods, and whenever Thursday is a holiday. There is no charge for camping permits.

Should you decide to camp in style, you may want to rent a camper (a truck with a little house on top) or a trailer (to which you attach a car). Both campers and trailers come equipped with everything from pots and pans to blankets, have their own toilets, stoves, and running water, and offer a family of four or more a terrific way to save money. For details on where and how to rent, see Chapter IV. See the Readers' Suggestions, ahead, for a warning from a local resident.

READERS' SUGGESTIONS IN WINDWARD OAHU: "Mention should be made about the hazards of camping in certain areas overnight. People come here expecting 'Paradise' and find that violence is the same all over. Many bad incidents have recently occurred to overnight tourist campers in the **Waianae** and **Waimanalo** areas. These two areas have many people of low economic situation who know tourists have money and are easy marks. Local folks don't even camp alone on the beaches in these two areas. A warning should be given" (Alton Rogers, Honolulu, Hi.). . . . "We took a pleasant drive to **Lanikai,** on the Kailua side. At the end of Highway 61, turn right, instead of left to Kailua. We sat overlooking Kailua Beach Park and the ocean at Alala Point, watching the small sailboats in the bay. It was hard to believe that busy Honolulu was so near" (Mrs. E. J. Parker, Jr., Hawthorne, Calif.). . . . "The **Kukui Nut Factory** in Haleiwa welcomes tourists and will show you their factory and processing of nuts" (Darlene Guidney, Dover, Del.).

"Rather than take one of the big tours, where there are so many people and the whole experience is so impersonal, I strongly recommend that people take the small 8- to 11-person tours. I went with **E Noa Tours** (tel. 941-6608) on an around-the-island tour and it was the best day I spent in Hawaii. Since the cost is $34 including lunch and snorkeling lessons, it's not cheaper than renting a car, but I would not have learned as much as I did about the Hawaiians, their land, culture, and values. Not only that, but when you get on the bus, the driver asks if there are any places in particular you would like to see, so you don't miss a thing. There were eight of us on our tour, and in that full day of traveling I made some beautiful friends. Ask to have Nelson for your driver. He knew so much about everything—there wasn't much he couldn't answer—and he had us constantly rolling with laughter. The tour is complete with snorkeling at Hanauma Bay and a multitude of sights" (Kristin Fry, Calgary, Alberta, Canada). . . . "I took a Circle Island Tour with **E Noa Tours** (without the snorkeling), following the advice of your book quoting Kristin Fry of Calgary, and found my experiences about paralleled hers. I had asked for Nelson, the driver, as suggested, and found he is no longer with them. A request for someone like Nelson elicited the response "We're all like Nelson!" They sent a lovely gal called Rhonda—who was surely Nelson's counterpart. She even shinned up a tree so we could sample a fresh guava, and set the tone for a beautiful day with a very international little group who ended up all loving each other so much we all had a turn at snapping a picture of the group beside our bus!" (Mary Risdon, Calgary, Alberta, Canada). [*Authors' Note:* Rhonda is gone now too, but the tours are still great! The question of whether or not companies like E Noa can teach snorkeling was up in the air at this writing.]

"Pass up the hike to **Sacred Falls,** Hauula, unless you're a vigorous and determined hiker. Even experienced hikers cannot reach Sacred Falls in an hour's hike. The trail has been neglected and jungle has leaned over the path; one must duck under and climb over trees. The path is indeed rough, rocky, and usually muddy. Plan an hour and a half up, an hour back. Local Hawaiians still pay their respects to the deities formerly resident at the **Puu O Mahika Heiau** by wrapping a ti leaf around a stone and placing it on the ruins. There are thousands of them here in various states of weathering. The road is no longer suitable for two-wheel-drive vehicles. It's 1.1 miles from Kam Highway to the heiau; the first part is a fine paved road, but there are great mudholes on the unpaved part, deep enough to swallow a Datsun! At Punaluu there's **Kahana State Park.** An excellent trail starts up the mountain toward the Koolau range. It quickly becomes pitted with mudholes, but is still a good foot trail and gives a good opportunity to see Hawaiian mountain jungle. There are a few papaya and banana plantings, and some oldtime-style Hawaiian dwellings. An hour's hike brings one to a freshwater swimming hole; it is possible to cross a dam here for an extended hike. Allow half an hour to return to Kam Highway. A permit to hike is required, but may be obtained, free, at Kahana Park Headquarters" (David Moore, Phoenix, Ariz.). . . . "On our first full day in Hawaii, six of our party rented a full-size, air-conditioned Lincoln and used your book as a guide. The highlight of the day was our lunch stop in a little town named **Wahiawa,** and the name of the restaurant was **Kemoo Farms.** It was a great, relaxing spot, overlooking a small lake, with a pineapple field beyond. The food was superb. If you like fresh pineapple, what a spot! Pineapple on the salad bar and large wedges of pineapple in the iced tea. We just had to let you know how much we enjoyed Kemoo Farms" (Richard and Angie Ager, Hyattsville, Md.).

"At **Sunset Beach,** beside the waves, which *did* reach 30 feet, we joined in with beachcombers who were sifting puka shells in the sand. We stayed here for about half an hour sifting the sand through our fingers and found several dozen beautiful shells" (Dave Kaiser, Fort Lauderdale, Fla.). [*Authors' Note:* A word of caution: Shell-hunters should never turn their back to the ocean when the surf is high; more than one person has been swept out to sea by a high wave.] . . . "We tried to get to **Kaena Point** on the primitive dirt road described in your book but found that after having negotiated a long stretch of moguls and potholes we were faced with a segment of the road so narrow that our car (a Pinto) simply would not have enough room between a rock on the one side and a precipice on the other. We had to turn back. To get to Kaena Point you need a motorbike or possibly a very small car with high suspension" (K. J. Orlik-Rückemann, Ottawa, Canada).

"If one is planning a trip around May and the **Polynesian Cultural Center** is on the agenda, plan to be there on May 1, Lei Day. There are special-occasion costumes representative of the different islands. Many are entire dresses made from leaves, painstakingly and beautifully sewn or tied together. Flowers are everywhere. The biggest surprise is that this is the day the people who work there bring *their* cameras and movie equipment; I saw as many people in PCC costume taking movies as did the tourists" (Shirley Gerum, Haleiwa, Hi.).

"We disagree with your advice to pass up the trail to **Sacred Falls.** Bearing in mind that it *is* a trail, not a sidewalk, we found it really easy going and the swim in that cool, freshwater, unchlorinated pool was the most pleasant and refreshing dip we had in Hawaii—a reward well worth the hike" (Lloyd and Shirley Kilby, Hope, B.C., Canada). . . . "All the fruit that you see on the trees and on the ground along the trail to Sacred Falls is good to eat. The fruit is called mountaintop apple and is absolutely delicious. It's great refreshment during the long hike" (Bonnie Chambers, Sherman Oaks, Calif.).

"One of the best kept secrets on the windward side is the **Kahuku Municipal Golf Course** overlooking the beach at Kahuku. The greens fees are a mere $2 for nine holes (no extra charge for the second nine holes). Since no signs direct the traveler from Kamehameha Highway to this secret treasure, visitors should turn toward the ocean at Kahuku High School (streets have no names here). This challenging 2725-yard course is uncrowded" (Mr. and Mrs. R. H. Pulley, Scotts Valley, Calif.). [*Authors' Note:* There's no pro shop, no restaurant. The course is occasionally crowded on weekends; tee times are required only on weekend mornings. Office phone: 293-5842.] . . . "Your readers should know about the new park at **Kualoa,** near Chinaman's Hat. It is marked on the makai side of the road just past Kualoa Ranch. The road is pretty poor (purposely so). Take the first turn right after you pass the gates. Soon you will reach one of the most respected places: this is where the Hoku L'ea was launched, just because of this. Be sure to take a look" (Mrs. Clarence Gaber, Kailua, Hi.). [*Authors' Note:* Swimming is poor here, but it's a beautiful park, a place where island families like to camp.]

Chapter IX

THE ABC'S OF HONOLULU

HERE'S A CAPSULE LIST of names and numbers to help you find your way around town. Some is a recap of what you'll find explained in more depth in other chapters, some of it new.

AAA HAWAII: The local office of the American Automobile Association is at 730 Ala Moana Blvd. (tel. 537-5544).

AIRPORT: Honolulu International Airport, about five miles from Waikiki, is easily reached by bus no. 8 ("Airport") or bus no. 20 from Waikiki and Ala Moana Center, without luggage. With luggage, try Airport Motor Coach (tel. 955-1446), or Waikiki Express (tel. 942-2177).

ANIMAL HOSPITAL: Twenty-four-hour emergency care for pets is provided at **Care Animal Hospital,** 1135 Kapahulu Ave. (tel. 737-7910).

AREA CODE: All telephone numbers in the State of Hawaii have one area code number: 808.

BANKING HOURS: 8:30 a.m. to 3 or 3:30 p.m., until 6 p.m. on Friday.

BABYSITTERS: Check first at your hotel desk. You can also try **Patch**—People Attentive to Children (tel. 523-6436), and **Aloha Babysitting Service** (tel. 732-2029).

BUSINESS HOURS: Most office workers in Hawaii are at their desks by 8 a.m., sometimes even earlier, and it's *pau hana* (finish work) at 4 or 5 p.m., the better to get in an afternoon swim or round of golf. Hawaii may be the only place where even executives can be reached by 8:30 a.m.!

BUS INFORMATION: Call **MTL,** which operates TheBUS, at 531-1611, or visit their information booth on the street level of Ala Moana Center, open daily 9 a.m. to 5:30 p.m., to 4:15 p.m. on Sunday.

CAR RENTALS: Major car-rental companies, which rent automobiles on all four major islands, include **Holiday Rent-A-Car Hawaii,** 2918 Ualena St. (tel. 836-1974, or toll free 800/367-2631); **Budget Rent-A-Car,** 2379 Kuhio Ave. (tel. 922-3600, or toll free 800/527-0700); **Tropical Rent-A-Car Systems,** 550 Paiea St. (tel. 836-1041, or toll free 800/367-5140); **American International Rent-A-Car,** 2880 Ualena St. (tel. 833-3355); **Avis Rent-A-Car,** Honolulu International Airport (tel. 836-5511, or toll free 800/331-1212); **Hertz Rent-A-Car,** 233 Keawe St., Room 625 (tel. 836-2511, or toll free 800/654-8200). See Chapter IV for details.

CLIMATE: Among the best in the world. Hawaii's climate is subtropical, which means that temperatures average about 75 degrees, rarely going more than six or seven degrees above or below that point. In summer months, the temperature is usually in the 80s; winter months, November through March, can bring slightly lower temperatures and occasional rain.

CONSUMER PROTECTION: To reach the Office of Consumer Protection, phone 548-2540.

DENTISTS: **Waikiki Medical and Dental Services,** Waikiki Medical Building, 305 Royal Hawaiian Ave., Suite 203, has a dentist on call 24 hours a day: phone 922-2323. For 24-hour emergency dental service, you can also call **Dr. Franson Tom,** Ala Moana Building, 1441 Kapiolani Ave. (tel. 946-1681; after-hours, the emergency number is 524-2575).

DOCTORS: House calls are available from **DOC (Doctors on Call),** 24 hours a day, seven days a week (tel. 922-9966 or 536-6318), charging $54; and from **Waikiki Medical and Dental Services** (tel. 922-2323), charging $35. For office visits, the latter is at Room 203, Waikiki Medical Building, 305 Royal Hawaiian Ave., by appointment. Or try **Waikiki Medi-Mart** in the Royal Hawaiian Shopping Center, Building A-401A (tel. 922-2335). Appointments are not necessary; medical doctors are on duty from 8 a.m. to 8 p.m.

DRY CLEANERS: Quick service is available from **Al Phillips the Cleaner,** 224 McCully St. (tel. 949-2935), and in the **Waikiki Market Place,** 2310 Kuhio Ave. (tel. 923-1971).

EMERGENCY: Dial 911 for fire, ambulance, or police; if you cannot reach 911, dial 0 and the operator will assist you.

HOLIDAYS: Just about all businesses and banks will be closed on the major holidays: Christmas, New Year's, Easter Sunday, Thanksgiving Day.

In addition to the legal holidays observed throughout the United States—Memorial Day, July 4th, Labor Day, Columbus Day, Election Day, and Veterans Day—there are specific Hawaiian holidays on which many business establishments close: Prince Kuhio Day (March 26), Kamehameha Day (June 11), and Admission Day (the third Friday in August).

HOSPITAL EMERGENCY ROOM: **Queens Medical Center,** 1301 Punchbowl, has 24-hour emergency room service and offers outstanding trauma care.

LAUNDROMATS: Should your hotel not provide washers and dryers (most do), try **Waikiki Landromats,** with four central locations. They also provide irons, ironing boards, and hair dryers. Addresses are 2335 Kalakaua Ave., across from the International Market Place; Outrigger West Hotel, 2330 Kuhio; Outrigger East Hotel, 150 Kaiulani Ave.; and Edgewater Hotel, 2168 Kalia Rd. Phone: 923-1711. Open daily from 7 a.m. to 10 p.m.

PHARMACIES: In Waikiki, try **Outrigger Pharmacy** at the Outrigger Hotel, 2335 Kalakaua Ave. (tel. 923-4466), or **Kuhio Pharmacy,** Outrigger West Hotel, 2330 Kuhio Ave. (tel. 923-4466); at Ala Moana Shopping Center, **Long's Drug Store,** 1450 Ala Moana (tel. 949-4010). **The Pillbox Pharmacy,** 1133 Eleventh Ave. (tel. 737-1777), is open seven days a week until 11 p.m. and provides 24-hour emergency service (for prescriptions only).

POISON CENTER: 941-4411.

POST OFFICE: The main post office in Honolulu is at 3600 Aolele St. (tel. 422-6564), open 1 a.m. to 4:30 p.m. Monday to Friday, until noon on Saturday. In Waikiki it's at 330 Saratoga Rd., next to Fort DeRussy (tel. 941-1062).

PUBLIC PHONES: Cost of a local call is 15¢ from any one part of an island to another. Inter-island calls are billed as long distance.

SHOPPING MALLS: Most shopping malls are open Monday to Friday from 9 or 10 a.m. to 9 p.m., Saturday until 5 p.m., and for a shorter period on Sunday, usually until 4 p.m. Individual establishments at these malls will vary their hours, some closing earlier than others.

SUNDRIES: **ABC Discount Stores** offer a little bit of everything one might need under one roof, from suntan lotion to sandwiches, from groceries to gifts, from postcards to photo processing and film, and much more, all at bargain prices. There are at least two dozen ABCs in town, and most of them are open from 7:30 a.m. to midnight. Walk a block or two from where you are and you'll find one.

SURF REPORT: 836-1952.

TIME ZONES: From the East Coast of the United States to Hawaii, one crosses five time zones. That means that when it's noon Hawaiian Standard Time, it's 5 p.m. Eastern Standard Time, 4 p.m. Central, 3 p.m. Mountain, and 2 p.m. Pacific. Hawaii does not convert to Daylight Saving Time as the rest of the nation does, so from May through October, noon in Hawaii would mean 6 p.m. Eastern, 5 p.m. Central, 4 p.m. Mountain, and 3 p.m. Pacific Time.

VISITOR INFORMATION: **Hawaii Visitors Bureau,** 2270 Kalakaua Ave., eighth floor; they also have a booth at Ala Moana Center and the Royal Hawaiian Shopping Center.

WEATHER REPORT: In the Honolulu area call 836-0234; for the rest of Oahu, phone 836-1021; for the Hawaiian waters, dial 836-3921.

Chapter X

TO THE NEIGHBOR ISLANDS

Polynesia with Plumbing

TOO MANY TOURISTS start and end their island holidays in Honolulu—and think they've seen Hawaii. Yes—and no. They've seen the one major city and the major resort area, but far more awaits: a Hawaii at once more gentle and more savage, where the old gods still have powers. To see the desolate moonscapes of the volcanoes and Hawaiian cowboys riding the range, to see beaches so remote and pristine as to make Waikiki seem like Times Square, and to visit South Seas villages just coming into the modern age, you'll have to venture to the three other important Hawaiian islands: the Garden Island of **Kauai,** the Big Island of **Hawaii,** and the Valley Isle of **Maui.** You may also want to visit **Molokai,** which remains much as it was 50 years ago; it is also the home of **Kalaupapa,** the settlement for the treatment of Hansen's disease—leprosy. The island of **Lanai** is almost wholly given over to growing pineapples and does not have much to interest the average tourist; but you may want to splurge on one of the sailing-ship cruises out of Lahaina, Maui, that spend half a day or so there for a figure of about $80. Going to the neighbor islands requires a little effort for the budget traveler, but we strongly urge you to try.

THE MONEY FACTOR: Most people do it the easy way, by simply taking one of the various package tours around the islands. A flat fee, paid in advance, covers your plane fare, hotels, meals, sightseeing. There is, of course, nothing wrong with this method except that it's expensive, even when you go as an economy tourist. We think you can do much better on your own. Besides, on a tour you've got to go where you're taken—in a group—thus missing all the fun of discovering the off-the-beaten-pathways that appeal to *you!*

Another alternative is to "flightsee" the islands from the air, landing briefly for meals and hurried sightseeing, and returning the same night; theoretically, you've "seen" five islands, but that's just a once-over lightly, about as satisfying as those European jaunts that take you to seven countries in six days. And the one day costs about $175 to boot!

The best way to see the neighbor islands is on your own; and doing that will cost you just a little more than you've been spending in Honolulu. You should be able to stay within a reasonable budget here. You can almost always find a good hotel room averaging $30 to $35 (you should, of course, be traveling with a companion); there are plenty of restaurants where you can get $5 to $8 meals; and the supply of kitchenette condo apartments (where you save money by doing your own cooking) is growing.

A money-saving plan is to check the special car-hotel-breakfast deals that the major airlines—Aloha, Hawaiian, and Mid-Pacific—often make in conjunction with the leading car-rental companies and some of the island hotel chains. If the airlines are sold out on any of these special programs, try a local travel agency; they'll often be able to help you.

Your major expense on the outer islands will be transportation. Only one city on one island—Hilo, on the island of Hawaii—has anything resembling a public transportation system, and even that is not very extensive. There is also bus service in Lihue, Kauai, and in the Lahaina-Kaanapali and Kihei areas of Maui, but none of the buses run for any great distances. So unless you want to stay put, you have only two choices: taking expensive sightseeing tours or renting your own car. The latter is not cheap either, especially on days when you must pile on a lot of mileage, driving from one end of an island to another. If you're a couple or a family, of course, your car costs per person will be fairly low. And you won't be sorry you made the trip.

WHICH TO CHOOSE: Each of the three major neighbor islands is fascinating and important to visit, and we strongly recommend that you make the circuit tour. (We suggest Molokai as an added attraction, after you've seen the others.) If you decide to go to only one island, read carefully the chapters ahead on the sights of Maui, Hawaii, and Kauai before you make your decision. Each has its special fascinations. **Maui** has become the most popular of the neighbor islands, especially appealing to an affluent condo crowd; it has some of the best golf courses in the state of Hawaii. Its great natural wonder, and its chief claim to fame, is Haleakala, the largest dormant volcano in the world, with a moon-like crater that you can explore on foot or horseback. The popular, picturesque old whaling town of Lahaina, remote and lovely Hana, and a succession of golden beaches are strong lures. The Big Island of **Hawaii** is the most varied, geographically, of the islands, almost like a small continent in miniature. It has few beaches (except in the Kona area), but it has the islands' second-biggest city (Hilo), the volcanic wonderlands of Manua Kea and Mauna Loa (Volcanoes National Park is a must on any itinerary), and a cattle ranch big enough to belong to Texas. **Kauai,** our personal favorite, is perhaps not as well known as it should be; it is still refreshingly rural, small, beautiful, and easily assimilated. The damage done by Hurricane Iwa in 1982 is largely repaired. Waimea Canyon, a smaller version of the Grand Canyon, is its principal natural attraction. It also has a string of unforgettable beaches (you've seen them as Bali H'ai in the movie version of *South Pacific* and as Matlock Island in the television production of *The Thornbirds*). For advice on itineraries, see suggestions on inter-island travel in Chapter I.

CAMPING ON THE NEIGHBOR ISLANDS: Camping is becoming increasingly popular on all the outer islands (as well as on Oahu, of course), and throughout these pages you will find various references to camping. For information on renting a camper (make arrangements in Honolulu), see Chapter IV. You can, of course, bring your own equipment (see the Readers' Suggestions ahead for some interesting tips), but note that permits in advance are required. Check with the offices of the Hawaii Visitors Bureau (you can write them in advance; their addresses are given in the Introduction) to find out where to get permits for each island. And note references to various special camping grounds and cabins in the pages ahead. Note too, alas, that camping is no longer as safe as it used to be: see the comments by Barbara and Val Menendez in the Readers' Suggestions.

AND KEEP IN MIND: Driving distances on the neighbor islands can be great, particularly on the Big Island of Hawaii, and you may have a lot of trouble finding gas stations, especially ones open on Sunday: keep the tank full. Be sure to check your U-Drive carefully before going on a long trip, and get a phone number where you can reach the agency at night in case of problems. Remember, too, to ask the agency for some good road maps indicating distances, and don't hesitate to ask questions and directions before you take off.

Also, even though it's easier than it used to be to find inexpensive places to eat as you scoot around the islands because of the rise of fast-food outlets, it can be a long drive between meals. It's always a good idea to throw a few sandwiches and some fruit in your beach bag, along with the suntan lotion and the road maps.

A NOTE ON PACKAGE TOURS: If you do decide on a package deal, remember that there are all kinds, sizes, and shapes. The most expensive ones park you at the luxury hotels and take you sightseeing in private limousines; the cheapest put you up in standard hotels, take you sightseeing in motor coaches, and may not provide meals. If they don't, you have a chance to shop around for inexpensive restaurants, which will charge much less than what the tour companies figure on as the cost of three meals. Do some careful studying and comparing before you sign up for one. Here, to aid in that task, are some of the major travel companies that offer tours to the outer islands:

Island Holiday Tours, 2255 Kuhio Ave. (P.O. Box 8519), Honolulu, HI 96815 (tel. 945-6000).

Hawaiian Holiday Tours, 2222 Kalakaua Ave., Honolulu, HI 96815 (tel. 923-0733).

Trade Wind Tours of Hawaii, 150 Kauilani Ave. (P.O. Box 2198), Honolulu, HI 96815 (tel. 923-2071).

MacKenzie Tours of Hawaii, 2222 Kalakaua Ave., Honolulu, HI 96815 (tel. 923-1116; toll-free reservation number: 800/421-0990).

American Express and World Travel, with offices in all major mainland cities, can also arrange comprehensive inter-island tours for you. And every travel agency in Hawaii will deal, if you wish, with these companies.

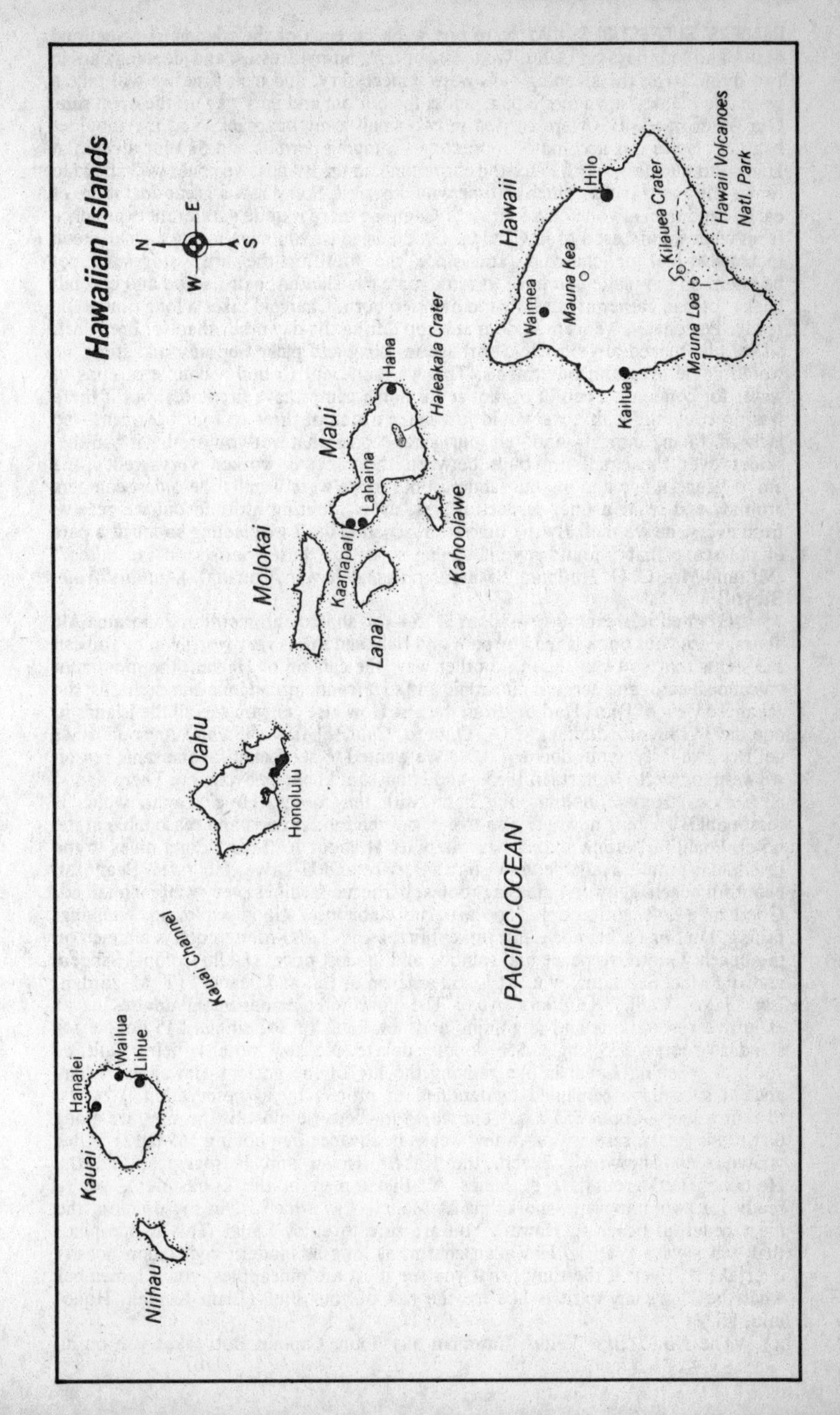
Hawaiian Islands
N
E
S
W
Hawaii
Hilo
Kilauea Crater
Hawaii Volcanoes Natl. Park
Mauna Kea
Waimea
Mauna Loa
Kailua
Maui
Hana
Haleakala Crater
Lahaina
Kaanapali
Kahoolawe
Molokai
Lanai
Oahu
Honolulu
PACIFIC OCEAN
Kauai Channel
Kauai
Hanalei
Wailua
Lihue
Niihau

READERS' SUGGESTIONS: "We were one week on each of the islands of Kauai and Maui, and four days on Oahu. We took our tent, air mattresses, and sleeping bags in two duffle bags; the sleeping bags were unnecessary, and next time we will take a washable blanket sewn into a bag, across the bottom and part way up the open side. Our other necessities were carried in two small army knapsacks and my shoulder bag. . . . Since our accommodation costs—camping permits and $10 for a cabin at Hana—totaled less than $25 for the entire time on the islands, we could well afford to rent a car and travel as much as time would permit. So we saw a great deal more of each island than anyone on a tour. . . . Camping there is quite a different experience from what we are used to in Canada. On the islands, you have to use a small stove that uses fuel or charcoal, and since the fuel for the little stoves cannot be taken on the plane you have to refuel on each island; the driftwood and coconut husks you can gather are usually too damp to burn. Charcoal takes a long time to be ready. Personally, we were seldom at camp during the day other than for breakfast, so we just tucked any burnable garbage in a bag and picked up any odd sticks we would come across in our travels. This was sufficient to boil a couple of cups of water for coffee or a cup of instant soup. Some camps have fireplaces, but if there was no cooking facility, we would just make a ring of three or four beer cans—no lack of them, either!—and put our small cook-whatever-you-are-having-in-the-skillet over the small fire built between the cans; it worked very well. . . . I am 55 years of age and my husband past 60, so we were usually the oldest campers around, and what a fine, respectful, yes, even admiring attitude did we receive from everyone we met. By the time we reached Oahu I was feeling so much a part of the scene that I found myself feeling sorry for those tourists on the buses!" (Mr. and Mrs. C. G. Huffman, Saskatoon, Saskatchewan, Canada). [*Authors' Note:* Bravo!]

"Granted it is expensive—about $175—you should still mention **Panorama Air Tours,** since your book is read by poor and rich, and this is very worthwhile. You can see sights that you can see in no other way: the canyon of Hawaii; the mouths of volcanoes; acres and acres of pineapple and sugarcane; macadamia-nut orchards; the Japanese view of Pearl Harbor, from the air. How else can you see all the islands in one day?" (Simon Klitenic, M.D., Ontario, Calif.). [*Authors' Note:* As soon as we get rich, we'll join you, doctor.] . . . "We wanted to see **Lanai** for the same reason we went to Puerto Vallarta in 1955—and Lanai should not be bypassed. There's good air service from Honolulu, one hotel with ten rooms, Hotel Lanai, which is reasonable. There is nowhere else to eat, but the food is good and reasonable at the hotel. Beautiful setting among Norfolk pines at about 1600 feet. Eight miles to the beach, car rentals available via Oshira's Service and U-Drive, fair rates. Beautiful, beautiful beach, showers, dressing rooms, barbecue facilities, very well maintained. Good nine-hole golf course, no carts, no clubhouse. Good exploring, climbing, fishing, hunting (deer, pheasant, turkey) in season. A 200-room motel is planned on the beach. Good-bye peace and solitude and modest prices. Hello Colonel Sanders and Big Mac! See Lanai while it is still a haven of rest and beauty" (T. M. Jordan, Los Gatos, Calif.). [*Authors' Note:* The new hotel management advises us of extensive renovations and upgrading and new rates of $42 single, $45 double for standard rooms; $55 single, $58 double, deluxe. No new motel is being built, as yet.] . . . "Seeing Lanai is like reliving the life of the ancient Hawaiians. Many ancient sites have remained unidentified to protect their preservation. It's best to rent a Jeep—about $55 a day but worth it—because most of the sites are along dirt roads (make reservations a few weeks in advance by phoning 565-6952). After you've seen Shipwreck Beach, the Kahe'a Heiau and Petroglyphs, and the Ho'Okio Battlegrounds (get James A. Bier's map in the bookstores), you're ready for swimming and snorkeling at Manele Bay which is, in my opinion, the most beautiful beach in Hawaii. You are sure to enjoy Lanai. This is one place that will always keep its Hawaiian charm, as long as modern civilization doesn't overtake it. Even if the things that you see most are pineapples, you'll remember what the Hawaiian spirit is like for the rest of your life" (Liam Kernell, Honolulu, Hi.).

"The No. 1 Best Value: **Hawaiian Sky Tour.** Captain Bob takes you on an adventure that really gives you a taste of Hawaii and its culture, as well as its beauty. The cost is $175 for a three-island stopover and a flight over eight islands. Molokai is by far my favorite. We had a tour of the leper colony at Kalaupapa by a patient who's been there all his life. The man is 75 and tells you the story. Fascinating. I know everyone is on a budget, but work on it before you fly to Hawaii" (Rob Phillips, Lames, Calif.).

Chapter XI

THE ISLAND OF KAUAI

1. Island Hotels
2. Island Restaurants
3. The Night Scene

ABOUT 15 JET MINUTES out of Honolulu and 110 miles to the west, your plane lands you in a tropical Switzerland. This is Kauai, the northernmost and oldest of the major Hawaiian islands, one of the lushest tropical spots on earth.

Kauai (pronounced correctly Kah-*wah*-ee, lazily Kah-*why*) is the oldest Hawaiian island in both geologic and historic time. The fantastic verdure of its cliffs and canyons was formed over millions of years of volcanic growth and collapse, by the endless workings of streams and ocean waves on its bleak cinders and craters (contrast these with the newly formed volcanoes on the island of Hawaii for an idea of the awesome powers of nature). In island lore, Kauai was the original home of Pele, the goddess of fire and volcanoes, before she moved southward. It was also the homeland of a race of pre-Polynesians, whose origins are anybody's guess—including anthropologists. Some believe they were the survivors of the lost continent of Lemuria. In legend they're called Menehunes, South Sea leprechauns who stood about two feet tall, worked only in darkness, and accomplished formidable engineering feats in the space of a night's work.

The first Polynesian settlers chose Kauai too, landing at the mouth of the Wailua River somewhere between A.D. 500 and 900. They had crossed the Pacific in outrigger canoes in a voyage of many months, probably from the Society Islands. Other Polynesians came later, but time stood still on Kauai and the rest of the Hawaiian Islands until 1778, when Captain Cook arrived at Waimea and the modern history of Hawaii began.

So much for history. Geographically, Kauai is a small island, about 32 miles in diameter. Its central mountain receives an average of 500 inches of rainfall a year, making it one of the wettest spots on earth, which accounts for the lushness of the surrounding landscape. You can see all the important things in Kauai in three days—but the longer you stay, the luckier you are.

Although Kauai bore the brunt of Hurricane Iwa in November of 1982, the storm and the damage it wrought are largely only memories now. Kauaians picked up quickly and made their beautiful island more beautiful than ever before.

ARRIVAL: Your plane will land in **Lihue** on an airstrip amid towering sugarcane. From here to town, which will probably be the base of your operations, you'll either have to drive in your own rented car or take a cab.

U-DRIVES: For information on the major budget U-Drive companies—offering excellent flat-rate packages on all the islands—see Chapter IV, "Transportation Within Honolulu." If, however, you haven't done so, or prefer a time-plus-mileage deal, simply walk up to any of the car-rental agencies just across the road from the airport. **Watase's,** a local company, offers $9-a-day, 10¢-a-mile rates for a standard-shift Datsun, $10 plus 10¢ a mile for an automatic-shift Datsun. **United Car Rental,** Booth 4, Lihue Airport, offers flat rates on standard-shift compacts of $18.95 a day, $21.95 for automatics. Their phone is 248-8894. Rates at **Aloha Rent A Car Kauai** begin at $21.95 for standard-shift cars; at **Alamo** (tel. toll free 800/327-9633), an automatic compact is $19.95 a day, $79.95 a week, with advance reservations. And **Westside U-Drive** (tel. 332-8644) offers free delivery and pickup in the Poipu Beach area, as well as good rates: standard compacts at $17.95, automatics at $19.95. Remember that in busy tourist seasons, advance reservations are always advisable.

1. Island Hotels

IN LIHUE AND ENVIRONS: The tiny town of Lihue and its immediate surroundings are the most centrally located places to stay in Kauai, since they're the starting point for your eastern and western tours of the island. Lihue is also the county seat and the center of Kauai's government, commerce, and culture. For so small a town, Lihue boasts a surprising number of budget accommodations.

The **Ahana Motel-Apartments,** at 3115 Akahi St. (tel. 245-2206), are a longtime favorite with budget travelers to Kauai. Located in the center of town and about a three-minute drive from the Kauai Surf Hotel and beautiful swimming at Kalapaki Beach, they offer clean and cozy rooms that are comfortably, if quite modestly, furnished. There's TV in every room, and a picnic and recreation area outdoors in the garden away from the street. The tab is low: singles and doubles, $16; singles and doubles with kitchenette, $22. A one-bedroom apartment is $22. Some of the apartments are connected units and can be used as two-bedroom suites. There's an extra charge of $4 for each additional person. Children are heartily welcomed. Two two-bedroom units, each with two bathrooms, rent for $38 for four, okay for two couples who want to share the cooking. Mr. and Mrs. Ah Sau Ahana's little place is very popular, despite its lack of fanciness, so write well in advance for reservations to P.O. Box 892, Lihue, Kauai, HI 96766.

Not far from here, where Kalena Street makes a sharp curve, is the **Hale Lihue Motel** (tel. 245-3151 or 245-2571), simple, plain, well worn, with 18 rooms, a comfortable lobby, and an orchid garden just outside the building. Singles here are $14; doubles, $16. Three air-conditioned kitchenette units go for $18 single, $23 double. For an extra bed, the tab is $4. The upstairs rooms, which go for $18 single, $24 double, are a little larger than the downstairs ones (150 square feet as against 120), but you won't be able to play tennis in any of them. Children are welcome. The location is good, on a quiet, tree-shaded street, just five minutes from the center of town. It's a smart idea to reserve several weeks in advance during the busy summer season. (See the Readers' Selections, at the end of this chapter, for a "rave review.").

Motel Lani, at Rice Street where it meets Kalena (tel. 245-2965), is a pleasant place patronized by both island people and tourists. The ten small but modern rooms rent for $16 to $18 single or double, $22 to $26 triple. All have small refrigerators. There's an extra charge of $6 per person for any number over three, with rollaway cots provided. Rates are subject to change without notice. Two nights' deposit required. Janet Naumu suggests that you reserve in advance by writing to P.O. Box 1836, Lihue, Kauai, HI 96766.

A few blocks away, at 3173 Akahi St., the **Tip Top Motel** (tel. 245-2333) offers 34 rooms at $18 single, $24 double. All rooms are air-conditioned. It's right above the Tip Top Restaurant, Bakery, and Cocktail Lounge, big favorites with the locals. The rooms are pleasant if plain, and the place seems to us more efficient than resorty, but it's comfortable, and the price is right. Prices may rise this year. The reservations address is P.O. Box 1231, Lihue, Kauai, HI 96766.

Two miles out of Lihue, in Nawiliwili, is another budget place, the tiny **Oceanview Motel,** located three miles from the airport on the corner of Highway 51 (Rice Street) and Wilcox Road (tel. 245-6345). The small complex was conceived and built by the owner/general manager Spike Isamu Kanja. Spike's rooms are plain, but they are clean and comfortable, and the first and second floors have recently been renovated. These rooms are $16 single, or $18 double. There's also a new and pleasant third floor with more spacious rooms at $19 single, $20 double. It's $5 for each additional person in the room, and also cheaper by the week. All the rooms have small refrigerators. The location right near the Kauai Surf Golf Course and the superb swimming and surfing of Kalapaki Beach, plus easy walking access to the Harbor Village Shopping Center and several good restaurants are pluses here. There's a carp pool on the side of the building and a communal TV room. For reservations, write to Mr. Kanja at 3445 Wilcox Rd., Nawiliwili, Kauai, HI 96766.

For a bit of luxury in the Nawiliwili area, there are the attractive one- and two-bedroom condominium apartments at **Banyan Harbor** (tel. 245-7333). Nicely decorated, these apartments feature complete kitchens with dishwashers, washers, and dryers, and each one has a private lanai. There's a lovely big pool, a tennis court, shuffleboard, and a barbecue area. Both the beach and the golf course are just a short walk away. From April 1 through December 14, the two-bedroom units are $42 garden view and $55 harbor view for up to four persons, $7 for each additional person (maximum six persons). During the high season, rates are $13 higher. For reservations, write to Banyan Harbor, 3411 Wilcox Rd., Lihue, HI 96766.

COCONUT PLANTATION: Nine miles out of town, near where the Wailua River meets the ocean, is the site of the Coconut Plantation complex of hotels in Wailua. These are more expensive than the ones in the Lihue area since they are situated directly out on the ocean, but here on the

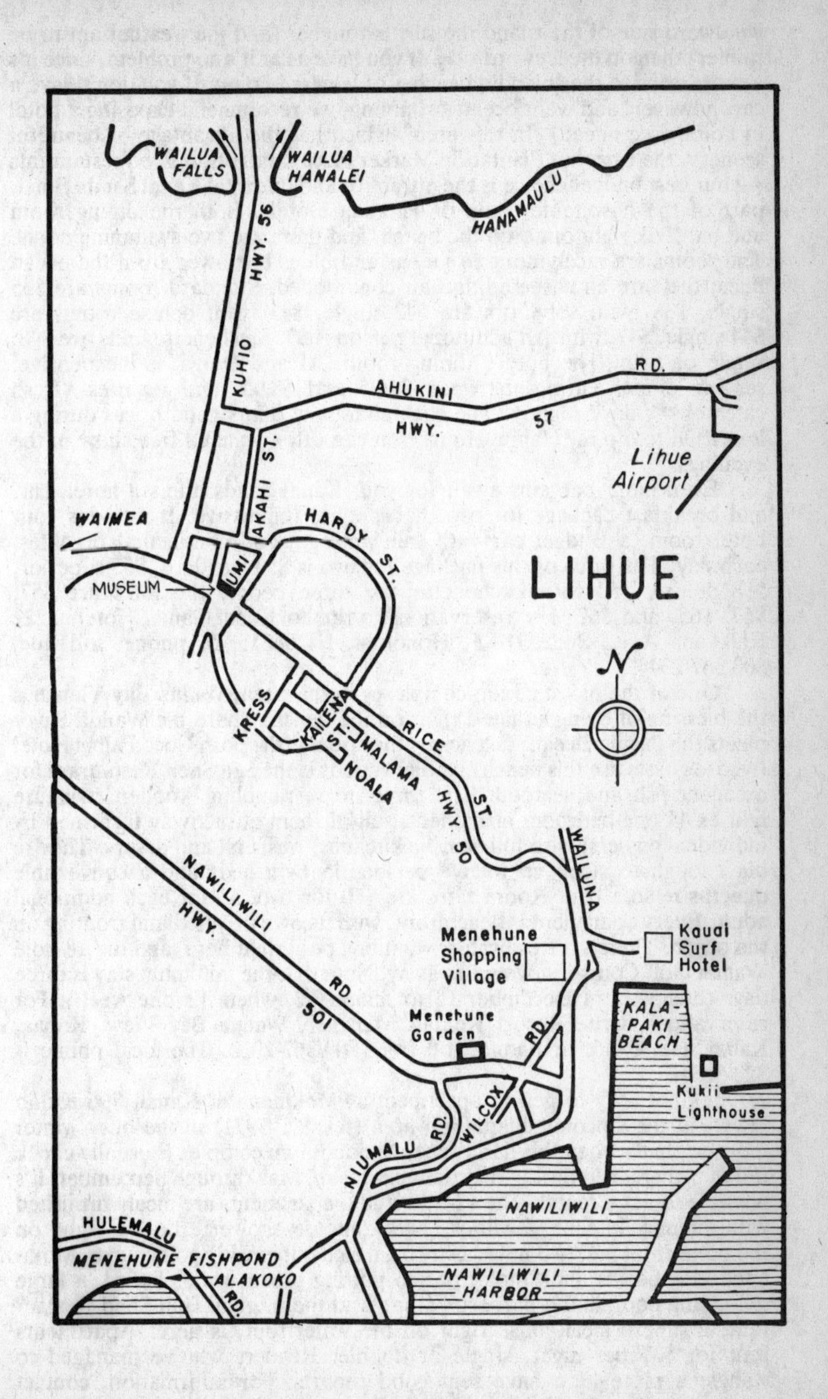
WAILUA FALLS
WAILUA HANALEI
HANAMAULU
HWY. 56
KUHIO
AHUKINI
RD.
HWY.
57
Lihue Airport
AKAHI ST.
HARDY ST.
WAIMEA
UMI
MUSEUM
LIHUE
N
KRESS
KAILENA ST.
MALAMA
NOALA
RICE
ST.
HWY. 50
WAILUNA
NAWILIWILI
HWY.
RD.
501
Menehune Shopping Village
Kauai Surf Hotel
KALA PAKI BEACH
Menehune Garden
RD.
WILCOX
Kukii Lighthouse
RD.
NIUMALU
NAWILIWILI
HULEMALU
MENEHUNE FISHPOND
ALAKOKO
RD.
NAWILIWILI HARBOR

windward side of the island the surf is rougher (and the weather apt to be rainier) than on the leeward side. If you have a car it's no problem, since it's a short drive to the splendid beaches of leeward Poipu. If you don't have a car, however, and want ocean swimming, we recommend choosing a hotel in Poipu (see ahead). In this area—which has the advantage of beautiful scenery, the Coconut Plantation Market Place, and lots of good restaurants—your best budget choice is the attractive and informal **Kauai Sands Hotel,** part of the hospitable chain of Hukilau Hotels. Both the dining room and bar look right out onto the beach, and there are two swimming pools. The rooms are nicely done in greens and blues borrowed from the ocean hues; they are all carpeted and air-conditioned. Standard rooms are $35 single, $38 twin; superiors are $42 single, $45 twin; deluxe rooms are $44 single, $47 twin. An additional person is $7. Kitchenette units are $48, single or twin. The hotel's dining room, Al and Don's, is inexpensive, serving dinner entrees between $4.95 and $8.75, and features "fresh catch of the day" nightly. The cocktail lounge offers good prices during a long 2:30 to 6 p.m. Happy Hour. You can often watch a free show in the evenings.

Even more bargains await for you: Kauai Sands offers a hotel, car, and breakfast package for two that is quite impressive. It includes your hotel room, a Budget car with free mileage, and continental breakfast each day. The price of this package for two is $50 standard, $55 superior, $58 deluxe, $60 with kitchenette; for three people the rates are $57, $62, $65, and $67. For reservations, write to Kauai Sands Hotel, 2222 Kalakaua Ave., Suite 714-F, Honolulu, HI 96815; or phone, toll free, 800/367-2344.

One of the nicest condo complexes in this area, **Wailua Bay View** has the blessing of being situated right on the beach, where the Wailua River meets the Pacific Ocean; just across the street is the posh Coco Palms Hotel (whose guests use this beach), and next door is the Sea Shell Restaurant for excellent fish and seafood. The three-story, rambling wooden structure houses 44 one-bedroom apartments, all of them attractively furnished by individual owners, with full electric kitchens, washers, and dryers. They're big enough to sleep up to five persons in twin beds and a convertible queen-size sofa bed. Room rates are $60 for two, $5 for each additional adult. Every apartment is beachfront, with its own private lanai fronting on the ocean. There's a freshwater swimming pool right here, and the 18-hole Wailua Golf Course is two miles away. Note that the minimum stay is three days (except from December 15 to January 2, when it's one week). For reservations, write Resort Rentals Manager, Wailua Bay View, Kapaa, Kauai, HI 96746; or phone, toll free, 800/367-2912. The local phone is 822-3651.

It's not easy to get an apartment at **Mokihana of Kauai,** 796 Kuhio Hwy., in the Coconut Plantation area (tel. 822-3971) in the busy winter months; that's when this handsome condominium complex is usually chock full of owners. But during the summer season, May through September, it's possible to get a rental. The 81-odd studio apartments are nicely furnished with limited kitchen facilities, bath, and/or shower; they're right on the oceanfront and two miles away from a championship golf course. Mokihana also boasts an 18-hole, par-36 putting green, shuffleboard, a large swimming pool, and a barbecue area. And the original Bull Shed Restaurant, a superb steakhouse right on the waterfront, is here. Apartments rent for $37 per night, single or double. Readers who've managed to wangle a place here have sent good reports. For information, contact

Hawaii Kailani, 119 N. Commercial, Suite 1400, Bellingham, WA 98225 (tel. 206/676-1434).

KAPAA: Farther up Highway 56 you'll hit the area of Kapaa, which boasts the cute little **Hotel Coral Reef** (tel. 822-4481), right on the ocean and close to everything. You could even make do without a car here, as within minimal walking distance is a pretty good public swimming beach (the hotel's own stretch of oceanfront is rather rough), a freshwater swimming pool, a tennis court, a library, and a laundromat—and several great little budget restaurants. Owner Mrs. Mae Matsumura will proudly lead you to the 16 units in the newer wing—very good buys at $27 double. These are beautiful modern rooms with two beds, large vanity dressers, refrigerators, and lanais with fantastic ocean breezes that were cooling the rooms on a day when everywhere else in Kauai felt oppresively humid. The floors are made of big colorful tiles and all rooms on the second floor are carpeted. Ten rooms in the older building have been fixed up and are now acceptable (although not nearly so nice as the ones in the new wing). They have showers (no tubs), twin beds, are carpeted, and rent for $19 double. Write Hotel Coral Reef, 1516 Kuhio Hwy., Kapaa, Kauai, HI 96746.

For a touch of luxury in Kapaa at a very good price, **Kapaa Shore,** 4-0900 Kuhio Hwy., may be just the ticket. This 81-unit condominium complex is right at the beach, and each and every apartment has a view of ocean, garden, or pool. They are beautifully furnished, many in avocado-and-white decorative schemes, with full electric kitchens, washers and dryers, and patio furniture to make dining on your lanai a treat. To help you prepare your meal, the kitchen is fully equipped, and includes a frost-free refrigerator, automatic dishwasher, and garbage disposal. The one-bedroom apartments can sleep up to four people in two twins or a queen-size bed in the bedroom and a queen-size sofa in the living room. Six people can be cozy in the two-bedroom apartments, which are duplexes with vaulted ceilings; they have a queen-size bed in one of the bedrooms, two twins in the other, and a queen-size sleeper-sofa in the living room. One-bedroom apartments are $59 for garden view, $65 for ocean view, and $69 for oceanfront; two-bedrooms are $79, $85, and $89. Pluses include the tennis court, 40-foot swimming pool, sunbathing deck, and barbecue area. For information and reservations, you can write Kapaa Shores directly at 4-0900 Kuhio Hwy., Kapaa Kauai, HI 96746; or phone 822-3055.

NEAR POIPU BEACH: In the other direction from Lihue, 12 miles south, stretches the idyllic Poipu Beach area, dry and sunny, where the surf crashes a Mediterranean blue-green on palm-fringed, white-sand beaches. This area is, of course, more expensive than Lihue, but you are right at the beach, and a glorious one it is—in our opinion, the best on Kauai. Any place you choose here will be lovely, but perhaps the best combination of value and charm can be found at the **Garden Isle Cottages,** a group of private cottages that offer island ambience and are scattered within a two-block area along the Poipu coast. The hospitable owners, Sharon and Robert Flynn, an artist, work hard at preserving the feeling of old Hawaii in all of their cottages by using batiks, ethnic fabrics and furniture, and Bob's paintings and sculpture. The cottages are set in Hawaiian flower gardens which include bougainvillea, banana, and hibiscus. Hale Melia, across the lane from a small sunning beach and gentle lagoon for floating and snorkeling, has three accommodations: two studios, each with bath and lanai overlooking the ocean; the smaller is $34 and the larger runs $38, double. You'll be in heaven if you can land the apartment below; it has a very large living/dining room with an open-beamed lahala ceiling, kitchen, and bath, surrounding an enclosed tropical garden patio that you will probably never want to leave. It rents for $50 double. A bedroom and extra bath can be added for two extra people, making it $68 quad.

Then there are the Sea Cliff Cottages, whose unique location—perched on a cliff over Koloa Landing, where the Waikomo Stream meets the ocean—gives them an ambience that can only be described as idyllic. They each have not one, but two lanais—a morning lanai for watching the sun come up over the water, an evening lanai for watching it set over the mountains. They are beautifully furnished with a spacious living/dining room, kitchen, one bedroom, and bath, plus washer-dryer. At $55 double, this is one of the best values around.

Kilohana Kai overlooks its own swimming pool and has a partial ocean view. The lower and upper one-bedroom apartments each have a living/dining room, kitchen, bath, and lanai, with washer and dryer, $50 each, double. Each additional person in all of the units is charged $6 per night.

The office of Garden Isle Cottages is located in Robert's gallery at 2666 Puuholo Rd., Koloa (open from 9 a.m. to noon), and Sharon is happy to give directions to out-of-the-way beaches and gardens. Good restaurants are nearby, but remember that you'll need a car to get around here. Write well in advance—these beautiful cottages are immensely popular—to Garden Isle Cottages, RR #1, Box 355, Koloa, Kauai, HI 96756. The phone is 742-6717.

A short distance down the road from Garden Isle is **Prince Kuhio,** which offers nicely furnished apartments overlooking either Prince Kuhio Park or a pool in a garden setting; there's a beach known for good snorkeling right across the road, and there are good swimming beaches nearby. A variety of studios and apartments are offered. Studios are $39 double daily, $195 weekly; one-bedroom apartments are $46 to $51 double daily, $230 to $255 weekly; $6 per extra person daily. All the units are fully equipped for light housekeeping with kitchens and comfortable living space; all have cable TV. There is no maid service unless requested upon arrival. The central barbecue is a popular spot here, and owners Den and Dee Wilson, who live on the premises, provide plenty of aloha spirit. Contact Prince Kuhio Rentals, P.O. Box 919, Koloa, HI 96756. The phone is 742-1409.

The **Poipu Beach Hotel** (tel. 742-1681), blessed with a perfect location right on the beach, has long been one of our favorite places on Kauai. While its rates are not quite budget, they are excellent value for a resort hotel of this caliber. Standard rooms are $60, single or double, and since all the rooms in this hotel are exactly the same, the only thing that determines the difference between a $60, $68, or $79 room is its location: at the higher prices you'll be facing the pool or the ocean; at the lower, the mountains. But the rooms are all good, spacious, nicely furnished, with private lanais, a huge dressing area, and best of all, a compact little kitchenette unit that makes fixing breakfast or a quick meal a breeze. The three buildings surround the pool and grassy area, the dining room is right in the middle of it all, and several nights a week there's a Polynesian show; sit out on your lanai and you'll hear the whole thing. There are six tennis courts, with a pro shop next door. The management is attentive, service prompt. The neighboring property, Waiohai, has been completely rebuilt and is now an exquisite resort hotel, all of whose guest services you can use, including the Clark Hatch Physical Fitness Center (gym, Jacuzzi, sauna, massage, etc.). Reservations: Amfac Resorts, P.O. Box 8519, 2222 Kalakaua Ave., Honolulu, HI 96815.

The furnishings in the **Poipu Shores Resort Condominium** are luxury-plus: in fact, the same may be said of the whole complex. Rattan and cane furniture with oceany-colored upholstery in Oriental leaf prints highlight the cool, spacious apartments. Each unit has an all-electric kitchen, a color TV set, and a lanai. The low-rise buildings are surrounded by lush gardens and located in a secluded area right on the ocean. The one-bedroom/1½-bath apartments are $75 a day, placing them out of our budget range, but savings can be realized in the larger units, if you're bringing the family or are two couples traveling together. The two-bedroom/two-bath apartments are $100 for up to six people; the three-bedroom/two-bath units and the two-bedroom town houses, with 2½ baths, are $120 and $110 respectively, for up to six people. Summer rates are $10 less. If you truly want to get away from it all, this is the place to do it—in style. For reservations, write Poipu Shores Resort Condominium, R.R. 1, Box 95, Koloa, HI 96756 (tel. 742-6522), or call toll free 800/367-6522.

PRINCEVILLE: Think of Princeville, on the north shore of Kauai, and you think of luxury living, of championship golf and tennis amid a green sweep of mountains and valleys. You don't think of budget accommodations here, and yet we've found some of the best values on the island right in the middle of otherwise pricey Princeville. First is a place called **Sandpiper Village,** a 75-unit condominium complex that features *only* two-bedroom-two-bath apartments, and two-bedroom-plus-loft/2½-bath apartments—but at prices comparable to what you'd expect to pay for just a studio room elsewhere: $44 for the smaller units, $56 for the larger during the long off-season (April 15 to December 14), and $56 and $66 the rest of the year. (An extra person is charged $7; kids under 12 free; rollaways and cribs, $7.) And each unit is like a lovely little house, high-ceilinged and fully carpeted, with ceiling fans, handsome dark bamboo furniture, superb decorator's touches wherever you look. Kitchens are of generous size, with dishwashers and washer-dryers. A cable hookup can be rented for the television set. From your windows you can sometimes watch the waterfalls coming down the mountains. The units are set in shaded gardens and clustered around a central area where the whole family can have fun—large swimming pool, sauna, Jacuzzi, recreation building, barbecue pits.

From your apartment here you're a short distance from the Princeville Makai golf course, rated among "America's Top 100," and its six outdoor tennis courts. There are half a dozen enjoyable restaurants right at Princeville. You can drive down to the beach at Hanalei in about five minutes, or get your exercise hiking down to the shore. For reservations, write Sandpiper Village, Princeville, Hanalei, Kauai, HI 96714; or call toll free 800/367-5314. Canadians can call Keith Cooke & Associates toll free. The local phone is 826-9613.

There's another top-flight choice right here whose modest prices hardly reflect its luxurious accommodations, surroundings, and services. That's **The Cliffs at Princeville,** the largest condo complex in the area (210 units). Set amid graceful lawns and gardens, and perched atop cliffs overlooking the ocean far below, it offers as much of peace and privacy, sports or excitement as one would wish. On the grounds are four tennis courts, a putting green, a large pool area with Jacuzzi, and a recreation pavilion complete with a huge fireplace, wet-bar, an indoor whirlpool bath and sauna, Ping-Pong and pool tables. All of the suites are perfect little one-bedroom-two-bath houses, fully carpeted, beautifully and individually furnished in bamboo and oak, with oak doors, completely equipped kitchens, and cable TV. All have been decorated in excellent taste. These suites can be divided to provide the following possible combinations: a hotel room with a garden view (small executive-size refrigerator instead of kitchen) for one or two people at $45; a studio with garden view for two at $45; a one-bedroom-two-bath unit with garden view for one to four people at $65 ($10 more for ocean view); and a one-bedroom-with-loft-two-bath unit for one to four people at $95. Four-bedroom-four-bathroom ocean-front or garden units that can sleep eight are $180. Weekly rates are available. Whatever the size of your family or group, the very helpful management will work with you to provide a highly livable and affordable setup.

There are amenities and service aplenty at the Cliffs. These include daily maid service, beach mats and ice chests for taking to the beach or touring, daily morning coffee klatches with slide presentations and after-noon cocktail parties, charcoal barbecues available at the pool area and at the Gazebo. And the Gazebo is something special—a romantic spot overlooking the water, the ideal place to watch the sunset or the crashing surf far below.

Again, the Princeville Makai Golf Course, designed by Robert Trent Jones, is right at hand; the sandy beach at Hanalei is about a five-minute drive; and opportunities for horseback riding, surfing, windsurfing, scuba diving, and much more are all close by. It's a good choice for Na Pali Coast hikers, as they will store your luggage while you're off hiking the trails.

For reservations, call 800/367-6046 toll free, or write to Colony Resorts, 733 Bishop St., Suite 1600, Honolulu, HI 96813.

KOKEE: Forty-five miles away from Lihue, in Kokee State Park (just beyond Waimea Canyon), you'll find **Kokee Lodge,** 3600 feet up in bracing mountain air. The cabins are owned by the state but operated by a private firm, and the prices are low—a practice we'd like to see imitated all over Hawaii. This is a place only for those who have enough time to really linger in Kauai (on a two- or three-day trip, a stay would be impractical, since the time and cost of driving to the other sights of the island would outweigh the savings here). The cabins vary in size from one large room, which sleeps three, to two-bedroom units that will accommodate seven. Each cabin rents for a flat $25 per night. The cabins are furnished with refrigerators, stoves, hot showers, basic eating and cooking utensils, blankets, linens, and pillows. You can buy a pile of wood and make a fire in the fireplace when the night air gets nippy in this cooler northern Kauai, that seems a world away from beaches and coconut palms.

Daytime activities at Kokee include driving or hiking on gorgeous trails and swimming in hidden freshwater pools. You can also hunt boar and wild goat, fish for trout in the nearby mountain streams, or just laze in the sun. Kokee Lodge Restaurant serves breakfast, lunch, and snacks daily from 8 a.m. to 5 p.m. Gourmet dinners are sometimes served on weekends and holidays. The restaurant provides take-out orders and snacks for outdoor picnics, and for those wishing to cook, there's a simple grocery store on the premises. (Bring your own supplies, however, if you're planning on cooking anything fancy.) There's also a cocktail lounge and a gift shop. For reservations: Kokee Lodge, P.O. Box 819, Waimea, Kauai, HI 96796 (tel. 335-6061). Management advises making early reservations, since holiday weekends are very popular here, and so is the trout-fishing season in August and September.

BED AND BREAKFAST: For information on bed-and-breakfast lodgings in Kauai, see details at the end of Chapter II, "Honolulu Hotels."

2. Island Restaurants

IN LIHUE AND ENVIRONS: Lihue has some excellent budget restaurants frequented mostly by the local people, and you'll be glad you joined them. One of the best is the **Lihue Barbecue Inn** on Kress Street (tel. 245-2921), where the cuisine is Japanese, American, and Chinese—and very good too. There's a bar and lounge off to one side of the restaurant. You'll know why the Barbecue Inn has been going strong for some 45 years now when you have a look at the prices: a typical dinner menu lists 17 complete dinners—and that includes soup or fruit cup, tossed green salad, vegetable, beverages, and Jell-O for dessert, accompanying such main courses as shrimp tempura, baked mahimahi, broiled teriyaki pork chops, corned beef brisket with cabbage, chow mein chicken with spare ribs—for under $7.95! (Complete meals start at just $4.85). Seven more dinners go up in price to as high as $14.95, for baked lobster tail with steak and fried rice. Fresh fish is served whenever it is available. Complete lunches are even cheaper; we counted 32 of them for under $3.95! These often include stuffed cabbage, tofu salad, taco salad, mahimahi sandwich, or pastrami on rye. The menu changes daily, but whatever you have here will most likely be good—especially the freshly made pies. Do try the green tea—the hospitable owner Henry Sasaki let us in on the secret; it's brewed with rice and popcorn! One of the most appealing inexpensive restaurants in Lihue, the Barbecue is patronized by family groups; and over the years we have had consistent letters of praise from our readers about it. It's open from 7:30 a.m. to 1:30 p.m. and from 4:30 to 8:45 p.m.; closed Sunday.

Another place that's long been popular with the locals is the **Tip Top Café,** in shiny air-conditioned quarters at 3173 Akahi St., just north of the Lihue Shopping Center. It's a family-style restaurant, the prices are modest, and while the food is not of gourmet quality, it's dependable. Service is apt to be on the slow side. We often have breakfast here (pancakes are served all day, and the macadamia nut ones, $2, are delicious). There's a Chinese plate lunch for $3.85, and lunch entrees like pork chops for $3.50. Dinner entrees such as teriyaki pork, breaded fish filet, and ground round steaks with eggs average $5.50, and that includes soup, salad or potato salad, rice or potatoes, and coffee. The Chinese combination plate dinner is $5.75. This is a good place to remember if you need a box lunch for an all-day excursion; either American- or Oriental-style take-out lunches are available at $3. Before you leave, take a look at the omiyage (gift) department. Besides pastries, orchids, and souvenirs, it has some memorable homemade jams; you might want to pick up a bottle of passion fruit, pineapple, or guava-macadamia nut to take to the folks back home. And the Tip Top Bakery is famous for its macadamia-nut cookies and Portuguese sweet bread, baked fresh daily. The Tip Top stays open from 6:45 a.m. until 9 p.m. daily (tel. 245-2343 or 245-2333). There are clean motel units next door (see above).

A new favorite with the local folks is **Ho's Garden Restaurant,** at 3016 Umi St., corner of Rice Street (tel. 245-5255). The atmosphere is plain, but it's the food that counts, and fragrant and tasty it is. Most lunch entrees run from $3.80 to $4.50; the day we were there we enjoyed two delicious specials at $3.80 each: tempura mahimahi in a black bean sauce, and roast duck with rice and oyster sauce. Dinner entrees such as lemon chicken, almond duck, abalone with black mushrooms, and squid with sour cabbage are mostly under $5, and often include specials like crab with black bean sauce at $4.50. Peking duck lovers—three of them—can feast for all of $23.50. Vegetarians take note: specialties like tofu tomato flower—golden-browned tofu and tomato sauteed in a scrambled-egg sauce—are quite tasty; most are under $4. Ho's is open Monday through Saturday from 10:30 a.m. to 2:30 p.m. for lunch, from 4:30 to 9 p.m. for dinner; Sunday, it's 5 to 9:30 p.m.

For authentic Hawaiian food—and American and Japanese dishes as well—local people recommend **Dani's,** at 4200 Rice St., where you can get a really early breakfast (doors open at 5 a.m.) and lunch up to 2 p.m. Breakfast and lunch specialties include a dish of lau lau, poi, and lomi salmon for $3.10; kalua pig and lomi salmon with rice for $3.60; and beef or tripe stew with poi at $3. You can also have main dishes like teriyaki beef, fried shrimp, breaded mahimahi, or broiled chicken, from $2.60 to $3.50. Don't be surprised if you're the only tourists here. On Sunday, Dani's closes at 11 a.m.

One of the most popular eating places in Kauai has long been the Bull Shed, a waterfront restaurant in Mokihana of Kauai at Waipouli. Now there's the **Bull Shed 2,** right in Lihue, in the Harbor Village Shopping Center, 2501 Rice St. (tel. 245-4551), and it's just as good—and that means very good indeed—as the original. The attractive lanai restaurant is three-tiered for coziness, warmly decorated with wood, hanging plants, overhead fans to keep everything cool. The house specialty is the finest midwestern beef, as well as chicken, seafood, and fresh catch of the day. If you're watching the budget or your waistline, you can make do with visits to the salad bar alone (it's ensconced in a canoe!) for $5.95. Spend just a bit more and you can have teriyaki chicken or a small sirloin at $7.95, Korean kal-bi for $8.95. The excellent prime rib is $12.95. All entrees include the salad bar, hot rolls, and steamed rice. There's a good wine list. Dinners only, every day from 5:30 p.m. [*Note:* The original **Bull Shed** is just north of Coconut Plantation, on Route 56, behind the Mokihana of Kaui condos (tel. 822-3791).]

The local people also rave about another restaurant at Harbor Village: **Kauai Chop Suey** (tel. 245-8790). Our favorite local couple love this place, and take all their visiting friends to dinner here. Despite its unimaginative name, it serves superior food, all in the Cantonese style. There are about 75 items on the menu, at least 70 of them under $5, so the budgeteer cannot go wrong here. There's something for everyone: roast duck, egg foo yong, squid with vegetables, shrimp with broccoli, lemon chicken, stuffed tofu, sweet pork, or char sui (an island favorite), and much more. If you come here on Tuesday, you can have the baked manapua; on Thursday, steamed manapua. And the soups—seaweed, scallop, abalone—are quite special. The place is large and comfortable, decorated in typical Chinese style.

Large parties are seated at round tables with revolving centerpieces, similar to our "Lazy Susans," the better to sample all the delicacies. Kauai Chop Suey serves lunch Tuesday to Saturday from 11 a.m. to 2 p.m.; dinner, Tuesday to Sunday from 4:30 to 9 p.m. Closed Monday.

Denmar's Pancakes & Things, also at Harbor Village (tel. 245-3917), took over the quarters of a handsome Mexican restaurant and has kept the open-air feeling here. Pancakes are the specialty—delicious concoctions like papaya-nut or banana-macadamia pancakes—but they also have other "things": at lunch and dinner they whip up moderately priced Mexican specialties like quesadillas at $4, and the burrito deluxe at $5.50. Other specialties include pineapple chicken, short ribs, and pork chops, $5.95 to $6.25.

One of the old-standby restaurants in Lihue is **Club Jetty,** overlooking the Pacific at Nawiliwili Harbor; it's the only restaurant and cabaret in Hawaii partially built on the water. Try to get a window seat here, so you can keep an eye on harbor activity: Coast Guard boats, a freighter swaying gently at anchor, small craft, the luxury liner *Constitution* if it happens to be Thursday. The food here is a combination of American and Chinese, with good values in both. American-style dinners start at $6.95, and that includes an all-you-can-eat salad bar and beverage. A hearty Cantonese dinner plate which includes chicken chow mein, egg foo yong, and sweet-and-sour spare ribs with fresh pineapple, among others, is about $5.25. Chinese entrees alone are mostly $5 and up. Music is on from 9:30 p.m. to 3:30 a.m. Wednesday through Saturday. Club Jetty is at the end of Route 51 South (tel. 245-4970). Dinner only, 5 to 9 p.m.; closed Sunday.

Going strong for over ten years now, **La Luna,** one of Kauai's few Mexican restaurants, occupies handsome, smartly decorated indoor and outdoor quarters at 4261 Rice St. (tel. 245-9173), after many years just out of town. The food here is *muy bueno,* as they say in Hawaii. You could start off with bean dip and crispy tortilla chips, $3.50; then proceed to the La Luna Especíal, a combination of cheese enchilada, bean burrito, beef taco, and rice for $7.50; or choose the Hanalei Rush, consisting of two cheese enchiladas, refried beans, and rice, $6.50. Even cheaper is the Pobrecito—a plate of Spanish rice, refried beans topped with melted cheese, guacamole, and chips, $6. Combination plates run from about $4.25 to $5.75. The margaritas are great. There's entertainment seven nights a week, from 8:30 until closing. Lunch is on from 11:30 a.m. to 4:30 p.m., "Sour Hour" from 2:30 to 5:30 p.m., with special prices on margaritas; nachos are available, but chips and hot sauce are free. Dinner is served from 4:30 to 10 p.m. Closed for lunch on Sunday.

The **Eggbert's: Kauai's Family Specialty Restaurant** is a long name for a friendly little restaurant at 4483 Rice St., in the Haleko Shops. It's an attractive place, with water fountains, colored lights, and ceiling fans to keep the trade winds moving. The day starts here at 6 a.m. (7 a.m. on Sunday) with a variety of terrific omelets at $2.65 to $4.95 for the two-egger and $3.25 to $5.95 for their "three-egg-wonder." Also excellent: Eggbert's Benedict at $5.25 for the vegetarian version, $5.95 with country ham and turkey. Their handmade hollandaise is quite special. All breakfast/brunch items are served until 2 p.m., but lunch dishes are added on at 11 a.m. That's when you can have soups, salads, sandwiches, and island favorites like tasty pork and cabbage ($3.85) or fried rice served on a "crêpe-like" open omelet, the chef's special ($3.25). A limited menu and bar service continue until dinner, served Wednesday through Saturday from 5:30 to

9:30 p.m., which features fish, chicken, beef, pork, and omelet specialties along with good salads, freshly made soups, and desserts. Entrees run from $5.95 to $12.95. Reservations are suggested (tel. 245-6325). Bar prices are very reasonable. Eggbert's is almost always open, and you can always get something tasty and decently priced here.

Be prepared to wait your turn in line before you gain access to a lunchtime table at **Kenny's** (tel. 245-6522), in the Lihue Shopping Center: this is a madly popular place with the local business people. When you finally settle down at your table in the big, bustling room with paintings on the wall, you can have dishes such as chuck ground steak, filet of mahimahi sauté, or shrimp tempura, from $3.50 to $4.95. Kenny's special sandwiches —hot pastrami on rye, supreme burgers, Reubens, and steak, run $3.50 to $5.50 and are very hearty. Dinnertime is a lot more peaceful, and that's when you can have regular entrees (similar to those served at lunch), plus some nightly char-broiled items—boneless breast of chicken, New York–cut steak, prime rib roast, and the like—from $4.50 to $16.95. All entrees come with rice or fries, hot dinner rolls, and a turn at the salad bar; the salad bar alone is just $5.25. Kenny's also serves good breakfasts, and between lunch and dinner, the action centers around the bar and cocktail lounge, where, from 11 a.m. to 2 p.m. they serve freshly carved meat sandwiches for $5.50; the lounge itself stays open until 1 a.m. Closed Sunday.

Swimming at Kalapaki Beach is sheer heaven, so it's nice to know you won't have to leave the scene if you get hungry: the Kauai Surf, which fronts right on the beach, has recently opened the large, cafeteria-like **Surfside Snack Shop** that's the answer to a beach lover's prayer. Step up to the counter and help yourself to saimin at $2.50, grilled cheese sandwich at $2.25, chile dog at $3.25, lox, bagel, and cream cheese at $4.95, or fish 'n' chips at $4.50. Vegetarian plates, chef's salad, friend shrimp are also good. And if you just want something sweet, sodas, sundaes, and banana splits are available—so are wine and beer. Birds fly in through the open doors, and the glass windows provide a view of all the beach activity. Open every day between 11 a.m. and 5 p.m.

The tiny **Restaurant Kiibo** at 2991 Umi St. (tel. 245-2650) is a comfortable, prettily furnished place where the food is outstanding. There's a low wooden counter surrounded on three sides by little stools with cushions. Japanese lanterns supply the soft lighting, and photos of kabuki actors and examples of Japanese folk art adorn the walls. Two of us had a lovely dinner here recently for less than $9. Our meals included a flavorful miso soup, rice, tsukemono (pickled salad), and tea. We enjoyed our $5 chicken sukiyaki and $4 beef teriyaki to the accompaniment of soft Japanese music in the background. For dessert—a very un-Japanese strawberry shave ice. (They have about ten flavors of shave ice; with ice cream, it's $1.80 and delicious.) Other good choices include a big plate of shrimp and vegetable tempura at $5, and donburi, a huge bowl of rice topped with sukiyaki or teriyaki or something equally interesting, at $3.75. Lunch offers similar dishes at slightly lower prices. Chances are good that you'll be the only haoles at the Kiibo; it's a local favorite, off the usual tourist beat. Have a look at their beautiful Japanese T-shirts. Closed Sunday.

Kukui Grove

Kauai's new multi-million-dollar shopping center, **Kukui Grove,** just outside Lihue on Route 50 toward Poipu Beach, has several attractive eating possibilities for us. Our favorite is not a traditional restaurant at all, but a café area in the middle of Rainbow Books called **Rainbow Coffees.** Freshly roasted coffee is sold by the pound and its fragrant aroma makes everything you eat here—at the cozy counter or tables—taste wonderful. There are always coffees of the day, a variety of espressos and cappuccinos and coffee specialty drinks (coffee cream soda, coffee grog, café mocha, etc.), black and herbal teas, croissants and bagels (filled with various spreads), plus some incredible, freshly baked pastries—bearclaws filled with almond paste, florentines, rum balls, and the like. Our nomination for sybarite's heaven goes to Rainbow Coffees' extraordinary brownie dessert: that's a heated brownie topped with a scoop of espresso ice cream, then smothered in fudge sauce Grand Marnier from the Silver Palate and whipped cream, $3.50. A lovely place for a sophisticated snack.

Probably the most popular specialty restaurant here is **Rosita's Mexican Restaurant** (tel. 245-8561), in an attractive indoor-outdoor setting: many plants, stained-glass lanterns, ceiling fans, stucco walls, cozy booths. You can dine leisurely here, at lunch and dinner, on Mexican and American favorites and sometimes a combination of both, like the hamburger ortega and hamburger ranchera lunch specials at $4.50. Combination plates run $5.25 to $6.75. Their seafood tostada, filled with shrimp, crab, and red snapper, is good at $6.75, and so is the arroz con pollo at $7.95. Dishes tend to be highly spiced. Don't pass up Rosita's famous margaritas—when was the last time you had a *strawberry* margarita? Rosita's is open every day but Sunday, serving meals from 11:30 a.m. to 10 p.m. The bar is open from 11:30 a.m. to midnight.

At the rear of Rosita's is **Taco Tia,** a five-table snackbar where you can dine Mexican in a hurry. Beef or chicken tacos are $1.25, beef tostadas are $2.35, an order of nachos is $3.50, and a plate lunch is $3.95. Open 11 a.m. to 6 p.m. Monday to Saturday, to 3 p.m. on Sunday.

The **Kukui Nut Tree Inn** (tel. 245-7005) is a family restaurant, serving all three meals in a summerhouse atmosphere. Latticework arching over the booths and on the ceiling make this nicer than your average coffeeshop. The food is American with island touches, and prices are quite reasonable. The day starts at 7 a.m. (8 a.m. on Sunday) with eggs and pancakes (try the strawberry pancakes at $2.60). Lunch features entrees like the mahi tempura and teri combo at $4.95, honey-stung fried chicken with corn on the cob at $5.95, grilled beef liver with onions and bacon at $4.95, and mahi macadamia sauteed with macadamia-nut bits in a butter sauce at $5.95. Entrees are served with a hot vegetable or starch; they are preceded by soup or fruit cocktail, and accompanied by salad, rolls, and beverage. At dinner the bill goes up about $1, but dessert—ice cream, pudding, pie, or cake—is added. With prices like these, it's no wonder this place is always crowded! Drinks are available. The kitchen closes at 8 p.m., except on Friday (9 p.m.) and Sunday (3 p.m.).

If you're in the mood for a quick Japanese lunch, join the locals here at **Joni-Hana,** a neat little red-and-white spot, where you can get sushi to go, sushi bento (a box lunch of assorted sushi with chicken and steak teriyaki for $3), or hot lunches like beef cutlet or sesame fried chicken wings for $3 for one choice, $3.50 for two.

Meals on the Run

For quickie meals at low prices, there are a few places in the center of town you should make note of. The **Big Save Snack Bar,** in the Rice

Shopping Center on Rice Street, has a variety of plate lunches that are much more than a snack, from $2.60 to $3.50. Good breakfasts too. . . . Across from the Kress Shopping Center, there's a **Dairy Queen** with a full lunch and dinner menu, like char-broiled butterfish for $4.95. . . . The food is good, too, at **Colonel Sanders Kentucky Fried Chicken,** at the corner of the airport road and Route 56. The prices are pretty much in line with those at his other chicken emporiums. . . . If you need to pick up an inexpensive lunch on your way to Kalapaki Beach, try **Keoki's Snack Bar** at 3474 Rice St., just past the entrance to the Kauai Surf Hotel. Chili dogs are $2, chili bowls run $2.25, and plate lunches include teriyaki steak, curry stew, and teriburger, from $2.95 to $4.25. . . . Absorb a bit of local color with your meal at **Hamura Saimin,** a super-plain lunch counter in an ancient woodframe building on Kress Street. A large sign over the counter proclaims: "Do not stick gum under counter." Specialties are saimin, $2.40 for a large bowl, and wonton min at $2.75.

Hanamaulu

It's well worth making a short trip from Lihue (about two miles north on Highway 56) to dine at the **Hanamaulu Restaurant and Tea House.** It's an attractive place, and the Japanese garden is really something to see, beautifully landscaped with stone pagodas, pebbled paths, and a pond filled with flashing carp. We suggest you call a day in advance and reserve one of the charming ozashiki, or teahouse, rooms; you take off your shoes, sit on the floor at a long, low table, and the shoji screens are opened to face the lighted garden. (You may be able to get one of the rooms without reservations, but it's best to call ahead; tel. 245-2511). The food here is excellent and inexpensive; the Chinese and Japanese plate lunches at $5.50 are good buys. You'll get soup, fried chicken or shrimp, chop suey, spare ribs, rice, and tea on the Chinese menu; miso soup, pork tofu or teriyaki steak, takuwan, rice, and tea on the Japanese. For dinner, the special plates start at $5; entrees like chicken sukiyaki go for $4.50; and you can feast on a veritable Oriental banquet for about $10 per person. An excellent sushi bar is an attraction here. Owner Roy Miyake is a cordial host. The restaurant is open from 11 a.m. to 1 p.m. and from 5 to 9 p.m.

Just next door to Hanamaulu Café is **Beef 'n' Pasta** (tel. 245-6832), located inside the 100-year-old Hanamaulu Trading Co. Building and Museum. It's a cozy little place with a tiny six-person bar (that way, no one stays a stranger for long), great food, friendly service, and reasonable prices. David and Carol Espinda, the owners, are right there to see to it that everything is congenial. Together they make up the soups, sauces, salad dressings, and desserts. And their salad bar (evenings only, $6.50 for salad bar alone) is wonderfully fresh, without a trace of those overmarinated, canned dishes that appear on too many salad bars. Dinners are decently priced: the house specialty, beef 'n' pasta, which consists of top sirloin plus a choice of spaghetti, rigatoni, or ravioli, is $8.95, and comes with unlimited salad bar and garlic bread. Other dinner favorites include lasagne; veal, eggplant, or chicken parmigiana; fettucine Alfredo; and scampi—from about $8.25 to $10.95. Fresh fish is served when available. Come at lunchtime and you can have some tasty sandwiches—like meatballs or chicken breast topped with melted mozzarella—at $3.75 and $4.75, or various salads and pasta, served with small salad and hot garlic bread, for about $4.75 to $5.50.

Beef 'n' Pasta is open for lunch Monday through Friday from 11:30

a.m. to 3 p.m., for dinner every night except Tuesday from 6 to 10 p.m. David can be found playing piano Wednesday through Saturday nights—anything from Golden Oldies on up.

RESTAURANTS ON THE EASTERN AND NORTHERN ROUTE: On this route, there are many budget restaurants to choose from.

In Wailua and Kapaa

Several of our readers wrote this year to praise **Restaurant Kintaro,** at 4-370 Kuhio Hwy., between Coco Palms and Coconut Plantation (tel. 822-3341), for its exquisite Japanese cuisine. We tried it and couldn't agree more: exquisite is the word for the dining experience at this sparkling bright restaurant, authentically Japanese down to the prettily wrapped chopsticks on the table. The rather bland exterior does not even suggest the harmonious Japanese scene inside: kites and kimonos on the walls, blonde woods, shoji screens, a long sushi bar from which the chefs turn out tender marvels. Have a seat, read the menu, sip a glass of sake or a cocktail while you're reading, and you'll be pleasantly surprised: a complete dinner runs from about $9.75 to $12.75 and includes a variety of delicious small dishes. First you are served chilled buckwheat noodles in a flavorful sauce, presented on a *zora,* a wooden box with bamboo top. Next, also served on traditional wooden platters, arrive miso soup, rice, Japanese pickled vegetables, and your main course—it could be the delicious chicken yakitori (boneless broiled chicken, onion, bell pepper, and teriyaki sauce and salad) or salmon yakitori that we sampled. Or it could be the yosenabe, a Japanese "bouillabaisse" of many kinds of seafood cooked with vegetables and served in a clay pot; a tasty tempura combination, or fresh fish of the day. Green tea ice cream, which we find delicious, is included with the meal; it was even more delicious topped with Suntory Green Melon Liqueur ($2.95)! A pot of green tea accompanies your meal. There are various sushi and sashimi combinations for appetizers or for those who wish to eat at the sushi bar. All in all, an ah-so harmonious experience.

Kintaro serves dinner only, Monday to Saturday, from 5:30 to 9:30 p.m.; closed Sunday.

At lunchtime, when the hungry crowds come off the boats from the Fern Grotto, the **Wailua Marina Restaurant** at Wailua Marina (tel. 822-4311) is the kind of place we like to avoid. But at dinnertime, when the mobs have gone, it's an entirely different story. Then, all is peaceful and quiet in the huge dining room with its slanted ceiling, murals, stuffed fish and turtleshells on the wall— and it's then that you can really enjoy the good food and attentive service at prices that are ridiculously low. How they manage to serve some 16 dishes from $4.75 to $7.50—and that includes boneless chicken stuffed with crab and pork, crispy teriyaki chicken, salmon steak, fried mahimahi, baked stuffed pork chop, and breaded veal cutlet—is a mystery to us, especially since every meal includes delicious hot rolls with butter and a green salad with choice of dressing (the bleu cheese is excellent), plus vegetables and potatoes for that same low price. Our teriyaki chicken was quite good, and the salmon steak, although frozen, was nicely done. Another dozen or so entrees, including seafood specialties like Alaskan snow crab claws and broiled lobster tail, range from $9 to $16.50. Homemade pies cost $1.25. Dinner is served from 5:30 to 9 p.m. daily, lunch from 11 a.m. to 2 p.m., breakfast from 8:30 to 11 a.m.

free transportation from Wailua area hotels in the evenings only. A find.

Hotel dining rooms are often overpriced, but we'd call the **Hale Kai Dining Room** at the Kauai Beachboy Hotel (tel. 822-3441) a very pleasant exception: the $8 to $13 it will probably cost you to have dinner here is well spent, considering the graciousness of the room and service, dinner music in the background, and tables well spaced for relaxed conversation. Best buy in the house is the generous salad bar (we don't doubt it's "the most popular on Kauai"), laden with many good things, more than enough for a full meal, and just $5.75. But house specialties like honey-dipped fried chicken, barbecue-style beef ribs, chicken 'n' ribs combo, filet of mahimahi, priced from $7.95 to $10.25, are also very good buys, considering that they include the salad bar and a choice of steakhouse fries, rice, or whipped potatoes. We started a recent salad bar meal here with one of the tempting pupus—potato skins stuffed and baked with cheese and bacon ($3.95)—and ended with a cooling mint-chocolate-chip mousse ($1.50). There's a full-service bar, and an attractive list of coffee and liquor drinks too. Dinner is served nightly from 6 to 9 p.m.

If you're in the mood for a treat now, stop and have lunch with the rich at the glorious **Coco Palms Hotel.** Considering that lunch is an extravagant buffet with several hot entrees—usually including chicken and roast beef—and many, many choices of vegetables, potatoes, salads, breads, yummy desserts, and fresh fruits, it's sensibly priced at about $8.50. And it's so nice to sit in the lovely open dining room overlooking the palms and the lagoon, where, in the early evening, their famous torch-lighting ceremony is held. Lunch is served 11:30 a.m. to 2 p.m., salads and sandwiches between 2 and 4:30 p.m. Be sure to walk around the beautiful grounds and browse through their museum and shops.

Waipouli Chop Suey, in the Waipouli Shopping Plaza at 4-901 Kuhio Hwy. (tel. 822-3911), caters to Chinese, Japanese, and American tastes. The menu and prices are always the same, except for the plate lunch/dinner special, $3.85 at lunch, $4.10 at dinner. À la carte choices include almond duck, crispy ginger-fried chicken (their specialty), shrimp Canton, from $3.90 to $5.70. American tastes can be satisfied with sizzling prime ribs (eight ounces for $7.50), broiled steak dinners, and even fish and chips or oysters and chips, $2.75 and $3.75. The best Japanese dishes here are chicken sukiyaki, beef teriyaki, and special saimin with shrimp and vegetables, from $3 to $3.90. Open from 7:30 a.m. to 9 p.m. daily. Take-out orders to nearby hotels and condos.

If you've developed a taste for real Hawaiian food, you can satisfy it in plain surroundings at the **Aloha Diner** in the Waipouli Complex, 4-971 Kuhio Hwy. (tel. 822-3851). Best bets are the lunch special for $4.50, including kalua pig or laulau, lomi-lomi salmon, rice or poi; and the more elaborate dinner special at $6.50—kalua pig or laulau, lomi-lomi salmon, chicken lau, poi or rice, and haupia (coconut pudding). À la carte entrees, from $2.50 to $3.50, include beef stew, squid lau, and other favorites. Several readers have praised this one. Open Monday to Saturday from 11 a.m. to 9 p.m.; closed Sunday.

The little town of Kapaa offers a bonanza of budget restaurants, all on or near the main street, Highway 56. A real favorite here is **Kountry Kitchen** (tel. 822-3511), a dressed-up diner with carpets, Tiffany-type lamps, gingham curtains at the windows, and a flavor of olden times. The flavor of the food is pretty good too: you can have complete dinners like fresh local fish, all-vegetable quiche, barbecued spare ribs, Kountry beef ribs, sesame shrimp, or steak and shrimp, from $5.75 to about $8, and your entree is accompanied by soup (homemade beef bouillon and chowder are special) or salad, vegetables, rice or potatoes, and a board of home-baked bread. Beer and wine are available at dinner, which is from 5 to 9:30 p.m. Lunch, served from 11 a.m. to 5 p.m., runs to sandwiches, superburgers, and dishes like fried chicken, grilled mahimahi, shrimp and crab salads, and roast beef, from about $3.65 to $5.25. Breakfast, from 6 a.m. to 1 p.m., offers crispy hash-browns, a big favorite with all omelets and egg orders on the complete breakfast. The omelet bar is popular at breakfast, especially the build-your-own combination, since such unusual ingredients (for omelets) as water chestnuts, tuna, raisins, and kim chee are all ready and waiting. On our last visit we breakfasted on the chef's sour cream omelet—filled with sour cream, chopped bacon, and tomatoes, served with hot corn bread and hash browns, it was a huge filler at $4.25. The coffee was great too.

For more exotic fare, there's **Norberto's El Café** (tel. 826-9568), a simple but welcoming little place, right off Highway 56 in the Roxy Theater Building. Its decor is Mexican posters and artifacts amid fresh-cut flowers and potted tropical plants. Norberto's is family owned and operated, and its meats and vegetables are largely supplied by the family farm in Kapahi, so you know they're fresh. Dinners range from $5.95 to $8.50, and include a main-dish combination of an enchilada (chicken, beef, eggplant, or bean) with your choice of chili relleno, tostada, or burrito. Included are bean soup, a fresh vegetable salad, Spanish rice, refried beans, corn chips, and plenty of hot Mexican salsa. As if that weren't enough, they also feature award-winning homemade chocolate cream pie and rum cake for dessert. And their margaritas are great! Ole! Open Monday through Saturday for dinner only from 5 to 9:30 p.m.

"Ono" means "delicious" in Hawaiian, and that's what to expect—delicious food for the whole family—at **Ono-Family Restaurant,** 4-1292 Kuhio Hwy. in old Kapaa town (tel. 822-1710). Pewter plates and fancy cookware hang on the wood-paneled walls; ceiling fans create a pleasant breeze; European and Early American antiques and paintings add to the charm. This is a family-owned operation, and it shows in the care and attention that the Smith family lavish on their guests (they even part with their special recipes for papaya-seed dressing and Portuguese bean soup). Omelets are featured at breakfast, and so are Canterbury eggs (grilled English muffins topped with turkey, ham, veggies, eggs, and cheese), at $4.35, and quite a way to start the day. The lunch menu has "Special Delights" from $3.05 to $4.95 (the $3.55 fish sandwich we dined on recently, with vegetables, cheese, sprouts on grilled Branola bread, was a meal in itself), superburgers from $2.85 to $4.05, and shrimp, fish, burger, and chicken plate lunches from $3.95 to $4.95. Dinner is nicely priced between $6.75 and $8.25 for dishes like teriyaki chicken, southern pork chops, barbecued ribs; all dinners are served with Portuguese bean soup or salad, rice pilaf or french fries, plus fresh vegetables and bread. Prime ribs of beef, some tasty Mexican specialties, fresh fish, burgers, and sandwiches round out the dinner menu. Desserts can be fun, especially apple strudel and coconut or banana pie. Open daily.

Many of the vegetables, herbs, and spices you eat at **Kauai Gardens,** 4-1639 Kuhio Hwy. at the north end of Kapaa town (tel. 822-1482), are grown organically right in their own gardens, and that's a big part of the reason why the food is so good at this combination farm center, botanical garden, plant nursery, and of course, restaurant. And the skill of the chefs matches the freshness of the ingredients, all of which makes Kauai Gardens one of the nicest things to happen to the local dining scene in many a year. You sit at pleasant wooden tables amid dozens of hanging plants, Tiffany-style lamps, and flowers everywhere. And you dine reasonably from an imaginative, gourmet menu. For lunch, have a cocktail or a glass of wine while you nibble on lavosh (Armenian cracker bread) and order, perhaps, the antipasto salad ($5.75 vegetarian, $6.25 with cold cuts) or the soup de jour at $2.25. Or proceed right to the main course: it could be spicy and delicious stir-fried vegetables with cashews and brown rice, served with salad (try their creamy pepper dressing), for $4.95. Tuna melt, burgers, fruit and cheese plate, seafood crêpe, a good mahimahi sandwich are all priced around $3.95 to $5.25. For dinner you can start with large plates of appetizers that are meant to be shared: stuffed mushrooms, sashimi, or sauteed scampi, from $4.75 to $5.95. Fresh fish of the day is excellent here, and so are such low-side-of-the-menu entrees as the lasagne with fresh vegetarian ingredients at $9.25, the stir-fried vegetables with macadamia nuts at $8.75, and the beef kebabs at $9.75. (Steak, scampi, and veal stuffed with crab run $11.75 to $16.50.) On Friday and Saturday nights there's a prime rib dinner for $12.95. Desserts? Certainly. You could have cheese-cake with strawberry topping for $2.50, and to go with it, something called "American Expresso—Don't Go Home Without It," a combination of espresso and brandy. On your way out, stop at the deli department up front for gourmet take-out and picnic fare—tabouleh, marinated artichokes, dolmades, Lebanese spiced olives, plus homemade apple pie. You can also get organic produce up here and take home plants or hanging lamps—just about anything you see in the restaurant can be purchased. Kauai Gardens serves lunch from 11 a.m. to 3 p.m., dinner from 5:30 to 10:30 p.m. Reservations are recommended.

There are a few places fine for quick sandwiches and snacks. At **Kinipopo Pizza and Subs** (tel. 822-9222), the locals will be sitting out on the porch indulging in "toadstool pizzas" (from $6.40) and hamburgers under $2. The tidy little dining room has hoagies, subs, chicken pieces, meatball sandwiches. . . . **Chic's Café,** a block from Pono Kai in Kapaa (tel. 822-9816), has pizza pies from $2.60, charburgers from $2.10, submarine sandwiches at $4.50, plus plate lunches, cold beer and wine—and they'll deliver it to your Kapaa-Wailua hotel or condo. . . . Next door to the Kapaa Post Office in the Kapaa Shopping Center, **Tropical Taco,** a little take-out spot, offers terrific tacos, burritos, and other Mexican dishes in the $2 to $4 range. They're the same people who've had the famous green van in Hanalei on the other side of the island, for years (see below).

At Coconut Plantation

It's hard to decide what's more fun, shopping or eating at the Coconut Plantation Market Place, but there are temptations aplenty in both areas. There's an international assortment of restaurants and snackbars here, and most are in the budget range. You can enjoy a reasonably priced lunch or dinner on the shaded lanai of **Create A Steak** if you're willing to take matters in your own hand. That means bringing your own portion of beef ribs ($5.50), mahimahi ($5.75), beef kebabs ($6.75), Italian sausage kebabs ($6.75), or top sirloin ($7.50) over to the grill and broiling your own.

Entrees are accompanied by salad bar and baked beans. Lunch is on 11 a.m. to 5 p.m., dinner from 5 to 9 p.m. . . . See the people at **Don's Deli & Picnic Basket** if you need a picnic lunch. They'll custom-make it for you, with meats, cheeses, breads, fresh fruits, and give you directions to secluded beaches as well. They also have good sandwiches to eat right there. Sandwiches are under $3; picnic baskets for two are under $10. . . . Jim Jasper, the very one who owns the more expensive J.J.'s Broiler in Lihue, and J.J.'s Boiler Room in the Market Place, both very popular for steak, fish, and salad bars, also runs a quality low-budget operation at **J.J.'s Dog House.** Ground fresh USDA choice chuck hamburgers start at $2.30, all-beef hot dogs are $1.95, and they cut fresh potatoes for natural french fries. Chili sausage dogs and kraut sausage dogs are $2.60. Wine coolers and ice-cold draft beer are at the ready, and there's a pleasant shaded terrace for eating.

The **Saimin Inn and Salad Bowl** is the home of the Kauai fresh fruit salad with all local fruits ($1.98 to $3.95), plus crab and shrimp salads ($2.98), as well as saimin ($1.50), fried saimin, clam chowder, soup, chili, and plate lunches for around $3.50. . . . The **Fish Hut** has lots of tasty goodies: fish and chip platters from $2.75 to $3.75, fish puffs at $1.65, plus homemade clam chowder, tuna and shrimp melt sandwiches, and more entrees under $3. . . . Complete lunch and supper plates such as chili dog, fish, and fresh chicken, range from $3 to $4 (breakfasts too) at **Plantation Cookhouse. . . .** And for tacos and burritos, try the "Outrageous Burrito"—from $3 at **Ramona's Mexican Foods. . . .** Tempting Hawaiian ice creams and macadamia-nut waffles for breakfast are the special treats at **Sugar Mill Snacks. . . .** And you can always count on **Farrell's of Kauai** for a snack or a meal or a super hot-fudge or passion-orange sundae. It's open from 8 a.m. until 10 p.m. every day.

RESTAURANTS ON THE WESTERN AND SOUTHERN ROUTE:

You should have no problem dining on your trip around the southern and western end of the island, for there are several excellent choices. Not all, however, are in the budget category.

Koloa

If you don't like the way your food is done at the **Koloa Broiler** (tel. 742-9122), on Koloa Road, a few miles from Poipu Beach, you have no one but yourself to blame. This cute little place is one of those broil-it-yourself affairs—and that way, they really manage to keep the prices down. You can choose from mahimahi at $5.95, barbecued chicken or beef kebab at $6.95, top sirloin at $7.95; and with your entree come salad bar and baked beans. Lunch offers the same choices, plus a $3.50 hamburger. At the time of this writing, the only dessert on the menu was macadamia-nut ice cream, so you may want to skip the dessert here and walk over to the Koloa Ice House (see below) for mud pie. This is a lively, fun kind of place, simply decorated (try to get a seat out on the lanai), with a jolly bar and lots of local people enjoying their meals. You will too. Koloa Broiler is open from 11 a.m. to 10 p.m. every day.

The **Koloa Ice House,** a few doors away from Koloa Broiler, is housed in a green wooden building and has just a few tables inside, but it's also fun to sit at any of the four large tables in the garden lanai. You can get a good variety of deli and veggie sandwiches here, as well as quiches, nachos, bagels and cream cheese, burritos, homemade soup, veggie burgers, and the like (most items are under $3), but our favorites are the superb ice creams, shave ices, frozen yogurts, and mud pies—the latter a cookie-crust ice cream pie—$3, but luscious!

Taquería Norteños, next to the Kukuiula Store in Koloa, is a tiny take-out taco bar that packs a mighty wallop. Owner Ed Sills, former chef at the prestigious Plantation Garden Restaurant, and his wife Morgan, decided to do their own thing: turn out excellent food, but keep the prices low. When you want some good Mexican munchies for a picnic at the beach or a meal on the run, come and see them. Tacos are $1.15 and $1.85; burritos, $1.60 and $2.60; tostados, $1.40 and $2.25; chips and salsa, 70¢ ($1.35 with cheese). Ask them to heat the tacos up; they're even better that way.

Poipu, Kalaheo, and Hanapepe

Poipu's famed **Beach House Restaurant** was destroyed by Hurricane Iwa in November of 1982, but by the time you read this the place should be completely rebuilt at the same oceanfront location on Spouting Horn Road and ready for business. Since the restaurant is nestled right on the sand, the waves lap the outer walls of the big dining room, while inside there's a veritable jungle of lush plants (a full-time gardener is needed to care for all that beautiful greenery). Alas, dinner only is served here, and it's a splurgy affair (up to $16.95); but the food is delicious, and if you order one of the lower priced entrees, like chicken teriyaki, sirloin kebab, teriyaki steak, or sukiyaki steak, you can dine for under $11; and that price includes soup or salad, rice and delicious bread. Children's dinners are half price. Don't miss the wonderful homemade desserts. Come to see the sunset; it's spectacular. Reservations are requested to assure the best tables (tel. 742-7575).

The same management also has things well in hand at **Kona's Restaurant** at Poipu Kai Resort (tel. 742-6433). The open-air setting affords a view of the ocean, so it's great fun to come here for sunset dining. Kona's caters to a family trade, and keeps the prices in a moderate range: from $5.95 to $12.95 for dinners, which include salad bar and homemade hot rolls. On the low side of the menu, you could have fish 'n' chips, mahimahi, teriyaki chicken, teriyaki steak, and top sirloin, from $6.95 to $8.95. Good, at both meals, are the burgers, with a variety of toppings, served on a sesame bun, from $5.25 for a cheeseburger to $5.75 for the "pig-out burger" (create your own combination). Lunch specials (from $4.95 to $6.50) include fresh fish and other sandwiches, "notorious beach burgers," homemade vegetable or seafood quiche, and salad bar at $5.25. You can start your meal with potato skins, end with luscious hula pie. Kona's serves lunch from 11:30 a.m. to 2:30 p.m., dinner from 5:30 to 10 p.m., every day. Reservations are requested.

The buffet lunch, served every day from 11:30 a.m. to 2 p.m. at the **Sheraton Kauai** at Poipu Beach, is a special treat. The lavishly laden groaning board features salads, fish, vegetables, a hot dish, and an irresistible dessert table. After you've spent your $8 or so for lunch here, you won't need to eat much dinner. Be sure to walk out to the pool and beach area for one of the most beautiful beach scenes in Kauai.

On the main highway in Kalaheo, you'll find **Mañana's** (tel. 332-9033), a bright, cheery Mexican restaurant where the food is good and the prices are quite reasonable. Enchiladas, for example, are priced from $2.50 to $3.25 and offer choices of cheese, veggies, beef, or chicken. Burritos are priced from $4.25 to $5. Combination dinners, all served with beans, soup or salad, and rice, from $4.95 to $8.50. The lively cocktail lounge opens at 5:30 p.m. Mañana's dishes out some very good breakfasts from 5:30 a.m. to 10:30 a.m., is closed for lunch, and serves dinner from 5:30 to 10 p.m. Open every day.

Farther on in Hanapepe, 18 miles from Lihue on Route 50, are two restaurants under one roof: **Conrad's Restaurant** and **Wong's Chinese Restaurant.** Oldtimers will remember this place as Mike's Café; now Mike's son Conrad and his partner Jackson are in charge, and the food is still good; the restaurant is nicely redone with plants, ceiling fans, white tablecloths, and still crowded at lunchtime when the tour buses pull in. When you sit down you are handed two separate menus: it's up to you to decide if you want Wong's Chinese dishes (most, like chicken with cashew nuts, shrimp with black bean sauce, or almond duck, are in the $4.25 to $5.50 range; the lunch plate is $4.25; the dinner plate, $3.75), or Conrad's more eclectic American-Japanese-Korean menu. At dinner, dishes like shrimp tempura, chicken kal-bi, buttermilk-fried chicken, sauteed filet of fish, and roast prime rib of beef go from $6.75 to $12, with many items in the under-$7.50 category. Dinner includes salad bar, starch, and vegetables du jour. Similar dishes are offered at lunch, for lower prices. Whatever you order, be sure to have the lilikoi chiffon pie for dessert, a happy holdover from the days of Mike's Café. For a quick meal, you can stop in at the **Omoide Deli** right off the main dining room, which offers plate lunches ($2.40 to $3.60), cold sandwiches, and Hong Kong–style roast duck and pork, local delicacies, as well as pies, pastries, and cakes.

Both Conrad's and Wong's are open every day, but close at 2 p.m. on Monday. Conrad's opens at 6 or 7 a.m., Wong's at 10 a.m., and both close at 9 p.m. Reservations recommended (tel. 335-5066).

About 40 years ago, Gwen Hamabata's parents and her grandmother started a simple little restaurant in Hanapepe and called it the **Green Garden** (tel. 335-5422). It's doubled and redoubled its size many times over in those years, and today it's one of the most charming lcoal spots around, with the kind of flavor and tradition that can only come from a family business where everybody cares. Gwen and her mother Sue are the "working bosses," who make sure that all of the guests, whether they be the faithful locals or the scores of visitors (we get letters every year praising this place) enjoy their modestly priced and delicious Oriental, American, and Hawaiian food. (As for the locals, we were told that in the aftermath of Hurricane Iwa in 1982, when much of the island had no electricity, Green Garden, which had its own generator, fed everyone in the neighborhood nonstop—and refused to accept payment!) You'll feel as if you're sitting in the middle of a greenhouse, with orchids on the tables, plants surrounding you everywhere, an entire screened wall facing a garden, bamboo chairs, and white walls. For a real treat, do as the locals do: have a family-style Oriental meal. Just tell them what you like and what you want to spend, and they'll create a meal for you. We did this recently and were treated to an incredible banquet; highlights were the luscious barbecued chicken, the shrimp wontons, the vegetable-stuffed eggrolls, tempura aki, shrimp omelets, and scallops with noodles. Reserve this meal at least half an hour in advance.

More simply, you can dine on a complete hot lunch for $4.50 and under (beef cutlet, roast beef Korean style, boneless barbecued chicken), or a complete dinner for $4.25 and up, choosing from such entrees as sweet-and-sour spare ribs, breaded filet of mahimahi, or shrimp tempura. Broiler specialties are also reasonable, like teriyaki steak at $6.25, filet mignon at $9.50, and the East-West Special (char-broiled petite teriyaki steak and shrimp tempura) at $6.75. With your main dish comes soup or fruit cup, a crispy green salad with a good dressing, hot dinner rolls, rice or potatoes, plus tea or coffee. And whatever you do, be sure to save room for Sue's homemade pies, $1.25; we'll vote for the macadamia nut and lilikoi. Open from 6 a.m. to 2 p.m. and from 5 to 8:30 p.m.

Brick Oven Pizza, on the main road in Kalaheo, is a nice cozy little place with red-and-white gingham tablecloths: it stays open until 11 p.m., so you can stop here just about anytime hunger pangs strike as you're driving this road. Pizzas start at $4.25 for a 10-inch plain cheese pie, and go all the way up to $14.35 for a 15-inch Canadian-bacon-with-tomatoes version. In addition to pizza, there's a vegetarian sandwich with cheese, mushrooms, olives, squash, etc., for $2.60, and a Hot Super Sandwich with Canadian bacon, salami, and a variety of cheeses and vegetables, for $2.95. A spicy Portuguese sausage sandwich is also $2.95. Green salads are available, and so are wine and beer. Open 11 a.m. to 11 p.m., every day except Monday.

In Princeville and Hanalei

The setting of the **Bali Hai Restaurant** in the Hanalei Bay Resort at Princeville is one of the most purely beautiful we've come across in many a tropic moon. Open on three sides, perched on a hill, the angled wooden building affords glorious vistas of the mountains and Hanalei Bay nestled far below; it was on this site, in fact, that the movie *South Pacific* was filmed in 1957. The artful interior decor—batik banners, bamboo chairs, palm fronds on the table—vies with the outside view for your attention. Dinner is expensive here (from $11.95 for marinated cubes of beef, up to $21.50 for surf and turf, scampi and filet mignon), but you can enjoy all that beauty earlier in the day at lunch or breakfast. The lunch buffet, served from 11:30 a.m. to 2 p.m., costs $6.95 for adults, $4.50 for kids: you help yourself to all you want of the salad and sandwich bars, plus soup of the day, daily entrees, and dessert. Or have the WikiWiki Lunch at $5.25, which consists of the salad and sandwich bars, soup of the day, bread, choice of luncheon meats, and fine cheeses. If you're staying in the Princeville area, come for the breakfast buffet between 7:30 and 10:30 a.m., at $6.50 for adults, $4.50 for kids. For dinner reservations, phone 826-6522, ext. 1018 or 1019.

Chuck's Steak House (tel. 826-6211) is rightfully one of the most popular places at Princeville. An attractive porch, plants, ceiling fans, dark walls, secluded booths, paintings, and antiques everywhere, set a cozy scene, and dinner prices are not bad, considering that dinner includes salad bar, hot bread, steamed rice or rice pilaf, and such entrees as mahimahi at $8.95, and teriyaki chicken breasts, shrimp Hanalei, and beef kebab from $9.25 to $9.95. Lunch is a good buy, with burgers starting at $3.95, garden salad at $3.25, teriyaki sandwich at $4.50. Chuck's is also known for great tropical drinks and fine wines. Open daily from 11:30 a.m. to 2:30 p.m. and from 6 to 10 p.m. Cocktails are served all day, from 11:30 a.m. to 11:30 p.m. Chuck's is right at Princeville Center.

A new restaurant at Princeville Center will look familiar to anyone who's been to Maui: it's a sister restaurant to Lahaina's popular **Tortilla Flats.** Stucco walls, tile floors, plants, ceiling fans, and a lively cantina lined with *ojos de dios* on the walls create that south-of-the-border mood, and partitions create a feeling of privacy around the tables. The food is very tasty and well priced: dinner combination entrees are accompanied by soup or salad, plus beans and rice, and run from $7.95 to $8.95. Specialties in the same price range include enchiladas suizas (chicken and green chile enchiladas topped with sour cream) and chile verde (pork chunks simmered in sauce with hot tortillas). The appetizers are fun too, especially an American-Mexican hybrid called Mexi-Skins: crispy deep-fried potato skins with either chicken or beef and melted cheese, plus sour cream for dipping, at $4.95. For dessert, a very un-Mexican mud pie. Tortilla Flats serves all three meals.

At the time of our last visit, **Godfrey's** had just taken over from the Princeville Lanai Restaurant and was pretty much hard-hat country. Plans were for a turn-of-the-century Hawaiian decor with rattan furniture, bay windows, canopies, plants everywhere, and historical photos on the walls. The general price range will be $12 to $14 for entrees (dinner only), about $5.25 for dinner salad.

The Hanalei area has been woefully short of budget eating places, but the opening of the **Ching Young Village Shopping Center** has helped a bit. Now we have a decent Chinese restaurant and several snack shops to choose from. **Foong Wong** is a large, simple restaurant, rather sparsely decorated, but with good Cantonese food: plate lunches run $3.50 to $5.50, and dishes like char siu, beef with oyster sauce, and chicken with black bean sauce are all under $5. **Norberto's El Café,** whose main restaurant is in Kapaa (see above) has a take-out counter and four tables out front, where you can get an enchilada plate lunch for $3.50, huge burritos from $3 to $3.50, and nachos for $1.75. The **Village Snack and Bakery Shop** has plate lunches like fried chicken and teriyaki beef for $3.50, but the real treats here are the home-baked pies: guava, lilikoi chiffon, lemon cream cheese, at $1.25 a slice. Then there's the **Healthy Jones Snack Bar,** which sometimes offers sandwiches, daily specials (perhaps vegetable burritos, Greek salad, quiche), plus freshly pressed tropical juices—mango, pineapple, papaya—for "a taste of Hawaii."

The **Hanalei Shell House,** on the main street in Hanalei, is just a little place with a few tables and simple, home-cooked fare prepared by owner Thelma Cooper. We found it rather hot on a steaming summer day, but a full-house lunch crowd didn't seem to mind. Breakfast, served from 8 a.m. to noon, specializes in omelets, strawberry waffles, and homemade bran muffins. At lunch, noon to 4 p.m., you can dine on specials like Hawaiian chicken baked in Thelma's own pineapple sauce, with baked beans or salad and bran muffins, at $4.95; plus quesadillas, hamburgers, and sandwiches, with baked beans or salad, at $3.45 to $4.25. An "off-the-wall" menu, served between 4 to 6 p.m., has tasty pupus—potato skins, sashimi, wontons—to go with cocktails. A new menu for dinner (4 to 10 p.m.) was being planned at the time of our last visit. Don't miss Thelma's homemade macadamia-nut and coconut-cream pies. There is either piano music or a combo playing "light jazz" from 9 p.m. until closing, which could be anytime between midnight and 2 a.m. Closed Sunday.

Hanalei also has a couple of food stands that are fine for quick snacking. You'll usually find Mike Williams and Roger Kennedy and their **Tropical Taco** on the main highway in front of the Dolphin Restaurant, where they dish up gourmet-quality, all-organic burritos, tacos, and the like, a complete lunch for around $2 to $4. Take your food over to the shady riverbank just a few steps away and enjoy your "picnic."

3. The Night Scene

There's more nightlife in Kauai than you would expect such a sleepy-looking little island to offer.

IN LIHUE: The center of activity in Lihue is the romantic Kauai Surf Hotel at Kalapaki Beach. As you sit in the **Planters' Bar and Lounge,** listening to the gently lapping waves below you, sipping a drink, and watching a languid Polynesian show, you'll feel you're in picture-postcard Hawaii. There is no cover charge for the revue *Adventures in Paradise,* which goes on nightly at 8:45; mixed drinks start at $2.75, and there is no minimum. During the 5 to 7 p.m. Happy Hour, there are free hors d'oeuvres, reduced prices on drinks, plus entertainment. The **Destination** piano bar at the Surf is a more intimate room, where you can sing along with Kathy Kay, from 10 p.m. on.

Down the road a bit from town, in Nawiliwili Harbor, is the **Club Jetty,** on the wharf, where things start to jump about 10 p.m. It's live-band entertainment and disco sounds Wednesday through Saturday with D.J. Aunt Betty and bands imported from Honolulu. Beer is $2 to $2.50; mixed drinks, $2 and up. There's a cover charge every night except, for the ladies, on Wednesday's "Ladies Night."

The best cantina in town is **Rosita's** at Kukui Grove Center, a beautiful bar and lounge, where you can admire the artwork, listen to local entertainers, and sip Rosita's "world-famous margaritas." You can have them by the pitcherful for $6.50, or individually at $3. The strawberry margarita is $3.75. Come by during the 4:30 to 6:30 p.m. Happy Hour, when everything costs 20% less. Open daily from 11 a.m. to midnight.

Watch the papers for news of free shows put on at the **Kukui Grove Center.** They often take place on Friday nights or Saturday mornings, right on the mall. These shows by local entertainers are sometimes every bit as good as those at the high-priced clubs.

IN WAILUA: You must see the **Coco Palms Hotel** at night. Five miles out of town on Wailua Bay, it's on the site of an ancient coconut grove and lagoon, where Hawaiian royalty once lived. Flaming torches cast eerie shadows on the water, there's much blowing of conch shells and other ritualistic goings-on, with an effect that reassures the visiting movie stars here that they've never left the set. Come around sunset time for a drink at the gorgeous cocktail lounge overlooking a natural lagoon (drinks at the Lagoon Terrace start at ($2.85) to catch the impressive and very moving torch-lighting ceremony—a Kauai must.

Come back to Coco Palms around 9 p.m. and you may be able to see their excellent dinner show—free! Of course, if you have dinner here (complete meals from $13.25), the show is included. But many people stand at the open sides of the dining room to catch glimpses of the show, and once, friendly hotel people even brought us chairs! The Larry Rivers Show is on every Tuesday, Thursday, Saturday, and Sunday. The Singers and Dancers of Niihau appear on Monday night, and Na Hoalaha O Coco Palm entertain on Wednesday night.

The best **luaus** in Kauai are held at two hotels in this area on Sunday, Tuesday, Wednesday, Thursday, and Friday at the **Sheraton Coconut Beach Hotel** ($28.50) and the **Kauai Resort Hotel** ($29). Reservations are suggested: phone 822-3455 at the Sheraton, 245-3931 at the Kauai Resort, which also provides free shuttle service from many hotels and condos in the Lihue and Wailua areas.

The **Kauai Beach Boy,** out in this same area, offers the best luau bargain: $19.75 for a luau dinner buffet and KTC's Songs and Dances of Polynesia. It's held every Wednesday from 6:30 to 8:30 p.m. Reservations: 822-3441. The Beach Boy also has an inflation-fighter Happy Hour between 5 and 6 p.m. (all drinks half price) and reduces prices on blended tropical drinks between 6 and 9 p.m. The same hotel is the scene of the **Boogie Palace,** which draws the disco set in every night except Tuesday from 9; cover charge of $1 on weekdays, $1.50 on weekends. Newest, noisiest disco in town is the **Vanishing Point** at Waipouli Plaza (just past Coconut Plantation), where the disco action gets under way around 10 p.m. and lasts until 4 a.m. There's live music too, from 8 to 10 p.m. You'll pay a $1 cover charge on weekdays, $2 on weekends.

AT POIPU BEACH: This side of the island is a bit quieter after the sun sets. Undoubtedly the liveliest place is the **Poipu Beach Hotel,** where there's usually a variety band playing for dancing on Friday and Saturday nights; various groups entertain the rest of the week. Drinks are moderately priced at the big and rather unglamorous Mahina Lounge. . . . It's lovely to walk down to the beach here at night and along the waterfront to the neighboring **Waioha Hotel.** Its Terrace Restaurant is right out on the beach, overlooking the breaking surf. You can catch the sounds of dinner music, enjoy the view, and perhaps decide to come back here for a meal the next night (their $10.50 salad bar is expensive, but one of the best around, and their $15.95 Sunday champagne brunch is renowned far and wide. . . . Our favorite spot at the Sheraton Kauai is the **Pareo Pub,** bordered by a lagoon filled with exotic Japanese koi fish. During the Menehune Magic Hour, between 5:30 and 6:30 p.m., "drink prices are as small as the legendary little people of Hawaii." There are specials on mai tais on Monday, Wednesday, and Friday, on margaritas on Sunday and Thursday, and on Singapore Slings on Saturday and Tuesday. If you're in Kauai on a Sunday, you'll enjoy Chief Taeza and his Polynesian Revue, along with a buffet feast, starting at 6 p.m. (phone 742-1661 for reservations). . . . The setting for drinks is pure tropical magic at **Plantation Gardens Restaurant,** once the gracious home of a plantation manager.

THE PRINCEVILLE–HANALEI AREA: **Tahiti Nui,** on Highway 56, just before Aku Road and a stone's throw from Hanalei Shell House, is so popular that it has to turn people away almost every night. The place has been done up with pareau fabric, Tahitian woodcarvings on the walls, bamboo, and a thatched ceiling. The atmosphere is super friendly. Jackie Onassis liked it so well that she came here two nights in a row and stayed until closing. The entertainment is impromptu; local entertainers often come in and sing, and owner Louise Marston, a bubbly Tahitian, can usually be persuaded to sing and do the hula. All this, and reasonable prices for drinks too. Beer starts at $1.75. Louise serves dinner too, with a limited menu including items like chicken curry with fresh papaya or pineapple at

$8.95, or smoked ribs at $10.95, served with rice, bread, and salad. There's a delightful luau Friday night only at 7:30 p.m., for $18. Reservations are a must (tel. 826-6277). We're told that this show is so popular that people even call from the mainland for reservations!

READERS' SELECTIONS IN KAUAI: "The following suggestion is probably the best I have found in years of traveling with your books. It is even more desirable than you describe it. Several times we have stayed in Lihue, Kauai, at the **Hale Lihue Motel.** Lihue is centrally located, as we chose the town for this, but the Hale Lihue Motel was a real find. It is on a very quiet street, it is spotlessly clean (no bugs in all our trips there), our double room had a nice little kitchen and an air conditioner, all for $24 a day. It is plain, but the hospitality makes you feel as if you belong there. Mr. and Mrs. Morishige are friendly and helpful. Rooms without a kitchen are small but are $15 double. There are many good, inexpensive restaurants within walking distance" (Jean Sharpe, Lake Oswego, Ore.). . . . "Our big splurge on our trip, but well worth it, was our stay at the **Hanalei Bay Resort** in Princeville. We stayed there with another couple. We split the cost of the entire package, which included a 1000-square-foot one-bedroom condominium and a rental car; each couple paid $55 a night. It is by far the best hotel complex I have ever stayed at. This place has its own restaurant, cocktail lounge, sauna, 11 tennis courts (some lighted), and is a short walk to indescribably beautiful Hanalei Bay" (Richard Marks, Lodi, Calif.).

"After yearly trips to Hawaii checking out your tips and those of your readers, we have discovered a real jewel to pass on to others. The **Koloa Landing Cottages** in Poipu turned out to be the most pleasant place we've ever stayed in the islands. They are well decorated, sparkling clean, and roomy. The Zeevats—Hans and Sylvia—made sure we saw some unusual sights. They even led us in their truck. Sylvia shared all the fruits grown on their grounds (bananas, limes, lemons, mangoes, etc.). Tell your readers not to miss an experience far removed from the big hotel scene, but close enough to check it out" (Gretchen and Ron Cowan, Huntington Beach, Calif.). . . . "I stayed at the Koloa Landing Cottages and had a great experience. The husband-and-wife owners are extremely helpful and friendly. Hans gave me an informative guided tour of Koloa and Poipu Beach, including a snorkeling lesson. This kind of human touch is something lacking in the mass tourism scene that is Hawaii, despite the great friendliness of most individual Hawaiians" (J. Dennis Harcketts, Falls Church, Va.). [*Authors' Note:* Two two-bedroom/two-bathroom cottages, which can accommodate up to six people, rent at $50 for up to two, $60 for three or four, plus $5 for each additional person. They have cable color TV, telephone, and dishwasher. A studio apartment is $30 for up to two people; it also has color TV, kitchen, and telephone. Write to Dolphin Realty, RR 1, Box 70, 2827 Poipu Rd., Koloa, HI 96756, or phone Sylvia Zeevat at 808/742-1470.]

"The **Green Garden** was as fantastic as you had said. My husband and I had salad, homemade rolls, grilled lobster, rice, vegetables, dessert, and drinks for under $30, and the service and atmosphere were great" (Beth and Chris Baine, Chicago, Ill.). . . . "I'm from San Francisco, and I found **Casa Italiana** in Lihue just as excellent as some of our great Italian restaurants. Prices are fairly high, but there were quite a few delicious dishes in a lower price range" (Kathy Doudiet, San Francisco, Calif.). . . . **"Kauai Chop Suey** in the Harbor Village was crowded every night, and for a reason. My wife and I had only one order of Kauai chow mein and two bowls of rice, spending a grand total of $6.15 plus tax, and were completely full. The majority of their customers are the folks who live there. There's plenty of capacity and the Chinese lanterns hanging from the ceiling are colorful. Their rug takes a beating because of the heavy traffic. But the quality of their food keeps you coming back" (Jack and Doris Toussaint, no address given).

"Our room at a more expensive hotel turned out to be very noisy, so we looked in your book, called the **Coral Reef Hotel** in Kapaa, and spent the next ten days feeling glad it didn't work out at the first place. The rooms were $26 a night instead of $62, and the people who run and clean the Coral Reef are wonderful. The view was dream-like and we could walk almost anywhere from there. We'd stay there again. And with the money we saved, we took the helicopter ride around the island. What an amazing place Kauai is! That was worth every penny. . . . We've never had better food anywhere than on Kauai. We really enjoyed **Kintaro's** for Japanese food and the **Aloha Diner** for Hawaiian food, both in Kapaa. Also, **Ono's Restaurant** in Kapaa is where we took most of our breakfasts—excellent food and service and prices" (Carolyn Pursley and Thomas Rubick, Eugene, Ore.). . . . "The **Coral Reef Hotel** in Kapaa was a quiet, peaceful place, overlooking park-like grounds and ocean. Mr. and Mrs. Matsumara and their conscientious staff made us feel at home. We chose this place over the 'sterile' atmosphere at Princeville" (Mr. and Mrs. Peter Guertler, Huntington Station, N.Y.). . . . "**Restaurant Kintaro** is a particularly wonderful, small restaurant. The food was exceptionally well prepared. The combination dinners allowed us to sample a variety of delicious dishes. The seafood, both raw and cooked, was fresh and tasty. All courses were served in beautiful lacquer bowls and trays. They have a sushi bar for those preferring that service. We are avid fans of Japanese fare, which is readily available in our home city of Sacramento. However, none really compares with the quality, diversity, or beauty of presentation at the Restaurant Kintaro" (Trudy Klein, Orangevale, Calif.).

"We stayed at Poipu in a great little place called the **Sunset Kahili.** Our condo was freshly redone as the hurricane had damaged it, and so it was especially nice. The walk to the beach is *maybe* five minutes. They have a small but immaculately clean pool, recreation room complete with pool table, lots of reading material, and comfy couches for relaxing and snoozing in the afternoon. The managers are more than helpful and we really felt we were at home. They also have a barbecue available. The rate for a two-bedroom/two-bath apartment was $60 per night and worth every penny" (Bart and Lynda Esterley, Capistrano Beach, Calif.). . . . "We enjoyed our weekend in Kauai at the **Kauai Sands,** right at the beach, for $34 a day (three adults, the third and fourth persons go free!). The $34 included our room and a Budget rental car—no mileage. A good deal" (Dorothy R. Astman, Levittown, N.Y.).

"Our **condo at Princeville** at Hanalei is available for rental at $205 per week or $33 per day. It is a detached, fully broadloomed, two-bedroom, two-balcony, two-entrance home, suitable for two couples. It is completely furnished with linen and all appliances, including washer, dryer, and dishwasher. Built on a hillside, this villa faces the mountains and overlooks Princeville's 27-hole championship golf course and backs onto the beach below. The golf course, designed by Robert Trent Jones, is rated among the ten best in America. A picture of the course with the villa in the background was printed in the November 1977 issue of *National Geographic.* For further information, please call 416/749-0519, or write Mrs. Sandy Jacobs, 26 Manswood Crescent, R.R. #8, Brampton, On L6T 3Y7, Canada" (Mrs. Sandy Jacobs, Ontario, Canada). . . . "We rented Mrs. Sandy Jacobs' condo for a week and highly recommend it. It was clean and very comfortable. It overlooks the golf course and is across the street from the ocean, which you get to down a steep, long, cemented pathway" (Mrs. Lyle Beach, Citrus Heights, Calif.).

"On your way to the north side of Kauai, stop at the **Big Save Market** in Kapaa, in the shopping center where the post office is located, and pick up some inari (cone sushi). The proprietor of the small food stand in this Big Save makes the best. Then, as you continue north on Highway 56, between Kapaa and Kilauea near Anahola, you will spot on the right-hand side of the road a rather new square brown fruit stand standing by itself next to the sugarcane fields. It's not well marked, but there is a Hawaii Visitors Bureau sign by the side of the road near the stand. You can get delicious fruit smoothies to drink made on the spot and luscious papaya fruit bowls—large watermelon-like papaya halves overflowing with fresh fruit. Take your sushi and fresh fruit to one of the beautiful beaches near Hanalei for some unforgettable pleasure" (Signe L. Boyer and Edwin F. Laak, Palo Alto, Calif.).

"The **Lihue Café** (kittycorner to the museum, behind the intersection with the traffic light) was a delightful place to eat. For $6.60, the three of us had beef and broccoli, wontons, and lots of Chinese tea for dinner. We fairly rolled out of there, we were so stuffed. I think I will never eat Chinese food again as nothing could even begin to compare with this. . . . The **Ahana Motel Apartments** on Akahi Street were very basic, but the charm of its proprietors and location make it luxurious. Our kitchenette came with a large closet, full bath, TV, kitchen with many, many dishes and utensils, and a view of the flowers and banana trees. The manager is quite charming. She spent some time telling me about Japan and what it was like to be Japanese on Hawaii during World War II. The apartments are close to two shopping centers, which have many fine, varied, and reasonable shops, and several nice eateries are close by" (Nancy Goertz, Sandia Park, N.M.). . . . "The **Kauai Resort Hotel,** above Lydgate Park, has a nice dinner show including a good salad bar, $10.50 and up. Be sure you see the Japanese gardens in daylight: one of the most charming Japanese gardens we have seen anywhere, with several small waterfalls, carp-filled pools, and truly shibui rock and plant arrangements" (Ulla Friedmann, Mercer Island, Wash.). . . . "We dined at the **Plantation Restaurant.** Ambience and decor were the best in all the islands. Delicious" (Connie Hendricks and Sandra Betner, New York, N.Y.).

"We stayed at the **Plantation Hale,** which is located in the Coconut Plantation area. These are older condos with two full-size beds in the bedroom and a sofa bed in the living room that also sleeps two adults. This lovely place has a fully equipped kitchen, a lovely view, three swimming pools, plus all the extras, including maid service. Right across the parking lot is the ocean! $60 a day included a rented car. Their address is 484 Kuhio Hwy., Kapaa, Kauai, HI 96746. **Don's Deli** in the Market Place, was great for a quick sandwich. You pick the bread, plus cheese, meat, or chicken, etc., and all the extras. Prices are around $3" (Sheri La Roche, Anaheim, Calif.). . . . "On Kauai, our long weekend stay at the **Sheraton Coconut Beach** was the highlight of our vacation. The facility is extremely comfortable and luxurious. The breakfast buffet is fantastic, and their luau, advertised as 'the best luau on Kauai,' we felt to be the best in Hawaii. Food delicious, atmosphere jovial, and entertainment very good. Also to be recommended is the **Captain Cook Lounge,** whose bartender blends the best Blue Hawaii cocktail in the state, with his own unique recipe, using Cream of Banana" (Cynthia Marie Dahlgren, Concord, Ill.). . . . "Whenever I'm in Kauai I never fail to indulge in coconut ice cream or a hot-fudge sundae at the ice cream shop at the **Kauai Surf.** It's delicious!" (Louise Alberti, Modesto, Calif.). . . . **"Lappert's Aloha Ice Cream** at Hanapepe, right on the main highway, is a new, clean, walk-up stand serving the *best* Hawaiian-flavored ice cream we found. Their hula pie (a blend of coffee, fresh coconut, fresh macadamia nuts, and chocolate in vanilla ice cream) can't be beaten! Their fresh pineapple ice cream is just smashing too" (Mr. and Mrs. Lorne Alton, Edmonton, Alberta, Canada).

"The **Aloha Diner,** off Kuhio Highway in Kapaa, has authentic and excellent Hawaiian food—lomi-lomi salmon, Kalua pig, lau lau, and poi or rice. Lunches and dinners are reasonable, $3.50 and $5.50. It's a small place, but well worth the visit" (Harold and Vicky Madsen, Penticton, B.C., Canada). . . . "We played at **Polihale State Park** and **Kokee State Park.** One needs permits to camp at any state park. On Kauai, the permits are issued at the State Building in Lihue, or one can write to Division of State Parks, P.O. Box 1671, Lihue, HI 96761. Rangers checked our permits. To stay at **County Campgrounds,** go to the County Building in Lihue. If it is after 5 p.m., one goes to the police station. The county permits are $3 per person per night; the state permits are free, but the office is closed by 3:30 p.m. As for restaurants, I recommend **Pancakes and Things** in Lihue (good, cheap breakfasts) and **Tahiti Nui** in Hanalei" (Rebecca Kurtz, Anchorage, Alaska). . . . "The only car-rental agency on Kauai presently willing to rent to campers is **Tony's** at Lihue Airport (tel. 245-2774). Vandalism is scaring the other companies off. When applying for a permit, campers should ask how many others are currently camping at each spot, and which have indicated plans to remain there for a bit. There is safety in numbers: don't camp alone" (Frank and Joyce Terwilliger, Swarthmore, Penna.).

"The **Sheraton Kauai** has an absolutely super buffet and Polynesian show on Sunday. The food is delicious, with many ethnic dishes, and selections too many to count. Service is courteous and efficient. A lovely way to spend an evening, under $40 for two people!" (Jessie Lahm, Glendale, Ariz.). . . . "The **Sheraton Kauai** luncheon buffet is great: around $8, with eight salads, two hot dishes, and four choices of dessert. Eat for the whole day here!" (Nancy and Tom Johnson, Croton-on-Hudson, N.Y.).

"There's no cover charge at the **Coco Palms Lagoon Dining Room,** where you can get complete dinners from $13.50, plus the impressive torch-lighting ceremony and dinner show. A real must" (Evelyn McCune, Topeka, Kans.). . . . "Brunch at the **Coco Palms Hotel,** overlooking the famous lagoon, and feeding the dozens of birds, is a must. The food is delicious and reasonably priced—a lovely experience. Buffet breakfast is enjoyable too" (J. G. A. Baelmans, Surrey, B.C., Canada). . . . "At the **Tip Top Bakery**—which we agree is marvelous!—try 'pipi kaula' with your eggs or pancakes. It is Hawaiian smoked beef, sort of halfway between beef jerky and smoked ham and very lean. . . . You can eat Hawaiian food by going to the local markets, which are generally considerably cheaper than markets in the tourist areas, especially on Kauai. You can get takeout lau lau, lomi-lomi salmon, and of course, poi. Many exotic Japanese delicacies are readily available, plus more standard things like saimin noodles plus dishes that are very cheap" (Ernest Callenbach, Berkeley, Calif.).

"I highly recommend the **Kauai Kailani Condominium Apartments,** about 1½ miles from Coco Palms toward Kapaa. We had a lovely suite for four—two bedrooms, living room area, fully equipped electric kitchen, lanai overlooking the ocean, and a delightful pool. There was a recreation room with a library and Ping-Pong. Out by the pool was shuffleboard—all for $55 per night. A great place for a family" (Mrs. Anna Woods, Costa Mesa, Calif.). [*Authors' Note:* For information and current rates, inquire of Hawaii Kailani, 119 N. Commercial St., Bellingham, WA 98225. From May through September only, the phone is 206/676-1434.].

"Probably the best all-around restaurant that we encountered in all of the Hawaiian Islands was the **Barbecue Inn** in Lihue. Four very hungry children, ages 11 to 18, and two adults had everything from soup to tea for a total bill of $36. It is comfortable, air-conditioned, and the service was simply unbelievable. The Japanese dishes were sensational. . . . We were delighted with the courteous, efficient service and fine facilities at the **Poipu Beach Hotel,** but swimmers should be warned that the beautiful lagoon at their beach is filled with treacherous rocks and razor-sharp coral just a few feet from the shoreline; three of us received nasty cuts" (Bob and Doris Ryan, Grand Island, N.Y.).

"The **Big Save—Ben Franklin Store** in Waimea, directly across the street from Captain Cook Memorial, has a very clean cafeteria, with a large number of very clean booths, which serves reasonable breakfasts and full-course meals. There is a wide variety of sandwiches to eat there or take out, $1.25 to $3" (John A. Sutherland, Calgary, Alberta, Canada). [*Authors' Note:* The management writes that they also have "delicious home-baked-style cookies—macadamia, sesame, chocolate chip, almond, cinnamon—that the tourists have gone wild over!"] . . . "The **Golden Cape Room** of the Kauai Surf Hotel has fine dance music every night; it's on the tenth floor, overlooking the ocean, so the view is great. Drinks are not much higher at the other hotels, and there is no cover or minimum. It's a lovely way to splurge" (Linda Buescher, Kirksville, Mo.). . . . "The **Tip Top Restaurant and Bakery** in Lihue sells a delicious mango loaf in season" (Fred C. Nelson, Plymouth, Mich.).

"The **Hanalei Dolphin** in Hanalei, does everything to perfection. Prices: seafood and steaks at dinnertime, $10.50 to $25. Hospitality, drinks, fine wines, food, atmosphere, decor, service, and cleanliness will stand up to anything that we have seen. The food is excellent and there's plenty of it—bread, salad dressings, and desserts are homemade" (Marvin L. Ponsar, Palmdale, Calif.). . . . "If you stay at the Ocean View Motel—a great place—or anyplace in the area, go across the street to the beach just as the sun goes down and watch the torch-lighting ceremony put on for the diners at the **Kauai Surf Hotel.** Just stand on the beach about 100 feet or so from the big drum" (Allen Zimbleman, Omaha, Neb.). . . . "The **Big Save Supermarket** in Kapaa Shopping Center, Koloa and Waimea, and at Rice Shopping Center, has an excellent take-out section for hot and cold foods. Plate lunches like pot roast or beef teriyaki go from $2.50 to $3.50. But get there by 4 p.m. for the hot foods; the kamaainas like them too" (Arthur Hakenen, Okemos, Mich.). [*Authors' Note:* There's now a new addition to the chain, the **Kauai Kitchen** in Hanapepe, with a take-out section, plus a coffeeshop. And they sell those delectable Kauai Kookies.]

"The **Bull Shed** at Mokihana of Kauai, 796 Kuhio Hwy. (Route 56), has fantastic food. A seven-course Brazilian lobster dinner, complete with salad bar, rice, and honey-wheat rolls, was well priced" (John Gender, San Diego, Calif.). . . . "One of our very best meals was at the **Kountry Kitchen** in Kapaa. We had a coupon given us with our rental car for a steak and shrimp dinner for two people for $11.90. We were a bit skeptical, so left that for our last night. When we did eat there we wished we had gone the first night so we could have gone again! It was the best steak since we'd left home! The atmosphere was very homey, a fresh-baked mini-loaf of bread was brought immediately to our table. The salad was fresh and crispy and the entire evening was delightful" (Mrs. Duane Sheets, Salina, Calif.).

Chapter XII

SEEING KAUAI

COUNT ON AT LEAST three days to see Kauai. After Lihue, the first two should be devoted to separate all-day trips, which between them circle the island: (a) an eastern and northern trip all the way to Hanea and the Na Pali cliffs, and (b) a southern and western trip, whose high points are Waimea Canyon and the magnificent end-of-the-road climax, Kalalau Lookout. To skip either would be unthinkable. The remaining third day is for side excursions, swimming, and going back to all the idyllic little spots you discovered on the first two trips. Even with three there's hardly enough time.

1. Lihue

Starting place for your adventures is Lihue, an overgrown plantation village that is beginning to look startlingly modern what with shopping centers, supermarkets, and the like. Near the Lihue Shopping Center, you'll note a restoration area; four old concrete homes of German architecture, formerly occupied by Lihue Plantation employees, have been restored and are now known as the **Haleko Shops,** with several interesting shops and restaurants on the grounds. We think a visit to the **Kauai Museum,** 4424 Rice St., adjacent to the shopping center and across from the post office, is well worth your while. Stop in first at the Wilcox Building to examine the changing art, heritage, and cultural exhibits of both Orientalia and Hawaiiana. The **Museum Shop** here is one of our favorites, with its fine collections of South Pacific handicrafts, tapas, baskets, rare Niihau shell leis, Hawaiian books, prints, and missionary dolls. The Rice Building, entered through a covered paved walkway and courtyard, contains the permanent exhibit, "The Story of Kauai," an ecological and geological history complete with photographs, dioramas, and an exciting six-minute film shot from a helicopter. Be sure to see the Plantation Gallery, a permanent showcase for a collection of splendid Hawaiian quilts, plus koa furniture, china, etc. The museum is open from 9:30 a.m. to 4:30 p.m., Monday through Friday. Closed Saturday and Sunday. Admission is $3 for adults; children through age 17, free when accompanied by an adult.

A few blocks away from the museum, on Hardy Street, stands the **Kauai Regional Library,** a handsome contemporary building, where the latest audio-visual aids, including closed-circuit television, are available.

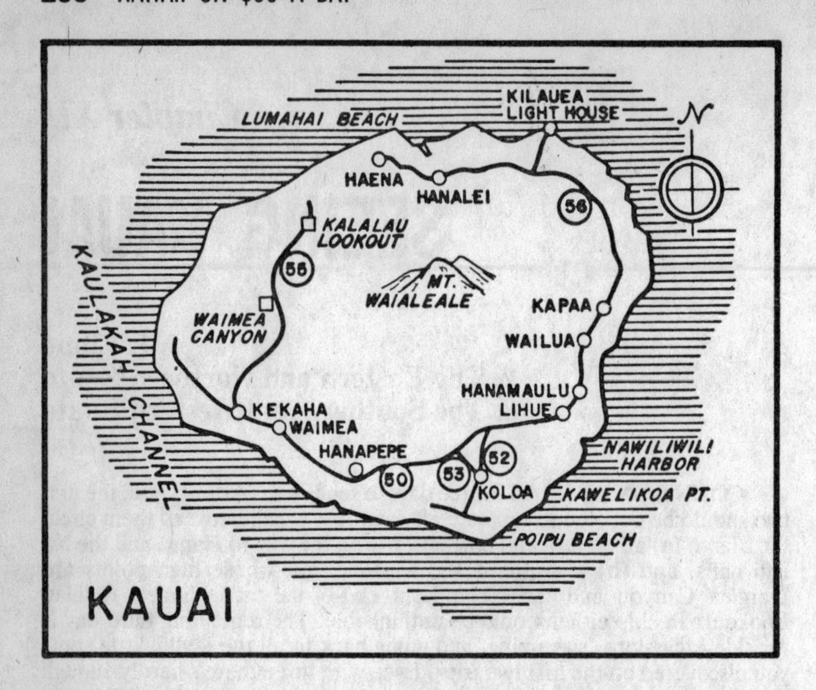

Note Jerome Wallace's impressive abstract batik mural measuring 10 feet high and 27 feet long. Library hours vary with the season but are usually 8 a.m. to 4:30 p.m., plus some evening hours. Ask about their free programs, which include films, art shows, story hours, and ethnic programs.

At 3016 Umi St., Suite 207, on the second floor of the Lihue Plaza, is the headquarters of the **Hawaii Visitors Bureau** (tel. 245-3971); stop in to chat with two charming ladies, Maile Semitekol and Sue Yoshishige, if you need any help in getting around the island. They have details on just about everything, including tips on where to play tennis and golf, hunt, fish, and go camping.

ON THE BEACH: If you follow Route H-50 a mile toward the sea from Lihue up until its junction with 51, you'll come to the deep-water port of **Nawiliwili** (where the wiliwili trees once grew), Kauai's largest harbor and the site of a bulk-sugar plant that looks out on **Kalapaki Beach** across the bay. Although it's on the grounds of the luxurious Kauai Surf Hotel, this is the town beach, and you are welcome to use it. The surf, similar to that at Waikiki, is fairly gentle, with enough long rollers to make surfing or outrigger canoe rides great fun. There's a marvelous cocktail lounge practically inside the pool of the Kauai Surf Hotel, and a snack shop on the beach. You can approach the beach from the hotel or, more directly, go past the Fisherman Restaurant, cross a little bridge, and you're there.

LIHUE SHOPPING: Pint-sized Lihue now has the largest of all neighbor island shopping malls, the $25-million **Kukui Grove Center.** Since it's just four miles from the airport on Route 50 (headed toward Poipu), it makes a logical first stop in town to stock up on food and vacation needs. **Star Market** has everything from boogie boards to gourmet take-out foods. At **Sears** you can shop for the whole family, rent a car, survey a good selection of Hawaiian wear and island souvenirs. Such other trusty island familiars as **Long's, Woolworth's, Liberty House, Waldenbooks,** and the **Fernandez Fun Factory** are here. If you need a good book to read on the beach, don't miss **Rainbow Books,** by far one of the most literate and tasteful bookstores we've come across in a long time. Their selection of books is so appealing that you might be tempted to spend your whole vacation right here. Under the same roof is **Stone's Gallery** for tasteful graphics, ceramics, jewelry, and other fine crafts, most by local artisans. This might be the place for you to buy that print by Pegge Hopper (her portraits of Hawaiian women with haunting faces and abstracted bodies are very popular in the islands right now), that runs into the hundreds, a hand-painted T-shirt for $25, or a variety of posters that begin at $10, unframed. In the center of the store, perched between books and art, sits **Rainbow Coffees,** with wonderful teas and coffees to take home or sip in the store along with heavenly pastries (see Chapter XI).

See You in China is another of our favorite Kukui Grove boutiques. This gallery and gift shop shows jewelry, totes, tiles, and other crafts by local artists, and beautiful clothing, most of it in 100% cotton. . . . **Butterflies Too?** is a love of a store. The buys here are excellent on such items as reversible handmade baby bibs appliquéd with butterflies, $5; cloisonné pendants from Taiwan, $5.98 and looking as if they were worth lots more; fossil beads and silk brocade jewel boxes from mainland China; butterfly tote bags for about $15, and more. You'll solve many gift problems here.

While most of the items at **Kauai Gifts** are of the usual garden variety, we did spot some handsome Niihau shell leis at 20% to 25% off regular prices. And they have a large collection of charming dolls and stuffed animals. . . . **Jack 'n' Jill** has cute clothing for the keikis, **Tad & Mary's** and **Déjà Vu** are fashion shops for women, and **Great Gourmet** has attractive kitchenware for the condo crowd. **General Nutrition Center** runs many specials and is a good place to replenish your vitamin supply.

The **Kukui Nut Tree Inn** for family-style meals and **Rosita's Mexican Restaurant** for spicy south-of-the-border fare are the big restaurant draws here, but also fine for an inexpensive meal is **Woolworth's Harvest House Café** and a small Mexican snack shop, **Taco Tia.** Free entertainment is often presented on the mall stage; check the local papers for details. Kukui Grove Center is open weekdays from 9:30 a.m. to 5:30 p.m., Friday night until 9 a.m., Sunday from 10 a.m. to 3 p.m.

Right across from the Kauai Surf Hotel in Nawiliwili is **Harbor Village,** a tasteful area with fountains and plantings and a cluster of shops that seem to come and go. At the time of our last visit, Harbor Village had just taken over from the old Menehune Shopping Village, and most of the stores were still a-building. We were, however, much impressed with **Golden Dolphin,** whose owner, Rosemary Oganeki, not only makes dresses to order for around $50, but carefully selects such lovely items as one-of-a-kind silkscreened cotton pareaus from Hawaii and Tahiti (about $32), baby quilts at $100, hand-painted prints by local artists, and a wide variety of interesting jewelry, from $4 cebu chipped shell necklaces to ivory necklaces that go up to about $200. Best time to visit Harbor Village is on a Monday or Friday at noon, when you'll see local hula halaus (schools) perform the dances, meles, and chants of old Polynesia, all free. We were lucky enough to catch a performance by Auntie Lovely and her troupe; her show is charming, and not even the good-natured participants from the audience minded when they were awarded their PhDs—Poor Hula Dancers.

Restaurants at Harbor Village are a big draw: just about everybody agrees that **Kauai Chop Suey** has the best Chinese food on the island, and a new branch of the popular **Bull Shed** restaurant is fast gaining in popularity.

The best budget shopping for resort fashions in Lihue is the big **Hilo Hattie's Fashion Center** at 3252 Kuhio Hwy. Phone them at 245-3404 and they'll take you out to the factory, where you can buy men's aloha shirts from $18, women's long muumuus from $30, plus monkeypod dishes, macadamia-nut candies, and the like, all at excellent prices.

JUST OUTSIDE OF TOWN: A visit to the **Grove Farm Homestead** in Nawiliwili takes a little advance planning, either by mail or by phoning 245-3203 for reservations. But it's worth the effort, as this is a trip backward in time, to the days of the old Hawaiian sugar plantations. Grove Farm itself is still fully operational; the Homestead has been lovingly preserved and still has a lived-in look. The plantation was founded by George N. Wilcox, the son of teachers who arrived with the fifth company of the American Board of Missions sent to Hawaii in the 1850s. (Part of Wilcox's original sugar plantation is now the site of Kukui Grove Center; see above.) His niece, Miss Mabel Wilcox, who was born and lived on the plantation all her life, left her estate as a living museum. The Homestead tour is leisurely, with stops for light refreshment along the way in the big kitchen. The old homes are lovely, furnished with antiques, Oriental rugs, and handsome koa wood furniture; there is an abundance of books, and sheet music is open on the piano. You'll visit the very different servants quarters too. Tours are held only on Monday, Wednesday, and Thursday, last about two hours, and get under way at 10 a.m. and 1:15 p.m. The cost is $3 for adults, $1 for children. To make mail reservations, up to six months in advance, write to Grove Farm Homestead, P. O. Box 1631, Lihue, Kauai, HI 96766.

THE SPORTING LIFE: There are plenty of opportunities for hiking, fishing, camping, golf, water sports, and the like on Kauai for those who have the time to stay and enjoy them. Check with the Hawaii Visitors Bureau or write to them at P.O. Box 507, Lihue, HI 96766. Hiking information is available at the Department of Land and Natural Resources, State Building (P.O. Box 167, Lihue, HI 96766), in Lihue. If you are writing for maps, please enclose $1 in stamps.

KAUAI ON HORSEBACK: A great way to enjoy the sights of Kauai is on horseback. **High Gates' Ranch** (tel. 822-3182) at Wailua Homesteads in Wailua rents horses for $13 per hour ($9 for children), and offers several guided rides; a special favorite is a five-hour trip to Keahua Arboretum, stopping for a picnic lunch beside a lovely, clear pond perfect for a swim. (Daredevils can plummet into the water from the rope swing on the mango tree at water's edge.)

2. The Eastern and Northern Route

Now you're ready for one of the big trips, an excursion around the glorious north and east shores of Kauai. Highway 56, which starts at Kuhio

Highway in town, takes you the entire length of the tour. The distance is 40 miles each way, and it will take you a full day.

KAPAIA AND HANAMAULU: After you've gone a few miles out of town at Kapaia, you'll find a turnoff to the left to **Wailua Falls,** about four miles inland. Watch for the white fence on the right of the road and listen for the sound of rushing water; soon you'll see the HVB marker. After you've seen them, don't be tempted to drive farther; turn around here and drive back.

Look now, on the left as you're driving to Wailua on Kuhio Highway (Route 56), for a quaint store called the **Kapaia Stitchery,** especially appealing in that many things in it are made by hand. Owner Julie Yukimura makes items like wrap skirts, kimono tops, pareaus, and aloha shirts which she sells at low prices. She also asks local craftsmen, especially senior citizens, to make things for her; we found lovely handmade, crocheted shawls and bags, priced from $30 up. Her own 89-year-old grandmother, Mrs. Shima Yukimura, is the master crocheter who does all of the shawls and jackets. Most exciting of all are the patchwork coverlets made of modern Hawaiian fabrics by four local grandmothers. We spied one in the window and guessed that its price was at least $150; we couldn't believe that it was only $50. A darling baby quilt with a pattern of Oriental children was $45. We hope Julie has a few quilts on hand when you're there; we don't need to tell anybody who knows about hand work that they are fantastic buys at the price, and each represents weeks of painstaking work. She also carries Hawaiian quilt pillow kits, hand-painted needlepoint designs of local flowers and themes, and specially selected Hawaiian print fabrics for those who like to make things themselves.

You may want to stop off in Hanamaulu now, to see the **Hanamaulu Museum.** Have a look at some of the artifacts, most of them unearthed in this area and used in the early plantation days of the island. You'll see water gourds and tapa beaters, a collection of old Hawaiian bottles, ancient canoes and surfboards, ice grinders from the camp store, even an altar from a Buddhist temple. Feminists take note: There's a plow here "pulled by a buffalo or wife and used for watering taro patches." The museum is open more or less all the time and is surrounded by Beef 'n' Pasta (see Chapter XI), Hanamaulu Stained Glass, with stunning work by Paul Oliver, a leather craftsman, an oldtime working post office, and an ice-cream and sandwich parlor, so there's always something to see and do here.

Hanamaulu Beach, which you reach by turning right to Heni Road and following the signs, is a pretty spot with a Japanese-style pavilion, slides for the keikis, and a picnic grove under the evergreen trees. The surf is gentle and inviting. Island families like this one; it's great for kids.

WAILUA: Continuing on Highway 56, you'll soon come to the mouth of the **Wailua River** and one of the most historic areas in Hawaii. Here, where the Polynesians first landed, were once seven heiaus, or temple sites, by the sacred (wailua) waters. Just before you get there, you'll come to **Lydgate Park,** on the right, a grassy picnic area directly on the water, in which are the remains of an ancient "City of Refuge." You'll get a better idea of what a City of Refuge actually looked like when you see the restored one at Kona on the Big Island. But the concept here was precisely the same. In the days when the Hawaiians still carried on their polytheistic nature worship, life was bound by a rigid system of kapus, or taboos, violations of which were punishable by death. But if an offender, or a prisoner of war, could run or swim to a City of Refuge, he could be purified and was then allowed to go free. Not too much of the City of Refuge remains, but if you wade out into the river you may discover some ancient carvings on the rocks, once part of the heiau. More practically, **Lydgate Park Beach** is one of the best beaches on Kauai for children. Two natural "pools," created by rocks, make it safe for them to swim and play in the ocean. The snorkeling is lovely, there are stripies and butterfly fish feeding on the rock, the water is clean and clear, and the sand is white. There are rest rooms, showers, and barbecue pits near the beach. Alas, there have been recent reports of vandalism here.

A relatively new Hawaiian ghost story got started out here. It seems that the old jail across from the Wailua Golf Course (now replaced by a new facility) may have been haunted. Local people tell us that it was once a burial ground and, before that, a battleground. Whatever the reason, the building shook, the lights went on and off by themselves, and strange mumblings were sometimes heard from the top floor. The police really did not like to draw duty there. Seems that once one of Lihue's Finest was so shaken up in the middle of the night that he took all the prisoners, put them in his car, and took them to the police station in Lihue!

The Wailua, one of the two navigable rivers in Hawaii, is also the place where you can rent a tour boat for an idyllic three-mile trip to the fantastically beautiful **Fern Grotto**—an enormous fern-fronted cave under a gentle cascade of water, unapproachable any other way. Personally, we'd love to take this trip in our own private craft and instead of being "entertained," spend the time contemplating the rare tropical trees and flowers that line the bank and pondering on the old Kauai alii whose bones still lie undiscovered in the secret burial caves of the cliffs above. But the tour boats are well run, the captains are entertaining, and the musicians' singing of the "Hawaiian Wedding Song" in the natural amphitheater of the Fern Grotto is a unique experience.

The cost of the 1½-hour boat trips is $7 (children, half price), and both **Waialeale Boat Tours** and **Smith Motor Boat Service** make the cruises. Their phone numbers are 822-4908 and 822-3467 and you should phone in advance to make a reservation.

If you decide to skip the river trip, you might want to visit **Paradise Pacifica,** just beyond the marina and toward the mountains. This 31-acre attraction displays Pacific cultures, gardens, and structures in an exquisite setting. For a $5 admission charge, $2.50 for children under 13 (rates subject to change), you can hop aboard one of the mini-trains for a narrated tour. You'll see five acres of lagoons filled with native fish, water fowl, and sea turtles, surrounded by gardens planted with tropical fruits and flowers (all labeled). Open daily from 10 a.m. (tel. 822-4911).

At this point on Highway 56, a side road called the **King's Highway** (named after the kings who had to be carried uphill in a litter, lest their sacred feet touch the ground) leads to the restored heiau, **Holo-Holo-Ku.** It's so serene here now that it's hard to realize that this was once a site for human sacrifice—where bloodthirsty deeds were done to calm the ancient gods.

Now you move on from Hawaiiana to observe some of the history of the Japanese settlers in Hawaii, recorded in a quaint cemetery just up the wooden stairs to the right of the heiau. If you continue driving along the King's Highway, you'll pass a rice field and soon, **Poliahu Heiau,** now a park that affords you a splendid view of the Wailua River. Next is **Opaekaa Falls,** plunging down from a high cliff (the name, quaintly, means rolling shrimp); there is talk of a Hawaiian village being restored here.

When you retrace your path to Highway 56, you'll see a little group of buildings on the right, across from the Coco Palms; it's the site of the **Rehabilitation Center Shop,** which features handcrafted coconut and woven lauhala products, made by the disabled, at reasonable prices. Wood roses and tinkly wood chimes, both inexpensive, make delightful gifts.

At some point you're going to want to visit **Coco Palms** itself, perhaps for its splendid evening torch-lighting ceremony. Have a look at some of the attractive shops here; they are more reasonably priced than you might expect. **Treasury,** for one, has many tasteful artifacts like banana-bark paintings, feather jewelry, and hand-crocheted pillow cases, which were just $7. Long silk Chinese beads sell for only $2.95.

The Market Place

Back on the highway now, continue toward the Coconut Plantation hotels and there, near the Islander Inn and the Kauai Beach Boy, you'll find Kauai's prettiest answer to the shopping complex craze: the Market Place at Coconut Plantation. It's a handsome setup, with concrete planked walkways, country decor, flowers and shrubs everywhere, and enough diverting shops (over 70 at last count) to keep you busy for an hour or two. We have a few special favorites, like **Waves of One Sea,** with such international gifts as batik table lines from Java, lacquer boxes from Kashmir, miniature "Trouble Dolls" from Guatemala, Fukagawa porcelain from Japan, Hawaiian tapa mâché dolls, Russian stone carvings, and the island's largest selection of fans from around the world. Jewelry handmade of peacock and pheasant feathers begins at $8. And handmade on Kauai, pressed seaweed and floral notecards and bookmarks, $1 to $2, make charming small mementos. . . . **Plantation Stitchery** specializes in needlepoint and patterns. . . . We saw some great sundresses for around $30 at **Batik Boutique. . . .** You can get leather sandals made in Hawaii at **Hele-On Sandals,** and all kinds of aloe products at the **Aloe Connection. . . . Plantation Artistree** features unique stoneware windbells by island craftsman Jim Larriva, from about $10 to $30. . . . **Tahiti Imports** sells beautiful clothing and hand-screened fabrics for very reasonable prices. . . . **Ye Olde Ship Store** is the place for maritime gifts, antiques, and scrimshaw. Hand-cast solid brassware goes for surprisingly nice prices, and the plaque that reads "On this site in 1897 nothing happened" ($17) appeals to our crazy sense of humor . . . The range of arts and crafts made from butterfly wings, or in the shape of butterflies, at **Julie's Butterflies** is amazing: most are done by local artisans, but there are also wall plaques from Brazil, rugs from Peru and Bolivia, and cloisonné from mainland China.

Be sure to visit the exquisite **Kahn Gallery,** where a consistently high level of taste is evident in the selection of paintings, woodcuts, watercolors, pottery, and crafts by Hawaiian artists. We admired the paintings of O. J. Metzner, the Hawaiian scrimshaw, and the unusual collection of Niihau shell necklaces, which begin at $30 and go up to $4500. Small paintings to carry home and limited-edition prints could start as low as $25, although most are in the several-hundred-dollar range . . . Lovely Niihau shell necklaces are also shown at the **Necklace Gallery . . .** If you'd like to fly a kite on a Kauai beach, the people at **High as a Kite and Toy Company** have some beauties for you. Huggable handmade dolls, made on Kauai, are a store exclusives. . . . You can get scrimshaw, 14-karat gold charms, and

Niihau leis at **Kauai Gold,** nuts and candies at **Nut Cracker Sweet,** and a huge variety of woods and wicker—fans, baskets, jewelry, carvings, from many countries—at **Tramp Steamer Trading Company,** one of our old favorites in the Market Place. . . . **Crazy Shirts** is here, full of whimsical T-shirts with silly sayings. Our favorite: "Here Today, Gone to Maui." . . . Stop in to see the rare thousand-armed golden Buddha (not for sale) at **Golden Buddha,** which does sell jewelry. . . . Observe the ocean's treasures at **Shells International** and at **Coral Grotto,** which abounds in all kinds of coral, including beautiful black, from about $40. . . . They'll roast and grind Kona coffeebeans as you like them right on the premises at the fragrant **Kona Kope Coffee & Nut Roasting Center,** which calls itself the only store in the world to offer 100% Hawaiian coffee in Viennese, French, Italian, or Turkish styles, plus a rare Hawaiian blend called "Malia." Prices vary, but regular Hawaiian coffee was around $10 per pound when this was written. They also have some very special gourmet teas grown at various elevations in the Hawaiian islands, as well as herbs, dried fruits, nuts (Hawaiian macadamia nuts roasted fresh every day), coffee grinders, teapots, et al., which can be gift-wrapped and sent to the mainland. Don't pass up their famous "Cappuccino Kauai" at their espresso bar.

LM Jeans carries jeans for everyone—in sizes up to 46 for women and 54 for men. . . . Need luggage, handbags, tote bags, flight bags, etc.? Check in with **The Bag Shop** owners Liz and Diana, who will guide you through their tremendous selection. . . . We saw elegant muumuus for kids, as well as many other lovelies, at **Happy Kauaiian**—which also has special selections for queen-sizes, petites, and sells fabrics too. . . . **Coco Resorts Shop** has great things for the whole family. . . . And **Hale Keiki** specializes in tasteful things for the kids: Hawaiian toys, games, souvenirs, dolls, and books, plus a good selection of Hawaiian T-shirts and aloha wear.

The kids will get a kick out of playing with the heavy equipment from the defunct **Kilauea Mill** that has been transformed into sculptural fountains they can control. When they tire of that, they may enjoy running to the top of the high wooden tower to see the beautiful view. And they'll be delighted with the children's hula show presented by the local hula schools every Thursday, Friday, and Saturday at 4 p.m.

Hungry? No problem. The Market Place abounds in snackbars and restaurants offering inexpensive meals, like **Don's Deli and Picnic Basket, Create A Steak,** and **J.J.'s Dog House** (see preceding chapter). And if you want to catch a first-run movie, Cinema I and Cinema II (Kauai's only air-conditioned movie houses) are right there. The Market Place opens daily at 9 a.m. It closes at 5 p.m. on Sunday; at 9 p.m. on Monday, Tuesday, and Wednesday; and at 8 p.m. on Thursday, Friday, and Saturday. Free hula shows are held Thursday, Friday, and Saturday at 4 p.m.

KAPAA AND KEALIA: From Highway 56, back on the northern drive, you'll soon see a remarkable formation on the left as you enter Kapaa, the **Sleeping Giant**—the subject of another Menehune tall tale. The old fellow, so the story goes, was a kind of Gulliver whom the South Sea Lilliputians inadvertently killed.

On the opposite side of the road, look for a little store shaped like a Samoan house and called **Marta's Boat.** Marta Curry, who has three young children of her own, understands the needs of mothers and children and has stocked her place with items both pretty and practical, much of it handmade. Her specialty is 100% cotton (or silk or rayon; she will not carry blends) aloha clothing for children. Cotton batiks for infants and toddlers are especially lovely. She also has a large selection of bags (for carrying kids' essentials), wind-up water toys, and for mom, mainland clothes in aloha fabrics—the kinds of things you'll be happy to wear back home too. Two-yard pareaus, hand-printed in traditional Hawaiian and Samoan designs, range from $15 to $25; and $39 Japanese antique rayon scarves could be made into handsome blouses. Next door is a natural-foods store run by her husband, Ambrose Curry; pick up a cooling bottled fruit drink here, or stock up if you need anything, for it's one of the few-and-far between health-food shops on the island.

Nearby, in a Chinese frame store building, also oceanside, at 788 Kuhio Hwy., Zan Fojas stocks the **Awapuhi Emporium of Hawaiiana and Orientalia** with all sorts of pretty things of good design. We saw some beautiful American Indian-style beaded jewelry made by a local craftswoman, priced from $13.95, and loved the ornamental hair-combs carved of local woods for about $5. **Zan** has also assembled a lovely collection of clothing in cutwork cotton from Bali—blouses, skirts, and dresses. Hand-painted T-shirts with bird and floral designs, and embroidered wearables, are also outstanding.

Some of the most beautiful fish in Polynesian waters live in the rocks and reefs around Kauai. The professional staff at **Sea Sage,** a friendly little dive shop at 4-1378 Kuhio Hwy. in Kapaa, sell and rent every conceivable item of snorkeling and scuba equipment, often at lower than mainland prices. They also carry boogie boards and all manner of beach accessories. Mask, snorkel, and fins still rent for $7 a day, and the half-day charters for certified scuba divers are still $25 plus gear rental. Sea Sage instructors are available daily, by reservation, to take you by the hand and gently introduce you to the basics of snorkeling safely in nice, shallow water for $13, plus $7 for equipment rental. Their most popular activity is a three-hour introduction to scuba; it's $60, including all equipment and individualized instruction, and your partner gets to go for half price. Call them at 822-3841 for details.

Continuing on, now, turn half a mile up the hill just before the bridge over Kealia Stream and you'll come to **St. Catherine's Catholic Church,** which boasts murals by leading Hawaiian artists: Jean Charlot, Juliette May Fraser, and Tseng Yu Ho.

Beyond Kealila, watch for the turnoff to **Anahola Beach** for a glimpse of one of those golden, jewel-like beaches that ring the island.

KILAUEA: The first church you'll see as you drive into Kilauea town, **Christ Memorial Episcopal Church,** has an only-in-Hawaii architecture. It's made of lava rock. Its windows, executed in England, are of the finest design and workmanship. On the other side of the road you'll soon see **St. Sylvester's Catholic Church** in Kilauea—something new in church architecture. This octagonal "church-in-the-round," constructed of lava and wood, has a beautiful, open feeling. You'll recognize the work of Jean Charlot again, this time in the fresco paintings of the stations of the cross.

Now follow the road for two more miles to **Kilauea Lighthouse** (turn right into Kilauea, past the sugar mill, and along the left side of the post office), high on a bluff that drops sharply to the sea on three sides. From here you get a magnificent view of the northern coastline of the island and of green sugarcane fields stretching to the mountains. Birds drift effortlessly in the wind like paper kites sent up by schoolboys; below, the turquoise sea smashes against the black lava cliffs. In spring and summer, you'll see the aptly named, blue-faced "boobies," which have a nesting ground on the rocks and don't seem to mind the tactless stares of tourists. The area has recently been taken over as a National Wildlife Bird Sanctuary, and the lighthouse, formerly manned by Coast Guardsmen (and once open to visitors) is now fully automated. For the record, the light is the largest clam-shell-shaped lens in the world (12 feet high) and the brightest in the Pacific. The area is open to the public from noon to 4 p.m. Monday through Saturday.

On the way to Kilauea Lighthouse, you might want to stop at **Old Kilauea Town,** which includes the **Kong Lung Company,** Kauai's oldest plantation general store (1881); the Farmer's Market; Grandma's Grocery; and the Filling Station Lunchwagon. The buildings are turn-of-the-century plantation, and the atmosphere charming. Kong Lung is very special, with beautiful antiques, cookware, tasteful craft items, even Chinese yo-yos for the kids. You can shop for local island wear and gifts, or pick up some cheeses and imported wines for a picnic at the beach, or dine on simple local and American foods in a lovely garden setting—or all of the above. Around the bend is **Jacques Bakery,** whose breads and pastries you'll find in many island supermarkets and restaurants. Stop in and treat yourself to some garlic and pepper bread right from the ovens.

Continue, now, past **Kalihiwai Bay,** whose sleepy little village was twice destroyed by tidal waves, in 1946 and 1957, a reminder that the much-celebrated mildness of Hawaii is a sometime thing; the violence of nature (or is it the old gods?) is always here, a sleeping beast that can spring to life at any moment.

HANALEI: The glorious views continue. Keep watching for the lookout at **Hanalei Valley,** where you will be treated to one of the special sights of the islands. The floor of Hanalei Valley, which you see below, is almost Asian, with neatly terraced taro patches and the silvery Hanalei River stretching through the dark greens of the mountains. (A sunset visit here is spectacular; plan it for a later trip if you have time.) You may want to drive through the luxury resort development of **Princeville at Hanalei**—surely a sportsman's idea of paradise—and perhaps have lunch here at the **Bali Ha'i Restaurant, Chuck's Steakhouse,** or **Tortilla Flats** (see Chapter XI). Another good idea would be to pick up a gourmet picnic lunch at **Pot Luck,** which offers soups, salads, sandwiches, entrees such as chicken Dijon or enchiladas, cheesecake, etc. Back on the road, you'll soon come to **Hanalei Beach,** one of the most imposing beaches in the islands, but swimming is safe only in summer months and only at the old boat pier at the river mouth. In winter, beware of high surf and undertow. To get to the beach, turn right at St. William's Catholic Church (another Jean Charlot mural is inside). There's a public pavilion, dressing rooms, and picnic facilities; your fellow bathers will include many island families.

In Hanalei Valley itself, history buffs will want to note the old **Waioli Mission.** The church, built in 1841, is now used as a community center. More interesting, we think, is the old Mission House, restored in 1921 and full of fascinating furniture, books, and mementos of 19th-century Hawaii. It's open Tuesday through Saturday for guided tours.

We loved the funky old Ching Young General Store that had sat in the middle of Hanalei town forever, so we looked upon its demise and the construction of the new **Ching Young Village Shopping Center** with mixed emotions. While none of the boutiques here seems remarkable, the center is certainly practical: it has a Big Save Market, a good Chinese restaurant, a health-food store and snackbar, and several fast-food operations (see Chapter XI). The **Native Hawaiian Trading and Cultural Center** was just being built at the time of our last visit, so let's hope this is going to be more exciting for visitors.

Our favorite shop in this area is called **Ola's,** and it's right next door to the Dolphin Restaurant in Hanalei. This is a serenely tasteful environment, stocked with beautiful handmade craft items. Silkscreened purses were $5 and $10; hand-blown oil lamps began at $37. We were especially taken with the silk-screened totes by Carol Mortenson of California at $17 and $25. A serendipitous spot.

Lumahai Beach is next, and you'll recognize it immediately from pictures appearing in dozens of books, postcards, and magazines. It's probably the most widely photographed beach on the island, and deserves its fame: golden sand, a long tongue of black lava rock stretching to the sea, a background of unearthly blue-green mountain. If the surf is not high, swimming will be safe here. It's a little difficult to find the entrance to the trail down to the beach (not indicated by any signs), but once you do it's easy to get down. If the surf is up, admire the view and continue on.

HAENA: Beyond this point stretches the Haena region, where the shoreline gets dreamier by the mile. You can swim anywhere along here with the local people, but be very careful of surf and undertow in the winter months. Many people consider **Haena Beach Park** one of the best beaches on the island (although we personally prefer to swim at Ke'e, ahead), and you won't go wrong swimming, camping, or picknicking here. Haena is what you always imagined the South Seas would be like—golden curving beaches, coconut palms and lush foliage, jagged cliffs tumbling down to the sea. Is it any surprise that this spot was chosen as Bali Ha'i for the movie *South Pacific*?

On this drive through the Haena region, watch on the left side of the road for the **Manimi-holo Dry Cave,** which was supposedly dug by the Menehunes to capture an evil spirit that had stolen some fish. This is the area from which the Menehunes were also said to have left Hawaii. A short distance from here, up a small rise, is the first of two **Wet Caves,** the **Waikapalae;** about 200 yards farther on is the second, the **Waikanaloa.** For once, the Menehunes were not responsible—the caves were reputedly dug by Pele in a search for fire. Finding freshwater instead, she left in disgust. It's reported that you can swim in these pools (the old Hawaiians used to jump off the ledges into them), but we think you'll do better to wait for the end of the road a few hundred yards ahead and an out-of-this-world beach, **Ke'e.** This is one of those gentle, perfect beaches that's almost impossible to tear yourself away from. As you loll on the sand under the towering mountains, listening to the Pacific, which has quieted down to a ripple beside you, it's not hard to picture this spot when it was the site of a most sacred temple of Laka, the goddess of the hula. Nearby are the remains of a heiau that guarded the sacred hua halau, to which novitiates came from all over the islands to study the dances, meles, and religious traditions of their people. From the cliffs above, specially trained men would throw burning torches into the sea (possibly in connection with temple rites). To your left are the cliffs of the **Na Pali Coast** and the end of your auto trip.

If you'd like to see the spectacularly beautiful Na Pali Coast in detail, however, you have three alternatives: by foot, by boat, and by helicopter. For the first, see Readers' Suggestions, ahead, for tips on hiking around the cliffs. Of the many boat trips offered, two are very special. **Ancient Hawaiian Adventures** is a "barefoot cruise for the adventurous," according to Capt. John Roon, who is dedicated to promoting the consciousness of ancient Hawaiian culture. He takes six passengers at a time out on a smaller, single-masted version of an ancient Hawaiian catamaran. This has to be the next-best-thrill to surfing as the captain guides the boat inside the waves and rides them to shore under sail power! Be sure to wear your bathing suit. These trips are "family priced": around $25 per person for a 2½-hour trip, $15 for 1½ hours. For information and reservations, phone 826-6088 between 9 a.m. and 5 p.m. The second, **Na Pali Zodiac** boat expeditions takes small groups out in boats similar to those used for shooting the rapids on the Colorado River. (The trip is usually smooth and gentle, but can be as wet and wild as the Colorado River on occasion; a licensed Coast Guard captain is in command.) A full day's expedition costs $80; camper drop-offs are $50 one way to Kalalau, $95 round trip leaving from Hanalei. Morning and sunset sightseeing cruises are $50. There may soon be a slight rise in prices. For information and reservations, contact Na Pali Zodiac, P.O. Box 456, Hanalei, HI 96714 (tel. 826-9371).

Helicopter Trips: Perhaps the most exciting way of all to see Kauai, to experience the grandeur of its remote and isolated areas, is to take a helicopter flight. These are not inexpensive: prices start at $90 and go up to $200 per person for trips over Waimea Canyon and the Na Pali Coast, into the wilderness areas of Kauai, often swooping down the canyon walls to make stops at pristine beaches. Early-morning and sunset flights can be the most beautiful of all. A number of companies are now offering tours, and competition can be fierce. Local people speak extremely highly of the tours run by **Jack Harter Helicopters** (tel. 245-3774), since Jack himself pilots all trips and provides a superb, informal, and warm commentary on his island. The price is around $90 for a 1½-hour flight that could be the high point of your stay on Kauai. Other popular companies include: **Papillon Helicopters**, the largest in the state (tel. 826-6591); **Kenai Helicopters** (tel. 245-8591); **Island Helicopters Kauai** (tel. 367-5183); **Menehune Helicopters** (tel. 245-7705); **South Sea Helicopters** (tel. 245-7781); and **Will Squyres Helicopters** (tel. 245-7541). Photographers are advised to bring plenty of film and a wide-angled lens if possible.

3. The Southern and Western Route

This tour is about as long as the northern one and requires another full day. Since the highpoint is Waimea Canyon, you might check with the forest ranger on duty before leaving (tel. 335-5871) to find out if there's fog over the canyon; if so, it might be preferable to save this trip for another day, if you have one. You may, by the way, want a sweater for the slightly cooler (but not at all unpleasant) 4000-foot altitude of the Kokee region.

KOLOA AND POIPU BEACH: With its glorious dry climate, golden sandy beaches, and breathtakingly beautiful surf, this is one of the choice areas of Kauai. Your first stop here might be at a place rich in both Hawaiian history and horticultural splendor, **Moir's Gardens,** surrounding the **Plantation**

Garden Restaurant in Kiahuna Plantation Resort. As for the history, it was supposedly on this site that **Laka,** goddess of the hula and sister of Pele, goddess of the volcanoes, trained her initiates. For whatever it's worth, the vibrations are very good, and the gardens are spectacular; many of the monstrous cactus plants look like something out of Middle Earth. There is no charge to walk around the gardens. Tours are held every day at 10 a.m. (tel. 367-7052 for information). To reach the gardens, drive roughly 14 miles from Lihue on Highway 50; then take Highway 52 to Plantation Gardens.

Now it's time to stop for a swim. **Poipu Beach,** which you'll reach soon after turning left past Plantation Gardens, is probably the best swimming beach on the island and one of the loveliest anywhere. Youngsters can swim in a shallow little pool; there's rolling surf farther out, and a picnic area and pavilion here too. A word of advice: Don't spend the **entire** day here, as there's plenty to see coming up ahead.

We've had good reports this year about a new diving facility in this area: **Fathom Five,** on Poipu Road, next to Koloa Chevron. They offer snorkeling lessons plus a snorkeling tour for $20, an introductory scuba dive (no experience necessary) for $55, and a variety of exciting adventures for certified divers, from $35. They'll rent you equipment, and even take photographs of you underwater. All tours are conducted in small, personal groups. Call them first to make reservations at 742-6991.

GEYSERS AND GARDENS: Trace your way back now to the fork in the road and this time take the other branch, the one on the right. Continuing past Kuhio Park (on the site of the birthplace of Prince Kuhio), you come to Kukuiula Small Boat Harbor, more familiarly known as **Sampan Harbor.** Be sure to walk out on the wharf for an absolutely gorgeous view; about a mile ahead to the right is **Spouting Horn,** where the water spurts up through several holes in the lava rock, and to your left is an uncannily blue-green Pacific hurtling itself against the black rocks. You might be tempted to just stand here for hours, but keep going and watch the Spounting Horn geysers from a closer vantage point farther up the road.

Just outside of Kalaheo, watch for enchanting **Kukui-O-Lono Park.** The entrance is through a majestic stone gate, just south of Kalaheo. The name means light of the god Lono; at one time kukui-oil torches here provided a beacon for fishermen at sea. Now the place is a public golf course (greens fees are just $5) and a small park, where you can see a Stone Age Hawaiian exhibit and a charming Japanese garden. There are birds everywhere.

Our next stop is again for lovers of gardens, and this is **Olu Pua Gardens,** past the intersection of Highway 50 and 54. Olu Pua overlooks the town of Kalaheo, sugarcane fields, and the tropical sea. Its 12½ acres of gardens surround a former plantation house, built in 1929. Among this setting are beautiful gardens that range from jungle to palm garden to Oriental garden. The most enchanting area is the one called the Kau Kau Garden, where you can see tropical fruits and vegetables such as papaya, mango, taro, lichees, and other exotic edibles. Admission is $4. Olu Pua closes at 5 p.m.

HANAPEPE AND WAIMEA: Another of the wondrous scenic views of Hawaii awaits you as you approach the town of Hanapepe. Stop at the overlook for a glorious vista of **Hanapepe Valley** below, where rice shoots, guava trees, and taro patches cover the fertile floor. Waimea Canyon is off in the distance to the left. Hanapepe, where you ought to stop for lunch at the **Green Garden** (see Chapter XI), is quaint, with old wooden, balconied Chinese shops and an air not unlike that of an Old West town. Just past the Green Garden, an old gas station has been converted into a charming gift shop called **The Station,** specializing in original, hand-painted Hawaiian-designed needlepoint, colorful appliqué quilt cushion patterns and kits, plus distinctive gift items from around the world as well as artwork by talented local residents.

Just past Hanapepe, off to the left on a side road, there's another HVB marker, labeled "Salt Pond." Follow Route H-543 here, take the first right turn past the Veteran's Cemetery, and you'll find yourself at **Salt Pond,** where the calendar seems to have stopped. It looks like a marsh dotted with strange covered wells, and it is here that salt is being mined and dried (some of the drying beds in operation date back to the 17th century) as the Hawaiians have been doing it for centuries. You may be lucky and arrive while they are working. Then you can head for **Salt Pond Pavilion,** a great swimming and picnicking beach, with safe, calm water. This beach is a good place to recoup your strength for the next big series of sensations coming up at Waimea Canyon.

But first you arrive at the town of Waimea, which, like Wailua, is steeped in history. A favorite deep-water harbor in the olden days, it was the center of government before the coming of the white man, and the place where old Captain Cook decided to come ashore. Whalers and trading ships put in here for provisions on their long voyages in the Pacific. It was also here that the first missionaries landed on Kauai, in 1820. And it was on this site that an employee of the Russian Fur Company, Dr. Anton Scheffer, built a fort and equipped himself with a Hawaiian retinue, promising Chief Kaumaualii help in defeating Kamahameha. The latter got wind of the scheme and gave Kaumaualii orders to get his foreign ally out of Hawaii—which he did, pronto. But the ruins of the old fort, a stone wall mostly hidden by weeds, are still here; an HVB marker points the way on your left, before you come to the Waimea River. The fort will soon be restored—already rest rooms and parking facilities have been built, and some of the old stonework is now visible. Until then, however, there's not much else to see here; the interest is mostly historical.

Again on the right, back on the main street of town, after you've passed the Captain Cook Monument, look for the turnoff to the **Menehune Ditch.** Follow the river about 2½ miles, past some Japanese shops, a Buddhist temple, taro patches, rice paddies, and tiny houses; where you come to a narrow bridge swinging across the river, stop and look for a stone wall protruding above the road for a few feet on the left side. This is all that remains visible of the Menehune Ditch, a remarkable engineering accomplishment that brought water to the neighboring fields several miles down from the mountain. The curious stonecutting here has convinced anthropologists that some pre-Polynesian race created the aqueduct. Who else but the Menehunes? They did the whole thing in one night, and were rewarded by the pleased citizens of Waimea with a fantastic feast of shrimps, their favorite food. They later made so much noise celebrating that they woke the birds on Oahu, a hundred miles away. While you're busy creating some legends of your own, you might see some Hawaiian Huck Finns, placidly floating down the river on rafts made of logs tied together, little bothered by either Menehunes or tourists.

The main highway now continues beyond **Kekaha** to the arid countryside around **Mana,** and beyond that to some enormous sand dunes known as the **Barking Sands.** The Kauaians swear they say "woof" when you slide down them, but that's pretty hard to prove. The U.S. Navy has now closed the area, so take the shorter drive to the canyon; you turn off the highway just past Waimea to Route H-550. (A possible side trip at this point could be to **Polihale State Park** for a picnic: just continue on Route 50, past Mana.)

KOKEE: For your first view of the canyon, drive on to the Kaana Ridge, which leads you right to **Kokee Park and Camp,** very different from anything you've seen on Kauai. You're in the midst of bracing mountain country now, with wonderful hiking trails, freshwater streams for trout fishing and swimming, wild fruit to pick in season, wild pigs and goats to hunt. The forest ranger here will give you details on trails. You can relax for a few minutes at the **Kokee Museum,** right next to the **Kokee Lodge Restaurant** and **Kokee Camps** (once again, see Chapter XI), where you could spend a long, blissful holiday.

Now it's just four miles for a spectacular climax to this trip, the view from the **Kalalau Lookout.** Driving the winding road for these last few miles, you will pass the Kokee tracking station, now world famous for its part in the success of the Apollo 11 mission to the moon. It was from this site that a laser beam was flashed to reflectors that Neil Armstrong had set up on the lunar surface. At Kalalau, the thick tropical forest suddenly drops 4000 feet down to the breathtakingly blue sea beyond, where it melts imperceptibly into the horizon. Below, on the knife-like ridges, are the remnants of irrigation ditches, taro patches, and signs of careful cultivation that have been long since abandoned to the elements. Read Jack London's story, "Koolau the Leper" (in *A Hawaiian Reader*) for a fictional rendering of the indomitable Koolau, who hid in the ridges here and, single-handed, held off the Hawaii National Guard in its attempt to get him to the leper colony at Molokai. His heroic wife crossed the dizzyingly narrow ridges hundreds of times in five years to bring food to her husband and son until they both died of the fearful disease and left her to return to her people alone.

This marks the end of your trip; depending on whether you want an early or late view of Waimea Canyon, you might schedule some of the other sights for the return trip. It's about 40 miles back to Lihue.

Now the road goes up, quite rugged in parts, through forests of eucalyptus, silver oak, and koa; soon you'll see the white ohia trees with their red blossoms of lehua (you'll see lehua again when you visit Volcanoes National Park in Hawaii). On you go, to the first lookout (and the best) in **Waimea Canyon,** Puu Ka Pele. Park your car and prepare yourself for one of the most spectacular views in all Hawaii. You're standing now at the top of a 3657-foot gorge, about a mile wide and ten miles long. Millions of years ago this was the scene of a tremendous geologic fault, a great crack in the dome of the island; erosion, streams, and ocean waves cut the cliffs into jagged shapes whose colors change with the sun and the clouds—blue and green in the morning, melting into vermilion, copper, and gold as the sun moves across it and finally sets. The gorge is comparable to the Grand Canyon, smaller than its Arizona sister, but sometimes outdoing her in the violent rainbow of its colors.

READERS' SHOPPING AND SIGHTSEEING SUGGESTIONS: "We discovered the **People's Market** in Puhi. This roadside stand provides local goodies like bananas, coconut meat ready to eat in Baggies, as well as ready-to-eat pineapple. This treat served as a great lunch and many a late-night snack. I highly recommend that anyone, and especially those trying to save dollars, make this a stop. You will come away with a bag of island delicacies for very little money and maybe an orchid for your hair!" (Holly McAlpen, Half Moon Bay, Calif.). . . . "Our helicopter flight to Waimea Canyon with **Papillon Helicopters** was a fabulous experience, well worth the price. They were playing Bach at full volume on the headsets as we swooped in and out of the canyon. Unforgettable!" (Bob Harrison and Hal Goodstein, Provincetown, Mass.). . . . "We suggest taking the **catamaran ride** on Poipu Beach. It costs $10 per person for half an hour of pure physical excitement. Only two passengers go out with the owner. We not only felt the excitement of riding the huge waves, but we saw a huge turtle and had a wonderful view of the mountains. A real thrill. . . . The best **snorkeling** we've ever seen—including the Caribbean—was in the little bay directly in front of the Poipu Beach Hotel. The water is a little wavy here, but if you go out in the morning, it is manageable. The fish are absolutely unbelievable. . . . There is a little market of **jewelry** vendors by the Spouting Horn near Poipu Beach almost every day. We picked up some gorgeous coral and shell necklaces of good quality at three for $5!" (Susan and Terry Young, Crystal Lake, Ill.). . . . The **Kauai Museum** in Lihue was wonderful. We stopped to take a 'quick' look around and left three hours later—and could have stayed longer" (Bart and Lynda Esterly, Capistrano Beach, Calif.).

"I would like to put in a good word for **Holo Holo Tours.** I took the Holo Holo tour to Waimea Canyon and had a most wonderful excursion. The driver went out of his way to make the experience memorable. Although I had paid for a half-day tour that did not include lunch, I was invited by this driver to join the others for a roadside lunch consisting of teriyaki steak, baked salmon, salads, and fresh fruit. I shall never forget that driver's aloha spirit" (Sheldon J. Karlan, Buena Park, Calif.). . . . "We recommend the **Kukuiolono Golf Course** at Kalahao as the best and cheapest golfing anywhere on the islands. And the scenery is beautiful too" (Ken and Dolores Dugan, Boise, Idaho). . . . "Do arrive early at **Waimea Canyon.** At 8:30 a.m. on a Saturday I shared the glorious view with only a family of mountain goats. It was a peaceful and very special moment of my vacation. At noon, when I passed the viewing point on my way out of the area, I counted eight buses in the parking lot! . . . Do take the **Fern Grotto Cruise** in the late afternoon. It's less crowded and more relaxing" (Paulette Getschman, Cudahy, Wisc.). . . . "We visited the **Rehabilitation Center for the Mentally Retarded** across the road from Coco Palms. For many reasons, going through the workshop and then checking out the gift store is a good thing to do. It enables a nonprofit enterprise with positive results to continue, the gifts are great, and the prices very good" (Ruth Hunter, Watsonville, Calif.).

"A note of caution to travelers: Our camera bag with camera equipment was stolen from our car, even though it was locked, while we watched the free Polynesian show at the Market Place at Coconut Plantation, which is held on Thursday, Friday, and Saturday afternoons between 4 and 5 p.m. Local police advise that all equipment—even in car trunks—can be a target for theft, since most people enjoy the show and thieves know they won't be returning to the car at that time" (Karolyn Fairbanks, Oroville, Calif.). . . . "Our son was the envy of all his friends after coming home with a real baby shark in a jar. He had purchased it at **Shells International** in the Coconut Plantation Market Place for $2.25" (Ingo Platzer, Omaha, Neb.).

"Yoneji's on Rice Street in Lihue is a local grocery store that carries a little bit of everything and is favored by the locals—not your usual tourist shop and a place for good buys. . . . Church bazaars not only offer good food at very reasonable prices, but they also present the visitor with an excellent opportunity to mingle with the local people. Plants, fruits, and fresh vegetables were for sale and there was also a rummage sale" (Louise Alberti, Modesto, Calif.).

"After having lived on Kauai almost two years and made a wide acquaintance among the local population, I feel qualified to tell others how to achieve a rewarding stay on the island—much more rewarding than the sterile, 'prepackaged' entertainments offered to tourists. Plan to stay a minimum of two weeks, and find a hotel that caters to the local people. Next day, explore. You can do this without a car, for a while. Find people with similar interests. Do you like to fish? Check with people at Lihue Fishing Supply. Whatever your interests are, there are people here who will enjoy sharing them with you. Photography? Hiking? See the people at the Forest Service in the state building. Ask questions. Be courteous, friendly. Talk to people—and learn to listen and to understand their slightly different way of speech. Away from Lihue there are 'mom and pop'-style grocery stores. Go there in preference to supermarkets. Learn to wear local-style clothes and especially footwear. . . . Island people are very easy to get acquainted with. Eye contact, a smile, and almost any attempt to make conversation will suffice to start an acquaintance" (David C. Moore, Phoenix, Ariz.).

"There is an undiscovered spot on Kauai called the **Pacific Tropical Botanical Garden** in Lawai, in the Koloa-Poipu Area. This is an absolute delight for garden lovers. The botanical garden's size is 186 acres. It adjoins 100 acres of the Allerton Gardens, a private estate. It was chartered by Congress in 1964; this particular site was chosen and dedicated in 1971; it is extremely well tended with a sizable staff and many volunteers. The botanical garden can only be viewed through escorted tours, which are limited and by reservation. There are two tours on Tuesday (at 9 and 10:15 a.m.) and tours on Wednesday, Thursday, and Saturday mornings at 9 a.m. More tours are planned for the future. Reservations should be made in advance by calling 808/332-8131 or 332-8901, or writing: Reservations Secretary, P. O. Box 340, Lawai, Kauai, HI 96765. The cost of the tours is $10 per person (Dimitri Moursellas, Manhattan Beach, Calif.). . . . "We had reservations to tour the Pacific Tropical Botanical Garden. We left our hotel early and it was good that we did. There are no HVB markers or signs to tell you where to turn. We finally got directions: take 53 from Koloa and turn left on Hailima Road. It was well worth the difficult time we had finding it. The tours are limited to about ten people, so there is plenty of time to stop, take pictures, and ask questions" (Mrs. Janet Bristow, Vasalia, Calif.). . . . For those who are doing a substantial amount of cooking, we suggest shopping at the **Kukuiula Store** (Jimmy's, to the locals), located on the road between Koloa and Poipu. We comparison-shopped over a several-week period at stores in Lihue and Koloa and found the Kukuiula Store the lowest overall. For liquor, we recommend **City Liquor** on Rice Street in Lihue" (Robin and Bert Brumett, Seattle, Wash.). . . . "**Wailua Falls** in Kauai—near the Fern Grotto area—are the falls you see at the beginning of the "Fantasy Island" television show. Also, some of it was filmed at Coco Palms, on their beautiful grounds in the coconut grove. . . . The torchlight ceremony at Coco Palms is still the best one to see" (Mrs. Elliot Gray, Cerritos, Calif.).

"We found the best **snorkeling** on Kauai was at the west end of the **Poipu Beach Hotel,** about 15 feet offshore, in two or three feet of water. Ke's Beach was not nearly as good" (Betty and Bud Eldon, Los Altos, Calif.). . . . "Poipu Beach is excellent for snorkeling—and bad for serious ocean swimming because of the volcanic rock on the ocean floor close in. It's easy to bruise and cut yourself because it is shallow for quite a way out" (Jack and Doris Toussaint, no address given). . . . "Please warn people of the coral and rock on the ocean floor of Poipu Beach in front of the Sheraton Hotel. It's very hard to see and several people cut themselves. Fins are a necessity" (Beth and Chris Baines, Chicago, Ill.). . . . "We were somewhat disappointed in the bird life until we got to **Kokee Camp.** We stayed overnight in one of the cabins, had a very active morning bird walk—this was the best birding area we saw—and spent a very informative afternoon in the museum there" (Linda Adair Wasson). . . . "Serious hikers should take along Craig Chisolm's **Hawaiian Hiking Trails** (Touchstone Press, 1976), $5.95, which is carefully researched and has reproductions of relevant topographical maps with the trails drawn in, as well as detailed verbal directions. Several hikes on Kauai are described. We took two and found the book most helpful and accurate" (Dan Keatinge, M.D., Santa Monica, Calif.).

"If readers decide to hike on the Kalalau Trail, beware of theft in cars left there My gas tank had been drained when I got back and I knew of people whose windows had been smashed. . . . Campers and backpackers should be sure to bring all supplies; there are few camping supply stores in Kauai. Campers should be warned that Kauai's camping permits must be purchased in Lihue; it's $3 a night for county campgrounds. I strongly recommend taking a look at the campgrounds before getting a permit" (Linda Haering, Santa Rosa, Calif.). [*Authors' Note:* There have been recent reports of vandalism and rowdyism at Kauai campgrounds.]

"We have just returned from an extensive trip to Kauai and we implore you to inform your readers of the dangers of the **Haena-Kalalau** 11-mile trail. Despite the fact that we are experienced hikers, in good shape, and had thoroughly read all available material on the trail, we were not prepared for some of the narrow ledges along the cliffs. In three or four places between Hanakoa Shack and Kalalau Valley, the trail narrows to one or two feet with a sheer drop of over 1000 feet to the rocks below. Children and hikers who are not in the best of shape should not venture past Hanakoa. Locals told us that some hikers had been killed along the trail, but we did not confirm this. A good, safe, round-trip hike would be from Haena to Hanakoa Stream (just past Hanakoa Shack). This can be done in one day. Hanakoa Stream runs rapidly, and it is a good place to fill your canteen and cool your feet. Along the 11-mile trail, there are only three places to camp: Hanakapiai Beach, two miles in; Hanakoa Shack area, six miles in; and Kalalaua Beach, 11 miles in. The Hanakoa Shack area is hot, humid, and loaded with mosquitoes. The entire trail takes at least seven hours, and more like ten hours if you rest along the way. Hikers should not be on the trail after dark" (Bob Rose, Ted Januszewski, and Reed Snyder, Oxon Hill, Md.). . . . "We spent two days making day hikes along the **Na Pali Cliffs** trail. It is a fairly easy foot trail extending 11 miles along this most magnificent coastline. Of course, it isn't necessary or even advisable to go the full 11 miles; a two-mile walk to spectacular **Hanakapiai Beach** is really quite negotiable for all but the lame and infirm, providing they have stout footgear. This means heavy-soled tennis or deck shoes or 'desert' boots, and hopefully, socks. The trail is not difficult, but it is rocky, and slippery in spots. A word of warning about the beaches along the trail. Those who are very modest or upset by nudity should be forewarned: the mode of dress at these beaches is undress. Hanakapiai has a marvelous stream flowing right into the ocean at the beach, so after a swim in the invigorating surf, one can rinse off in cool, fresh water. It is also a good idea to bring a canteen or a cup as the walker will get thirsty. There are a number of little springs that are safe to drink from along the way, but we wouldn't drink from the larger streams without using Halazone tablets" (Joann Leonard, Los Angeles, Calif.).

"If you approach **Moloaa Beach** from the northernmost of the two roads, watch for the derelict church on your left. Interesting photographs are possible here" (Fred C. Nelson, Plymouth, Mich.). . . . "While driving to Kokee, I picked up a young man with a tight necklace who said that he lives in the wild part of Kauai, which he reached by a two-day hike from Kokee Camps. He gets supplies by boat. I asked him if he owned land there, but he said the land didn't belong to anyone. I asked him why he lives there. He said, 'Because it's like the Garden of Eden, with fruits and flowers' " (Mark Terry, Honolulu, Hi.).

"We drove on from Kalalau Lookout for about one mile of paved road to the **Pau O'Kila Lookout,** about a third around the canyon rim, from where the view of the ocean far below is completely different. The trail to **Pihea,** along with four other trails, starts from here" (Mrs. Parker Hollingsworth, Pacific Grove, Calif.). . . . "**Polihale Beach** is not good for swimming, but it's a marvelous picnic-sketching-walking beach. There are long vistas of white sand, cliffs coming down to the ocean, fire pits, picnic pavilions—and no one there. Camping is allowed farther on. Go past Kekaha on Route 50; when 50 goes left at the intersection, turn right on the narrow, paved road. Turn left at the HVB marker that reads 'Polihale Sacred Springs,' and follow the dirt road through the sugarcane field five miles to the beach" (Mrs. J. C. Chognard, Menlo Park, Calif.). . . . "**Polihale Beach** is very beautiful, a nice place for picnics, sunning, or just loafing. But we've been hit by sand fleas every time we visited it. Every year it's a toss-up—do we suffer the bites or forget it all. The beauty of the beach always wins out. There's some nudity at the far end of the beach near the cliffs, but it can be avoided by staying near the main section" (Michale J. Toennessen, Bellingham, Wash.).

"Catholics visiting Lihue should not miss the 9 a.m. Sunday Mass at the **Immaculate Conception Church,** a mile out of town past the hospital. We heard the most magnificent choir at a folk mass there, consisting of 50 voices, five guitars, two electric guitars, two ukuleles, and an organ, singing Hawaiian tunes given religious lyrics" (Ray Van Vorse, Maynard, Mass.). . . . "We rented a VW camper that came with a tent for our boys. This is the best way to travel on Kauai, for you can stay at many of the beautiful beaches and parks, and if the north side gets rain you can easily drive to the sunny side. We went in winter, and the weather was often stormy and windy. We met many lovely Hawaiians at the parks nd were invited to join in a local feast and party; it was the highlight of our trip. w loved **Polihale Beach:** good puka hunting, good wading, and our favorite camping each—and it's the warmest one in winter" (Phyllis Montague, San Diego, Calif.).

Chapter XIII

THE ISLAND OF HAWAII

1. Hilo
2. Between Hilo and Kona
3. Kailua-Kona

EVER HEAR OF a tropical island with black beaches, snow-capped mountains, cedar forests, and one of the largest cattle ranches in the world? This is **Hawaii,** twice as large as all the other Hawaiian Islands combined (4030 square miles), the orchid capital of America, and the residence of Pele, the goddess of volcanoes, who still stages some spectacular eruptions every couple of years. The islanders usually call it the Big Island, sometimes the Orchid Island or the Volcano Island; all the names are appropriate and all suggest part of the fascination of this astonishing continent in miniature. To know the 50th state, you must know the island of Hawaii.

Like all the neighbor islands, the Big Island is more expensive for the budget tourist than Oahu; nevertheless, you should be able to stay fairly close to your $35-a-day budget. Your car rental—unless it's split up three or four ways—is your biggest expense here, for driving distances are sizable, especially from one side of the island to the other (about 100 miles).

Hawaii is about 200 miles southeast of Honolulu, and either Hawaiian, Mid-Pacific, or Aloha Airlines will take you to **Hilo** on the east or to **Kailua-Kona** on the west in roughly half an hour. You can also fly directly to or from Hilo or Kona from the West Coast (United is the only carrier bringing in the big jets from the mainland at this writing). Which city should you choose as your first stop? We've done it both ways and our considered opinion is that it doesn't make a particle of difference. Let your itinerary and the airline schedules—the ease with which you can make connections to the next island on your agenda—be the determining factor. Hilo, the only real city on the island and the second largest in our 50th state, is the takeoff point for the imposing Volcanoes National Park and the lava-scarred Puna area. Hilo has been experiencing a slump as of late, but it still has its own gentle charm. Kona is fishing and the beach. From either you can drive across the island and see all the sights. We prefer to stay in one hotel in Hilo and one in Kona, but it's possible to make one side of the island your base if you don't mind long drives (please limit your driving to daytime hours for safety!). Read up on the hotels, restaurants, and nightlife in each area in this chapter, the particular sights in the next, and you'll know just where you want to stay and for how long.

U-DRIVES: Most agencies on the Big Island offer a flat rate with unlimited mileage—you buy the gas. You have your choice of the trusty and popular inter-island outfits like **Holiday Rent-A-Car Hawaii, American International, Budget,** etc., whose main offices are all in Honolulu (see Chapter IV, "Transportation Within Honolulu," for details), or local agencies like **Phillip's U-Drive** (tel. in Hilo, 935-1936; in Kona, 329-1730) which offer rates beginning at $16.95; and **Liberato's U-Drive** (tel. in Hilo, 935-8089; in Kona, 329-3035), whose cars can begin at $17.95 in winter, $14.95 in summer. These prices are for economy, standard-shift cars, mostly Datsuns and Toyotas. Automatics and American cars are higher. You can make advance reservations by writing to any U-Drive company in Hilo but there are usually plenty of cars available (except at the peak tourist seasons), and the budget-minded driver can often do best by some careful on-the-spot shopping.

Keep in mind that the U-Drive business is a highly competitive one here as elsewhere, with rates in constant flux; you may be able to get a flat rate or a better deal than you expected just by asking. Also note that there is usually a ferrying charge of $15 to $25 if you drive a car from Kona to Hilo, usually no charge if you take it from Hilo to Kona and leave it there. Which may be a good reason for putting Hilo on your itinerary first and then flying out of Kona to your next port-o'-call.

1. Hilo

ARRIVAL IN HILO: You'll know why it's called the Orchid Island as soon as you arrive at General Lyman Field: rain may be helping those orchids to grow. But don't despair; it's just a "Hawaiian blessing" and probably won't last long. Nobody in Hilo lets a little drizzle interfere with comings and goings. There's no public transportation into town, so pick up your car or get a cab (about $4) to take you to your hotel.

CITY BUSES: After talk of it for many years, Hilo finally has a mass transit system. Having a car is, of course, more convenient, but if you want to reach local destinations by bus, be advised that the bus operates Monday through Saturday, costs 50¢ per ride, and can be picked up at Mooheau Terminal on Kamehameha Avenue, Kaiko'o Hilo Mall, Hilo Shopping Center, Lyman Museum, and Rainbow Falls, among other points. You can see many of the major sightseeing attractions by taking the **Hele-On** ("Moving On") Banyan Shuttle bus, which makes five round trips daily. The cost is 50¢ per ride, or $2 for an unlimited pass. Pick up a bus schedule at your hotel, or phone 935-8241.

There is also a bus that goes cross island, from Hilo to Kona, leaving at 1:20 p.m. and arriving in Kona at 4:30 p.m. (The other way around, it leaves the Kailua-Kona Post Office at 7 a.m., arriving in Hilo at 10:10 a.m.) The cost is about $4 one way; for information call the **Mass Transportation Agency** at 935-8241 or 961-6722. The Hawaii County Transit System (same phone numbers) runs one bus a day to the museum at Volcanoes National Park, leaving Hilo at 2:30 p.m. Bus schedules are sometimes available at the terminal or at the **State Visitor Information** booths in the airport. The **Hawaii Visitors Bureau** is in the Hilo Plaza Building, Suite 104, 180 Kinoole St. (tel. 961-5797). Mrs. Lei Branco is the helpful lady to contact.

HOTELS IN HILO: Every now and then you come across a little hotel where you know you could comfortably settle down for a long, long time. Such a place is the **Dolphin Bay Hotel,** at 333 Iliahi St., Hilo, HI 96720 (tel. 935-1466), in a quiet residential neighborhood of Hilo, that's just a four-block walk to town. The 18-studio unit meanders in and out of a lush tropical garden resplendent with papayas, breadfruits, bananas, and the like; it's the only hotel we know where you are invited to step right outside your room and pick your breakfast! The rooms are all modern, quite large, and nicely furnished, with full kitchens and large tub-shower combinations in the bathrooms. The carpeting in the rooms extends into the bathrooms and even up to the front and back doors—yes, most rooms have both. The standard studios, which rent for $20 single, $27 twin, sleep one or two comfortably. The superior studios, usually with a twin and a double bed (plus a built-in Roman-style tub!), are larger and can easily sleep three; these are $35 double. There's also a marvelous honeymoon room with an open-beamed ceiling and a large lanai for $35; and some really spacious one- and two-bedroom apartments, perfect for families, are $45 and $49 double, $7 for each extra person. Favorable weekly and monthly rates are available. Since the hotel is near Hilo Bay, a cooling breeze keeps the units pleasant all year long. Manager John Alexander dispenses the same kind of warmth and hospitality that have made this one of our best island finds over the years. Write in advance, if you can, since the number of guests who come back each year—many from Canada and the Midwest—keeps this place hopping. Lots of readers hurrahs for this one, even though there is no pool (see the Readers' Selections, ahead).

Hilo's original budget hotel, the Palm Terrace, which had fallen below our standards for some years, has been taken over by a new management, and things are going nicely. Now it's called the **Lanikai Hotel,** 100 Puueo St., Hilo, HI 96720 (tel. 935-5556). There are just 31 rooms here, about six of which have small refrigerators with hotplates. The hotel has been repainted, carpeted, and good second-hand furniture from the late, lamented Kona Inn has been used for the refurnishing. Rooms are a decent size, with orange or mustard spreads, nice prints on the wall, open closets, showers (but no tubs), no telephone, radio, or TV. Since it is just above the highway, there might be some traffic noise. Since the hotel does not require a lease, people looking for a place to live in the area find this a good choice for a month or two. Rates go from $15 to $18 single, $18 to $21 double, daily; $75 to $95 single, $90 to $100 double, weekly; and $200 to $240 single, $240 to $265 double, monthly. Ting Hao Chop Suey, a delightful little local restaurant (see ahead) is on the premises, as is Lopaka's, a friendly little lounge.

The **Hilo Hukilau Hotel** (tel. 935-0821), near Hilo Bay, has long been a pleasant place to stay. The local branch of the kamaaina-owned Hukilau Hotels (there are others on almost all the islands) has attractive rooms with lanais, TV, and phones—rooms that look out either over the freshwater swimming pool or lush tropical gardens. The lobby is decorated with lauhala-weave walls, bamboo, and tapa cloth. Wood fenceposts, Polynesian murals, and tikis permit you to forget the mainland. There's a dining room and cocktail lounge. Singles go for $27, $32, and $36; twins for $31, $35,

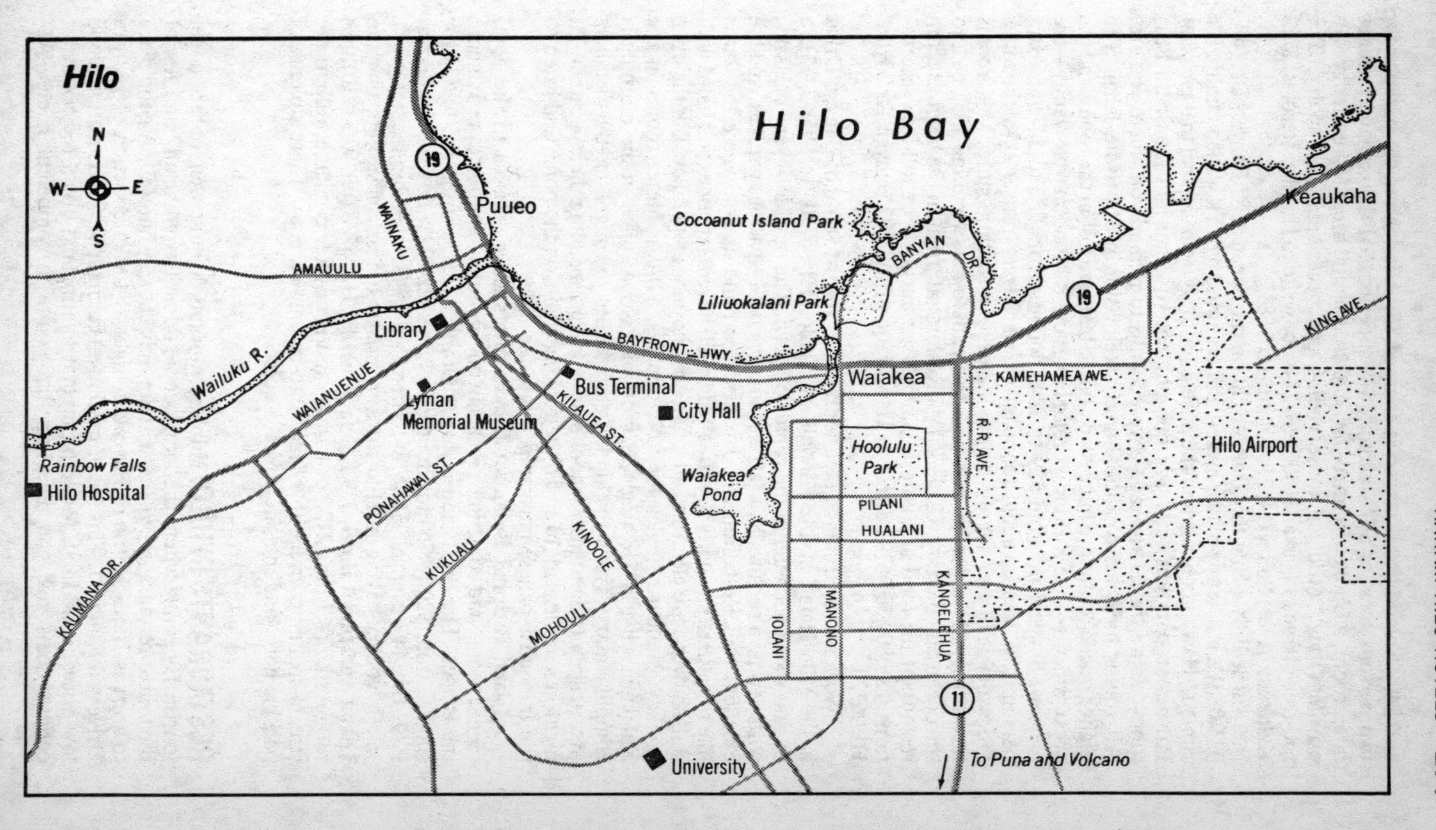
Hilo
N
W
E
S
Hilo Bay
19
Puueo
WAINAKU
AMAUULU
Cocoanut Island Park
BANYAN DR.
Keaukaha
19
Liliuokalani Park
KING AVE.
Library
BAYFRONT HWY.
Wailuku R.
Waiakea
KAMEHAMEA AVE.
WAIANUENUE
Bus Terminal
Lyman Memorial Museum
KILAUEA ST.
City Hall
R.R. AVE.
Hilo Airport
Hoolulu Park
Rainbow Falls
Hilo Hospital
PONAHAWAI ST.
Waiakea Pond
PILANI
HUALANI
KINOOLE
KUKUAU
KAUMANA DR.
MOHOULI
IOLANI
MANONO
KANOELEHUA
11
University
To Puna and Volcano

and $40. An additional person is charged $5. A hotel-and-car package for two persons goes for $47 standard, $49 superior, $51 deluxe, and includes hotel room, a Budget Rent-A-Car, and continental breakfast each day. An excellent buy, although housekeeping can occasionally be spotty. The toll-free phone to Hawaii is 800/367-2344, or write to Hukilau Resorts, 2222 Kalakaua Ave., Suite 714, Honolulu, HI 96815.

Uncle Billy's Hilo Bay Hotel, right on the ocean at 87 Banyan Dr. (tel. 935-0861), is a happy place, owned and operated by a Hawaiian family. It's run on "Hawaiian time" and the pace is leisurely; you can feel that pleasant Polynesian paralysis setting in the moment you step into the South Seas lobby, with fishnets and tapa-covered walls to remind you where you are. All rooms have air conditioning and television plus private lanai. The higher priced rooms are huge: two double beds are lost in the room, and the appointments—like a Princess telephone and a broad marble vanity—are elegant. Singles run from $29 to $44, doubles from $32 to $47; an extra person is $7. Inquire about room and car packages, from $49. Kitchenettes are available in superior and deluxe rooms for an additional $5. Most rooms face a tropical fish garden that leads to a path to the swimming pool, next to the ocean on Hilo Bay. Uncle Billy's Restaurant, right in the hotel, is a fun restaurant for food and entertainment (see ahead). For toll-free reservations, call 800/367-5102 direct to Hawaii, or write to 87 Banyan Dr., Hilo, HI 96720.

Worlds away from the pleasantly hokey tourist world of Banyan Drive is the **Hilo Hotel,** at 142 Kinoole St., Hilo, HI 96720 (tel. 961-3733), a businessperson's hotel in the center of town. The outside is very pleasant, with new lava-rock walls, a large swimming pool, spacious gardens, and the excellent Fuji Restaurant for Japanese food and drinks, where the locals like to gather. The hotel rooms, all of which have telephones and baths with stall showers, are clean and adequate, but nothing at all fancy. But the price is okay: standard singles for $14; doubles, $18; or larger rooms in the Kalakaua wing at $18 single, $20 double. Kona coffee in the morning is complimentary. This is the kind of place where you might find the members of a neighbor island high school baseball team spending their vacation. At night, it's so pleasant to sit on the rocking chairs on the porch and listen to the tranquil Japanese music piped into the lobby.

Island Bed and Breakfast Hawaii offers an alternative to the hotel scene: rooms and sometimes meals in charming private homes throughout the islands. The Big Island is no exception. Rates go from $15 to $35 for singles, from $20 to $60 for doubles. Phone 822-7771, or write to them at P.O. Box 449, Kapaa, HI 96746. There is a $5 membership fee per year.

If you're staying in Hilo for a month or longer, make note that the **Lehua Apartment Hotel,** 349 Lehua St., Hilo, HI 96720 (tel. 935-1210), has roomy studios from $242 per month, and is just a five-minute walk to the stream-spanning bridge that leads into downtown Hilo. There's plenty of parking here, and the side street is quiet.

RESTAURANTS IN HILO: Hilo's restaurants do quite well for the budget tourist. By eating where the local people do and avoiding all but a few of the tourist restaurants, you can eat not only cheaply but well. A good place to start is **Ken's House of Pancakes,** right at the intersection of Banyan Drive and Route 11. This is a prime budget eating spot: good location, good low prices, good food. Modern pinpoint lighting and bright-red booths or counter seats give you a feeling that you're in competent hands. At breakfast, pancakes start at $1.90, waffles at $2.95. Once you start adding berries to the batter and meat or whatever on the side—the varieties and combinations seem endless—prices go up; but they manage to stay around the $3.20 mark. Good news: Lunches and dinners (which include a tossed green salad, potatoes, and hot roll) are the same price. They begin with filet of mahimahi at $6.10 and move up through such choices as veal cutlet, prawns, fried chicken, to a broiled steak at $7.75. Pop by from midnight until 6 a.m. and you'll be treated to an early brunch—all the pancakes, plus imaginative omelets with an international touch, in the $3.65 to $5.50 range. Our kind of place.

Also our kind of place is **Smitty's,** in the Kaiko'o Hilo Mall, a brightly modern cafeteria with orange Formica tables, wooden chairs, and murals on the wall. Although Smitty's makes very good pancakes and waffles (most $2.75 or under), the star here is authentic Chinese food, served deli-cafeteria style. Order one of the $3 plate lunches or dinners and you'll get a choice of any two of the nine tasty entrees (roast duck, shoyu chicken, beef broccoli, etc.), plus rice or noodles. For $3.50 you can have three entrees. Smitty's stays open until 8:30 p.m., and the prices do not go up. This place caters mostly to local people and is usually thronged with busy shoppers, so you know the values have to be good. Even if you're not eating here, you might want to stop by for some of those luscious Chinese cookies—spice cake, wedding cake, black bean cake—in the window.

Over at **Kow's Won Ton and Noodle House** in the same Kaiko'o Hilo Mall, the Smitty's management concentrates in depth on luscious Chinese offerings. Surroundings are similar to Smitty's—orange Formica and captain's chairs—and the atmosphere is no-nonsense, so you can concentrate on steaming platters of, say, boneless chicken fritters with pineapple or beef with oyster sauce or crisp wonton vegetables with crispy noodles. Price range is about $2.75 to $5. Chinese pastries here too. Local people love this one. Open from 10 a.m. until midnight, Monday to Thursday, until 3 a.m. on Friday and 2 a.m. on Saturday, Sunday until 3:30 p.m.

Mexican food served in a clean, healthful (there's a health-food store adjoining), and cheery atmosphere is what you'll find at **Norberto's El Café** at 11 Waianuenue Ave. Prices are modest: complete dinners run from $6 to $7.50, and along with entrees like burritos rancheros, enchiladas grandes, or rellenos tampico (cheese-stuffed fried chilis) come soup, a good green vegetable salad, refried beans, rice, corn chips, and salsa. Vegetarian ingredients can be substituted in any dish. Kids have their own special plate at $4.50, which makes Norberto's a good family choice. Try the guacamole to start, the chocolate cream pie to finish. Margaritas can be had by the glass or pitcher. Norberto's serves dinner from 5 to 9:30 p.m. Monday through Saturday. Closed Sunday.

For a true taste of Japan, the place to go is the **Nihon Cultural Center,** newly opened at 123 Lihiwai St. (tel. 989-1133), overlooking Hilo Bay and lovely Liliuokalani Gardens. Authentic to the last detail, the Nihon Cultural Center houses an art gallery, a traditional tearoom, an auditorium for cultural events, and at the heart of it all, a restaurant where traditional Japanese chefs ply their art. Of course there is a sushi bar—the menu describes these dainty morsels of fish and rice as "health foods"—and a dining room for regular Japanese meals. Sashimi, tempura, and tonkatsu lunches, as well as hanami bento (a one-tray luncheon) run $8; beef curry and pork cutlet curry each cost $4. Dinner specials, from $7 to $13, include sukiyaki, a broiled fish meal, a broiled eel meal, and shabu shabu, a fanciful beef dish. Traditional Japanese soup, pickled vegetables, fruits, and rice dishes accompany the meals. Of course there's sake or Japanese beer to wash down your meal. You can take all three meals at Nihon, beginning with breakfast from 7 to 10 a.m., lunch from 11 a.m. to 2 p.m., dinner from 5 to 9 p.m.; the sushi bar is open from 5 to 10 p.m. Reservations are advised.

You can relax in a very pretty setting at the **K. K. Tei Restaurant,** 1550 Kamehameha Hwy. between Hilo and the airport (tel. 961-3791). K. K. stands for the late K. Kobata, who was Japanese, and the food is mostly Japanese, with some American specialties. Lunch is an especially good buy; our favorites are the complete Japanese ozen lunches, served on a lacquered tray. With your under-$5 main course—perhaps tonkatsu or beef teriyaki—come miso soup, rice, pickled vegetables, mukozuke, raw fish or salad, and tea. Seafood salads, sandwiches, and noodle dishes are also available. Dinners are a bit more expensive but still a good buy: beef or chicken sukiyaki on the Japanese menu is about $8.50. American-style seafood and steak dishes start at around $8. If there are at least six of you, call for reservations to sit in one of the pretty ozashiki rooms; from here you'll see the authentic Japanese rock garden and pool. The bar begins dishing out free pupus from 11 a.m.

There's another K. K. restaurant that you should know about. At 413 Kilauea Ave. (tel. 935-5216), next to the Safeway, is **K. K.'s Place,** a Japanese-American fast-food operation, sparklingly clean, and offering tasty plate lunches—with two entree choices like fried fish, chicken hekka, pork cutlet, and meat cutlet—for $3.50. Meals are served day or night at the same price. A good place to remember whenever you feel hungry and in a hurry. You'll usually find Mrs. Kobata at the Place, and son Paul at the K. K. Tei.

We can't resist a Mexican meal at **Reuben's Mexican Food,** 336 Kamehameha Ave., across from the waterfront (tel. 961-2552), every time we're in Hilo. Recently moved to spacious quarters (after a tiny storefront restaurant and more crowds than it could handle), Reuben's is run by Reuben and Sue Villanueva (he's from Mexico, she's from Hilo), and his brother Vicente, who is the fantastic chef. The new place has a pretty pink curtain up at the window and paneled brown walls, otherwise minimal decor (brown plastic tablecloths, orange chairs, a few murals on the walls), but there's plenty of breathing room between the tables, and the cooking is what counts—so good you'll want to come back for more. Our appetizer of nachos ($2.40) was hot and tasty; so was our chicken sour-cream enchilada combination plate for $5. At least 19 combination plates, which include beans and rice, run $5 to $7. À la carte orders, like the tasty bean and beef burrito that we enjoyed, with stripped beef, frijoles, chilis, grated cheese, lettuce, and guacamole in a flour tortilla, are around $3.25. You'll find lots of local families here, savoring the great food and low prices. Open daily from 10 a.m. to 11 p.m., except Sunday from noon to 4 p.m., same menu all day.

Local people insisted we have a meal at **Ting Hao Chop Suey,** in the lobby of the Lanikai Hotel, 100 Puueo St. (tel. 935-9697), and we're glad we did. Not many tourists know this place yet, but the Chinese population has discovered it, and you can often see Mercedeses and other fancy cars parked here, even though the surroundings are simple—you sit at stone tables in the partially open lobby of a very plain hotel—and the prices are very modest. What brings the gourmets here is the cooking talents of Ting Cheng, the master chef, recently arrived from Taiwan, whose repertoire includes some 200 banquet dishes; he cooks Peking, Mandarin, Szechuan, and Cantonese style, so there is quite a variety on the menu. Here's your chance to try pot stickers, those tasty dumplings that are both steamed and fried (on one side), at $3. Our party dined mostly on Mandarin cuisine: Phoenix shrimp (like shrimp toast with a whole shrimp on top), at $5.50, and the shredded pork with fungus and golden egg, at $4.50, were both outstanding. The most popular items on the menu are the shredded pork with garlic sauce (watch out, it's hot!) and the eggplant with garlic sauce, each $4.50. We started our meal with a superb tureen of hot-and-sour soup. While specialty dishes may go up to $5.50, most of the menu is very inexpensive: combination lunch and dinner plates are $2.50, and hearty enough to fill you for many hours. Chef Ting is assisted in the restaurant by his family—three sisters and their husbands, and children of various ages—some of whom will usually be scurrying around to see that you are happy. Service is not totally professional, but warmth and willingness go a long way. Ting Hao is open Monday through Saturday from 11 a.m. to 8:30 p.m., closed Sunday.

Another local place where you can't go wrong is the ten-table **Tomi Zushi,** 68 Mamo St., where $5 to $6 buys you a good Japanese dinner, in the company of lots of local people who are heartily lapping up the food. There is no attempt at decor here: walls are institutional green, and tables are just tables: you come for the food. Here's what the average $5 to $6 buys: a choice of any two main courses like fried shrimp Tokyo style, shrimp tempura, wok sashimi, beef or pork or fish tempura, accompanied by soup, pickled vegetables, rice, and tea. Plate lunches are $3.50. Plan on this when you want to eat quickly, as it's no place to relax and visit. Taki Zushi closes at 8 p.m., and is open every day but Wednesday.

In the Waiakea Kai Warehouse at 100 Kanoelehua St. (tel. 961-5884), you'll find **Apple Annie's,** of the popular island chain. Like all Apple Annie's, it's artfully decorated: this one has attractive antiques, old street lamps, wrought-iron chairs, and a cobblestone floor up front leading to partitioned booths that give a feeling of privacy. And like all Apple Annie's—perhaps even more so—it has a huge menu, offering the literal something for everybody, from pizzas to prime ribs. Favorite choices are the Mexican specialties (combination plates about $5.25 to $7), plenty of omelets, super salads, pizzas, burgers, and luncheon specials for under $6. There's a 26-item salad bar for $7.95. Bar prices are reasonable and ladies usually get an extra little treat on Wednesday.

Like to dine at one of the best restaurants in town for just $5.95? You can do so at **Rosey's Boathouse,** 760 Piilani St. (tel. 935-2112), if you pass up the seafood and meat specialties and concentrate instead on the copious salad bar, as we recently did. This is one of the better salad bars around, with cottage cheese, sprouts, mixed beans, a good green salad, fresh pineapple spears, etc. Rosey's rates high for atmosphere (panels of rough-hewn woods, crystal chandeliers, black leather booths, subdued nautical decor), service by the friendly young waiters, and very good food. If you're in the mood for a splurge, meat and fresh local fish seafood dishes go from $8.95 to $16.95. Specialty of the house is chilled mainland beef, and all broiling is done over a Ki'awe charcoal fire. Rosey's is open for dinner only, from 5:30 to 10 p.m. every day; and the bar does not close down until 1 a.m. Entertainment nightly, with a musical mix that goes from jazz to contemporary Hawaiian. Reservations are suggested.

Tou Inn, 172 Kilauea Ave. (tel. 935-6030), is one of the newer Chinese restaurants in town, and it's a favorite with local Chinese families. The place is attractively decorated, the Cantonese-style food is quite good, and the price is right—most dishes are $2.50 to $4, and that includes the likes of lemon chicken, crab roll, mahimahi in a sweet-and-sour sauce, and shrimp fritters with vegetables. A six-course dinner for two is just $9. Open daily, 11 a.m. to 9 p.m.

Sun Sun Lau, 1055 Kinoole (tel. 935-2808), is a large, family-type place that also serves pleasing Chinese meals. The pineapple shrimp done with sweet-and-sour sauce, $4.25, is quite good. Even less expensive choices might be watercress pork or beef bitter melon, each $3.50. Lunch specials, which include chop suey, tomato beef, spare ribs, and crisp wonton, run $3.50 to $4.50. While you're here, take a look at the fascinating seed and candy section. Cracked seed, a Chinese specialty, has become popular all over the 50th state and here you see one of the best selections anywhere: salted lemon seed, cherry seed, shredded mango, even something called footballs, which are made out of olives! The restaurant is open Friday, Saturday, and Sunday until 9 p.m., every other day (closed Wednesday) until 8 p.m.

We wouldn't go so far as to call **Sachi's Gourmet,** 250 Keawe St. (tel. 935-6255), a gourmet restaurant; rather, it's a simple place popular with local Oriental families happily eating away at the few booths separated by bamboo slats and the tables in the center. The food is tasty, and a few dollars buys a lot (three of us ate dinner here for $14!). We ordered oden, a seaweed-based broth with chicken, fish, tempura, tofu, and daikon; with it came a plate of barbecued beef, various pickled vegetables, a bit of sashimi, delicious miso soup, rice, and tea—not bad for $5.20. Our oyako donburi—chicken, onion, and egg, served over rice—plus extras, was also good at $4.75; and there are various makunouchi (combination plates) starting at $5.20. At lunch, American dishes join the menu, and prices are lower, around $3.35 to $4.65. Open for breakfast from 8 to 10 a.m., for lunch from 10 a.m. to 2 p.m., for dinner from 5 to 9 p.m.

Local people consistently praise **Leung Chop Suey House,** 530 E. Lanikaula (corner of Kaneolehua Avenue, Route 11). Wooden tables with bamboo chairs, Chinese lanterns and Chinese pictures on the walls, and fresh flowers on the tables are the background for very good food served cafeteria style. There are about eight different Oriental selections daily, like beef and broccoli, sweet-and-sour pork, chicken, duck, and egg foo yong; any two will cost you $2.90; any three are $3.25; and four run $3.65. Lemon chicken, boneless chicken with oyster sauce, and a seafood plate at $3.55 to $5.50 are treats; cake noodle is a specialty. Leung's is open Wednesday through Monday from 9 a.m. until 8:30 p.m., but closed on Tuesday.

Jimmy's Drive Inn, at 362 Kinoole St. (tel. 935-5571), is a popular local place offering some of the best prices in town. The "drive inn" is misleading; you don't eat in your car but at clean chrome tables or at the counter. Japanese meals go from $4.40 to $4.75, and there are daily dinner specials like chicken-katsu, beef stew, fish tempura, breaded scallops, and captain's platter, which go from $4.25 to $5.35, quite a bargain considering that they are accompanied by rice, vegetables, tossed salad, dessert, and coffee or iced tea. On the regular menu, there are at least a dozen dishes between $4.25 and $5.50, and that could include breaded mahimahi, butterfish with lemon, and liver and bacon, $5 for breaded tenderloin cutlets and grilled island pork chops. There are daily lunch specials at $3.85 to $4.85, regular meals up to $5. Open from 8 a.m. to 10 p.m., daily except Sunday.

Eating at the Hotels

The popular **Hukilau Restaurant** in the Hilo Hukilau Hotel, Banyan Drive, is managing to hold the price line on three good meals a day. They have a lunch special every day at $2.55, which includes entree, salad bar, rice or potato; and at least a dozen à la carte entrees (filet of mahimahi steak, stuffed tomato salad, etc.) are just $2.85 to $5. Dinner features two menus, seafood and regular. The seafood dinners start at $6.50 for fried oysters or mahimahi, and there are half a dozen choices like salmon steak or rainbow trout for $6.95 to $9.95. On the regular dinner menu there are at least eight choices—including calf liver, fried chicken, pork chops, and teriyaki steak—under $6. Main dishes come with soup of the day and salad bar. Breakfast here is a treat; we always have either the pineapple hotcakes or french toast with macadamia nuts for $2.40 (price goes up 15¢ after 10:30 a.m.). The dining room is soft and pretty, and the staff has plenty of aloha.

You may not be able to afford the luxury rooms at the Hilo Hawaiian Hotel, 71 Banyan Dr., but their restaurant, **Queen's Court** (tel. 935-8361), is another story. A good time to try this room, with its monarchy decor and panoramic waterside view, is at lunch. Then you can have a hot sandwich like the fishburger melt (with cheese on a sesame bun) or the french dip prime beef) or a Reuben sandwich from $4.25 to $5.75. Salads like chef's salad bowl are $4.75. If you're willing to splurge a bit, come back some evening for an excellent buffet meal. It's a Hispanic-Italian-Portuguese buffet on Monday for $11.25; a seafood buffet with fresh fish prepared to order on Tuesday for $14.95; an international buffet with typical Japanese food, including sake, on Wednesday for $11.25; a prime rib buffet on Thursday for $14.25; a seafood buffet on Friday for $14.95; a steak buffet, including champagne, on Saturday for $14.25; and a Hawaiian buffet, with beer, on Sunday for $11.95. Some 15 salads accompany the main dishes, and there are at least ten desserts, all made in the hotel's own kitchens. Italian wines and Mexican beers are available. Live harp music accompanies dinner and brunch. The $10.75 Sunday-morning champagne brunch is also a treat.

For a traditional Japanese meal—and for an excellent bargain as well—don't miss the **Restaurant Fuji,** in the Hilo Hotel, 142 Kinoole St. (tel. 961-3733). This is one of those gracious, relaxed places where you can really get comfortable; you can sit either at the tempura bar (where you watch your dishes simmer and sizzle), at the comfortably spaced tables in the dining room, or at tables with hibachi grills overlooking the pool. The hotel is owned by Japanese interests and caters to a Japanese clientele, so you can be sure the food is authentic. At lunchtime recently, we sampled the very good butterfish ($6.40), and the barbecued chicken and egg ($5.50) with green salad, soup, vegetables, rice, and tea. There are a number of dinners under $8—yosenabe teishoku for $7.90 and pork ginger teishoku for $7.50, to name two you might want to try.

Meals on the Run

One of the most popular coffeeshops in town is **Dick's** in the Hilo Shopping Center, a lively local place with sporting pennants on the walls. Many of our readers write to recommend it. The menu is varied, with prices ranging from about $2.65 for ground beefsteak to $5.35 for New York–cut steak; pork chops are $3.05. Seafood specials are mostly under $4.50. All entrees come with soup or salad, rice or potatoes, rolls, and butter. For lunch, sandwiches go from $1, and there are five weekday lunch and dinner specials at $2.25: shoyu chicken, turkey, roast pork, fresh corned beef and cabbage, meat loaf; steak and rice is $2.35. Breakfast is inexpensive too: you could have a complete breakfast of deep-fried mahimahi, with toast, and hash browns or rice, for $1.95. Dick's serves all three meals, Monday through Saturday; Sunday it's breakfast and lunch only.

The Kaiko'o Hilo Mall, behind the government buildings, is a boon for hungry, hurried budgeteers. In addition to Smitty's and Kow's Won Ton (see above) there's the **Kaiko'o Coffee Shop,** small and cozy with deep-cushioned booths, stained-glass lamps, a pleasant atmosphere. Breakfast features extra-thick french toast with meat and coffee for $1.99. Some of the other specialties are homemade New England clam chowder, a very good chili, honey chicken, and hearty sandwiches, all under $3.65. Complete dinner too, $3.95 to $5.95. . . . The **Sure Save Snack Bar and Bake Shop** at the Mall is also good to know about, for its 75¢ teriyaki beef on a stick, tacoburgers at $1.60, and seafood platters and veal cutlets at $2.75. . . . Lunch specials in the $2 to $4 category are featured at **Mr. Ben's,** the coffeeshop adjacent to the Ben Franklin store here.

Just across from Kaiko'o Mall, at 804 Kilauea Ave., you might want to remember **Kawika's** if you're planning a picnic lunch. It's a real deli-type place where you can pick up pastrami, corned beef, turkey, or ham with sides of potato salad, pickles, and the like, at reasonable prices.

Whenever we'd drive by **Cafe 100,** 969 Kilauea, opposite Kapiolani School, we'd notice huge lines of local people at the windows of this popular drive-in. We joined them one day and found out why: it's hard to spend more than $2.95 for a full hot lunch. Fried chicken, beef stew, breaded mahimahi, and teriyaki steak are all served with rice and vegetables. The natives swear by the local favorite: loco moco, a hearty meal of a hamburger patty and fried egg on rice, topped with brown gravy; it's $1.25. They even have loco moco T-shirts! Chili with rice and sandwiches of all kinds start at 65¢. Good to remember when you're in a hurry and the travelers' checks are running low.

McDonald's of Hilo, at the corner of Haili and Ululani Streets, is an enclosed, air-conditioned restaurant, with tables and swivel chairs, hanging plants, and tiled floors. The Big Mac is $1.45, a cheeseburger is 80¢, and saimin is 95¢. . . . You'll find a familiar **Dairy Queen** on Wainuenue Street, just up from Kinoole Street: hamburgers are 80¢; hot dogs go for 70¢; shakes and malts are $1.10 and $1.55. There's another Dairy Queen on Banyan Drive at the Kamehameha intersection. . . . You'll find salads, spaghettis, sandwiches, and, of course, those thick and crusty pizzas waiting at **Pizza Hut,** 233 Kilauea. . . . **Wendy's** and **Burger King** have opened just one block from Kaiko'o Hilo Mall, at 348 Kinoole St.

Although we weren't much taken with the shops at the **Waiakea Kai Shopping Plaza,** 88 Kanoelehua, there is a collection of fast-food places here that could prove useful. Nicest of all is a big, family-style **McDonald's,** with Tiffany-type stained-glass dividers, lamps, booths, a cheerful atmosphere, and the usual low prices. . . . **Magoo's Pizza** has sandwiches and baked chicken dinners in addition to tasty pizza pies, plus beer, a jukebox, booths, and a moderate-to-high noise level. . . . Not only can you get all kinds of frozen yogurts and toppings at **Ono Yogurt,** but also some pretty good sandwiches like chicken, tuna, pastrami, corned beef, salami, and cheese, from $1.50 to $1.85. And their $1.92 breakfast specials—quiche, toast, and fruit cup or croissant, juice, fruit, and coffee—are deservedly becoming very popular. . . . **Robert's Bakery** can supply you with their wonderful Portuguese sweet breads or their famous macadamia and coconut "cookies from Hawaii," packed ready to carry or mail.

In the mood for a coffee and a danish, sandwich or hot dog, or a luscious ice-cream soda or sundae? Join the guests of the lovely Naniloa Surf Hotel on Banyan Drive at the cute little **Ice Cream Factory,** a snackbar on the lower level, where you can relax in soda chairs and lounge seats. Open from 11:30 a.m. to 7 p.m. daily.

More ice cream treats and other goodies await you at the **Old Fish Market Sandwich & Ice Cream Shop** at 89 Lihiwa, in the same building as the Suisan Fish Market (where early risers can watch the local fishermen bring in their daily catch between 7:30 and 8 a.m. and the late sleepers can get very fresh fish, whole or cleaned, for great sashimi or a cooked feast). The best part about this bright and clean-looking ice-cream shop with its ice-cream chairs and tables is the Sundae Bar, outrageously tempting with at least seven toppings to choose from as you build your own sundae: one scoop is $1.35; two scoops, $2.15. The homemade ice cream offers tempting island flavors like pineapple, coconut, and macadamia nut. Sandwiches here are built by price: choose one meat for $2.05, two meats for $2.15, or three meats for $2.25 served on french rolls. Very nice.

If you're driving Volcano Highway 11 and need a good sub or pizza, stop in at **Snappy's Family Restaurant,** 421 Kalanikoa St., in the industrial area just off the highway. Subs are $3 to $4.25; pizzas begin at $3.30. They also offer chicken, ribs, and pork chop dinners at reasonable prices. Monday through Friday, between 11 a.m. and 2 p.m., there's an all-you-can-eat buffet, with salad bar, chicken, ribs, rice, and garlic bread. Delivery service is also available to hotels. Note that it's right next to Hilo Airport Flowers, a good stop for inexpensive fresh anthuriums.

For a yummy natural snack, remember **Hilo Natural Foods,** 306 Kilauea St., the big health-food store in town. Inside, you'll find **Hilo Natural Foods Kitchen,** with table and counter seating, as well as take-out. Daily offerings include veggie burgers, avocado bean burritos or tostadas, vegetarian chili, and homemade soups, plus hot lunch specials like quiche, baked stuffed potatoes, and enchiladas. Prices range from $1.75 to $3.50. There is also fresh lemonade, carrot juice, smoothies, and incredibly delicious fruit freezes. Stop in on a Friday for their special clam chowder. Food is served only on weekdays, from 10 a.m. to 3 p.m., but there are sandwiches, salads, and other treats in the cooler on Saturday. Closed Sunday.

Lovers of freshly brewed coffee, espresso, and heavenly desserts have *bearly* been able to wait for the openings of **Bear's Coffee,** adjoining the Most Irresistible Shop in Hilo at 110 Keawe St., but it's here at last. This cozy and cheerful little café with its marble-topped tables and hand-stenciled walls is just the place to sample 12 kinds of coffee drinks, as well as indulge in the likes of chocolate eclairs, coconut macaroons, croissants (plain and cheese), pies, cakes, and quiches, plus Bare Bear's Brownies and Frosted Bear Brownies. You can also buy fresh roasted coffee beans by the pound to take home. House coffee is 65¢ per cup, and pastries are about 90¢ to $1.35. Bearvo! Open from 8 a.m. to 4 p.m. Monday to Saturday; closed Sunday.

THE NIGHT SCENE IN HILO: Nightlife is quieter than it used to be in Hilo, with the closing or conversion into condominium apartments of several major hotels. However, there's still enough to keep you busy making the rounds of some of the favorite places.

For an inexpensive, family-style evening in Hilo, try **Uncle Billy's Restaurant** at the Hilo Bay Hotel. The hotel and restaurant are owned and operated by Uncle Billy and his Hawaiian family, and each night at 6:30 and 7:30 there's a free hula show, a totally nonslick, warm-hearted revue. Helpings from the large salad bar are included with dinners. Most meals are priced from $5.95 to $9.95; the menu includes fish catch of the day, island steaks, shrimp, teriyaki chicken, and daily chef's specials. The restaurant has been redecorated in South Seas decor with shells and large grass chandeliers, and is more attractive than ever.

The other dinner shows in Hilo will all be more expensive, but if you can forgo the shows for just drinks and music, there are a number of good spots around Hilo. It's no cover, no minimum, and complimentary pupus (from 5 to 7 p.m.) at the Hoomalimali Bar of the **Naniloa Surf Hotel,** with Roy Anthony playing from 9 p.m. to closing, for listening and dancing. The Naniloa Surf also goes in for disco in its Polynesian Room, from 9 p.m. on, Thursday, Friday, and Saturday. There is a cover charge plus a two-drink minimum. . . . The plush **Hilo Hawaiian Hotel** has a Menehuneland Lounge with the little people scrambling all over the walls. Most nights, it's Hawaiian music beginning at 5 and contemporary music from 8:30 p.m. until closing, no cover, no minimum, and some of the best beer prices in town. Free pupus are served from 4 to 6 p.m. . . . The nicest place for handholding and a quiet drink is **Rosey's Boathouse,** 760 Piilani St. Entertainment varies nightly from a four-piece jazz group to a solo guitarist playing old-style Hawaiian music. All drinks are poured with premium liquor, and start at $1.85. . . . There's no entertainment and scarcely any atmosphere at the **Hukilau Hotel** bar, but always a local crowd full of fun. A no-nonsense female bartender dispenses drinks at some of the lowest prices in town. . . . A lively crowd hangs out at **Apple Annie's** at the Waiakea Square Warehouse, where the prices are low and you can treat yourself to a Kona MacRoyale (Kona coffee liqueur and macadamia-nut liqueur with hot coffee and whipped cream, $2.50). On Friday it's live Hawaiian music; on Saturday, contemporary music.

If you're still game for more, drive nine miles out of town to Keaau and the Keaau Shopping Plaza, where you'll find the **Keaau Korral,** with high-decibel disco action. Perhaps for safety's sake, the office of the local chiropractor is right next door. . . . When the bars close down, you can get some nourishment over at **Ken's House of Pancakes** (see above), where they serve pancakes and omelets through the wee hours of the morning.

2. Between Hilo and Kona

In our next chapter we'll describe the drive from Hilo to the resort center of Kona, a trip you should take. Right now we'll tell you about some hotels and restaurants at which you might stop en route.

HOTELS AND RESTAURANTS ON THE NORTHERN ROUTE: Forty-four miles north of Hilo on the northern, or Hamakua Coast route, and not far from the cattle country of the Parker Ranch, is the venerable **Hotel Honokaa Club,** Honokaa, HI 96727 (tel. 775-0533). A favorite with businesspeople and hunters for some 50 years now, this very plain hotel has low-priced rooms: $8 for a single with adjoining bath, $12 for a double, $18 for a double with private bath, $20 for a triple. Wall-to-wall carpeting and

TVs have been added to all the rooms with private bath. The hotel's inexpensive restaurant and bar are very popular with the local people. If you're driving through on a weekday, between 11 a.m. and 2 p.m. you can get a big meat-and-cheese hero, with salad bar and beverage, or plate lunches, between $3 and $4.

From Honokaa, it's 15 miles on Highway 19 to Kamuela (or Waimea), heart of the Parker Ranch cattle kingdom. The best budget place to stay in this deliciously cool mountain town is the **Kamuela Inn** (tel. 885-4516), a modest but pleasant place. The 19 rooms have showers, but no baths. Singles go for $20; doubles, $26; kitchenette units, $32; and full kitchen units, $35. Scenic grounds (there are "bottle brush" trees with red flowers that really look like bottle brushes) just outside the hotel and a friendly management are pluses here. Write to Kamuela Inn, P.O. Box 1994, Kamuela, HI 96743. There are restaurants nearby and good swimming 12 miles away at Samuel M. Spencer Beach Park, near Kawaihae.

A newer, more spacious and expensive accommodation in this area is **The Lodge** (tel. 885-4100), Parker Ranch's modern ten-unit motor hotel within walking distance of the Parker Ranch Center and all its sightseeing, shopping, and eating facilities. Horseback riding and golf are nearby, some excellent beaches a reasonable drive away. Each room boasts quality furnishings, attractive decor, a beamed ceiling, and a fully equipped kitchenette. From this cool, 2500-foot elevation you have a view of rolling green meadowlands and mountains. Singles are $33; doubles (king-size beds) are $38; twins (two queen-size beds) go for $43. Reservations advised: The Lodge, P.O. Box 458, Kamuela, HI 96743.

On Kawaihae Road across from Edelweiss you'll find the **Great Wall Chop Suey** (tel. 885-7252), which looks like nothing at all from the outside, but is really quite attractive inside, with a large mural of—you guessed it—the Great Wall of China. Most dishes are between $3.95 to $4.50, and a filling lunch plate, laden with chicken, rice, mixed vegetables, egg foo yong, and sweet-and-sour mahimahi, is $3.95, served only on weekdays. The dinner plate, $8, includes soup of the day, pineapple chicken, beef with oyster sauce, fried rice, and eggroll.

The place for a big splurge in this area is the **Parker Ranch Broiler** (tel. 885-7366), sitting majestically at the head of the Parker Ranch Visitor Center. Its interior is plush turn-of-the-century saloon vintage. Dinner is a pricey affair, in the $11 to $16 range, but the roast beef dinner, served with bread, salad, vegetables or rice, is very popular at $13.75, regular cut. Lunch offers hot sandwiches and dishes in the $3 to $7.50 range, and there's an excellent luncheon buffet at $5.95 from 11 a.m. to 2 p.m. Dinner is on from 5:30 to 9 or 10 p.m. On Sunday, brunch only.

Another pleasantly splurgy stop here might be at **Edelweiss,** on Kawaiaihe Road (tel. 885-6800), a new restaurant with a continental flair. This is a homey place with a European country feeling, and chef Hans Peter Hager's cuisine does not disappoint. Bratwurst and sauerkraut, a mere $3.95, is very popular at lunch, as is the Puu Haloa ranch burger at $5. Dinner starts with a light meal at $5.75; most entrees range from $9.50 (for roast duck) and go up to $28 (for a rack of lamb for two). The Edelweiss specialty of sauteed veal, lamb, beef, and bacon with pfifferling (wild mushrooms from Europe) is $15 and very tasty. You can start your meal with appetizers like melon prosciutto and crouton champignons, and end with a satisfying Bavarian cream pie or Bavarian cassis (each $2) or simply fresh Kamuela strawberries. Edelweiss serves daily from 11:30 a.m. to 2:30 p.m. and from 5:30 to 9:30 p.m., Sunday until 8:30 p.m.; closed Monday.

A deliciously inexpensive favorite lunch stop nearby is **Homer's** (on the left side of the road on Route 19), a wholesome-looking, spanking-clean establishment with polished wooden benches and seats, and a few tables on the porch outside. The self-service menu is simple but delicious, and everything is homemade. Every day they have Portuguese bean soup and corn chowder for $1.50 (the latter was thick and chunky, delicious). A cup of soup, plus their salad with a choice of gourmet dressings (bleu cheese, house, vinaigrette), makes a satisfying lunch for $2.50. Or have a sub or a sandwich plate with tossed greens or potato salad; these run from $2.50 for egg salad to $3.75 for a Buffalo Bill—a fanciful combination of roast beef, cheese, sprouts, and creamed horseradish. Honey lemonade and apple juice supplement the usual beverages, and desserts like French cheesecake with strawberries or chocolate Bavarian cream pie are special.

For a meal on the run in this area, you can join the local families at the **Kamuela Drive-in Deli,** next to the Parker Ranch Center. It's a plain, unpretentious spot where you can eat either in your car or at the indoor tables. The prices are low and the portions big. They open at 5 a.m. for breakfast, when they cook up a storm of hotcakes, and bacon and eggs. But have the Portuguese sausages instead; they're the real thing. The rest of the day they serve sandwiches like roast beef, $1.75 to $1.95 (no doubt from the Parker Ranch); and hot platters like curry or beef stew or teriyaki steak for around $3. The only thing high here is the elevation—almost 3000 feet.

You can get other quick meals in this area at **Massayo's,** across from Edelweiss, a luncheonette with hearty local specialties like curry stew, loco moco, and pigs' feet soup, from $2.75 to $3.75; at the **Wild Horse Pizza** (on the Honokaa side of town), with good salads, sandwiches, and French onion soup, as well as pizza pies; and in the Parker Ranch Mall at **Kamuela Delights Ice Cream Shop,** which also serves salads and sandwiches in addition to ice cream treats, and at **Mauna Kea Pastry Shop,** which has pastrami, ham, and tuna sandwiches under $3 and decadent pastry goodies!

Prefer a light, natural-food snack? **Rainbow Mountain Natural Foods** (next door to Kohala Coast Properties) has a small snackbar in the midst of what is mostly a health-food store: soups, smoothies, salads, chili, and the like, are made only with natural ingredients and are all inexpensive. Try the soup and cornbread at $1.95, the huge garden salad at $3, or a chapati, burrito, or carrot juice shake. There are sandwiches too, and always daily lunch specials. You take your food to the benches outside.

If you branch off from Waimea for an excursion into the Kohala district, you might want to experience a bit of local color by staying overnight in Hawi at the **Old Hawaii Lodging Company,** where a new management has freshened up the rooms a bit and taken over from the venerable Luke's Hotel (tel. 889-5577). Nothing fancy at this simple local hotel, but then neither are the rates: $17 single, $20 double, $26 triple. There's a 10% discount on two rooms sharing a bath, and on weekly rates. **Kohala Inn,** right on the premises, offers burgers from 95¢, lunch and dinner specials at $3.50 to $4, and T-bone steaks from Parker and Kahua ranches at $6.50. You're at 500 feet in altitude here, so expect warm days and cool nights. Write to Old Hawaii Lodging Company, P.O. Box 308, Hawi, HI 96719.

A new hotel in this area offers possibilities for a retreat-like vacation. The **Hawaiian Plantation House,** also known as **Aha Hui Hale** (tel. 889-5523), was once a sugar plantation manager's home; now it has been converted into a guest house with just four two-bedroom suites, each of which includes a living room, bathroom, and color TV. Guests share the communal living and dining rooms and kitchen. There's a pool out on the tropical grounds. Rates per suite are from $50 for one or two persons, $10 for each additional occupant. For reservations and information, write to the owners in, yes, Alaska: Aha Hui Hale, P.O. Box 2118, Fairbanks, AK 99707; or locally, to P.O. Box 10, Hawi, HI 96719.

Since the construction of the Queen Kaahumanu Highway it is now possible to drive along the seacoast from the Mauna Kea Beach Hotel to the Kona Airport and on to Kona. And it is also possible for those who want to experience the charms of this area to stay in their own luxury apartment just three miles past the glorious resort (and near the new Sheraton-Waikoloa) at the **Puako Beach Condominiums,** as isolated a retreat as one could want. These condominiums are deluxe apartments with complete kitchen, large living room, and all the amenities of home, including electric appliances and a color TV; each is furnished differently by its owner. There's a large swimming pool as well as good ocean swimming nearby. Rates for one-, two-, and three-bedroom apartments run from $42 to $46, $67 to $71, and $81 to $86. Weekly and monthly rates on request. Not inexpensive, but a bargain compared to the rates at Mauna Kea! Reservations: Puako Beach Condominiums, 3 Puako Beach Dr., Kamuela, HI 96743 (tel. 882-7711).

Should you want to wait until you get to Kawaihae, on Route 19, to make your lunch stop, we have a neat suggestion. Right across from the deep-water harbor, looking like something out of a Somerset Maugham novel, is the **Harbor Hut** (tel. 882-7783). Walk past the nondescript front, a liquor store and fast-food take-out, and you'll find a bamboo-walled garden restaurant, thickly overhung, with a real boat (the *Harbor Hut Cruiser)* in which local types will be lounging about. Relax, have something cool to drink; this is the tropics the way it used to be. Local people swear by the food, and the price is right. Full meals include a catch of the day at $5.95, a seafood plate at $6.95, and dishes such as chicken teriyaki, chicken Cordon Bleu, and the like, most between $4.50 and $8.95. Good sandwiches, salads, burgers, and desserts too—carrot cake, cheesecake, and homemade apple pie. There are lots of imported beers and an extensive wine list. Harbor Hut serves all three meals, and is open from 6:30 a.m. to 9 p.m. every day.

HOTELS AND RESTAURANTS ON THE SOUTHERN ROUTE: Driving the southern route (Highway 11) from Hilo to Kona, or vice versa, you have several delightful possibilities if you want to spend the night. First there's the famed and venerable **Volcano House,** now under Sheraton management, right on the brink of Kilauea Crater, where the ancient kahunas (priests) once gathered to make sacrifices to Pele. Standard rooms are $36 single, $39 double; superiors are $43 and $46; and deluxe accommodations, with a view of the crater, are $47 and $50; an extra person is charged $10. Where else can you take a bath with live volcanic steam? A breakfast here in the early-morning mountain air, seated at a table near the window where you can gaze right into the volcano as you savor your ono french toast and poha preserve, is one of the special treats of Hawaii. Reservations: Volcano House, Hawaii Volcanoes National Park, HI 96718; or phone Sheraton toll free at 800/325-3535.

Any former Boy Scouts or Girl Scouts in the crowd? You might try one of the ten cabins at **Namakani Paio Campground,** in Volcanoes National Park, three miles beyond Volcano House. Designed for those "who desire true outdoor living," they are of Polynesian design, frame construction, and they're furnished with a double bed, two double-decker bunks, and your own lanai. You share a common bathhouse with your neighbors. The tab is minimal: about $16 per night for up to four people. Write to Volcano House (the concessionaires) at Hawaii Volcanoes National Park, Hawaii, or call them at 967-7321.

You have several interesting choices of atmosphere for lunch on this trip. The traditional lunch stop here has long been **Volcano House** (tel. 967-7321), noted for its lovely buffet—a tempting array of salads, fruits, and main dishes, served with beverage and dessert, in a spectacular setting overlooking Halemaumau Crater. The cost is under $7. The dining room at Volcano House has been attractively enlarged and now seats 400 people, so there is no longer a crowding problem as in the past, when tour buses disgorged their hungry mobs all at the same time. Busy, but very pleasant.

Two miles south of Volcanoes National Park entrance, watch for the sign that reads **"Volcano Golf and Country Club"** (tel. 967-7978). Here's where local people take visitors to avoid the Volcano House crowds. The clubhouse, open to the public, has a rustic modern dining room with glass windows, huge ceiling, and wood-burning fireplace. Their hamburger, considered by some as "the best hamburger in the State of Hawaii," *is* good, and so are the homemade kettle soup, and the Reuben and french dip sandwiches, which go from $3.95 to $4.50. There are usually several specials at $4.95, like honey-stung chicken, chili and rice, and Salisbury steak. Open most days from 7:30 a.m. to 4:30 p.m. only; on weekends, it turns into the International Sportsman Restaurant at dinnertime and entrees go way up, from $9.95 to $16.95. Soup and salad bar at $6.95 would be the only item in our budget range.

Less polished than the country club, but with all the fun of a real general store and the people who frequent it, is the Volcano Store in Volcano Village. Make your way up to the big ramshackle porch, half of which is given over to the simple tables and chairs of the **Volcano Country Kitchen** (tel. 967-7223). Nothing fancy about this place, but if the sun (or rain) is beating down on you, you'll be quite cozy at the little indoor café with wooden floor and walls, sunlight slanting in off the roof, and works by local artists on the walls. You place your order up front, then sit down and wait. Although the staff has not mastered the art of speedy short-order cooking, they do well enough, and the food is good and reasonable; specialty burgers like "The Eruption" (with cheese and salsa and a choice of soup and salad at $4.95) are tasty, and so is the mahimahi on sweet bread sandwich at $3. You can nibble on a chili dog, have a smoothie or a "Volcano Melt," or come back for dinner, when entrees like ground round, chicken, and mahimahi, served with choice of rice or potato and soup or salad, go from about $4.75 to $5.80. Open daily, 8 a.m. to 7:30 p.m.

Inside **Volcano Store** itself, you might want to pick up some cone sushi or hard-boiled eggs or other munchies to nibble on as you drive along. This is one of the best places to buy orchids and anthuriums, which can be mailed anywhere. To get to Volcano Store, reached before Volcanoes National Park, stay on Highway 11 until Haunani Road; then go straight ahead to the stop sign, and it's right there.

On your way to the Puna area of the Big Island (see "Seeing Hawaii," Chapter XIV), you'll pass through the little town of Keeau. An enjoyable new restaurant here is **Mama Lani's,** in the shopping center (tel. 966-7525). Actually, Mama Lani and Papa Lani are a young couple with four active children. They've created a charming, two-story Mexican restaurant with a warm feeling and a clean, crisp look: dark-wood tables, white stucco walls, tile floors, archways, and orchid-lined window sills. For lunch or dinner you can have specials like tacos or enchiladas for $3.75, chimichangas for $5.50, burritos for $5.25. Or create your own plate for $7.50. Desserts like chocolate cheesecake and Mexican flan are homemade, and they boast the "best margaritas around." Mama Lani's is open Monday to Saturday from 11:30 a.m. to 9 p.m., and for Sunday brunch.

In about ten miles, you'll come to another little town, Pahoa, about a 40-minute drive from Hilo. The most enjoyable restaurant here is **Miguel's Place,** across from Gallery Unique (tel. 961-9729), a dimly lit, atmospheric Mexican restaurant with dark wooden tables. There's a homey, pleasant atmosphere here, and it's popular with local artsy types for luncheon and dinner platters from $2.50 to $5.50, luncheon tacos at $1.20 to $1.75, and Mexican breakfast specials at $2.25 to $3.35. Doors close at 9:30 p.m. Next door is **Trade Winds,** a pleasant coffeehouse and bakery, featuring coffee and espresso, cakes, ice creams, smoothies, and shakes.

An older restaurant in town is **Pahoa Chop Suey,** a few hundred yards on the Hilo side of Pahoa, which has a clean, tiny (ten-table) eat-in section and a busy take-out window from which issues forth an endless variety of tasty Cantonese Chinese dishes, all from $3.25 to $4.50. Open Tuesday through Sunday. Its next-door neighbor, the **Circle J Restaurant,** features Magoo's Pizza (very tasty), foot-long subs, reasonable breakfasts (pancakes begin at $1), and reasonable dinners too: oven-baked half-a-chicken at $4.25, and a mahimahi fish dinner at $3.95. Honey shakes are 95¢; banana or carrot cake is 45¢. Good places to stop on your way back from the Black Sand Beach at Kalapana.

Just about halfway between Hilo and Kona, you come upon an oasis in the lava flows. This is the beautiful town of Naalehu, the southernmost community in the United States. To us, stopping off here at the **Naalehu Coffeeshop** is one of the highlights of the drive, since it's much more than an eatery, and Roy and Arda Toguchi—the people responsible for the restaurant/gift shop/art gallery in this historic old building—are more than just proprietors. The Toguchis are artists in their own right, and they number the greatest among their friends. You'll see Roy's artistry in his fabulous bonsai garden (which he'll be delighted to show you), in his mural of Mauna Loa behind the counter, and on the handmade menu. The same fresh and delicious foods are available at both lunch and dinner. We've never been disappointed in the fish, the beef cutlet, or the teriyaki beef barbecue. The entrees come with salad, vegetable, bread, rice or potatoes, and the total cost is $7.95; other entrees go to $9.95. Don't miss the homemade banana cake. The sandwiches are good too: the Hawaiian fishburger, the Farmer John baked ham, oven-baked turkey sandwich, and others are all served with relishes and salad, $3.25 to $4.75. After your meal, check out the art gallery and Menehune Treasure Chest, and browse among the local handicrafts. If it's anytime between September and March, be sure to see the flaming sphere poinsettias, blooming out back. If you approach from Naalehu, make your third left when you pass the school; from Kona, turn right when you pass the theater. The coffeeshop is just 100 feet on the left-hand side, across from the shopping center—where, incidentally, Roy's brother runs the **Green Sands Snack Bar,** a little take-out place for plates like chicken hekka, pork tofu, chopped steak, and chili, from about $1.95 to $4.25.

Your last chance for a bite to eat for the next two hours' drive from Hilo to Kona is at the **Ocean View Restaurant** (tel. 929-9985), up on a knoll that affords an expansive view of the shore to South Point. Watch for the 76-mile marker. New owners have taken over here recently, and we've had enthusiastic reports on Gerry (who does all the cooking, specializing in home-baked pies), and his wife Mary Ann, hostess and waitress. Readers Mark and Kay Irwin of Phoenix, Arizona, commented on their delicious breakfast of "fluffy omelets with cheese, homemade biscuits and homemade hash browns for $3.50. Coffee was special, made with rain water as they have a water shortage here." Entrees like roast beef, pork teriyaki, or spaghetti average $4.25; hot meat and fish sandwiches run from $2.95 to $4.95. French dip is a specialty at $3.95. At dinner, entrees run from $4.95 for meat loaf, chicken breasts, or shoyu chicken, up to $9.50 for sirloin or tenderloin, all served with soup or fruit cocktail, rice or potatoes, salad, and beverage. The bar provides a mai tai at a reasonable $2. Open from 9 a.m. to 7 p.m. Tuesday to Saturday, to 2 p.m. on Sunday; closed Monday.

3. Kailua-Kona

The Kona Coast is to the Big Island what Waikiki is to Oahu—the beach resort. Unlike Waikiki, though, it still has a small-town charm. Once the playground of the Hawaiian alii, Kona lures deep-sea fishermen (its marlin grounds are the best in the Pacific), families, anyone looking for relaxed, tropical beauty. A handful of hotels offer pretty decent budget rates.

HOTELS: A neat bargain, right in the center of town on Alii Drive, is the **Kona Bay Hotel,** a sister establishment to Uncle Billy's Hilo Bay Hotel, and run by the same family management. Kimo and Jeanne Kimi are the friendly folks in charge here. They have landscaped their newer hotel (formerly the garden wing of the Kona Inn) with bridges and ponds and a Polynesian longhouse restaurant surrounding a large circular swimming pool. All rooms are of comfortable size, smartly done up in green, gold, and brown color schemes, with Polynesian prints on the walls, air conditioning, bathrooms with full tubs and showers, and good-size lanais. Most have refrigerators, and many have two double beds. And all this comfort is at a realistic price: singles, $30 to $43; doubles, $37 to $46. Add $7 for an extra person, $5 for a studio kitchenette. Car, room, and breakfast packages are available at good rates, starting at $49 for two. For reservations, phone direct to Hawaii, toll free, 800/367-5102, or write Kona Bay Hotel, 87 Banyan Dr., Hilo, HI 96720.

If you want more luxury and still a good price, try, also on Alii Drive, the **Kona Islander Inn,** a rambling, plantation-style complex that boasts some of the nicest hotel rooms in the area, plus a pool set in a glorious garden and a barbecue pit out by the pool. All rooms here are identical, but the price is $38 for garden or poolside rooms, $46 for ocean-view rooms. Third and fourth persons in the rooms are not charged extra. Rooms are beautifully decorated in earth tones, with rich orange carpets; all have two twin beds, plus a queen-size sofa bed, showers (no tubs), and a private lanai furnished with a table and two director's chairs. There's a coffeepot and refrigerator in every unit, and for an extra $5 you can command the kitchenette package of hotplate and utensils. For reservations at Islander Inn, call, toll free, 800/922-3311, or write to Islander Inn, 75-5776 Kaukini Hwy., Kailua-Kona, HI 96740 (tel. 329-0711).

A good choice, smack in the center of town, is the **Kona Hukilau** (tel.

329-1655), whose sister hotel we've told you about in Hilo. This is a very similar place, with most of the rooms overlooking the large lovely pool. The rooms are smartly furnished, have twin- or king-size beds, and from many, you can see the harbor across the road. Or you may just want to laze on the sundeck, which looks out on Alii Drive and the harbor, and watch the world go by below you. Standard, non-air-conditioned rooms are $27 to $30, single or twin; it's $32 and $35 for superior rooms. For $36 and $40 you're in the garden wing, which provides both air conditioning and TV. An extra person is $6; there is an additional charge of $3 per room from January 1 through April 1. An economical package plan includes hotel room for two, a Budget Rent-A-Car, and continental breakfast, at rates of $47 standard, $49 superior, $51 deluxe, for one or two persons. For reservations, write Kona Hukilau Hotel, 2222 Kalakaua Ave., Suite 714-F, Honolulu, HI 96815, or call, toll free, 800/367-2344.

The same Hukilau management is also in charge at the 240-unit, five-story **Kona Seaside Hotel** (tel. 329-2455). Although it's off the main drag, at the intersection of Kuakini Highway (Route 11) and Palani Road (Route 19), it's just a parking lot away from the shopping and restaurant excitement of Alii Drive. Size is the byword of the Seaside—large rooms, spacious lanais, and an extra-large pool. Blue is the theme of the well-appointed rooms, all of which are equipped with television, air conditioning, and switchboard-serviced telephones. Prices are excellent, considering the comfort. Rates are $29 and $36 standard, $35 and $40 superior, $39 and $44 deluxe. For a similar car package as above, the rates are $50, $55, and $60 (rates subject to slight increase). Extra persons are charged $6 each. Write to them at Kona Seaside, 2222 Kalakaua Ave., Suite 714-F, Honolulu, HI 96815; or call, toll free, 800/367-2344.

In a garden setting overlooking the ocean, a bit away from the bustle of Alii Drive and very close to the Kona Hilton, is the petite **Kona Tiki Hotel** (tel. 329-1425), a longtime budget favorite in Kona. All the rooms have private oceanfront lanais looking out on the blue-green pounding surf (and it really does pound—noisily—against the sea wall). The ocean is great for fishing and snorkeling; there's a freshwater pool for gentler swimming. So popular has this small, unpretentious hotel been over the years, that its rooms have seen a great deal of use; at the time of our last visit, owners Mr. and Mrs. Garrette L. Matlock had completed a renovation, with new furnishings, ceiling fans, and a small refrigerator in every room, even those without kitchenettes. And since they are old friends of this book, they have advised us that they will give guests who write directly to them and bring this edition a discount of $2 a day from the regular prices of $27 single or double for a standard room, $30 for a room with a mini-kitchenette, $5 for each extra person; maximum of four in a room (and that's a bit small, except for a very close family). Prices may be subject to change. Friendliness abounds at the Kona Tiki; in the morning you can help yourself to Kona coffee and doughnuts; it's the kind of small hotel where guests usually get to know each other. You can drive from here to the center of town in 3 minutes, or walk it in 15 minutes. For reservations, a month in advance usually, two months in advance in busy seasons, write: Manager, Kona Tiki Hotel, P.O. Box 1567, Kailua-Kona, HI 96740. Specify first and second choices on rooms with or without kitchenette; very few kitchenettes are available. Minimum stay is three days.

Condominiums are very big in Kona these days, and surely one of the nicest is the **Sea Village,** an idyllic spot overlooking the ocean just outside of town at 75-6002 Alii Dr. This is a large resort complex, with a tennis court, a swimming pool, and Jacuzzi whirlpool bath on the premises, good snorkeling off the rocks in front of the hotel. Living quarters are outstanding: each apartment is beautifully furnished, ultra-spacious and luxurious, with huge living rooms, one or two bedrooms, shiny modern kitchens fitted with every appliance including dishwashers, washer-dryers, and refrigerators with automatic ice makers. Bathrooms are lovely, and there is ample closet and storage space, weekly maid service, private lanais. Although rates here are higher than our usual budget ones, if you come during off-season (April 16 through December 15), you can get a one-bedroom garden apartment for two persons for just $38; it's big enough to sleep four, at $6 per extra person. A two-bedroom apartment for up to four persons is $54; it can sleep six. Ocean-view apartments go up to $48 and $66; oceanfront apartments even higher, to $54 and $72; high-season rates add $6 more per unit. For reservations, write to the Sea Village Condominium Resort, c/o Paradise Management Corp., Kukui Plaza C-207, 50 S. Beretania St., Honolulu, HI 96813 (tel. 538-7145); or call, toll free, 800/367-5205.

Thirteen miles south of Kailua, on Highway 11—and 1400 feet high in the coffee country—is the place where you'll find the cheapest accommodations in the Kona area, the **H. Manago Hotel** in the village of Captain Cook (tel. 323-2642). This family-run hotel was founded in 1917, and the old rooms show their age; they're very, very plain. Singles are $13, doubles are $15, and triples run $17, and you share the bathrooms. This is for those who don't mind roughing it. The new wing, however, is quite another story; the rooms have private baths and lanais, are modern and comfortable, and overlook a lovely court and gardens; they rent for $18, $19, and $21 single; $21, $22, and $24 double. It's delightfully quiet and cool here throughout the year. The hotel restaurant is a favorite with local people for its home-style Japanese and American cooking; breakfast starts at $3.50, lunch and dinner about $5 to $8.25 (a typical meal is beef or fish with three kinds of vegetables, and beverage). And incidentally, the three-story frame building looks down the foot of the mountain to Kealekekua Bay, where Captain Cook met his end. The hospitable owner, Mr. Manago, advises reserving about three weeks ahead in season, two weeks other times. Address: P.O. Box 145, Captain Cook, Kona, HI 96704.

RESTAURANTS: You won't break the budget by eating at the **Spindrifter** on Alii Drive (tel. 329-1344), and you'll be treated to some great views along with the good food; since the rustic building is right on the water, you can watch the crashing sea from your table. Dinner is an attractive package that includes an appealing salad bar and crudités of fresh cauliflower and broccoli for dipping (among other items), plus hot bread and butter. Salad bar alone is about $5.95. We had enough to eat even before they brought our main courses, chicken and mahimahi, each $9.95. Other seafood and meat entrees run higher. Lunch also features a salad bar, sandwiches, and a few Mexican specialties. Locals claim Spindrifter's terrific omelets make it the best breakfast place in town. Drinks are special here too, especially during Happy Hour when mai tais are only $1.25.

Every time we dine at the **Ocean View Inn,** just north of the Kona Hukilau on Alii Drive (tel. 329-9988), we realize why it has survived and thrived for so many years while other newer, flashier establishments come and go. It's a big, comfy place, nothing fancy, the view across the road is ocean all the way, the tables are filled with local residents, and the waitresses are oldtimers who know their trade. Best of all, it can always be counted on for a generous, inexpensive, and delicious meal, either American or Chinese. And it has a wide variety of Chinese vegetarian dishes that are surprisingly delicious. Vegetarians bored with yet another salad bar had best make tracks for this place. Dishes based on vegetarian beef and tofu run from $2.75 to $3; the sweet-and-sour crisp vegetarian wontons rank with the tastiest Chinese food anywhere. Dinners have to be the best buy in town: they include soup or fruit cup, rice or mashed potato or fries, green salad (with a choice of dressings, including bleu cheese), tea and coffee. At a recent meal we dined on broiled ahi (the fish of the day), and for the same $5.95 could have had broiled ono, breaded mahimahi, salmon steak, or butterfish. There are at least 18 other choices between $4.95 and $8.25, including corned beef and cabbage, fried chicken, and roast pork with apple sauce. And there are over 80 Chinese dishes beginning at $3; a Chinese plate dinner is $4; roast duck and roast chicken are $4.25 each. Lunch is also a good buy, with many hot plates to choose from: shoyu chicken, teriyaki steak, from $3.95 to $4.50. These are served with rice or potato, salad, and beverage, as are the dinner entrees also. Breakfast too, starting at $1.50 for two eggs, $3 for eggs and Portuguese sausage.

So you want to live the good life dining at the **King Kamehameha Hotel** restaurants? Treat yourself to a big-splurge Sunday brunch, held every week between 9 a.m. and 1 p.m. in the hotel's lovely Moby Dick room, overlooking the ocean (tel. 329-2911). For around $11 you can make as many trips as you wish to the enormous buffet table, laden with fresh island fruits, a variety of egg dishes, home fries, buttermilk pancakes; either custom-made omelets or roast sirloin or Virginia ham carved to order is featured every week. The dessert table is an amazing array of cakes and pies and muffins and ice cream . . . and more. Wonderful! The rest of the week, try the pretty Kona Veranda Coffee Shop, which offers many dishes—on the order of Polynesian chicken, mushroom burgers, sandwiches—from $4 to $6. Open for breakfast and lunch only.

There's an outpost of Middle Earth right on Alii Drive, across from the Kona Hilton Hotel. It's known as **Tom Bombadil's Food and Drink,** born in the uplands of Kuakini Highway and now in a land by the sea. And while murals and decor and names on the menu are mythic (Aragorn pizza, Misty Mountain sandwiches, Smeagol's Fine Fishes), the food is downright substantial, filling, and delicious. Tom Bombadil's is known for its wonderful broasted chicken (the unique taste is a result of its being deep-fried under pressure), about $3.35 for two pieces; for excellent pizzas, from $2.90 (small); and for nifty hot or cold sandwiches (ham, roast beef, avocado and cheese, and such), direct from Goldberry's Pantry, served with potato chips and a kosher pickle, from $3.65 to $6.75 for the huge submarine. There are also neat appetizers like batter-fried zucchini and an antipasto platter that two or three hungry hobbits could share, beautiful salads, spaghetti, and lasagne, and a full line of cocktails, including a spectacular mai tai. Enjoy ocean-view dining from the covered lanai, or relax in the cozy pub area while the friendly Middle Earth people are preparing your picnic. Tom Bombadil's is open daily, serving continuously from 11 a.m. to 10 p.m. All food is available for take-out by phoning 329-1292 or 329-2173.

The best Mexican restaurant in Kona is found "up mauka," where a lot of transplanted mainlanders have followed the Hawaiian rainbow. Close to town, about a five-minute drive out on Kuakini Highway is **Jose's** (tel. 329-6391), where the Martinez family serve up some marvelous, *muy auténtico* Mexican cuisine. It's a big restaurant, attractively decorated, with black velvet Mexican paintings on the wall. Try to sit out on the lanai on the beach chairs. The waiters and waitresses are attentive, the margaritas just fine, and the food well priced as well as well seasoned. You can have several combination plates for $6.95 to $7.45 and under (taco, tostada, beans and rice, etc.), or specialties like enchiladas suizas (sour cream and chicken enchiladas, beans and rice) at $6.45, or burrito del mar (a delicacy of flour tortillas stuffed with Alaskan king crab meat and garlic butter, topped with cheese and sour cream) at $8.45. Among the appetizers, nachos (tortilla chips covered with a tangy melted cheese sauce) were delicious, and so was the unusual dessert called capiortada: vanilla ice cream topped with Mexican bread pudding and whipped cream. The Mexican sundae—coffee ice cream topped with coffee liqueur and sprinkled with coconut—is another sweet treat. Jose's is open weekdays and Saturday from 11 a.m. to 10 p.m.; on Sunday there are seven different brunches (at about $5.25), from 10 a.m. to 3 p.m., and dinner from 3 to 9 p.m.

There's another good Mexican restaurant right in town, and that's **Reuben's Mexican Food** (tel. 329-7031), just off Alii Drive on Sarona Road. This is a sister establishment to the one we've told you about in Hilo (see above), and the food is just as delicious. The setting here is a little classier—an indoor-outdoor dining area furnished with darkly polished woods—so prices are a bit higher too: from $5 to $7 for lusty combination plates and specialty dishes. Reuben's is open Monday to Saturday from 11 a.m. to 11 p.m., Sunday from 3 to 11 p.m.

Cousin Kimo's Steak 'n' Seafood Restaurant (tel. 329-1393), on the garden lanai of Uncle Billy's Kona Bay Hotel on Alii Drive, is a popular and pretty spot, owned and operated by a local Hawaiian family. It features the same kind of reasonably priced dinners as the Hilo Bay does; the house specialty is fresh fish caught off Kona daily on their own boats. Four to five varieties of fish are offered, at prices ranging from $7.95 to $10.95. Other choices include shrimp, scampi, nut chicken, and New York–cut steaks. Your entree includes fried rice, and as much as you want from the soup and salad bar (salad bar alone is $4.95). There's Hawaiian entertainment every day starting at 6:30 p.m., with no cover charge; dinner is on from 5:30 to 9 p.m. Remember this place too for delicious breakfasts, with plenty of island fruit and pancakes.

Just across the street from Cousin Kimo's, at the Kona Inn Shopping Village, is Uncle Billy's newest venture, a charmingly quaint restaurant called **Hurricane Annie** (tel. 329-4345). The decor might be described as Early Hurricane—the idea being that you might be on a ship out at sea in a hurricane. All of the interior boards were taken from very old plantation houses in Hilo and left unpainted, along with the corrugated aluminum roofing. Naturally, there's a salad bar, and while you help yourself, the cooks will be whipping up your orders of anything from spaghetti with tomato sauce at $4.75 to New York–cut steaks at $10.95 for the large cut. In-between, among others on a long menu, are spare ribs, scampi, fresh Kona fish of the day, roast beef with barbecue sauce, and various Italian dishes. Dinner is served from 5 to 9 p.m.; lunch, with a collection of sandwiches, salads, and hot dishes, from 11 a.m. to 2 p.m. Open daily.

There are lots of places for quick meals in town. **World Square Shopping Center,** right on Alii Drive, boasts a large picnic area with tables under umbrellas out in the back, near the bus stop. Pick up a tasty snack from any of the fast-food stands and enjoy an inexpensive meal. . . . World Square also has its own branch of **Colonel Sanders Kentucky Fried Chicken,** with all the trimmings, three pieces for $3.48. . . . There's a Kona underground that swears by the sushi (Japanese seaweed stuffed with rice and vegetables) made by one Mrs. Blondie and sold at several local stores. You can pick up two of these for about $1.15 at **Union Jack,** an internationally minded (and rather high-priced) grocery store in World Square. Add a can of juice and you've got a neat lunch.

Some of the tiny snack shops are surprisingly good, even exotic. At **Sibu Café,** for example, in Banyan Court on Alii Drive, you can sample the mood and food of Indonesia. Blue tile tables, wooden chairs, revolving fans overhead, and Balinese decorations set the scene. Served all day, 11 a.m. to 8 or 9 p.m., are satés—skewers of marinated meats or vegetables broiled over an open flame, from $3.75 to $3.85. Balinese chicken, chicken curry, and stir-fry vegetables are also reasonable ($3.65 to $3.70), and everything is accompanied by marinated vegetable salad and fried rice. Healthy portions and a great taste for the price. Closed Tuesday.

As its name implies, the **Farm Restaurant,** in the arcade below Buzz's Steak House, concentrates on fresh and natural foods, most made from scratch; the results show in the tasting. Lunch dishes (served 11 a.m. to 5 p.m.)—like homemade vegetarian chili with brown rice, crunchy farm salads, heapings of nachos, real roast turkey sandwiches (not made with that pressed stuff!), Mexican pizzas, homemade soups—run from about $1.30 to $2.95 and are super. Dinner is on from 5 to 9 p.m., and that's when the Farm prepares delicious entrees like walnut chicken (chicken breast and veggies quickly sauteed in the wok), french stir-fry vegetables (with cheese), enchilada supper, and sweet-and-sour boneless chicken, served along with soup or salad and brown or white rice, from $4.95 to $5.50. Seafood specials are similarly reasonably priced: from $5.25 to $7.95 for the likes of red snapper filet, scallop stir-fry, or prawns in wine and garlic. The only dessert is Häagen-Däzs ice cream, but herb teas and smoothies are available. Three-egg omelets make a terrific breakfast at $2.99 (7 to 11 a.m.). Eat at one of the half-dozen tables in the cozy little room with parquet floors and farm implements on the wall, or phone for take-out (tel. 329-5547). Closed Sunday.

Our award for the most scenic snack shop in Kona has to go to **Billy Boy's Fast Foods** in the Kona Inn Shopping Village. Its eight or nine tables are perched right on the garden and beach, in the kind of setting usually reserved for much fancier establishments. In the middle of a broiling Kona afternoon, this place is c-o-o-l. Daily plate specials at $3.25 might include chicken long rice, sweet-and-sour pork, hamburger with cabbage or fried ahi, all served with rice and salad. Saimin, fish and chips, omelets, and good salads are modestly priced. If you're not ready for a meal, just stop by for ice cream and ocean breezes. You can also pick up sandwiches, fruit, and gourmet goodies to go.

Should you prefer to rest and relax from your shopping labors while listening to classical music at a sidewalk café and sipping some espresso or cappuccino or a freshly roasted coffee of the day, take your cue from **Coffee Cantata.** They also have good pastries and attractive packages of Kona coffee to take with or mail home.

The lovely **Kona Inn Restaurant** (tel. 329-4425) in the Kona Inn Shopping Mall is a splurge for us at dinner: meals in the $8 to $20 range. But it's such a special spot, with a spectacular view of the bay and some tables perched right at water's edge, that it's worth your while to have a light lunch here: a soup and salad special is just $4.25, an inexpensive way to dine with the upper class. Come by for cocktails on the lanai on Tuesday, or Thursday for a free hula show.

Yes, folks, **McDonald's** is here. It's nearby. A spic-and-span one on Kuakini Highway, just a block from the center of things. Hamburgers at 75¢; cheeseburgers, 87¢; filet fish, $1.25; and the Big Mac is $1.60. Breakfast includes scrambled eggs and sausage, $1.99.

For inexpensive dining in the big Keauhou-Kona hotel area, try the **Kona Koffee Mill** in the lovely Keauhou Beach Hotel for either breakfast or lunch. Three different kinds of omelets (including bay shrimps and chili and cheese) from $3.95 to $4.75 are pleasant for breakfast. Meat and fish sandwiches from $3.75 to $4.75, and a Chef's Pot Luck Special for around $5.50 and up, are the lunch offerings. The decor is coffeehouse-pleasant—nothing extraordinary, but the prices are good for this posh area. Open 6:30 a.m. to 2 p.m.

At the **Sunset Rib Lanai** of the same Keauhou Beach Hotel (tel. 322-3441), you can, indeed, watch the sunset—the dining room overlooks the ocean—and have a very reasonable meal. Most of the guests will dine on the house specialty of roast prime rib of beef ($14.50), but their 12-item salad bar, a meal unto itself, is just $6; add some Portuguese bean soup, and it's still only $8. Sunday brunch is a delight: from 10 a.m. to 2 p.m., they lay out a huge spread of Hawaiian, Oriental, and American goodies, including omelets made to order, fresh fruit, desserts, and more, all at $10.25. There's live music every evening.

Dinner is also a good buy at the **Keauhou Golf Club Restaurant,** above the Kona Surf Hotel (tel. 322-2700). Large bay windows overlook the golf course, Kona Surf, and the bay. Regular dinner entrees include everything from spaghetti and catch of the day to broiled chicken, teri-beef kebab, and barbecued pork spare ribs—and begin at $6.25. Side orders like sauteed mushrooms, garlic cheese bread, and fritters are great fun, and the desserts are delicious. There's a special senior citizens' menu of spaghetti, spare ribs, fish, and more, from $3.50 to $9. Best buy at lunch is a cup of soup and half a sandwich, at $4. Live contemporary Hawaiian music is featured from 7 to 11 p.m. Wednesday through Saturday, and there's drop-in entertainment Monday. Free transportation is provided within the Keahou-Kona resort area. Dinner is from 5:30 to 10 p.m.; lunch, 11 a.m. to 3 p.m.; breakfast, 7 to 11 a.m.

For a change of ambience from the tourist world of Kailua, drive out on Route H-11 (one block mauka from the main street of Kailua), a few miles south to **Teshima's** at Honalo—a very popular place for many years with the local Japanese, Hawaiians, Filipinos, and haoles. This is the area where they grow the coffee. You can have a complete teishoku lunch of miso soup, sashimi, sukiyaki, plus various side dishes, served on an attractive black lacquered tray, from $4.25 to $6. At dinner, vegetable tempura and shrimp tempura run $5 and $7.50, and there are plenty of dishes like oyako donburi, beef teriyaki, and sashimi from $3.75 to $5.75, all served with miso soup, tsukemono, rice, and tea. Breakfast is on from 7 to 11 a.m.; lunch, from 11 a.m. to 2 p.m.; dinner, from 5 to 10 p.m.

Take your choice of mood and food at **Kona Ranch House** (tel. 329-7061) on Highway 11, just after the intersection with 190. The same people who run the popular Bibbs Family Restaurant in Honolulu have completed a loving restoration of this old ranch house, and have quickly won a following among locals and tourists alike for excellent food, friendly service, and a gracious atmosphere. There are two distinct dining areas. Our favorite is the Plantation Lanai, so pretty in wicker and green, which serves lunch from 11:30 a.m. to 3 p.m. and dinner from 6 to 10 p.m., featuring steaks, from about $9.50 to $14.95. There is always a complete dinner special at $12.50. The adjoining Paniolo Room, also attractive with white booths and blue fabrics, open from 5 to 10 p.m., offers more modestly priced, family-geared menus. Best buy in the house is the $6.95 Paniolo Platter: along with the entree which changes every night (mahi-mahi, sliced roast beef, chicken, barbecued ribs, etc.), come salad, cornbread, corn on the cob, a choice of rice, fries, or baked beans, even a small dessert. We also like the tasty Taco Grande evening salad at $5.85 and the vegetarian ratatouille at $4.85. Barbecues and steaks are around $6.95 to $8.50. Children's menus, burgers, good drinks, luscious desserts—Kona Ranch House has all of this and more. Their $7.50 Sunday brunch, which includes a champagne cocktail, bloody mary, or screwdriver, is a treat at $6.95; it's served from 8:30 a.m. to 1 p.m. Kona Ranch House is open every day from 6:30 a.m. to 10 p.m.

The lively **Kona Coast Shopping Center,** near the intersection of Highways 11 and 19, offers you a chance to mingle with the local folk at some inexpensive restaurants. There's a branch of the **Sizzler Steak House** national chain here: a big handsome place where steaks are cooked to order and you serve yourself. Prices are always low: fish platter, $4.29; teriyaki steak platter, $5.99; quarter-pound hamburgers, $1.79—served with Sizzler toast and baked potato, french fries or rice. Salad bar too. Open 6 a.m. to 9 p.m. Sunday to Thursday, till 9:30 p.m. on Friday and Saturday. The answer to a hungry family's prayer. . . . **Paniolo Pizza** is more than just a pizzeria. Their South of the Border specials—burritos, enchiladas, tostadas, quesadillas, and the like—are priced from $2.25 to $6.95 and *muy bueno.* Sandwiches like the Turkey Tom—sliced turkey smothered with tomato, onion, melted cheeses, and sprouts—are all served on hot rolls with Hawaiian chips; at $3.95 to $5.25, they make a small meal in themselves. Salads are good too; the large ones, at $5.25 to $6.75, can feed two to four of you if you want to make a whole meal of them; the small ones are too meager. Pizza pies begin at $2.05. . . . Unusual Japanese dishes are what you'll find at a take-out spot called **Mr. Tonkatsu.** We know you've always wanted to try shrimp ebi, tonkatsu, and kushikatsu, so step right up: à la carte items are about $2.75, and plate specials from $3.95. (In case you didn't know, tonkatsu is Oriental breaded pork loin.) They serve beef teriyaki too. Open for both lunch and dinner. . . . **Betty's Chinese Kitchen,** small but sparkling, offers Oriental food in serve-yourself cafeteria style; most dishes are $2.95 for two portions, $3.45 for three, $3.95 for four.

On your way to City of Refuge at Honaunau (see Chapter XIV), there are some good places to stop. The **Aloha Café** (tel. 322-3383), in the lobby of the Aloha theater in Kainaliu, has wonderful, healthful food and an unusual atmosphere. The counter service café is in the lobby of the theater. Navajo rugs on the wall, plants, handsome wooden chairs and tables, and fresh flowers set the scene for homemade vegetarian soups, veggie salads, eggplant sesame burgers, vegetarian burritos, lots of sandwiches, and even a non-health-food item or two like turkey and avocado sandwich or hot brisket of beef. Sandwiches run about $3.95 to $5.50. If you get there in time for breakfast, you'll be treated to three-egg omelets, pancakes, and whole-wheat french toast, $3.25 to $5.25. Even if you don't have a meal here, stop in for some of the homemade fresh baked goods. The day we were there it was raspberry linzer tortes. Ono! Their baked goods, sandwiches, and burritos are also served at the World Square Theater in Kailua, and you don't have to pay admission to the theater to get the food. Aloha Café, by the way, seems to be local headquarters for transplanted mainlanders to hang out, so it's always a fun stop. Open every day except

Sunday from 7:30 or 8 a.m. to 3:30 p.m. only. Their adjoining health-food store can provide picnic ingredients—sandwiches to go, cheeses, organic fruits and vegetables; on our last visit we stocked up on locally grown, organic lichees. Delicious!

A few hundred yards up the road, on the opposite side of the street, is the **Garden Café,** which roasts Kona coffee fresh every day and sells it by the pound. Outside are two tables with director's chairs, where you might sit and snack on a $1.25 croissant or a 50¢ cup of Kona coffee, among other light fare.

The dining room of the **H. Manago Hotel** in Captain Cook (tel. 323-2642) is the place to catch a slice of local life. This big, family-style restaurant has enjoyed a good reputation for years among the local people, although very few tourists make their way here. Everything is served family style: big plates of rice, salad (macaroni salad is especially good), vegetables, whatever the cook has made that night are brought out and served to everyone at the table, along with such entrees as pork chops, barbecued liver, ulu, ahi, or steak; the prices go from about $5.50 to $8.25. The menu is limited and the food is not fancy, but this is a good chance to experience the nontourist life of the Kona Coast. Very pleasant. They serve all three meals, dinner until 8 p.m.

Everybody likes **Canaan Deli** in Kealekekua, across the street from the Bank of Hawaii. It's a New York-type deli started in 1972 by several young Christians with a mission: high-quality food served with aloha. The deli features kosher-style sandwiches using fresh island beef and locally baked breads (hot pastrami and rare roast beef run around $3), homemade salads, and Italian specialties. All sandwiches come with a choice of salad and kosher pickle. They even have lox and bagels! Scrambled eggs and omelets are breakfast favorites, with a $1.99 breakfast special from 7 to 9 a.m. And the homemade Italian dinners are fun: accompanied by minestrone soup or salad, and garlic bread, entrees of fettucine Alfredo, ravioli, spaghetti, and pesto run from $3.75 to $7.50.

There are two more places in Kealekekua that you may want to keep in mind. Next door to Canaan Deli is one of the three **Rolf's Sandwich Islands** in the area, fine for a special Captain Cook burger ($1.85 to $2.25) or a $3.50 lunch plate. You'll like the wire-and-wicker decor. A short way down the street, on the mountain side, **Crazy Mary's Ice Cream Parlor** has some interesting local ice cream: poha, macadamia nut, and Kona coffee. The owners here (who also run the Farm Restaurant in Kailua) are not so crazy; they feed you concoctions like the Grasshopper Pie (a brownie topped with mint-chocolate-chip ice cream, hot fudge, and whipped cream) and hang a fun-house mirror to create the illusion that you're still skinny! They also serve Hawaiian-style barbecued ribs and chicken with cole slaw and rice for about $3. Bring some quarters for the kiddies; they'll want to play the video games in the rear of the shop. Open daily until 9 p.m.

If you're ready for a big-splurge meal now, we can't think of a more idyllic place to have it than at **Kona Village,** a glorious hideaway resort on an oasis in the lava flows at Kaupulehu, about 15 miles from Kailua-Kona. The lunchtime buffet, served outdoors in a garden setting at this luxurious Polynesian village, where guests live in private thatched huts, is yours for $16, and so filling that you probably won't want to eat again until the next day. We counted something like 37 dishes on the smörgåsbord. You line up, first, for the cheeses (good bries, cheddars, and the like) and breads, including crisp Armenian lavash and hot rolls. Then on to the salads, which include raw tuna (sashimi) and hot tuna (delicious). We found nothing overly marinated or mayonnaised, as is so often the case with buffets. Next comes the fruit tray where, pausing among the kiwis and cherries and melons and papayas and such, you could linger indefinitely. But don't stop here: five or six hot dishes might include breaded shrimp, fried rice with bacon, chicken, and sweet-and-sour fish. For dessert, you could have home-baked banana bread and malasadas—as much as you want of everything, of course. Beverages and cocktails are served at your table. Be sure to call in advance for reservations (tel. 325-5555), as only expected guests can get past the guardhouse and gain access to this special Hawaiian place.

THE NIGHT SCENE IN KAILUA-KONA: Luaus, as you will soon discover, are the biggest form of nighttime visitor entertainment in Kona. Almost all of the big hotels—the **King Kamehameha,** the **Kona Hilton,** the **Keauhou Beach,** and the **Kona Surf**—have them, and the current going rate is about $30. At the exotic **Kona Village Resort** at Kaupulehu, the price is $36, but it is considered the best and most authentic luau here. If, however, you don't mind skipping the pig and poi, you can catch the "Night in Hawaii" show in the Poi Pounder Room of the sumptuous **Kona Surf** free—and that's every night except Sunday, at 7:45. It's worth the drive just to see the Kona Surf anyway. Happy Hour, from 4 to 6 p.m., at the **Nalu Terrace** pool bar is particularly pleasant—there is always a group playing soft music as the sun sinks into the sea. And, oh yes, most drinks cost less at that time. From 6 to 9 p.m., it's regular bar prices and contemporary Hawaiian music.

Even if you don't make it to a luau or a show, you must at least see a torch-lighting ceremony. Happily, there's no charge at all for that. Just take yourself to the beach in front of the **King Kamehameha Hotel** on a Sunday, Tuesday, Wednesday, or Friday evening just before sunset and watch the beautiful ceremony, as torches are lit on land and sea, in the shadow of an ancient heiua. Then you might proceed to the **Billfish Bar,** situated around the lovely pool, to hear music until 10 p.m. During the 5 to 6 p.m. Happy Hour at this popular spot, prices are lower. You may decide to have dinner in the atmospheric **Moby Dick's** at this hotel (there are several dishes like mahimahi and chicken on the low side of the menu, $7.50 and $8.25), and then you can enjoy music and dancing while gazing at the hefty marlin (weight: 1146 lbs.) mounted on the wall: no wonder the fishermen flock to Kona! There's Hawaiian music for dancing on Thursday, Friday, and Sunday from 9 p.m.

One of the most atmospheric small lounges in town is the **Spindrifter** on Alii Drive, where the tables and chairs are *that* close to the ocean. Hot pupus are served from 4 to 7 p.m. daily at half price, standard drinks and beers from $1.25, exotics at $2.50, but more when the entertainment is on (nightly from 9 p.m.). Spindrifter has the longest Happy Hour in Kona: from 11 a.m. to 6 p.m. daily, it has delicious pupus half-priced and mai tais for only $1.25. . . . Another very popular lounge overlooking the water is **Don Drysdale's Club 53,** where the exotic drinks—like Frozen Baboon, Fuzzy Willie, and Hawaiian Sunset—are unique, and where the pupus—shrimp scampi and deep-fried zucchini—are really special. There are burgers and sandwiches too, to go along with the drinks. . . . If dancing is your thing, check out the new **Eclipse Restaurant** on Kuakini Highway (across from Foodland). Dancing to a variety of music begins nightly at 10 p.m.; there's backgammon too. . . . At the **Pool Bar** of the Keahou Beach

Hotel, it's Happy Hour between 4 to 6 p.m. every day; mai tais are $2.25, and all drinks are half price.

If all you want is a drink, the bar at the **Kona Hukilau Hotel** is a good place to remember. Beer is 95¢ to $1.25 (25¢ less during Happy Hour, when they often serve pupus), and mixed drinks go from $1.50. . . . And if you're in a romantic mood, breeze over to the **Windjammer Bar** at the Kona Hilton, where you can listen to the sound of the surf smashing up against the rocks as you sit out on the patio and watch the Pacific perform. Tuesday through Sunday, there's dancing from 8 p.m. until closing—contemporary Hawaiian disco, and oldies. Sing-alongs take place with Tony Savone at the Piano Bar during the Garden Bar's Happy Hour, 4:30 to 6 p.m., nightly except Sunday. Walking around the big hotels like the Hilton, examining their gardens and lagoons by moonlight and floodlight, is a show in itself.

If you're having a private party down at the condo or wherever, and really want to surprise the guest of honor, get in touch with Yasmina Lakshanni. Yasmina, a professional belly dancer whose motto is "Have finger cymbals, will travel," delivers a Bellygram that is unlike anything else on the Big Island—or anywhere else, for that matter. You can call her at 325-6213.

The best place to catch free entertainment is at the shopping centers, and the **Kona Inn Shopping Village** on Alii Drive happily obliges. Every Tuesday and Thursday at 6 p.m., the delightful Ka'pionali Butterworth and her students (you may have caught them at the Ala Moana Shopping Center in Honolulu on a Sunday morning) present a free hula show on the oceanfront lawn of the Kona Inn. The show may be a little less than professional, but it's always charming, and you're welcome to pose with the dancers afterward. Bring your cameras.

READERS' SELECTIONS ON HAWAII: "We stayed at the **H. Manago Hotel** in Captain Cook. Our room on the third floor of the new wing was nicer than the one we had at Kona Village the night before at five times the price. The vegetables served with the fresh fish were Japanese and delicious, and the bed quilts were hand-knotted patchwork, sewn by grandma, I'll bet" (Arlene Bernstein, Napa, Calif.). [*Authors' Note:* It pays to go budget!] . . . "The H. Manago Hotel in Captain Cook is really unique and conveys the character of a big hotel of bygone times. An experience in itself! There seemed to be plenty of space, advance booking was not necessary, although March is considered high season for Hawaii" (Jurgen Simon, Bloomington, Ind.).

"I welcome travelers looking for a unique experience at my quiet retreat among the big trees overlooking meadlowland and the South Kona coast. This is an exquisitely beautiful place near the Honaunau Painted Church, within walking distance of the beach at Pu'uhonua O'Honaunau National Park. It is possible to stay in my luxury two-bedroom home with outdoor waterbed, hot tub, and private sunbathing deck at $300 a week for two, $350 for four. Individuals or couples on a smaller budget may contribute $30 to $50 a night for the use of a private studio apartment with cooking facilities and shower. Write to **Barbara Moore** or Caretaker, P.O. Box 675, Honaunau, HI 96726; or call 808/321-2159. . . . **Jessie Hillinger** has rooms available in her quaint sugar shack with steambath and bathhouse, located next to Wood Valley Temple (Tibetan) and not far from the Volcano and the Black Sand Beach at Punaluu. She would appreciate $25 a night. Her address is P.O. Box 37, Pahala, HI 96777, and her phone is 808/928-8212" (Barbara Moore, Honaunau, HI.). . . . "Our great find this summer was a lovely, superior room at the **Hilo Hawaiian Hotel** for only $45 per night, because they do not charge for young children 10 and under" (Mrs. Don Rushton, Scottsdale, Ariz.). . . . "Although ours has not been a low-budget trip, we'd like to report that one of our most satisfying meals was enjoyed at Sibu Café in the Kona Banyan Court on Alii Drive. Excellent combination dishes of curry, saté, stir-fried vegetables, cucumber salad, and exceptionally good fried rice plus tea came to $10.40 for two" (Constance Wallace, Bennington, Vt.).

"We stayed at **Uncle Billy's** in Hilo and I can't say enough about the aloha spirit they generate. Their rooms are very roomy and clean, their restaurant and entertainment were a lot of fun, and they are close to many attractions. . . . **Ken's House of Pancakes** has excellent food for breakfast: I especially give their macadamia-nut pancakes a 10" (Anna Stricherz, Bellflower, Calif.). . . . "We stayed at the impressive **Hilo Hawaiian Hotel** for $39.50 per night double, which also included a rental car. This is a very fine hotel with attractively furnished rooms looking out on a beautiful lagoon. We considered this the outstanding travel bargain of our trip" (Bill Halliday, Fair Oaks, Calif.).

"We would like to endorse your mention of the **Spindrifter Restaurant.** The waterfront location is terrific, the food is good, and the prices reasonable. We enjoyed the Happy Hour with its $1.25 mai tais and half-price ono pupus" (Ed and Joan Butterline, North Brunswick, N.J.). . . . "We decided to eat at the **Kamuela Drive-In Deli** in Waimea. It was packed with folk from around the area: cowboys, Hawaiian and Oriental, all so friendly and interesting. We had a delicious teriyaki dinner for $3.10, and met lots of good friends" (Mark and Kay Irvin, Phoenix, Ariz.). . . . "I have been spending some time in Hilo and would like to draw your attention to a great restaurant that is unbelievably reasonable and serves good food. I have eaten there regularly and never gotten sick of it. This is the **Mun Cheong Lau Chop Suey Restaurant,** at 126 Keawe, corner of Kalakaua Street. Most dishes are between $2 and $3, and the hearty lunch and dinner plates are the same price ($2 to $2.80), unlike some places where the food goes up two or three dollars more just because it is the evening meal. Mun Cheong Lau also stays open pretty late, much later than most of the restaurants in this sleepy big city" (George Daugiro, Utrecht, Holland).

"We found **Suzanne's Bake Shop** on Alii Drive in Kona, a few doors from the Mokuaikaua Church. All the local people seem to know about Suzanne's. They open at 5 in the morning and have all kinds of breads, rolls, doughnuts, and danishes. We loved the caramel/macadamia-nut danish. They also sell coffee, milk, juices, tea, and soft drinks, and even have a few small tables and chairs outside, with a great view of the ocean. Prices for danish were 55¢ to 85¢ each. . . . We stayed at the **Keauhou Beach Hotel** and were very pleased. The staff is helpful and friendly and the view is unbelievable!" (John and Lana Keck, Glendale, Calif.). . . . "There is an excellent restaurant behind the Kona Hukilau Hotel called **Stan's.** There are 28 different entrees to pick from, with prices starting at $4.85. They serve mainly seafood, but also steaks and chicken. The fresh catch of the day (I had ahi) was only $6.75. All entrees come with a large salad bar and soup. The salad bar includes delights such as kim chee and papaya. The meal is excellent, service very good with a smile!" (Kevin and Theresa Lew, San Francisco, Calif.).

"At the Kona Coast Shopping Center, **Betty's,** which you recommend, is good for Chinese food. But right around the corner is **Roy's,** a Japanese restaurant. We had a wonderful fresh fish dinner there which we carried out to our condo" (Howard and Joan Hunter, Omaha, Neb.). . . . "The current car-rental drop-off charges are $18.50 for the Kona-Hilo trip. However, if you have a little time, take your inter-island flight into Hilo. Take the northern route to Kona and the southern route back to Hilo. With a stay in Kona at the halfway point, you not only save $18.50, you also see more of the island. This worked great for us since we were going to the mainland from Hilo. . . . On the outer islands, we stayed at the **Hukilau chain** of hotels. When we called for reservations using their toll-free number, we received accommodations for $39 to $49 per night (car and breakfast). However, when we were in Honolulu, we were able to get our reservations for $33 to $39 per night. You may consider waiting to make your reservations. . . . You may consider flying standby to the outer islands and realize considerable savings. We flew to each island on standby, and never had to wait for a flight. Also, note that Hawaiian Airlines flies the biggest planes (727s) between the islands and would have more available seats for this system" (John Sinclair, Louisville, Ky.). . . . "On our previous visit to the island of Hawaii, we stayed at the Mauna Kea Beach Hotel, a lovely, expensive hotel. This time, we took your advice and stayed at the **Puako Beach Condominiums,** a mere five-minute drive from Mauna Kea. What a delightful surprise we had when we arrived. Not only was it a luxurious apartment, it was clean and well stocked with linens. The personnel were friendly and our stay was magnificent. We have recommended this place to many friends who are going in the near future" (Dr. and Mrs. Barry J. Slipock, Bonita, Calif.).

"The **King Kamehameha Hotel** in Kona has so much to offer visitors. The Kona Veranda Coffeeshop had the best hamburger of any—the new Mauna Loa Burger with a fine garnish of onion curls and the best steak fries, adorned with a Vanda orchid. Across the street, **Quinn's**—plain out front but with a pleasant dining area out back—had an outstanding vegetable omelet with mushrooms and a mouth-watering sandwich of fresh avocado, beansprouts, and delicious cheese. In fact, Kona restaurants served the most reasonable and delicious food we had on our trip" (Beth and Bake Baker, Englewood, Fla.). . . . "Tell your readers to look into the very good rates that are occasionally offered at the lovely **Kona Lagoon Hotel.** I live for less than I would pay in an apartment, including utilities and maid service even!" (Barbara King, Kailua-Kona, Hi.).

"**Rosey's Boathouse** in Hilo is sensational for a low price, the salad bar, and dinner is wonderful. The special of the day, usually fish, should be tried. I had ono, which was my best meal of the entire trip" (David Abraham, Forest Hills, N.Y.). . . . "Above all else, **Volcano House** must not be missed. Sitting on the rim of Kilauea Crater, it invokes the feeling of a mountain lodge. Volcano House is small and intimate with a friendly staff. It has a wood fireplace in the lobby, but no TVs (who needs them here in this setting!). We live in the mountains of New Mexico, but I have never seen stars like those at Volcano House. Where else but in Hawaii can you stand on a tropical island shivering in the chill below a 10,000-foot-plus mountain with snow in early October" (Nancy Goertz, Sandia Park, N.M.). . . . "We would like to recommend breakfast at the **Kona Lagoon Hotel.** The french pancakes, wrapped around blueberries and covered with orange butter, were fantastic" (Linda Huetinck, Alhambra, Calif.).

"The **Naniloa Surf** not only has free pupus during Happy Hour, but a beautiful orchid corsage arrived with my single drink" (Pat Lu, Hickory, N.C.). . . . "At the **Galley Restaurant,** located across from the King Kamehameha Hotel, one can eat a delicious chicken salad in half a papaya for $4.75, while getting the extra bonus of an ocean view and feeling the ocean breezes" (Jan Bell, Florissant, Mo.). . . . "We had breakfast at **Dick's** in the Hilo Shopping Center and the cost was only $5 for two of us and we were very full. The service was the fastest and friendliest we have experienced in a long time, and the food was excellent—hot and perfectly prepared. It was a nice change from food that is prepared and allowed to sit too long under heat lamps" (Tina and Mike Kyrias, Anchorage, Alaska).

"Our outstanding dinner was at the **Parker Ranch Broiler,** a worthwhile splurge. We had a top sirloin and London broil with mushrooms, each with hors d'oeuvres, baked potato, and salad and rolls. Great meat. Such a first-rate, memorable dinner would probably have cost much more in Washington or New York, and would not have had such friendly, informal service and spacious surroundings" (Ian O. Huebsch, Berkeley, Calif.). . . . "The buffet lunch at the **Mauna Kea Beach Hotel** is $16.50, $8.75 for children, but it is still excellent and worth the price. Incidentally, they do not start serving until noon [*Authors' Note:* Mrs. Morris J. Finck of Shaker Heights, Ohio, recommends the almond cream soup at Mauna Kea—"fit for the gods."]. . . . We had to wait a long time for the buffet lunch at **Volcano House,** as tour groups were ahead of us" (Carl R. Zimmer, Tempe, Ariz.). . . . "A worthwhile budget-blower was the luau at the **Keauhou Beach Hotel** near Kailua-Kona. The price included a one-hour open-bar cocktail party, excellent buffet dinner, and terrific show. If you like smaller crowds, better food, and entertainment in a less hurried atmosphere, go to a luau here or one of the other outer islands, rather than on Oahu" (Judith and Louise Jacobus, Long Beach, Calif.).

"We particularly like the **Dolphin Bay Hotel** in Hilo. The travel tips we received there enhanced our visit greatly, and they offer a service to guests who are taking a night plane to the mainland: a shower for $1 before going to the airport, even though you checked out in the morning. After a day touring and swimming, it was great to have a shower before getting on the plane" (Mrs. J. S. Birtwistle, Houston, Texas). . . . "The **Dolphin Bay Hotel** was by far the best buy for the money. My studio with full kitchen and full bath was extremely clean and well furnished, and only cost $162 for the week (single). The taxi fare from the airport is now $7, so renting a car, which you need for sightseeing anyway, is the best idea. John Alexander couldn't have been nicer!" (Trude Hirsch, Sudbury, Mass.). . . . "We have just returned from Hawaii and want you to know that the **Dolphin Bay Hotel** in Hilo is the best, cleanest, and most friendly hotel we have stayed at in 12 trips to the islands. Fresh bananas, papayas, and mangoes each day free, and beautiful grounds to surround you, and very reasonable cost, $27 a day with kitchen. We have found that we can see Hawaii without paying a fortune. Thanks for telling us about the little hotels, especially the Dolphin Bay in Hilo and Kona Tiki in Kona. They are like old Hawaii" (Tom and Marg Keall, Surrey, B.C., Canada).

"My husband wore bermudas and sandals everywhere throughout the trip and was never refused admittance anywhere until we got to Hilo, where we were not allowed in any of the bars or restaurants in the big hotels" (Murray and Judy Via, El Monte, Calif.). . . . "Free entertainment abounds in Kona. On the days that the **King Kamehameha Hotel** puts on a luau (Sunday, Tuesday, Wednesday, and Friday), the budget traveler can enjoy the music and see the pig being removed from the imu by standing on the public beach in front of the hotel. Festivities begin just before sunset" (Pamela Chappele and Michael E. White, San Francisco, Calif.). . . . "Please warn your readers that it is not advisable to stroll along Alii Drive after dark. We observed a young man who had just been attacked—not a pretty sight. There were many articles in the local newspapers advising tourists to be very careful. It is hoped that the installation of more lighting on the street will help, but until that time it is well to be careful at night" (Patricia A. Monteath, Pleasanton, Calif.).

Chapter XIV

SEEING HAWAII

COUNT ON A MINIMUM of four days on the Big Island for relaxed sightseeing: the first day for touring in and around **Hilo;** the second for visiting the **Puna area** and **Hawaii Volcanoes National Park;** the third for driving across the island from Hilo to **Kailua-Kona** on the western coast; and the fourth for exploring the **Kona Coast.** This gives you two nights at a hotel in Hilo and one or more in Kona. You can, of course, add a few more days at either end. It's also possible to arrive at Hilo, drive immediately to the Volcano area for a few hours, and then continue right across the island to Kona, where you can then relax in the sun for as long as you want. Or fly into Kona and reverse the trip, from west to east. The following itinerary will give you the basic information, around which you can do your own improvising.

1. Around Hilo

Most of the residents of Hilo are convinced that this is the world's greatest little city, and they wouldn't consider living anywhere else. The fact that they live—quite literally—between the devil and the deep-blue sea, bothers them not a bit. See those huge mountains that dominate the skyline? The bigger one, Mauna Kea, is an extinct volcano, but her smaller sister, Mauna Loa, is still very much alive.

If you've read Michener's *Hawaii,* you'll remember how the Alii Nui Noelani went to Hilo in 1832 to confront Pele and implore her to halt the fiery lava that came close to destroying the town. Pele has toyed with the idea more than a few times since, as recently as 1935, 1942, and 1984, but she has always spared the city—even without the intervention of priestesses. The citizens are convinced she always will. They feel just as nonchalant about tidal waves—at least they did until 1960. On the May morning when seismic waves hurtled across the Pacific headed for Hawaii, the citizens of Hilo had hours to evacuate; instead, some of them actually went down to the bridge to watch the show. This time the gods were not so kind. Sixty-one people were swept into the waves and a big chunk of waterfront area was wiped out. For several years after, one could see the devastation along the ocean side of Kamehameha Avenue; now there is

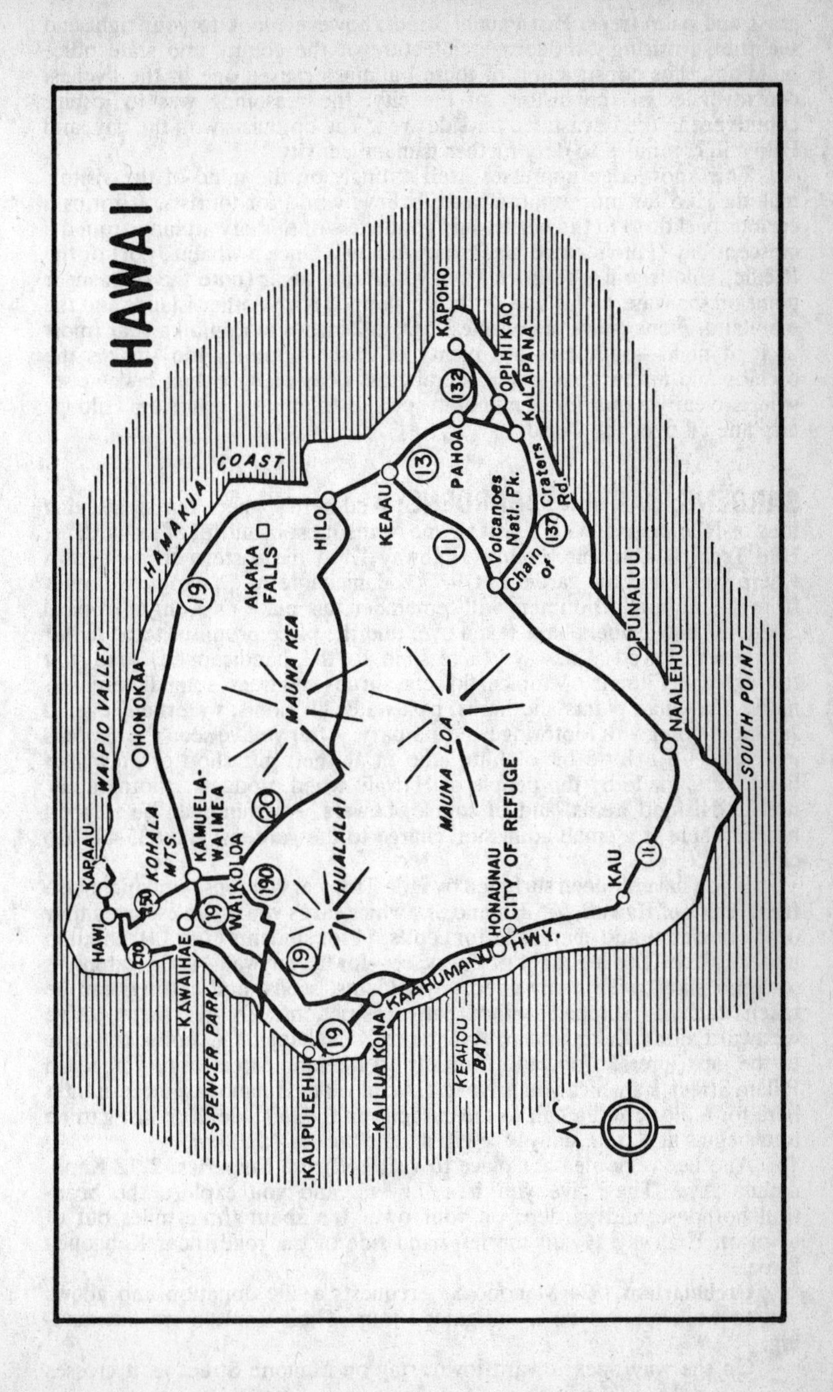
HAWAII
HAMAKUA COAST
KAPOHO
OPIHIKAO
KALAPANA
132
PAHOA
13
KEAAU
HILO
AKAKA FALLS
11
Volcanoes Natl. Pk.
Chain of Craters Rd.
137
PUNALUU
19
WAIPIO VALLEY
HONOKAA
MAUNA KEA
MAUNA LOA
NAALEHU
SOUTH POINT
KAPAAU
HAWI
KOHALA MTS.
KAMUELA-WAIMEA
WAIKOLOA
20
190
HUALALAI
CITY OF REFUGE
HONAUNAU
KAU
11
250
270
KAWAIHAE
SPENCER PARK
KAUPULEHU
KAILUA KONA
KAAHUMANU HWY.
KEAHOU BAY
N

grass and palm trees. Past Pauahi Street, however, look to your right and see the surprisingly modern architecture of the county and state office buildings. The construction of these buildings caused one of the liveliest controversies in the history of the city; the reasoning was to inspire confidence in the devastated bayside area. The optimists won the day, and Hilo still continues to defy further tsunami activity.

This knowledge impresses itself strongly on the mind of the visitor, making Hilo far more than a make-believe world for tourists. It forms a curious backdrop to the beauty and gentleness of this city arching around a crescent bay (Hilo's name means new moon). Once a whaling port of the Pacific, Hilo is still a seaport, from which raw sugar (note the bulk-sugar plant on the waterfront) and cattle are shipped to the other islands and the mainland. Flowers are big business too; 132 inches of rainfall a year (most of it at night—but there are plenty of misty mornings too) makes the orchids and anthuriums grow as crabgrass does on suburban lawns elsewhere. Nearly a quarter of million tropical blossoms are sent from Hilo via airplane all over the world.

GARDENS, GARDENS, GARDENS: And here's where our sightseeing tour of Hilo begins, with a visit to one of the most beautiful of its gardens, **Hilo Tropical Gardens.** Follow Highway 12 to the eastern strip of town where you'll find the gardens at 1477 Kalanianaole Ave., about two miles from the airport. Oldtimers will remember this place as Kong's Tropical Gardens; new owners have taken over and the place promises to be better than ever. Paved walkways (accessible to the handicapped) lead you through a tiny jungle of tropical flowers, shrubs and trees, splendid orchids, native Hawaiian plants and herbs, past water lily pools, waterfalls, even a Japanese pond with footbridge and statuary. After you've seen the gardens and used up a little bit of film, stop in at their gift shop of Hawaiian handicrafts made by the people of Hawaii: wood products, photographs, notecards, food items, and of course, flowers. Anything can be shipped home. There is a small admission charge to the gardens: call 935-4957 to check.

If you haven't been surfeited by Hilo Tropical Gardens, you might also try **Orchids of Hawaii,** 575 Hinano St., which takes you on an escorted tour of the nurseries and charges $2 for adults, $1 for students (7 to 14); children under 7, free. The highlight of this place—for us, anyway—is the extensive souvenir shop, with many good buys. Plants, seeds, and cuttings can be taken back or shipped without any restrictions. To get there, drive westward along Kalanianaole Avenue to Kamehameha Avenue, continue to the next intersection, and turn left on Manono Street until you reach Piilani Street, on which you drive left one block to Hinano Street; turn right here for a block and a half to the gardens on the left side. The last garden tour begins at 4 p.m. daily; the gift shop closes at 4:30 p.m.

Another very pleasant place to visit is **Hirose Nurseries,** 2212 Kaneolehua Ave. They give you free flowers, and you explore the beautiful hothouse and gardens on your own. It's about three miles out of town on Highway 11, on the left-hand side of the road, near Kahaopea Street.

Orchidarium, 524 Manono St., requests a 50¢ donation and allows you to walk around on a self-guided tour. Their displays are outstanding.

On the way back toward town, stay on Manono Street as it crosses

Kamehameha Avenue and continue on the drive along Hilo Bay. Soon you'll spot the **Nihon Japanese Culture Center** which, in addition to serving authentic and excellent Japanese cuisine (see Chapter XIII), has an art gallery, a tearoom, and spaces for music, dancing, films, and other entertainments. Check to see if anything special is going on. Now there's **Liliuokalani Gardens** coming up on your right, lovely with its Japanese bridges, ponds, plants, and stone lanterns; you can picnic here. It's believed to be the largest such formal Oriental garden and park outside Japan. Look for the authentic Japanese tea ceremony house. Now on your left is **Coconut Island,** a favorite picnic spot for the local people. If you continue around the park, you'll find yourself on Banyan Drive, which takes you past many of the elegant resort hotels in the city. The magnificent trees are labeled in honor of the celebrities who planted them; James A. Farley was one, Amelia Earhart another; Cecil B. De Mille has a tree, and so does Mrs. De Mille. At the end of the drive is **Reed's Bay Park,** a cool picnic spot on the bay.

To see our favorite gardens, however, you'll have to drive in another direction, about three miles south on Highway 11 (the road to the volcano) from Hilo Airport, then turn left onto Makalika Street just after Highway 11 divides; drive in seven-tenths of a mile, and you'll soon find **Nani Mau Gardens,** a recently developed wonderland of 20 acres full of the fruits and flowers of many lands; orchids are only some of the growing things here. The gardens are a work of love on the part of Mr. Mac Nitahara and his family. The macadamia and coffee trees, the air plants, the incredible varieties of hibiscus, orchids, and ginger are some of the things you'll see. They'll let you smell everything too—from vanilla orchids to fragrant allspice leaves. Mr. Nitahara is working especially hard to grow Hawaiian herbs and to propagate their lore as well—it's fascinating to see and learn about the herb that helps heal broken bones (the noni plant), the one that clears up sinus trouble (olena), the one that cures coughs (ohaloa), and the one that heals cuts (ti leaf). Get Mr. Nitahara to tell you about the herb that cured his father of high blood pressure! When you come back from your tour, which takes about an hour, they bring you a cup of fresh fruit—perhaps papaya, pineapple, bananas, even fresh guava—whatever is in season. You can stay in the gardens as long as you like, to picnic or just relax. Open daily, from 8 a.m. to 5 p.m.; admission is $3 for adults, $1.50 for children 7 to 12; below 7, no charge.

A HAWAIIAN ZOO AND AN ENVIRONMENTAL CENTER: While you're out in this area, you might also want to take in a charming Hilo attraction: the **Panaewa Equestrian Center and Rain Forest Zoo** complex. It's just outside the city as you drive on Route 11; turn right on the Stainback Highway and watch for signs on the right to the zoo. This is by no means the big time, as zoos go; it's a small place but with its own special Hawaiian charm. You'll see denizens of the South American rain forest, the rare Hawaiian "nene" (goose), the Hawaiian "pueo" (owl), many brightly plumaged birds, and peacocks roaming the grounds; cutest of all are the monkeys, especially the capuchins, who seem to enjoy the funny humans walking about. Free admission. Open every day from 9 a.m. to 4:30 p.m. In this same area, stop in, if time permits, at **Honua Hawaii,** a nonprofit environmental center whose goal is to "reunite man and nature." Its 202 acres of forest reserve with labeled nature trails are lovely; educational displays show how the Hawaiians managed to live in harmony with their world by means of the strict environmental codes that were part of their kapu system. Open weekdays, 9 a.m. to 4:15 p.m.; free (tel. 959-6244).

Nearby is **Hale Manu Crafts,** featuring lauhala, chimes, and other gift items.

THE TRAIL OF KAMEHAMEHA: Now it's time for some Kamehameha lore, since the Big Island is where that doughty old warrior was born and where he first started dreaming his dreams of glory and conquest. Continue your journey on Kamehameha Avenue, turn left at Waianuenue Street (Norberto's Restaurant is at the corner), and drive three blocks to the modern County Library on the right side. See the two stones out in front? The bigger one, the **Naha Stone,** was Kamehameha's Excalibur. According to Naha legend, only a chief of the royal blood could even budge the gigantic boulder; any warrior strong enough to turn it over would have strength to conquer and unify all the islands of Hawaii. Kamehameha did the deed, but since the stone weighs at least a ton, no one has, as yet, bothered to repeat it.

HILO'S NATURAL SIGHTS: Best time to see the next sight, **Rainbow Falls,** is early in the morning. Come between 9:15 and 10 a.m., when the sun gets up high enough over the mango trees so that you're apt to see rainbows forming in the mist. But it's pretty at any time, and so are the beautiful yellow flowers growing near the parking lot. You reach the falls by taking Rainbow Drive off Waianuenue Avenue. If you'd also like to see the **Boiling Pots,** deep pools which appear to be boiling as turbulent water flows over the lava bed of the river, continue along Waianuenue about two miles, past some of the nicest homes in Hilo and a huge monkeypod tree, to Peepee Street. From the parking lot you can walk over to the edge and observe the show below. Both Rainbow Falls and the Boiling Pots are part of the **Wailuku River State Park.**

Now we head for the **Kaumana Cave** and a chance to see some of the work of Pele at close range. The cave is a lava tube, created in 1881, when Pele came closer to wiping out Hilo than at any other time. Lava tubes are sometimes formed when lava flows down a ravine or gully; the top and sides cool while the center keeps racing along. Millions of years of volcanic eruptions have left hollow tubes like this all over the islands; in many of them are hidden the bones of the alii, which were always buried in remote, secret places. Of the two tubes here, only the one on the right—whose entrance is an exquisite fern grotto—is safe for exploration. The one on the left is treacherous, and who knows—perhaps the bones of Kamehameha, never discovered, are buried here? To get to the caves, return to the fork at Highway 20 and turn right to the other branch of the fork, Kaumana Drive. The cave is about three miles out; an HVB marker indicates the spot.

A CHURCH AND A MUSEUM: On we go, from paganism to Christianity. When you get back to Kamehameha Avenue, watch for Haili Street; turn onto it in a mauka direction (away from the bay and uphill); cross Keawe, Kinoole, and Ululani Streets, and on the left-hand side you'll see **Haili Church.** Its architecture is pure New England, but its fame stems from its great Hawaiian choir. Continuing up Haili Street, you next cross Kapiolani Street, and on the right-hand side you'll find the **Lyman House**

Memorial Museum Complex at 276 Haili St. You can visit either the old missionary house and the new $1-million museum addition, or both. The original Lyman House is another of those old mission homes which the grandchildren and great-grandchildren turned into a museum, and this one, originally built in 1839, has now been fully restored and furnished as a home of the 1850-1870 period. Hilo's oldest structure, the white-frame building contains hand-molded New England glass windows, doors made of native koa wood, and the original wide koa floorboards. As you tour the rooms, you'll see how the missionary family lived: the clothes, old four-poster beds, white marble-top table stands and dressers. The fascinating Hawaiian artifacts and worldwide curios that used to be displayed here have now been transferred to the newly built Lyman Museum building. In this very modern museum, you begin at the Island Heritage Gallery on the first floor where a raised relief map shows routes taken by all the groups that came to Hawaii. Then you can see the artifacts of each group and study their cultures; the Hawaiian exhibit includes a full-size grass house, Stone Age implements, feather leis, etc. Other ethnic exhibits include an intricately hand-carved Taoist shrine brought to Hilo piece by piece in their luggage by early Chinese sugar plantation workers. There are also Japanese, Portuguese, Korean, and Filipino displays.

The second floor also has fascinating exhibits, among them the Earth Heritage Gallery with its display of volcanic eruptions and worldwide mineral collection, one of the finest and most extensive such collections in the Pacific; a large Pacific shell collection, covering many examples of beautiful and rare shells; and Man's Heritage Gallery, containing beautiful collections of old glass, Oriental furniture, screens, and a large collection of Oriental art.

Lyman House is open from 9 a.m. to 4 p.m. Monday through Saturday; closed major holidays. Admission is $2.50 for adults, $1.25 for children; subject to change.

SHOPPING IN HILO: The big local shopping center is the **Kaiko'o Hilo Mall,** just behind the County and State Buildings, with everything in it from a supermarket to a drugstore to souvenir shops, plus some more sophisticated shops. Have a look at **Book Gallery,** where you can learn a lot about Hawaii; pick up some island cookbooks, books for the keikis back home, or some of the unique Petroglyph Press paperbacks, printed right here in Hilo. . . . **J.C. Penney's** has a branch here and, as usual, value and selections are excellent. . . . There's a **McInerny's** too. . . . **A Different Drummer** (entrance outside the mall) has lovely muumuus at $50, and children's clothes too. . . . We like the cheeses, candied herbs, and teas at **Gourmet Hut Hawaii.** (Their take-out sandwiches are really good.). . . . **The Puka** and **The Puka Too,** two gift huts located in the center of the mall, carry better-than-usual merchandise.

Although **Hilo Hattie's Resort Shop** here has prices that are below average for island wear, you can do even better by going directly to **Hilo Hattie's Fashion Center & Factory** at 933 Kanoelehua (tel. 961-3077 for free transportation), on the main highway going out of town, just a few blocks past the airport. Not only can you see the garments being made, but you can get them at a lower price than in the retail shops. It's open seven days a week, from 8:30 a.m. to 5 p.m.

Just down the street from the mall, between Long's and Safeway, craftsminded people should stop in at **Kaiko'o Modelcraft,** a great hobby store for kids of all ages. The people here freely dispense hospitality and travel tips to visitors along with know-how on local crafts.

Uncle Billy's Polynesian Market Place, at the Hilo Bay Hotel, 87 Banyan Dr., is an enormous clothing-gift-souvenir store, with low prices on just about everything. Some of the clothing is made in their own garment factory. We saw rather nice muumuus beginning at about $25.

For health-food buffs, we're happy to report that small Hilo has two big and exciting health-food stores. The oldest of the duo is **Hilo Natural Foods,** 306 Kilauea St., stocked to the brim with natural foods, herb teas, cheeses, natural vitamins and supplements, honeys, home-baked breads, pastries, books, plus a Natural Foods Kitchen for snacks and light meals. You'll find plenty here that you'll want to bring back to your kitchenette apartment or nibble on right here at the store.

Newer on the Hilo scene is **Abundant Life Natural Foods Store,** which has taken over the premises of an oldtime pharmacy (and still retains much of that feeling) at 90 Kamehameha Ave. They consider themselves to be one of the state's most complete natural-foods stores, and indeed the selection is fascinating: over 200 varieties of herbs, teas, and spices; fresh, locally grown produce; plus natural vitamins, groceries, and quality skin-care products, including suntan oils and lotions with sunscreens. There is also a nice assortment of locally crafted items. You may want to try some of their tropical fruit jams, all made locally with Hawaiian honey. Freshly pressed carrot juice and sandwiches are prepared daily for take-out. And you'll probably find it hard to resist some of their delicious snack items on the way out.

If you'd like to take some anthuriums home with you, be sure to stop at **Anthuriums of Hawaii,** 1605 Ainaola Dr., where you can see anthuriums of every color and description (green and red "hula dancer" or "lipstick" anthuriums, for example) being grown, and enjoy the friendly hospitality of the owners. They're the kind of people who, simply because we inquired about different varieties of ginger, rushed to our car as we pulled out with a big stalk of fresh ginger to take with us—compliments of the house. They'll pack and ship anthuriums anywhere, and prices are reasonable. Everyone gets two anthuriums and whatever fresh fruit is in season free—just for visiting. The owners ask that you call 959-8717 for directions before you come.

For local color along with good bargains, stop in at the **Miyao Gift Shop** at 182 Kilauea, a very plain, jumbled little shop that usually has a few orchid plants for sale. We picked up some lovely Japanese rice-paper wallets at $1.85 that made fine small presents, and beautifully painted egg shells at $2.45. Small brocade coin purses are $2.25. A nice touch of nonplastic Hawaii.

Across the street from the Hawaii Visitors Bureau, at 201 Kinoole St., is **Old Town Printers & Stationers,** the retail store of the Petroglyph Press, which has been publishing books on Hawaiiana since 1962. Drop in to browse through the books, cards, and an outstanding collection of maps.

There's an artistic touch to a handful of downtown shops, all of them close to each other on or near Keawe Street. **Moon Lily's,** 270 Keawe St., shows original designs in handmade women's clothing, cut lacework done in Bali, plus casual, island-style earrings. . . . Their new shop, called **Maggie Mae's,** at 169 Keawe St., is a very feminine, lacy "ladies shop." They carry a large selection of bath capsules and soaps, lingerie, fans, unique greeting cards, hair ornaments, all in an antique setting. . . . The **Potter's Gallery,** located in the Mamo Mart, 176 Mamo St., shows pottery done with an Oriental flair. It always has a selection of functional stoneware by Randy Morehouse, plus rotating shows by Big Island artists (Mamo Mart, by the way, mostly of interest to local people, is the only indoor parking lot we've ever seen surrounded by shops!). . . . **Imagination,** at 264 Keawe St., is a charmer, a fantasy spot that abounds in the likes of soft sculptures, rainbows, unicorns, animated music boxes, and porcelain dolls. Our favorites here are the adorable little furry mice, beautifully dressed (for example, Red Riding Hood, a bride and groom, a clown, a witch, a nurse, etc.). They are created by—of all people—a retired marine officer! The mice are just $5; soft sculptures, $12 to $50; and stuffed animals in satins and laces, from $17.

We have to agree with owner Sally Leuer-Mermel that her place at 110 Keawe St. is indeed **The Most Irresistible Shop in Hilo**—at least for people like us who love fine crafts. Sally has superb taste, and she has chosen the work of over 125 artists and craftspersons from all over the islands. We saw stained-glass mirrors and lamps, watercolors, Hawaiian needlepoint kits, baby blankets, patchwork quilts, fantastic soft dolls by local dollmakers (from $12), hand-screened canvas bags, luggage, and Hawaiian quilt patterns for pillows, all cut out and ready to go ($10.50). Children will love the dollhouse furniture, books, handmade wooden toys, and lots of cute T-shirts. There is also a huge selection—over 100 designs—of adult T-shirts. Note the kitchen section, with delightful ceramic (stoneware juicers, colanders) and koa wood utensils (rolling pins and bowls) by island potters and carvers. Sally also has one of the most tasteful postcard and card selections on the Big Island. Her new shop, Bear's Café (see Chapter XIII) is now ready to go, with coffees and luscious desserts, all with a bear theme—Bear Claws, Teddy Bear Pie—and more.

The newly renovated and quite attractive Pacific Building, which houses The Most Irresistible Shop in Hilo, is also home to several other tasteful boutiques. The **Picture Frame Shop** features prints and paintings by local artists like Pegge Hopper, Richard Thomas, Doug Lindsay, and Dietrich Varez. Some of his tasteful block prints of Hawaiian legends begin around $15. . . . A lot of the items at **The Futon Connection** are too big for you to carry home, but do have a look at their silk brocade makeup cases at $4.95, their hand-painted parasols at $12.95, and beautiful large paper fans at $25. . . . **Chef's Heaven** is just that—in a bright and cheery interior, made mostly of knotted pine wood, home cooks can find a complete line of gourmet herbs and spices; aprons, potholders, and dish towels in the $3.50 to $4.50 range; a variety of teas; and more. . . . Don't miss **The Chocolate Bar,** you chocaholics out there. All candies are made on the premises, and begin at 25¢ apiece. There are many novelty Hawaiian candies, like chocolate sushi, chocolate aloha greeting cards, and macadamia-nut candies. If you'd rather, they have a full range of ice creams.

WAILOA CENTER: The building that looks like a volcano, just behind the State Office Building, is actually the **Wailoa Center,** a continuing free exhibit that accents the natural history and culture of the Big Island. Wall niches and free-standing displays are changed every month or two, so you might get to see an exhibit of Hawaiian-born artists, a display of the history and culture of the island, or one on ancient Hawaiian antiques. They're happy to provide information and suggestions for visitors. Services and admission are free. The entrance is on Piopio Street, between the State Office Building and Kamehameha Avenue. It's open Monday through Saturday from 8 a.m. to 4:30 p.m.

TIME FOR A SWIM: Your ramblings have worn you out, your budget hotel doesn't have a pool, and you want a swim. Where do you go? We'd head out on Kalanianaole Avenue, drive three miles to **Onekahakaha Beach Park** or a mile farther to **James Kealoha Park,** where the swimming in the rocky bay is okay if not memorable. But it's pleasant to drive through this Keaukaha area, the most beautiful part of Hilo, to see the exquisite private homes, some with their own tranquil and Oriental fish ponds. Picnic and swimming spots continue until the end of the paved road. Watch for the signs pointing to **Richardson Ocean Center** at Waiuli Point, a modest but rather appealing public information center for marine affairs, where you can see aquarium displays of marine life from various parts of the Big Island, swim or snorkel in the waters out front, and have a look at marine organisms in their own natural habitats of coral reefs, lava surge zones, and tide pools. Open weekdays only, 9 a.m. to 4 p.m. Free admission.

If you favor pool swimming, join the local people at the Olympic-size **Kawamoto Pool** (tel. 935-8907) at Kuawa and Kalanikoa Streets, near the Civic Auditorium. Admission is free. Open from 11 a.m. to 1 p.m. for adults, from 1 to 4 p.m. for everybody. Good swimmers only can swim in the deep waters of the **Boiling Pots** at Wailuku River State Park (see above), but you are cautioned to ask about conditions on the day you're planning to swim. If the river is running high, the current may be too strong. Alas, there have been drownings here.

2. Puna and Volcanoes National Park

You must not leave the Big Island without paying homage to the goddess Pele. Not to visit her residence at Halemaumau, the firepit crater of Kilauea (this is the smaller volcano nestled along the southeastern slope of Mauna Loa), would be unthinkable. If Pele is entertaining, you're in for one of the world's great natural spectacles; if not, just a look at a volcano and what it can do will be a big experience.

Although everybody goes to the volcano, a lot of tourists miss one of the most fascinating places of all: the Puna region east of the volcano, where you get a feeling of what a volcanic eruption means, not as a geologic curiosity, but in terms of the farms and stores and orchards and graveyards and cucumber patches that got in its way. We'll also show you how you can continue right on to Volcanoes National Park—feasible if you get started early, as you'll be covering quite a bit of territory. It's easier, though, to break this up into two separate day trips.

THE DRIVE TO PUNA: This outing begins on Volcano Highway, Highway 11, which branches off from Kamehameha Avenue southward past the airport. About six miles out of town, you'll come to a possible stop, the **Mauna Loa Macadamia Nut Corporation,** the world's leading grower, processor, and marketer of macadamia nuts. Macadamias—Luther Burbank called them "the perfect nut," and they taste better than peanuts—are a big crop for the islands. On the drive from the highway to the Visitor

Center, you'll see hundreds of thousands of macadamia trees planted in this area. From an observation gallery, you can see the processing and packing operations, with taped audio explanation; you can taste sample macadamias and watch a slide presentation at the Visitor's Center. Visiting hours are 8 a.m. to 5 p.m. Monday through Friday, and 9 a.m. to 1 p.m. on Saturday.

At Keaau turn left off Volcano Highway and drive through town until you find Highway 13 and Keaau. If you're in the mood for shopping, you can stop in this old plantation town to sample the works of local artisans and craftsmen at the **Sugar Mill,** plantation quarters that have been reconverted into several crafts shops. Have a look at **Kalanikoa Studio,** owned by Glenn Severance, which makes very fine handmade furniture in island hardwoods, specializing in koa. Glenn is well known in these parts for his koa wood rocking chairs. **One of a Kind** is a gallery featuring a different solo artist each month. The latter also carries handmade cards, prints, and locally produced books. Sandwiches, salads, and beer are available at the laidback **Keaau Junction Deli.**

Just across the street is the **Christmas Store,** where everything and anything could turn up, from handmade Hawaiian Christmas tree ornaments to funky jewelry from the '20s and '30s. Interesting antiques here, and also at nearby **Gaughan's Emporium.**

Back on the road now, Pahoa is about ten miles farther along; here you'll enter the area that received the brunt of the 1955 eruption of Kilauea. This had been peaceful farm country for a hundred years, dotted with papaya orchards, sugarcane fields, coffee farms, pasture lands. Then a rift in the mountain opened and the lava fountains began to spout erratic cauldrons that here turned a farm into ashes, there left a gravestone or an old building untouched. You'll see cinder cones along the road and tiny craters still steaming. The most spectacular—and chilling—scenery comes later.

You might note that there are usually local vendors in downtown Pahoa selling anthuriums, puka products, papayas, and the like—all at very reasonable prices. Look for the one selling six papayas for $1.

Follow the signs now to Kalapana, which brings you to one of the most incredible beaches in the world; the black-sand beach at **Kaimu.** The unexpected color effects are the results of explosions of black lava hitting the sea. Graceful palm trees make the picture idyllic, but don't try swimming here, for the currents are treacherous. Continue on a short way to the right to **Harry K. Brown Park,** which ought to be a model for builders of seaside parks. The whole place looks like something out of *Alice in Wonderland,* with tables and enormous mushrooms of chairs carved out of lava rock; the lichen moss beginning to grow on them gives them a light-gray patina. There's a reconstructed heiau platform, and more practical things like a saltwater swimming and wading pool, rest rooms, cooking facilities, and showers. See those funny-looking trees that look as if they're resting on stilts? Those are the pandanus trees, one of the special glories of the islands.

A bit down the road, you'll pass the **Star of the Sea Painted Church,** one of the two painted churches on the island. Since the ancient Hawaiians were accustomed to outdoor worship of their pagan gods, the murals on the walls of these little churches were designed to create an outdoorsy feeling. (You'll see the other, much older, painted church just off the road to Honaunau, when you explore the Kona coast on the other side of the island.)

You could continue about five miles beyond this point to the **Queen's Bath,** a natural pond where the royal queens supposedly bathed *au naturel,* and where commoners peeped on pain of death. Today the alii have been replaced by local kids who use the spot as a swimming hole and the old bumpy road has been replaced by a new highway.

Continue on a few more miles to the **Wahaula Visitor Center.** This tasteful Polynesian museum on the site of an ancient heiau is the beginning of the coastal section of Hawaii Volcanoes National Park. The heiau has been restored and is worth visiting (tel. 965-8936). (Incidentally, just past the Visitor Center is the Royal Gardens subdivision, which underwent heavy damage in the 1983 eruptions of Kilauea.) Here you're going to have to make a choice. You can continue on this road, past the ancient Hawaiian village of Kamoamoa and on to Puu Loa, where hikers rave about the trail along a vast field of petroglyphs. This road links to the Chain of Craters Road, reopened after having been blocked by unexpected lava flows for several years. The Chain of Craters Road brings you directly to the center of Volcanoes National Park.

Let's assume, however, that you will take the Chain of Craters Road in the reverse direction from park headquarters, on another trip. For today, you might turn around and retrace your path to Route H-137, toward Kapoho and a fantastic 15-mile trip across one of the most exciting coastlines in Hawaii. From the red rollercoaster of a road, you'll see where the tropical jungle alternates with black rivers of lava that laid waste miles of earth before they reached their violent end in the steaming Pacific. The sea pounds relentlessly on the black lava rocks, eventually to grind them into more black sand; on the land the jungle creeps back slowly, reclaiming the land for itself and breaking it down into what will one day again be red earth. This is how the islands of Hawaii—and many of the earth's surfaces—were formed, and no textbook description will ever leave such a vivid picture in your mind.

There's a new visitors' attraction in this area: **Kalani Honua** is a cultural and arts educational farm and health spa, offering classes, special events, and performances; theater groups perform here. For information, phone 961-3529.

En route, there are two good spots for picnicking, fishing, or hiking (no swimming): **McKenzie State Park** near Opihikao and **Isaac Hale Park** at Pohoiki. If you continue in the direction of Pahoa on Highway 32, you'll reach **Kapoho,** a Hawaiian Pompeii that was buried under spectacular lava flows in 1960. The day-by-day fight to keep the village from being overwhelmed by the lava flow and pumice cinders from the new cinder cone (which now overlooks the sad remains of Kapoho) was one of the most dramatic episodes in recent Hawaiian history. A cinder cone on the concrete floor is all that remains now of Nakamura's Store, and nearby, a desolate lighthouse stands inland from the new coastline created by the lava flow. A few miles farther on, just before Pahoa, you'll pass **Lava Tree State Park.** An old lava flow encircled the trees here, and they were eventually burned out, but the lava trunk molds remain, surrealistic witness to the whims of Pele.

You'll note that you've now described a triangle almost back to Pahoa; from here it's Route 130, back to Keaau and then home to Hilo.

THE VOLCANO: It's more exciting than ever to visit the volcano, because for several years there has been a great deal of activity in Mauna Ulu,

Pauahi Crater, and others. These new eruptions on the flanks of Kilauea were big enough to spurt enormous fountains of fire 1800 feet up above the crater's rim. In 1984 both Kilauea and Mauna Loa were active at the same time, the first time this has happened since 1868. Lava flows came dangerously close to the city of Hilo. And just why has Pele been acting so uppity lately? Could it be that she's been angered by the prospecting for geothermal sources that has been going on in the Campbell Estate lands, where much of the recent activity occurred? Some conservationists and local people are saying so, and another Pele myth may be forming. Be that as it may, you're going to want to see what's happening. You can call the park rangers at 967-7311 before you start for news of the latest eruptions and viewing conditions. Call 967-7977 anytime for recorded information on eruptions. But whether or not anything is happening, the volcano trip is a must.

Your excursion to the volcano will start on Highway 11 out of Hilo, just as the Puna trip did, but this time you stay on that road all the way to **Hawaii Volcanoes National Park.** It's a drive of about 30 miles. Be sure to take a warm sweater; the air gets refreshingly cool 4000 feet up at Kilauea Crater.

Another possible stop for flower fanciers—and for lovers of local color—is **Volcano Store,** in tiny Volcano Village, reached just before you get to the park (on Highway 11, make a right at Haunani Road directly to the store). Half of the porch, as we've told you in the previous chapter, is devoted to the Volcano Country Kitchen; the other half is the place where local people go to scoop up reasonably priced sprays of orchids from late November through early May (a spray of about 18 orchids for $3.50 to $4.50). During the summer, we've seen anthuriums here for $2 to $3.75 per dozen. They will pack and ship anywhere.

Once you reach the park area, signs will direct you to the headquarters building, which should be your first stop. Check with the very helpful park rangers here for directions to the current eruption—if any. You may have to do some hiking over lava beds to see the show, but it's well worth it. (Bring heavy shoes.) And do note that sulfurous fumes are dangerous to those with respiratory problems and can be pretty repulsive even to those without; you may want a clothespin for your nose. It's possible, however, that you'll be able to drive right to an eruption, as we once did; simply get out of your car, and watch one of the most awesome shows on earth. The reason, by the way, that it is safe to watch a volcano like Kilauea erupt is that it produces lava that flows along the surface; Mount St. Helens volcano in Washington state and most others in the world, by contrast, produce steam and ashes that explode into the air.

The park rangers can also supply you with a driving map and information on hiking trails. You can learn a little bit about volcanology at the **Visitor Center,** and you should try not to miss the terrific color films of the latest eruptions; the show goes on at every hour on the hour from 9 a.m. until 4 p.m. The most popular display case here always seems to be the one of letters of people who took rocks from the volcano—despite being warned never to do so—hit a spell of bad luck, and sent them back. Many of the letters ask forgiveness of Madame Pele. For example: "My friends are no longer in my life, I am divorced, I've lost my business, my property is being foreclosed. Pele is surely angry about something. . . . I took the rock. . . . Pele is a very busy woman and surely she would not miss a handful of stones from the firepit. Right? Wrong!" Amazingly enough, this display is changed every three months with more letters and more rocks making their way back to Hawaii.

Now that you know not to break any Hawaiian kapus by taking lava rocks back home, walk a few doors from park headquarters to the **Volcano Art Center.** Here, in the 1877 original Volcano House Hotel, once host to Mark Twain, a nonprofit group shows the work of some 200 artists and craftspeople, most of them from the Big Island. Original works are for sale, as well as posters, and many small items that would make distinctive gifts: Barbara Irwin's herbal hot pads, for example, which give off the scent of cinnamon and clove when a dish is placed on them, $9. There are excellent fine and performing arts programs here for long-term visitors, as well as occasional concerts. A worthwhile stop.

Just across the road is **Volcano House,** which we've described in Chapter XIII. Situated as it is on the rim of the crater, it's also a great spot for sunset watching—best done from the cocktail lounge where the bartenders, volcanologists all, have whipped up something called "Pele's Delight," a combination of rum and lilikoi that manages to be pink at the bottom, fiery orange at the top. Eruption movies are shown in the lobby every night at 8:30 and 9 p.m. And it's so cozy just to sit here for a few minutes in front of the fireplace.

But enough of these man-made frills. It's nature you came here to see. There are some simple nature trails that begin right in back of Volcano House, and we urge you to take at least one. The upland air is fragrant, the vegetation glorious, the views spectacular. The silvery trees that look something like gnarled birches are ohia, and their red pompom blossoms are lehua, the flower of the Big Island, sacred to Pele. (It's rumored that if you pick one, it will rain before you arrive home.) That's the big bald dome of **Mauna Loa** towering 10,000 feet above you into the heavens; you're on **Kilauea,** which rises on its southeastern slopes. Pele hangs out in **Halemaumau,** the firepit of this enormous, 2½-mile-long crater.

To see the important views, you merely take the 11-mile circle road in either direction around the rim of Kilauea Crater. The ranger's map is easy to follow. We'll begin our trip around this wonderland of rain forests and volcanic desert at the **Sulfur Banks,** just west of park headquarters. The banks have that familiar rotten-egg odor. Farther along the road you'll see eerie wisps of steam coming out of some fissures, but don't be alarmed—they've been puffing along for centuries. You can stop to enjoy a hot blast from the steam jets, a natural underground "sauna."

Just beyond the Kilauea Military Rest Camp, there's a road that swings off to the right and across the highway that brought you here; if you follow this side path, you'll come upon an interesting clump of tree molds, formed in the same freakish way as the ones at Puna. The 100-acre **Bird Park** (Kipuka Pualu) is here too, a sweet spot for a picnic or a nature ramble through many rare trees; but you'll have to be sharp to spot the birds chirping away above your head.

Driving back to the rim of the crater road, turn right and continue the journey into the weird world ahead. You'll get your first view of Halemaumau, that awesome firepit 3000 feet wide and 300 to 400 feet deep, from the lookout at the **Volcano Observatory,** and a better view a few miles beyond. For a more intimate glimpse of Halemaumau, the three-mile (one-way) hike through a hushed forest to the eerie heart of the volcano is recommended. The walk, a tough one, starts at Volcano House; be sure to get the descriptive pamphlet at headquarters to guide you. Or you can simply drive along the well-marked Crater Rim Road to Halemaumau Overlook. When Halemaumau decides to act up, everyone from here to the Philippines seems to descend on the area; whole families sit bundled in their cars all night long watching the awesome fireworks. Nobody can say when Pele will blow her top again. It is still local custom to appease her, but now that human sacrifice is out of fashion, she is reputed to accept bottles of gin!

The drive now takes you to the area hit by the 1959 eruption of Kilauea Iki (Little Kilauea; all the volcanoes have little sisters here). A boardwalk has been set up over the cinder ash here; and a walk along this **Devastation Trail** will take you past the twisted ghosts of white trees felled by the lava. At the end of the trail you can look down into the **Kilauea Iki Crater.** (This walk takes about 15 minutes, so to conserve energy you might send one member of your party back to the parking lot to bring the car around to the lookout area at the end of the walk.) A favorite four-mile hike around the crater's edge begins here.

The forest takes over at **Thurston Lava Tube** a few miles farther on, and a magnificent prehistoric fern forest it is. The lava tube shaded by this little grotto is another of those volcanic curiosities, even more spectacular than the one you saw in Hilo.

What else you see on the road will, of course, depend on what Madame Pele has been up to. Again, be sure to check with the rangers to see that you haven't missed anything.

Note: If you haven't made the trip to Puna outlined above, you might wish to take Chain of Craters Road all the way to the Wahaula Visitors Center on the coast, then take Route 130 to the black-sand beach at Kaimu, then directly on this road to Pahoa (or for a more scenic trip, take Route 137, the coastal road to Pahoa), then home to Hilo on 130.

HUNTING AND CAMPING IN THE VOLCANO AREA: If you're brave enough to tackle Mauna Loa (the largest mountain in the world, more than 32,000 feet from sea floor to summit—18,000 of them below sea level), make your requests for information and permits for overnight trips to the superintendent, Hawaii Volcanoes National Park, Hawaii. The area is under the jurisdiction of the federal government and is administered by the National Park Service, U.S. Department of the Interior. There is an overnight camping area at the **Namakani Paio Campground,** two miles from Volcano House. Ten cabins, nicely furnished, with beds and cooking utensils, each sleep four people, at about $14.50 per night (more details in Chapter XIII).

In addition, Hawaii Volcanoes National Park manages three **drive-in campgrounds** on a first-come, first-served basis at no charge: these are the above-mentioned Namakani Paio on State Highway 11, 2½ miles west of park headquarters, with eating shelters, fireplaces, water, and restrooms; Kipuka Nene, on Hilina Pali Road, 11½ miles south of park headquarters, with eating shelters, fireplaces, water, and pit toilets; and Kamoamoa, one mile west of the Wahaula Heiau Visitor Center, with eating shelters, fireplaces, pit toilets, and water at a nearby area. You cannot reserve sites in these campgrounds in advance. There is no camping fee and no permits are required. However, your stay is limited to no more than seven days in any one campground.

Backpackers who wish to camp in the Volcano area must register at the

Kilauea Visitor Center or the Wahaula Visitor Center before beginning their trip (shelters and cabins are managed on a first-come, first-served basis at no charge). They may use the two Mauna Loa Trail Cabins (one at Red Hill at an elevation of 10,000 feet, ten miles from the end of the Mauna Loa Strip Road, and another on the southwest side of Mokuaweoweo, the summit caldera, at an elevation of 13,250 feet, each with bunks but no mattresses) or the Pepeiao Cabin, another patrol cabin on the Ka'u Desert Trail at Kipuka Pepeiao.

Oddly enough, Mauna Loa's sister, **Mauna Kea,** belongs to the state, and is administered by the State Department of Land and Natural Resources, which is responsible for the maintenance of the camping facilities on the mountain. This is great hunting country, and not a few of the sportsmen use bow and arrow. Mammal game consists of wild pigs and sheep; the birds are pheasant, chukar partridge, and quail. For all the details on seasons and licenses, write to Conservation Resources, 75 Aupuni St., Hilo, HI 96720.

Slightly higher up the mountain, in the saddle at 6500 feet, **Pohakuloa** is the base camp for recreational activities in the Mauna Kea area. It has seven housekeeping cabins that sleep up to six each, rates from $10 for one person to $30 for six people. Again, these are completely furnished and equipped, from bedding and dishes to an electric range and refrigerator. Also available are two immense barracks, each containing four units, each with eight beds—just great for a huge family or a U.N. convention. Prices range from $8 for one to $2 per person for 64 persons. One huge mess hall with a restaurant-size kitchen is shared by both buildings. You can write to the Department of Land and Natural Resources, Division of State Parks, P.O. Box 936 (75 Aupuni St.), Hilo, HI 96720 (tel. 961-7200).

For additional information on camping around the Big Island, details on current conditions of parks, fees, etc., contact the County Department of Parks and Recreation, 25 Aupuni St., Hilo, HI 96720. Remember that summers and holidays get booked far in advance.

3. Across Hawaii

There are three possible routes across the Big Island from Hilo to the Kona coast.

THE CHOICES: (1) If you're continuing on from the volcano, simply follow the excellent Highway 11 another 90 miles. You pass through the Ka'u Lava Desert (where an explosion of Kilauea in 1790 routed an army of Kamehameha's chief enemy, Keoua) and can stop off at Punalu'u to see the black-sand beach. You hit the pretty little village of Naalehu before encountering mile on mile of lava flows, until you get to the other side of Mauna Loa and the welcoming Kona coast.

(2) If you're starting from Hilo, however, and have already been to the volcano, it's impractical to take this 126-mile route, when you can reach Kona directly in 96 miles, and sample in-between terrain so varied that Hawaii seems more like a small continent than a large island. We're referring to the drive along the majestic Hamakua Coast, through the rolling pasture lands of the Parker Ranch, and then around Mauna Kea and Hualalai Volcano to Kona.

(3) An alternative route for the first 50 miles of this trip crosses over the saddle between Mauna Loa and Mauna Kea, giving you wild, unforget-

table views of both—but also a not-so-comfortable ride. Car-rental companies prohibit driving on this Saddle Road—Highway 20 out of Hilo—mostly because help is so far away. If your car breaks down, the tow charge is enormous, not to mention your being stranded in the wilderness! Not recommended.

(The drive in the opposite direction, from Kona to Hilo, is described briefly at the end of this section.)

THE HAMAKUA COAST DRIVE: The drive we prefer—and the one that we'll explore in depth—starts from Hilo on Highway 19, paralleling Kamehameha Avenue along the waterfront and heading for the northern shore of the island and the Hamakua coast. This is sugar-plantation country, miles of cane stretching inland to the valleys (the produce eventually goes to the bulk-sugar plant in Hilo and then to the mainland), the coastline a jagged edge curving around the sea, broken up by gorges and streams tumbling down from the snow-capped heights of Mauna Kea. The views from the modern and speedy Highway 19 are good, but if you really want to soak up the scenery, get off now and then on the old road that winds through the gullies and goes to the sea.

Ten miles out of Hilo, at Honomu, the HVB marker indicates the way to **Akaka Falls.** Four miles inland on a country road, you'll find not only the falls—perhaps the most beautiful in the islands, plunging dizzily 420 feet into a mountain pool—but also a breathtakingly beautiful bit of tropical forest turned into a park, lush and fragrant with wild ginger, ancient ferns, glorious tropical trees and flowers. It's a rhapsodic spot, very difficult to leave. Console yourself, then, with a brief stop at the **Honomu Plantation Store** in Honomu, a general store with a little bit of everything—groceries, liquor, Hawaiian woodcarvings, souvenirs—at good prices. Sandwiches at the snackbar are very reasonable, and the free sugarcane sample is quite tasty.

The little town of **Laupahoehoe**—you can drive down to it from the highway—is a "leaf of lava" jutting into the Pacific, its local park another idyllic spot for a picnic. But it's also a grim reminder of the savagery of nature that is always possible in Hawaii; a skeleton of a school building still stands where 20 children and their teachers were swept away into the sea by the 1946 tidal wave.

If you have time for a little hiking and nature study now, watch for the signs leading to **Kalopa:** this is a 100-acre Native Forest State Park containing trees, shrubs, and ferns indigenous to pre-Polynesian Hawaii, with trails through the ohia rain forest and many spectacular views—a nice spot for a picnic. Cabins are available for rental here, through the County Department of Parks and Recreation.

Thirty miles past Akaka Falls you reach **Honokaa,** second-largest city of the Big Island, the site of the **Hawaiian Holiday Macadamia Nut Factory,** where you can view the plant and visit the retail store, which features a mind-boggling array of 200 macadamia-nut products. Prices are factory-to-you. A macadamia-nut festival is held here in late August. Follow the warrior signs to the "Macadamia Nut Capital of the World." Open daily 9 a.m. to 6 p.m. On your way down the hill to the factory, you might want to stop in at **Kamaiina Woods;** handcrafted wooden products are available, and prices begin at just $3. Closed Sunday. If you need to stock up on health foods in Honokaa, stop in at the **Homestead Market,** which carries a variety of natural foods, fresh fruit and vegetables, and delicious raw, rennetless cheeses. Snackbar and gift shop too.

Honokaa is perhaps better known as the takeoff point to pastoral **Waipie Valley.** This side trip from your cross-island route takes you eight miles from Honokaa, branching off to the right on Route H-240. The best way to explore this spectacular valley (where 7000 full-blooded Hawaiians lived less than 100 years ago; today there are fewer than 10, plus a few hippie families) is by the **Waipio Valley Shuttle,** a 1½-hour Jeep tour starting and ending at the Waipio Valley Lookout. The tour takes you down into the valley, through taro fields, a $200,000 Ti House, the Lalakea fish pond, a black-sand beach, and the dramatic Hiilawe Falls (the water drops 1200 feet here when it's running). The cost is $10 for adults, $5 for children 2 to 12. Make reservations by calling 775-7121 in Kukuihaele. We've had excellent reports on Alan Shattuck and Brian Nelson, the new people who have taken over this service.

Whether or not you make the Waipio Valley trip, you should pay a visit to **Waipio Woodworks,** snuggled in the sleepy town of Kukuihaele which overlooks the valley (turn at the sign that reads "Kukuihaele 1 mile"). Here, at Waipio Woodworks, local craftsmen and artisans display some incredible island wood products, which begin at low figures and go up. Don't be shy: ask to see Joe, out back; he's the owner and resident craftsman, and a very friendly person. His three sons help him with the woodwork, and the family takes much pride and puts a lot of aloha into their work. Open every day, 9 a.m. to 5 p.m.

The Parker Ranch

On the next leg of your trip you'll begin to see why Hawaii is so often called a continent in miniature. West of Honokaa, winding inland on Highway 19, the sugar plantations of the tropics give way to mountain forests of cedar and eucalyptus as you climb up the slopes of Mauna Kea toward a vast prairie of rangelands and the plateau of Kamuela (also known as Waimea) and the 250,000-acre **Parker Ranch,** one of the largest cattle ranches in the United States under single ownership.

King Kamehameha started the whole thing, quite inadvertently, when he accepted a few longhorn cattle as a gift from the English explorer Capt. George Vancouver. They multiplied and ran wild until a young seaman from Newton, Massachusetts, John Parker, tamed them and started his ranch. The Parker family still owns it today, and many of the current generation of paniolos are descendants of the original Hawaiian cowboys. Parker Ranch is the biggest, but certainly not the only one; ranching is a way of life on the Big Island.

For years, visitors have wanted to tour the Parker Ranch, but it was so vast that this was impossible. A few years ago the ranch came up with a solution, and the **Parker Ranch Visitor Center** was opened. It's well worth an hour or so of your time to look around. The show starts with a 15-minute narrated audio-visual presentation in the Thelma Parker Theater, that describes the history and present-day workings of the ranch. Then you move on to the John Palmer Parker Museum, examining artifacts and mementos from the Parker Ranch and from Hawaiian history, plus a collection of trophies and mementoes of Duke Kahanamoku, Hawaii's great swimmer and Olympic athelete. You can visit the Parker Ranch Museum anytime between 9:30 a.m. and 3:30 p.m. Monday to Saturday. Admission is $2.25 each or $4 for two adults, $1.25 for active-duty military personnel and those between 12 and 18, 75¢ for those 7 to 11; 6 and under, free. Prices subject to change.

The newest gift to the community by the Parker Ranch people is the 500-seat **Kahilu Theater and Town Hall,** just across from the Visitor Center. It's a handsome facility for professional touring productions and contemporary films; you may be able to catch a performance while you're in town.

The Parker Ranch Visitor Center sits in the **Parker Ranch Shopping Center,** which has some attractive stores. At the **Paddock Shop,** adjacent to the Visitor Center, you can buy locally handcrafted gifts and mementos: handmade leather goods, Parker Ranch T-shirts, belt buckles, lauhala hats, and fabrics, plus unusual items such as handmade pheasant and peacock-feather hatbands (about $23), and unique feather pins, combs, and earrings. Elsewhere in the complex, **Waimea Sand Box** is more than the usual gift shop. Unusual paperweights featuring black and green sand, with shells and rocks embedded in them, would make fine mementos of the Big Island. And so would Elizabeth Frutiger's delicate banana bark artworks, which use no paint, and range in size from postcard ($6) to 12 by 16 inches.

Shopping and Sightseeing in Waimea

Now that you're in a shopping mood, take an hour or so to shop and look around this bright little mountain town. **Cost Less Imports** is the bargain mecca here, with vast quantities of imported wares at low, low prices: you could pick up anything from beads for handcrafts to a bentwood rocker, from porcelain hooks to tapa hangings, sheepskin rugs, and the latest oil paintings done by local artists. There are art supplies too.

Down the road a bit, we never miss a stop at the **General Store,** a tasteful bazaar with a highly sophisticated potpourri of merchandise: distinctive handicrafts—koa-wood bracelets, toys, stamp boxes, eggs, many by Le Tas de Bois—kitchen gadgets, toys and games, handmade baby quilts, and lovely Reyn Spooner clothing, for both men and women. Note the original photos of the Big Island by Jeffrey Leuer-Mermel.

The **Warehouse Shopping Complex,** one block off Highway 19, is a delightful new establishment, composed of many little booths catering to different interests, but all under the aegis of Hale Ku'ai, Gallery Extraordinaire. We spotted beautiful custom-made koa-wood tables, a well-stocked bookshop with many children's books and local cookbooks which are always fun, ceramics and gift items, plants and flowers, gourmet kitchenware and food, among many others. You can stop here to have a fancy coffee drink at the **Coffee Connection,** and, if need be, visit the local Western Union office, upstairs in the Computer Store.

New in the neighborhood, **Kamuela Country Store,** 64-1040 Mamalahoa Hwy., looks like a big winner. Browse among their very large selection of books on Hawaiiana (as well as equestrian books, cookbooks, and children's books), select some teas, jams, or coffees for gifting, and note their complete line of gourmet and regular kitchenware.

If you're an art collector, or simply appreciate beautiful work, stop in at **Martin & MacArthur;** it's a little difficult to find, on a side road just after Edelweiss and the '76 station. Changing shows by local artists feature hand-blown glass, batik, fiber, paintings and watercolors. When you come into your fortune, come back to furnish your home with exquisite originals of handmade koa furniture: dining tables, billiard tables, roll-top desks, and much more.

Your last stop in this area could well be the **Kamuela Museum** (tel.

885-4724), the largest private museum in Hawaii, founded and owned by Albert K. Solomon, Sr., and Harriet M. Solomon, great-great-grandaughter of John Palmer Parker. You'll see ancient and royal Hawaiian artifacts (many of which were formerly in Iolani Palace in Honolulu) alongside European and Oriental objets d'art, plus cultural objects brought to the islands by various ethnic groups in the 19th century. A charmer. The museum is at the junction of Routes 19 and 250; open daily, including holidays, from 8 a.m. to 5 p.m.; $2 admission for adults, $1 for children under 12.

A SIDE TRIP FROM KAMUELA: From the cool green oasis of Kamuela, you can make another side excursion, 22 miles to the little town of **Hawi,** on the northernmost tip of the Big Island. The drive is along Route 25, winding uphill through the slopes of the Kohala Mountains, and the sights are unforgettable—the Pacific on your left, looking like a blue-velvet lake lost in misty horizons; the shimmering, unearthly peaks of Mauna Kea, Mauna Loa, and Hualalei, their slopes a jumble of wildflowers, twisted fences of tree branches, and giant cactus. Your destination, Hawi, is an end-of-the-world spot, recommended for those who like to be far away from the nagging complexities of civilization. There's Old Hawaii Lodging Co., an inexpensive hotel, and a more expensive inn called Aha Hui Hale (see Chapter XIII), but that's about as much truck as they'll have with any new-fangled amenities. No drugstore, no fire station, and if you call the police, you may be told to ring up Hilo—90 miles away!

Hawi's riches—and those of its neighboring Kohala district—are in its memories. The great Kamehameha was born in this area, and if you travel east a few miles to **Kapaau,** you'll see a statue of the local hero that looks amazingly like the one you saw in Honolulu. Actually, this one is the original; it was made in Florence, lost at sea, and then found after another just like it had been fashioned for the capital. On your way back, take Route 270 out of Hawi and stop in at **Lapakahi State Historical Park,** a restored native Hawaiian village by the sea. The trip to this North Kohala area is thrilling, but remember that you've got to come down the road again (Highway 270, which links up to Highway 19 and the Kona coast), adding a total of 44 miles to your cross-island trip.

You have two routes to choose from now, as you head across the island from Waimea. If you take Route 190, you'll soon find yourself in Waikoloa Village, a newly developed area (it was once part of the Parker Ranch), where the riding, scenery, and golfing are all magnificent. (To find out about horseback riding, call 883-9335; for tee times, call 883-9621.) A short distance from the village is a glorious white-sand beach at **Anaehoomalu Bay.** Take time for a swim here, or at least for a few photos, perhaps by the fish pond, like the ones once sacred to the alii of old Hawaii. Two magnificent new luxury resorts have opened here, the **Mauna Lani Bay Hotel** and the **Sheraton Royal Waikoloa,** and yes, you're welcome to explore the grounds, the properties, and the archeological sites. The Mauna Lani is, to our way of thinking, one of the most purely beautiful resorts anywhere, especially in its landscaping and gardens, and well worth a stop. A plentiful buffet lunch is about $14.50 (tel. 885-6622). You can then continue along the coastal road, Queen Kaahuumanu Highway (Route 19), until you reach Kailua-Kona. Or you can leave Waimea on Route 19, and drive about 12 miles to the deep-water port of **Kawaihae,** where you descend through prairie land, cows grazing, and ocean vistas all about you, until you're suddenly in sultry tropics. On the road above the harbor is **Puukohola,** a well-preserved heiau and historical park that figures importantly in the history of the islands. It was here that Kaahumanu, the sweetheart-queen of the great Kamehameha, after his death began the breakdown of the dread tabu system by the startling act of eating in public with men (previously, such an act would have been punished by death). But the place is better remembered for a bloody deed that should forever disencumber you of notions that Stone Age warfare was all good clean fighting. Remember Keoua, Kamehameha's biggest rival, the one who lost an army at K'au? Kamehameha had decided to dedicate this heiau to the war god Kukailimoku, and invited Keoua to a supposed peace parley in the new temple. Instead, he had him speared as he approached the land and sacrificed to the god. Then he was free to unify Hawaii and the other islands.

After digesting this gory bit of history, you deserve a change of pace. A mile and a half back, on a right fork just past Samuel Spencer Park, is the much-touted **Mauna Kea Beach Hotel,** one of the in places for the beautiful people. The architecture and landscaping are elegantly imaginative, the rooms nestling along the brow of a hill overlooking the crystal waters of Mauna Kea Beach below. You can wander a little about the public areas of this seaside caravanserai, perhaps bumping into a celebrity or two en route to the golf course. Note the magnificent plantings, the authentic Hawaiian quilts, and the splendid art collection which ranges from Oriental bronzes and a gigantic seventh-century Indian buddha to primitive masks and woodcarvings from New Guinea. After many years, the beach has been opened to the public (but only ten parking spaces provided!) and you can also join the leisure class at lunch; a lovely, splurge buffet runs about $16.50. (Considering that there are hot dishes like stuffed Cornish hen and beef Wellington among the dazzling array of fresh fruits, salads, cheeses, hors d'oeuvres, home-baked breads, and scrumptious desserts, it's worth the money.) The Sunday buffet brunch is reported to be even more spectacular! Not far away are two public beaches where you might want to stop for a picnic: **Samuel Spencer Park** (popular with campers and sometimes a bit unkempt) and, about three miles farther south, the more spacious **Hapuna Beach** (watch, however, for signs indicating possible dangerous tides and rip currents). Continue on Route 19 through the lava desert, with the possibility, on clear days, of glorious views of all the volcanoes of Hawaii and perhaps of Haleakala on Maui too. Lava flows from Mauna Loa and Hualahai mark the eerie landscape, punctuating the miles until you emerge at last into the verdant world of the Kona coast.

(Note: We're sorry to have to issue this caveat, but we've been told that rowdies sometimes hide in the bushes near these beaches, wait for tourists to dutifully put their valuables in the trunks of their car, and then proceed to pick the locks while the tourists are out on the beach. If you're going to put anything in your trunk, do so a few miles before you reach your destination.)

FROM KONA TO HILO: If you've arrived at Kona first, you drive across the island to Hilo on Highway 11, through the K'au Desert and miles and miles of lava flows, desolate enough to be reminiscent of Dore's engravings. But before the landscape turns bleak, there's plenty of magnificent scenery. Should you make the drive in November or December, you'll see unbelievably beautiful poinsettias, riot upon riot of red color. For a swim, you might try **Hookena Beach Park,** 22 miles from Kailua. It's a long drive down the road to an almost-deserted, lovely sandy beach. **Manuka State Park,** farther on, with its arboretum of extraordinary plants and trees, is a good spot to stretch your legs and perhaps have a picnic lunch. The approach to the little village of **Waiohinu** is marvelously scenic, and the village itself, once a small farming center, is one of the quaintest on the Big Island. This is the site, too, of the Shirakawa Hotel, which we've told you about in the previous chapter. Just past the hotel is a monkeypod tree planted by Mark Twain, and a few miles farther on you can make a side trip (about a mile and a half off the highway) to the black-sand beach at **Punaluu.** Another favorite jaunt is the 12-mile drive off the highway outside Naalehu down to **Ka Lae** (South Point). Local people fish here on this wild shore of cliffs and surf, the southernmost point in the United States. Now you approach the desolate K'au region where Pele obligingly destroyed an army of Keoua, Kamehameha's archenemy, in 1790; the footprints of the victims can be seen under glass. The landscape is moon-like, and we don't mean that only poetically; space scientists are studying the lava fields of the Big Island in the belief that actual conditions on the moon may be similar. The lava flows lead you to Kilauea, Hawaii Volcanoes National Park, and on to Hilo.

4. The Kona Coast

A man we know in Kona, a refugee from the Bronx, swears he will never go back home. "I've found my bit of paradise right here, and I'm staying!" A lot of other people have waxed ecstatic about Kona, the vacation resort of Hawaiian royalty ever since the word got out that the sun shines here about 344 days a year. (Kona winds, that nasty stuff they get in Honolulu, should be properly called southerly winds, say the Konaites.) It's such a deliciously lazy spot that you may be very contented doing nothing at all in Kona. Of course, looking at the surf as it smashes along the black lava coast, noting the brilliant varieties of bougainvillea, the plumeria, the jasmine tumbling about everywhere, and lazing on the beach can keep you pretty busy. But we suggest that you take a day off from these labors and have a look at the sights. Kona is an important historic center; within the space of a few miles, Captain Cook met his end, the New England missionaries got their start, and Kamehameha enjoyed his golden age.

The tiny village of **Kailua-Kona** is the resort center, modern enough to be comfortable, but still unspoiled. Gene Wilhelm and Ami Gay, who run the Hawaii Visitors Bureau office, in the Kona Plaza Shopping Arcade, can help you with all sorts of practical information. At the Flea Market in World Square is a small post office.

TOURING THE TOWN: There's only one street, Alii Drive, running down the length of Kailua, so you won't get lost. Start up at the King Kamehameha Hotel, in the northern end of town, at the site of the monarch's heiau, which has been restored. There are tasteful museum-caliber displays highlighting Hawaiian history throughout the lobby and various free activities: ethnobotanical tours on Tuesday and Thursday at 10 a.m.; historical tours on Monday, Wednesday, and Friday at 1:30 p.m.; lei-making classes on Friday morning. Just about 150 years ago, Kamehameha ruled the Hawaiian Islands from a grass-roofed palace on this very site (Lahaina became the next capital; Honolulu did not become the capital until 1820). The old king died here in 1819, just a year before the first missionaries arrived from Boston, bringing with them the purposeful Protestant ethic that would effectively end the Polynesian era in Hawaii.

They were responsible for the **Mokuaikaua Church,** standing on the mauka side of Alii Drive, a handsome coral and lava structure that is the oldest church in Hawaii, built in 1838. Note the sanctuary inside; its architecture is New England, but it is made of two Hawaiian woods, koa and ohia. Just next door is **Hulihee Palace,** until 1916 a vacation home for Hawaiian royalty. Now it's a museum, full of Hawaiian furniture and effects, as well as more primitive curiosities like Kamehameha's exercise stone (it weighs about 180 pounds, so maybe that story about the Naha Stone isn't so crazy after all). The museum is open from 9 a.m. to 4 p.m. daily; closed federal holidays. Admission is $3 for adults, $1 for students 12 to 18, 50¢ for children under 12.

On the oceanfront at Kona Inn, **Uncle Billy's Grass Village** was just getting under way at the time of our last visit. You know Uncle Billy—his family runs the Kona Bay Hotel, Cousin Kimo's Seafood and Steak Restaurant, and Hurricane Annie's. Local students plus some from Samoa are building four grass shacks, or *hales,* to be the scene of demonstrations of the old Hawaiian crafts, which will also be sold here. An estimable project.

KONA "UP MAUKA": The shore road extends for about six more miles, but we're going to leave it temporarily, taking a left at Hualalai Street and heading out of town on Highway 11 (the mauka road). Kona "up mauka" is far removed from the tourist scene at Kailua. It is, for one thing, the place where Kona coffee, that dark, rich brew you've seen all over the islands, is grown. Hawaii is the only state in the union that has a commercial coffee crop. There are no big plantations, only small farms where everybody in the family pitches in to bring in the crop. Watch the road for the shiny green leaves of the coffee bushes with little clusters of red berries at harvest time. There are small cattle ranches here too, although they're not visible from the road. You'll see the local folk at places like the H. Manago Hotel in Captain Cook.

The drive is a beautiful one, winding through the cool mountain slopes, with fruit trees and showers of blossoms all around. If you're in the mood for a little offbeat shopping here, there are several possibilities. In Holualoa, **Pineapple Patch** offers quilting kits with free one-day instruction on Hawaiian quilting, and Rose Kimura has very reasonable prices on baskets, mats, boxes, rugs, and the like at **Kimura's Lauhala Shop,** just before Holualoa. . . . Look for the **Aloha Theater and Café** in Kainaliu now, and perhaps stop in for a tempting pastry or snack (see preceding chapter). . . . Across from it you'll find **Rainbow Light Works, Wool, Warp & Weft,** which combines stained-glass original artworks and fiber-craft supplies. . . . **Paradise Found** is the place for unique clothing, like beautiful cut lacework garments from Indonesia, as well as sought-after antique aloha shirts. Gift items by local artisans as well as Oriental imports too. . . . **Sterling Thimble** has Hawaiian quilts, straw hats, and custom dresses.

Next stop for shoppers should be the **Grass Shack** in Kealekekua, a real grass shack with bananas growing out front. The inside is laden with tasteful and authentic Hawaiian and South Pacific handicrafts, including one of the largest collections in the islands of locally made wood items. They also have original watercolors of local fish and birds at $7.95, black or brown kukui-nut leis at $6.95, coffee-bag purses at $8.95, plus Burmese jade at the most competitive prices around. The nice people here will give you some coffee beans for planting as you leave; within three to four weeks (the time it takes for the seed to germinate) you're on your way to having your own potted coffee plant, with its lush, gardenia-like fragrance.

After about 12 miles from the beginning, the road winds gently down the slopes of the mountain (watch for the HVB marker), past the **Captain Cook Coffee Mill,** the only remaining mill still in operation, through the lush tropical village of Napoopoo on to **Kealakekua Bay.** Visitors are welcome at the mill.

A monument to Captain Cook is visible across the bay, erected at a spot near where he was killed in 1779. It was here that Cook and his men pulled into the Kona coast a year after their first landing on Kauai, were again treated as gods—and wore out their welcome. When their ship was damaged in a storm and they returned to Kealakekua a second time, the men got into a fight with the natives and Cook was killed trying to break it up. You can't see the monument up close unless you approach it from the water. There's a **"Captain Cook Cruise"** that leaves Kailua wharf daily; it gives you a good look at the monument and lets you swim and snorkel in the bay. It's a good way to combine a suntan and a history lesson for about $12 for adults, $6 for children 2 to 12 (tel. 329-3811).

There are two plaques you can see on the Napoopoo shore: one of which commemorates the first Christian funeral in the islands, the other in honor of the remarkable Opukahaia, a young Hawaiian boy who swam out to a ship in 1808, got himself a job as cabin boy, converted to Christianity, and convinced the missionaries that they were needed here in the pagan, ignorant Sandwich Islands. Right near the shrines are a few jewelry stands that offer good buys in clothing and necklaces of local seeds and kukui-nut leis.

THE KONA SHORE: Continuing along the shore road now to Honaunau, you'll pass **Keei Battlefield,** a lava-scarred stretch where Kamehameha started winning wars. In the tiny fishing village of **Kei,** there's a beach with good swimming.

But the best is yet to come: Honaunau and **Pu'uhonua o Honaunau National Historical Park.** This ancient, partially restored Pu'uhonua still has about it the air of sanctuary for which it was built over 400 years ago. In the days when many chieftains ruled in the islands, each territory had a spot designated as a place of refuge to which kapu breakers, war refugees, and defeated warriors could escape; here they could be cleaned of their offenses and return, purified, to their tribes. (There is another such place on the island of Kauai, near Lydgate Park, but this one is far better preserved.) The heiau, **Hale-o-Keawe,** the temple of the purifying priests, has been reconstructed (it was in such temples that the bones of the high chiefs of Kona—which had mana, or spiritual power—were kept), and so have the tall ki'i built for the god Lono. After you've driven into the park and left your car in the parking lot (an improvement over the old days when the only way to get here was to run, or, if one came from the north, to swim, since the feet of commoners were not fit to tread on the Royal Grounds on the north side of the place of refuge), we suggest you take in one of the orientation talks given daily at 10, 10:30, and 11 a.m., and at 2:30, 3, and 3:30 p.m., in the spacious amphitheater staffed by the National Park Service, which administers this facility. Besides explaining the concept of refuge, the park ranger also talks about the plants and trees of the area. Then you're free to have a swim (but sunbathing is not allowed), a picnic, go snorkeling or fishing—or just absorb the peace on your own. Or you can tour the area by yourself with a self-guiding leaflet. "Cultural demonstrators" are usually on hand, carving woods, pounding poi, and performing other such ancient Hawaiian tasks. Canoes, fishnets, and traps are on display, and often are being used outside the huts.

There's one more curious sight in Honaunau, which you reach by turning north on a side road as you go back up the highway. This is **St. Benedict's Church,** which everybody calls the "Painted Church." The Catholic missionaries, more adaptable than their Protestant predecessors, created biblical murals that gave a feeling of spaciousness to the tiny church, presumably so that the congregation would have more of a feeling of the out-of-doors—to which pagan nature worship had accustomed them.

Between Pu'uhonua o Honaunau and the Painted Church, you might want to stop in at **Barry's Nut Farm.** Barry Gitelson and Arlene Wakefield, transplanted mainlanders, not only sell macadamia nuts reasonably ($5 buys three pounds in the shell), they also offer guided and self-guided tours of a lovely five-acre botanical garden, with some 1000 varieties of plants and flowers. Be sure to see the Fuku-Bonsai collection, the first and only public display of bonsai trees on the island. The gift shop features items made only in Hawaii, and the snackbar offers moderately priced soups, salads, and nut treats. They're on Highway 160, open daily (tel. 328-9930).

Nearby, at the junction of Middle Keei Road with Highway 11 in Honaunau, is the **Kona Coast Macadamia Nut Company,** where you can get good prices on air-dried macadamias made up into luscious chocolates; irregular chocolate-covered nuts may run as low as six for 75¢, and you can often buy a pound of nuts—edible rejects—for $1. The sign reads "Buy at your own risk"; we did, and they were slightly burnt-tasting, but not bad. Open daily (tel. 328-2201).

Back on Highway 11 and headed toward Kailua now, you continue for about 11 miles until you come to a turnoff to the left that brings you back to the shore at Keauhou Bay. If you'd like to see how the other half lives, drive on and explore the ground and public areas of the fabulous **Kona Surf Hotel.** The Oriental and Polynesian art objects scattered about, the glorious use of natural materials, the 14½ acres and 30,000 plants on the property make it a sightseeing stop in its own right. Complimentary garden tours are given Monday, Wednesday, and Friday at 9 a.m., but you're welcome to come on your own and have a look. Opposite the Keauhou Beach Hotel in this area is **Kona Gardens,** a new attraction. On the site of an ancient Hawaiian village where heiaus, petroglyphs, lava tubes, and gravesites have been excavated, a handsome cultural and botanical park has been created, featuring plants, trees, and flowers from the Pacific Islands. In addition to touring the grounds, you can purchase plants and flowers, visit the gift and snackshops, maybe catch a special entertainment in the large amphitheater. Pleasant, but a bit overpriced we think, at $5 for adults, $3 for children 7 to 12, free for those under 7. If, however, you're in Kona on a Saturday morning, this is a "must" stop. Between 7:30 a.m. and 2:30 p.m., there's a colorful flea market; 75 to 100 vendors sell everything from fruits to Frisbees, and a great time is had by all. There is no admission fee for buyers.

Continuing back to Kailua now, the old vies with the new for attention everywhere. To your left is a modern small-boat harbor; to your right, faintly visible on the mountain slopes, the remains of a rocky royal slide down which the alii of Hawaii scooted into the water below. Coming into sight soon is Kahaluu Beach Park, and your sightseeing labors are over.

THE LAZY LIFE: Now you can concentrate on the important business of Kona, sun-worshiping. **Kahaluu Beach Park** is a fine place for swimming, snorkeling, and picnicking. There's a pretty lagoon, the swimming is safe, and the sand, once a fine white, is now salt-and-pepper, thanks to an ancient lava flow that came pounding across it. But we are partial to **White Sands Beach** (sometimes called "Disappearing Beach," since the high surf occasionally removes and then returns the sand), a gorgeous, if tiny, spot. Palm trees arch across the sand, the surf is a Mediterranean blue, and the brilliant reds, yellows, and purples of tropical blossoms are everywhere. Be careful, though, when the surf is rough. Back in Kailua, you can swim in front of the luxurious King Kamehameha Hotel; the beach here is a public one, something that old King Kam would probably have approved of.

THE SPORTING SCENE: There is, of course, no dearth of sporting activities in Kona. Deep-sea fishermen consider Kona their favorite place in the world. Deep-sea fishermen must also be rather affluent, since they think nothing of calling **Roy Gay** (tel. 369-6041) and having him arrange a fishing boat charter at about $300 a half day, $400 a full day. Split two or three ways, it's considered a bargain! Meanwhile, us ordinary folk can view the catch. The morning weigh-in of the giants is from noon to 1 p.m., the afternoon one from 4 to 5 p.m., at the pier in front of the King Kamehameha Hotel.

A number of our readers have written over the years to recommend an idyllic snorkeling adventure aboard the *Kahlua,* a 26-foot double Malibu outrigger run by **Pacific Sail and Snorkel** (tel. 329-2021 for reservations, or write to P.O. Box 2021, Kailua-Kona, HI 96745). The great thing about this trip is that it's just as simple for nonswimmers as it is for Red Cross lifeguards, since those who wish to may enter the water in an inner tube. Jay Lambert, who runs the tours, claims that snorkeling is even easier than swimming, requires little exertion or water knowledge. And everybody likes to hand-feed the many varieties of small tropical reef fish abounding in the crystalline waters where the boat drops anchor. Those who only want to sail without getting wet are welcome too. One of our readers, Marty Iabis of Prospect, Illinois, wrote us: "The cruise was organized by two very congenial fellows who make each trip cozy and informal, unlike the mass atmosphere most tourists have to put up with—this was on a first-name basis and only 10 to 15 persons aboard. My husband and I found it to be one of our most memorable experiences on the island!" You receive free transportation by van to the boat, then sail to an isolated reef; equipment, professional instruction, and even a glass of guava juice and some freshly cut pineapple are provided, all for $20. Plan on about three hours for the total experience.

Golf? That's easy too. The place to play is at the beautiful **Keauhou Kona Course,** six miles south of Kona; make arrangements at your hotel. If it's tennis you're after, try the free public court at the **Kailua Playground** near the Kona Sunset Hotel, or the four courts at the Old Airport Tennis Court. Courts are also available at nominal cost at the Hotel King Kamehameha, the Keauhou Beach Hotel, the Kona Hilton Beach and

Tennis Resort, and the Kona Surf Hotel. And you can make arrangements for many different activities at various branches of the **Kona Activities Center;** you'll find them in the lobbies of the King Kamehameha and Kona Hilton Hotels and at the Kona Inn Shopping Village. The Hawaii Visitors Bureau can provide you with complete listings of island sports facilities.

SHOPPING IN KONA: The Kona shopping scene has blossomed like everything else in this bubbling resort town. At last count, there must have been something like 100 stores and shops, some in quaint arcades, some in small centers and hotels, others just there, all on or just off Alii Drive.

A good place to begin might be the shopping arcade in the **Hotel King Kamehameha.** New Guinea artifacts—carved figures, woven bags, masks, shields, and spears—abound at **Tribal Arts Gallery.** We also spotted tapa cloth from Tonga and Fiji from $7 up, and cloisonné jewelry from mainland China, from $4.25 and up.

Proceed to the Seaside Mall across from the King Kam, to the **Butterfly Boutique,** where they'll show you shorts, skirts, and sarongs in subdued Hawaiian prints. Plenty of bikinis, one-piece bathing suits, and a large selection of dresses. There's always a sale rack. . . . A sign at **Island Silversmith** reads "We only look expensive," and they're right. A good-looking sterling-silver tiki on a chain was just $18.

In the Akona Kai Mall, art lovers should check out the **Akona Kai Gallery,** which shows beautiful work by Hawaiian artists. You may not want to spend $300 to $400 for brass sculptures by such Hawaiian names as Spanky and Craig Fuller, but small wall sculptures start under $100, and there are charming coffee mugs for $8.

If you haven't brought the right walking shoes with you (doesn't it always happen?), stop in and see Jack and Marge Mulhall at the **Sandal Basket** on Alii Drive. They have a very large selection for both men and women, the prices are excellent, and the service first-rate. No wonder they've been here for over 21 years!

There's one first-run movie theater right in this area, at **World Square** (there are three more at Hualalai, up mauka). A London doubledecker bus takes you here, free, from any of the hotels in the Keahou Beach area on a frequent shuttle schedule. Of the shops here, we like **Smuggler's Loft** for its nautical giftware, and **Showcase,** a gallery-shop offering paintings, hand-blown glass, prints, woven baskets, and island wood products. Prices for prints begin around $4 and go up to about $40.

Cross the street now to the ocean side where you'll find another big shopping arcade: **Kona Inn Shopping Village,** with 50 shops and a bevy of restaurants (Kona Inn, located directly on the waterfront, is outstanding). Some favorites are **The Shellery,** where you can get gold-plated shell pendants for $7, petroglyph charms for $10, lots of lovely jewelry, many fine specimen shells. Kids will love the large aquarium with its amazing fish. . . . You can get an Indian fighter kite for $3.95, T-shirts with their names, and much more for the kids at **High as a Kite Toys and Kites.** . . . Boys' and girls' Hawaiian clothing is priced reasonably at **Kona Inn Children's Wear,** whose selections go from infants through young teens. . . . A few doors down, the same people run **Fare Tahiti Fabrics,** a fabric shop with Hawaiian and Tahitian prints in cotton, polyesters, and the new rayon "silkies." Prices are reasonable, from $5 up. Note too the beautiful silkscreen-printed Alfred Shaheen panels at competitive prices. . . . The **Kona Gold Mine** specializes in those 14-karat solid-gold pineapple charms that everyone seems to like so much. Prices begin at $5 and go way up, but they often run 50% discount sales . . . If calories are irrelevant, pick up some coconut shortbread or macadamia-nut cookies ($3.75 the dozen) at **Mrs. Barry's Kona Cookies.** One of our readers, Charles Rabin of New York, writes that "These cookies were one of the many reasons I regretted departing Kona!" . . . Don't miss saying hello to Joe, a real live mynah bird who lives in a cage at **The Mynah Bird.** He says "aloha" and a few other things while you're busy viewing a collection of lovely fabrics. . . . We found stylish modern and vintage fashions for women at **Flamingo's,** and classy items for men at **Flamingo's for Men.** . . . The **Wild Orchid** specializes in women's swimsuits and clothing; and at **Noa Noa,** you can come away with a different look. Indonesian clothing, hand-printed cotton batiks, jewelry, and sandals, plus Indonesian artifacts. . . . Take a coffee break, have some espresso or cappuccino, and maybe buy some coffees as gifts at **Coffee Cantata.** . . . Or have an ice cream or snack on a breezy lanai overlooking the ocean at **Billy Boy's Fast Foods.**

Running out of things to read? Help is at hand in the **Middle Earth Book Shoppe** across the road, stocked with an excellent selection of paperbacks, plus lots of Hawaiiana.

Near the intersection of Highways 11 and 19 is the **Kona Coast Shopping Center.** Here, the old **Taniguchi's,** razed when the King Kamehameha Hotel was rebuilt, has been relocated in a modern supermarket setting. The store is slick and modern now, with none of its pretourist local character, but it's still a good place to stock up on food for your kitchenette apartment. It also might pay to join the local folks at places like **Pay 'n' Save,** a huge drugstore with very low prices for film and other items, and **Kona Health Ways,** with a large selection of herbs, roots, teas, spices, and some fresh produce.

Island Cheese Shop and Delicatessen, located in the industrial area at 74-5552A Kaiwi St. (take your first right after the intersection of Highways 11 and 190), is a real find. Phone ahead (tel. 329-4646), or just come by to pick up some good cheese, a pickle, bagels (or one of their $2.60 to $3.95 sandwiches) and head for a picnic down the road at the old airport beach. . . . Or patronize the competition, **Belli Delli,** right across the street at 74-5543 Kaiwi St., which has all the delights of a New York deli, with sandwiches from about $2 to $4. You can call in for special or large orders by 10 a.m. for a noontime pickup (tel. 329-9454).

If candy is your passion, be sure to visit the **Kailua Candy Company** at 74-552C Kaiwi St., where you'll be taken on a tour of the kitchen and given lots of free samples of chocolates and dry-roasted macadamia nuts. It will be hard to resist buying some to take home with you, even though the average price is $12 a pound, for these are handmade and hand-packed candies, made with real butter, no preservatives, and a great deal of pride by the family who operates the business. They call them the best tasting candies in Hawaii, and you might just agree.

A BIG ISLAND CALENDAR: Can't decide when to come to the Big Island? Here's a list of some events that may help you make your plans. Late in April is the time for the **Merrie Monarch Festival,** including competitions, workshops, and mini performances at Wailoa Center, lots of free shows at the tennis stadium, and more hula than you can shake a hip at. . . . May Day is **Lei Day:** there's usually lei making in the hotel lobbies. . . . A major event for local artists is the **Big Island Spring Arts Festival,** held in May or June. A wonderful chance to see the best of island arts. . . . **July 4** is a big time for community gatherings: rodeos in Waimea and Naalehu, rough-water swims in Hapuna, and an anniversary celebration for the Pu'uhonua o Honaunau in Kona, showing off old Hawaiian crafts in a cultural festival. . . . Also in July is the **International Festival** in Hilo, including free Shakespeare in the Park performances, parades, dances, and displays of the multiethnic peoples of Hawaii. . . . **Bon Dances** are big events in both July and August. . . . In late July or August, sportsmen from all over gather for the **Billfish Tournament** in Kona. . . . The **Honokaa MacNut Festival,** featuring unusual races with macadamia-nut bags, nut balls for a golf tournament, and more, is held in late August . . . **Aloha Week** festivities in October are special on the Big Island: the opening ceremony is at Halemaumau with dance performances and offerings to Pele. . . . The **Kona Coffee Festival** is held in mid-October.

READERS' SIGHTSEEING AND SHOPPING SUGGESTIONS ON THE BIG ISLAND: "One of our favorite side trips was the **Waipio Valley Jeep Ride,** with our guide, Kamiko. This area is untouched by hotels and beautiful in its natural state. It is land that is owned and protected by native Hawaiians. An ancient zigzag trail leads up a mountain to valleys that are yet untouched by too many litterbugs; and quiet beauty abounds to strong, steady, and prepared backpackers. There are wild avocado, papaya, mango, mountain apple trees, etc. The Jeep saves you a steep trek up and down a winding road that finally leads to a wild beach. We were happy to pay the $10 because we learned much about the history of the area. . . . In Hilo, we found the **Island Seed Shop** close to the waterfront. There are jars and jars of crackseed candy, some of which we had never before seen or tried" (April Kashaveroff and Ian McDonald, Oakland, Calif.). . . . "At **Fare Tahiti Fabrics** in the Kona Shopping Village I found tapa cloth print fabrics for making a muumuu. I learned that for $1 one can get a catalog of patterns for Polynesian and Hawaiian clothes from Pattern People, P.O. Box 11254, Honolulu, HI 96828. If you're handy with needle and thread and sewing machine, you can quickly run up exactly the gladrags you want. My fabric cost about $5.25 a yard for 3½ yards and $3.25 for the pattern which is adaptable to five sizes, from extra-small to extra-large" (Ilma Rosskopf, Baltimore, Md.). [*Authors' Note:* Patterns are also available right at Fare Tahiti.] . . . "I would like to recommend **The Fairwind,** a 50-foot sailing trimaran cruise to Captain Cook Monument underwater park. You can learn to snorkel and hand-feed the tropical fish, or view from the glass bottom. Scuba is available for certified and beginner divers. You can plunge into the water from a 16-foot slide, if desired. Cost, including pickup and return to your hotel, is $30 in the morning with lunch, $18 in the afternoon with snacks, gear included both times. The boat was absolutely spotless. One has to see the fish and the underwater scenery for oneself" (Katherine Seaman, Victoria, B.C., Canada).

"In my opinion, the best shop in all of the Hawaiian Islands is the **Volcano Art Center** on the Big Island which sits next door to Volcanoes National Park headquarters and across the road from the current Volcano House. This art center, housed in the original Volcano House built in 1877, contains handcrafted items of the finest quality from island artisans. Beautiful koa, mango, milo, and other native wood bowls, boxes, and cutting boards, may be purchased, as well as feather leis, ivory jewelry, petroglyph notecards and postcards, among others. They will package and mail any item purchased there" (Teresa M. Zent, Taneytown, Md.). . . . "**Photo Express** in World Square, Kona, will have films developed in 24 hours—including slides. We were very pleased with the service and with the quality of the developing" (Rosemary and Kent Brauninger, Port Angeles, Wash.). . . . "**Anthuriums of Hawaii** was a delight; the man in charge was so enthusiastic about the flowers. And the prices were unbelievable: we bought two dozen anthuriums, at $2.50 a dozen. The shopkeeper even packed them for us so they would safely make the trip back to St. Louis that evening" (Jan Bell, Florissant, Mo.). . . . "A United Airlines employee at Kahului gave me this helpful tip. If your plane stops in Hilo en route home, buy flowers at the airport—fresher and cheaper. I bought a beautiful orchid, carnation, and plumeria lei for $2, and orchid plants were $1 to $2 less than at other flower stands elsewhere. The saleswomen were extremely helpful and cordial" (Elizabeth C. Greer, El Cerrito, Calif.). . . . "On our way home we stopped at **Hawaiian Flower Gardens,** on the road from the volcano to Hilo in Mountain View to get several dozen gorgeous anthuriums at *$1.50 a dozen.* They packed them beautifully, stamped them with an agriculture stamp, and they came through without incident. We paid extra for the packing box. In our area, anthuriums run approximately $2.50 per flower" (Mrs. Donna Hoyt, Fountain Valley, Calif.). . . . "There isn't too much to do for evening entertainment in Kona. But the triple movie theater, **Hualalai Theater,** plays first-run movies for only $2! On Thursday, admission is a bargain $1. The theater is clean and air-conditioned" (Kevin and Theresa Lew, San Francisco, Calif.).

"We snorkeled at Hanauma Bay in Oahu, and Popiu Beach and **K'ee Beach** in Kauai, but we found the best snorkeling by far to be at **Kahalou Beach Park** in Hawaii, about three miles south of Kona. One day I took out some bread and when I let some pieces go, we had hundreds of fish within reaching distance of us. This definitely was a highlight of our entire trip" (Richard Marks, Lodi, Calif.). . . . "We found shopping in Kona to be cheapest and least crowded of any place we visited. The shopping mall of the **King Kamehameha Hotel** was a very pleasant experience, both in price and selection. We found good buys on Kona coffee and macadamia nuts in the local grocery on Kona (Foodland). But we really got hooked on dry-roasted macadamia nuts from the **Kailua Candy Co.** right on Alii Drive. Your book directed us here to taste Kona coffee, but their candy and nuts were also superb" (Mrs. Hugh Tyree, Dallas, Texas). . . . "Our favorite pastime on the Big Island was snorkeling. We found **Jack's Diving Locker** in the Kona Inn Shopping Village (tel. 329-7585). The young owners were personable and most helpful, not only with snorkeling information, but also local news. They were great" (Alice L. Dufresne and Venice V. Keyes, Gilroy, Calif.). . . . "One of the big athletic events in the islands is the **Triathalon.** It's said to be the single most grueling athletic contest in the world; it's much harder to be a participant in this than in the Olympics. Over 600 brave souls entered the contest twice last year. Briefly, it is a 2½-mile swim, then a 117-mile bike race, then about a 50-mile run with no resting in between. It starts about 8 a.m., and many do not finish until the wee hours. . . . There's an interesting **Fourth of July Rodeo** in Waimea. Instead of the typical bucking broncos you would expect from a mainland rodeo, they have hilarious 'wild cow milking,' and also relay races on horseback. . . . Kailua Kona's annual **Billfish Tournament** in July features a parade bearing floats and entries from countries like Samoa, Fiji, and New Zealand" (Barbara King, Kailua-Kona, Hi.).

"John Alexander, the delightful host at the **Dolphin Bay** in Hilo, gave us a helpful hint that we want to pass on. He told us to buy our flowers at an inexpensive place, such as a grocery store or small florist, obtain a carton, and pack them carefully with shredded, wet newspapers, covered with plastic, to keep them moist. We did this, and carried them on the plane with us. I am writing this over a week later and they are still in good shape. I have four dozen anthuriums and six birds of paradise to give to my friends, and all for just a little over $15" (Mrs. Dean James, Celina, Ohio). . . . "We found a great deal of unshelled macadamia nuts in the supermarket at the shopping center at Waimea. Their price was 89¢ a pound—by far the cheapest of anything we found elsewhere. There is another shop in the same shopping center selling nothing but macadamia nuts, just a few doors from the Parker Ranch Visitor Center, and its price is higher. Budget shoppers beware! The next best deal was at the **Green Sands Coffee Shop** in the delightful untouristy town of Naalehu, the southernmost town in the U.S.A." (Donald T. Hawkins, Berkley Heights, N.J.).

"While visiting Kailua-Kona we took a dinner cruise on **Captain Beans's Royal Canoe.** It cost $30 per person, but it was the most we received for our money on the entire trip. The bar was wide open, the food was good—all the food and drink you wanted—and the entertainment was excellent and continuous. If you take a cruise, be sure to take your camera. You'll be sorry if you don't" (I. F. Komoroske, Sun Prairie, Wisc.). [*Authors' Note:* Captain Beans also runs some excellent glass-bottom sails.] . . . "The Kailua-Kona **McDonald's** has a new playground next to it for its small customers. The play equipment includes the McDonald characters. There is also a 'train' for the children to sit in while dining. Our children loved it" (Kay Baur, Hollywood, Calif.). . . . "Snorkeling can be done by anyone! Jay Lambert of **Pacific Sail and Snorkel** runs a trimaran for the young at heart. He and his mate, two serious and intelligent young men, took us out, taught us how to snorkel, and were as concerned and safety-conscious, and careful of our well-being as our favorite grandchildren. I urge all older people to join the young in experiencing the wonderful underwater world off this coast in complete safety. If you can wade out in water to your knees to get on the boat, put your swim suit on and go! And the sail back to Kailua was beautiful" (Bridget Paddock, Elmendorf AFB, Alaska). [*Authors' Note:* See text, above, for details on Pacific Sail and Snorkel.] . . . "For those who enjoy snorkeling, we would like to recommend a lagoon only five miles south of Kailua-Kona at milepost 5. **Kahaluu Beach Park** has picnic tables, showers, rest rooms, and a beautiful large lagoon from one to three feet deep. Part of the lagoon is closed from the sea by a row of rocks. According to the local groundskeeper, the Menehunes were to create a fish pond in trade for some land. Since the Hawaiian who bargained with the Menehunes had second thoughts about the deal, he would crow like a rooster from a coconut tree every morning at 3 a.m. The Menehunes, who worked by night, thought morning was approaching, so they stopped work, never completing the fish pond. All types of fish are present in this lagoon, including a few Crown of Thorns" (Charles Kinney, Hayward, Calif.). . . . "When visiting the petroglyphs at Puako, be sure to take along some material suitable for making rubbings. Burlap and wax crayon (seen in the Lyman Museum) were very effective. There are two sites; the second one, about a quarter mile past the first, has a much wider variety of carvings" (Patricia Scruggs, Chino, Calif.). . . . "At the **Coffee Mill Museum Kona,** a two-ounce can of Kona Blend Freeze Dried Coffee was $3.60. At the **K. Taniguchi Super Market** in Kailua, the same can was $1.40, and it wasn't on sale: that was the regular price . . . **K.T.A. Supermarket** had great prices on macadamia nuts: I paid $2.09 for a five-ounce can on sale" (Martha F. Battenfeld, Brighton, Mass.). [*Authors' Note:* This is a family-owned supermarket, with one branch here, two more in Hilo. They have good sales all the time.]

"We took a nice side trip to Pololu Valley Lookout on the northern tip in the **Kohala** district. After viewing the beautiful valley we stopped about three miles back down the road from the lookout on Highway 27 at **Keokea Park,** which had a lovely view, picnic tables, outdoor showers, and a little sea pool. There is a sign off Highway 27; you drive in from the road about one mile" (Mr. and Mrs. Donald Plumlee, Santa Clara, Calif.). . . . "We found canvas shoes much more desirable than sandals when we visited Volcanoes National Park and the Pu'uhonua o Honaunau at Kona; the volcanic pebbles are difficult to walk on and get between your toes, and the canvas shoes give you a firm footing. Since we were in Hawaii in November and December we did have rain, and my washable canvas shoes were not ruined by the red mud I encountered several times or the deluge of rain we had to paddle through in Hilo" (Mrs. Jack Morgan, Vacaville, Calif.). . . . "The fishing pier across from Liliuokalani Gardens Park has a very interesting fish auction at 7:30 a.m. weekday mornings, when the boat operators sell to licensed fish markets. The auction takes only a few minutes, and visitors may ask questions. In Kona, the weighing in of marlins and tuna is very interesting and starts at 6 p.m." (Mrs. Charles H. Gould, Seattle, Wash.). . . . "It is interesting to drive up the 13-mile road on the slope of Mauna Loa for the view. From there the trail leads to the summit. On this ride in the morning at 7 a.m., I saw plenty of wild pigs and wild goats. Before Waiohini, it is worthwhile to drive nine miles down to the left to the South Point (Ka Lae), the southernmost point of the U.S. There is a lighthouse and steep cliffs. The fishermen have to tow the fish over the cliffs from their boats" (Prof. Dr. W. K. Brauers, Berchem-Antwerp, Belgium).

"For children's gifts, we picked free coconuts under the trees at Kalapana Black Sand Beach. You remove the bud, write the address with black marking crayon on the hard outer shell, and mail. Postage from Hilo is about $1 and passage takes three weeks. The kids on our street loved them" (Arthur Hakenen, Okemos, Mich.).

Chapter XV

THE ISLAND OF MAUI

1. Hotels
2. Restaurants
3. The Night Scene

EVEN THOUGH SHE LIVES two blocks away from highly celebrated Waikiki Beach, a woman we know in Honolulu regularly spends her vacations in Maui. The reason? To go to the beach! In addition, however, to possessing some of the world's most marvelous beaches, this second-largest island in the Hawaiian archipelago boasts one of the great natural wonders of the planet: **Haleakala,** the world's largest dormant volcano. Add to all this a string of gorgeous little jungle valleys where the modern world seems incredibly remote, a picturesque whaling town kicking its heels after a long sleep in the South Seas sun, and a wonderfully hospitable local citizenry intent on convincing you that Maui no ka oi—Maui is the greatest. You just might end up agreeing.

Maui has been going through the throes of enormous expansion. But while new hotels and condominium apartments have been and are being built at a formidable rate, the island still manages to retain a graceful, unhurried feeling. The laws here are stricter, and nowhere on Maui has there been such wanton destruction of natural beauty as there has been in Waikiki.

Although most of the new condominium apartments are in the luxury category, some are fine for us. But even with these additions to the hotel scene, a room in Maui is probably going to be more expensive than one in Waikiki. Meals, however, are reasonable, and there are more kitchenette apartments than in the other neighbor islands. Again, your biggest expense will be car rentals or guided tours, your only alternatives on an island with very limited transportation. A bus service and an oldtime tourist train run between the Lahaina and Kaanapali areas, and there's another bus service from Kahului to Kihei, but that's about the extent of it.

CHOOSING A BASE: Maui is small enough so that you can logically make your headquarters at one hotel and take off each day for various sightseeing and beach excursions: to **Haleakala Volcano,** to the historic old whaling town of **Lahaina,** and to remote romantic **Hana.**

The **Wailuku-Kahului** area, closest to the airport, is centrally located

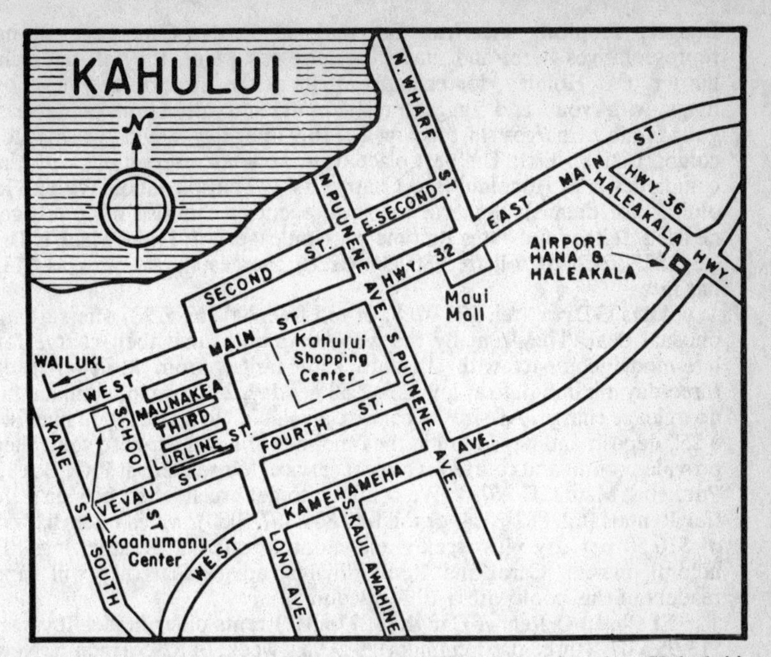

for sightseeing excursions but lacks a beach. The closest beach to Kahului is **Kihei** (about a 15-minute drive) and this also enjoys a central location. The liveliest and most beautiful area, to our taste, is the **Lahaina-Napili** region, about 40 miles from Kahului. All of these places work as a base; the only place on the island that is inconvenient as a base if you want to move around is **Hana;** you might want to plan an overnight stay there as the drive each way is a long one, although most people do it on a one-day trip.

ARRIVAL IN KAHULUI: Your plane will land at the very modern and airy Kahului Airport. The terminal is located in the seven-mile-wide valley that binds together the two great volcanic masses of Maui—the West Maui Mountains and Haleakala on the east—and accounts for the name Valley Isle. You're just a few miles here from modern Kahului and graceful old Wailuku, neighbor towns competing peacefully for the title of largest city. From the airport, you'll have to take a taxi to your hotel, unless you're going to rent a car. If you need assistance, stop by the state information kiosk at the airport.

If you're flying directly to the Kaanapali area and not continuing on a round-the-islands itinerary, you can have a bit of low-cost adventure by hopping a commuter air-carrier right to the Kaanapali strip. On one trip we flew in a twin-engine Cessna of the Royal Hawaiian Air Service (Gate 1, Honolulu International Airport; tel. 836-2200), sat up next to the pilot, and caught some fantastic scenery at the low altitudes. The cost of the trip from Honolulu should be about $45.

U-DRIVES: As in all the neighbor islands the major low-cost, all-island car-rental companies are represented in Maui. **Holiday Rent-A-Car Hawaii,**

Budget, Tropical, American International Rent-A-Car, etc., all have representatives here, and maybe because it's Maui, they all try a little harder. (At Holiday, for example, right at the airport, they'll go over maps with you, and suggest restaurants and attractions suitable for your family. Charges start as low as $16.95 per day, $69.50 weekly, for a compact stick shift.) The best place to make your reservations with these companies is in Honolulu (see Chapter IV, "Transportation Within Honolulu," for details). Some of the local agencies can also offer you good deals, at either flat rates or time plus mileage. At **Trans Maui U-Drive** (tel. 877-5222, or toll free 800/367-5228) charges start as low as $13.95 flat rate.

Atlas U-Drive (tel. 877-7208, or toll free 800/367-5238) offers a rather unusual deal. They rent by the week or month, and their charge for a late-model compact with standard shift ranges from $16.50 per day, three-day minimum, to as low as $12.50 per day, 28-day minimum, flat rate, no mileage charge. All sizes of cars are available. To qualify, you must send a $50 deposit and pay in full at the time the car is delivered to you. They'll provide prompt and courteous airport service. Write them at P.O. Box 126, Puunene, Maui, HI 96784. We continue to get excellent reports on **V.I.P. Car Rentals** (tel. 887-2054, or toll free 800/367-6080), which offers flat rates of $16.50 per day plus weekly and monthly rates at great savings. The helpful owners, Carol and Ron Williams, advise that they will supply readers of this book with a 10% discount.

El Cheap-O Rent-A-Car (tel. 877-5851) rents older model Toyotas at $13.95 a day (three-day minimum), $89.95 a week, or $295 a month. Newer models and four-wheel-drives are also available. Insurance is an extra $4 a day. Reservations are suggested and will be acknowledged by return mail upon receipt of a $50 deposit. Free airport shuttle is available. Write them at P.O. Box 1065, Puunene, HI 96874.

In the Lahaina-Kaanapali area, you can get a good deal on flat rates from **Rainbow,** 161 Dickinson St., Lahaina (tel. 661-8734), which charges $12.50 per day for Toyota Corolla compacts.

1. Hotels

IN KAHULUI-WAILUKU: Kahului has a string of four hotels within minutes of the airport and across the road from three very attractive shopping centers dotted with inexpensive restaurants. The beach here, however, is barely swimmable, with rough tides and rocks. With the development of a very good beach area in Kihei, just 15 minutes away, these hotels have become largely the place for local business travelers and for very large tour groups, since Kahului does offer a central location for touring all of Maui. If you choose to stay here, your best budget bets are the **Maui Hukilau** and its sister hotel, the **Maui Sands.** At the pleasingly Polynesian-style Maui Hukilau, standard singles are $28 and standard twins are $31; higher priced rooms go for $23 and $35 single, $35 and $38 double. Like another wing of the Maui Hukilau (same swimming pool, same restaurants, etc., and under the same management) is the newer **Maui Seaside,** with large, light, tastefully furnished rooms, all boasting air conditioning, color TV, refrigerator (but no cooking facilities), and two double beds. There are no lanais, but most of the rooms have lovely views of mountains, sea, or garden. Standard rooms go for $35 single, $38 twin;

higher priced accommodations are $38 and $41 single, $41 and $44 twin. Their hotel-car-breakfast package for two runs from $48. The toll-free reservation number is 800/367-7000.

Two good apartment-hotels in Wailuku now rent mostly on a long-term basis. If you're planning to stay in the area for quite a while, you might consider the **Puuone Gardens Apartments** at 471 Liholiho St. (tel. 244-5240) or **Fong's Apartment Motel** at 509 Pio Dr. (tel. 878-1525).

IN KIHEI-WAILEA: The closest beach area to Kahului (about 15 minutes away) is the Kihei-Wailea section of Maui—a windswept stretch of sea and sand, with miles and miles of unspoiled ocean beach, the waves lapping at your feet, air warm and dry, and the mighty volcano of Haleakala and its changing cloud colors to gaze at from the shore. Full-scale tourist development began here not so long ago, and the area has blossomed mightily since then, with scores of condominiums, plus new restaurants and small shopping centers opening to keep pace. There are two luxury-class hotels in Wailea, and even a private bus line (Bee Lines; tel. 877-3382), which shuttles visitors back and forth from Kahului for a fee of about $1.50 each way. Beaches here can be rather windy in the afternoon (get your swims in the morning and save sightseeing for later). Despite its beauty, the Kihei-Wailea region remains less glamorous and exciting, at least for us, than the Lahaina-Kaanapali region (see ahead), but if you like a quiet vacation, you'll do well at any of the places described below.

Two former readers of this book, Milt and Eileen Preston, started traveling to the islands a few years ago and then decided to settle there. Now they have their own place in Kihei, and will give you a warm welcome at the **Sunseeker Resort,** across a tiny road from Kihei Beach. There are just half a dozen studios, plus one- and two-bedroom apartments here, and although the studios are not lavish, they are nicely furnished with a cheerful color scheme, upholstered furniture on the lanais, cross-ventilation, and a full kitchen. These go for one of the best prices in the Kihei area: $29, single or double. The one-bedroom apartments, with a couch in the living room that opens to a double bed, require a stay of three days. They rent for $39, single or double, $5 for each extra person; the two-bedroom apartments are $50 per day. The Prestons will provide you with free barbecue equipment. For reservations, write them at P.O. Box 276, Kihei, Maui, HI 96753 (tel. 879-1261).

A very pleasant neighboring place is **Wailana Sands Resort Apartments.** Inland and off the main road about 100 yards, it's quiet and secluded, and as you sit on your lanai overlooking the green lawn and lovely swimming pool, you can just feel yourself unwind. There are ten one-bedroom apartments, each of them individually furnished (and some nicer than others), but all are comfortable. The bathroom, with its tub-shower combination, can be entered from either the bedroom or the living room, which doubles as a second bedroom. The kitchen is fully equipped, and the TV has excellent reception. Rates are from $26 double in summer, $39 double in winter, $5 for each extra person. Write at least a few weeks in advance to Wailana Sands, 25 Wailana Pl., Kihei, Maui, HI 96753 (tel. 879-2026).

Close by, the **Nona Lani** consists of eight individual cottages, each standing alone in a grassy tree-filled area. The cottages afford an ocean view, and there is a beach for swimming and walking 20 yards away.

Delightfully furnished and decorated, with rich wood panels and thick carpets, they feature a living room, full bedroom (with a queen-size bed), kitchen, bath, color TV, and an open lanai with dining table. Since there are two beds in the living room, a family of four could be comfortable here. Prices begin at $40 for two, $6 for each additional person. For reservations, write to Dave and Nona Kong, 455 S. Kihei Rd., Kihei, Maui, HI 96753 (tel. 879-2497). Three-night minimum stay.

All three of these places are near the beach at the stop where the 1792 arrival of Capt. George Vancouver is commemorated by an HVB marker and a Thunderbird totem carved by the Nootka Indians on Vancouver Island.

For those who can stay at least three days, the **Lihi Kai Cottages and Apartments** are another good choice in this wonderfully dry and sunny Kihei area. The complex of 25 one-bedroom cottages and apartment units is set in a lush tropical garden and looks out over a protected bay and small boat landing. Each of the suites is nicely furnished, and has wall-to-wall carpeting and a private lanai with floral landscaping. (If you're a light sleeper, ask for a room away from the road.) Kalama Park, a lovely, uncrowded swimming beach, is right at hand. Lihi Kai is especially popular with long-term residents, but transients are welcome. Daily rates are $35 a couple for a minimum of three days, $175 a week, $465 a month. Write to Lihi Kai Cottages and Apartments, 2121 Iliili Rd., RR1, Kihei, Maui, HI 96753 (tel. 879-2335). (See the Readers' Selections, ahead, for comments on Lihi Kai.)

We've always shied away from high-rise condominiums, but after we visited **Kahale Makai Resort (Village by the Sea)**, we were convinced that, in this case at least, bigger also means better. The two five-story buildings house some 168 units, and some have been superbly decorated by their owners. All have full kitchens, laundry, central air conditioning, and color TV. The two buildings, right on the ocean, are separated by a well-tended lawn on which there is a pool and putting green, Jacuzzi, barbecues. Also available are saunas and shuffleboard; tennis courts and golf are nearby. An in-house convenience shop makes housekeeping easy in case you've forgotten something at the supermarket in Kihei, or in Kahului, 15 minutes away. As with most condominiums, several rental agents handle units here, but the one offering the most reasonably priced units is Village Rentals, Azeka's Place, P.O. Box 1471, Kihei, Maui, HI 96753, which can also be reached toll free at 800/367-5634. Studios for one or two persons go from $25 a night during the off-season (April 15 to December 15), and from $35 the rest of the year. One-bedroom units begin at $29 off-season, $40 in; two-bedroom units at $53 a night off-season, $70 in; and two-bedroom deluxe oceanfront apartments for four people begin at $68 a night off-season, $85 in.

Kahale Makai Resort is right on the ocean, but you may want to walk a bit to a good swimming beach, as this one tends to be a bit rocky.

Can't choose between the tennis courts and the beach? **Leinaala Oceanfront Condominiums** makes life easy for you, since this cozy little complex of 25 apartments is sandwiched on both sides by public tennis courts and faces on a beautiful beach. And after your game, you can cool off in the freshwater swimming pool if you choose. All of these one- and two-bedroom apartments are nicely and individually furnished and all have complete kitchen facilities. When we visited, one-bedroom apartments were being discounted to $37, even lower than their usual off-season (May 1 through December 15) rates of $45. Two-bedrooms go for $55 during that season. In winter, the one-bedrooms are $55 and the two-bedrooms are $65. For reservations, write the managers, Norm and Nancy Sanders, Leinaala Oceanfront Condominiums, 998 S. Kihei Rd., Kihei, Maui HI 96753. The toll-free number is 800/367-5234, and the local phone is 879-2235.

The traditional big hotel in this area is the casually relaxed **Maui Lu,** a collection of low-rise, Polynesian-style buildings on 30 acres of tropical grounds, complete with a large Maui-shaped swimming pool, two sandy beaches, tennis courts, and a spirit of "ohana" or "family" that gives a stay here the feeling of an older, more gracious Hawaii. Jesse Nakooka, the Maui-born singing star who presides over the weekly luaus, the Aloha Mele luncheon, and the Polynesian Revue in Jesse's Restaurant, is very much a part of that feeling. The hotel's Aloha Department regularly holds classes in lei-making, the hula, Hawaiian arts and crafts—and will even teach you to play the ukulele! The rooms are modestly priced by the standards of the larger hotels, especially when one considers that all have those handy conveniences, refrigerators and coffeemakers, as well as phones, color TVs, and air conditioning. Furnishings are attractive. Many units offer kitchenettes and some even have full kitchens. For those not cooking in, the Hale Kope Coffee Shop serves all three meals (Jesse's serves dinner only). Standard rooms, single or double, run $50; superior, $60; deluxe $65. An extra person is charged $8; add $10 to any category for a room-and-car package. For reservations, write Reservations Manager, Maui Lu Resort, 575 S. Kihei Rd., Kihei, HI 96753, or call collect from Canada 808/879-5808. The mainland toll-free number is 800/367-5244; the Hawaii toll-free number is 800/592-5808. The local number is 879-5881.

On the beach at Kihei, the **Menehune Shores** offers family accommodations in a big, beautiful condominium complex. You could almost stay here and not want to leave the grounds—there's the wonderful beach, a conventional swimming pool, and the "Royal Fishpond," a protected stone and reef formation built by the ancient Hawaiians, right on the premises—and Hong Kong, a Chinese seafood restaurant specializing in Szechuan and Cantonese cuisine as well. There's a whale-watching platform on the roof garden. All apartments face the ocean, are individually decorated, and have full electric kitchens, with refrigerator-freezers and washer-dryers. The one-bedroom/one-bath units rent at $60 for two, $65 for three. Two-bedroom apartments with two baths are $70 for two, $5 more for each additional person, up to $90 for six people. Three-bedroom units with two baths cost $95 for five, $105 for six. From April 15 to December 15 there's a 30% discount. Across the road are studios that rent for $25 a day all year round. For reservations, write Kihei Kona Rentals, P.O. Box 556, Kihei, Maui, HI 96753 (tel. 879-5828).

A unique hotel in this area—or in any area, for that matter—is the **Mana Kai Maui Condominium Hotel,** ten years old, 98 rooms big, and offering a combination of condominium apartments and regular hotel rooms in a lively, upbeat setting. Situated on a beautiful crescent of beach (it's known as one of the best snorkeling beaches around), with a pool, an airy, open restaurant, and all sorts of activities going on (like fitness classes, or free snorkeling lessons in the pool), it offers a lot under one roof. If you're watching the budget, stick to their $35-a-day hotel rooms; these are small bedrooms with twin beds under a king-size spread; louvered closet door, telephone, color TV, and an attractive bathroom with a large vanity-sink. If you want to splurge, take one of their one- or two-bedroom apartments, whose rental—$87.50 and $107.50 (with weekly maid service) or $92.50 and $110 (with daily maid service) per day—includes, in addition to handsome lodgings for four to six people, the use of a complimentary car with 50 free miles a day. (Add about $10 for winter rates.) For reservations from the mainland, write Mana Kai Maui Condominium Hotel, P.O. Box 1808, Fort Collins, CO 80522. Outside of Colorado, call toll free 800/525-2025. If you're already in the islands, write Mana Kai Maui Condominium Hotel, 2960 S. Kinei Rd., Kihei, Maui, HI 96753 (tel. 879-1561).

Note: Mana Kai Maui is also the scene of a five-day course, beginning every Sunday, known as the **Pritikin Better Health Program.** Based on the well-known work of Nathan Pritikin, it is an educational experience designed to change your lifestyle and prevent degenerative diseases. Daily lectures, exercise programs, and three meals a day that stress "foods natural to man," while avoiding fats, sugars, chemicals, and stimulants, are served. Rates begin at about $700 per week. Whether or not you're on the program, you'll learn a lot by attending the free weekly introductory lecture, open to the public, Sunday evenings. Write or phone the hotel for details.

Although it's across the street from the ocean, all units are oceanfront at **Shores of Maui,** an attractive, two-level condo complex of one- and two-bedroom apartments. Snorkeling is good right across the street, and there's a sandy swimming beach just a block away. You can relax in the good-sized swimming pool, soak in the Jacuzzi, play a little tennis, enjoy a barbecue here. Apartments are nicely and individually decorated, all with dishwasher, washer-dryer, TV, and summer rates, May 1 to December 19, are quite modest: $40 per day for a one-bedroom/one-bath unit, $240 weekly; $55 per day for a two-bedroom/two-bath unit, $330 weekly. The one-bedroom units can sleep up to four; the two-bedroom unit, up to six. It's $7 per night for each extra guest. In winter, the one-bedrooms are $55 daily, $330 weekly, and the two-bedrooms are $70 daily, $420 weekly. For reservations, write to Shores of Maui, 2075 S. Kihei Rd., Kihei, Maui, HI 96753, or phone toll free 800/367-8002. The local phone is 879-9140.

AT MAALAEA BAY: Down by the small boat harbor at Maalaea Bay, a few miles from Kihei, is a wonderful beach area, and perched here, at Maalaea Village, is a small group of condominiums. **Hono Kai Resort,** one of the most reasonably priced of the lot, would make an ideal place for a family vacation (minimum stay is five days). You can swim in front of your door or at the public beach 50 yards away—or try your luck with surf at the harbor which according to some of the locals, is "the fastest surf in the world." All units are on the ocean side of the street and have at least one or two bedrooms, and all are nicely furnished. Shoji doors separate the living room and bedroom; the two-bedroom units all have lofts. There are full kitchens, including dishwashers, cable TV with HBO on request, even use of boogie boards and surfboards free. There's a swimming pool, washers and dryers on every floor, and two good restaurants—Buzz's Steak House and The Waterfront, nearby. We've had several good reports from our readers about this place and about managers Jim and Jeanne McJannet, who also manage two adjoining properties: **Makani A Kai** and **Kanai A Nalu.** Rates at Hono Kai, slightly lower than at the others, average around $37 for the one-bedroom garden view, $43.50 for the one-bedroom ocean view, and $45 for the one-bedroom oceanfront during the summer; during the winter, the rates go up a few dollars. For reservations, write Hono Kai Resort, RR1, Box 389, Maalaea Village, Maui, HI 96793, or phone, toll free, 800/367-6084. The local phone is 244-7012.

IN KULA: **Kula Lodge,** in cool, up-country Maui, is composed of five A-frame chalets nestled on a hill. The best buys for us are the three smaller ones priced at $40 double: one features a fireplace and the other two have little sleeping lofts, which are reached by ladders. The two larger units, which rent for $50, have Swedish fireplaces and stairs leading to the "mezzanine." No kitchenettes here, but there's a restaurant on the premises, the chalets are clean and nicely furnished, and the bathrooms have both tub and shower. When the sun goes down, it gets quite chilly, so a heavy sweater or jacket is advised; the management tells us that the fireplaces are, at times, used even on summer nights. For reservations, write to RR1, Box 475, Kula, Maui, HI 96790 (tel. 878-1535).

IN LAHAINA, KAANAPALI, AND ON NAPILI BAY: The area surrounding the historic old whaling town of Lahaina, about 30 miles from Kahului, might be a good place to move on to after a day or two in the Kahului or Kihei areas; or it could serve as a base of operations for your entire stay in Maui. In the heart of it all, out on the wharf overlooking the harbor, is the **Pioneer Inn,** an island landmark and a historic sight in its own right. Kamaainas, tourists, movie stars, sailors, and beachcombers have been sitting out on the big lanai in front for years, wondering what's happening back in civilization. At this writing, the Pioneer Inn looks as if it's in need of a major renovation, which is being talked about. Our considered advice is to hold off on this one until the renovation is completed; although rooms are relatively moderately priced, you probably won't like what you get. The food, however, is still good here. The Harpooner's Lanai serves breakfast and lunch (and more potent stuff all day), and at night it's broil-your-own steak around the pool and patio.

Without a car, almost any vacation on Maui is difficult. But lack of wheels will not be a hindrance to anyone who chooses to stay at the **Maui Islander,** a hotel that affords peace and privacy (its units are spread out over nine acres of tropical grounds) while providing proximity to everything you could want in the area: it's a three-block walk to a sandy swimming beach, a two-block stroll to the activities of Lahaina Harbor, a block away from the shops and restaurants of Front Street, two blocks to the supermarket, and a short bus ride to the resort life at Kaanapali Beach. You can be picked up at the airport and taken to the Maui Islander at a cost of $8.30 per person. And the hotel-condo itself is lovely: the 324 units are simply but very nicely decorated in island style with light woods, tiled bathrooms, color TV, telephone, tidy kitchens (except in the hotel rooms). Right at home is a swimming pool, a tennis court that is lit at night, and a recreation room with a pool table, and board and video games. Guests can consult the staff at the activities desk for advice on planning their days, and partake of free lessons—in hula, lei making, scuba diving. And the price for all this comfort and convenience is really right: $42 for two people in a hotel room, $55 for three people in a studio, $65 for four guests in a one-bedroom apartment, $90 for five in a two-bedroom/two-bath unit, and $115 for seven people in a three-bedroom/three-bath unit. For reservations, write to Maui Islander, 660 Wainee St., Lahaina, Maui, HI 96761. The phone is 667-9766.

Slightly more expensive and very attractive is **Lahaina Shores,** overlooking Lahaina Harbor. It's composed of 200 units, all with complete electric kitchens, air conditioning, and lanais offering ocean or mountain views. The seven-story building, a charming example of Victorian architecture, is very much in keeping with the rest of old Lahaina—a welcome contrast to the burgeoning concrete high-rises flourishing all over the rest of the island. Decor in the rooms is in oranges and golds; the huge, airy lobby runs to leafy greens. A swimming pool with adjacent Jacuzzi sits ocean side, just off the lobby. The studios are priced at $49 and $54 single for mountain and ocean views, respectively; double rates are $52 and $57, with a charge of $6 for an extra person. In the luxury category are one-bedroom units for $72 and $84, single or double, and penthouses at $90 and $100, single or double. Children under 6 are free. You can swim in front of the hotel, play tennis across the street. For reservations, phone, toll free, 800/367-2972, or write to Lahaina Shores, 475 Front St., Lahaina, HI 96761. The Lahaina phone is 661-4835; in Honolulu, you may call 531-4442.

True budget-minded folks will find the **Lahainaluna Hotel,** an 18-room wooden building of uncertain but venerable age, acceptable if not at all glamorous. Rooms are small, furnished with cheap but serviceable furniture, and all are air-conditioned, have their own bathrooms (showers, no tubs), and black-and-white TVs. For $23 you get a single or double room with a lanai, two single beds, and mountain or ocean view; $21 gets you an inside room without a view, but quieter; half of these rooms have double beds. There is no maid service for stays of three days or less. The location is right in the midst of the busy Lahaina shopping-nightlife-restaurant scene; during the Christmas–New Year's holidays, confirmed reservations must be made two months in advance. Write to Lahainaluna Hotel, 127 Lahainaluna Rd., Lahaina, Maui, HI 96761 (tel. 661-0577). There is no parking space at the hotel.

A few miles outside of Lahaina, on Maui's exquisite west coast, you approach the Kaanapali-Napili region, one of Hawaii's most desirable vacation areas, blessed with miles of gorgeous beach and stunningly blue skies, with the famed Royal Kaanapali Golf Courses thrown in for good measure. The luxury hotels here are way beyond our budget, but just in case you're wondering which of the hotels has the lowest prices, it's the **Kaanapali Beach Hotel.** There are a number of standard rooms that go for around $79, single or double, $15 for each extra person. The rooms are large and well decorated, and have TVs, refrigerators, and private lanais facing into a garden. The Kaanapali Beach has a spacious open feeling, with its huge garden, a whale of a swimming pool (yes, it's in the shape of a whale), a beautiful ocean beach right next to the rock formation (which makes it good for snorkeling) on which the neighboring Sheraton Maui sits, and all the comforts of the luxury life. Certainly worth a splurge—if your pocketbook is up to it. Reservations: Amfac Resorts Hawaii, P.O. Box 8519, Honolulu, HI 96815 (tel. 661-0011 in Maui).

For families with lots of kids, or for two couples traveling together, an apartment at the **Maui Sands** is ideal. Imagine an enormous living room (about the size of two average hotel rooms put together), beautifully decorated, with two small but comfortable bedrooms, twin beds in each, a full electric kitchen, tropical ceiling fans, color TV, a view of gardens or ocean from your private lanai, and enough space for six people to stretch out in—for a cost of $85 (garden view) to $103 (oceanfront) per day for four and $6 for each additional body. You'd expect to pay twice as much for anything comparable at the luxury resorts. This attractive hotel, just past the Kaanapali gold coast area, also has one-bedroom apartments at $65 or $79 double; and apartments close to the road (for heavy sleepers) at $52 for the one-bedroom, $73 for the two-bedroom. There is a four-day minimum most of the year, longer at the peak of the winter season. Since the Maui Sands was built when it was feasible to buy large lots of land, there is plenty of it to spare; the grounds are abloom with lovely trees and plantings, there's a comfortable swimming pool and sunning area (free coffee is served there in the morning), a big laundry area, and oh, that wonderful beach! At sunset, it's pure enchantment as you watch the sun seeming to sink right between the islands of Molokai and Lanai off in the distance. A coral reef forms a natural ocean pool, and that white sand stretches off for miles in the distance; you could walk all the way to the Kaanapali strip if you had a mind to. The hotel is completely refurbished, including new furniture. Managers Kay and Adele Kunisawa are cordial hosts, and some weekends they provide Hawaiian entertainment and free mixers for a cocktail party. Don't plan on getting here for Christmas unless you make reservations a year in advance; other times, a short notice should do the trick. Readers continue to praise this one. Write to Maui Sands, 3559 Honoapiilani Rd., Lahaina, Maui, HI 96761. The toll-free reservation number is 800/367-5037 and the local number is 669-4811.

The same Maui Sands management is in charge at the select units at **Papakea,** right next door, and these little homes are even more luxurious. Creature comforts include two pools, two Swedish saunas, two tennis courts, shuffleboard, barbecues, putting green, and picnic areas. Of course it's all on the beach. During the summer season (April 15 to December 15), a group of three can stay in a garden studio for $75, a group of four in a one-bedroom for $95. Phone the same toll-free number—800/367-5037—anytime between 8 a.m. and 5 p.m. Hawaii time to make reservations. Also inquire about the attractive room-plus-car packages at both hotels.

You'll have to walk across the street to get to the beach from **Honokowai Palms,** but that little extra effort pays off well. Over the years, we've had consistently good reports from people who've stayed at this complex of spacious one- and two-bedroom apartments. Many write that this is the one place they'll be sure to go back to. Prices are good value received: $37 for two people in a one-bedroom apartment without lanai or ocean view, $40 for two in a one-bedroom apartment with lanai and ocean view, $52 for four in a two-bedroom apartment without lanai or ocean view. The one-bedroom apartments can accommodate four, the two-bedroom apartments can hold six: one additional person is charged $6 daily; two are charged $10. There's a large pool to dunk in, barbecue equipment pool-side, and ample kitchens to make cooking easy. Maid service only for an additional payment. A three-day minimum stay is required, and so is a $100 deposit. For advance reservations, write to Honokowai Palms, 3666 Lower Honoapiilani Hwy., Lahaina, Maui, HI 96761 (tel. 669-6130).

The condominium units, all oceanfront, at **Noelani,** in the Kahana area, are beautifully furnished, and the view from your oceanfront lanai—of Molokai Island, blue seas, and tropical gardens—is even more beautiful. There are two freshwater swimming pools at seaside, good snorkeling right in front, and many sandy beaches closeby. Managers Ken and Colleen Arntzen host mai-tai parties at poolside several times a month so that guests can get to know one another. The studios, which rent for $50, are furnished in Pacific decor, with dressing room, bath, and kitchen. The one-bedroom units at $65 have their own dishwasher and washer-dryer. There is an extra-person charge of $7 from December 15 through April 15, and $5 from April 16 through December 14. Two- and even three-bedroom apartments are available, and so are weekly and monthly rates; three-day minimum stay. Write Noelani, 4095 Honoapiilani Rd., Lahaina, Maui, HI 96761 (tel. 669-8374). The toll-free number from the mainland and Alaska is 800/367-6030.

Every time we have a look at the **Pohailani Maui,** it grows a little bit more. The original eight-unit complex now has 29 units at the water's edge, plus another 85 two-bedroom duplex apartments on the mountainside. Two tennis courts, two pools, and other facilities are spread out over eight acres—not to mention a stretch of sandy beach, perfect for gentle ocean swimming. Each of the seaside units is spacious, attractively furnished in studio style (with such touches as big, old-fashioned ceiling fans), and boasts large kitchenettes plus lanais that are perfectly enormous. Summer-season rates, May 1 to December 14, are $55 for two in the studios, $65 for two in the deluxe studios (all studios are beachfront); $75 with garden view, $85 with ocean view for four people in the two-bedroom town houses. Winter rates are $10 higher. There is an extra charge of $10 per night for each additional person. A three-night stay is required in summer, a five-night stay in winter. For reservations, phone, toll free, 800/367-6038, or write to them at 4435 Honoapiilani Rd., Lahaina, Maui, HI 96761.

Every year we get letters saying that the **Mahina Surf** is a fine place to settle in for real at-home living. We inspected the units on our last visit and found them to be not only charming and attractively furnished, but well priced for the area: from April 15 to December 15, it's $55 per night (minimum stay of three nights), $365.75 a week; during the high season, December 15 to April 15, it's $65 per night, $423.25 per week. These rates are for two people in a one-bedroom unit with complete kitchen and accessories, color TV, telephone, and an ocean view. These units can actually sleep four: each extra person is charged $6 per night. Two-bedroom units are available for an extra $5 per day, and two-bedroom/two-bath units for an additional $10. Sizes of the apartments vary, but all are little "homes"; the cutest are those with a loft area upstairs that serves as a second bedroom, and these are big enough to sleep six. The 56-unit complex is situated on a rocky strip of ocean, and snorkeling is fine, but there is no sandy beach; there is, however, a big pool as compensation. Write to Mahina Surf, 4057 Lower Honoapiilani Rd., Lahaina, Maui, HI 96761 (tel. 669-6068 or toll free 800/367-6086).

Now you're approaching Napili Bay, a gorgeous little stretch of sea and sand where not very long ago the breadfruit, papaya, and lichee trees ran helter-skelter to the sea. For us, this area is the end of the rainbow, and we don't mean the one likely to be arching across the sugarcane fields as you approach: the setting is perfect, and the swimming, from a gentle reef-protected beach, among the best in the islands. Here you'll find the **Mauian Hotel,** with 44 attractive studio apartments big enough for four, each with private lanai, all-electric kitchen, one queen and one trundle bed (that opens into two), and all the conveniences of home. From April 15 to December 15, rates are $49 single, $59 double; in high season, it's $59 and $64. For those capable of tearing themselves away from the idyllic beach, there's shuffleboard and a freshwater swimming pool (a big laundry and ironing area too). Write to Mauian Hotel, 5441 Honoapiilani Rd., Lahaina, Maui, HI 96761 (tel. 669-6205). Toll-free reservations: 800/367-5034.

A better choice for the budget-minded is **Napili Village,** where the rates are a bit lower and the 24 convertible studio-bedroom units are a bit larger (a family of five can be easily accommodated—but you'll have to do without a view of the beach). It's just a stone's throw away, however, and right on the grounds you have a big pool plus the Village Store, a Hawaiian supermarket (the shopping carts wear grass skirts) that offers ranch steaks and vegetables and tropical fruits grown a farmyard away. You can also pick up gifts and muumuus here. Each unit has a king-size bed plus twins, a full kitchen, color TV and radio, and a private lanai. Folding privacy doors can create two separate sleeping areas if you wish. Rates are $55 daily, $360 weekly from December 15 to April 1, and $50 daily, $300 weekly the rest of the year. An extra person is charged $5. Write Napili Village Hotel, 5425 Honoapiilani Hwy., Lahaina, Maui, HI 96761 (tel. 669-6228).

One of the very nicest places in this area is the **Napili Surf Beach Resort,** which has 54 soundproofed luxury units perched on the tip of Napili Bay, on a particularly lovely curve of beach. Each of these units is completely equipped for easy housekeeping, and has color TV and handsome furniture; the private lanais overlook the pool, garden, or ocean. You'll have to spend your hard-earned splurge money: $63 double for the studios, $81 for the huge one-bedroom units. But wait—managers Bob and Marge Putt also have newer garden units, at $53 double, $61 triple. These 18 off-beach studios, called Napili Puamala (garden of flowers) are small but super-neat and functionally designed; they come with color TV, radio with digital clocks (something rather rare in hotels), full kitchens, dishwashers, the works. All these units overlook the pool. No matter where you stay, though, it's fun to get together with the other guests out on the lawn in the evenings when Bob and Marge often bring in entertainment. It may be a well-known island group like the No Ka Oi Four or just some friends or guests who like to sit around with a guitar and sing the old songs. In such a gracious setting, with such warmly hospitable people in charge, the coconut palms swaying in the evening wind and the sea lapping gently at your feet, it's hard to remember what you were planning to worry about. Write to Napili Surf, Napili Bay, Maui, HI 96761 (tel. 669-8002). An advance deposit is required.

Napili Shores, at 5315 Honapiilani Hwy., is a condominium on Napili Bay with a number of accommodations in the hotel pool. It is a delightful low-rise group of buildings with its own sundries store and an attractive Thai restaurant, Orient Express, on the premises. When you watch the sunset from the pool deck, you'd swear you could reach out and touch Molokai. Studios are priced at $65, $75, and $85 double for garden area, ocean view, and oceanfront respectively. There's a charge of $8 for an extra person, a maximum of three persons in the studios. The one-bedroom apartments, with a maximum of four persons, are $80 for garden area and $95 for ocean view. Niceties include full kitchens, telephones, color TV, laundry, two freshwater pools (one with Jacuzzi), shuffleboard, croquet and of course, that idyllic Napili Beach bay. Free snorkeling lessons are given every Thursday; mai-tai parties are held on Friday. Write Napili Shores, 5315 Honoapiilani Hwy., Lahaina, HI 96761, or phone, toll free, 800/367-6046. The local phone is 669-8061.

IN HANA: Since Hana is one of the more remote, untouched areas in Maui (in all Hawaii, in fact), you might well want to spend a few days here just relaxing and being utterly away from civilization. But you'll have to look hard for reasonably priced accommodations, as there are very few places, and their rates are climbing every year. If you write well in advance (or happen to be lucky), you may be able to get a room.

The most inexpensive accommodations in Hana are available courtesy of the Division of State Parks. These are the housekeeping cabins in **Waianapanapa State Park,** a few trails away from a black-sand beach. The attractive bungalows are snuggled among the pandanus trees, some overlooking the ocean, and are supplied with bedding, towels, cooking utensils, dishes, electricity, and plenty of hot water. The only fly in the ointment may be mosquitoes: a reader who spent a hot August week here advised taking insect spray and repellent. And lately we have had reports here of more than the usual number of ants. Let's hope this situation is remedied speedily! Each two-room cabin has its own lanai, can sleep six persons, and rents for $5 to $10 per person a night, depending on the number of occupants. Rates may change soon. The maximum stay is five nights. For reservations, write to Division of State Parks, P.O. Box 1049, Wailuku, Maui, HI 96793 (tel. 244-4354).

For deluxe studio and one-bedroom apartments where you can prepare your own meals (almost a necessity in Hana, where there are very few eating places), the **Hana Kai Resort Apartments** are a fine choice. The rates for the studios are $50 single, $53 double, $6 for each additional person; no charge for children under 2. These studios, maximum of three persons, include a bath with bath-shower combination, dressing vanity, and private lanai—a spacious open room where you can enjoy the ocean just a few feet away. The kitchen comes fully equipped, even including staples like sugar, salt, and coffee. The two- and three-story buildings are scattered over a fairly wide area. One-bedroom apartments are $60 single, $63 double, and can sleep up to five. One oceanfront building has a barbecue lanai for everyone to use. The beach is stony, black, and better for surfers than swimmers, but there is a mountain pool on the grounds. For reservations, write Hana Kai, P.O. Box 38, Hana, Maui, HI 96713 (tel. 248-8435).

Mrs. Alfreda Worst, the owner of **Heavenly Hana Inn,** has created a miniature Oriental garden-like atmosphere in her four units, each of which has two bedrooms, a dining area, bath, screened lanai, and its own private entrance. The inn is small but charming, and the inside door of each unit leads to the lobby and lounge. Outside, leading to the street, is a winding walkway through a screened Japanese gateway guarded by stone lions, symbols of good fortune. Breakfast and dinner food service are available at reasonable prices. Rates are $50, single or double; $58 triple, $65 quad. An additional person is charged $6.50. Write to Mrs. Worst at P.O. Box 146, Hana, Maui, HI 96713 (tel. 248-8442).

Hana Bay Vacation Rentals started out five years ago with Hana Bayview and Kauki Cabin, both known to readers of this book. Now managers Stan and Suzanne Collins have branched out and are renting eight properties scattered throughout the Hana area, with a wide variety of locations, including on the beach, in town, out of town toward Kipahulu, plus some in very secluded and private places. They offer apartments, cabins, and homes, with either one, two, or three bedrooms, and ocean and mountain views. All are fully equipped with the essentials for comfortable vacation living. They can accommodate as few as one, as many as 15 in a group, at prices ranging from $35 to $85 per night for two people, plus $7 to

$10 for each additional person. Each cabin and home is private, and all have full kitchens; most have cable TV. For reservations or more information, write or phone Stan and Suzanne at Hana Bay Vacation Rentals, P.O. Box 318, Hana, Maui, HI 96713 (tel. 248-7727).

Located conveniently close to Hana Bay and the stores are the **Aloha Cottages.** Each redwood cottage has two bedrooms (queen-size bed in one and twin beds in the other), a living room, complete kitchen, and bathroom. Each has a view of Hana Bay. The recently built cottages are well ventilated, comfortably furnished, and clean. All necessities are provided. Rates are: $42 for two and $6 each additional person. Write to Mrs. F. Nakamura, P.O. Box 205, Hana, Maui, HI 96713 (tel. 248-8420). *Note:* See the Readers' Selections at the end of this chapter for several rave reviews this year.

2. Restaurants

IN KAHULUI: If you like buffet meals as much as we do, then you should know about the Rainbow buffet lunch served in the pretty main dining room and pool terrace of the **Maui Beach Hotel.** It's on daily from 11:30 a.m. to 2 p.m., and it's a real winner at $6 for all you can eat, $5 for salad bar alone. Local people like it because it includes many Oriental dishes not usually seen on buffet meals: we ourselves are partial to the tsukemono (pickled vegetable salad) and kamaboku (fishcakes). Also there for the taking—and still more taking—are those delicious Kula onions, Maui potato chips, lots of greens, sunflower seeds, rice, hot breads, three hot entrees daily (perhaps fried chicken, spaghetti and meatballs, beef stew), and rich desserts like chocolate pudding and cakes baked daily by the hotel's own bakery shop.

For a full-course, inexpensive dinner in this area, try **Vi's Restaurant** at the Maui Hukilau. The food is not gourmet quality, but who can argue with meals from $6.95 that include a free salad bar with 40 selections, rice or mashed potatoes, bread, and dessert, along with entrees like mahimahi, broiled ham steak, deep-fried scallops, filet of sole, and sirloin steak cutlet. Fresh fish is reasonably priced. Mai tais are only $1.50. Dinner is served from 6 to 8:45 p.m., and there are $2.95 breakfasts, but no lunch.

In and around the big shopping centers across the way from the hotels—the Kahului Shopping Center, the Maui Mall, and the Kaahumanu Shopping Center—are several places that are fine for a modest meal. The **Maui Mall** is fairly bursting with inexpensive places to eat. You could have a "home-cooked meal" for $2.95—barbecued spare ribs, hamburger steak—at **Hat's Restaurant;** a $2 teriburger at **Stephanie's Restaurant;** some good cheeses, $3 deli sandwiches, and soup of the day at **Irma's Bakery and Deli,** or Mexican chicken with salad and refried beans at $2.60 at cute little **Don Taco.** Don't miss the luscious, sugary buñuelos; they're three for 65¢. **Farrell's** always works for a family meal or a snack.

If your taste runs to pizza and grog, and a dimly lit, Tiffany-shaded atmosphere with good sounds on the stereo is just your thing, visit the **Pizza Factory** at Maui Mall. Pizzas run from $4.95 for small pies, and there are also plenty of burgers, from $3.25. Baskets of fried chicken or shrimp are around $5.95; and you can get salads and delicious sandwiches from $3.95 to $5.50. Dinner items go from $7.50 to $12.95, and include fish pesto and New York–cut steak. There's wine, beer, and drinks for those of age, and

"Under Eighteen Drinks" like "Snoopy" and "Charlie Brown" (fruit juice combinations) are available for the younger set to sip along with their supper.

The cutest restaurant in the shopping centers? Our vote would have to go to **Apple Annie's,** at Kaahumanu Shopping Center, whose terrific decor grows more exciting the farther back you move in the restaurant: from a stylish plant-filled up-front area with counter and booths, toward a dimly lit, mellow area in back, lined with a wall of books, on the other side of which is the cocktail lounge. The day starts with a "belly-warming" breakfast and continues through dinner. The food is as much fun as the atmosphere, dedicated to pleasing a variety of tastes: take your choice of omelets (from $5.95 for shrimp and sprouts, or dream up your own at a $4.95 base, plus $1 for each ingredient); burgers from $3.95 plain, with some fancy concoctions at higher prices; Mexican specialties (beef enchiladas, tacos, and chilis, starting at $2); or dinner specials (served from 5 p.m. until closing), like fried fish, broiled breast of chicken, Korean-style ribs from $7.95 to $13.95. All these are served with soup or a tossed green salad and choice of dressing, plus hot vegetable, fries, fruit cup, or rice. For dessert, have Apple Annie's Special: apple pie, of course, topped with cheddar cheese or whipped cream. The friendly young staff will oblige with beer, wine, harder drinks, even margaritas, served from the bar.

A favorite in the same Kaahumanu Shopping Center is **Idini's Liquor and Deli** (the liquor store is in the back, the deli part in front). Flowered tablecloths, director's chairs, lots of plants and paintings set a relaxed mood for big Italian sandwiches, hot corned beef and veggie sandwiches, croissant sandwiches, most from $2.75 to $5.95. Homemade soups are $1.50. We like the $3.50 salad bar and the French bakery products—shrimp and spinach quiches, croissants, even New York–style cheesecake. There's a variety of alcoholic and nonalcoholic beverages—wines, beers, cocktails, espressos. Owner Bob Idini is planning on doubling the size of this popular place soon. A pleasant stop.

Other tastes can be assuaged at Kaahumanu. **Ma-Chan's Okazuya** has both local and Oriental foods. . . . **Vim and Vigor,** the popular natural-foods store, has a new restaurant in the rear of their store. The Vigory is neatly decorated with booths and carpets, features an all-you-can-eat salad bar for $3.75, plus daily specials like meatless spaghetti, quiches, stir-fried or tempura veggies, around $2.95. Homemade soups, salads, smoothies, of course. Open Monday to Saturday from 9 a.m. to 4 p.m.

Those who have developed a taste for Hawaiian food should head for Puunene Avenue, on the other side of the Kahului Shopping Center, and join the local folks at the **Aloha Restaurant.** The place is quite plain, but it's air-conditioned and comfortable, and the menu offers more than a dozen dinners, from $3.50 (for omelets, rice and salad) up to $5.25. The kalua pig, lomi salmon, and poi dinner is $4. Or make up your own, from a large list of à la carte dishes that start at $2.35 for lomi-lomi salmon. Inexpensive American meals ($3.50 to $4.75) and sandwiches too, and plenty of beer and harder drinks at the bar are reasonably priced. Lunch hours are from 11 a.m. until 2 p.m., dinner from 5 until 9 p.m. daily.

Attractive, moderately priced Chinese restaurants are hard to find on Maui, so praise be for **Ming Yuen** at 162 Alamaha St., in the Kahului Light Industrial Park, off Highway 380. The specialties here are authentic Cantonese and the spicier Szechuan cuisine. We always like to start off with crispy wonton and Chinese spring rolls, $3 and $3.50. The menu here offers a very wide choice of entrees, like Mongolian beef, lemon chicken, mu shu pork Szechuan (a personal favorite), and sweet-and-sour shrimp, all about $4.95 to $6.75. Should you prefer something spicier, choose the Szechuan eggplant, $4.95. They have excellent vegetarian dishes too. The desserts here are a little different: we like the Mandarin mousse and fresh cream pies. Ming Yen serves lunch Monday through Saturday from 11 a.m. to 2 p.m.; dinner is served from 5 to 9 p.m. seven days a week. Reservations requested (tel. 871-7787). Look for Ming Court, their new restaurant at the Whaler's Shopping Village in Kaanapali.

IN WAILUKU: Lunch at **Naokee's Restaurant,** at 1792 Main St. (tel. 244-9444), is a long-time budget tradition in Wailuku. Naokee's is a modern, attractive three-level restaurant, with steakhouse decor, a bar, table service, and a very cozy feeling about it. At night, steak and fish dinners begin at $8.75 and go up, but lunch is another story, and that's where we come in. That's when just about everything on the menu goes for $4 and under—and that includes New York–cut steak, broiled filet of fish, sirloin butt, Korean barbecue, and chopped steak, all served with rice, vegetables, and a little kim chee on the side. The dinner prices are not bad, considering that everything is served with rice, soup, salad, a basket of delicious garlic bread, and beverage, and that there are a few entrees in the lower price categories—but you can't beat lunch. Naokee's is just past the bridge on the right, as you head for Wailuku from Kahului. Lunch is from 11 a.m. to 2 p.m., dinner from 5:30 to 9 or 9:30 p.m. every day.

Local people put us on to **Archie's,** at 1440 Lower Main St. (tel. 244-9401), and we're glad they did. It's a Japanese restaurant, with just a touch of the Orient in the fans lining the walls; otherwise, it's plain but pleasant enough, with orange booths and green chairs, Formica-wooden tables, and wood paneling. Dinners are a real bargain: along with the soup, pickled vegetables, rice, and tea that are mandatory for any Japanese meal, come such main courses as chicken tofu, fish nitsuke, teriyaki chicken, and shrimp tempura, from $4 to $8. Very popular at both lunch and dinner—it's only $3.90—is the nabeyaki udon: that's vegetables, chicken, fishcakes, and shrimp tempura. And also at lunchtime, the tempura udon at $4.20 is big enough to make a meal on. Open Monday to Saturday from 10:30 a.m. to 2 p.m. and 5 to 8 p.m. Closed Sunday.

PAIA AND ENVIRONS: Paia is one of our favorite little towns—full of seekers from everywhere who've found the natural lifestyle they were looking for in these Hawaiian uplands. Since the area is only a 15-minute drive from Kahului, at the beginning of the road to Hana and just past the cutoff to Route 37 (the Haleakala Highway), a visit to the restaurants here can be worked into almost any itinerary.

Our favorite place in Paia—at 89 Hana Hwy.—is **Dillon's Restaurant** (tel. 579-9113), which calls itself "a tropical hideaway," and that's just what it is. The bamboo walls, tropical decor, outdoor garden, and orchid paintings on the wall are all the art and craft of Casimir (Charles Powell), an island painter; the inspired menu is the work of his wife, Nancy Powell. The Powells are transplanted New Yorkers who have brought a touch of both sophistication and hominess to their restaurant, and the local people and visitors have responded enthusiastically. Travelers on their way to Hana often stop by between 8 and 9 p.m. for the eggs Benedict special at $3.95, or french toast with Kahlúa. The kitchen and bar are open every day for breakfast, lunch, and dinner, with a continuous pupu menu available until closing. There is always a wonderful quiche with salad, a superb frittata (an open-faced vegetable omelet topped with hollandaise), excellent burgers, and the Coral and Jade sandwich, veggies, and cheese on whole-wheat bread, which comes nicely presented, with french fries and a slice of orange; all are under $5. Portions are very large. New England–style clam chowder, made from scratch, is a welcome treat out here in mid-Pacific. For a more extensive meal, you might have a mahimahi lunch at $6.95 or a complete mahimahi dinner at $11.95, the homemade pasta dinner at $9.95, or New York steak, with salad, vegetables, and french bread. Also very popular the is the "Lite Dining" meal, which includes meat or vegetarian lasagne and "really Italian" spaghetti with meatballs, $5.95. Desserts are a must: Nancy brought her recipe for New York–style cheesecake and Kahlúa cheesecake too. Service at Dillon's is apt to be a bit leisurely, as everything is cooked to order; best to sit back and sip one of the fresh tropical fruit drinks of the day; the day we were there it was passion fruit daiquiri! This food is worth waiting for.

Piero's Garden Café, 120 Hana Hwy. (tel. 579-9730), has its own quaint charm. It's a mom-and-son-and-grandsons operation. Artist Piero Resta hails from Florence, Italy; mamma does all the cooking at home and every day she brings it down to the restaurant, which is run by the grandsons, Stefano and Luigi. It's a cute little place with just a few tables inside, a few more in the garden and on the porch. The setting is modest, and so are the prices for fresh and tasty food. Fettuccine with clams, veggie quiche, frittata with garlic bread and salad, green lasagne, and the like, all go from $4.50 to $6.50. Fresh fish, served with a small salad and garlic bread, is $6.50. Many of the vegetables are grown in the garden outside; Greek salads and green salads are artistic creations. Fresh papaya shakes, beer, cappuccino, and espresso provide the liquid refreshments; you can also bring your own bottle. If you're here early, you can have cappuccino and croissants for breakfast.

Piero's is open every day from 9 a.m. to 10 p.m. On Thursday nights, visiting poets, wandering minstrels, musicians, and entertainers of all sorts provide impromptu entertainment; according to the local paper, Thursday nights at Piero's can be "an extraordinary cultural happening." Call first to see if anything is scheduled: you might luck into something very special. Also inquire about dinner and a show on Sunday at $10. Adjoining Piero's is the East Maui Gallery.

If you need a picnic lunch for your trip to Haleakala or Hana, the place to stock up is **Pic-nics** on Baldwin Avenue right in Paia (you'll recognize it by a bright orange-and-yellow awning), a very plain, clean, Formica-table-and-benches place which is, nonetheless, known all over the area for its sandwiches: especially the spinach-nut burgers, served on whole-wheat sesame buns, and piled high with lettuce, tomato, sprouts, and dressing; they are $2.95 and terrific. They also serve a filet of mahimahi for just $3.95. Iced mint tea is refreshing. Good for a satisfying light meal. Excursion lunches include sandwiches, Maui potato chips, homemade cookies (Maui-Zowees), a Coke, and a picnic map (that offers detailed information about the trips to Hana and Haleakala), and are priced at $4.50. Open daily from 7:30 a.m. to 3:30 p.m.

EN ROUTE TO HALEAKALA: Since there is no food to be had in Haleakala National Park, you might want to eat on your way to—or from—the crater. Two places in Pukalani, about halfway between Kahului and the park entrance, do very nicely. Your best bet for an inexpensive snack is **Bullock's of Hawaii,** a snack shop where you get delicious hamburgers, cheeseburgers, "moonburgers" (a meal in themselves), from $1.75 to $3.25. Be sure to try the sensational shakes, a combination of nectars, juices, and ice cream; we loved the guava, but they also have pineapple, mocha, and coffee, each $2.25. Full breakfasts, complete with coffee, juice, toast, rice, and up-country jumbo eggs delivered fresh daily, range from $2.75 to $5.95, for steak and eggs. Open daily from 7:30 a.m. to 9:30 p.m.

T-Bone Junction, in the Pukalani Terrace Center, will be closed as you start your early-morning trip to Haleakala (it opens at 11 a.m.), so remember it for the way back. It's smartly decorated, with lots of wood, glass, and plants creating a rustic, airy feeling. Lunch offers interesting sandwiches like barbecue ham, a Reuben, spicy hot pastrami, from $3.60 to $3.95, plus hamburgers from $3 and salads and omelets. Dinner is served from 5 to 10 p.m., and with entrees like ground sirloin at $7.25 or New York steak at $14.95 come clam chowder or dinner salad, vegetable of the day, rice or potato or baked beans, and paniolo toast. Open every day.

The **Dairy Queen** next door has a varied snacking menu: chicken in a basket, nachos, and lobster or chicken eggrolls. And they also have ten malasadas for $1.50, and shave ice for 75¢—$1 with ice cream (just in case you get an urge for the local goodies).

Another enjoyable place to eat is in nearby Makawao, a few miles off your route to Haleakala, but worth making a little detour for; turn right at Pukalani. The most inexpensive place to grab a bite in this quaint little cowboy town is **Mountainside Liquor & Deli,** in a big blue frame building at 1188 Makawao Ave. (tel. 572-9723). The broasted chicken is outstanding; you get two pieces for $1.49, eight pieces for $5.99. The chicken plate lunch, with rice and salad, is $3; there's a teriyaki plate lunch for $3.25. Also well priced are a french dip sandwich, crab sandwich, a foot-long hot dog and chili dog. The wine shop specializes in old and rare wines. The Deli is open seven days; our Makawao friends swear by it.

A newer restaurant in town, at 1202 Makawao Ave. (tel. 572-7808), is **Polli's Mexican Restaurant and Cantina,** a cute little place at the corner of Olinda Street, which specializes in "cold beer and hot food." The decor is Mexican, the clientele is local, the music is loud, and the food is very tasty. Taco salad is $4; cheese enchiladas, $5; a bowl of chili, $2.25. We love their desserts, especially the buñuelas: Mexican pastries topped with vanilla ice cream, drizzled hot pure maple syrup, and cinammon, $2.50. *Muy bueno!* Polli's is open daily, with entertainment on Wednesday, Friday, and Saturday from 9:30 to 11 p.m.; "cantina hours" are 2 to 5:30 p.m.; and Sunday brunch is on at 10:30 a.m. There's a great new Polli's in the Kihei area (see below).

IN KIHEI AND WAILEA: Remember the name **Azeka's Place:** this lively new shopping center is the best spot for budget watchers to get a good meal in Kihei. In addition to pancakes, omelets, waffles, burgers, and such, the **International House of Pancakes** here offers some 16 dinner specialties from $4.95 to about $8.95—and these include mushroom crêpes, breast of chicken parmigiana, country-fried steak, breaded pork chops, and delicious spit-roasted chicken. The big, high-ceilinged dining room has comfortable booths and a pleasant atmosphere.

Off in a corner of Azeka's Place are some outdoor tables. Since they're conveniently located between Philadelphia Lou's and Kihei Natural Foods, you can satisfy some different tastes in your party. **Philadelphia Lou's** (also in the Kahului Shopping Center) can dish up Philadelphia hoagies, famous Philadelphia cheesesteaks (fried beef with melted cheese, fried onions, and pizza sauce on a hot, homemade french loaf, $3.95), as well as other "East Coast sandwiches" like bagel, Nova, and cream cheese. There are beeping electronic game machines in back, and we'd guess that Lou comes from South Philly, what with all the sports and *Rocky* posters about. The snackbar at **Kihei Natural Foods** can oblige with juices, sandwiches priced from $2.95 to $3.50, smoothies, salads, frozen yogurt, freshly baked muffins, and tempeh burgers—that's an Indonesian soy food. (They also carry a large assortment of natural-food bulk items, fruit, beauty aids, and supplements.)

In the same shopping center, **Sailmaker,** a lively, nautically decorated watering spot, is part of the Apple Annie family and has a menu similar to the Apple Annie's we've told you about in Kahului (above). You can get those good omelets here, pizza pies, lots of fanciful burger combinations (topped with ham or cheddar or mushrooms or even shrimps), from $2.95 to $5.95, and a full range of dinner specials (served from 5:30 to 9:30 p.m.). Best buys for dinner are the stir-fried dishes, from $7.95 to $8.95 for stir-fried vegetables, shrimp, mahimahi, beef, and chicken, all combined with garden vegetables. Most other dishes hover around the $9.95 to $10.95 mark. Dinner is served until 10 p.m., a limited menu until 1 a.m. A lively crowd hangs out at both the raw bar and the regular bar. From 9:30 p.m. until 2 a.m., it's disco ($1.50 cover) in the sail loft upstairs. Take a little time to study the nautical-comical paintings, and the plaques on the walls of the booths, with both sage and silly sayings. Open daily from 8 a.m. to 11:30 p.m. for all three meals.

Next door to the Kihei Store is a Maui institution known as **Suda's Snack Bar,** where the local people rave about the low-priced hamburgers and the chow fun. If you're thirsty, pop into the store itself and get a bottle of Maui Juice, a natural fruit drink (pineapple, coconut, lilikoi, banana, guava, and combinations), already chilled. They are made on the island and available in many Maui supermarkets too.

Old Maui hands will remember **La Familia,** a name synonymous with great Mexican food for over ten years in Wailuku. La Familia Wailuku has closed now, but in its place have sprouted two great new La Familias—one in Kihei, another at Kannapali Beach. The Kihei La Familia, in Kai Nani Village at Kamaole Beach Park (tel. 879-8824), is probably the happiest spot in Kihei; once the 2 to 6 p.m. Happy Hour gets under way and they start pouring those frosty margaritas for 99¢, the large, circular tiled bar and its lanai look to be the "in" place in town for a smart young set. Dinner service starts at 4 p.m. and continues to 10 p.m. Come around sunset time and you're in for a special treat: the dining room is glassed in on three sides, affording a splendid view of the ocean. You might even catch a view of humpback whales. Mexican specialties are reasonably priced, from $5.50 to $8.95 for such dishes as huevos rancheros, Judy's sour cream enchiladas, crab tostada, and chimichangas. If you're not feeling all that Mexican, you could have burgers, soup and salad, fresh fish, spinach quiche, or saddle-back sandwiches, from $4.95 to $6.95. The mini-desserts are delicious: chocolate pudding laced with Kahlúa, homemade pies, and a delectable mud pie (cookie crust topped with ice cream, fudge sauce, and whipped cream). Beverages include imported and domestic beers, super margaritas, and "Maui Wowies." La Familia is open every day and serves cocktails until midnight.

In the same Kai Nani Village, **Kihei Prime Rib House** (tel. 879-1954) has long been an island favorite. It's a bit high for our budget, but arrive early—between 5 and 6:30 p.m.—and enjoy their early-bird special: prime rib dinner or fresh island fish at $7.95. Their salad bar, which you can have alone at $7.95, uses only locally grown fruits and vegetables. And beautiful woodcarvings and paintings add to the warmth and charm.

You may remember Polli's Mexican Restaurant from upcountry Makawao; you'll be even happier to find the same good food and good drinks here in a perfectly wonderful location at Kihei, at the Kealia Beach Center, 101 N. Kihei Rd., at the entrance to Kihei (tel. 879-5275). **Polli's on the Beach** has tall, beamed ceilings, wooden tables, straw chairs, tiled floor, plants, and piñatas; best of all is its huge dining lanai with umbrellaed tables that juts right out over the beach, so that you feel *that* close to the water. What a spot for sunset watching, whale watching, people watching, or just sitting in perfect contentment as you sip your margaritas and munch on delicious Mexican food with an island flair! The *entremesas* (appetizers) are a bit unusual here: spicy, deep-fried zucchini; Mexican pizza; and a new invention called baked bajas—that's potato shells filled with taco, bean, or cheese dips at $4.50, and a great way to start a meal. Most combination plates are $6.50 to $7.50 (there are tofu enchiladas for vegetarian types); à la carte entrees average about $2.50. Try the house dressing with your salad; it's an unusual blend of cashews and garlic. Los niños can have their own plate at $5. Good desserts include buñuelos and amaretto cheesecake. Polli's is open every day from 11 a.m. to midnight, serves lunch from 11 a.m. to 3 p.m., dinner from 5 to 10 p.m., drinks throughout the day. Happy Hour is on from 3 to 5 p.m., and there's Sunday brunch too, from 9:30 a.m. to 2 p.m.; try the bueno toast with cream cheese and jalapeño jelly. *Ole!*

If you're in Kihei on a Tuesday or Thursday afternoon between 11 a.m. and 3 p.m. and you're feeling really hungry, pull in at **Gaspare's Place and Pizza,** in the Island Surf Building at 1993 S. Kihei Rd. (tel. 879-8881). That's when you can partake of the Italian lunch buffet—pizza, pasta, garlic bread, soup, and salad bar—all you can eat for $4.95. Gaspare's also keeps the budget diner well in mind at dinnertime with its "Inflation Fighting Dinner Menu": spaghetti, fettucine, lasagne, ravioli, with garlic bread and salad bar, $6.50 to $8.25. Other times there are always good pizza pies, and sandwiches served hot from the oven, with french fries: submarines, meatballs, burgers, vegetarian submarines, most in the $3.50 to $4 range. There are both booths and tables here, a cocktail lounge and bar, and a casual mood. Open Tuesday through Saturday until midnight.

Wailea, just beyond the Kihei area, is wealthy condo country, and the home of two stunning hotels, the Hotel Inter-Continental Maui and the Westin Wailea Beach. At the Hotel Inter-Continental Maui, you might try the salad bar of the otherwise pricey **Kiawe Broiler;** a good selection of locally grown vegetables and greens is $7.25. . . . The **Wet Spot,** located at the Luau Pool (open only from 11 a.m. to 5 p.m.) is a health-food snackbar, featuring freshly squeezed juices, snacks, salads, and sandwiches. . . . And you can have reasonable specialties like chicken pot pie, fish and chips, or mahimahi, from $4.50 to $10 (most are in the $6 and $7 range) at the very beautiful **Makani Coffee Shop,** overlooking the ocean and pool. The room is done in earth tones of beige and terracotta; handsome Indian straw baskets line the walls and serve as a centerpiece; and you can sit in tall, high-back wicker chairs as you enjoy the super-friendly service and delicious food.

Although the **Ocean Terrace Restaurant,** overlooking the beach at the Mana Kai Maui Condominium Hotel, is out of our price range (fresh fish, steaks, and the like from about $11 to $15), you should know that they serve Pritikin Better Health meals, excellent for those on a health regime. Dinner features entrees like breast of chicken, Oriental vegetables, local fresh fish, from $7.95 to $11.95, all prepared without fats, sugar additives, or preservatives, accompanied by salad (except Monday), rolls, and herb tea. Healthy breakfasts and lunches too. Local bands play nightly (except Monday), and Happy Hour is 3 to 6 p.m. daily.

Remember **Ed and Don's** at the Wailea Shopping Center for a pleasant snack or lunch in this area: they have gourmet sandwiches of tuna, ham and cheese, veggies, smoked ham, etc., from $2.50 to $3.25, and lots of good ice creams. Open from 9:30 a.m. to 3:30 p.m. only.

IN LAHAINA: Lahaina's restaurants reflect its easy, relaxed approach to living. The food is not gourmet, but the **Harpooner's Lanai** of the Pioneer Inn is always fun. At one of the pretty tables on the terrace across from the boat landing, you might order a sandwich lunch—mahimahi burger, Reuben on Russian rye, or teriyaki steak, from $4.65 to $5.50—all served with potato salad or french fries. A big bowl of seafood chowder is $1.95. Lunch is served only until 2:30 p.m. For breakfast, you get pineapple or guava juice, a hot pastry, and all the coffee you desire for $1.95, wiki wiki. Your fellow diners are likely to include local people, the boating set, tourists, and perhaps a lone beachcomber.

For dinner at the Pioneer Inn you move onto the **South Seas Patio** (tel. 661-3636) surrounding the lovely pool for a broil-your-own steak, ground beef, or mahimahi treat on the open grill. The price of your entree, from $6.95 to $14.95, includes all you can eat at the salad bar and baked barbecued beans. The **Snug Harbor Restaurant** here has four complete dinners—eggplant and zucchini, deep-fried chicken, rib bones, and pork chops from $7.95 to $9.95, including salad bar, baked beans, vegetable, rice or potatoes, plus fresh catch of the day at $12.95 and other higher priced entrees.

One of the prettiest garden settings in Lahaina now houses **Hamburger Mary's** (tel. 667-6989), which serves—you've got it—a variety of hamburgers. Mary's also dishes up omelets, beginning at $4 for the basic one, with a variety of fillings possible, and a mahimahi, broiled chicken, or steak dinner for $8.75, including rice or home fries. Fresh catch of the day is available at market price. The garden looks like a small jungle of hanging plants, with a fountain in the middle, a big bar, and cozy director's chairs pulled up to natural-wood tables. On the stereo, usually played at high volume, you'll hear a variety of taped music that ranges from Hawaiian jazz to blues, rock, and reggae. To find Mary's, head for 608 Front St., walk down a graveled path bordered by huge potted avocado trees, and you're there. The full menu is served continuously every day from 10 a.m. to 11 p.m. The bar is open daily until 2 a.m. (tel. 667-6989).

A venerable Lahaina favorite, the **Banyan Inn** (tel. 661-4489), across from the town's landmark, Banyan Court, has recently been done over; now it has a high cathedral ceiling for coolness, a pretty wood front, and, as before, some of the tables near the garden in the large, semi-open dining

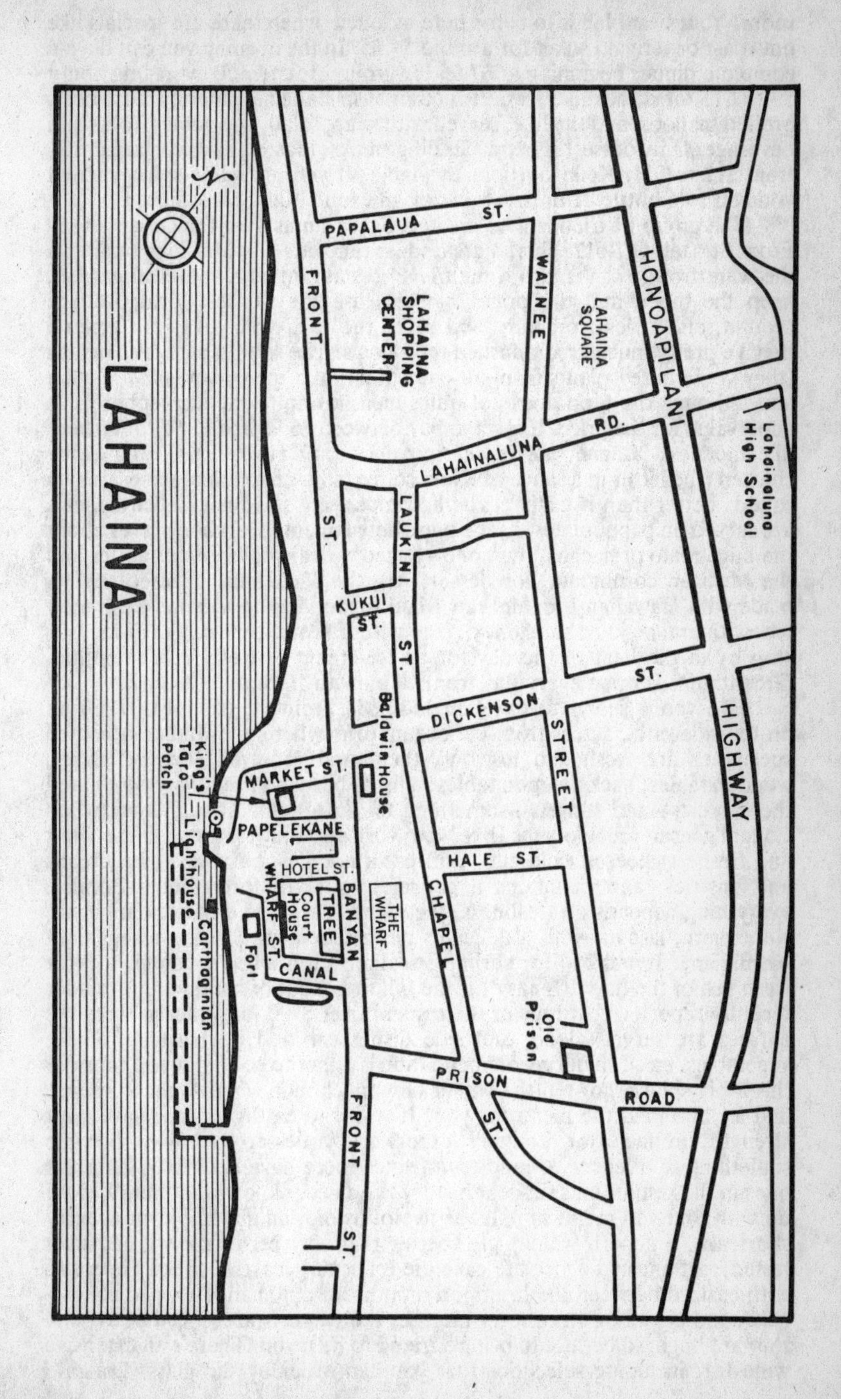
LAHAINA
N
FRONT ST.
PAPALAUA ST.
LAHAINA SHOPPING CENTER
WAINEE
LAHAINA SQUARE
HONOAPILANI HIGHWAY
Lahainaluna High School
LAHAINALUNA RD.
LAUKINI ST.
KUKUI ST.
DICKENSON ST.
Baldwin House
MARKET ST.
King's Taro Patch
Lighthouse
PAPELEKANE
HOTEL ST.
WHARF ST.
Court House
TREE
BANYAN
THE WHARF
Carthaginian
Fort
CANAL
STREET
HALE ST.
CHAPEL ST.
Old Prison
PRISON ROAD
FRONT ST.

room. Your best plan is to come here at lunch, when there are specials like pot roast or teriyaki steak for around $4.25. In the evening you can have a complete dinner beginning at $7.95 for ground round and averaging about $9 to $11 for dishes like fresh fish (caught in Lahaina waters), roast beef, broiled scallops, and the like, served with soup, salad, vegetables, rolls, and beverage. Only dessert is extra. Sizzling steaks, lobster, and crab are great, from $12 to $14. Keiki portions available. If you're feeling splurgy, treat yourself to a bottle of French wine or an exotic island cocktail.

The group of friends who created **Greenthums over the Ocean** at 839 Front St. (tel. 667-6126) had a great idea: renovate an old fishing house on the waterfront, turn it into a multilevel restaurant-cum-botanical garden, keep the menu and the prices modest, use the freshest local produce around, and "bless, prepare, and serve the food with love." In general they've pretty much accomplished their goals. The setting here is charming (they've gathered plants from all over Maui, and the ocean is *that* close), and although the food does not quite measure up to the atmosphere, it's good value for the price. Expect to pay between $6.95 and $8.95 for entrees like meatless lasagne, curried shrimp in a puff pastry shell, and Kona chicken (the latter in a sauce of Kona coffee, sour cream, and spices, which sounds better than it tastes). The accompanying salad is excellent. Meals are served on paper plates. In the pupu department, everybody raves about the huge plate of nachos, the honey-glazed teriyaki chicken drumettes and the Mexican cornbread. For dessert, try the Menehune cheesecake; it's made with Hawaiian rum and raw Maui sugar. And have some fresh mint tea, with orange juice and honey, to go with it. Come for a sunset dinner, or stop by in the heat of the day for an ice-cream or fresh-fruit smoothie. Greenthums is open every day from 10 a.m. to 10 p.m.

Everybody seems to like **Longhi's,** 888 Front St. (tel. 661-0911), an on-the-sidewalk, across-from-the-ocean café where the Italian-accented specialties are fresh and luscious, the mood convivial (lots of plants, wooden tables, backgammon tables, a lively bar, and friendly service), and the desserts—and sunsets—something to write home about. Owner Bob Longhi goes to great lengths (like New York and Italy) to bring in the finest and freshest cheeses, cold cuts, and pasta noodles, bakes his own breads and pastries, and maintains a gourmet standard throughout. Because everything depends on freshness, the menu is always verbal: the night we were there, lasagne with a delicious pesto sauce was $9, as was eggplant parmigiana. It was $14 for shrimps, scallops, and lobster scampi, $16 for fresh fish of the day. It's easy for the bill to get out of hand here (a reader recently reported that four of them spent over $100 for a meal), since the entrees are served alone, and side dishes can add up (salad at $3.50, vegetables, etc.), so our recommendation is either to go all out and consider this a big splurge, or tell the waiter how much money you want to spend, and let him plan the menu for you. It's wise to eat lightly and save your strength, in fact, for Longhi's otherworldly desserts; they've become something of a legend around town, since there have been 1000 different ones in the restaurant's six-year history. You never know what they'll come up with, but you might sample, as five of us did, an incredible strawberry shortcake, a superb walnut pie (better than any pecan pie we had ever tasted), an unusual chocolate cake pie (chocolate cake between pie crusts with custard between the layers), a mouthwatering mango-topped cheesecake, and a cooling strawberry mousse. All desserts are priced at $4, and they are huge, so be sure to bring a friend to help you. There's an extensive wine list, including selections that you can order by the glass. Longhi's opens at 7:30 a.m. for breakfast (frittatas, omelets, homemade coffeecake, and strudel), and serves continuously till about 10:30 p.m. or later.

Perhaps the most atmospheric restaurant in Lahaina, overlooking the ocean and handsomely done in South Seas beachcomber style, is the **Lahaina Broiler** (tel. 661-3111), just opposite the Lahaina Shopping Center at the intersection of Front and Papalua Streets. Dinner entrees are apt to be high (although you can get chicken curry, broiled salmon steak, broiled teriyaki, and poached red snapper between $7.95 and $12.50), but lunch is inexpensive and well worth the tab. There is always a daily special—perhaps Hungarian beef stew—for $5.75, and the mahimahi almond sherry sandwich is practically a meal in itself, at $4.95. Breakfast starts at 7:30 a.m., lunch is on from 11:30 a.m. to 2:30 p.m., dinner from 6 to 9:30 p.m., and the bar swings until midnight. Should you run into a huge tour group being served here, as occasionally happens, better come back another day.

Moose McGillycuddy's Pub & Café, 844 Front St., which you may remember from Waikiki, offers the same brand of good food, good booze, and good fun here in Lahaina. It's one flight up, with a big bar, a lively atmosphere, and some tables set out on the lanai overlooking busy Front Street. The menu is the same for lunch and dinner. Maybe you'll go for one of the char-broiled-to-order burgers, anything from your "friendly, unassuming basic burger" at $4.75 to a University Burger ("highly ranked bacon and intelligent cheddar") at $5.40, or even an Air Burger ("no meat, no cheese, a vegetarian's delight") at $4.95. Four-egg omelets are served with country fries or rice, Texas toast and fruit, and cost $5.50. Looking for something different in a sandwich? How about deep-fried mahimahi and banana on whole-wheat bread at $4.95. The Moose's hot 'n' juicy pizzas (from $4.95 small) are good; so are salads and munchies like hot Texas chile, fish 'n' chips in beer batter, stuffed potato skins—all from $3.50 to $4.95. Margaritas and daiquiris at $3.50 are the big booze selections here, along with coffee drinks, Hawaiian exotics, and way-out house specialties like the Mooseberry—vodka, amaretto, cranberry juice, sweet-sour, and Grand Marnier, 22 wicked ounces for $4.25. Moose McGillicuddy's opens early for hearty breakfasts and hangover helpers, and stays open until late, late.

Fujiyama, in the Lahaina Shopping Center (tel. 667-6207), is our favorite Japanese restaurant in the Lahaina area. It's not fancy, but it's clean and cozy and definitely has atmosphere. For an exotic appetizer, try the ikura oroshiae at $4.95—that's grated radish topped with salmon roe! We like the chicken yakitori, barbecued chicken on a stick, and the kani sunomono—that's crab with cucumber. The combination dinner, of various teriyakis and shrimp tempura, served with soup, salad, vegetables, rice, and tea, is a winner at $9.75. For two or more and a tab of $13.75 each, you can have dinner cooked right at table by a lovely waitress; choose from the likes of sukiyaki, shabu shabu (all beef), or yosenabe (fish), served with all of the above accompaniments. Or try the sushi/sashimi platters, priced between $4.50 and $7.25. Fujiyama is open for lunch, weekdays only, from 11 a.m. to 1:30 p.m.; and for dinner every day, from 5 p.m. on. A sushi bar is open at both meals.

Not only does **The Wharf,** a nifty shopping complex at 658 Front St., have some of the most tasteful boutiques in the area, it also has restaurants serving some of the tastiest food—and prices are reasonable. An attractive little *fonda Mexicana* on the ground floor of the Wharf, **Tortilla Flats** (tel. 667-9581) is a colorful room with banquettes, wooden tables, Mexican lanterns on the walls, and flowers on the tables. Portions are generous, almost more than one can eat. We can vouch for the enormous plate of nachos (beans, chips, and melted cheese, with sour cream and green onions) at $3.75, and the gigantic guacamole tostado (stuffed with beans, cheese, and lettuce, and topped with guacamole, more cheese, and sour cream) at $5.50. Combination plates are served with refried beans, Spanish rice, hot corn chips, soup, and salad, and run about $7.25 to $8.75 at dinner. There are quite a few fish and seafood dishes too: shrimp, scallops, fish and chips, and a combination seafood platter, from $5.75 to $6.95. Strawberry and pineapple margaritas (17 ounces!) from the bar add a tropical, if not strictly Mexican, touch. Lunch is served from 11:30 a.m. to 5 p.m., dinner from 5:30 to 10 p.m.

If you enjoy having breakfast or lunch al fresco, **Lani's Pancake Cottage** (tel. 661-0955) at the Wharf is the place to go. The indoor area with its counters and booths is pleasant enough, but they also serve on a large umbrellaed terrace. Breakfast is on all day, so anytime is fine for banana or strawberry pancakes ($2.65 and $3.50) or the omelet to end all omelets: the Chef's Mess Omelet, made of five eggs and filled with the likes of Ortega chili and cheese, bell peppers, Swiss cheese, etc.—$11 for two of you, $12 for three. Their tuna melt sandwich—grilled tuna and cheese with a small green salad—makes a good lunch at $3.50, and so do such fanciful entrees as a chili relleno burger (meat plus cheese and chilis on sourdough, dipped in egg batter with relleno sauce—not bad!) or more usual items like a bowl of chili or honey-dipped fried chicken, from $3.45 to $5.75.

Next door to Lani's, sharing the same outdoor terrace area, is **Mama's Original Maui Pizza** (tel. 667-2531), where you can get pizza by the slice for $1.25 and partake of the salad bar ($3.49), or stuff yourself at the all-you-can-eat buffet of pizza, spaghetti, garlic bread, and salad bar, $4.95 at lunch, $6.95 at dinner. Lunch from 11 a.m., dinner from 5 p.m.

We like the motto of **Skippers Seafood 'n Chowder House,** up in the front area of the Wharf: "Get good seafood without getting soaked." They're quite right: you're too far from the ocean to worry about the salt spray, and the prices are very good. Call this one a medium-fast-food operation: you place and pay for your order at the cashier's, then proceed to sit either indoors at booths or outdoors under umbrellaed tables in the very pretty patio bar (tropical mixed drinks are excellent here). The servers will bring the food to your table. All of the fish is deep-fried and served with fries or rice, plus cole slaw. You have a choice of cod and mahimahi: one piece of fish is $2.59; two pieces are $3.59; four pieces, $4.59. Shrimp, clam, or salmon dinners are $5.29; the Skipper's Platter of shrimp, clams, and fish filets is $5.59. There's fried chicken in a basket too, chicken and fish combo, family meals, a children's menu, New England clam chowder, a salad bar (one serving at $1.99, all-you-can-eat at $4.99), carrot and chocolate cakes for dessert, and wine and beer. All in all, a safe and scenic harbor for a family meal.

For those who savor the bookish life, the most charming place at the Wharf will have to be **Upstart Crow Co., Bookstore and Coffee House.** Here, in a shady corner at the top of the Wharf, people are sitting quietly on the patio engaged in such pursuits as reading or writing letters—all the while munching on light snacks like quiches ($4.25) and sipping some wonderful coffees, English teas, hot Ghirardelli chocolate, iced cappuccino, and the like. Drinks are 65¢ to $1.75, and there are good homemade quiches, cookies, cakes, and pastries to accompany them. You can also buy Kona coffee here by the pound—and books, of course, to give you something to do out on the patio.

Stick to the pasta and chicken dishes on the low side of the menu, and you can have a very reasonable and atmospheric meal at **Bettino's,** at Lahaina Shores Village, 475 Front St. (tel. 661-8810). Bettino's is tucked away in the rear of this little shopping complex, affording you a view from its lanai of the oceanfront at Lahaina Harbor. The menu is mostly Italian, and the food is good. Along with your orders of, say, pasta ala vongole (clams in a white-wine-and-garlic sauce), fettucine Alfredo, Italian sausage and chicken, chicken breast parmesan, or broiled breast of chicken, all from $6.95 to $8.95, you'll get soup or salad, fresh vegetables, and a loaf of their delicious fresh-baked Italian bread. Fish and steak dishes are higher. Lunch is moderately priced, and specials include mahimahi, fish and chips, fettucine marinara, Maui-style ribs, and pork chops, from $4.95 to $6.95, plus a goodly array of burgers and hot sandwiches. Bettino's serves breakfast from 7 a.m. to 2 p.m. (full bar service starts at 8 a.m.), lunch from 11 a.m. to 2 p.m., and dinner from 5:30 to 10 p.m. Open every day.

Lahaina Square (just behind Lahaina Shopping Center) is a good place for hungry budgeteers to note. Here you'll find **Amilio's Delicatessen,** which has good sandwiches, some with an Italian flair, to take out or eat here; the price range goes from $2.85 for tuna or cheese, to $4.25 for Amilio's special of many meats and cheeses. There's a choice of good breads. Small pizzas start at $4, and there are deli meats and cheeses if you wish to make your own sandwiches. Open most days from 9 a.m. to 1 p.m., until 9 p.m. on Friday, on Sunday from 10 a.m. to 4 p.m.

Stacks of kiawe wood and Hawaiian ranch decor set an upcountry mood, but here we are in tropical Lahaina, at **Chris' Smokehouse BBQ** in Lahaina Square (tel. 667-2111). The baby back pork ribs and kiawe chicken are good and tasty—they're marinated overnight in barbecue sauce, then smoked over kiawe wood and broiled over kiawe charcoal to give them a very special flavor. There are four complete dinners on the menu between $7.95 and $8.95—and that means that along with your four-rib rack of baby back pork ribs, smoked sausage links, half a smoked kiawe chicken or three smoked beef ribs, you also get freshly baked cornbread muffins with honey macadamia-nut butter, cole slaw, and two choices among ranch-style baked beans, sweet potato fritter, homemade steak fries, or steamed rice. Higher priced dinner entrees include various combination plates, New York strip steak, and charcoal-broiled fresh fish at $11.25. À la carte dishes run from $1.50 (for one smoked rib) to $11.50 (for steak). Come at lunchtime and you can sample Chris' tasty smoked meats in open-face sandwiches with barbecue sauce at $3.50 to $4.50, served with cole slaw, cottage cheese, or steak fries. Chris also serves some nice cool specialties, like Mauian seviche, a tomato and Mauii onion salad, papaya or avocado salad, and an avocado and orange salad, from $3.50 to $4.95. You're given a plain, white paper placemat and crayons for doodling while you're having a drink and waiting for your meal. Our Häagen-Däzs hula pie was a bit of a disappointment at $3, so next time we'll try the giant chocolate-chip cookie at $1. Chris' serves dinner every night from 5:30 to 10 p.m., lunch Monday to Saturday from 11:30 a.m. to 2:30 p.m.; Happy Hour is 2:30 to 5 p.m.

Christine's Family Restaurant at Lahaina Square (tel. 661-4156) is just the place to bring a hungry family; they'll eat heartily and well, and there won't be a big dent in the budget. It's very popular with the local people for its home-style cooking. Readers have written to praise their breakfasts: you get two eggs, your choice of meat, either hash browns or two scoops of rice, plus toast, for about $4.25. Lunch features lots of burgers and meat sandwiches around $4, plus plate lunches—beef teriyaki, roast pork, ham steak, and the like—in the $4.50 to $4.75 range. At dinner, served from 4:30 to 9:30 p.m., prices run from $5.85 to $8.25 for dishes like chicken cutlet, beef teriyaki, tonkatsu (deep-fried breaded pork, an island favorite), top sirloin, and lemon chicken. Along with the main course come rice or potato, tossed green salad or soup. There's nothing fancy about Christine's, but it is large and comfortable, with a smaller counter up front, and booths and tables in the back, a large sunset painting on the wall. It's open weekdays from 6 a.m. to 9:30 p.m., Saturday and Sunday 24 hours.

There's just a counter and a few outside tables at **House of Canton** in Lahaina Square (tel. 661-5408), but is the food ever good! This is Hong Kong–style Chinese cuisine, and the chef knows his way with dishes like chicken with black mushrooms, sauteed chicken Cheng Tu style (hot!), Mongolian beef, and shrimp fried rice, all of these priced from $3.95 to $4.95. Come here anytime between 11 a.m. and 2 p.m. for lunch, between 4 and 8 p.m. for dinner.

An ice-cream counter with a health-food flavor—that's what we'd call the **Wizard of Aah's** at Lahaina Square. The gentleman behind the counter can fix you up with yogurt, smoothies, fanciful ice-cream flavors like Alaskan wild blueberry and Georgia peach, but he also has his own brand of nondairy ice cream (delicious!), and if you're feeling out-of-sorts, he'll offer you a Flu Buster—that's green magma, powdered Vitamin C, and apple juice plus catalyst altered water. It's $2, and he swears it works! Fun for a chat and a snack. There are two tables with deck chairs outside.

"We're the alternative to the Big Mac," says the owner of **The Fish Fry** in the Lahaina Shopping Center. This cute little eatery with its wooden chairs and tables has blossomed from a fish-only place to one serving local food, all of it home-cooked, at all three meals. They boast the "best fish and chips in Hawaii," and we'd say they are pretty good: fish and chips, scallops and chips, shrimp and chips start at around $3.25 for a small fry, go up to $4.50 for a plentiful Captain's Plate. Zucchini and onion rings, called "Zings," are fun, and cold lemonade and Maui-made ice cream are welcome on a hot Maui day. Local plates—kalua pig, roast pork, teriyaki, etc.—are under $4. Open every day.

Also popular at Lahaina Shopping Center: **Colonel Sanders Kentucky Fried Chicken, McDonald's,** and **Ron's of Hawaii,** a local chain that features quick breakfasts, sandwiches, ice cream, and "mainland-style doughnuts" made fresh every day.

Just past the railroad depot on Honoapiilani Highway you'll spot a familiar building: it's a **Pizza Hut,** the home of those thick, crusty pizzas with the chewy, cheesy taste. This attractive spot, with its red curtains at the window, cozy booths and tables, attracts a large family crowd, since both pizza and pasta are filling, tasty, and inexpensive. If you come between 11 a.m. and 2 p.m. Monday through Saturday, they'll guarantee that your personal pan pizza ($2.09 for the supreme, $1.79 for the pepperoni) will be ready in five minutes, or the next one's on them. As for the regular pies, create your own with any two ingredients chosen from the scores available at $7.10 small, $10.95 medium, $13.90 large. Beer and wine by the glass and the pitcher. Open from 11 a.m. to midnight, until 1 a.m. weekends, no lunch on Sunday.

Besides being a top-flight health-foods store, **Lahaina Natural Foods,** 1295 Front St. (at the edge of town, Kaanapali side), has long been serving hot lunch specials every day, along with sandwiches, burritos, soyburgers, and other natural specialties. But now they've outdone themselves and opened the **Waterfront Café** for "international cuisine au natural." Here's how it works. You go up to the counter on the side of the building and place your order, then take your food to one of the several picnic tables under Cinzano umbrellas, overlooking the waterfront. It's one of the breeziest spots around (Lahaina can be very hot during the daytime), very casual, and the food is delicious and inexpensive. For dinner, served between 4 and 7 p.m., you could have stir-fried vegetables, a tofu plate, homemade lasagne with salad, a Mexican plate, or chicken Milano, all from $3 to $4.95. For a splurge, there's lobster tail at $9.95 with rice and salad. Lunch, served from 11 a.m. to 3 p.m., offers lentil-and-grain burgers, a Mexican plate, buñuelos, vegetables, salads, sandwiches, and soup of the day. Even if you don't eat here, run in for a cup of toffuti—the chocolate peanut butter flavor we sampled was fabulous. Note: If the food counter happens to be closed, you can still go inside the store, pick up a good sandwich and some bottled juice in the cooler, eat outside at the picnic tables, and enjoy those ocean breezes.

A door or two away at 1307 Front St. is **Naokee's Too,** which has been offering one of the best deals anywhere on a one-pound New York steak: with salad, rice, and vegetable, it is $6.95. Naokee's is a very plain little luncheonette right on the ocean, but the food is excellent. For $3.95 you can get such selections as Korean barbecue, beef stew, roast pork, roast beef, hamburger steak, and fried chicken, along with rice and salad. Neighborhood kids like to come here to play Pac-Man.

Next to the train depot (the Lahaina-Kaanapali Railroad) at 991 Limahina Pl. are two spots you might keep in mind if you need food to take out. **Café Allegro** has Italian and Mediterranean gourmet food to take out or eat at a few outside tables: enchilada casserole, chicken pizzaiola (baked with marinara sauce and cheese), lasagne, vegetarian dishes, most under $4. **The Bakery,** next door, is a popular spot, crowded with locals, who come early in the morning for croissants, brioches, pain au lait, hot from the oven. Butter bread and cheese butter bread, $1.25, is their specialty.

BARGAINS AT KAANAPALI BEACH: The strip of luxury hotels along Kaanapali Beach boasts a goodly share of luxury restaurants, but just a few where the budget dinner can relax. So it's good news that the **Moana Terrace** of the beautiful new Maui Marriott Resort has inaugurated a $7.95 Sundowner Dinner, served only between 5 and 6:30 p.m. Three or four entrees—perhaps beef, mahimahi, or teriyaki—are featured each night. All entrees come with soup or salad, dessert, and beverage. Some other time, when you're ready for a little splurge, come back to the Moana Terrace for the spectacular buffet served between 6 to 9:30 p.m. every night, one of the best on the island. The tables are laden with more dishes than you could eat in a week, and the dessert selection alone is mind-boggling. The price is $12.50 for adults, $8.75 for children under 12. The room is exquisite, open to the sea, furnished with airy wicker: plants abound (tel. 667-1200 for reservations).

There's another popularly priced eating spot at the hotels: the **Kaanapali Beach Hotel Coffeeshop.** Breakfast begins at 6:30 a.m., lunch at 11 a.m., and dinner at 5 p.m. Be sure to check the luncheon specials, perhaps pot roast, barbecue ribs, beef stew, or roast chicken, plus hot and cold sandwiches, $3.95 to $4.95. At dinner you can have hot platters such as roast turkey, fried shrimps, breaded veal cutlet or New York–cut steak, from $5.95 to $6.95, plus a nightly dinner special at the same price, which includes entree, vegetable, potatoes or rice, rolls and butter, and salad.

Service is cafeteria-style, and since the coffeeshop is at the entrance side of the hotel, you can walk right in after parking your car, without having to go through the hotel lobby.

We've already told you about La Familia in Kihei (see above). **La Familia Kaanapali** (tel. 667-7902) serves the same delicious menu of moderately priced Mexican food specialties and good drinks, but has its own distinct *muy simpático* atmosphere—it's at the entrance to the Kaanapali Resort area, across from the Hyatt Regency Maui, overlooking the 18th hole of the Royal Kaanapali Golf Course. The huge lanai is great for drinks, especially during the 4 to 6 p.m. and 10 p.m. to midnight Happy Hours, when frosty margaritas are only 99¢, and other drinks are similarly discounted. Interesting specials are offered for dinner every night: the night we were there it was ahi sashimi for $6.95, top sirloin for $12.19, shrimp scampi provençale at $14.95, and fresh sauteed ahi at $12.95. La Familia Kaanapali serves breakfast, lunch, and dinner every day from 7 a.m. to 10 p.m.

You keep running into Apple Annie's all over Maui these days, but it's especially nice to find one of these upbeat, medium-priced eateries in the normally expensive Kaanapali area. Just at the entrance to Kaanapali Resort (Lahaina end) is **Apple Annie's Beach House,** a breezy, sophisticated spot, where it's pleasant to sit out on the porch and have a drink while you're waiting for a table (and there usually is a wait). Dinner specialties begin at $6.50 for a steamed-vegetable plate, and various mahimahi and chicken dishes start at $7.95. There are also plenty of omelets, salads, pizzas, burgers, Mexican dishes, and such at moderate cost. Breakfast begins at 7 a.m. and the door stays open until 1 a.m. Sunday to Thursday, to 2 a.m. on Friday and Saturday.

AT WHALER'S VILLAGE: There's a salty but slick flavor to the handsome complex of shops and museum attractions at Maui's Whaler's Village, and you can be sure that oldtime seamen never had food as good as you'll find in the village's restaurants. From the Cinzano umbrellas over the outdoor tables to the espresso coffee-maker and banners inside, the flavor of **Ricco's Old World Delicatessen,** on the lower level of Whaler's Village, is definitely Italiano. Their sandwiches, generous and tasty, are served on a choice of french roll or rye, with tomatoes, marinated onions, and their own "secret sauce." They range from meatballs, pastrami, Italian sausages, corned beef, vegetarian (cheeses, mushrooms, bell peppers), roast beef, and turkey breast, and cost $3.59 for the "Mama" version, $3.99 for the "Papa." Ricco's pizzas are great too (try the "world-famous" pineapple pizza or Ricco's "Magnifico" for something different). Wine and a huge selection of ice-cold beers are available. A fun place, good for a quick and tasty meal. Open daily from 11 a.m. to 10 p.m.

On the upper level of the village is the **Rusty Harpoon,** where it's so pleasant to sit out on the shaded oceanfront lanai gazing at Molokai and Lanai right there across the blue water—that is, unless the live entertainment is a bit too lively. But Rusty's is fun. Big sandwiches like the Stevedore's Sandwich (turkey with sprouts and tomato on a sesame-seed bun) or the First Mate's Ham and Cheese Sandwich are priced at $4.45, and are served with chips. Dinner is usually a broil-your-own affair: best bets for budgeteers are Rusty's Swashbuckling Burger (a half-pounder) at $6.75, and Captain Ahab's Delight (teriyaki boneless chicken breast) at $8.50. Rusty's calls itself the "Daiquiri Capital of the Western World," and its fresh-fruit daiquiris (how about banana, pineapple, or peach?) are memorable, $3.50. Drinks and food from 11 a.m. until closing.

For a quieter mood, there's **Yami's Soft Frozen Yogurt,** with a few outside tables to sit at on the lower level of Whaler's Village. Relax with one of their yogurt shakes like the Queen's Quencher, yogurt plus lemon and coconut, $1.55; or snack on a papaya stuffed with yogurt and topped with fruit, $2.45; or try one of their good sandwiches—tuna, avocado, raw milk cheese, and egg salad—served on cracked-wheat bread with tomato and alfalfa sprouts, for $2.75. Their cheesecake frozen yogurt is a winner.

The only restaurant we know of with its own pool, right on a glorious beach, is **El Crabcatcher** at Whaler's Village. This is a glamorous place, with dinner too pricey for us, but you can make do at lunch with sandwiches starting at $4.95. Sit at an outside table, relax, have a drink and pupus, and enjoy a swim in the pool or ocean.

AT KAPALUA: We hardly expected to find a moderately priced eating place in the posh pastures of Kapalua Bay Resort, but find one we did, and so charming and tasteful is the **Market Café** that it's become one of our special Maui favorites. The Market Café, at the Kapalua Shops, is a tiny little place (no more than nine tables, three booths), with the flavor of a European sidewalk café—and with the flavor too of cheeses and wines (over 400 to choose from), espressos and cappuccinos, imported beers (we counted at least 50), luscious ice-cream drinks, rich desserts, and good sandwiches—everything from bagels and cream cheese to baked ham or roast beef, from $3.85 to $5.95. Sandwiches are served with lettuce, tomatoes, and a choice of cheese. Sandwiches, burgers, homemade soups and chowders, cheese nachos, and chili nachos are fine for a light meal, but for something a bit more substantial, try one of their specials of the day at $7.95: it might be lasagne with garlic bread, quiche with fruit, spinach pie, barbecued chicken, served with a choice of soup or salad. Home-baked spice, zucchini, and banana breads, croissants, and pastries—like their award-winning fudge brownies—are special treats here. Breakfast is good too. Between 7 and 11 a.m., there are many items to choose from: pancakes cooked with fresh fruit are especially good, as are the café's own homemade biscuits, which are served with every meal. Open daily.

IN HANA: There are very few public restaurants in Hana, and **Tutu's at** Hana Bay is about the only one in the budget category. People swimming and sunning at the Hana Beach Park keep their eye on the door, and when it opens they line up in front. At Tutu's you can buy large saimin bowls for about $2, grilled-cheese sandwiches, cheeseburgers, milkshakes, ice creams, etc. Tutu's is in a large beach pavilion where some of the best luaus on the island are held.

There's a fabulous buffet lunch every day for $10 at the **Hotel Hana Maui,** more expensive dinners, and less expensive meals at the Hotel Hana Maui Coffeeshop located away from the hotel in the Hana Ranch complex.

3. The Night Scene

IN KAHULUI: Nightlife is relatively quiet in this area. Your best bet, as usual, is in the big hotels. The **Maui Palms** has music every night except

Sunday and Monday, from 9 p.m. on by varied groups, and there's no cover. On Friday and Saturday from 9:30 p.m. you can catch the sounds of the Sakuras in the East West Room (dress code). . . . At the Red Dragon Room of the **Maui Beach,** the mood is more mod than Hawaiian: **Stylus Point Disco** swings into action weekend nights and continues until the wee hours; cover charge and a two-drink minimum. Friday night is Ladies Night (half price), and during summer and school vacations there's Teen Disco on Monday nights, with a $5 cover and a two soft-drink minimum. . . . The coziest place for just a drink is **Apple Annie's** in the Kaahumanu Shopping Center. You can sink into a sofa or a soft wicker chair, and join the small convivial crowd at the bar. "Do you have entertainment here?" we asked one night. "Yes," answered one of the habitués, "but it's not from entertainers." It's that kind of place. Sports fans can watch their favorites on the 48-inch color TV set. . . . Check the shopping centers for free Polynesian shows, presented several times a week. Maui Mall, for one, sometimes presents top revues from Honolulu clubs—free.

IN LAHAINA: Lahaina at night is the place for the drinking set, with no shortage of swinging bars. For a start you might try the **Harpooner's Lanai** at the Pioneer Inn; salty atmosphere and moderate prices. The bartender is a pure Hawaiian, famous for his harpoons and mai tais. . . . Visiting celebrities from the music world usually head for **Bluemax,** 730 Front St., where there's an entire monoplane hanging from the ceiling. This is one of the liveliest contemporary music clubs in Hawaii ("the most popular nightspot on Maui," according to *Time* magazine), featuring jazz and occasional mainland rock. Highballs are about $2, and the food ranges from $4.25 sandwiches at lunch to way up for elite dinner entrees. . . . The **Whale's Tale Restaurant** on Front Street always attracts a lively crowd. Beer from $2.25, plus good burgers and sandwiches from $4.25. . . . **Moose McGillycuddy's Pub & Café** has a half-price sale on during its 4 to 8 p.m. Happy Hour: all drinks and draft beer are 50% off, and 11 flavors of margaritas are just $1.75. In case you can't wait that long, there's an Early Happy Hour between 11:30 a.m. and 4 p.m., when draft beer is $1, standards are $1.25, and mai tais or chi chis are $1.75. . . . Happy Hour prices are *muy simpâtico* at **Tortilla Flats,** on the first floor of the Wharf. From 3 to 6 p.m., it's 99¢ for frosty margaritas, beer, and house wine, $1.25 for well drinks. . . . **Blackbeard's** 5 to 8 p.m. Happy Hour at the Wharf means $1.25 prices on draft beer, house wine, and well drinks; tasty pupus (baked brie, stuffed potato skins, sashimi) run $3.95 to $6.95.

IN KIHEI AND WAILEA: The **Maui Lu Resort** is a favorite entertainment address out in these parts. In Jesse's, the renovated and renamed supper club, Jesse Nakooka presents his Hawaiian Revue Tuesday through Saturday at 8 p.m., with dinner service beginning at 6 p.m. There is usually a cover charge. An old-style Hawaiian luau is held Monday, Wednesday, and Friday at 5 p.m.; the tab is $28 per person (reservations for dinner or the luau are recommended: tel. 879-5858). At either the luau or the dinner show you'll see Kawika, whose Samoan Fire Dance is, to say the least, unique: he stands, sits, and actually dances in the flames! How he does it, nobody knows. For more ordinary kinds of dancing—the kind the rest of us mortals can do—it happens here every night from 9:30 p.m. on a spacious dance floor. . . . Another beautiful luau ("Maui's Merriest Luau") is held every Thursday at 6 p.m. on the oceanfront lawn of the **Maui Inter-Continental Wailea,** complete with lavish feast and Polynesian revue; this one is priced at $26 for adults, $13 for children (reservations: 879-1922). . . . If it's Tuesday, it must be the luau at **Stouffer's Walea Beach Resort,** held in a beachfront garden setting at 6 p.m. The "Hawaiian Hula Revue" is the featured entertainment. Adults pay $29.50; children 12 and under, $16.50 (for reservations, phone 879-4900). . . . At the same Stouffer's Wailea Beach Resort, the **Lost Horizon nightclub** offers live entertainment nightly except Sunday. Entertainment ranges from contemporary, '20s and '50s music, rock, country, and Hawaiian. No cover charge (reservations not taken). . . . The disco spot in this area is **Sailmaker Saloon,** in Azeka's Place, every night from 9:30 p.m. until 2 a.m.

If you're not a night person but want to see a lovely Hawaiian show, you might like the **Aloha Mele** luncheon, which happens each Thursday at **Jesse's** at the Maui Lu resort. The mistress of ceremonies is one of Hawaii's most beloved entertainers, Auntie Emma Sharpe. The entertainment is preceded by a Hawaiian blessing. This luncheon is a favorite with local retired people: the tutus get all dressed up in their most beautiful muumuus, and Auntie Emma calls many members of the audience up to sing or dance. Jesse Nakooka and the Local Connection provide the music. As for food, you may order the Hawaiian plate, featuring kalua pig, or anything else on the menu. At the end, everyone rises, holds hands, and sings "Hawaii Aloha." As islanders say, it's "chicken-skin" (goose-bumps) time. Cocktails begin at 11 a.m. For reservations, phone 879-5858. The price of the lunch is $12.50 including tax and tip; cocktails are extra.

For a free Hawaiian show in this area, the place is the **Wailea Shopping Village,** and the time is Saturday afternoon, from 1:30 to 2:30. You can have a modestly priced sandwich or an ice cream at Ed and Don's when it's over.

AT KAANAPALI BEACH: More fun and games await you at the big beach hotels at Kaanapali. One of the greatest shows in town takes place every night at the **Sheraton Maui,** and it costs absolutely nothing to be in the audience. As the sun begins to set over the water, torches are lit all the way to the point. A native Hawaiian boy stands atop Black Rock (that eerie perch from which the souls of the dead were supposed to depart to the other world), throws his leis into the water, and then looks down some 20 feet or so to the waiting ocean below. The crowd—on the beach, lining the lobby floors—holds its breath. He plunges in, surfaces, and the evening festivities are under way.

If you need something to steady your nerves after that spectacle, make your way to the nautically decorated **Barkentine Bar.** The ship models, volcanic rock floor-to-ceiling columns, and the tables with compass designs are all unusual and handsome, but somehow we never notice anything except the view; from the crest of this black lava cliff overlooking the sea it's a spectacular one, a must for us collectors of Hawaiian sunsets. . . . One of the most romantic cocktail lounges, here or anywhere else, is surely the **Pequod Bar and Cocktail Lounge** at the Maui Surf Hotel. The bar resembles an old sailing ship, even to its figurehead, and while you're sipping your "Equator Exotics" (about $4), you can gaze at a moat filled with waterfalls, flashing carp, and water lilies. The big show at this hotel, in the **Kapa Room,** is *Here is Hawaii,* a musical Hawaiian history lesson with outstanding performances by Keola Beamer and Audrey Meyers. Dinner and show cost $22.50 for adults, $14.50 for children under 12. For reservations, call 661-4411.

Choosing among all the luau and dinner shows in the Kaanapali area can be difficult: all of them are good, none is inexpensive (most run from $27 to $34). Only one, the *Drums of the Pacific* production at the **Hyatt Regency Maui,** offers a cocktail show: the $20 tab includes a mai tai and a souvenir lei, tax, tip, and a chance to see a spectacular production of Pacific dancing (Samoan slap dances, Tahitian drum dances and shimmies, spear and knife dances, fire dances, etc.). The dinner show is $24 for adults, $28 for juniors (6 to 12), $18 for children 5 and under. Call Hyatt at 667-7474 for reservations.

The New Ohana Polynesian Revue at the Plantation Room of the **Kaanapali Beach Hotel** has been drawing rave reviews. You can take in both the prime rib dinner and the show at $29.50 for adults, $15 for children under 10. Or see the show only (no drinks) for just $10. It's an imaginative and exciting production, with a slide-show background and narration adding dramatic excitement to the songs, dances, and history of Hawaii and the South Pacific. Reservations: 661-0011.

For us, just walking around the Hyatt is another kind of show: its displays of Oriental art, gracefully situated throughout the public areas, are worthy of any fine museum. Be sure to stroll the grounds, too, of its exquisite next-door neighbor, the **Marriott Resort.** Stop to sit in the lobby and you can enjoy the sounds of music coming from the open Lobby Bar. For something a bit more organized, try the **Banana Moon nightclub** here, where disco is usually the order of the night. The two-level club allows you to dance and/or talk. Remember the big bands? The same hotel plays their music for tea dancing with Island Magic, from 7 to 10 p.m., in either the **Lobby Bar** or **Banana Moon** (tel. 667-1200).

A longtime favorite disco spot is the **Foxy Lady Dance Emporium** at the Royal Lahaina Hotel. Cover charge varies. . . . Happy Hour (4:30 to 6:30 p.m.) is the time when all well drinks are $1.50 at **El Crabcatcher** at Whalers Village, right out there on the waterfront, perfect for sunset watchers. . . . Happy Hour (4:30 to 5:30 p.m.) prices are a bargain at the salty **Rusty Harpoon** in the Whaler's Village: beer from $1.25, regular drinks at $1.75, fresh-fruit daiquiris (like mango or banana) and chi chis all reduced. Or have a "Doc Baldwin": rum, Galliano, and banana, named in honor of Doc, the resident—and very amiable—macaw. Happy Hour dinner specials for around $5.95 are offered at the same time. Live music every evening from 7 p.m. . . . We've heard good reports about the **Aloha Luau,** held Tuesday, Thursday, and Sunday at 5:30 p.m. on the grounds of the Sheraton Maui, featuring "Chief FAA," Samoan fire-knife dancer. Price is $30 for adults, $17 for children (for reservations, tel. 667-9564).

READERS' HOTEL AND RESTAURANT SELECTIONS ON MAUI: "We highly recommend the **Napili Bay,** close to Kaanapali Beach and Lahaina. These are studio apartments with one queen-size bed and two singles and kitchen; they are reasonably priced. We had clean, fresh linens each day, including beach towels; the rooms are not air-conditioned, but have adjustable shutters so you can feel the incredibly refreshing trade winds and hear the ocean at night. It cost us $50 for groceries for two people for a week and we ate well. Efficiencies are great! The owners were like grandparents to us, extremely friendly and accommodating" (Francine Schept, White Plains, N.Y.). [*Authors' Note:* Napili Bay's address is 33 Hui Dr., Lahaina, Maui, HI 96761 (tel. 669-6044).]

"The **Aloha Cottages** that you mention in Hana are wonderful. When we arrived, Mr. Nakamura gave us a basket of local fruits. He immediately suggested some good places to see in the area. He is also the barber in Hana, and I got a good haircut for $3.50 and learned all about Hana from him: he has lived here 30 years. The Nakamuras have built another cottage and may expand to a third. We highly recommend it. Be sure to ask Mr. Nakamura how to get to the secluded *red sand* beach in Hana. . . . We also enjoyed our stay at the **Mana Kai Maui Condominium Hotel.** They have washing machines and dryers on each floor, and all local calls are free—in contrast to our experience elsewhere" (Peter Sinclaire, New Britain, Conn.). . . . "I want to thank you for listing Mr. Nakamura's Aloha Cottages at Hana. We had not even unpacked before he shinned up a papaya tree and plucked the ripe fruit for our pleasure. We stayed in his larger cottage and can hardly express the feeling. It is large, and as the old saying goes, 'you could eat off the floors' and I really mean it. The furnishings are spare, but it is one of the most peaceful places we have ever stayed. One could easily stay a week instead of just overnight" (Bart and Lynda Esterly, Capistrano Beach, Calif.). . . . "We stayed one night at the **Hana Kai Resort Apartments** in Hana, a real tropical hideaway. We did cook our own steak in the barbecue, with several other couples. We wish we had planned to stay there longer. . . . The Japanese buffet dinner at the **Maui Palms** was superb and reasonable. About the only inexpensive restaurant was the one at the **Maui Hukilau;** the grilled mahimahi was the best we had on the island, and at $5.95 a real bargain. I take that back—**The FishFry** in Lahaina was another outstanding place. The scallops were delicious and downright cheap!" (Peter and Mary Tannen, Albuquerque, N.M.).

"We loved our cottage at **Nona Lani** on Kihei. Mr. and Mrs. Kong were so gracious and helpful. For complete relaxation, this is the place to go. We hope to return someday. No crowds—just lovely, peaceful, long beaches" (Margaret and Don Mead, Ontario, Calif.). . . . "I called **Maui Sands** on their toll-free number (800/367-5037) because their rates were among the best in the Kaanapali area. And I thought I'd ask them if they had a discount rate for clergy. As it turned out, they gave me a 20% discount. Other clergy would, I'm sure, be glad to know this" (Rev. Bob Waliszewski, no address given). . . . "A bouquet to the **Maui Islander** in Lahaina. Although it was more pricey than we had planned, the atmosphere was great and the staff was just super! . . . **Apple Annie's** in Kahului spoiled us for any other macadamia-nut pancakes. Theirs are just out of this world, as were all the meals we ate there. The staff here too is just great. . . . The **Chart House Restaurant** in Lahaina serves probably the best food we found in Maui with a wonderful atmosphere. Dollar for dollar, the Chart House is a pretty tough act to follow" (Mr. and Mrs. Lorne Alton, Edmonton, Alberta, Canada).

"We want to strongly recommend **Ma-Chan's** at the Kaahumanu Shopping Center in Kahului. It is a clean, attractive, simple restaurant that serves breakfast, lunch, and dinner at very low prices. Sandwiches run from $1.25 to $2.95. Lunches and dinners range from $2.85 to $3.50 (except for a $6.50 steak). These are full meals—soup, salad, and entree (no beverage)—but very generous servings. In addition, in the back is a self-service steam table where you can order and eat all kinds of treats—sushi, chow fun, luncheon plates, sandwiches, etc. All good food" (Melvin Mann, Berkeley, Calif.). . . . "We found good buys for lunch and dinner along the Kihei Road. Several restaurants have Early Bird dinners from 5 to 6:30 p.m., ranging from $5.95 to $8.95. We thoroughly enjoyed the **Maui Outrigger** at 2980 Kihei Rd., a stone's throw from Wailea. The fresh snapper with a sumptuous salad bar was priced at $8.95, but with wine, tip, and tax, the bill for two came to $26.50. It was truly a memorable experience to enjoy one of the better sunsets from our beachside table, with a view of the late-evening swimmers and snorkelers" (Melvin H. Boyce, Corte Madera, Calif.). . . . "We recommend the **Maui Sunset** in Kihei. Four of us stayed in a large, two-bedroom condo with washer/dryer for under $80 per night. It was on the top floor, with the ocean just beyond our lanai. The furniture was a bit worn, and the service not the best I've seen, but the lovely grounds and the view made up for it. Its name is just what we hoped for. . . . We discovered why condos are so much cheaper than hotels; their services are meager. Maid service is usually every other day. It is harder to obtain touring advice and assistance than in a full-service hotel. We recommend that first-timers stick to hotels, unless they have their trip very well planned" (Jeff and Chris Jacobsen, Rinton, Wash.).

"We found two restaurants in Maui that we would like to share with others. The first is the **Bar and Grill** in Kapalua. It is moderate to expensive, but if you make reservations for a window seat, you will have a fantastic dinner and a beautiful sunset view. The second place is a very inexpensive restaurant on Vineyard Street in Wailuku called **Hazel's.** All of the local people congregate here for socializing and eating. Complete breakfasts were $2.45 to $3.25. Lunches and dinners were $3.50 to $4.50 for a full-course meal. They have specials posted on a blackboard every day. The food is home-cooked and they have very generous servings. A great place to stop while out sightseeing" (Charleen and Wally Chornby, Portland, Ore.). . . . "We were well pleased with the food, service, and atmosphere at **La Bretagne,** located in an old house just off Front Street, facing Malu-ulu-o-lele Park. Prices are medium to high" (E. J. Felton, Largo, Fla.). . . . "**Lahaina Natural Foods** on Front Street is the most delightful restaurant, very inexpensive, overlooking the beautiful Pacific Ocean with tables outside, flowers and palm trees. The food is marvelous. The chef is amazing. Fresh fish, natural foods" (Gilda Wynne, Old Saybrook, Conn.). . . . "**Kahana Keyes Restaurant,** next to the Royal Kahana at Kahana Beach, three miles north of Kaanapali Beach, has one of the best salad bars we encountered. Dinners range from $8.95 to $18.95 for rack of lamb, seafoods, prime rib, steaks, lobster, etc. However, they also offer an Early Bird special for $8.95, including salad bar, served from 5:30 to 7 p.m. nightly. On this special, which changes nightly, they offer eight-ounce New York steak, steak and six-ounce lobster tail, prime rib, BBQ chicken and spare ribs. There is live music and dancing nightly. Nice atmosphere and great food" (Mrs. David Millison, Bellevue, Wash.).

"Special recommendations of the **Aloha Café** in Kahului as the only restaurant on the island where one can obtain a good à la carte selection of really characteristic Hawaiian foods. They are not 'blanded down,' either, as they are at the so-called luaus at the big hotels; moreover, the prices are so ludicrously low that one is tempted, after eating well and very amply, to offer to pay more. . . . The **Maui Lu** is mediocre for food, but it serves very good tropical drinks for the price. The fashion shows are a drag, but the **Jesse Nakooka Show** is surely one of the best on Maui for the money" (Frank R. Dollard, San Francisco, Calif.). . . . "I suggest that everyone spend some time visiting the **Hyatt Regency** on Maui, an absolutely luxurious hotel which, in my opinion, after having traveled all over the world, is probably the most beautiful hotel I have ever had the privilege of staying at. Highlight is the buffet breakfast at the **Swan Court,** approximately $9 per person" (Dr. Martin L. Jaffe, La Palma, Calif.).

"For those who enjoy a deli, our best find in Kihei was the **Surfside Spirits and Deli** in the Island Surf Shops, just past Kihei town center and across the street from picnic tables at Kalama Park. We got lunch and dinner there several times and were always pleased with the quality, selection, and reasonable prices. It was terrific eating at Kalama Park, with a very beautiful view of the coastline. The park also has playground equipment, a soccer field, basketball hoops, and rest rooms." (Julie Martin, Huntington Beach, Calif.). . . . "The **Napili Surf Beach Resort** was as charming as you described. We had a lovely little one-room apartment in the Puamala wing, with full kitchen, dressing room off a large bathroom, and living room, lanai; beautiful pools, and the beach the best we found. Laundry room, paperback library, beach towels, and so many extras made our stay a dream—so much so that we are returning for ten days. Barbecues are available with charcoal furnished, so outdoor cooking will be great" (Mrs. Leonard Lundgren, Boise, Idaho). . . . "We figured out how to beat the system at the **Chart House,** which serves a terrific dinner but never takes reservations. Put your name down on their list and then go shopping in Lahaina; they'll let you know when to be back" (Bob Harrison and Hal Goodstein, Provincetown, Mass.).

"My wife and I spent a week as guests—and we felt more like guests than customers—of Jeanette and Joe DiMeo at the **Lihi Kai** in Kihei. Everything about the place was delightful and comfortable, plus the best beach on East Maui only 50 yards away, an ample and convenient parking lot, and a line on the roof for hanging wet bathing suits, etc. And all this for $175 a week—the best bargain in the islands! Jeanette DiMeo, the chatelaine of this exemplary utopian home-away-from-home, is a model of friendliness and discretion, always available when needed, but with a distinct disinclination to hover. And when I developed a dental problem, she went out of her way to obtain an emergency appointment with her own dentist in Kahului. Maui no ka oe! And that goes for all innkeepers named DiMeo and all inns named Lihi Kai, which rates four stars in our travel book" (Frank W. Lindsay, Schenectady, N.Y.).

"We found staying in a condo in Kihei a relaxed experience that was not expensive (we had a condo that slept two couples for $60 a night), and we were aghast when we went to Kaanapali and saw the big, high-priced hotels with helicopters overhead and millions of people. It was a zoo!" (Christopher David Peters, Balboa Island, Calif.). . . . "**Gaspare's Place,** in the Island Surf Building in Kihei, has excellent pizza, a nice salad bar, and many other things on their menu. Everything is fresh and clean and the owner and staff are friendly and try very hard to please. It is a bright and attractive place with a cocktail lounge—not a pizza joint. . . . We went to Raffle's at the Wailea Beach Hotel for Sunday champagne brunch, $19.50 each, but well worth it, the best we've ever seen anywhere" (Joy Faust, Burnaby, B.C., Canada). . . . "**Golden Jade** is a favorite Chinese restaurant in Wailuku, known for their cake noodles and crispy kau chee min with vegetables. Garish decor" (Zulie Hasdris). . . . "For Maui, you may add another cheap accommodation for those who have rented a car. About halfway between Kahului and Hana, the YMCA runs apparently well-kept accommodations for $4.50 per night—the lowest you can find on Maui! For reservations, call **Camp Keanse** (tel. 248-8355) or one of the Kahului YMCA phone numbers (tel. 244-3253 or 242-9007). The risk that this place is already fully booked seemed to be low, but without a car or hitchhiking luck, one might get stuck there. The camp, however, is located at a most scenic spot at the coast" (Jurgen Simon, Bloomington, Ind.).

"A good restaurant we think, is the **Kihei Prime Rib House.** An impressive salad bar, good service, and excellent fish dishes" (Rhoda and Eugene Kaellis, Victoria, B.C., Canada). . . . "We enjoyed **Buzz's Wharf** near Lahaina, where we had excellent chicken teriyaki. It was all delicious, with hot homemade bread, crisp salads, excellent service, lovely atmosphere, and a harbor view—one of our cherished Hawaiian memories" (Mrs. John R. Maxwell, Iowa City, Iowa). [*Authors' Note:* Buzz's, open for dinner only (5:30 to 10 p.m.), is at the small-boat harbor at Maalaea, approximately 12 miles from Lahaina. Complete dinners range from about $8.95 to $16.95 for such entrees as roast chicken, scallops kebab, and steak.] . . ."We tried the **Chart House** on Front Street, Lahaina. The menu was à la carte; they had all the salad you wanted in a large chilled bowl from which you served yourself, two kinds of homemade bread (all you wanted), and choice of homemade salad dressings. Generous servings of excellent top sirloin steak for $10.75 and teriyaki steak for $10.95 were some of the entrees on the menu" (Kay Furst, Livingston, N.J.).

Chapter XVI

SEEING MAUI

1. Kahului-Wailuku and Kihei-Wailea
2. Haleakala, the House of the Sun
3. The Road to Hana
4. Lahaina
5. Kaanapali and Kapalua

THREE DAYS are the absolute minimum for savoring the varied charms of Maui, figuring one day in the **Kahului-Wailuku** and **Kihei-Wailea** areas, and **Haleakala,** another at **Lahaina** and **Kaanapali** in West Maui, and a third day for the trip to and from **Hana.** And this is going at a pretty rugged pace. If you can manage a few more days, we strongly urge you to do so. It's so pleasant to relax here after you've seen the sights. *Note:* Excellent maps are available in the *Maui Drive Guide,* which your car-rental company will give you free.

1. Kahului-Wailuku and Kihei-Wailea

THE KAHULUI AREA: A little more than 30 years old, **Kahului** is too new to have any historic sights, but it's considered a good example by city planners of what a model city should be. You can spend a pleasant hour or so browsing through its shopping centers. Maui's biggest shopping complex, **Kaahaumanu Shopping Center,** opened a few years back, and a better name for it might be Ala Moana No. 2. Like its Honolulu counterpart, it has **Sears** at one end, **Liberty House** at the other, and that fascinating Japanese department store, **Shirokiya,** in between. Most of the 50-odd stores here are geared to local residents, but there are a few places catering to gift buyers, like the **Gift Horse,** with beautiful windchimes, lots of brass, figurines, ceramics, jewelry, Pegge Hopper graphics, and novelty items like a slice of pineapple soap for $2. . . . **Toda's** has all kinds of souvenirs, plus Japanese dolls. . . . And **Karen's** will airmail fruit, anthuriums, and other tropical flowers to your friends back home. . . . **eye-T-ease** specializes in silkscreen designs by local artists on its T-shirts for men, women, and kiddies. Sayings might include "She Sells Sashimi by the Seashore" for grownups, and "Purple Pupu Eater" for the kids. . . . The **Alexander Collection** is a stylish interior design shop that exhibits and sells the work of local artists. Handsome posters by Otsuka were on sale during our last visit. . . . The **Center for Performing Plants, Nani Pacifica,** not only has certified Hawaiian cuttings, bulbs, and plants, but Maui's largest collection of miniatures for dollhouses and collectors. . . . You can get island and

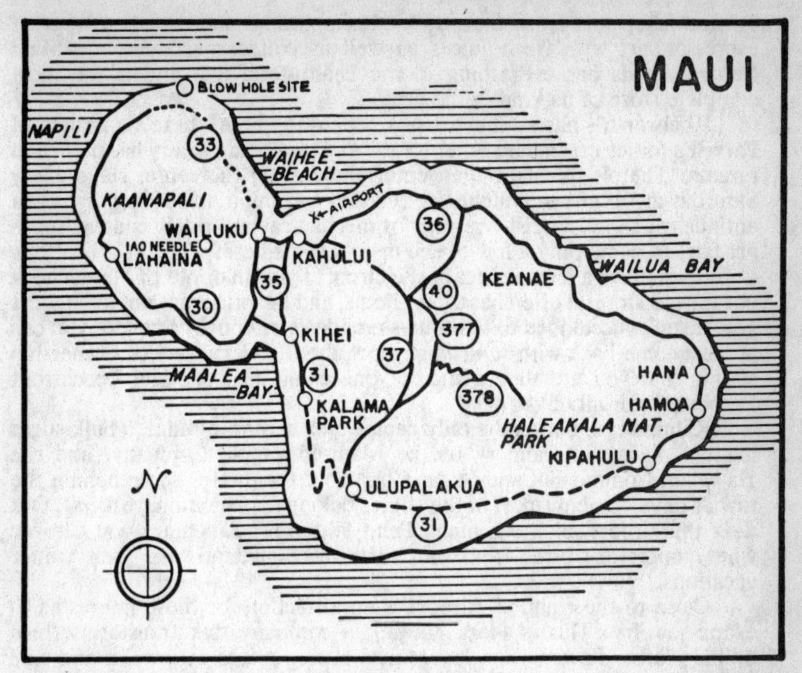

Oriental prints by the yard, well priced, at **Sew Special. . . . Foxmoor Runway 7** and the **San Francisco Rag Shop** have the latest in foxy threads. . . . The **Book Cache** abounds in Hawaiiana, as well as all the bestsellers. . . . In case you haven't sampled crackseeds yet, **Camellia Seeds** is the place; or you can munch on freshly baked cookies at **David's Cookies,** or on gourmet franks at **Orange Julius.** For a glass of cold, organic fruit juice, **Vim 'n' Vigor,** the local branch of the Honolulu chain, is the place. They also have a natural-foods restaurant in the rear. And **Apple Annie's,** plus several other places (see Chapter XV), are fine for meals. Check the local papers for news of frequent entertainments on weekends; if it's the first or third Thursday of the month, you can enjoy "Hawaiian Thursdays" at 7 p.m., a free show of local, Hawaiian, and Polynesian entertainment.

The newest of the shopping centers is the **Maui Mall,** a busy scene with its frequent sidewalk sales. Have a look at the Petroglyph Garden. The petroglyphs are carved into boulders, and are representative of ancient ones. Prof. Edward Stasack, noted authority on petroglyphs, supervised the work: you're invited to make rubbings of them if you wish: all you need is cotton fabric and a big felt-tipped marker. . . . We saw beautiful long muumuus at the **Second Look** and **Jerri-Jane's Fashions,** mod clothes at the **Jeans Factory** and **L.A. Boardwalk. . . . Long's Drugs** offers some of the best values for souvenirs and sundry items. . . . And you can stock up on groceries at **Star Super Market,** where the locals shop; if you're going to be cooking in your kitchenette apartment, it pays to stop here after getting off the plane before driving on to the more expensive resort areas. . . . You can pick up a T-shirt that reads "Eat, Drink and Be Maui" at the **T-Shirt Factory. . . . Roy's Photo Center** has probably the most complete supply of camera accessories and film on Maui. . . . **Sir Wilfred's Coffee, Tea,**

Tobacco shop has more than its name implies; it also boasts a fragrant espresso bar, with fresh juices as well as coffee specialties. . . . **Maui Natural Foods** has everything in the health-food line and is the most complete store of its kind in the area.

Woolworth's has an inexpensive coffeeshop here, there's a branch of **Farrell's** for ice cream and other treats, and the **Pizza Factory** has pizza and pizzazz. There's free Hawaiian entertainment on the center stage every Saturday at 1 p.m.; you might also run into an exhibit on oceanography, an antique car show, a wrist-wrestling or mechanical bull-riding contest, or an art fair, to name only a few of the many events here.

If you have a few minutes at the airport flying in or out of Maui, check out the gift store; it often has clever items, and the prices are not inflated. If you haven't succumbed to the time-share deals or bought a condo, you can at least come back with *something:* how about a Certificate of Ownership stating that you are the "owner of one cubic inch of Maui Beachfront Property," for all of 98¢?

Kahului also boasts the only deep-water harbor in Maui, a bulk-sugar loading plant, the cannery of the Maui Pineapple Company, and the Hawaiian Commercial and Sugar Company, the driving force behind the town's development (most of the homes belong to plantation workers). Out near the airport, at the **Kanaha Pond Waterfowl Sanctuary** you can see where migratory birds from our northwest mainland take their winter vacations.

Close to the Kahului Airport is an attraction for those interested in exotic jewelry. This is **Flora Hawaii,** a company that transforms fresh orchids, other flowers, and leaves into lasting pieces of jewelry and wall decor through the electroplating process: some are finished in gold plate, others preserved in their natural color and shape. Visitors are invited to tour the factory showroom and orchid nursery from 9 a.m. to 5 p.m. weekdays; free pineapple juice is served. Flora Hawaii is located two minutes from the airport, just between the intersection of Highway 38 with Highways 36 and 35 (tel. 877-7958).

THE WAILUKU AREA: Historic old Wailuku, the commercial and professional center and the seat of Maui County (which also includes Molokai and Lanai), is quite different from Kahului—even though it's right next door. Drive westward along Kaahaumanu Avenue out of Kahului about three miles; you'll pass the Maui Professional Building at High Street on the right, and then, about one block farther on to the left on Iao Road, you'll reach the **Hale Hoikeike,** the Maui Historical Society Museum. These buildings, on beautiful shaded grounds, once housed in the Wailuku Female Seminary (where young females could be kept safely "away from the contaminating influences of heathen society") and the home of Mr. Edward Bailey, the seminary instructor. Today they are full of fascinating bits of Hawaiiana, from ancient petroglyphs and necklaces of human hair worn by the alii of Maui to missionary patchwork quilts and furnishings. Dating back to 1834–1850, the building itself was completely restored in 1974–1975, and is an excellent example of Hawaiian craftsmanship and Yankee ingenuity. This smaller building, once the dining room of the school and later Mr. Bailey's studio, has been restored as a gallery of his paintings of Maui in the late 1800s. The museum is open daily from 9 a.m. to 3:30 p.m. Admission is $2 for adults, 50¢ for students.

Just off Kaahaumanu Avenue, across from the Wailuku War Memorial on Kanaloa Street, you may want to make a stop at the **Maui Zoological and Botanical Garden.** Beautifully and lovingly maintained, the Botanical Garden contains an abundance of native Hawaiian plants, many of which can no longer be seen anywhere else. At the very front of the garden is the Maui Zoo, a new little zoo that has been stocked largely by its big sister, Honolulu Zoo. The majority of the collection consists of lovable farm animals—we like the noisy feral sheep or "hipa" as they're called here; there are also some very happy monkeys and a few tropical birds, notably peafowl and parrots. Admission is free.

Not far from Wailuku, in the sugar plantation village of Waikapu, **Hawaii Tropical Plantation** was planning to open at the time this book went to press. Designed as a showplace for tropical agriculture, HTP offers the visitor a chance to learn about Hawaii's agriculture, take a Plantation Tour Express trip of some 50 acres planted in bananas, papayas, coffee, pineapple, macadamia nuts, sugarcane, and other crops, and buy fruits, plants, and gifts to take home. There's a market, restaurant, visitors center, and shops on the premises. Admission to the complex and to the exhibits is free, but there will be a charge for the Plantation Tour Express.

Now if you need to stock up on avocados, yogurt, papayas, honey ice cream, tofu, and the like, you can do so at bargain prices at **Down to Earth Natural Foods,** 1910 Vineyard St., which has one of the largest selections of natural foods on Maui. Their snackbar is open Monday to Saturday. For super bargains in fruits and vegetables, attend their Farmer's Market, every Saturday from 8 a.m. to 5 p.m.

Back to sightseeing: Continue on now in the direction of Iao Valley, and about two miles from Wailuku, on the right, you'll note a sign reading **"Black Gorge President Kennedy Profile."** The jagged mountain cliff ahead of you, which does bear a resemblance to JFK's profile, has been there for centuries, but not until relatively recently, of course, did people begin to notice its timely significance. In another mile you'll come to **Iao Valley,** a wildly beautiful gorge dominated by the **Iao Needle,** 2250 feet of green-covered lava rock reaching straight up into the sky. In this dramatic setting, Kamehameha won the battle that was to give him the island of Maui; the local warriors, accustomed to spears and javelins, were no match for Kamehameha's forces supplied with cannon by two English sailors. The carnage was so intense that the waters of Iao Stream were dammed up by the bodies of the conquered, giving the stream its present name: Kepaniwai, damming of the waters. Now all is tranquil here, save for the shouts of happy keikis wading through the pools at **Kepaniwai Park,** where present-day Mauians love to go for a picnic or a swim. Beautifully landscaped gardens with Oriental pagodas, swimming, and wading pools provide a palatial playground in this crisp mountain valley.

KIHEI-WAILEA: If you're staying in Kahului, Kihei is your nearest beach, about a 15-minute drive, via Route 38 and then Route 35 right to Kihei. Both Kamaole Beach and Kalama Park are fine, but the beach is public everywhere, and you can swim where you like. Look for **Azeka's Place,** a lively shopping center on the ocean side of the road, where you can have a snack or a drink at **Sailmaker's Saloon** or **International House of Pancakes** and browse among a collection of tasteful shops. Our special favorite here is **Alchemists' Garden,** a store with an old-world look: we loved their cards, soaps, herbs, china, fine custom-made jewelry, crystals, and lots more. . . . Be sure to stop in at **Vagabond,** where you can not only rent a surfboard, but also stock up on bags, tank shirts, and all kinds of necessities for the beachcomber's lifestyle. **Wow Swimwear** has something for "every body." . . . **Maui Dive Shop** can outfit you for scuba or snorkeling and take you on a tour. . . . **O'Rourke's Tourist Trap** is a good place to stock up on any necessities you forgot to pack, as well as postcards, monkeypod souvenirs, and the like.

Rainbow Connection abounds with pretty and useful things with a rainbow theme: T-shirts, tote bags with silkscreened or appliquéed rainbows, soft-sculpture hangings of satin clouds and rainbow, and rainbow windchimes and mobiles. . . . **Lobster & Roses** has pretty clothes, gauzy dresses and tops, and those tiny High Voltage bikinis. . . . There are tasteful books and cards at **Silversword. . . . Liberty House** has its usual excellent selections. . . . **Pingo's Yardarm** featurs muumuus and aloha shirts in tapa and palaka prints. . . . And **Ben Franklin** has a little bit of everything.

On the mountain side of the street, at 1301 S. Kihei Ave., is the new **Gallery Makai,** a distinctive small gallery that represents such well-known artists as Guy Buffet, Pegge Hopper, Richard Nelson, and Shige Yamada. And if a visit here wets your appetite for art, continue on to **Stouffer's Wailea Beach Resort** and have a look at the splendid artworks in the public areas, noting especially Ruthadell Anderson's weavings adjacent to the front desk, Nancy Clark's banners in the Palm Court, Tom Van Sant's concrete intaglio work on the Wailea Terrace, and his superb mural in the main lobby, an impressionistic colored paper collage of a volanic eruption and the streams of lava cascading down the mountains into the sea. Quite a stunner.

2. Haleakala, the House of the Sun

Any schoolchild on Maui can tell you the story of the demi-god Maui, the good-natured Polynesian Prometheus, who gave man fire, lifted the Hawaiian Islands out of the sea on his fishhook, and trapped the sun in its lair until it agreed to move more slowly around the earth—so that his mother could have more time to dry her tapa before night came! And where did this last, most splendid achievement take place? Why, right at **Haleakala,** 10,023 feet up in the sky, just about the closest any Stone Age man—or god—ever got to the sun.

With or without benefit of legends, Haleakala is an awesome place. The world's largest dormant volcano (its last eruption occurred two centuries ago), its 33-mile-long, 24-mile-wide, 10,000-foot-high dimensions make Vesuvius seem like a mud puddle. Even more spectacular is the size of the volcano's crater: 7½ miles long, 2½ miles wide, big enough to swallow a modern metropolis or two within its moon-like desert. Haleakala is one of the grat scenic wonders of Hawaii.

TO THE SUMMIT: Plan on at least three hours for the Haleakala excursion (37 miles from the airport each way) and bring a warm sweater or jacket with you (it gets surprisingly cold and windy two miles up). We feel it's best to get an early start on this trip, since there's less likelihood of clouds early in the day. You might call the park headquarters (tel. 572-7749) to check on cloud, road, and weather conditions before you start out. There's no place to eat once you enter **Haleakala National Park,** but you might pack a picnic lunch and stop at Hosmer's Grove on the lower slopes. You can have a very good breakfast, or get sandwiches or a snack at **Bullock's of Hawaii,** in Pukalani, about halfway between Kahului and the park. You might also stop off at the **Pukalani Superette,** a real upcountry store, where you can get mangos for about half of what they cost in town, plus delicious homemade sushi and lumpia, and local Japanese and Filipino delicacies. The drive starts in Kahului on Route H-32; head eastward to Haleakala Highway (Route H-36), on which you turn right. Shortly after Route H-36 swings left, it's intersected on the right by Route H-37, which takes you to Route H–377, the Upper Kula Road, where you head up into a cool forest of flowers, cactus, and eucalyptus.

Among the most striking flowers that bloom in this mountain soil are protea, and you may have noticed that protea are becoming a new commercial crop for Maui. If you'd like to see them growing in their natural habitat and perhaps buy some to take home or have shipped, turn left on Ihe Place on Highway 377 and proceed about seven miles up the road to **Dean's Proteas** at 355 Ihe Pl., the second large house on the left. The Deans sell a wide variety of protea from their home at wholesale prices, and will give you instructions on how to dry them. *(Note:* There won't be much to see from mid-June through September, the dormant season for protea.) For information, phone Verna Dean at 878-6386.

Now watch for the turnoff to Route H-378 to the left, Haleakala Crater Road, a snaky two-lane highway curving through the clouds. You'll see cattle and horses on the pasture lands of Haleakala Ranch as you climb the slopes of the volcano. At 6700 feet, you reach the entrance to Haleakala National Park. You'll then see **Hosmer's Grove** on the left, a scenic place to picnic (or camp) among rare trees and plants. Temperate tree seedlings from around the world have been planted here, along a half-mile trail of native shrubs and trees that are home for a variety of birds; you may see a pueo (short-eared owl) or a ringnecked pheasant. Stop at park headquarters a mile ahead at 7030 feet, where the friendly and knowledgeable rangers will give you maps, instructions, directions for hiking the trails, and camping permits. The way to see Haleakala is to go into the crater on foot or horseback, but you must check with the rangers before you do.

Now you're ready for the ascent on this South Seas Everest, to the **Haleakala Observatory Visitors Center,** two miles up on the edge of the crater. Inside the octagonal observatory, you learn that the early Hawaiians used the crater as a highway across East Maui, camping in its caves and building rock shelters. The last eruption from the crater was prehistoric, although there was an eruption from the flanks of Haleakala just 200 years ago, and very likely the volcano will erupt again; it is dormant, not extinct. But the most thrilling show is what lies beyond the glass: a dark kaleidoscope of clouds and colors and light played against what might well be the deserts of the moon. On a clear day you can see over a hundred miles to the horizon, your field of vision encompassing 30,000 square miles of the Pacific; from this altitude, the volcano's vast cones look like so many sand dunes. Their rust-like colors change as the day grows old. At sunrise the crater is in shadow; it seems to give birth to the sun. From midday to sunset the play of sun and shadow is more subtle, and sunset, according to some, is the most muted and lovely of all. One of the easiest ways to get a spirited controversy going among Mauians is to ask whether sunset or sunrise is more superlative at Haleakala; suffice it to say that both are considered among the great natural sights of the world.

The summit of Haleakala is a half mile beyond at **Red Hill,** atop a cinder cone 10,023 feet high. Nearby, there's a satellite-tracking station and a **Science City** complex (the clear air here in mid-Pacific permits research that could be done nowhere else) which you reach via the Skyline Drive.

On the way down from Kaleakala, you should stop for some different —and spectacular—views of the crater at **Kalahaku** and **Leleiwi** lookouts. (Because of safety hazards, you cannot stop at these places on the drive uphill.) At Kalahaku, you view the vast crater on one side; on the other you'll spot West Maui and your first silverswords (unless you've seen some on the Big Island). The silversword is a botanical rarity, a plant that will grow only on lava rock, at the highest altitudes. These curious, oversize cousins of the sunflower have sword-like leaves, and when they're ready to blossom (between June and October) they shoot up a stalk the size of a man. The whole thing turns into a tower of pink and lavender flowers, blooms once, and dies, scattering its seeds into the cinders to begin the phenomenon all over again. At the next lookout, Leleiwi, you may, with great luck, get to see the rather spooky specter of the Brocken; the sun must be strong at your back with misty clouds overhead in order for you to see your own shadow in the rainbow-mist of the crater. It doesn't happen often, but when it does, it is unforgettable; a ranger told us that he has seen it many times, and with as many as seven rainbows!

CAMPING AND RIDING IN HALEAKALA: Hiking buffs take note: you can spend a magnificent two or three days in Haleakala for spectacularly low prices. At Haleakala there are three dormitory cabins, each sleeping 12, for overnight lodging. The cabins have running water, wood-burning stoves, and cooking and eating utensils. All you need bring is food, water, a sleeping bag, and matches! The three form a sort of triangle in the crater, and you can go from one to the other on your exploration. **Kapalaoa Cabin** is at the middle of the southern end of the crater, **Paliku Cabin** is northeast of Kapalaoa at the eastern tip, and **Holua Cabin** is northwest of Paliku across at the western tip of the crater. Write to the Superintendent, Haleakala National Park, P.O. Box 369, Makawao, Maui, HI 96768, to make reservations for use of the cabins. Give the details of your proposed trip, the number in your party, dates of the stay, and names of the specific cabins you wish to use each night. The price is minimal: $4 per person per night, $2 for children 12 and under, with a minimum of $12 per night, plus a $12 key deposit. Cabins may be occupied for no more than three consecutive nights, with a maximum of two nights' stay in any one cabin. So popular are these cabins that assignments for each month are chosen by lottery 60 days prior to the beginning of the month. In other words, if you want a reservation sometime in the month of July, be sure your request is received before May 1.

We should note that these cabins—and these trails—are for experienced hikers in good physical condition: the Park Service warns that "wilderness travel is arduous; the elevation and exertion required to return from the crater floor place excessive physical demands upon the body. Pits, cliffs, caves, and associated sharp rocks are dangerous."

For more information on overnight trips into the crater, get in touch with Charles Aki, Jr., of **Charley's Trailrides & Pack Trips,** c/o Kaupo Store, Kaupo, Maui, HI 96713 (tel. 248-8209). Charley provides everything, including horses, guides, and food. Rides begin in Kaupo, near Hana. Trips require two to six persons, and cost from $100 to $175 per person. Pony Express Tours will meet you at the rim of Haleakala Crater at 9:30 in the morning, and take you for a 12-mile ride into the crater and

Kapalaoa cabin. The full day ride, which includes a hot lunch at Kapalaoa Cabin, costs $110 per person. There's also a 3½-hour ride for $75 per person. Contact **Pony Express Tours,** P.O. Box 507, Makawao, Maui, HI 96768, or through any of the Activity Desks in Lahaina and Kaanapali.

Did you know that you can coast downhill on a bicycle, all the way from the 10,000-foot summit of Haleakala to sea level below? You must be a skilled rider and in good physical condition, and it helps if your nerves are in good shape; but **Cruiser Bob,** who runs these tours, claims that this is a safe ride and is approved by the National Parks Service. For reservations, call 667-7717.

MAKAWAO: On your way back down from Haleakala, it's easy to make a visit to Makawao, Maui's very own cowboy town, the scene every Fourth of July of the famed Makawao Rodeo. Turn right at Pukalani for just a few miles and you'll find yourself on the main street of what looks like something out of the Old West. This is a good place to stop off for a snack; local people swear by the fried doughnuts on a stick at **Komoda's General Store**—as well as by their great macadamia-nut cookies. You can also have a bite at the **Mountainside Deli** (see preceding chapter), or splurge on dinner at the **Makawao Steak and Fish House** at 3612 Baldwin Ave., which has long been popular in these parts. Have a look at **Sea Dreams** on Baldwin Avenue; it carries lovely clothing plus island arts. Unless you're planning to stop at **Paia** on the way to Hana (see below), we recommend that you do so now. Instead of taking the road back to Pukalani, just take Baldwin Avenue a few miles into Paia, where you can shop for gifts and antiques and hobnob with the local people before heading back home.

HAWAIIAN VINEYARDS: Another little side trip you might want to take on the way back from Haleakala is to the **Tedeschi Vineyards,** on Highway 37, in the beautiful Maui upcountry, at the Ulupalakua Ranch, not far from the town of Kula. The vineyard welcomes you for a free, self-guided tour daily from 10 a.m. to 5 p.m. After experimenting with 140 different varieties of grape, Emil Tedeschi found the one he was after. Maui's Carnelian champagne should be ready by the time you read this. A sparkling pineapple wine, christened Maui Blanc, is already very popular in the islands. The bottling area was once a dairy, the aging cellar is in the basement of the old jail, and you attend your wine-tasting session in the jail proper. After your tour, you can buy Maui wine T-shirts or gold-dipped grape blossoms as mementos.

3. The Road to Hana

Ten thousand feet down from the moon canyons of Haleakala, curving around the base of the old volcano, is a world light-years away, a place of such tropical lushness and splendor that it conjures up the word "primeval." This is remote Hana and the curving road leading to it—a road carved under the fringe of the lava cliffs, plunging down on one side to the sea, emerging on the other from overhanging jungle watered by the thousand streams of Haleakala.

In all of Hana, there are just a few dozen modestly priced hotel rooms. (The town's chief industry is the exquisite Hana Maui Hotel, which caters to wealthy travelers only.) If you can reserve one of these (see the preceding chapter), it would be worth your while to stay overnight;

otherwise, you'll have to do Hana in a one-day trip. Count on two to three hours each way, more if you want to savor the magnificent scenery. And be sure to check with the Highway Department about road conditions before you take off. If the weather has been wet, you could get stuck in landslides or mud. If it's raining heavily, forget the Hana trip altogether. Parts of the road are easily washed away, and it may take hours for you to be rescued (which happened one year to friends of ours). There's always tomorrow, or the next visit to Maui.

There are two roads to Hana. One is the primitive southern route (H-31), about 80 miles from Wailuku. Only a Jeep or other four-wheel-drive vehicle can traverse the entire road, some of it a dusty, bumpy stretch over old lava flows. The northern route (H-36) is shorter (59 miles), has a hard surface, and is reasonably smooth. You can make a return-trip circuit over the southern route if you like, but we recommend the northern road both ways; you won't be bored retracing it on the return trip. But we want to emphasize again that about half the 50-mile Kahului to Hana road is rugged and winding. There are plenty who love it and some who think that, despite the glory of the scenery, it's just not worth the effort. A picnic lunch is essential, unless you want to eat at the expensive Hana Maui or one of the little snackshops in Hana. Besides, you'll be traveling through the kind of country for which picnics surely were originally invented.

Hana glories in its remoteness. Rumor has it that a new road is not being built because the local people like to keep Hana the way it is—difficult to get to. The current road was not completed until 1927, and by that time, the Hasegawa General Store had already been in business 15 years and a hotel was already operating there. Hana's lush isolation attracted the late aviator and environmentalist Charles Lindbergh, who spent his vacations in Hana and is now buried there.

Because of its remoteness, Hana has been slow in accepting change. Throughout its history it has assimilated new cultures, new religions, and new institutions, but Hana has not become part of them; rather, they have become a part of Hana.

STARTING IN PAIA: Start eastward on Route H-32 in Kahului or Wailuku and switch (right) to H-36. You may want to stop at **Dillon's Restaurant** on the Hana Highway, or **Pic-nics** on Baldwin Avenue in Paia, to pick up a picnic lunch (see Chapter XV), or take some time now, or on the return trip, to browse some of the antique, decorator, and gift shops that have sprung up in this unspoiled, upcountry community. Be sure to visit the **Maui Crafts Guild** at 43 Hana Hwy., a cooperative gallery showing outstanding work by local craftspeople. Prices can go way up for some of the furniture, wall sculptures, stained glass, paintings, etc., but there are many small items too, like coconut baskets at $4 and tiny ceramic avocado planters at $7. We loved Steve Smeltzer's "Maui Menehumes"—figures of the little people in outrigger canoes or riding dolphins—and the superb wooden bowls by Takeo Omura. In the rear of the wooden building is **Touchstone Ceramics,** which always has a few bargain shelves on the ou

On either side of Dillon's Restaurant on Hana Highway are attractive shops: **Rhonda's** for children's clothes, toys, notions, and fabrics; the **Treasury Antiques** for charming gifts and jewelry. . . . **Summerhouse,** 124 Hana Hwy., is an old favorite here. Their specialties are casual island wear in natural fibers, Oriental imports, and a swimsuit collection extraordinaire.

The owners travel to Asia twice a year to buy silks and collectibles. . . . At the **Paia Art Center,** 120 Hana Hwy., you'll find **Clementine's One of Da Kine** boutique, **Anuene** for gifts and cosmetics, and **Rona Gale,** who shows some beautiful kimonos, hand-printed dresses and tops. . . . The **Paia General Store** has everything a general store should have—including, because this is Maui, those wonderful macadamia-nut brownies and chocolate-chip macadamia nuts. Resist, if you can, and continue on your trip.

Now it's back on the road to Hana. The highway runs straight and easy, through cane fields, until you get to Pauwela. Here's where the road becomes an Amalfi Drive of the Pacific; the view is spectacular, but keep your eye on the curves. The variety of vegetation is enough to drive a botanist—or photographer—wild. Waterfalls, pools, green gulches beckon at every turn. You'll be tempted to stop and explore a hundred times, but keep going, at least until you get to **Kaumahina Park,** where you might consider picnicking high on the cliff, looking down at the black-sand beach of Honomanu Bay below, watching the local folk fish and swim.

Believe it or not, from here on the scenery gets even better. From the road, you can look down on the wet taro patches and the peaceful villages of **Keanae** and **Wailua,** to which a short side trip, to see the old Catholic church built of lava rock and cemented with coral, is eminently worthwhile. It seems that this coral was strewn ashore after an unusual storm in the 1860s, providing the villagers with the necessary material to construct their church. To commemorate this miracle, they constructed the **Miracle of Fatima Shrine,** which you will see on the Wailua Bay Road, at the 18-mile marker (turn left at the road sign).

Across from the shrine, take a little time now to stretch and visit Anna Kapuana at her home, which houses **The Shell Stop!,** a quaint country store specializing in shells and carved coral jewelry. Anna tells us that they do all their own diving for food (no stores here), and they come up with beautiful ophi, lehua, vana, and other shells. Since it's a home operation ("We don't have to pay the $4000 a month rents in Lahaina," says Anna), they manage to keep prices very fair. A worthwhile stop.

In a little while, you get another vista of Keanae from Koolau Lookout. In the other direction you look through a gap in the cliff over into **Haleakala.** A little farther on is **Puaa Kaa Park,** another made-in-heaven picnic spot. The flowers are gorgeous here, and so are the two natural pools, each with its own waterfall. You might have a swim here before you continue. On you go, past grazing lands and tiny villages, to **Waianapanapa Cave,** another possible side excursion. This lava tube filled with water is the place where a jealous Stone Age Othello was said to have slain his Desdemona. Every April, the water is supposed to turn blood-red in remembrance. Near the cave is a black-sand beach (not always safe for swimming), another great place for a picnic. Just before reaching Hana, you arrive at **Hana Gardenland,** a lovely tropical nursery. You can visit the garden free, watch lei-making demonstrations, and purchase plants and local crafts at the gift store. They also have rest rooms and a picnic area.

HANA: Your first vision of heavenly Hana may be a letdown, if the black-sand beach is not as neat as it should be. But you can explore the views, watch how the other half lives over at the big hotel, or make a few historical pilgrimages.

Not a little history was made at Hana. The Big Three—Captain Cook, the Protestant missionaries, and the vacationing Hawaiian royalty—were all here. You can even follow the road to a historic Stone Age delivery room near the cinder cone of **Kauiki Head,** where Kamehameha's favorite wife, Kaahaumana, was born (there's a plaque near the lighthouse). Or you can just walk around the town for a while and soak up the atmosphere. A must on your list of sights should be the **Hasegawa General Store** where, it is reported, you can get anything and everything your heart desires (just like at Alice's Restaurant) in one tiny shack. A song was written about the place some years ago, and it has not changed in spite of all the hullabaloo. As for practical matters, the store has clothing, books, film, wine, and sporting goods, but because of the scarcity of restaurants in Hana, the food department—plenty of local fruit, some vegetables, mostly sausage meats, and some staples—will be of most interest to you. And you may not be able to resist—as we couldn't—the bumper stickers that read: "Fight Smog—Buy Horses, Hasagawa General Store" or "We visited Hasagawa General Store—far from Waikiki."

Unfortunately, the Hana Maui Hotel, the town's chief industry and source of employment for most of its citizens, has preempted the best beach, Hamoa, but you can use the public beach on Hana Bay. Drive to the hotel's parking lot and then up the private road (which closes at 6:30 p.m.) to the **Fagan Memorial Cross** on Lyon's Hill. The cattle will let you by, grudgingly, and from the top you'll get a great view of Hana and the coastline.

Most visitors drive about ten miles past Hana on to Kipahulu, an unspoiled extension of Haleakala National Park and the **Seven Sacred Pools,** a gorgeous little spot for a swim. Here the pools drop into one another and then into the sea. But it's a roller-coaster ride on a rough, narrow road filled with potholes, and again, unless you dote on this kind of driving, it may not be worth your nerves. (Incidentally, look for the sign reading "Stream"; that's the correct name for the Seven Sacred Pools; many visitors miss it).

En route to the Seven Sacred Pools, you'll pass **Wailua Gulch** and a splendid double fall cascading down the slopes of Haleakala. Nearby is a memorial to Helio, one of the island's first Catholics, a formidable proselytizer and converter. A tribute to his work stands nearby—the *Virgin of the Roadside,* a marble statue made in Italy and draped every day with the fragrant flower leis of the Hawaiians. The good road runs out a little farther on at Kipahulu, so it's back along the northern route, retracing your way past jungle and sea to Wailuku.

Now for the fourth of your day-long trips:

4. Lahaina

If Haleakala and Hana are nature's showplaces on Maui, Lahaina is man's. It was there that some of the most dramatic and colorful history of Hawaii was made: a hundred years ago Lahaina was the whaling capital of the Pacific, the cultural center of the Hawaiian Islands (and for a time its capital), and the scene of an often-violent power struggle between missionaries and sailors for—quite literally—the bodies and souls of the Hawaiians.

Your trip to Lahaina and the West Maui coast happily combines history with some of the most beautiful scenery in the islands. Take your bathing suit and skip the picnic lunch, since there are plenty of places en route where you can eat. Since there's no paved road completely circling the western tip of Maui, we'll take the road as far as Honokahua, and return by driving back along the same road to Kahului—a route that is more interesting and comfortable than the drive on the unpaved portion between Honokahua and Waihee on the northern shore. The trip begins on Highway 32, which you follow through Wailuku to Highway 30 (High Street), where you turn left. At Maalaea the road swings right at the sea and continues along the base of the West Maui Mountains, along a wild stretch of cliffs pounded by angry seas, until it reaches Lahaina, 22 miles from Kahului.

THE SIGHTS OF LAHAINA: Lahaina today is a comfortable plantation town, with pretty little cottages, a cannery, sugar mill, and acres of cane and pineapple stretching to the base of the misty West Maui hills. It is currently in the process of a restoration that will cover the 150 years or so during which Lahaina rose from the Stone Age to statehood—from the reign of King Kamahameha I to the annexation of Hawaii by the United States. Re-created will be the days when Lahaina was the capital of the Hawaiian monarchy (before the king, in 1843, moved the palace to Honolulu, where there was a better harbor); the coming of the missionaries; the whaling period; and the beginning of the sugar industry. The restoration is being lovingly and authentically carried out by the Lahaina Restoration Foundation, a devoted group of local citizens and county and state interests. The project is proceeding at caterpillar-like speed, but there are enough historic landmarks around to keep you busy.

Begin your exploration out on the old pier in the center of town, where you can gaze at the famed **Lahaina Roads;** from the 1820s to the 1860s this was the favorite Pacific anchorage of the American whaling fleet. Over on your left are the soft greens of Lanai, to the north the peaks of Molokai, on the south the gentle slopes of Kahoolawe. During the winter and early spring, you may get to see some nonpaying tourists sporting about in the water; these are the sperm whales that migrate from their Aleutian homes to spawn in the warmer waters off Lahaina.

For the whalers, this place was practical as well as beautiful; they were safe here in a protected harbor, they could come or go on any wind, there was plenty of fresh water at the local spring, plenty of island fruits, fowl, and potatoes. And there were also Hawaiian women, who, in the old hospitable way of the South Seas, made the sailors feel welcome by swimming out to the ships, and staying a while. To the missionaries, this was the abomination of abominations, and it was on this score that violent battles were fought. More than once, sailors ran through the streets setting houses on fire, rioting, beating up anyone who got in their way, even cannonading the mission house. You can see the evidence of those days at **Hale Paaho,** the old stone prison (on Prison Street, off Main), where sailors were frequent guests while the forays lasted.

Across the street from the waterfront, you'll see the **Pioneer Inn,** which may look oddly familiar—it's been the set for many a South Seas movie saga. Back in 1901 (it has since been tastefully renovated and enlarged) it was quite the place, the scene of arrival and departure parties for the elegant passengers of the Inter-Island Steamship Company, whose vessels sailed out of Lahaina. And since it was too difficult to make the hot trek to central Maui immediately, arriving passengers usually spent the night here. Walk in and have a look around: note the lovely stained-glass window one flight up from the entrance to the **Harpooner's Lanai** and the grandfather's clock at the foot. The lanai itself is a wonderful place to waste a few years of your life while soaking up the atmosphere.

Across Wharf Street from the hotel, a little to the north of the lighthouse, is the site of a palace used by Kamehameha in 1801, when he was busy collecting taxes on Maui and the adjoining islands. And across from that, where the Lahaina Branch Library now stands, is another spot dear to the lovers of the Hawaiian monarchy, the royal taro patch where Kamehameha III betook his sacred person to demonstrate the dignity of labor.

The huge banyan tree just south of the Pioneer Inn covers two-thirds of an acre; it's the favorite hotel for the town's noisy mynah bird population. In the front of the tree is the **Court House,** a post office, and police station, the post office part of which has been functioning since 1859. Between the Court House and the Pioneer Inn, you'll see the first completed project of the Lahaina Restoration, the **Fort Wall.** It's built on the site of the original fort, but since rebuilding the whole fort would have destroyed the famed banyan tree, the authorities decided to reconstruct the wall instead, as a ruin—a ruin that never existed.

Now that you've seen how the whalers lived, let's see how their arch opponents, the missionaries, fared. Walk one block mauka of the waterfront to Front Street and the **Baldwin Home**—so typical, with its up and downstairs verandas, of New England in Polynesia. The old house, built in the late 1830s with walls of coral and stone, served as a home for the Rev. Dwight Baldwin, a physician and community leader as well as a missionary (and incidentally, the founder of a dynasty; the Baldwins are still an important family in Maui). Thanks to the Lahaina Restoration Foundation, the house has been faithfully restored; you can examine Dr. Baldwin's medical kit (the instruments look like something out of a Frankenstein film), kitchen utensils, and china closets, old photographs and books, the family's furniture and mementos, all the little touches of missionary life 100 and more years ago. Open daily. Admission is $2 for adults and free for children accompanied by their parents for a personally guided tour.

The Restoration Foundation also operates the floating museum ship *Carthaginian,* moored opposite the Pioneer Inn. Its "World of the Whale" exhibit features a series of colorful multimedia displays on whaling, whales, and the sea life of Hawaii. Maui's own humpback whale, which comes to these waters each winter to mate and calve, gets special treatment through videotape presentations made on the spot by the National Geographic Society, the New York Zoological Society, and others. The ship is being restored as a 19th-century brig and is open daily from 9 a.m. to 4:30 p.m. Admission is $2 for adults, free for children with their parents. (If you visit between January and May, when the whales are "in town," be sure to drop by the Whale Report Center at the *Carthaginian* berth where sightings pour in by phone and radio and you can add your personal observations to the scientific data being being compiled.)

Head now for Wainee Street (to the right of Lahainaluna Road); here, where the recently built **Waiola Church** now stands, is the site of Wainee, the first mission church in Lahaina, to which the Reverend Baldwin came as pastor in 1835. The old cemetery is fascinating. Buried among the graves of the missionary families are some of the most important members of the Kamehameha dynasty, including no fewer than two wives of Old King Kam: Queen Keoupuolani, his highest born wife, and Queen Kalakaua.

Outside of Lahaina proper, opposite Wahikuli State Park, is the new **Lahaina Civic Center,** an auditorium and gym, with a dramatic mosaic by one of Maui's most famous artists, Tadashi Sato.

Five miles east of Lahaina, on the highway headed toward Kahului, are the well-preserved **Olowalu Petroglyphs.** Two to three hundred years old, these rock carvings depicted the occupations—fishing, canoe-paddling, weaving, etc.—of the early Hawaiians. Unfortunately, they are rather difficult to get to.

On the other side of Lahaina, on the road leading toward Kaanapali, is another historical spot, the **Royal Coconut Grove of Mala.** Mala, one of the wives of Kamehameha, brought the trees from Oahu 137 years ago. They are now being replaced by local citizens as part of the restoration.

For collectors of Orientalia, it would be unthinkable to leave **Lahaina** without a visit to the **Japanese Cultural Park** of the Lahaina Jodo Mission. In a beautiful spot perched above the water is a 3½-ton statue of Amitabha Buddha, erected to commemorate the centennial anniversary of Japanese immigration in Hawaii. You can meditate here as long as you wish, strike the huge temple bell, and perhaps leave a small donation in the offertory (there is no admission charge.) *Note:* It's easy to miss this place. As you drive along Front Street, look for the big sign that reads "Jesus Coming Soon." Then turn makai on Ala Moana Street and you'll find the Buddha.

If you want to continue your sightseeing out in the Kaanapali resort area now, there are two ways to go, in addition to driving your own car. The first is the Shoreline bus, which connects Lahaina and Kaanapali for 75¢, leaving Lahaina from the Shopping Center every hour and half hour most of the day. It's more fun, however (and also more expensive: $6.50 round trip, $4.25 one way, half fare for children), to hop the oldtimey **Lahaina-Kaanapali & Pacific Railroad**, a reconstructed, turn-of-the-century sugar-cane train for the 12-mile round trip between Lahaina and Kaanapali. You'll be entertained with songs and stories en route by a singing conductor, and kids will get a kick out of the hoot of the locomotive's whistle. The railroad terminal is on Honoapiilani Highway, one block north of Papalaua Street; the bus service from the Pioneer Inn, Boat Harbor, Shopping Center, etc., to the terminal is free.

SHOPPING IN LAHAINA: We must confess: the thing we love to do most in Lahaina is shop. While the reconstruction of the historical sights is proceeding slowly, Lahaina (and Whaler's Village at Kaanapali Beach, see below) is fast emerging as one of the best shopping areas in the islands, second only to Honolulu. On each one of our visits there are new and exciting shops, boutiques, galleries to visit. Perhaps it's the influence of the young people and other newcomers moving into the area; they keep everything constantly stimulating and alive.

First, let's get your car parked. Finding a spot on the street is not easy, although it's often possible on Front Street, on the ocean side. Also try the Lahaina Shopping Center. If that doesn't work, however, drive in to one of the commercial parking lots like the one behind Baldwin House, at the corner of Luakini and Dickinsen Streets: charges are $1 for half an hour, $7 per day. Across from the parking lot is a place where you can get fresh island produce to take home, and in front of that is a stand selling ice-cold coconut juice for $1.50.

Cool and refreshed now, let's start our wanderings, perhaps at **Perils of Pauline,** 697 Front St., a shop a bit different than most others in Hawaii. The emphasis here is on good-quality, handmade clothing at reasonable prices. We like their cotton kimonos from Japan ($30 to $40), sundresses ($29 to $90), and hand-painted shirts and dresses ($30 to $60; Balinese tops are $60). . . . Batik lovers should not miss **Fabrics From Paradise** on Front

Street; in addition to authentic Indonesian batik and Hawaiian tapa prints, it carries the largest selection of Tahitian pareau prints in the Western Hemisphere (let alone Hawaii); buy it by the yard, from $5. . . . We loved the great T-shirts at **David's of Hawaii,** 815 Front St.—especially "Happily Mauied" and "Just Mauied." . . . The **Waterfront Gifts Gallery,** 825 Front St., sports alpaca and sheepskin rugs, in addition to coral and pearl jewelry.

Not too many places like the **South Seas Trading Post** at 851 Front St. are left in Lahaina, places where the owners still search out and find authentic South Seas and Oriental treasures. Although there are many collector's items here, like 17th- and 18th-century antique jewelry from Sri Lanka, 100-year-old jade carvings from China, and woodcarvings that can go up into the thousands, there are many items of good quality at modest prices, like made-in-Maui Christmas tree angels (at $2.75), authentic pili grass skirts from Samoa ($15 for adults, $12 for children), evening bags made of pineapple fiber ($28.50), and hand-polished boar's teeth pendants from the Big Island ($4.50). This is one of the few stores carrying "Maui Diamonds." They are real diamonds and quite lovely: a one-carat gold ring is $183. . . . **The Whaler, Ltd.,** at 866 Front St., is just about the only honest-and-true nautical shop in the old whaling port of Lahaina. They have lanterns that run on oil, brass lamps and hooks in various shapes, scrimshaw and ivory carvings, whaling prints and boxes, carvings of whales and whalers, and more. . . . **Lahaina Florists,** in the Lahaina Shopping Center, will send leis, tropical flowers, pineapples, and inspected plants back to the mainland for you.

The newest addition to the Lahaina shopping scene is **The Wharf,** 658 Front St., a stunning three-story arcade built around a giant tree, with a fountain and a stage on the lower level, a glass elevator, a number of attractive eating places, and dozens of shops reflecting high quality and taste. Soft contemporary music plays throughout the complex as you shop. Here you'll find places like **Ocean Magic,** which has casual wear plus beautiful hand-embroidered tablecloths from China, eel-skin wallets, and other treasures. . . . **Alberta's Gazebo** does have a real gazebo, and also has some absolutely knockout imported handmade clothing: we loved the appliquéed jackets from Thailand. Asian crafts and miniature China groupings vie for attention with a collection of extraordinary beads: 200- to 800-year-old African trading bead necklaces (from $50 to $60) and 2000-year-old Inca and Aztec beads (up to $200). Local shell necklaces, bracelets, and earrings begin at just $1.50. . . . **Blue Ginger** is the native spice that grows wild in Singapore, and it's the name given to a women's fashion shop showing distinctive, very subtle designs. Pure-cotton batik dresses begin at $55. . . . Silks for women are featured at **Amy's Boutique,** and **Luana** also has lovely women's fashions. . . . The people at **Ecology House** are doing such good work that you really ought to buy something here. How about an Endangered Species T-shirt for $9, a tape of whale sounds recorded off Maui waters for $8.95, some 14-karat-gold whale jewelry, a stuffed whale or seal, or some synthetic scrimshaw. Their main focus is saving the whales and seals, but they also have magazines and literature on animal rights, vegetarianism, and world food policies.

Gold-plated parsley rings (real parsley!) for $8 and gold-plated seahorse charms (real seahorses!) are some of the surprisingly lovely jewelry at **Flora Hawaii. . . . Captain Wood Pecker Wood Carvings** is carving a name for itself hereabout, what with laser-light carvings, custom-carved name boards, and more. Massage away those traveling tensions with the Maui Massager, $15, handmade from distinctive Maui woods. . . . Have you always wanted a genuine Panama hat? The **Maui Mad Hatter** has them, plus scads of other chapeaux—every known type of hat weave, including Maui lauhala, for men, women, and children. Proprietor Shell Hansen, who invites visitors to his factory in Paia, claims, "If you've got the head, I've got the hat!" . . . Children can be outfitted with island clothes at **Little Polynesians,** and they'll love the hand-carved toys and the stuffed animals at **Geppetto's Workshop.**

We've already told you about the restaurants at the Wharf, but if all you want is a cookie to nibble on, or perhaps a coffee drink to go with it, try the delicious homemade goodies at **Upstart Crow & Co.,** a combination bookstore-European café, where you can sip your cappuccino in un-Lahaina-like peace. (Our favorite cookies are the chocolate no bakes at 30¢ each.) And check the papers for news of frequent entertainments at the Wharf; shops stay open late, so a visit here can be a good evening's activity.

Strolling along Front Street and the side streets, one comes across many serendipitous findings. At 730 Front St., for example, is **Jade and Jewels,** a museum-quality store where you must stop to at least have a look at hand-carved ivory masterpieces from the Orient, opal rings, rosewood carvings from China, and fine art. . . . Stop too to admire the superb coral necklaces at **Olah Jewelers,** 839 Front St. . . . Even though **Alexia Natural Fashions** has other shops in pricey Palm Springs and Scottsdale, don't presume that her things are out of reach. We saw charming dresses in the $50 to $60 range, many from Greece and Cyprus, most in natural fabrics and fibers. . . . **Pacific Visions,** 819 Front St., has gifts made by local artisans: sterling silver and hand-etched crystal—very tasteful.

You've always wanted a sarong, and you've finally gotten up your nerve to get one. Then go to **Tropical Batik,** 819 Front St., which will not only sell you a sarong made of beautiful handmade Indonesian batik, but will teach you the gentle art of wrapping it around you and having it stay wrapped! Their hand-batiked clothing from Indonesia is unique, and not expensive for the quality: rompers at $39, dresses about $54, sarongs for $37.

Some of Hawaii's leading artists show their works at the **Lahaina Gallery,** 117 Lahainaluna Rd. Stop in to see some of our favorites: mystical Chinese landscapes by David Lee, charming Hawaiian primitives by Guy Buffet. The same artists show in two sister galleries, **Casay Gallery** at the Wharf, and **Kapalua Gallery** in the Kapalua Shops at the Kapalua Bay Hotel; the latter two galleries also handle (surprise!) the works of that prominent Hawaiian artist, Jack Lord—whom you may know better as Steve McGarrett of "Hawaii Five-O."

You can hardly miss the ads for **Hilo Hattie's Fashion Center** at 1000 Limahina Pl., in the industrial area near the sugarcane train. Hilo Hattie's provides free bus service from the courthouse at Lahaina Harbor seven times daily, and once you're there, they'll give you free leis, refreshments, and take you on a factory tour. You can choose from some 10,000 garments at good prices. Phone 661-8457 for information. While you're in the industrial area, have a look around too at some of the outlet stores. There's a **Coral and Gifts** outlet, and a **Lobster and Roses** sportswear outlet. Merchandise varies from day to day, but value can be excellent.

5. Kaanapali and Kapalua

Head out of Lahaina now for a bit of sightseeing at some glamorous hotels, shopping, and swimming. Your first stop should be at the splendid new **Hyatt Regency Maui,** where you can be taken on a free guided tour of the $80-million, 20-acre complex, lush with waterfalls, gardens, tropical birds, an acre-long swimming pool with its own bar in a lava cavern, an atrium lobby surrounding a 70-foot-tall banyan tree, and an elegant shopping arcade that rivals Rodeo Drive. Or simply walk around on your own; it's like touring a park-botanical garden and an indoor-outdoor museum of priceless Oriental art. This aesthetic and architectural tour-de-force offers gorgeous vistas wherever you look. You might want to pause and have a drink at the Weeping Banyan Bar beside a lagoon—and please don't throw crumbs at the penguins! Note too the unusual ceilings in the shops—there is one in stained glass—and perhaps pick up a trinket at a place like **Elephant Walk,** where prices go way up for safari exotica, but are relatively down-to-earth for elephant-hair jewelry.

By all means, pay a visit to the **Maui Marriott Resort** on Kaanapali Drive, next to the Hyatt Regency. This is an example of modern hotel architecture and landscaping at its best, especially beautiful at night, when lights, flowers, and tropic moon over the ocean create dazzling effects. Stop in at the **Friendship Store** in the lobby: everything here is from mainland China, and prices are surprisingly low: we purchased $10 necklaces here that had cost us $20 in New York! Note the cork sculpture, a unique folk art from Foochow, among many other lovely items.

As you continue driving, you may want to stop at the **Sheraton Maui Hotel,** which sits atop **Black Rock,** the perch from which the souls of the dead Hawaiians were said to leap into the spirit world beyond. The majestic hotel, not in the least bit haunted, is worth having a look at, especially for the 360-degree view from the top, a sweeping panorama of ocean, islands, and mountains. The tasteful Polynesian formal lobby is on the top floor; you've got to take the elevators down to everything else, including Kaanapali Beach.

WHALER'S VILLAGE: The main shopping attraction out here is Whaler's Village. The one- and two-story buildings are of uniform design and materials, authentic reproductions of the type of buildings that the New England missionaries constructed in Lahaina between 1830 and 1890. As you pop in and out of the shops, you can stop to examine museum display cases of old whale bones or mariners' tools or old ship models, or what-have-you. After you've boned up on history and soaked in some gorgeous views, you can concentrate on the serious business of shopping, and there's plenty to concentrate on.

You never can tell what you'll find at **Whaler's Mercantile:** we recently saw stunning necklaces of macramé, beads, and fungi—yes fungi—at $4.25. They also had fragrant Hawaiian sandalwood beads, from $14.50 to $24, pewter mugs starting at $21, scrimshaw ivory teeth and jewelry, and even pewter spoons, $5.95. They also have scrimshaw treasures and Niihau shell leis under lock and key. . . . The **Narwahl Shop** has lots of shells, brass, darling glass whales for $3.95. You could also pick up a handy fan for 99¢, or a pair of fancy chopsticks for $1.75. . . . **Ka Honu Gift Gallery** is a delight, with lots of handmade works, like Hawaiian dolls, baskets from the Marshall Islands, ceramics, bowls of milo and koa wood, and handmade Hawaiian Christmas ornaments that would look great on the tree back home. . . . Scrimshaw collectors should head straight for the **Lahaina Scrimshaw Factory,** Pier 49, where there's an impressive selection of quality art executed by over 20 different scrimshaw artists, most of them residents of Maui. There's a prize antique collection as well, with prices going up into the thousands. Do-it-yourself scrimshaw kits are available too, from $8.95 to $15. Since the people here are fervent "Save-the Whale" supporters, they will continue to create fine-quality scrimshaw on nonendangered fossil walrus ivory. They've become so popular that they've opened two additional stores in Lahaina—at 718 and 811 Front St., and a third at the Maui Marriott Resort. . . . There are acres of souvenirs—hand-carved candles, Hawaiian notepapers, wood products, seashells, scrimshaw, mother of pearl, and costume jewelry—at **Internatonal Bazaar.** . . . You can catch up with the lore of sailing ships, whaling days, and just about everything else at the **Book Cache.** Note their large selection of magazines, paperbacks, and Hawaiian books, as well as books to help you identify the local fish, coral, flora, and fauna. Should you get homesick, you can purchase the *Wall Street Journal,* the Sunday *New York Times,* and daily San Francisco and Los Angeles papers. The people here are experts on giving directions to lost tourists. . . . **Lahaina Printsellers** has some fascinating antique maps and prints that would look great on those walls back home. . . . Don't miss **Super Whale Children's Boutique** if you have your own kids with you or some back home to buy presents for. They have one of the best selections of Hawaiian-made children's clothing we've seen in the islands, including malos for infants and a big selection of T-shirts for both keiki wahines and keiki kanes. The size range goes from infants to size 14 for girls, to size 18 for boys. Styles are unique and prices fair: bikinis from $10.50, short muus from $9, long muus from $18. The rage of the moment is Magnum P.I. shirts, in boys' sizes 3 to 20, $17 to $21.

We've told you about some of the restaurants—**Ricco's, Rusty Harpoon, El Crabcatcher,** and **Yami's Soft Frozen Yogurt**—in the preceding chapter. There's also a wonderful over-the-water reataurant called **Leilani's on the Beach,** plus **Coco Loco's Mexican Cantina** and the **Ming Court** (a sister restaurant to the excellent Ming Yuen in Kahului (see preceding chapter), all of which should be ready and waiting for you as the reconstruction of Whaler's Village is completed.

TIME FOR A CRUISE: If you need a little break from sightseeing and shopping, you might want to board a bright-red Chinese junk called the **Lin Wa,** which is really a glass-bottom boat in disguise. It makes five fish-feeding cruises daily, the first at 9:45 a.m., the last at 4:15 p.m. Their Dragon Wagon will pick you up at any Kaanapali hotel and take you back after the cruise. The tab is $9.50 for adults and $4.75 for children.

TO KAPALUA AND THE NEARBY BEACHES: One of the nicest things about the Hawaiian islands is that all beaches—even those at the fanciest hotels—are open to the public. As you stroll by the beachfront hotels (the Sheraton Maui, the Royal Lahaina, the Kaanapali Beach, the Marriott, the Maui Surf, the Hyatt Regency), you can stop by for a snack or a drink and treat yourself to a swim. Kaanapali Beach is superb, and we can personally recommend the swimming at both the Royal Lahaina and the Sheraton. The swimming is also good right behind Whaler's Village. Should you happen to pass this area during sugarcane harvest time, the hotels overlooking the sea may look like huge haunted palaces, uncannily spooky through the dense smoke.

On to more practical matters: **Honokawai Beach Park** is another good place for a picnic or a swim. If you're a shelling nut, get out your bucket and trek along the Kaanapali beaches, which are also good for more ambitious sports like skindiving and spearfishing. A mile or two past this is Kapalua where you should definitely stop to see Regent International Hotels' **Kapalua Bay Hotel,** the ultimate luxury resort. You probably won't want to book a room here (doubles start about $150), but take time out to explore the grounds and to visit **The Shops at Kapalua,** one of the most serenely tasteful of island marketplaces. **Auntie Nani** (of the Super Whale family) is here, and can outfit young teens as well as children. **Trouvaille** means "hidden treasures" in French, and that's precisely what you'll find at the boutique of the same name. The price range goes from $1.50 mother-of-pearl charms, up to $3000 for rare masks and shells from the North and South Pacific, Asia, and the Himalayas. You could get a cone-carved snuff bottle from China for just $7.50, Hawaiian reed bracelets for $6.

Have a sandwich and an espresso now, at the European-style **Market Café** (see Chapter XV), which also purveys a multitude of baskets, antique copperware, cheeses, and deli items—as well as Famous Amos Macadamia Nut Cookies. Or in the precincts of the hotel itself, join the leisure class at what is perhaps the best buffet lunch in the islands (some say it now surpasses the one at Mauna Kea on the Big Island, since it has garnered the former Mauna Kea chef!). That's the **Mayfair Buffet,** served in the hotel's graceful dining room every day between noon and 2:30 p.m., a feast of such lavish and delicious proportions that it is well worth the $15 tariff. Or more simply, wander out to the **Bay Club.** Here you can have a medium-priced lunch, a drink, or simply walk out to see the breathtaking views, with blue sea at every vista. **Fleming Beach** is fine for swimming and snorkeling. Let the peace and beauty stay in your memory as you turn around and go back the way you came—the road contiuing around the island is a poor one—driving the 32 miles back to Kahului.

READERS' SIGHTSEEING AND SHOPPING SUGGESTIONS ON MAUI: "We discovered protea flowers, a variety of beautiful blossoms that grow on the slopes of Haleakala; they are the native flower of South Africa, and grow only there, in Australia, and now in the volcanic soil of Maui. The place to get them is at the **Hawaii Protea Cooperative** on Kula Highway 37, almost opposite the post office. Prices for these fabulous flowers, which can be dried and last a very long time, go from 90¢ to $9 a blossom. You can also order flowers by mail. Send them $25, and they will send you whatever is currently in blossom—much cheaper than buying similar flower arrangements at home. Their address is Hawaii Protea Cooperative, P.O. Box 68, Kula, Maui, HI 96790" (Bob Harrison and Hal Goodstein, Provincetown, Mass.). . . . "We really enjoyed our **Windjammer Cruise** from Lahaina to Lanai from 8:30 a.m. to 4:30 p.m. It includes continental breakfast, all the beer and soft drinks you want, and a tour of the island. Two vans and an old green schoolbus are waiting to take everyone on a tour of Lanai when you get off the boat. The old man with the green schoolbus is getting very popular; aside from his delightful humor, he, unlike the rest, takes everyone to see his 'Hawaiian home.' His wife brought out fresh, sweet pineapple for all and showed off all her beautiful handmade Japanese dolls. What an extra-special occurrence to remember! After an hour, we all went to the beach for swimming and snorkeling. Then a barbecue lunch, more swimming, and then time to go. Mai tais were served on board. If the sails are up, you're in for an exciting trip back. The crew was delightful! [*Author's Note:* Several letters this year praising Windjammer Cruises.] . . . It is an expensive excursion but worth the price of $90—every penny. I booked a day sailing with the Coon Family on the *Trilogy* out of Lahaina to Lanai. About 12 to 15 people were on board, the trip was very personalized. We spent all morning on a private beach on Lanai with snorkeling, a delicious barbecue, a private tour of the island and Lani City. So native, no tour buses. In spite of the expense, well worth it! **Trilogy Excursions** (tel. 661-4743)" (Sheryl Ziegler, Elyria, Ohio).

"Free tennis! You can pay anywhere from $2 to $18 to play tennis on Maui, but we discoverd five **public tennis courts** in back of the main post office a mile or so north of Lahaina. They are in fair shape and quite a friendly group hangs out around there. Crowded, yes, but if you care to play in the middle of the day there is almost no wait. I understand the courts are lighted until 9:30 p.m." (James Sanderson, Del Mar, Calif.). . . . "There is a new store on the road to Haleakala. This is the little **Sunrise Country Market,** on the road at about 3500 feet. They serve fresh Kona coffee, snacks, sandwiches, which are a boon on the long drive. They also have protea and other fresh flowers and local fruits" (Marilynn Hirashima, Kula, Hi.). . . . "The best price we found anywhere for renting snorkeling equipment was at the **Hawaiian Reef Divers** in Lahaina. Rental for 24 hours was $4.50" (Cindy Battis, Eagen, Minn.). . . . "If your readers wish to rent tents, backpacks, sleeping bags, etc., so that they can really see Haleakala or Hana, they might want to try **Outdoor Sports,** located in the scenic old paniolo town of Makawao. They can phone 572-8736 for availability and reservations" (Neida Cahoj, Lahaina, Hi.). . . . "The Japanese department store, **Shirokaya,** at Kaahumanu Center in Kahului, has great buys in tea sets and lacquerware" (Peter and Mary Tannen, Albuquerque, N.M.). . . . "One suggestion we might have for others is to buy a one-hour video of Maui called *Moods of Maui,* from **Video Concepts, Inc.,** Kihei, HI 96753 (tel. 808/879-4226). It was well worth the $39.95 we spent. It's fun to have and to show relatives and friends where we have been" (Gina Baum, Dorset, Ontario, Canada).

"Our most enjoyable snorkeling spot was near the rocks below the Maui Sheraton. The area is so beautiful, and public walkways lead right to the beach. Our daughter loved it here because she didn't have to go out too far to snorkel, and the water was calm, so we could lay acros an air mattress to see the fish. This is a perfect way for youngsters or beginning swimmers to view the underwater world. It was also fun watching the windsurfers and natives diving off the cliffs. . . . Regarding the trip to Hana and the **Seven Sacred Pools.** We had the most enjoyable time swimming under the waterfalls on the drive there, and we were very glad we stopped on the way. At the Seven Sacred Pools it was so crowded that it really detracted from the fun and beauty of the place. But at the waterfalls on the way, we were usually the only ones there, and that made it seem very special. Swim here earlier in the day as there are apt to be mosquitos later" (Julie Martin, Huntington Beach, Calif.).

"It's becoming very popular to get up early to catch **sunrise on Haleakala.** The total experience of leaving the motel at abut 3 a.m., driving up the mountain in pitch blackness, meeting other other people with the same crazy idea, then slowly waiting for the sun to rise over the crater is absolutely breathtaking. At that hour, however, a sweater, jacket, and blanket *may* suffice for only some. It was cold! Bring breakfast/lunch and enjoy amid other sun/nature worshipers or on your own" (Francine Schept, White Plains, N.Y.). . . . "In Lahaina, a great shop is **One World Family** at 762 Front St. They have lovely, hand-painted clothing—T-shirts, skirts, jackets, baby clothes. Books and toys too. . . . On the early-morning drive to **Haleakala Crater** for sunrise it took me an hour and ten minutes from Kahului, and I am a cautious driver. It was freezing at the Visitors Center—about 45 degrees in late August—so I would suggest gloves, especially for photographers; my 'shutter finger' was stiff from the cold! First light—30 to 40 minutes before sunrise—is as lovely as the sunrise and should not be missed. On the way down, I was the only person to stop at Leleiwi Lookout, sharing it with a park ranger for two hours; I think the view from the lookout is superior to the one at the Visitors Center" (Martha F. Battenfeld, Brighton, Mass.).

"We would like to recommend buying fresh fish at **Lahaina Fishery** across the street from McDonald's in the Lahaina Shopping Center. It is a small place. We barbecued ono and ahi by placing the fish directly on the grill after sprinkling it with pepper and lemon juice. It's simply delicious, and so much less expensive than eating in restaurants!" (Ed and Rebecca Beaver, La Mesa, Calif.). . . . "For clam and shallow snorkeling, pull off Highway 30, south of Olowalu General Store. This is not a park, just a shallow beach. So good, they give beginner scuba lessons here" (Vic and Bev Suzuki, Thornhill, Ontario, Canada).

"Our four nights at **Waianapanapana Park** were our No. 1 idyllic spot. Hana was having a week-long Aloha Week festival. We went to a real Hawaiian luau with great performers for $6; the previous night the ladies of the village gave a real hula show at the village soccer field—free. October is a great time to go to Hana, as there are very few guests. Try the red-sand beach for snorkeling at **Hana Park,** near the old frame school house, now a library, and follow the trail down a meadow, around a cliff, to a secluded beach behind a natural lava breakwall. Caution: Young couples still swim in the buff here! For golf in Maui, go to **Wailuku Golf Course:** 18 holes, most overlooking the ocean. A real fun place!" (Richard Welse, Westfield Center, Ohio). . . . "If you follow the river upstream from the **Seven Sacred Pools** near Hana, you will find a very spectacular waterfall around 75 feet tall. There is a large natural pool at the bottom to swim in. It takes approximately 30 minutes to walk up from where the river crosses Highway 31" (Carol Harper, Felton, Calif.). . . . "Visiting **Alberta's Gazebo** at 658 Front St. in Lahaina was a wonderful experience. She is very informed about the old beads she loves so much and sells in her shop. They are slave-trading beads up to 600 years old, from Africa, Persia, Italy, and other countries, in Venetian glass, silver, very beautiful, and not expensive" (Nita Brown, Okalahoma City, Okla.).

"The book *Hiking Hawaii* by Robert Smith (Wilderness Press, Berkeley, 1977) is excellent. It has lots of hikes from family outings to those that are very tough going. . . . One of the nicest waterfalls and swimming holes is located exactly 2.8 miles toward Hana from the Seven Sacred Pools at a bridge. It was still going even when lots of others were dry" (Dr. Michael Baron, San Francisco, Calif.). . . . "We found the prettiest part of Maui to be that short section of Highway 30 that goes past the **Napili Bay** area: towering cliffs, crashing waves, lush valleys. Few tourists seem to drive up here because they know the road ends. We packed a picnic dinner and ate it in total isolation on a cliff overlooking the water. It was one of the best moments of our honeymoon" (Sue and Terry Young, Crystal Lake, Ill.). . . . "The road past **Nakalele Point to Kapuna** marked impassable on most tourist maps is definitely just that! The trip is 14 miles, not 5 as stated in most brochures, and a total disaster. We ventured a couple of miles on the road ourselves and had to turn around when the road became too narrow for our car. However, a couple we were traveling with covered the entire 14 miles, and it took them several hours which they say were harrowing at best. The scenery is not any more spectacular than you can find on other island roads and the driving is so nerve-wracking it is unlikely you will be able to spare any time to view the scenery anyway. The road to Hana is described as treacherous in some brochures, but it is no comparison to this road—save youself some time and nerves and just don't bother with this route" (Mr. and Mrs. Wes Alton, Edmonton, Alberta, Canada).

"As far as Kona coffee, Hawaiian plants to take home, and coconut syrup, **Long's Drugs** in Kahului is the cheapest we found on Maui. Both make good gifts that are sturdy, a packing plus" (Gary Morgan, Greeley, Colo.). . . . "My wife found an excellent shop called **Palani's** in the Kihei Town Center for handmade bikinis that were only $18. It's on the way to the new hotels below Kihei on Highway 31" (Maurice Elmore, Etiwanda, Calif.). . . . "The trip to **Haleakala** for the sunrise (in early August) required more than a heavy sweater. Some people used blankets as cloaks. The rangers give a very fine explanation of the development of the volcanoes. It's worth hearing" (Rhoda and Eugene Kaellis, Victoria, B.C., Canada). . . . "We found the municipal beach between Lahaina and the hotel beach comlex great! Protected and much less surfy than in front of our hotel" (Mrs. Morris Finck, Shaker Heights, Ohio). . . . "The best snorkeling beach on Maui (we discovered it ourselves and it was later pointed out to us by islanders) is **Honolua Bay** on the north end of the island near the end of Highway 30. Overnight camping permits should be obtained from the Maui Pineapple Company in Lahaina, but we did not have one and had no problems" (Sandra Johnson, Santa Paula, Calif.). . . . "South of Kihei is **Kamaole Park,** which is actually three beaches. Each is calm, sandy-bottomed, and almost deserted on weekdays. On this and a previous visit we saw a whale frolicking just offshore" (Bob and Doris Ryan, Grand Island, N.Y.).

"We made the drive to the **Seven Sacred Pools** past Hana on Maui. It took four hours to reach because of intermittent stops to see the beautiful views. Unfortunately, we didn't start soon enough to return by dark and our return trip was nerve-wracking. Advise anyone who wishes to take the drive to heed the warning to start early enough to return before dark" (Mr. and Mrs. Michael Ward, Mt. Morris, Ill.). . . . "I would like to put in a good word for the road to Hana and the Seven Sacred Pools. I don't think it deserves the bad publicity it's gotten. I am a new driver and had no problem with the road. As far as mudslides are concerned, I don't doubt that they occur occasionally, but we saw little evidence of old ones and no evidence of recent ones. It was raining off and on the whole way to Hana, so we knew we were risking a mudslide, but when we called the Highway Department before leaving, they didn't seem concerned about mudslides, even though they said it was overcast and would probably rain. I was very glad that I drove to the Seven Sacred Pools because the scenery was lovely and the road was fine—except for the potholes, which weren't much worse than those in New York City streets. My only recommendation would be to rent a small car, not a large one, because the road seems worse in a larger car. I would also drive to Haleakala, or Waimea Canyon on Kauai first, to get a feel for mountain roads if you've never driven on one. Let's hear it for the Hana road!" (Virginia W. Pfeiffer, New York, N.Y.). . . . "The road to Hana is an absolutely incredible 30 miles of curvy winding road with frequent one-lane bridges. I always seemed to meet the largest trucks at a one-lane bridge. I wouldn't have missed it for the world, but it was a harrowing experience and a trip that should be done in two days. One day to go there, stay overnight (arrange accommodations before going—they are limited), do your sightseeing, and leave the next day. It would really be nerve-wracking to drive that road twice in the same day" (Jane C. Kenney, Kingston, N.H.).

"**Camping** is still inexpensive. On Maui, you pay for County Park, Hookipa, and Baldwin Park, $3 per adult and 50¢ per child. State parks are free. For County Park permits: War Memorial Gym (next to Baldwin High School), Kaahumanu Avenue, Wailuku, Maui, HI 96793. Office hours are 7:45 a.m. to 4:30 p.m. Monday to Friday. For State Park permits: State Office Building, Wailuku" (Frank Bogard, Pasadena, Calif.). . . . "Taking the road to Hana, we stopped at the **arboretum,** which is on the main road just before the turnoff to the rock and coral church mentioned in the book. This was the highlight of our Hana trip, as the gardens were beautiful with the exotic trees and plants clearly labeled for the haoles. There are about two miles of path to hike (all level), it's free, and would make a lovely place for a picnic—there are some picnic tables available" (Barbara L. Mueller, Tucson, Ariz.). . . . "For those who wish to swim in the buff, the most beautiful beach in West Maui is **Makena,** a bumpy 45-minute ride down from the airport but well worth it. It is also a lovely beach to bodysurf at in the buff" (Jeffrey Gale, San Rafael, Calif.). . . . "The best snorkeling we found was at the southern edge of the **Kaanapali Airport.** The water was clear and safe for children, the coral plentiful and well below the surface, and the variety of fish amazing. Even beginning snorkelers will enjoy this beach, which is reached by turning in at the last Kaanapali sign going north, then walking about 50 yards down to the beach" (Nick Howell, Camp Springs, Md.).

"If you're staying in the Napili Beach area, we suggest you stock up on groceries at the **Foodland** in Lahaina before going to Napili. The prices at the 'Village Store' at Napili were out of this world!" (William H. Blue, Seattle, Wash.). . . . "The road to Hana is much improved. We were there five years ago and two years ago. I mention this so people will not be scared off by prior reports. We found out how to get to the exquisite red-sand beach in Hana only to find out that it has been allowed to become a nude beach" (S. F. Dreesen, Metuchen, N.J.). . . . "I'd like to pass on some information I learned the hard way. I mentioned to a clerk in a market that I was planning to drive to Hana the next day. He said, 'If it's raining when you get halfway, turn back, or you can get stuck out there.' I assumed he was being overly cautious. It sprinkled off and on as we drove to Hana, but it's a long trip and we didn't want to waste our day. The sun was shining as we visited the Seven Sacred Pools, and water rushed from the very top pool to the ocean. On our way back, cloudy but no rain, we were stopped in a line of about 30 cars, trapped by a landslide on a narrow, cliff-hugging road. Rescue crews had been called, but it took two hours with men, shovels, and a bulldozer to clear the road so we could get by. It could have been a tragedy, and we learned to take seriously what the Hawaiians say. They know best!" (Mrs. Donald B. Newton, Saratoga, Calif.).

Chapter XVII

THE ISLAND OF MOLOKAI

1. Island Hotels
2. Island Restaurants
3. The Night Scene
4. Shopping
5. Seeing the Sights

OF THE THOUSANDS and thousands of visitors who come to the islands every year, only a small percentage visit the island of Molokai. Known in the past mostly for its treatment center for Hansen's disease—leprosy—at Kalaupapa, and as a pineapple plantation island, Molokai in the past few years has gained a reputation as a hideaway island for hunters, golfers, and sportsmen (facilities for water sports are, to put it kindly, less than ideal; its beaches can be beautiful, but most are unsafe for swimming). Somehow, the tidal wave of progress that has swept the islands since statehood has left Molokai behind; it appears, at first glance, like a midwestern town in the Depression '30s. Yet there's a down-homeness and a realness here that most people find appealing, and a genuine friendliness among the locals. Artists and craftsmen, seeking a last refuge from overpriced civilization, are beginning to seek it out. If you'd like to see what Hawaii was like perhaps 50 years ago, a visit to Molokai is a rewarding experience. And you won't have to break the bank to do it. Because Molokai itself is experiencing hard economic times, now that the pineapple industry is being phased out, prices here are somewhat lower than elsewhere.

GETTING THERE: Molokai is easily reached via either **Hawaiian** or **Aloha Airlines.** The commuter airlines of **Air Molokai, Royal Hawaiian Air Service,** and **Air Hawaii** also call at Molokai. It lies between the island of Oahu and Maui (it can easily be seen from West Maui) and is, in fact, part of Maui County. Route it on your way to either Maui or Hilo.

MOLOKAI, PAST AND PRESENT: Although Molokai is known as "The Friendly Isle," that friendliness has really not been tested yet, as far as tourism goes. You might easily be the only mainland visitor on the few minutes' flight from Oahu or Maui, and your fellow passengers will more than likely be island people visiting relatives, or plantation men arriving on business.

Since tourism has not yet reached Molokai in any significant proportion, its charm is that of discovery and adventure. Picturesque valleys and veritably unexplored coves wait to be found by you—and your camera. Fishermen attend to their nets, farmers work in their taro patches, and paniolos (cowboys) ride the ranges, not for the benefit of the visitors, but for real.

The Friendly Isle was once known as the Lonely Isle. The power of Molokai's kahuna priests was feared throughout the other islands. Warring island kings kept a respectable distance from Molokai until, in 1790, Kamehameha the Great came to negotiate for the hand of the queen, Molokai's high chieftess, Keoupuolani. Five years later he returned with an army to conquer Molokai on his drive for Oahu and dominion over all of Hawaii.

Today Molokai presents a tranquil scene, a Polynesian island untouched and unspoiled. A thickly forested backcountry makes life exciting for the huntsman. For those of you who just like to look and sightsee, there is magnificent Halawa Valley with its healing pools at the foot of Moaula Falls; the less rugged Palaau Park with its Phallic Rock; Kalaupapa Lookout and Kalaupapa itself, an isolated peninsula, refuge for the victims of the once-dreaded leprosy, which today you can visit on a guided tour. But more about that later.

You won't have to rough it on Molokai. The few hotel facilities are excellent, the roads are for the most part quite good, and you'll be able to get whatever comforts and supplies you need—from rental cars to color movie films. The drinking water is as pure as you'll find anywhere in the world, and the restaurants, most located in the three major hotels on the island, serve very good meals.

One word of advice: Go directly to your hotel from the airport and get comfortable and adjusted to Molokai before visiting its nearby principal town, Kaunakakai. This sleepy village, made famous by the song "Cockeyed Major," is best appreciated once you're in the Molokai mood. Especially after Waikiki.

U-DRIVES: You're going to need a car if you want to explore Molokai on your own. The popular **Tropical Rent-A-Car,** with a booth right at the airport, offers a $20.95 rate for a compact stick shift, $23.95 for a compact automatic, with no mileage charges. Rates are subject to change. The local number is 567-6118 (make reservations in Honolulu at 836-1041). For toll-free reservations and information, call 800/367-5140.

We've had several good reports from readers this year on **Avis.** Rates are about $24 for a stick-shift Chevette, $31 for an automatic compact with air conditioning. Their local phone is 553-3866; their toll-free reservation number is 800/331-1717. See, too, details on their $119-a-week "Aloha Special" in Chapter IV.

A local firm based at the airport, **Molokai Island U-Drive** (tel. 567-6156), offers good flat rates. They do not rent to campers, and only to those between 25 and 70.

1. Island Hotels

Molokai at this moment has a grand total of six hotels—and that's more than twice what they had seven years ago! Since there are so few,

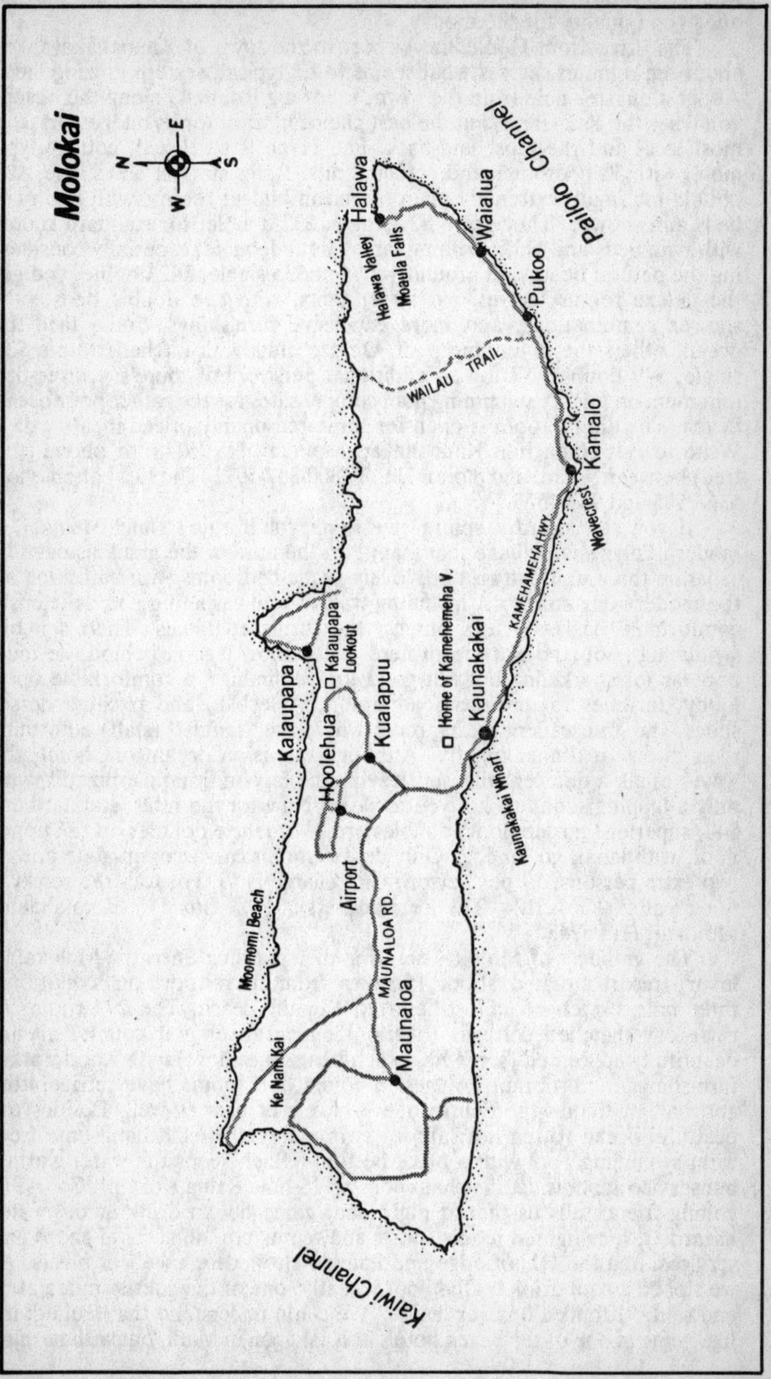

Molokai
N
E
S
W
Halawa
Halawa Valley
Moaula Falls
Waialua
Pukoo
Pailolo Channel
WAILAU TRAIL
Kamalo
Wavecrest
KAMEHAMEHA HWY
Kalaupapa
Kalaupapa Lookout
Home of Kamehemeha V.
Kaunakakai
Kualapuu
Hoolehua
Kaunakakai Wharf
Airport
MAUNALOA RD.
Moomomi Beach
Maunaloa
Ke Nani Kai
Kaiwi Channel

we'll give you the details on all of them; they're not all budget, but they all offer good quality for the money.

The drive from Hoolehua Airport to the town of Kaunakakai takes about ten minutes, across what seems to be typical western grazing land. About a quarter mile from the town, following Route 45 along the beach, you'll see the **Pau Hana Inn,** the best choice in town for us budgeteers, the most local and the most laid-back. Pau Hana is a relaxed, cottage-type motel with 50 bedrooms and cottage units. Rates start at $20 single, $25 double for small, extremely plain but clean budget rooms, with two twin beds and shower. They go to $27 single, $32 double, for standard rooms with twin beds and bath; nothing fancy, but adequate, especially considering the natural beauty all around you. For $35 single, $42 double, you get the deluxe rooms, newer and larger units, with two double beds, tub-shower combinations, and more expensive furnishings. Some face the ocean, others the swimming pool. Deluxe units with kitchenette are $39 single, $49 double, $7 for an additional person, but there's a three-day minimum on this. A swimming pool compensates for the rather poor ocean beach. The dining room is open for three reasonably priced meals a day. Write to Pau Hana Inn, Kaunakakai, Molokai, HI 96748; or phone (toll free) between 9 a.m. and 8 p.m. E.S.T. 800/367-5072. The local phones are 536-7545 and 941-1555.

If you can afford a splurge we think you'll enjoy **Hotel Molokai,** a modern Polynesian village that maintains the aura of the gracious past. In separate three-unit cottages are lovely rustic bedrooms with baths and all the modern-day comforts, including wall-to-wall carpeting and deliciously comfortable basket swings out on the furnished lanais. There's a big swimming pool (the waterfront here is a shallow lagoon behind the reef, popular for snorkeling but not good for swimming), a comfortable open lobby, facilities for croquet, badminton, volleyball, and pitching horseshoes, and an excellent dining room where the "family" (staff) entertains their guests at dinner nightly. Although this is an oceanfront hotel, the waves break a quarter mile out, leaving the lagoon tranquil and still, with only a lapping sound to lull you to sleep. Now for the rates: standard are $42; superior (garden floor) doubles are $44; deluxe doubles on the upper floor, with lanai, go for $52. Only deluxe rooms can accommodate one or two extra persons, $9 per person. Crib charge is $9. For toll-free reservations, call 800/367-5124. The local address is P.O. Box 546, Kaunakakai, Molokai, HI 96748.

The grandest of Molokai hotels is the sparkling **Sheraton-Molokai,** a luxury resort situated about 15 miles from the airport on a glorious, three-mile stretch of almost-deserted Kepuhi Beach. The 292 rooms in two-story thatched cottages (overlooking ocean or golf course) all are beautifully appointed (some have high-beamed ceilings) with wood, rattan furnishings, and vibrant Polynesian colors. All rooms have refrigerators and half of them—the deluxe ones—have wet bars as well. Besides the beautiful ocean (often not safe for swimming), there's a handsome free-form swimming pool with a black bottom (which keeps the water warm), bar service at poolside, the championship 18-hole Kalua Koi Golf Course (a golfing friend tells us that at night deer come out to drink at the water hazards!), four lighted tennis courts and tennis pro, all sorts of shops and services, and the Ohia Lodge and Paniolo Broiler for excellent meals. As we sipped a cool drink by the pool recently, one of the guests smiled at us and said: "I think I'll never leave." We could understand that feeling; it's like being at one of the beach hotels at Kaanapali in Maui, but with nothing else around. It's luxury all the way here, and that includes the rates too: $70, single or double, in standard rooms; $90 for a deluxe garden, $95 for a partial ocean view, $100 deluxe ocean view. From April 30 to December 20, it's $5 less per category. Guests paying published rates can play tennis and golf free. Reservations are available from the mainland U.S. by phoning Sheraton's toll-free number: 800/325-3535. From eastern Canada, the number is 800/261-9393; western Canada, it's 800/261-9330.

If you want to settle into your own apartment in this area, **Paniolo Hale** is the place. Next door to the Sheraton, on Kepuhi Beach, it is adjacent to the Kalua Koi Golf Course (in fact, one must cross the fairway to get to the beach). Wild deer and turkeys are frequently seen on the grounds. There is a swimming pool and a paddle tennis court, and guests receive a reduced rate when golfing at Kalua Koi. The Sheraton also offers its four lighted tennis courts to Paniolo Hale guests for a nominal fee. This is a luxury condominium complex. Best buys here are the one-bedroom, two-bath units, at $75 for up to four persons. Studios rent for $60 for two, and two-bedroom, two-bath units go for $95 for up to four persons, with a maximum of six; extra persons over four in a unit are charged $8. Car and condo packages are also available at very good rates: $75 for the studio for one to two persons, $85 for the one-bedroom for one to four persons, and $110 for the two-bedroom for one to six persons; $25 more is charged for oceanfront accommodations. Hot tubs are available on the lanais of all two-bedroom units for an additional charge. All the apartments have full kitchen, TV, telephone, and attractive island furnishings. Each unit has its own screened lanai (a touch of old Hawaii), which you walk right onto from your room, without going through a door. The nearest restaurant is the Sheraton, about one block away along the sea wall, and the nearest grocery store five miles away (it closes at 5 p.m. and all day on Sunday). We've had several good reports this year on this one. For reservations, phone, toll free, 800/367-2984. From Canada and Hawaii call collect 808/552-2731 for reservations, or write to Paniolo Hale, P.O. Box 146, Maunaloa, Molokai, HI 96770.

Molokai's two other condominium complexes are a bit older, and more reasonably priced. **Molokai Shores** is located just a mile from Kaunakakai, between the Pau Hana Inn and the Hotel Molokai. The three-story, 102-unit oceanfront apartment building has very pleasant one-bedroom, one-bath and two-bedroom, two-bath units, all with ocean views, color TV, well-equipped kitchens, and private lanais overlooking tropical lawns. Picnic tables, barbecue units, and a putting green make outdoor life pleasant, and there's a pool for swimming (the beach is not particularly good here). The one-bedroom units rent at $50 daily for two people, and most can accommodate four ($6 for each additional person per night); and the two-bedroom, two-bath units are $62 for two. A one-bedroom apartment with an additional loft bedroom, and one bath, is $57 for two, and can accommodate up to six. A minimum stay of two nights is required. For reservations, write Molokai Shores, Star Route, Kaunakakai, Molokai, HI 96748 (tel. 553-5954).

On the east shore of Molokai, a new area for tourist development, is **Wavecrest Resort,** with tennis courts, a swimming pool, and all the amenities necessary for at-home resort living. There's not much of a beach, but it's okay for fishing. The 126 one- and two-bedroom condominium apartments are all smartly furnished with fully equipped electric kitchens and color TV. From your private lanai you can see Maui, right across the water. One-bedroom apartments run $35 to $50 for two people; two-bedroom units are $50 to $65 for up to four persons. For reservations, call, toll free, 800/367-7040.

2. Island Restaurants

There aren't many restaurants to choose from in the only business district on Molokai, on Ala Malama in Kaunakakai. Local friends advise that you keep your eyes peeled for the Filipino lady who parks her bright-blue station wagon in town around lunchtime and sells local delicacies from the back of the wagon. All dishes are cooked in a certified kitchen, and you can usually get shoyu or teriyaki chicken, vegetable tempura, coconut candy on a stick, and other goodies, at very reasonable prices. Another local lady also sells food from her station wagon, this one an older model but also painted a shiny blue. Her lunches too are both affordable and delicious. **Molokai Buyers,** a natural-foods cooperative, sells tasty salads plus a meal in a sandwich for $2.50 or less, and the **Kanemitsu Bakery** has takeout lunch food as well—plus its famous and flavorful cheese and onion bread.

For a sit-down meal in Kaunakakai, you have two pretty good possibilities: a Chinese restaurant quaintly called **Hop Inn** and Mid-Nite Inn. Don't let the dreary outside appearance of Hop Inn put you off; just about every building in town shows its age, and inside you'll find a clean place and good Chinese cooking. The à la carte dishes are reasonable: we spent $4.50 for shrimp chop suey, $3.95 for an interesting chicken with cashew nuts, the same for sweet-and-sour pork. Watch for Hop Inn on the left as you drive up Ala Malama Street from Kam Highway.

We don't know why they call it **Mid-Nite Inn,** since it's never open at midnight: 5:30 a.m. (they get up early on Molokai) to 1:30 p.m. and 5:30 to 9 p.m. are more like it at this venerable local establishment, with tables, booths, and counter, and tasty, inexpensive food. Owners Art and John Kikukawa, father and son, are super-friendly, and you know they've got to be nice people if they're offering delicious fresh fish dinners, steamed or fried and served with rice and pickled vegetables, for all of $3.95 to $4.25! The highest price on the menu is $9.75 steak, while most regular dishes like fried chicken with fries, fried aku, shrimp, or corned beef and cabbage go from $3 to $4.75. You're welcome to bring your own bottle of wine: they'll gladly uncork it and provide glasses at no charge. Breakfast is also available at good old-fashioned prices like $1.35 for hotcakes and coffee. (For a solution to the name mystery, see the Readers' Selections, at the end of this chapter.)

If you're driving the long 25 miles out to Halawa Valley, there's a **Neighborhood Store** some 18 miles out on Route 45, your last possible stop for provisions. Bananas and papayas are reasonable, and you can also buy eggs, vegetables, and other produce as well as cold drinks. Not a restaurant by any stretch of the imagination, but an important stop if you're hungry and thirsty.

Now for the best restaurants on Molokai—starting at the three major hotels. They can rise into the slightly splurgy category but are well worth it. The Hotel Molokai's restaurant is superb. Its name, **Holo Holo Kai** (tel. 553-5347), means to sail in the sea—appropriate, since the restaurant is right on the edge of the ocean and open to its charms. It's easy to imagine you're off in Tahiti or some other South Seas isle (you are) as you enjoy the peaceful Pacific mood. You can stay right within our budget here if you stick to the all-you-want soup-and-salad buffet (the fruits and vegetables are fresh from the garden), which includes that wonderful Molokai french bread. It's $5.50. Add another few dollars and you can have the soup-and-salad buffet, plus rice or potatoes or pilaf, plus fresh island vegetables (beans or carrots grown on Molokai), and entrees such as savory pepper steak or roast pork loin at $6.95, mahimahi at $8. Beef stew, a local favorite, at $6.95, is served with rice or poi, and elicited from one of our readers, Jack Lindberg of San José, California, the comment that "it is a bottomless bowl of hearty munching: it approaches my Irish mother's blend—ummm!" Fresh catch of the day (usually pricing out to around $12) is a dinner specialty, and there are weekend steak specials at $12 to $14. Lunch features a daily special at $5.50, the soup-and-salad buffet, and a Hawaiian menu at $2.75 to $4 that includes sashimi, lomi salmon, and that homemade beef stew. Island-style entertainment accompanies dinner, served from 6 to 9 p.m., and often lunch too. Box lunches, around $5, are, to our appetite, big enough for two.

The mood is different at the **Pau Hana Inn Restaurant** (tel. 553-5342); you dine indoors in a big rustic dining room with a tremendous fireplace. Doors open to the outside, where a seaside café provides evening dancing and entertainment. Dinner is well priced, with most entrees in the $6.25 to $14.95 range: you might have catch of the day, southern fried chicken, barbecued beef short ribs, teriyaki steak with crab legs, or New York strip steak. Your entrees are served with potato or rice, bread, and beverage. Coconut cake or cheesecake is fun for dessert. At lunch there are entrees like spaghetti with garlic bread and salad, fried chicken, plus sandwiches, from about $3.95 to $5.25. This room is generally open from 6 a.m. to 1:30 or 2 p.m., and again from 6 to 8:30 or 9 p.m., but it's all "Hawaiian time."

The most expensive of the hotel dining rooms is the glamorous **Ohia Lodge** of the Sheraton-Molokai (tel. 552-2555), a South Seas spot overlooking the water, where there's music for dancing every night. Many of the local people feel the dining room is the best on Molokai. Be prepared to spend from $8.50 to $17 for tasty fish and seafood entrees, plus veal Oscar, rack of lamb, chicken, and a variety of steaks, chops, prime ribs, and birds. With your entree, always beautifully prepared, come potatoes or rice and a fresh vegetable. Lunch is more reasonably priced; there are specials like island-style beef stew and cannelloni, plus a variety of salads, burgers, and hot and cold sandwiches from $4.25 to $8.25.

For a real budget meal in this area, dine with the islanders at **Jo Jo's Café,** not far from the Sheraton; it's in Maunaloa, in the tavern section of the old Pooh's Restaurant. The old antique bar is still here. The menu is the same all day, and the prices are low for the likes of chopped steak, breaded fresh tuna, fried akule, butterfish, Korean ribs, from $3 to $4.50. Fish is usually $3.50. You can have a hamburger for $1, cheeseburger for $1.35, a super-teriyaki steak sandwich for $1.65, plus hot dogs, saimin, and salad. Funky and fun. Open daily, except Wednesday, from 11 a.m. to 7:30 p.m., Sunday only to 2:30 p.m.

3. The Night Scene

Nightlife on Molokai, as we travelers know it, is almost all in the major hotels. A dance band plays every night except during dinner at the **Ohia Lodge** of the Sheraton-Molokai. You might want to try a Molokai Mule (it has a kick!) in the cocktail lounge of the Ohia Room; it's $6, and you take home the mug. . . . The bar at the **Hotel Molokai** is a pleasant place to be, since it's in between the pool area and the open-at-the-sides dining room; so you can have a drink and watch the entertainment, usually a duo, every evening except Sunday. They have hula shows too, but only about once a month. During the 11 a.m. to 6 p.m. Happy Hour, beer is $1.25 and $1.75, drinks run $2 to $3.50. At the **Pau Hana Inn** a musical group plays until 1 a.m. on Friday and Saturday in the huge seaside cocktail garden, and a piano bar is in operation on Thursday. During another long Happy Hour—11 a.m. to 6 p.m.—beer is $1, and call drinks run $1.95; in the evening, beer is $1.50, and call drinks cost $2.10.

4. Shopping

This is one place in the islands that is *not* heaven for the shopping buffs. The local supermarkets, grocery shops, and liquor stores on Ala Malama, the main street of Kaunakakai, and a general store here and there in the country just about do it—but there are a few places of interest to visitors. To stock up on local produce—papayas, bananas, avocados, sprouts, etc.—try **Molokai Buyers** (next door to the laundromat), which sells the usual natural-food store fare plus other items at the lowest possible prices. They're the only natural-foods coop on Molokai. For the best selection of books on the island, try **Port of Call,** also on Ala Malama. Their strength is in Hawaiiana and paperbacks, and they also have a big selection of Hawaiian tapes and records—and a unisex hairstyling salon as well. To learn where the fish are biting, and to get fishing, diving, and camping gear, the place to go is **Molokai Fish and Dive,** also on Ala Malama Street.

Our favorite Molokai shopping is out in **Maunaloa** (not far from the Hotel Sheraton). Once a thriving plantation town, Maunaloa has been declining since Dole closed shop in 1975; however, young artisans are seeking it out and showing their wares here. The people at **Dolly Hale** create charming handcrafted dolls, priced from $6.75 to $18.75. One, a real Molokai doll, is made of coconut fiber with a macadamia-nut head; others are decorated with dried flowers, shells, ti leaves. . . . Across the street from Dolly Hale are several more interesting places to visit. Stop in at the **Big Wind Kite Factory** if you're in need of some beautiful, high-flying kites. Chinese birds, hand-painted on silk or paper over bamboo, are $7.95 in paper, $24.95 in silk, and pretty enough to use for decorations. The friendly owners, Jonathan and Daphne Socher, even offer free flying lessons with modern, 80-m.p.h. "aerobatic kites." Nylon windsox in rainbow colors, at $19.95, are very popular, and so are their kite kits for kids, to color, cut out, and fly, at $2.95. A great browsing spot.

Next door to the Kite Factory, take time to explore the work of several island artisans. You'll probably find Butch Tabano and his deerhorn jewelry made from the axis deer of Molokai at **Plantation Gallery**—unless the surf is up. Prices begin around $15. While you're at Plantation Gallery, inquire about Hawaiian smoked kiawe chips, to use in place of hickory chips, for real island-flavored barbecuing. Twelve-ounce packages are about $3. . . . The master woodcarver of **Tao Woodcarver** does custom koa-wood furniture and accessories. . . . Hand-wrought rings, charms, bracelets, and pendants are custom-made at **Molokai Mountain Jewelry. . . . Jay's Boutique** (behind Plantation Gallery) has clothing and shoes, plus attractive children's clothing.

5. Seeing the Sights

Sightseeing on Molokai requires a bit more determination on the part of the visitor than it does on the other islands. A great deal of the island, including its best beaches, belongs to private ranches. A visit to the island's most spectacular scenic spot, Halawa Valley, involves some rugged driving and an hour's hike. To reach Kalaupapa, the major point of interest on the island, you either have to fly, hike, or ride a mule down a steep pali. But if you're willing to put up with a few obstacles, you might find sightseeing on Molokai among the most rewarding adventures of your trip to Hawaii. Sightseeing tours and local guides are especially helpful on this island.

THE TRIP TO HALAWA VALLEY: For a beautiful day on Molokai, get up early, have your hotel pack you a picnic box lunch (or put one together from the supermarkets in town), hop into your car, and head for Halawa Valley. The trip is just about 25 miles from Kaunakakai along Highway 45, but it will probably take you two hours to get there, since the last part of the driving is rough going. This is Molokai's southeastern coast, dotted with ancient heiaus, old fish ponds (some of which are used for scientific studies), and many coastal churches built by Father Damien and others. You won't be able to see the heiaus unless you get permission to go on private property, but you can stop in at **St. Joseph's Catholic Church** in Kamalo and at Father Damien's **Lady of Sorrows Church** a little farther along the way, where you'll see a statue of Damien in a pavilion near the church. About 20 miles out, past Pauwalu, the broad country road begins to narrow, and soon you're on a one-lane road where the sharp turns force the car to practically creep along while the scenery becomes more beautiful every minute. Then you begin to climb up, up, through the ranchlands of **Puu O Hoku Ranch,** from which a narrow road takes you into the Halawa Valley.

We hope you do make it into the valley, because this is veritably a tropical paradise, a remote Shangri-La that one may find difficult to believe still exists. Once a populous area, it was swept by a tidal wave in 1946 and largely deserted. You can explore the valley (a few people still live here), have a swim in the bay, or make a roughly two-hour hike to the valley's most spectacular point, **Moanaloa Falls.** You'll probably need mosquito repellent. The rewards are a picnic or a swim at the base of a waterfall that plunges relentlessly down from dizzying heights. The water is cold and delicious, but according to Molokai legend, it is only safe to swim here if the ti leaf that you throw in floats. If it should sink, you'll have to make your own decision. Remember to make this trip in the morning, since, after a hike back to your car, you'll have to drive another two hours or so back to your hotel at Kaunakakai. *Note:* Since so many people have difficulty finding the falls, we refer you to Mr. and Mrs. Wayne Ditmer's letter in Readers' Selections, ahead.

KALAUPAPA LOOKOUT: Even if you don't get to Kalaupapa itself, you should pay a visit to the Kalaupapa Lookout on Palaau Park. It's an easy trip on very good roads, about ten miles from Kaunakakai on Highway 46. After you make your right on 47 and begin to climb to Upper Molokai, the air becomes fragrant with eucalyptus and pine. Park your car at **Palaau State Park,** a well-maintained and popular camping and picnicking spot for the local people. A short walk through towering cypress and pine and suddenly you're high, high up, looking down immense cliffs to the Kalaupapa peninsula below. A marker tells the Kalaupapa story, but official descriptions seem superfluous. Just standing here, gazing down at the peninsula below, you are caught up in some of the tremendous sorrow of those who lived their lives of exile at Kalaupapa.

There is another trail, this one a bit longer (and steeply uphill some of the way) that leads to the **Phallic Rock.** According to legend, barren women who made offerings to the rock and spent the night here would then become capable of bearing children. Supposedly, an unfaithful husband of one of the minor goddesses was transformed into this rock and his mana still remains there.

While you're pondering this story (wrongdoers were often turned into stone in Hawaiian mythology), get back into your car and drive down the hill. A right turn on Route 48 will take you through a Del Monte pineapple suburb (pineapple and cattle provide the island's muscle) and Hawaiian homestead lands. Turn left on Puupeelua Avenue and you arrive back at the airport road.

If you're in the mood for traveling, continue west on Route 46 past the airport, and you're on Maunaloa Road which goes ten miles past a Dole pineapple village to Maunaloa, about 1300 feet high.

MOLOKAI RANCH WILDLIFE PARK: Yes, you can go on a safari of sorts in Molokai, a camera safari to see the giraffes, antelopes, ibex, Barbary sheep, axis deer, and other unusual animals that live on the grounds of the 800-acre wildlife preserve known as Molokai Ranch Wildlife Park. The cost of the hour-and-a-half tour is $12 for adults, $6 for children, and arrangements can be made at the Sheraton Hotel or by phoning 553-5115.

FISHING AND SAILING: You'd like to live the sporting life on Molokai? It can be easily arranged. **Molokai Charters** (tel. 553-5045) can take you out for a half-day trip, set you up for either fishing or snorkeling, let you watch the whales in season, and provide pupus and other refreshments. The cost is around $40 for a half day, $75 for a full day. The same company also runs a two-hour sunset sail aboard a 42-foot sloop, for about $30.

THE TRIP TO KALAUPAPA SETTLEMENT: Even those who have never been to Hawaii have heard about Father Damien and what he did for the destitute lepers on Molokai about a century ago. Kalaupapa is where he performed his labors, and it is still in operation as a center for the treatment of leprosy—which is now politely called "Hansen's disease." Some 151 patients and former patients are still left on Kalaupapa, and to visit them—and their island home—is an extraordinary experience. It is not, however, a trip we advise everyone to make. It is not for those who get nervous just thinking about diseases (although leprosy has been arrested by modern drugs and is presumably not contagious), and it is definitely not for those with idle curiosity. The people of Kalaupapa do not wish to be patronized. It is for those with genuine interest and concern, for those who would like to meet some of the most gentle and remarkable people in the islands. Getting to their beautifully but tragically isolated home takes a bit of doing, and the emotions the trip can raise have been overwhelming to more than one visitor. We can promise only one thing: it is a special kind of experience, and one not easily forgotten.

There are a couple of ways to get to Kalaupapa. The one that's the most excitin the famous mule trip. It's run by **Molokai Guided Mule,** which picks you up at your hotel or airport by 8 a.m. and drives you to the corral to pick up your mule. Mule riders should be between 16 and 70 years of age and weigh no more than 225 pounds. It's an unforgettable experience as the mule descends a spectacular, steep switchback trail 2000 feet below the towering cliffs at Kalae into Kalaupapa. You are met at the peninsula, given a tour and a picnic lunch, and then returned to the trail for the ride to the top at 2 p.m. Cost is $52, including tax. Call the travel desk at the Sheraton Molokai (tel. 555-2662, or in Honolulu, 526-0888). You can make reservations in advance by writing to **Rare Adventures, Ltd.,** 1188 Bishop St., Suite 1605, Honolulu, HI 96813.

It's more economical, of course, to hike down the trail; it's a scenic 3⅛-mile cliff walk which should take about an hour and a half. It's safe for most hikers; the hike *up* the pali, however, is arduous, so best to come back by mule or fly back. You must be at Kalaupapa by 9:45 a.m.

There is, of course, an easier way to get to Kalaupapa, and that's by air. Call Richard Marks' **Damien Molokai Tours** at 567-6171 (the only tour service operated by former patients who know Kalaupapa from the inside out) and they will arrange for you to fly in via a nine-passenger shuttle flight for $24 round trip. (You could also fly to Kalaupapa from any airport in Hawaii—except Kauai—via Royal Hawaiian Air; call 836-2200 for details). Keep in mind that you cannot walk past the gate at the top of the cliff trail or around the peninsula without a permit, according to Health Department rules (Damien Molokai Tours will handle all permits). Minors under 15 are not allowed at Kalaupapa. Bring some lunch, as there are no stores or restaurants open to visitors at Kalaupapa. Yes, you may bring your camera and binoculars. To make advance reservations for the tour, you can phone, from Honolulu, 946-7506 or 524-5658, or write Damien Molokai Tours, Box 1, Kalaupapa, Molokai, HI 96742. The full, four-hour grand tour costs $13.50 per person. What you'll see on that tour—the early settlement at **Kalawao** where Father Damien's church remains, the cemetery where he was buried before his remains were returned to Belgium, the grave of Mother Marianne, the healing springs of **Siloama,** the **Kauhako Crater** with its glorious view of Molokai's towering mountains, the ancient caves of the rocky east shore—is just the beginning. All the tour guides are ex-patients, people who can give you a look at Kalaupapa off the record. It is a magnificent sight—a testimony to the patients who took barren lands and turned them into Eden, a testimony to the medical pioneers and missionaries who preserved so many lives; and yet it is a strangely paradoxical place. Despite the fact that many of the inhabitants live in cozy little houses and spend much of their time boating and swimming, Kalaupapa is one of the most silent places on earth. There are no children on Kalaupapa. Only a small minority of the residents have their spouses living with them; when pregnancy occurs, the expectant mother is usually flown from the island for the delivery, where she either remains to raise her child without its father or chooses to return to Kalaupapa alone. And this is the deepest of sorrow of all the sorrows of Kalaupapa.

There is another sorrow of Kalaupapa—the fear that, since there are so few patients left and since all of them have been cured or at least "arrested"—that Kalaupapa will one day soon give way to the gods of progress. The state government once talked about phasing out the patients at Kalaupapa and eventually turning the area into another giant tourist facility. Although the former patients may be physically able to return to society, it is hard for them to imagine a society in which their disfigurement

—many are fingerless, toeless, scarred—would not, indeed, turn them into the social lepers of biblical days. Most are silent about this, a few are vocal and protesting. As wards of the state, they have little voice in determining their own future. Happily, their dream has come true: under legislation recently passed by Congress, Kalaupapa will be left as it is until the last of the residents has died. It is now known as Kalaupapa National Historic Park.

Like so many visitors who come to Kalaupapa, you may want to stay here a few days to really get to know the people. But it is almost impossible; except for family members and "officials having business in the Settlement," overnight stays have not been permitted. However, we have been informed that Damien Tours may have overnight accommodations available for selected groups or couples—not for mule train passengers. Inquire to see if these are available.

READERS' SELECTIONS ON MOLOKAI: "We highly recommend a visit to Molokai. For those on a short vacation, we recommend a simple one-day trip the way we did it. We made it our second stop, after Maui. We caught Hawaiian Air's 7 a.m. flight from Maui to Molokai which stopped en route to Lanai City, giving us a bonus view of that island as we landed and took off. Upon landing on Molokai, we rented a car and drove immediately to the **Kalaupapa Lookout** (less than a half-hour drive from the airport), then to the **Hotel Molokai** for check-in—and we even got there in time for breakfast! After the late breakfast, we took the long drive to **Halawa Valley,** and even made it all the way to the valley. There is a natural parking area and turnaround when you reach the bay with the ocean on your right and **Moanaloa Falls** on your left, a pretty good hike away. This drive was one of the most spectacular of our trip, with the scenery so natural and unspoiled by man's intervention. A highly recommended trip—it takes your breath away (so do some of those mountain curves). We were able to make it back to Kaunakakai for a light midafternoon lunch, then to the hotel for a late-afternoon swim. The sunset view from our lanai was beautiful, and the dinner and entertainment at the hotel superb. We had done the entire island—with the exception of Kalaupapa—in a day" (Roger H. Luscombe, Salem, Ohio). . . . "Regarding the trip to **Kalaupapa Settlement,** my wife and I recommend that for a couple in average physical shape, a hiking trip of 45 to 50 minutes down the pali will allow a leisurely view of the beautiful surroundings. After touring with Richard Marks (a former patient himself) and possibly the mule skinner, Clarence, you can request a mule ride up the trail (one hour). A hike up the trail is very tedious and difficult and should not be attempted by those lacking good physical conditioning. My wife rode up and I hiked. We both made it in an easy hour. My wife told me that the mule ride was a great deal of fun" (Dr. Robert W. Elliott, Hermosa Beach, Calif.).

"The **Wave Crest Resort** has an excellent view of Maui's Gold Coast from the lanais at night. Handy grocery store, lovely, well-groomed grounds, friendly personnel—especially Pauline in the office who is smilingly helpful" (Mr. and Mrs. Peter Guertler, Huntington Station, N.Y.). . . . "The **Molokai Ranch Wildlife Safari** is a great tour. The animals come right up to your van—fantastic. You can sign up for horseback riding at the Hotel Sheraton, even if you are not staying there. We were picked up for our ride by H. 'Nobu' Shimizu, who took us on a personal tour of the island after our horseback ride. He showed us the true aloha spirit" (Nancy Grant, South Easton, Mass.).

"Molokai is no place for swimming. Heavy surf along the north and western shores during winter months makes the beaches unswimmable except for experienced surfers. Residents claim that swimming is unsafe even in summer because of undertow and riptides. The local swim team has to practice off the wharf in Kaunakakai, as there is no other real swimming area. Hurricane Iwa has almost completely destroyed the beach at Kepuhi, removing almost all the sand and leaving, instead, piles of jagged rock. You can still walk the beach for several miles on the south side of the parking overlook near the Sheraton, but there, too, as much as six feet (in depth) of sand has been lost and the beach is down to bare rock in many places and very steep. It would be very unsafe for swimming. The best beach we found is **Kawakili,** the public beach on the west coast. It's spectacular, still has lots of sand and extends back into a wooded area. Camping is permitted there weekends. Of course, swimming conditions are not good in winter (locals tell us they are better in summer), but there is a saltwater pond that seeps in behind the beach, which is clear and quiet—ideal for children and sometimes deep enough for a swim. To reach this beach, however, you must look for a small sign on the north side of the highway at about mile 12½ which says 'Beach,' and drive the narrow dirt road for about *seven miles!* Snorkeling enthusiasts coming to Molokai should also be prepared for the fact that there really isn't any of note. You can get out to the reef from the Jay Cees beach on the south shore at about mile 20 if the tide is not too low. There is also a good spot at a tiny piece of beach just over the rocks to the east of Jay Cee, where a channel through the rocks takes you to deeper water and some nice coral heads. The current there, however, is very strong. . . . The **Mid-Nite Inn** doesn't look like much, but we had their Oriental fried fish—$3.75 for the full dinner!—which was much better prepared than at the Sheraton, and unlike the Sheraton, service was prompt and food arrived at the table hot" (Judy Rosen, Alexandria, Va.).

"Visit the **Big Wind Kite Factory** in Maunaloa. The charming, hospitable owners are also technical giants when it comes to explaining the aerodynamics of various styles of kites. These are not the remembered paper-and-stick creations of long ago, but modern, jet-age wonders. With kites imported from all over the world, the shop is a delight, even if just to browse. If you are fortunate, the owner may take out his 'triple-decker' stunt kites and bedazzle you with dives and twists as the kites rattle crisply in the breeze. Beware, though—it is tough not to buy at least two! . . . It is still possible to be the 'only one' on a beach in Hawaii. Take a stroll along three-mile **Popolaku Beach,** just south of the Sheraton. Most of the water farther along is free of coral and slopes gently to wave level—good for body surfing, but the undertow may be dangerous, so 'know your water.' Snorkel toward the east end, past the 19-mile marker at a pretty little park. Lots of coral. Very shallow, lots of interesting fish. Great for poor swimmers since it is only waist deep way out. . . . Be sure to eat at the **Sheraton** on buffet nights—outstanding food and selection. Reasonable by *Maui* standards" (Jack Lindberg, San José, Calif.).

"**Hotel Molokai** is under new management and they are making improvements. Manager Peter outdid himself in making Molokai the highlight of our ten-day trip to Hawaii. The hotel gift shop, **Jo's of Molokai,** has beautiful, inexpensive clothes and souvenirs. The hotel employees were all friendly and helpful. . . . We enjoyed shopping at **Takes,** a variety store on the main street in Kaunakakai. After returning our Datsun station wagon to **Avis,** their employee drove several miles out of her way to show us some sights we had missed. Molokai is indeed 'the friendly isle'" (Marion Montgomery, St. Paul, Minn.).

"I advise your readers to forget their budget when visiting Molokai, for if bound to the budget they would not have the experience of visiting **Kalaupapa.** I flew to the settlement on Polynesian Airways for $24. The Damien Tour cost $13.50. The returns from the investment will continue, for the experience was filled with love, sensitivity, and affection for a special group of proud people who ask for nothing but their dignity. I suggest that your readers read *Holy Man* by Gavin Daws, published by Harper & Row, prior to their trip. It will give them a broader insight and background fasil A. Willet, Jr., Redwood City, Calif.). . . . "We found out why they call it **Mid-Nite Inn** in vol. 160, no. 2, August 1981 issue of *National Geographic Magazine* in an excellent article, 'Molokai.' I quote: 'Art Kikukawa's restaurant, the Mid-Nite Inn, began as modestly as the bakery—with a saimin stand his mother opened. Four nights a week, departing travelers would eat the zesty noodle dish while waiting until midnight to board the inter-island steamer. Hence the name'" (Marceile Gresch, Waukesha, Wisc.).

"I went **snorkeling** just south of the Sheraton by the golf course after 5 p.m. The water was not clear enough to see the vivid colors of the fish (which I had remembered from prior snorkeling at Hanauma Bay on Oahu), but I wanted to give it a try anyhow. What I had not counted on, however, was the unpredictable currents near the large rocks. I barely avoided being swept into them, and/or out to sea. In discussion with the locals later, I learned that such experiences are not uncommon there. A safer area would be about 20 to 22 miles east of town on the route to Halawa Valley. I rented full snorkel gear at **Molokai Fish and Dive** in downtown Kaunakakai for $5 per day (tel. 553-5926)" (Mr. and Mrs. Ronald Sandberg, Pleasanton, Calif.). . . . "The mule ride to **Kalaupapa** was a highlight of our trip: such beautiful and strong animals, a breathtaking view, as well as a high experience touring the community with a patient-guide" (Mr. and Mrs. Paul Shaver, Murray Isle, N.Y.).

"If you are leaving Molokai to go back to the mainland, there is no agriculture inspector there. Consequently, you must check all your luggage to Honolulu, pick it up there and take it to the agriculture inspectors, then to your airline back to the mainland. This is a real chore as both Aloha and Hawaiian Air are miles from the main terminal and a porter costs $4 and a taxi about the same, to say nothing of the walk you have to put in! In other words, if you're doing Molokai, don't do it last before you return" (Howard S. Walker, Sequim, Wash.). . . . "We found it very difficult to locate the trail to **Moanaloa Falls,** and could never have done it without the help of some of the local people. The hike was definitely worthwhile, however. I made the walk down into the **Kalaupapa Settlement.** The trail is a little over three miles long, and descends about 1700 feet over 26 switchbacks. It is a difficult, trail, rocky but if you are in good hiking condition, you will find it well worthwhile. Coming up took a little longer, but wasn't as difficult as I had imagined, when going down. The tour through the area was a fascinating experience" (Rev. H. W. Schneider, Church of St. John the Apostle, Minot, N.D.).

"To get to **Moanaloa Falls** you must go up the dirt road in front of the small green church on the left side of the river as you face the falls. The small parking lot across from the church is the best place to leave your car. As you go up the road, stay on the main road until it ends; you go by several houses on the way. A trail takes over where the road ends. Go up this trail *only* about 100 yards and you will come to a row of rocks across the trail. Turn to the right here and follow the trail down to the stream. You have to cross *both* forks of the stream here. When you get to the other side, find a trail that goes up the hill perpendicular to the stream. (When you cross a mud flat, you will see an orange mark on a tree. Here, go right through some heavy grass. When you leave the grass, look behind you as you go up the trail. If you see some more orange marks, you know you are on the trail.) Shortly you come upon a major trail that has been blocked off to the right. Turn left and now follow the white plastic pipe and white arrows marking the trail to the falls for a spectacular hike and view of the falls and the pool below. The trail by the houses and through their fields on the right side has been closed off" (Mr. and Mrs. Wayne Ditmer, Mott, N.D.). . . . "We were thankful to 'Johnny of the Valley' for information on how to find Moanaloa Falls. This incredibly interesting man who is a 'kahuna' seems to look after the park grounds. He is a philosopher and a man to be respected both for his knowledge and spirit. Perhaps other readers might meet him and be inspired by his stories" (Gwenyth Phillips, Wolfville, N.S., Canada).

And so this 20th edition of *Hawaii on $35 a Day* is *pau.* As every writer knows, no travel book is holy writ; establishments go out of business, owners change, prices go up, quality improves or falls off. Don't become angry with establishments if their prices are higher than those quoted as we went to press; inflation is a fact of life. The book is brought up-to-date every year; be sure you are reading the latest edition available. And we will be grateful to all readers who give us their up-to-the-minute reports on the places mentioned in the book. If you've discovered something new—a hotel, a restaurant, a shop—we hope you'll share it with us and with readers of future editions of this book. Send your suggestions, comments, criticisms to us, Faye Hammel and Sylvan Levey, c/o Frommer/Pasmantier Publishers, 1230 Avenue of the Americas, New York, NY 10020. We regret that we cannot personally answer the many hundreds of letters we receive each year. You can be certain, however, that your letter is carefully noted and appreciated. We will be glad to send a free copy of the next edition of this book to each reader whose suggestion is used.

And now you're ready to strike out on your own, to sample for yourself the charms of what Mark Twain called "the loveliest fleet of islands anchored in any ocean." Ahead of you lies the newest, and most unique, of the United States.

Aloha!

Appendix

A HAWAIIAN VOCABULARY

From AA to Wikiwiki

AS WE POINTED out in the introduction, there are just 12 letters in the Hawaiian alphabet: the five vowels—*a, e, i, o, u,*—and seven consonants—*h, k, l, m, n, p, w*. Every syllable ends in a vowel, every vowel is pronounced, and the accent is almost always on the next-to-the-last syllable, as it is in Spanish. Consonants receive their English sounds, but vowels get the Latin pronunciation: *a* as in farm, *e* as in they, *i* as in machine, *o* as in cold, and *u* as in tutor. Note also that when a *w* comes before the final vowel in a word, it is given the "v" sound, as in Hawaii. Purists say Ha-vye-ee for Hawaii, but most people call it Ha-wye-ee.

The following glossary will give you a pretty good idea of what the Hawaiian language sounds like. No one, of course, expects you to go around spouting phrases like "Holo ehia keia?" to ask what time it is, but a familiarity with the most important words is what distinguishes the kamaainas from the malihinis.

aa	rough lava
aikane (eye-kah-nay)	friend, as in "Aloha, aikane"
ai (eye)	eat
ala (al-lah)	road, as in Ala Moana (ocean road)
akamai (ah-kah-my)	smart
alii (ah-lee-ee)	noblemen, the old royalty of Hawaii
aloha (ah-low-hah)	welcome, farewell, love
aole (ah-oh-lay)	no
auwe (ow-way)	alas! woe!
ewa (ehvah)	in the direction of Ewa, a town on Oahu "Drive ewa five blocks."
hala (hah-lah)	the pandanus tree, the leaves of which are used for weaving

halakahiki (hah-lah-kah-hee-kee)	pineapple
hale (hah-lay)	house
hana (hah-nah)	to work
haole (how-lay)	Caucasian, white
haolewahine (how-lay-wah-hee-nay)	white woman
haolekane (how-lay-kah-nay)	white man
hapa (hah-pah)	a small part, a half
hapai (hah-pie)	pregnant, originally "to carry"
hauoli (how-oh-lee)	happiness
heiau (hey-ee-au)	ancient temple
hele (hey-lay)	to go, to walk
haimoe (hee-ah-mow-ay)	to sleep
hilahila (hee-lah-hee-lah)	ashamed
holo (ho-low)	to run
holoholo (ho-low-ho-low)	to have fun, to relax
holoku (ho-low-koo)	formal dress with train
holomuu (ho-low-moo)	a cross between a holoku and a muumuu, long and without a train
honi (ho-nee)	to kiss, as in "Honi Kaua wikiwiki! ("Kiss me quick!")
hoomalimali (ho-oh-mah-lee-mah-lee)	to flatter
huhu (hoo-hoo)	angry
hui (hoo-ee)	a club, an assembly
hukilau (hoo-kee-lau)	a fishing festival
hula (hoo-lah)	a dance, to dance
imu (ee-moo)	underground oven lined with hot rocks, used for cooking the luau pig
ipo (ee-po)	sweetheart
ka (kah)	the
kai (kye)	sea
kala (kah-lah)	money
kalua (kah-loo-ah)	to bake underground
kamaaina (kah-mah-eye-nah)	oldtimer
kane (kah-nay)	man
kapa (kah-pah)	tapa, a bark cloth
kapakahi (kah-pah-kah-hee)	crooked
kapu (kah-poo)	forbidden, keep out
kaukau (kow-kow)	food

keiki (kay-kee)	child
kokua (ko-koo-ah)	help, cooperation
kona (ko-nah)	south
la (lah)	sun, light, day
lanai (lah-nye)	porch
lani (lah-nee)	heaven, sky
lauhala (lau-hah-lah)	leaf of the hala or pandanus tree
lei (lay)	garland
lolo (low-low)	stupid
lomilomi (low-mee-low-mee)	massage
luau (loo-au)	feast
mahalo (mah-hah-low)	thank you
ma'i ka'i (mah-ee kah-ee)	good, fine
makai (mah-key)	toward the sea
malihini (mah-lee-hee-nee)	stranger, newcomer
manawahi (mah-nah-wah-hee)	free
mauka (mau-kah)	toward the mountains
mele (may-lay)	song, chant
menehune (may-nay-hoo-nay)	a mysterious race who inhabited the islands before the Polynesians. Mythology claims they were pygmies.
muumuu (moo-oo-moo-oo)	loose dress, Hawaiian version of missionaries' "Mother Hubbards"
nani (nah-nee)	lovely
niu (nee-oo)	coconut
nui (noo-ee)	big, as in mahalo nui (big thanks)
ono (oh-no)	sweet taste, delicious
opu (oh-poo)	belly
paakiki (pah-ah-kee-kee)	stubborn
pali (pah-lee)	precipice
paniolo (pah-nee-oh-low)	Hawaiian cowboy
pau (pow)	finished
pilikia (pee-lee-kee-ah)	trouble
poi (poy)	crushed taro root
puka (poo-kah)	hole
punee (poo-nay-ay)	couch
pupu (poo-poo)	hors d'oeuvre
pupule (poo-poo-lay)	crazy
ua (oo-ah)	rain
waha (wah-hah)	speech, mouth

wahine (wah-hee-nay)	female, woman, girl
wai (why)	fresh water
wikiwiki (wee-kee-wee-kee)	to hurry

Phrases

Be careful	**Malama pono** (mah-lah-mah po-no)
Bottoms up	**Okole maluna** (oh-ko-lay mah-loo-nah)
Come here	**Hele mai** (hey-lay my)
Come and eat	**Hele mai ai** (hey-lay my eye)
Come in and sit down	**Komo mai e noho iho** (ko-mo my ayno-ho-ee-ho)
For love	**No ke aloha** (no kay ah-low-hah)
Go away	**Hele aku oe** (hey-lay ah-koo oh-ay)
Good evening	**Aloha ahiahi** (ah-low-hah ah-hee-ah-hee)
Good morning	**Aloha kakahiaka** (ah-low-hah kah-kah-hee-ah-kah)
Greatest love to you	**Aloha nui oe** (ah-low-hah noo-ee oh-ay)
Happy birthday	**Hauoli la hanau** (hah-oo-oh-lee lah hah-nah-oo)
Happy New Year	**Hauoli Makahiki Hou** (hah-oo-oh-lee mah-kah-hee-kee ho-oo)
Here's to your happiness	**Hauoli maoli eo** (hah-oo-oh-lee mah-oh-lee oh-ay)
How are you?	**Pehea oe?** (pay-hay-ah oh-ay)
I am fine	**Ma'i ka'i** (mah-ee kah-ee)
I love you	**Aloha wau ia oe** (ah-low-hah vow ee-ah oh-ay)
I am sorry	**Ua kaumaha au** (oo-ah cow-mah-hah ow)
It isn't so	**Aole pela** (ah-oh-lay pay-lah)
I have enough	**Ua lawa au** (oo-ah lah-wah ow)
Let's go	**E hele kaua** (au hey-lay cow-ah)
Many thanks	**Mahalo nui loa** (mah-hah-low noo-ee low-ah)
Merry Christmas	**Mele Kalikimaka** (may-lay kah-lee-kee-mah-kah)
Much love	**Aloha nui loa** (ah-low-hah noo-ee low-ah)

No trouble	**Aole pilikia** (ah-oh-lay pee-lee-kee-ah)
What is your name?	**Owai kau inoa?** (oh-why kah-oo ee-no-ah)

AND THEN THERE'S PIDGIN: Despite the earnest efforts of educators to stamp it out, pidgin, that code language of the islands, continues its not-so-underground existence. The Chinese developed it in their first contacts with English-speaking people, but you'll hear it spoken today by all the racial groups, from haoles to Hawaiians. Beachboys, cab drivers, university students, a few who don't know better and a lot who do, all occasionally descend into pidgin. Although its subtleties are unintelligible to the newcomer (that's part of the idea), you'll be able to pick up a few words: *wasamala, wasetime, lesgo, da kine.*

You'll hear all kinds of theories about the indestructibility of pidgin. Some sociological types feel it's a subtle form of rebellion by the dispossessed Hawaiian, not unlike the jargon of mainland blacks. The psychological types call it more of an adolescent code, a desire for teenagers to have their own language. Others say it's just plain bad English. Take your choice, whatever *da kine* reason, pidgin is "in" in Hawaii.